THE CASE OF LEON TROTSKY

The case of LEON TROTSKY

Pathfinder

New York London Montreal Sydney

BEINECKE LIBRARY, YALE UNIVERSITY

Dewey Commission hearings, April 1937. Left to right around table: Jean van Heijenoort, Leon Trotsky, Jan Frankel (behind him in corner, Natalia Sedova), Otto Ruehle, Carleton Beals, John Dewey, Suzanne La Follette, Benjamin Stolberg, John Finerty, Albert Glotzer, Albert Goldman. At far right, standing with sketchbook, is artist Dorothy Eisner.

BY PERMISSION OF CHRISTIE McDONALD

Preliminary sketch for painting by Dorothy Eisner of Dewey Commission hearings. At bottom right, muralist Diego Rivera, in whose house the commission was meeting.

ISBN 978-0-87348-868-6
Library of Congress Catalog Card Number 68-7089
Manufactured in the United States of America

First Merit/Pathfinder edition, 1968
First paperback edition, 2006
Fourth printing, 2010

Cover design: Eva Braiman
Cover painting: "Dewey Commission and Leon Trotsky" by Dorothy Eisner, 1937, oil on canvas, 25" x 30". By permission of Christie McDonald. Photograph of painting courtesy of Center for Dewey Studies, Southern Illinois University, Carbondale.

Pathfinder
www.pathfinderpress.com
E-mail: pathfinder@pathfinderpress.com

Contents

List of exhibits

Introduction

This book contains the verbatim transcript of the hearings held by the Preliminary Commission of Inquiry into the Charges Made Against Leon Trotsky in the Moscow Trials. The Dewey Commission, as it is known, was an independent, impartial body initiated in March 1937 by the American Committee for the Defense of Leon Trotsky. Its sole purpose was to ascertain all the available facts about the Moscow Trial proceedings in which Trotsky and his son, Leon Sedov, were the principal accused and to render a judgment based upon those facts.

Its subcommission conducted thirteen hearings at the home of the exiled revolutionary in Coyoacan, Mexico, D.F., from April 10 to April 17, 1937. During these sessions it received Trotsky's testimony and that of his secretary, Jan Frankel, cross-examined both witnesses, heard Trotsky's answer to the charges against him and his countercharges against the Soviet government. It accepted, subject to verification, such documentary evidence as he had to introduce.

The reasons for the commission's formation and its work were bound up with one of the most momentous and tragic political events of the nineteen-thirties: the prolonged blood purges and frame-up trials through which Stalin consolidated his personal terroristic tyranny over the Soviet Union.

His henchmen staged four key trials from 1936 to 1938. The first was "the trial of the sixteen," with Zinoviev, Kamenev, Smirnov, Mrachkovsky, and others as defendants; the second, "the trial of the seventeen," which included Pyatakov,

Radek, Sokolnikov, Muralov, Serebryakov, and others, took place in January 1937. Then came the secret trial of Marshal Tukhachevsky and a group of the highest Red Army generals in June 1937; and finally, "the trial of the twenty-one" (Rykov, Bukharin, Krestinsky, Rakovsky, Yagoda, and others) in March 1938.

The men in the dock included all the members of Lenin's Politbureau, except Stalin himself. Trotsky, though absent, was the chief defendant in these proceedings. He and the Bolshevik old guard were charged with plotting to assassinate Stalin and other Soviet leaders, of conspiring to wreck the country's economic and military power, and of killing masses of Russian workers. They were likewise accused of working, from the earliest days of the Russian Revolution, for the espionage services of Britain, France, Japan, and Germany and of making secret agreements with agents of Hitler and the Mikado to cede vast slices of Soviet territory to imperialist Germany and Japan. The defendants in Moscow abjectly confessed to their guilt; Trotsky alone did not.

The trials of these notables were accompanied and followed by a frightful purge of people from every walk of Soviet life: party members, military men, Comintern leaders, intellectuals, officials, ordinary workers and peasants. It is still undetermined how many were caught in its bloody net, since the post-Stalin regimes still refuse to divulge such facts. But the victims numbered in the millions.

Stalin did not spare his closest associates or members of his own family. Even the secret police chiefs, Yagoda and Yezhov, who organized the early trials, were later slaughtered.

Stalin arrested and executed almost every important living Bolshevik participant in the Revolution. Of 1,966 delegates to the seventeenth Soviet party congress in 1934, 1,108 were arrested. Of 139 members of the Central Committee, 98 were arrested. Along with the three Soviet marshals, one-third to one-half of the 75,000 Red Army officers were arrested or shot.

The purges of the nineteen-thirties were so sweeping that no major party figure of the October Revolution, which gave power to the Bolsheviks, survived to celebrate the fiftieth anniversary of the event, except Stalin's faithful lieutenant, Vyacheslav Molotov, who was retired in disgrace in 1958. The terror has left enduring scars upon Soviet society. There are few families there today which did not in one way or another suffer from its effects.

*

The subcommission hearings in Mexico took place in April 1937 between the second and the third Moscow Trials. In the trials of August 1936 and January 1937, Trotsky and Sedov had been declared convicted without any opportunity for their cases to be heard. They had denied their guilt through the world press and in their turn had accused the Soviet government of having based their "convictions" on false evidence. Indeed, the forced confessions of the defendants in the public trials were the only basis for the verdicts.

Trotsky was the only one among the accused Bolshevik leaders who was beyond Stalin's grip. When Zinoviev and Kamenev were put on trial, Trotsky had challenged Moscow to request his extradition from Norway, where he was then living as an exile from the Soviet Union. This procedure would have brought his case before a Norwegian tribunal. Instead, the Norwegian government, under heavy economic and diplomatic pressure from the Kremlin's ambassador, interned Trotsky and his wife. For six months he was gagged and unable to answer the monstrous charges against him.

As soon as he gained asylum in Mexico in January 1937, Trotsky publicly demanded the formation of an international commission of inquiry, since he had been deprived of any opportunity to reply to the accusations before a legally constituted court. He asked that such a body be constituted of unimpeachable personages who would take his testimony and consider documentary proofs of the innocence of himself and Sedov.

In a speech prepared for delivery by telephone from Mexico City to a large meeting at the New York Hippodrome on February 9, 1937, Trotsky made the following dramatic declaration: "If this commission decides that I am guilty in the slightest degree of the crimes which Stalin imputes to me, I pledge in advance to place myself voluntarily in the hands of the executioners of the G.P.U. [Soviet secret police]."

Such an inquiry was imperatively justified in view of the controversy and consternation stirred up by the trials, the widespread suspicion of their authenticity, the many lives at stake, and the gravity of the issues they posed. Trotsky was entitled to have his day in court and establish the credibility of the charges, not only to defend his honor and reputation as a revolutionist but to try and forestall further trials and executions.

The members of the full commission were John Dewey, its chairman, America's foremost philosopher and liberal; Otto Ruehle, biographer of Karl Marx and former member of the Reichstag who alone with Liebknecht had voted against war in 1914–15; Benjamin Stolberg and Suzanne LaFollette, American journalists; Carleton Beals, authority on Latin-American affairs; Alfred Rosmer, who in 1920–21 had been a member of the Executive Committee of the Communist International; Wendelin Thomas, leader of the Wilhelmshaven sailors' revolt in November 1918 and later a Communist member of the German Reichstag; Edward A. Ross, Professor of Sociology at the University of Wisconsin; John Chamberlain, former literary critic of the *New York Times;* Carlo Tresca, well-known Italian-American anarchist leader; and Francisco Zamora, Mexican journalist.

The first five made up the subcommission which went to

Coyoacan. John Finerty, famous as defense counsel in such great American political trials as those of Tom Mooney and Sacco-Vanzetti, acted as the commission's legal counsel. Albert Goldman of Chicago was Trotsky's attorney.

The commission members held widely divergent political and ideological views, and none was a follower of Trotsky. They were concerned with the interests of historic truth as well as the desire to ascertain the facts in the case. They had been mandated by similar committees in France, England, and Czechoslovakia to fulfill that responsibility.

The taking of testimony in Mexico was followed by months of assiduous investigation. The commission made its findings public in New York on September 21, 1937. It stated: "(1) That the conduct of the Moscow trials was such as to convince any unprejudiced person that no effort was made to ascertain the truth. (2) While confessions are necessarily entitled to the most serious consideration, the confessions themselves contain such inherent improbabilities as to convince the Commission that they do not represent the truth, irrespective of any means used to obtain them."

The commission therefore concluded that the Moscow trials were frame-ups and Trotsky and Sedov were not guilty of the eighteen specific charges of the prosecution against them. (The complete report of the findings was published by Harper & Brothers in 1938 under the title of *Not Guilty* in a companion volume to this one.)

*

That verdict was rendered thirty years ago. Since then enlightened opinion the world over, not only in the capitalist but in most Communist countries, has come to recognize the monstrous falsifications perpetrated by Stalin against his political opponents.

Stalin's successors at the head of the Soviet government have likewise acknowledged this truth in their own manner by their indictment of the dead dictator and posthumous rehabilitation of some of his victims (Trotsky is not yet among these). In his famous secret speech to the Twentieth Congress of the Soviet Communist Party in February 1956, Khrushchev partially disclosed the enormity of Stalin's pogroms and the means by which his agents extorted false confessions from the self-defamed defendants. Stalin now clearly emerges as the real criminal of the proceedings, the sinister figure who mounted to unrestricted supremacy over the mountain of corpses he had besmirched.

Thus history has already vindicated the work and conclusions of the Dewey Commission. A full and final accounting for these crimes will very likely have to wait until Stalin's bureaucratic disciples are themselves replaced by honest representatives of the Soviet people who will undertake a thorough review of the trials and purges and restore all their victims to honor. This volume will facilitate that task.

It has still another value. In the course of the thirteen-day countertrial, Trotsky was subjected to the most searching examination by his attorney and cross-examination by the commission members and their counsel. He had to do more than expose the falsity of Moscow's allegations. He had to recount the main events of his career, expound his beliefs, describe and explain the bewildering changes that had taken place in the Soviet Union from Lenin to Stalin. He had to analyze the issues in the factional disputes within Russian and world communism, portray the leading personalities in the struggles, and touch upon every phase of the terrible contest between Stalin and himself which led up to the trials.

I attended the hearings as national secretary of the American Committee for the Defense of Leon Trotsky and vividly remember the tension in the long, narrow, barricaded room as day after day Trotsky strained to answer all the questions directed at him in the unfamiliar English tongue. It was a prodigious intellectual performance.

"By the end no question had been left unanswered, no important issue blurred, no serious historic event unilluminated," wrote Isaac Deutscher in *The Prophet Outcast*. "Thirteen years later Dewey, who had spent so much of his life in academic debate and was still as opposed as ever to Trotsky's *Weltanschauung*, recalled with enthusiastic admiration 'the intellectual power with which Trotsky had assembled and organized the mass of his evidence and argumentation and conveyed to us the meaning of every relevant fact.' The incisiveness of Trotsky's logic got the better of his unwieldy sentences, and the clarity of his ideas shone through all his verbal blunderings. Even his wit did not succumb; it often relieved the gloom of his subject-matter. Above all, the integrity of his case allowed him to overcome all external restraint and constraint. He stood where he stood like truth itself, unkempt and unadorned, unarmoured and unshielded yet magnificent and invincible."*

The record of the hearings is therefore an extensive and valuable compendium of information about the events, personalities, and problems of the Russian Revolution and the Soviet Union. It presents the ideas and positions of Marxism, Bolshevism, and Trotskyism on a wide range of questions.

Trotsky made his summary speech on the last day of the sessions. It concluded with a reaffirmation of his confidence in the ultimate triumph of the cause of socialism to which he had dedicated his life. The tragic backdrop of circumstances against which his words were spoken made them all the more moving and impressive.

"Esteemed Commissioners! The experience of my life, in which there has been no lack either of successes or of failures, has not only not destroyed my faith in the clear, bright

---

* Isaac Deutscher, *The Prophet Outcast*, Oxford, 1963, pp. 381–382.

future of mankind, but, on the contrary, has given it an indestructible temper. This faith in reason, in truth, in human solidarity, which at the age of eighteen I took with me into the workers' quarters of the provincial Russian town of Nikolaiev—this faith I have preserved fully and completely. It has become more mature, but not less ardent.

"In the very fact of your Commission's formation—in the fact that, at its head, is a man of unshakable moral authority, a man who by virtue of his age should have the right to remain outside of the skirmishes in the political arena—in this fact I see a new and truly magnificent reinforcement of the revolutionary optimism which constitutes the fundamental element of my life. . . ."

A hush fell over the assemblage as the Promethean revolutionary ended his prolonged and passionate presentation. The shadows of late afternoon had begun to cut across the patio outside. "Anything I can say will be an anti-climax," the white-haired John Dewey remarked and pronounced the hearings closed. Their content is preserved in the following pages.

George Novack
MARCH 1, 1968

Foreword

This volume contains the report of the hearings of the Preliminary Commission of Inquiry, but none of the documents introduced in evidence, save for excerpts actually read into the record. A later volume will contain the report of the full Commission, together with records of further hearings both here and abroad, and documents finally accepted in evidence by the Commission.

The Preliminary Commission of Inquiry takes this occasion to thank Mrs. Robert Latham George for having generously permitted it to establish its headquarters in her house, and for having housed three of its members during their stay in Mexico City. It is indebted to Mr. Charles Rumford Walker for invaluable assistance in handling its relations with the press, and to both Mr. and Mrs. Walker for having undertaken, and discharged to the satisfaction of all concerned, the responsibility for the issuance of cards and the supervision of admissions to the hearings. Mr. and Mrs. Carlos Iturbe kindly undertook to interpret the proceedings to those representatives of Mexican labor organizations who were present at the hearings; and for their assistance in this matter, and also for that of Mrs. Otto Ruehle during those sessions which she was able to attend, the Preliminary Commission is deeply grateful.

John Dewey,
CHAIRMAN

Suzanne LaFollette,
SECRETARY

Report to the Commission of Inquiry into the charges made against Leon Trotsky in the Moscow Trials

Your sub-commission, which was empowered to go to Mexico and take Leon Trotsky's testimony on the charges made against him in the Moscow trials, has completed its task and now submits its report.

1. *Function.*—Your sub-commission was in Mexico neither as prosecutor nor as judge. We did not regard Mr. Trotsky as defendant or accused. Nor did he so regard himself. Indeed, so to regard him was impossible, since in the Moscow trials he was never indicted—only convicted. Therefore we were in Mexico solely as an investigating body, to take Mr. Trotsky's testimony on the accusations made against him in the confessions of the Moscow defendants; to accept such documents as he had to submit in his own defense; and to report to the full Commission on the basis of this evidence our decision whether or not Mr. Trotsky has a case warranting further investigation.

2. *Scope.*—The scope and content of our inquiry was necessarily determined by the proceedings in the Moscow trials.

According to the prosecutor, Mr. Vyshinsky, the testimony was of two kinds: "First there is the historical connection which confirms the theses of the indictment on the basis of the Trotskyites' past activity. We have also in mind the testimony of the accused which in itself represents enormous importance as proof." Equally important with the testimony of the defendants are Mr. Vyshinsky's final pleas, in which he went beyond the accusations to rewrite the history of the Russian Revolution and Mr. Trotsky's part in it. He also edited to suit his purposes Mr. Trotsky's writings both before and since the Revolution. Impartiality in this case does not of course require the abandonment by the Commission of its knowledge of the simple facts of history.

Accordingly, our inquiry fell into three categories:

a) The biography of Mr. Trotsky, with special reference to his relations with the defendants in the Moscow trials;

b) Factual material relating to the decisive accusations against him;

c) His theoretical and historical writings as they bear upon the credibility of the accusations, the testimony, the confessions, and the summations in the two Moscow trials.

3. *The Hearings.*—Your sub-commission held thirteen hearings, from April 10 to April 17, 1937—twelve of three hours each and a final one of five hours.

In order not to embarrass the Mexican Government by requesting the added police protection which public hearings in Mexico City would have required, we held the sessions in the large hall of Diego Rivera's house at Coyoacan, where Mr. Trotsky lives. This arrangement limited the audience to about fifty persons, almost half of whom were correspondents representing the Mexican and the foreign press.

4. *The Evidence.*—In addition to Mr. Trotsky's oral testimony, the evidence introduced consisted of such material as the following:

a) Documents purporting to refute the testimony given

in the Moscow trials concerning his alleged conspiratorial contacts with the defendants. This material includes affidavits of witnesses concerning Mr. Trotsky's activities, his movements, and his visitors at the periods when he was alleged to have had personal contact with Holtzman, Berman-Yurin, David, Romm, and Pyatakov. It includes letters written to him at Prinkipo by friends in Berlin, advising him against engaging Olberg as a secretary. It includes a photostat of the passport of his son, Leon Sedov, purporting to show that Sedov could not have been in Copenhagen at the time when Holtzman was supposed to have been conducted by him to Mr. Trotsky; and that Sedov did go to Paris to meet his parents immediately after their sojourn in Copenhagen. It also includes the telegram sent by Natalia Sedov-Trotsky to the French Foreign Minister, M. Herriot, requesting that her son be granted a visa, and the telegram of the French Foreign Office to its Berlin representative, authorizing it. It includes a statement by the head of the airport at Oslo that no foreign airplane landed there during December, 1935, the month of Pyatakov's alleged flight.

b) Citations from Mr. Trotsky's writings bearing upon his attitude, past and present, towards the defendants in the Moscow trials; also on such subjects as individual terror, fascism, the proletarian revolution, the Soviet Union, the Soviet bureaucracy, and the Communist International. Citations of letters and articles revealing the nature of his relations with Lenin both before and after the October Revolution. Also passages from the works of Lenin, Stalin, Radek and others concerning Leon Trotsky's role in the Revolution, the Civil War, and the various party struggles during the period which followed.

c) Letters and other writings showing the methods and the nature of Mr. Trotsky's communications with his sympathizers in the Soviet Union since his exile.

Such, in brief, is the nature of the documentary evidence

submitted to us. Mr. Trotsky also placed at our disposal his archives in Mexico, and offered to reveal to the Commission, whenever it shall so request, the location of his European archives and to give it access to them. Naturally, during our brief stay in Mexico we had time to examine very little of this material. We have therefore authorized one of our members, Otto Ruehle, who resides in Mexico City, to continue this work and to supply to the Commission certified copies or translations of such documents as exist there and as in his judgment or that of any other commissioner are pertinent to our further inquiry. Your European subcommissions will have the task of examining Mr. Trotsky's European archives. Altogether Mr. Trotsky's archives consist of many thousand documents.

5. *Mr. Trotsky as Witness.*—It is an established rule even in legally constituted courts that the bearing of the witness may be taken into account in weighing the value of his testimony. We are guided by the same principle in reporting our impression of Mr. Trotsky's attitude and bearing. Throughout the hearings he seemed eager to cooperate with the Commission in its efforts to ascertain the truth about all phases of his life and his political and literary activity. He answered readily and with every appearance of helpfulness and candor all questions put to him by the counsel for the sub-commission and by its members.

6. *The Case of Mr. Beals.*—Your sub-commission reports with regret the resignation, before the hearings were concluded, of one of its members, Mr. Carleton Beals. Toward the close of the hearing on the afternoon of April 16, Mr. Beals put to Mr. Trotsky a provocative question based on alleged information which the sub-commission could not check and place on the record. After the hearing our counsel, Mr. John Finerty, advised the sub-commission that questions based on private information were highly improper, would be sufficient cause for mistrial in any ordinary court, and that he

could not continue as counsel if they were to be permitted in future. Mr. Beals then angrily declared that either he or Mr. Finerty must leave the sub-commission. Still, he promised to attend a conference that evening to discuss the matter. But although we waited for him until midnight he did not come. The next morning, before the opening of the session, Mrs. Beals brought us his resignation, in which he charged that the Commission was not conducting a serious inquiry. He also made the astonishing statement that the sessions had been completed, although the cross-examination by the commissioners was only half finished and he had himself stated that he had "hundreds more questions" to ask. In view of the fact that Mr. Beals later gave to the press a series of statements which were widely published and in which he impugned the integrity of the other commissioners and made false accusations against us, we think it necessary to put before you the following facts:

a) From the first Mr. Beals held himself almost completely aloof from the sub-commission. Shortly after the hearings opened he moved from his hotel, and evaded our request for his new address. He was constantly with people who were known to be against the purposes of the Commission, and at no time gave his full attention to its work, as did the rest of us. We made every effort to secure his full cooperation. Obviously, we failed.

b) At no time before his resignation did Mr. Beals intimate to the other members of the sub-commission that he was dissatisfied with the attitude of any one of us or with the conduct of the hearings. As a member of the sub-commission he was under obligation to express frankly and honestly in private conference any dissatisfaction he may have felt, instead of springing it in public without warning. In this obligation he failed.

c) At no time, either during the hearings or in our private conferences, did any commissioner ever object to *any* question put to the witness by Mr. Beals. Even the improper question which precipitated Mr. Beals's resignation still remains in the record.

Much as we regret the resignation of Mr. Beals, it does not disturb us. The Commission is investigating a great historic controversy. Powerful interests are engaged in attempting to disrupt it and sabotage its work. More efforts of this kind may be expected.

7. *Recommendations.*—Your sub-commission submits the verbatim report of its proceedings, together with the documents submitted in evidence. This record convinces us that Mr. Trotsky has established a case amply warranting further investigation. Therefore, we recommend that the work of this Commission proceed to its conclusion.

JOHN DEWEY, *Chairman*
OTTO RUEHLE
BENJAMIN STOLBERG
SUZANNE LAFOLLETTE, *Secretary*

JOHN F. FINERTY,
Counsel, Concurring

TRANSCRIPT

of

PROCEEDINGS

in the

HEARINGS OF THE PRELIMINARY COMMISSION OF INQUIRY

into the

CHARGES MADE AGAINST LEON TROTSKY

in the

MOSCOW TRIALS

Held

April 10 to 17, 1937

at

Avenida Londres, 127

COYOACAN, MEXICO

Reported by
ALBERT M. GLOTZER
Court Reporter
of Chicago, Illinois

PRESENT

The Members of the Preliminary Commission

DR. JOHN DEWEY, Professor Emeritus of Philosophy, Columbia University. (New York City) Chairman of the Commission.

MR. CARLETON BEALS, Author and Lecturer. (California) *(Resigned after eleventh session.)*

MISS SUZANNE LAFOLLETTE, Author and Former Editor of *The New Freeman*. (New York City) Secretary of the Commission.

MR. OTTO RUEHLE, Former Member of the German Reichstag and Biographer of Karl Marx. (Mexico City)

MR. BENJAMIN STOLBERG, Author and Journalist. (New York City)

MR. JOHN F. FINERTY, former counsel for Sacco and Vanzetti and counsel for Tom Mooney, acting as counsel for the Preliminary Commission of Inquiry. (Washington, D.C.)

MR. ALBERT GOLDMAN, Labor attorney, acting as counsel for Leon Trotsky. (Chicago)

Witnesses:

LEON D. TROTSKY

JAN FRANKEL

REPORTER FOR THE COMMISSION: Albert Glotzer. (Chicago)

ALSO PRESENT: Representatives of the press and visitors.

First session

April 10, 1937, at ten o'clock a.m.

DR. DEWEY: The preliminary hearing is now opened. You will all notice the sign which says: "No smoking." There will be recesses in which there will be an opportunity to smoke. Also, as you have already been told, we will be glad to give the photographers an opportunity to take pictures, only we will have to ask that they do not do so during the sessions. After the adjournment of this session, at one o'clock, there will be arrangements made with the photographers for any special shots they wish to make.

I now declare the first session opened. I shall read a brief preliminary statement in English first, and then shall ask Mr. Carleton Beals to read it in Spanish:

It is with great pleasure that I find myself again in Mexico after a decade's absence. Like my fellow Commissioners, I have again found the capital of Mexico most agreeable. It is to all of us a regret that we do not today have with us as a colleague a Mexican representative, but before the full Commission is completed, to which we must report, we may hope that this deficiency will be remedied. The fact that hearings are being held in which a foreigner will defend himself before foreigners on Mexican soil is an honor to Mexico, and a reproach to those countries whose political system or current policy bars the holding of our meetings on their soil.

It is fitting, indeed, that representatives of several continents meet on this soil, which has granted asylum to many of the Old World who are persecuted for political views. This Commission, like many millions of workers of city and country, of hand and brain, believes that no man should be condemned without a chance to defend himself. It desires at the outset, therefore, to congratulate the Mexican Government on its broad interpretation of the meaning of political democracy, which makes our meeting possible.

(The opening remarks of Dr. Dewey were translated into Spanish by Mr. Carleton Beals.)

DEWEY: At the opening of this first session, I will read the introductory statement of the Commission.

(Dr. Dewey reads the opening statement for the Commission of Inquiry.)

This Preliminary Commission to inquire into the charges made against Leon Trotsky in the Moscow trials of August, 1936, and January, 1937, is here in Mexico neither as court nor as jury. We are here neither to defend nor to prosecute Leon Trotsky. We are not here to pronounce a verdict either of guilt or innocence. We are here as an investigating body. Our function is to hear whatever testimony Mr. Trotsky may present to us, to cross-examine him, and to give the results of our investigation to the full Commission of which we are a part, so that the results obtained here, in connection with those secured by other investigating bodies, may bring to light the objective facts upon which judgment in the case of Leon Trotsky must rest. Our sole function is to ascertain the truth as far as is humanly possible.

The Commission of Inquiry was initiated by the American Committee for the Defense of Leon Trotsky. Lest these two bodies be confused in the public mind, I think it proper here to define their separate functions.

In the United States, it has long been customary for public-spirited citizens to organize committees for the purpose of securing fair trials in cases where there was suspicion concerning the impartiality of the courts. Such committees are traditionally known as "defense committees," and include in their title the name of the defendant. I cite just two instances in this connection: The Tom Mooney Defense Committee and the Sacco-Vanzetti Defense Committee, with which many members of the American Committee for the Defense of Leon Trotsky cooperated. Membership on such committees does not, of course, imply anything more than the belief that the accused is entitled to a fair trial.

The present case differs from those I have cited in one important point. In this case there exists no legally constituted court before which the accused may plead his case. Twice, in their absence, both Leon Trotsky and his son, Leon Sedov, whose guilt or innocence hangs upon that of his father, have been declared guilty by the highest tribunal of the Soviet Union. And Trotsky's repeated demands that the Soviet Government ask for his extradition, which would automatically have brought him before either a Norwegian or a Mexican court, have been ignored. Therefore, it became part of the function of his defense committee to initiate the formation of an impartial body before which his side of the case could be heard.

The simple fact that we are here is evidence that the conscience of the world is not as yet satisfied on this historic issue. This world-conscience demands that Mr. Trotsky be not finally condemned before he has had full opportunity to present whatever evidence is in his possession in reply to the verdict pronounced upon him in hearings at which he was neither present nor represented. The right to a hearing before condemnation is such an elementary right in every civilized country that it would be absurd for us to reassert it were it not for the efforts which have been made to prevent Mr. Trotsky from being heard, and the efforts that now are being made to discredit the work of this Commission of Inquiry.

The impartiality of any investigating body can be judged by one test, and one test only: the way in which it conducts its affairs. From this test, the Commission of Inquiry neither can nor wishes to be exempt. However, until this test has been applied, we appeal to every fair-minded person to support the Commission in its effort to afford Mr. Trotsky the chance to be heard. We appeal particularly to the press, which bears the heavy responsibility of serving as intermediary between these hearings and the public, to safeguard our task by living up to its own highest tradition of scrupulous objectivity.

The facts from which any inquiry must start are found in the official records published by the Government of the U.S.S.R. According to these records, Leon Trotsky was charged with a series of counter-revolutionary crimes committed over a number of years. He was charged with instigating acts of individual terrorism having for their purpose the assassination of the leaders of the Communist Party and the Government of the Soviet Union; of organizing and giving direction to numerous attempts at industrial sabotage and "diversion"; of wreckage of factories and trains, resulting in great loss of life; of initiating and promoting espionage in the U.S.S.R. by agents of imperialistic nations; of entering into conspiracy with the "Gestapo" in Germany and, through his agents, with Japanese intelligence officers; of conspiring with official representatives of Nazi Germany and of Japan to assist, in every possible way, those nations to bring about and win a war in which they might engage against the U.S.S.R., these measures including the hindering of mobilization and the provision of necessary military supplies, the wrecking of troop trains, etc. Finally, he was charged with making an agreement with Germany and Japan to cede territories of the U.S.S.R. to those countries after their victory in the projected war; with arranging to grant special trade privileges to Germany, along with concessions of mines, forests, etc. It was charged that the object of these counter-revolutionary criminal acts was to restore capitalism in the U.S.S.R. and to bring to political power in that country the leaders of opposition factions, including Trotsky himself.

If Leon Trotsky is guilty of the acts with which he is charged, no condemnation can be too severe. The extreme seriousness of these charges is, however, an added reason for securing to the accused the full right to present whatever evidence is in his possession, in rebuttal of them. The fact that Mr. Trotsky has personally denied these charges is not of itself a matter of concern to the Commission. That he has been condemned without the opportunity to be heard is a matter of utmost concern to the Commission and to the conscience of the whole world.

The scope and content of the inquiry to be undertaken are determined by that part of the testimony given in the Moscow trials upon which Trotsky was condemned. With this testimony, so far as it bears upon the guilt or innocence of those who were present and had a hearing, we are not concerned. We are concerned with discovering the truth or falsity of the testimony given in so far as it implicated Mr. Trotsky. This testimony was, according to Mr. Vyshinsky, the prosecutor, of two kinds: "First, there is the historical connection which confirms the theses of the indictment on the basis of the Trotskyites' past activity. We have also in mind the testimony of the accused which in itself represents enormous importance as proof."

In accord with this definite statement of the prosecution, the Commission is compelled both to carry on its inquiry into the past activity of Mr. Trotsky and his faction, and to receive testimony, here and elsewhere, upon the factual material brought forward by witnesses and by the accused in the Moscow trials.

The Commission has no illusions concerning the extraordinarily difficult nature of its task. It is aware that much important evidence is inaccessible because of the impossibility of extending its inquiries to Nazi Germany and the Soviet Union as it will extend them to other European countries. It is aware that a long, tortuous course of events is involved, every stage of which is beset by bitter controversy. But even were the difficulties more serious than they are, we should find ourselves unwilling and unable to take the defeatist position of those who proclaim in advance that any attempt to ascertain the facts upon which judgment must finally rest is doomed to failure.

Speaking, finally, not for the Commission, but for myself, I had hoped that a chairman might be found for these preliminary investigations whose experience better fitted him for the difficult and delicate task to be performed. But I have given my life to the work of education, which I have conceived to be that of public enlightenment in the interests of society. If I finally accepted the responsible post I now occupy, it was because I realized that to act otherwise would be to be false to my lifework.

I will now ask Mr. Trotsky if he wishes to state anything before the commencement of the hearing.

TROTSKY: Esteemed Commissioners: Permit me to express my profound respect and my no less profound gratitude to you, as well as to your colleagues who remain in New York or who carry on their work in various cities of Europe. I am entirely aware that the members of the Commission are guided in their work by motives incomparably more important and more profound than an interest in the fate of a single person. But all the greater is my respect, and all the more sincere my gratitude!

I cannot but note here that only the magnanimous hospitality accorded to me in extremely difficult conditions by the Mexican Government, headed by President Cardenas, now makes it possible for me to appear freely and openly before you.

The composition of the Commission and the high authority of its chairman exclude the possibility of any apprehension that the work of the Commission might signify even indirectly an intervention in the internal life of this country or cause the slightest damage to its interests. I beg you to believe, Mr. President and ladies and gentlemen of the Commission, that on my part there cannot be and will not be the slightest pretext for apprehension of this sort. The obligation that I take upon myself before the Mexican Government is absolutely unshakable. I must note gratefully that the Mexican press, like the majority of the local representatives of the foreign press, has shown a complete understanding of the difficulties which produce for me the necessity, on the one hand, to struggle with all my energy against all the accusations which are familiar to you, and, on the other hand, to avoid any steps which might be unwelcome to the public opinion of this country. I express a sincere gratitude to the representatives of the press for their loyal and sincere regard for the peculiarities of my situation. Certain unfortunate exceptions need not be dwelt upon. Public opinion will judge them as they deserve.

I beg your indulgence for my English which—I must say in advance—is the weakest point of my position. For everything else I do not ask the slightest indulgence. I do not demand any *a priori* confidence in my affirmations. The task of this Commission of investigation is to verify everything from the beginning to the end. My duty is simply to help it in its work. I will try to accomplish this duty faithfully before the eyes of the whole world.

DEWEY: In accordance with the usual American custom, I will ask the lawyer, Mr. Goldman, for the defense of Mr. Trotsky, to state, before the direct examination of Mr. Trotsky begins, the points—the defense he expects to prove.

GOLDMAN: Ladies and Gentlemen of the Commission: What is it that Leon Trotsky and those of us associated with him in defending his honor and the honor of the revolutionary Marxist movement throughout the world aim to do before this sub-commission and through this sub-commission before the whole Commission which is yet to hear the case, and before the whole world?

We intend to prove that Leon Trotsky is absolutely innocent of the charges made against him by the Stalinist Central Executive Committee of the Soviet Union. We shall willingly assume a greater burden than we need to assume. For all that is required of us is to raise a reasonable doubt in the minds of men, and then we would be justified in asking for a verdict of not guilty.

But we are not satisfied merely to raise a reasonable doubt. That we can do on the basis of the prosecution's own evidence. We are determined to convince the members of this Commission, and everyone who reads and thinks with a free and independent mind, beyond all doubt that Leon Trotsky and his son are guiltless of the monstrous charges made against them.

What are the charges made against Trotsky and his son?

Since the time of the Kirov assassination, December 1, 1934, there have been seven trials in the Soviet Union, either directly connected with the assassination or directed against the Trotskyites in general. In all of the trials Leon Trotsky played the part of the principal defendant, if not directly, then indirectly. It is, however, in the last two trials, one held in August, 1936, and the last one in January, 1937, that direct and positive allegations were made in the indictments charging both Leon Trotsky and his son, Sedov, with violating certain sections of the criminal code of the Soviet Union. On the basis of these charges and the evidence presented in the last two trials, Leon Trotsky and his son were, in their absence, found guilty and were ordered to be arrested immediately in the event of their being discovered on the territory of the U.S.S.R.

Taken together, the indictments of the last two trials contain the following principal accusations against Leon Trotsky and his son:

a) Preparation of terrorist acts against the leading figures of the U.S.S.R., in particular the organization of the assassination of Kirov;

b) organization of industrial sabotage, with the aim of weakening the national economy of the U.S.S.R.;

c) organization of alleged "diversions," that is, explosions, catastrophes, destruction on a huge scale, including the mass assassination of workers and soldiers, with the aim of undermining the military strength of the U.S.S.R.;

d) secret relations with German fascism and Japanese militarism, with the intention of precipitating war and preparing the defeat of the U.S.S.R. and its dismemberment, involving the surrender of territory to these two powers;

e) finally—as the crowning point of all this activity and its fundamental aim—to destroy socialist economy and to reestablish capitalism in the U.S.S.R.

In this opening statement, I shall refrain from analysis and argument. I accept the accusations as they are and declare: We intend to prove that the accusations levelled against Leon Trotsky and his son in the Soviet court are false from beginning to end. We shall show that in all of Leon Trotsky's activities there is not the slightest trace of acts, declarations, or even thoughts which might serve in the slightest degree as a support for the accusations brought against him. Leon Trotsky has indicated more than once in the press, and we shall contend here, that it is a question not of a judicial error but of a malevolent frame-up prepared over a series of years and costing many human lives.

Because the trials of Zinoviev, Kamenev, Smirnov, *et al,* held in August, 1936, and of Pyatakov, Radek, *et al,* held in January, 1937, received the greatest publicity; because the indictments and evidence produced at these trials directly implicated Leon Trotsky; because reports of these trials (the first a summary of the evidence, and the second a verbatim transcript) were published in English and other languages and we have them at our disposal—because of these factors, it seems to me to be advisable and necessary to consider that whatever case has been made out by the prosecution on behalf of the Soviet Government against Leon Trotsky is contained in the evidence produced at these two trials, and our evidence will therefore be limited to meet the testimony of the defendants and witnesses of the last two trials. Before the members of the sub-commission are the official reports of the last two trials, and we shall assume that the Commissioners will consider those reports as the evidence of the Soviet prosecution.

We do not intend to ignore the other trials. On the contrary, we shall show, through an analysis of these trials, that the real objective of the last two trials was not to convict criminals, but to discredit in the eyes of the Russian masses, and of the workers throughout the world, the chief representative of the only consistent revolutionary opposition to the ideas and practices of the Communist Party of the Soviet Union and the Communist International.

The two trials were completely and exclusively based on allegedly voluntary confessions of the defendants. In actuality, that means, as we hope to demonstrate during the course of this proceeding, that to the defendant's bench were led only persons who had agreed beforehand to give testimony that was expected of them.

All of the accused in the two trials, without exception, as well as the witnesses, mentioned Leon Trotsky's name in one way or another, with the purpose of attributing to him the leading role in some criminal acts. However, by far the greater part of the testimony we shall be unable to meet, because the kind of testimony which was produced in the Soviet court is not subject either to verification or refutation by us. No representative of the real defendant—that is, Leon Trotsky—was notified to be present and to cross-examine the defendants—that is, the witnesses against Leon Trotsky. The testimony of most of the defendants was of such a vague and general nature as to be absolutely valueless. The slightest cross-examination would have been sufficient to destroy the tissue of lies created by these witnesses.

That is why we shall be compelled, for the most part, to limit ourselves to the evidence of those accused who, according to their own words, either met Leon Trotsky personally or received criminal instructions from him, or claimed to be in criminal correspondence with him. As far as Sedov is concerned, we hope that another sub-commission will be able to take his testimony.

In the Zinoviev-Kamenev trials, it was claimed by the defendants Holtzman, Berman-Yurin and Fritz David that they visited Trotsky in Copenhagen at the end of November, 1932, and received from him instructions with reference to committing terroristic acts against leading figures in the Soviet Union. It was further claimed by Smirnov, Dreitzer and Olberg that they received similar instructions from Trotsky in writing.

Our evidence will show that Leon Trotsky never met and never heard of Berman-Yurin or Fritz David; that the said Berman-Yurin and Fritz David never met Leon Trotsky at Copenhagen or anywhere else, and that Trotsky never had any correspondence with them.

Holtzman, the most important of the three witnesses

who claimed to have visited Trotsky in Copenhagen, testified that he met Trotsky's son in the vestibule of the Hotel Bristol and that from there he was brought by Sedov to Trotsky's apartment.

We shall show by written and oral testimony that Trotsky's son, at the time in question, was not in Copenhagen but in Berlin, and that Trotsky and his wife, Natalia, were able to see their son only in France, on the train returning from Denmark. We shall prove that Sedov made several efforts to reach Copenhagen, but without any success.

We shall offer testimony to prove that Leon Trotsky was never in any correspondence whatsoever with Dreitzer, and that he knew him only slightly and lost sight of him in 1928. The alleged contents of the correspondence, as testified to by Dreitzer and Mrachkovsky, sufficiently prove that they are the products of the not too vivid imaginations of the gentlemen of the G.P.U.

The evidence will further show that Leon Trotsky did not give any instructions from Turkey to Smirnov, who only by chance met Sedov, Trotsky's son, in 1931 in a street in Berlin where Sedov was then studying in a polytechnical institute.

The evidence will show that Leon Trotsky never met Olberg; that he was in correspondence with him for a time and that such correspondence contained nothing whatsoever on questions of terror. The evidence will further show that Trotsky in April, 1930, was warned against Olberg as an individual not worthy of the slightest confidence and probably an agent of the G.P.U.

In the last trial (January, 1937) the whole accusation against Trotsky, according to Radek's words in his last plea, words that were not denied by the prosecution (and their truth is evident from the record itself), rests entirely on the testimony of the two principal defendants, Radek and Pyatakov. Radek was supposed to have corresponded with

Trotsky through the intermediation of a certain Vladimir Romm, a correspondent of the *Isvestia*. Pyatakov, according to his testimony, came to Oslo by airplane in December, 1935, and there saw Trotsky.

Leon Trotsky has already declared in the press, and we shall show here, that the testimony of Radek, Pyatakov, and Vladimir Romm is pure invention from beginning to end. The testimony will show that Trotsky has had no connection either direct or indirect with Radek since the time of his expulsion from the U.S.S.R., and that he has neither received from Radek nor written to him a single letter. The testimony will prove that Vladimir Romm never met Trotsky in Paris, and therefore could not have received any letters from him to be delivered to Radek.

Pyatakov testified that at the request of Sedov he gave Soviet governmental orders to German firms with the understanding that part of the profit should go to him, and that he gave the money to Trotsky for "counter-revolutionary" work. We shall introduce into evidence Trotsky's accounts since his deportation from Russia, and they will show how much money Trotsky has received from various sources and how he spent that money.

Such is the nature of the evidence which we shall produce in opposition to the testimony of the most important witnesses—or, rather, defendants—testifying to the fact that Leon Trotsky directed the plot against the leaders of the Soviet Union. It will be made absolutely clear that the refutation of the most important sections of the evidence given by the defendants in both trials must in the end compromise the whole system of voluntary confessions, and by that very fact deprive the Moscow trials in their entirety of the slightest credibility.

However, even if we did not have in our possession the evidence necessary to demonstrate a perfect alibi in all the most essential instances, we would be far from disarmed in facing the false accusations brought against Leon Trotsky. We have at our disposal a whole series of supplementary proofs of a documentary, historical and political character, which, taken together, have a persuasive power not at all inferior to that of the alibis mentioned above, and in the eyes of many have an incomparably greater value. I shall enumerate very briefly the type of proof to which I have reference:

According to the spirit and the letter of the indictment, the accused—Trotskyites and Zinovievites—had, with Trotsky's consent, capitulated in order to penetrate into the ranks of the party and there, under cover of a false loyalty, conducted their criminal work. Leon Trotsky will present to the Commission hundreds of letters, dozens of articles, to prove that he and his genuine partisans *treated the capitulations as treachery and the capitulators as traitors;* that even in centers of deportation and in prisons these two groups would have nothing to do with each other; that Zinoviev, Kamenev, Mrachkovsky, Pyatakov, Radek and others became his most bitter enemies during the last nine years, and systematically carried out venomous missions in the service of Stalin and the G.P.U. in order to discredit the opposition in general and Trotsky in particular.

The indictment presents *Radek* and *Pyatakov* as people in whom Trotsky had the greatest confidence, whom he placed at the head of the special "purely Trotskyite," "parallel center," and to whom he had confided designs and plans which he kept hidden even from the members of the "unified center" (Zinoviev, Kamenev, Smirnov, etc.). Trotsky will place before the Commission dozens of articles, documents, and private letters, in which it is indubitably revealed that he regarded Radek and Pyatakov as the most demoralized representatives of the capitulators, and that he systematically expressed sentiments of hostility and contempt for them.

The accusation of *individual terror,* as will be shown on the basis of Trotsky's numerous articles, beginning in 1902, is in direct contradiction with the whole bent of his thought, with his political education, with the lessons of his revolutionary experience, and, finally, with the entire tradition of Russian Marxism. The citations given by Prosecutor Vyshinsky from the Russian *Bulletin of the Opposition,* edited by Trotsky, as proof of his "terrorist" propaganda represent, as can be seen from the relevant numbers of the *Bulletin,* a gross distortion.

We shall submit to the Commission a no less abundant literature and correspondence pertaining to Trotsky's attitude toward the *defense* of the *U.S.S.R.* From these materials it will be clear that Trotsky has never for a moment wavered on the question of the necessity of defending the Soviet Union, and that he immediately and openly broke with old partisans and political friends the moment they took a negative or even only an ambiguous position on the defense of the U.S.S.R. against imperialism.

We shall present to the Commission a collection of Trotsky's interviews and articles on *international questions,* for the whole period of his exile, as incontestable proof of the fact that Trotsky's main efforts in the domain of international politics were directed toward obtaining the recognition of the U.S.S.R. by the United States, toward *rapprochements* between the U.S.S.R. and France, toward the defense of China against Japan, toward the revelation of the war plans of German fascism and Japanese militarism.

From these interviews and articles, which appeared in the press throughout the world, it will be apparent that Trotsky considered, and that he considers at present, in the event of war, the military and social collapse of feudal-imperialist Japan as absolutely inevitable, and almost similarly inevitable a revolutionary upheaval in fascist Germany. The importance of this analysis for the understanding of Trotsky's real international "plans" needs no clarification.

On the basis of the Soviet press itself, we shall demonstrate that all the phenomena now alleged as special crimes of the Trotskyites, under the heading of "sabotage" and "diversions," actually represent the organized results of the absence of control and responsibility in the bureaucratic leadership of industry, and of the criminal lack of attention to the interests of the working masses on the part of the new aristocracy. We shall, on the other hand, demonstrate, on the basis of a series of Trotsky's articles, beginning in March, 1930, that he untiringly revealed these same diseases and cancers which only several years later received the name of "sabotage."

In connection with this, we deem it relevant to remind the Commission that Trotsky's younger son, Sergei Sedov, a twenty-eight-year-old engineer, who for several years has been engaged in pedagogical and technical work, has been arrested, in relation to the last trial, under the accusation of preparing a *premeditated mass poisoning of workers.* We shall place before the Commission the photograph of this "poisoner," because we think that it is a moral document not without importance as evidence against an accusation which, moreover, is destroyed by its own monstrosity.

On the basis of official Soviet documents and the commentaries of the Soviet press, we shall demonstrate that the false and venomous accusations against the Opposition have become a system, beginning with 1923, have assumed a more and more ruthless character since 1926, and have led to ferocious repressions; and the constant attempts of the bureaucracy in all this to impute "terrorist" and "defeatist" tendencies to the Opposition preceded by some years the Kirov assassination and the trials which followed it.

On the basis of the literature of the Opposition, particularly Trotsky's own articles and letters, we shall prove that the Oppositionists, through a series of facts and symptoms, had *foreseen* each new step of the bureaucratic repressions, and, beginning in 1927, had tirelessly warned public opinion that Stalin, in the struggle for the privileges of the new aristocracy and for his unlimited power, would be forced, like all Bonapartist autocrats, to crush the Opposition with more and more monstrous police frame-ups. And we shall show from an article written by Trotsky in the *Bulletin of the Opposition* on March 4, 1929, that Trotsky predicted that Stalin would proceed inevitably to future "terrorist" trials. *Six* years later, on January 26, 1935, Trotsky wrote in the same *Bulletin* that Stalin would not stop at the first Zinoviev-Kamenev trial (based on the accusation of "moral responsibility" for the assassination of Kirov), but would prepare a new, more vicious amalgam. After the execution of Zinoviev-Kamenev, Trotsky wrote on September 15, 1936, from his internment in Norway, to his lawyer Puntervold, that Stalin would not be satisfied with his incarceration only and that, with the aim of ulterior pressure on the Norwegian Government, he would prepare a new trial, this time transporting the base of the plot to Oslo. Pyatakov's fantastic flight was the exact confirmation of this prediction.

It is necessary and relevant to draw the attention of the Commission to the fact that on the night of November 7, 1936, a part of Trotsky's archives which were being kept by the Parisian section of the Institute of Social History was stolen by the agents of the G.P.U. in Paris. The deposition of Trotsky's son on this subject, as well as Trotsky's deposition to the French judicial authorities, we shall turn over to the Commission. The small part of Trotsky's correspondence stolen from the Institute, like all his archives, is valuable, not to confirm but to refute the accusations brought against him. That is why there can be no question of a public utilization of the stolen documents. But, having in their hands certain letters of the period of 1934–35, the organizers of the "German" amalgam, can, as far as conditions of time and place are concerned, avoid the most scandalous blunders, of which the preceding trials are full. To warn the Commission of this in advance and, through it, public opinion, is, to a certain extent, to paralyze the action of the new frame-up now in preparation.

Such is the nature of the proof which we shall lay before the Commission. We contend that it is only by an analysis of all factors, by a study of all the evidence, from the false testimony of those who claimed to converse or correspond with Leon Trotsky to an investigation of the nature of the Stalin régime, that one can really understand the character and the essence of the Moscow trials from the juridical, moral, political and historical points of view. We shall attempt, and I believe successfully, to unmask the nature of these judicial frame-ups, before world public opinion. The structure of falsehoods shamelessly erected in the Moscow trials will crumble before our attack with the weapons of truth.

DEWEY: I will state that the proceedings will go on as question and answer on direct examination. That will be conducted by Mr. Goldman. The cross-examination will be by members of the Commission and especially by Mr. Finerty as soon as he reaches here, which we hope will be very shortly.

We will adjourn now for a five-minute recess.

DEWEY: As I was saying just before the recess, the investigation will proceed by question and answer, beginning with direct examination of Mr. Trotsky by his lawyer, and then cross-examination by the Commission and by our lawyer, Mr. Finerty, as soon as he reaches here. Because of the complexity of the problems and issues involved, I wish to ask Mr. Goldman to conduct his direct examination by sections, so that the cross-examination may come after each section and not be postponed until the whole direct examination has been had. On this account, I wish to ask Mr. Goldman if he will provide the Commission in writing with a statement of the various matters which he intends to go into, putting them in the order in which he proposes to take them up, so that the Commission may, as far as possible, prepare itself in advance to cross-examine upon each section. There is only one further remark I wish to make before Mr. Trotsky takes the stand. I hope that Mr. Goldman will cooperate as far as possible with the Commission and save it from embarrassment by excluding all political material which does not have a direct and close relationship with the charges made against Mr. Trotsky. I think it is generally understood that we are not here to consider in any way the political issues involved in the struggle between the present-day Government and leaders of the Party in Russia and the Opposition element. Some of this material is, obviously, very directly related to the charges brought against Mr. Trotsky, but the Commission wishes it understood that, as far as possible, it will draw a line strictly between the political issues and the charges made against Mr. Trotsky.

GOLDMAN: I shall prepare a statement of the one or more sections which I will deal with from day to day. I shall give that statement to the Commission. As for asking questions on political matters not involved in this particular issue, I shall try my best to limit myself. Here I want to state that I have had some experience in political trials in the United States, and it is always difficult to say exactly where the political question ceases to be germane and becomes irrelevant. However, when I ask questions on matters which the Commission deems irrelevant, then I shall desist if asked to do so by the Commission, and proceed to other points.

WITNESS: LEON TROTSKY
DIRECT EXAMINATION
BY MR. GOLDMAN

GOLDMAN: Now, for the sake of the record, will you state your name, where you live, and your occupation?

TROTSKY: The name of my father was Bronstein. My name, my political name, has been my genuine name since 1902. It is Trotsky.

GOLDMAN: Your first name; what is your first name?

TROTSKY: Excuse me. Leon. I will explain also the fact that the name of my wife is Sedov and that is the reason the name of our sons is Sedov.

GOLDMAN: Where do you live, Mr. Trotsky; where do you live now? Let me make this statement to the Commission. Mr. Trotsky finds himself unable to express his thoughts quickly in English. I suggest that he speak German whenever he finds himself in difficulties. One of the Commissioners, I understand, knows German very well. The answers can be translated into English.

TROTSKY: I live here in Coyoacan in this house.

GOLDMAN: It is only for the purpose of the record, Mr. Trotsky. I assume that you know where you live. (Laughter) Everybody else does. I must also ask you what your occupation is at the present time.

TROTSKY: Author.

GOLDMAN: Would you kindly tell us who lives with you in this house at Coyoacan, Mexico?

TROTSKY: My wife, my collaborators—my secretaries.

GOLDMAN: How many secretaries have you?

TROTSKY: Three—or four. My Russian secretary does not live in this house.

GOLDMAN: How many years, approximately, have you been connected with the revolutionary Marxist movement?

TROTSKY: Exactly forty years.

GOLDMAN: Would you tell us exactly when it began?

TROTSKY: It began in 1887, in March, in Nikolaiev, where I organized the first illegal workers' organization in this town, called the "South Russian Workers' Union." It was 1897, I should have said.

GOLDMAN: I think in my opening statement I made reference to the beginning of your revolutionary career as 1902, and I was mistaken.

TROTSKY: It was the beginning of my fight against the terrorists. You mentioned the date of 1902. That was the date of publication in London of my first article against the terrorists. Because the question of terrorism became very important in the Russian revolutionary movement.

GOLDMAN: The record will show that I made a mistake in my opening speech in so far as I said that Trotsky's revolutionary activities commenced with 1902. Now, will you kindly give us a résumé of the main events of your political biography?

TROTSKY: After the creation of the illegal organization of workers in Nikolaiev, I was arrested. I remained two and a half years in prison, was deported to Siberia for four years, participated in Siberia in the creation of an illegal workers' organization of Siberia. I escaped from Siberia after two years' sojourn. At that time I gave myself the name "Trotsky," on a passport which I wrote myself. I went to London and I adhered to the organization of *Iskra,* directed at that time by Plekhanov and Lenin. I remained—it was my first exile—two and a half years. At this time I devoted myself to the revolutionary activity on the Marxist paper, the *Iskra,* and to agitation amongst the Russian émigrés, and studies of Europe. The most important topic of our discussions and struggles was the question of terrorism, individual terrorism, at this time from 1902 until 1905, the first revolution.

GOLDMAN: What did you do in 1905?

TROTSKY: At the beginning of 1905 I went illegally to Russia. I was busy for a year with revolutionary activity. At the end of a year, I became a member of the first Soviet in Petrograd, then a member of the Executive Committee, and, at the end, the chairman of the first Petrograd Soviet, in 1905.

GOLDMAN: How old were you at that time?

TROTSKY: Twenty-and-six. My revolutionary activity began in my eighteenth year.

GOLDMAN: What role did you play in the 1905 revolution, Mr. Trotsky?

TROTSKY: I was chairman of the—after the arrest of the first chairman, I was chairman of the Petrograd Soviet, editor of two papers, one a popular paper and the other one a theoretical paper. I played an active role. I was arrested with the Soviet, all of the Soviet together, and remained in prison one and a half years. I was condemned to deportation, perpetual deportation to Siberia. But I remained in Siberia only eight days. I escaped to Austria. I published during seven years in Austria a paper for the Russian workers called *Pravda,* "The Truth."

GOLDMAN: In Austria?

TROTSKY: In Austria. It was illegally introduced into Russia. I participated, also, in the workers' movement of Austria. At the beginning of the war—

GOLDMAN: The World War?

TROTSKY: The World War of 1914. I then left Austria for Switzerland. I participated in the workers' movement in Switzerland.

GOLDMAN: Were you expelled from Austria?

TROTSKY: As a Russian. All the Russians were notified by the police that they must leave the country or be put into a concentration camp.

GOLDMAN: You left Austria?

TROTSKY: For Switzerland. I began a campaign against chauvinism which invaded the Second International at that time. I wrote a book, "The War and the International," in Switzerland, which is translated in English and was published in the United States. Then I left Switzerland for France.

GOLDMAN: When was that?

TROTSKY: It was at the end of 1914, the first year of the

war. I believe it was October, 1914. In France I began publishing, with other friends, a Russian daily paper which remained under the surveillance of the military censorship for two and a half years.

GOLDMAN: So you were in France two and a half years during the war?

TROTSKY: Yes, during the war, and all the time I was devoted to the fight against the war. It seems now incredible, but at the beginning, the first years of the war, the democracy preserved and retained some rights in France. They expelled me from France only at the end of 1916.

GOLDMAN: Where were you expelled to, what country?

TROTSKY: To Spain. I was arrested by the police of His Majesty, Alphonso XIII, for a week's sojourn in the Carcel Modelo in Madrid. I remained under police surveillance for a month, and then was deported to the United States.

GOLDMAN: Approximately when was that, Mr. Trotsky?

TROTSKY: That was in January, 1917.

GOLDMAN: When did you reach the United States?

TROTSKY: It was in January; we met the New Year on the sea.

GOLDMAN: You arrived in the United States January, 1917?

TROTSKY: Yes.

GOLDMAN: How long were you in the United States, and what were your activities there?

TROTSKY: I continued the same activity—that is, the fight against war and chauvinism. I published—I participated in the publishing of—a Russian daily paper and also in the activity of the American Socialist Party. I had conflicts with Hillquit and with Algernon Lee, publishing the discussions, half in Russian, half in German, and in English.

GOLDMAN: Can you tell us something of the story to the

effect that you were a tailor in New York?

TROTSKY: Tailor?

GOLDMAN: Yes, there are some stories—

TROTSKY: Unfortunately, I did not learn any productive trade in my life. I regret that very much. (Laughter)

GOLDMAN: And when did you leave New York?

TROTSKY: After the first cable coming from Petrograd about the revolution. We began to take steps to get back to Russia—the revolutionary émigrés. That was in the beginning of March. But the British authorities arrested me on the way.

GOLDMAN: Where?

TROTSKY: It was near Halifax. They put me in a concentration camp as an alleged agent of Germany.

GOLDMAN: So this is not the first time you are an alleged agent of Germany?

TROTSKY: No, it is the second time.

GOLDMAN: Who got you out of the concentration camp in Canada?

TROTSKY: I remained in the concentration camp a month with German sailors—very good fellows—and we became very friendly on the basis of the agitation of Karl Liebknecht. I had full freedom in the camp of concentration to explain to the sailors my opinion about the war. Then the Soviet of Petrograd insisted on my release.

GOLDMAN: The Petrograd Soviet did not believe anything about your being a German agent?

TROTSKY: I think that the British Government did not believe it themselves, because a declaration made by the ambassador at the time tried to shift the responsibility upon the old Tsarist Okhrana, the Tsarist intelligence service, whose agent made such representations before the British authorities.

GOLDMAN: I want to go back a minute, Mr. Trotsky. What was the role played by the Tsarist police at the time you were expelled from France, if they played any role at all?

TROTSKY: Yes, they played an important role. They insisted through the French deputies—the embassy insisted—upon my expulsion before Briand, the prime minister; but he rejected this. I repeat, a certain measure of rights and democracy remained intact during the first years of the war. Then the Tsarist Okhrana made use of an incident in Toulon. There were Russian soldiers in Toulon. In the atmosphere of a freer country, they protested against their colonel, and the protest ended in the assassination of the colonel. I had nothing to do with the matter. But through the agent of the Okhrana—I believe his name was Vining—it was discovered that my paper was among the soldiers. An *agent provocateur* put my daily paper into the pockets of many soldiers. The police discovered that. It was an important story in the political life of France at the time. Nevertheless, I was expelled from France.

GOLDMAN: Did they accuse you of inciting the soldiers to murder?

TROTSKY: Officially, there was no accusation. The prefecture of police notified me—they explained to me that it was impossible for them to give me further hospitality because they were in friendly alliance with the Russian Government. I immediately left the country.

GOLDMAN: Now to go back to the time you were in the concentration camp. When did you leave the concentration camp in Canada?

TROTSKY: It was the second half of March or the first half of April, 1917.

GOLDMAN: Do you remember any statement that Lenin made at that time in reply to the charge that you were a German agent?

TROTSKY: Yes, I believe I have it here.

DEWEY: Will his relations with Lenin be gone into later?

GOLDMAN: I am asking certain questions that I deem important, and the Commissioners in the cross-examination can enter into any question that I have left out which they deem important.

TROTSKY: I believe it is—

GOLDMAN: Well, we need not spend time looking for the document.

TROTSKY: Excuse me, this is the document. I can read it if you wish.

GOLDMAN: It is dated April 16. Reading the quotation from the article written by Lenin with reference to the arrest of Leon Trotsky as an alleged German agent, on April 16, 1917. This is the beginning of the sentence, and refers to the time when he was in the concentration camp:

> Can one even for a moment believe the trustworthiness of the statement that Trotsky, the chairman of the Soviet of Workers' Delegates in St. Petersburg in 1905—a revolutionary who has sacrificed years to disinterested service of revolution—that this man has anything to do with a scheme subsidized by the German government? This is a patent, unheard-of, and malicious slander of a revolutionary. From whom did you get your information, Mr. Buchanan? Why don't you disclose that? Six men dragged Comrade Trotsky away by his legs and arms, all in the name of friendship for the Provisional Russian Government!

This is cited from *Pravda,* No. 34.

TROTSKY: Permit me the remark that it was in 1917. It was before the October Revolution; it was before the Civil War in Russia; and it was before my activity, together with Lenin, in the building of the Soviet state. At that time, Lenin stated to the Central Committee, on November 14, 1917, the following:

> As for a coalition, I cannot even speak about that seriously. Trotsky long ago said that a union is impossible.

Trotsky understood this, and from that time on there has been no better Bolshevik.

GOLDMAN: I will introduce a photostatic copy of the minutes of the Central Committee at which Lenin made this statement as Exhibit No. 1.

(Said document was introduced as Exhibit No. 1.)

GOLDMAN: Now, when did you arrive in Russia, Mr. Trotsky?

TROTSKY: It was the fifth of May, 1917.

GOLDMAN: Will you briefly describe the nature of your activities, the relationship with Lenin and the Communist Party between the time of your arrival and the October insurrection?

TROTSKY: I was working together with the Bolshevik Party. There was a group in Petrograd which was the same, programmatically, as the Bolshevik Party, but organizationally independent. I consulted Lenin about whether it would be good that I enter the Bolshevik Party immediately, or whether it would be better that I enter with this good workers' organization which had three or four revolutionary workers.

GOLDMAN: Three or four?

TROTSKY: Three or four thousand revolutionary workers. We agreed that it would be better to prepare for a merger of the two organizations at the Communist Party Congress. Formally, I remained in that organization and not in the Bolshevik Party, until August, 1917. But the activity was absolutely identical. This was done only to prepare for the merger on a larger scale.

GOLDMAN: What was the name of this organization to which you belonged?

TROTSKY: The name was a very long one. It was composed of workers' organizations in different parts of the city—*rayons*.

STOLBERG: That means "interborough."

GOLDMAN: This *rayon* is a section of the city?

TROTSKY: Yes.

GOLDMAN: It might be better to call it "interborough" as Commissioner Stolberg suggested.

TROTSKY: Politically we were internationalists.

DEWEY: Mr. Goldman, his relations with Lenin have been gone into. I want to know if later there is to be documentary evidence in support of his present statement.

GOLDMAN: Did you hear the question, Mr. Trotsky? Will you have documentary evidence supporting your statement about your relationship with Lenin in the various years?

TROTSKY: Yes, absolutely.

GOLDMAN: Then, we shall introduce this documentary evidence upon the completion of the cross-examination.

TROTSKY: The most important evidence is the works of Lenin and my works, which are published.

GOLDMAN: We shall furnish the Commission with a bibliography. Now, will you tell us what were your activities during that time, beginning with May, 1917? What were your official positions?

TROTSKY: The first thing, after two months or three months of activity, revolutionary activity, under the Bolshevik banner, I was arrested by the democratic Kerensky Government.

GOLDMAN: When was that?

TROTSKY: It was in July, in the middle of July.

GOLDMAN: What happened to Lenin at that time?

TROTSKY: He was obliged to hide in Finland. The accusation against him was the same as against me. The accusation was a plagiarism, taken from the accusation of the British authorities, to the effect that we were, Lenin and myself, agents of Germany.

GOLDMAN: You and Lenin were accused of that?

TROTSKY: Yes, and Zinoviev, Kamenev and Lunacharsky. If Stalin was not accused, it was only because nobody knew his name at that time.

GOLDMAN: When were you released from prison?

TROTSKY: In August, or about the beginning of September.

GOLDMAN: What was the occasion of your release?

TROTSKY: The occasion of my release was the upheaval, the insurrection of Kornilov against Kerensky. "The Bolshevik agents of Germany"—they became the best defenders of the revolution. From prison I went directly to the Winter Palace, and collaborated with the representatives of the Government who accused me of being an agent of Germany. I collaborated in the fight against Kornilov.

GOLDMAN: They accepted your service?

TROTSKY: Yes, with gratitude.

DEWEY: Mr. Goldman, the Commission thinks the previous remark with reference to Stalin, being purely a matter of Mr. Trotsky's interpretation, should be struck from the record.

TROTSKY: Excuse me. This was absolutely not directed against Stalin, but only to indicate that he could not have the same "honor" of his adversaries because he was not at that time sufficiently known politically. But he was a prominent member of the Bolshevik Party, and in that sense he merited the observations and accusations against us.

DEWEY: The point is, the reason Mr. Trotsky gave is a matter of his personal interpretation.

GOLDMAN: We will not quarrel with the Commission on these minor points. Now, after the Kornilov revolt, will you describe your activities and the activities of Lenin.

TROTSKY: Lenin remained in Finland in illegality, and then Petrograd, until the day of the insurrection. His great influence consisted in his letters to us, to the members of the Central Committee.

GOLDMAN: Were you a member of the Central Committee of the Communist Party?

TROTSKY: Yes.

GOLDMAN: When were you elected?

TROTSKY: At the merger Congress in August, 1917.

GOLDMAN: Now, go ahead.

TROTSKY: Permit me the remark: Lenin and myself, Zinoviev and Kamenev, had the same number of votes as members of the Central Committee.

GOLDMAN: How many were there?

TROTSKY: It was the total vote.

GOLDMAN: Unanimously?

TROTSKY: Unanimously. At the merger Congress, at the election of the Central Committee, four members received all the votes of the Congress. They were Lenin, Zinoviev, Kamenev, and myself—maybe with one or two votes' difference, or none at all.

GOLDMAN: Now, what were your activities after the Kornilov revolt?

TROTSKY: I became, in a short time, the chairman of the Petrograd Soviet. There was a great change in the mood of the workers.

GOLDMAN: Will you briefly tell us what were your activities during the insurrection?

STOLBERG: During the Kornilov insurrection?

GOLDMAN: I mean, during the October insurrection.

TROTSKY: If you will permit me, I will give you a short quotation from Stalin, who was an objective witness. In an article which he wrote a year after the insurrection, and he tried, I can say, to limit my role in the October Revolution, Stalin was nevertheless forced to write the following, which is a quotation from *Pravda,* the central organ of the Bolshevik Party:

> All the work of practical organization of the insurrection was conducted under the immediate leadership of

> the President of the Petrograd Soviet, Comrade Trotsky. It is possible to declare with certainty that the swift passing of the garrison to the side of the Soviet, and the bold execution of the work of the Military Revolutionary Committee, the Party owes principally and above all to Comrade Trotsky.

That is from *Pravda* of November 6, 1918.

GOLDMAN: It is a quotation from Stalin?

TROTSKY: Yes. Can you permit me another quotation from him, a very short one of six years later?

> Comrade Trotsky played no particular role either in the Party or the October insurrection, and could not do so, being a man comparatively new to our party in the October period.

That is six years later.

DEWEY: Where was that published?

TROTSKY: It is published in his book, "Trotskyism or Leninism," pages 68 and 69, of the Russian edition. I will submit it to the Commission.

DEWEY: That was in 1924?

TROTSKY: That was 1924.

GOLDMAN: Now, what official positions did you hold in the Soviet Government up to the time of your expulsion from the Communist Party?

TROTSKY: I remained for a certain time, after the seizure of power, President of the Petrograd Soviet, and secretary of the revolutionary military committee which directed the October insurrection. Then, I became People's Commissar of Foreign Affairs and then People's Commissar of War. I was busy with the organization of the Red Army, and for three years I passed my time in the military train. It was during the Civil War. After the Civil War I remained People's

Commissar of War and I was also busy with many economic questions, building up the state and state economy.

DEWEY: Will you ask him to give the date of this work?

GOLDMAN: Will you give us some dates with reference to your positions?

TROTSKY: Yes. I remained People's Commissar of War until 1925. I believe it was in May, 1925, that I was dismissed. After that—I forgot to say that all the time I remained a member of the Politburo. That is the most important position because the genuine ruling body is the Politburo.

GOLDMAN: Of the Communist Party?

TROTSKY: The Politburo of the Communist Party.

GOLDMAN: Who else were members of the Politburo of the Communist Party with you?

TROTSKY: On the Politburo at that time were Lenin, Zinoviev, Kamenev, Bukharin, Rykov, Stalin and myself.

GOLDMAN: What was the occasion of your removal as Commissar of War in 1925?

TROTSKY: It was the fight against me—the first Opposition fight with the majority of the Politburo. At that time Stalin was intimately connected with Zinoviev and Kamenev. They were called the "Troïka," or "Triumvirate." It was created especially against me. They had an illegal organization throughout the country, with codes for cables. Certain secretaries were involved. It was a blow, a genuine blow, against me, with the purpose of dismissing me from the Bureau.

GOLDMAN: Tell us what part you played in the formation and development of the Communist International.

TROTSKY: I played a direct and active role at all the first four Congresses. In the time of Lenin, the most important reports concerning the international situation and the tasks of the Communist International were shared between Lenin and myself. All the programmatic manifestoes of the four Congresses were written by me. Some important theses about the strategy of the Comintern were also written by us.

GOLDMAN: When were you exiled? First, when were you expelled from the Party?

TROTSKY: It was in October, 1928—I believe in October, 1928.

GOLDMAN: What was the reason for your expulsion?

TROTSKY: The reason was my fight against the new ruling caste, the new privileges and the uncontrolled power. That was the reason for the expulsion. It was the first *croquis* for this book. (Referring to the verbatim report of the trial of Radek-Pyatakov, *et al.*)

LAFOLLETTE: The first sketch, he means.

TROTSKY: If we put together all the accusations against the Opposition, you will see that the indictment is only the sum total of the accusations beginning in 1924.

DEWEY: Mr. Goldman, would it not be better to go into that as a separate matter?

GOLDMAN: Yes.

DEWEY: He gave his reason for his expulsion. Will you ask him what reason the Party gave?

GOLDMAN: What were the reasons, what were the pretexts which the Party gave for your expulsion?

TROTSKY: Many of them. There was a story about an officer of Wrangel. We published programmatic documents; they were written on a typewriter.

GOLDMAN: Who is "we"?

TROTSKY: We? The Opposition. The Party papers refused to publish our documents, absolutely loyal documents in which we criticized certain proceedings of the bureaucracy. We published them by mimeograph. It was done by young comrades. I don't know where, who, or how. But they then accused us of publishing the documents with the help of an officer of Wrangel. [Wrangel was a White-Guard general—Ed.] I was absolutely astonished. It was then established that the officer of Wrangel was an agent of the G.P.U. for many years; that he approached a young Oppositionist and proposed to get him a mimeograph and ink and service. The young man accepted. It was then the G.P.U. declared that he was not an agent of the G.P.U., but an officer of Wrangel. Perhaps it was correct that before he became an agent of the G.P.U. he was an officer, for a time, in the army of General Wrangel.

GOLDMAN: Just briefly, will you tell us the struggle on the fundamental, theoretical questions between the Left Opposition and the Party majority—very briefly.

TROTSKY: We were fighting the party bureaucracy, the Soviet bureaucracy, and the trade-union bureaucracy. We were in favor of cutting the privileges of the ruling caste in favor of the masses. We were for an international policy as the basis of revolutionary Marxism as against the new national, conservative policy of the State.

GOLDMAN: After your expulsion from the Party, where did you live, in what city?

TROTSKY: For a few weeks in Moscow. Then I was deported to Central Asia, to Alma-Ata, near the Chinese border.

GOLDMAN: What activities did you carry on there, in Alma-Ata?

TROTSKY: I wrote two books; many letters, political letters, to the comrades. The books are published now in English by the Pioneer Publishers of New York. They are: "The Third International After Lenin" and "The Permanent Revolution."

GOLDMAN: You wrote these books while you were in Alma-Ata?

TROTSKY: In Alma-Ata, with the help of my wife and my son, who were my secretaries.

GOLDMAN: How did you get the manuscripts out of Russia? How did you distribute the manuscripts in Russia?

TROTSKY: It was not published in Russia. But the Sixth Congress of the Communist International took place in August, 1928. The representatives from different countries were interested in my criticism of the official program of the Comintern. They asked for the manuscript. The manuscript was delivered to them, and there was the possibility of its getting abroad, to the United States, for example.

GOLDMAN: You said you were expelled from the Party in October of 1928?

TROTSKY: No, 1927.

GOLDMAN: You want to correct yourself?

TROTSKY: Yes, 1928 I passed in Central Asia.

GOLDMAN: Where did you go from Alma-Ata?

TROTSKY: To Turkey.

GOLDMAN: How did it happen that you went to Turkey?

TROTSKY: An agent of the G.P.U. came to me in Alma-Ata and presented me with a summons to abandon all political activities, my writings, and so on. I declared: "Only treacherous bureaucrats can ask such things from a revolutionary, only renegades can act in such a way." Then he declared that he must wait for a decision. After a week or so, he told me that I would be sent abroad.

GOLDMAN: And did you go abroad voluntarily?

TROTSKY: No, I believe the circumstances show that it was not voluntary. In my autobiography, I explain all the circumstances. I present that to the Commission.

GOLDMAN: Who was with you at the time you were deported from Russia to Turkey?

TROTSKY: My wife, and our older son, Leon Sedov, who is now in Paris, France.

GOLDMAN: How long did you live in Turkey?

TROTSKY: Four and a half years.

DEWEY: Would he give the dates of arrival and leaving?

GOLDMAN: When did you arrive in Turkey?

TROTSKY: February, 1929.

GOLDMAN: Will you tell us the nature of your activities while you were there?

TROTSKY: I began to publish a Russian monthly, the *Bul-*

letin of the Opposition, which I submit to the Commission because it is the most genuine expression of my political opinions—the genuine and permanent expression of my political opinions during my last exile. Then, I wrote some books which are also published in English in the United States. They are the story of my life, an autobiography published by Scribner's; "The History of the Russian Revolution," published by Simon and Schuster; and many pamphlets which present a new and particular interest in view of the accusations. I published, at that time, "Germany, the Key to the International Situation," written in 1931; "What Next, the Problems of the German Proletariat," published in New York; "The Only Road," a pamphlet. All of them are devoted to the fight against German fascism, and they were published in New York. Then articles—"The Impending Danger of Fascism in Germany," January 9, 1932; "What Is Fascism," January 6, 1932; "I See War with Germany," July 13, 1932; "How Can Fascism be Smashed in Germany," February 20, 1933; "The Tragedy of the German Proletariat," April 8, 1933; "Hitler and the Red Army," April 8, 1933.

DEWEY: Mr. Goldman, we have been handed this list. Can we receive that as his testimony?

GOLDMAN: Then we will introduce it into evidence.

TROTSKY: Permit me only to emphasize the number of articles directed against fascism, without reading them.

GOLDMAN: Then, we will introduce into evidence the bibliography of articles and books written by Trotsky at various points in his career, with special emphasis that these works were written by him while in exile in Turkey.

(Said Bibliography was introduced into evidence and marked Exhibit No. 2.)

GOLDMAN: Did you ever leave Turkey while you were in exile there?

TROTSKY: One time.

GOLDMAN: When was that?

TROTSKY: That was in November, 1932. I left for Copenhagen.

GOLDMAN: Who were with you at the time you left?

TROTSKY: My wife and my collaborators, during the entire travel to Copenhagen.

GOLDMAN: Here I want to state before the Commission that at another point in the introduction of my evidence I shall go into great detail with reference to this trip. At the present time, I simply want to make clear for the record and to the Commission that I am not going into great detail because I intend at the proper time to go into very great detail on this matter. Is that acceptable?

DEWEY: That will be satisfactory.

GOLDMAN: When did you arrive in Copenhagen?

TROTSKY: We started the 14th of November, 1932, and we arrived in Copenhagen the 23rd of November, 1932.

GOLDMAN: How long did you stay in Copenhagen?

TROTSKY: Eight days.

GOLDMAN: What did you do there?

TROTSKY: I was invited by the Social-Democratic Students for the purpose of giving a lecture on the Russian Revolution.

GOLDMAN: And did you deliver any speeches there?

TROTSKY: Yes, I delivered a speech on the Russian Revolution, at a meeting. Then, I gave a radio message to the United States on the Russian Revolution.

GOLDMAN: Have you a copy of the speeches?

TROTSKY: Yes.

GOLDMAN: Later on we shall introduce copies of these two speeches before the Commission.

TROTSKY: Then, I also made a gramophone record speech for the Left Opposition.

LAFOLLETTE: A phonographic record?

TROTSKY: Yes. It was a speech concerning the methods

of the Left Opposition, especially for the propaganda of the Left Opposition.

GOLDMAN: You can furnish the Commission with a copy of that speech?

TROTSKY: Yes. I can give important quotations, but it is not necessary.

GOLDMAN: It is not necessary now.

TROTSKY: I also spoke for the actualities, the film actualities.

LAFOLLETTE: The news-reels.

GOLDMAN: When did you leave Copenhagen?

TROTSKY: It was the 2nd of December, 1932.

GOLDMAN: When did you return to Turkey?

TROTSKY: On the 12th, I returned to Turkey. Our trip lasted a month.

GOLDMAN: When was the next time you left Turkey?

TROTSKY: Excuse me a moment. I will find my material. I received a French visa on the 12th of July, 1933.

GOLDMAN: When did you leave?

TROTSKY: I left the 17th of July, 1933, from Istanbul [Constantinople] on the Italian ship "Bulgaria," and I arrived at Marseilles on the morning of the 24th of July.

GOLDMAN: How long did you reside in France?

TROTSKY: I resided in France two years—yes, two years.

GOLDMAN: When did you leave France?

TROTSKY: On June 13, 1935, for Norway. On the 18th of June, 1935, I came to Oslo.

GOLDMAN: Where did you reside while you were in France?

TROTSKY: The first two months or more I resided in Saint Palais. It is a small village near Royan.

GOLDMAN: For the purpose of the record, I want to state before the Commission that I shall go into great detail with reference to this question later on, when I am dealing with the testimony of Vladimir Romm, the testimony that he produced at the Moscow trial. Now I am just going into this in a general way.

DEWEY: The Commission will reserve its cross-examination on this matter until you bring up that special matter.

GOLDMAN: After Royan, where did you live?

TROTSKY: In Bagnères, in the Pyrenees.

GOLDMAN: How long did you reside there?

TROTSKY: Four weeks.

GOLDMAN: And after that?

TROTSKY: I received permission from the Government to live near the center of France. It was in the town of Barbizon, which was about two hours by train or car from Paris.

GOLDMAN: Were you ever in Paris?

TROTSKY: Yes, during my sojourn I visited Paris two or three times, but it was in the winter.

GOLDMAN: I think you said you resided in France up to July or June of 1935?

TROTSKY: I left France the 13th of June, 1935, for Oslo.

GOLDMAN: Briefly, will you describe your activities while you were in France?

TROTSKY: I continued the same activities. I published the Russian *Bulletin*. I wrote some books, I worked on the biography of Lenin, I published some pamphlets and many articles in the world press.

GOLDMAN: All these books and pamphlets are contained in the bibliography I handed the Commission before?

TROTSKY: Yes.

GOLDMAN: Describe the circumstances under which you lived in France.

TROTSKY: My situation in France became very acute after the fascist uprising of February 6, 1934—of de La Rocque. At that time the fascist press in Germany accused me of preparing a revolutionary insurrection in France. Goebbels published—I believe it was Rosenberg, who stated in an issue of the *Völkischer Beobachter*, the central organ of the fascist Party—or, rather, accused me of being behind the preparation of an insurrection in France. The reactionary press in France reproduced all the accusations by special telephonic communication from Germany. There was a very great campaign carried on, and all the papers were greatly involved. The so-called Communist paper attacked me with the same vigor, only with the difference that the Communist paper, *l'Humanité*, accused me of being an agent of the French Government and of preparing a military invasion of the Soviet Union.

GOLDMAN: Did the French Government ask you to leave?

TROTSKY: That question is a very difficult one, because there was a declaration that I must leave France. But the authorities explained that it was only a concession to the press campaign, the agitation of the press. After this declaration I remained in France for more than a year, but incognito.

GOLDMAN: Where were you during that time?

TROTSKY: First in the department of Seine-et-Marne, then in the department de l'Isère, near Grenoble.

GOLDMAN: How did it happen that you finally had to leave France?

TROTSKY: Flandin was head of the Government at that time. When I came, it was the Government of Daladier which gave me the authorization to come in, principally through the intervention of the Radical Deputy Guernut. Guernut was Minister of Education. The authorization was given on condition that I remain in Corsica. They were a bit afraid of the possibility of demonstrations by the fascists and the Stalinists in France. The idea of Corsica was given by myself.

GOLDMAN: Pardon me, Mr. Trotsky, we will go into that question in great detail later on.

LAFOLLETTE: Will the exact dates in the *Völkischer Beobachter* and *l'Humanité* be given?

GOLDMAN: You can ask this question under cross-examination.

Now tell us exactly the circumstances under which you left France in June of 1935.

TROTSKY: The political event was the new Government in Norway, the Government of the Workers' Party. That was the first time that the Workers' Party took power—or rather, took office—in Norway. The Norwegian Workers' Party had the reputation of being a radical party. It did not belong to the Second International. In the past, it belonged to the Third International. I asked my friends if it would be possible to get a visa through the Government of the Workers' Party. It was a very quiet country. I received a very positive answer. Then I made a formal request and received a visa, and we left for Norway.

GOLDMAN: When did you arrive in Norway?

TROTSKY: It was the 18th of June, 1935.

GOLDMAN: Is that when you left France or when you arrived?

TROTSKY: When we arrived. I left France on the 13th.

GOLDMAN: Where did you live while you were in Norway?

TROTSKY: We lived in the village of Weksal, near a small town called Hönefoss, a town of 4,000 inhabitants. It is two hours from Oslo by car or train.

GOLDMAN: Will you briefly tell us the nature of your activities while you remained near Oslo?

TROTSKY: I wrote the book, "The Revolution Betrayed," many articles and pamphlets. They are enumerated in the documents.

GOLDMAN: Referring to Exhibit No. 2 presented to the Commission.

TROTSKY: I had correspondence with my friends in all countries.

GOLDMAN: What was the occasion of your leaving Oslo, and

where did you go from Oslo, from this place near Oslo?

TROTSKY: The Norwegian Government arrested me at the end of August, 1936, after the Zinoviev-Kamenev trial. The pretext was that I developed political activity, and as a proof of my political activity is quoted in the official statement of the police my article in the American *Nation* on France—a proof of my criminal activity. But the genuine cause was the pressure from the Soviet Union.

BEALS: Will you present proof of that pressure?

GOLDMAN: You say that the pressure of the Soviet Union was the cause of your removal—

TROTSKY: Of my arrest, together with my wife.

GOLDMAN: In what way can you prove that? Have you documents? Or logical proof?

TROTSKY: I have some friends in Norway—and my lawyer. Norway is not a large country. It has only three million population. Everything is known immediately. I knew of the visits of Yakubovich, the Russian ambassador, to the Foreign Minister of Norway, and of the intervention of the shipowners.

GOLDMAN: Were these published in any press at the time? That is, these facts?

TROTSKY: These facts were published in articles by Helge Krog, a very brilliant young Norwegian author who took up my defense in a liberal paper. He was a member of the Workers' Party. He defended me, not in the Workers' press, but in a liberal press which appeared there.

GOLDMAN: Which press?

TROTSKY: The *Dagbladet*. It is a great liberal paper of Oslo. He explained the situation in that paper.

BEALS: The only point that I was raising—you had mentioned this arrest and this prosecution were the result of pressure from the Soviet Government.

TROTSKY: Yes, I made a long deposition before the Norwegian court as a witness in the case concerning the theft of a part of my archives. I gave testimony under oath as a witness. It was behind closed doors. All my testimony was written up, and I will present it to the Commission. It is official testimony, and I explained that by the threats of the Soviet press everything is prepared against me. It was absolutely clear during July, before the trial, the August trial. I declared to Deputy Knudsen, in whose house I stayed—the Minister of Foreign Affairs of Norway was at that time in Moscow—"In Moscow there is conversation about my head." He answered: "You believe"—he was a member of the Government—"You believe we are ready to sell your head?" "No," I answered him, "I believe the Moscow Government is ready to buy my head." That was in July, 1935. The pressure from the Moscow—

GOLDMAN: July, 1935?

TROTSKY: No, 1936. And then, the best proof is the so-called Communist paper. The Communist papers are not papers of the revolution or of the international workers' movement, but organs of Moscow diplomacy, and especially the G.P.U. The Comintern papers are the official papers of the G.P.U. I say that on the basis of my experiences of years.

GOLDMAN: Mr. Trotsky, permit me to interrupt you at this point. Before August, 1936, were you molested by the Norwegian Government?

TROTSKY: Not yet molested, but I had the impression and also the information from my friends that something was being prepared against me in the bureaus of the Government.

GOLDMAN: When was the first time you were arrested in Norway?

TROTSKY: I was arrested the 27th of August.

GOLDMAN: Was that before or after the Zinoviev trial?

TROTSKY: It was after the Zinoviev trial.

GOLDMAN: And the pretext was the article you wrote for *The Nation*?

TROTSKY: One of the pretexts. The pretext, or the point

of departure of the prosecution, was the night attack of the fascists on my home.

GOLDMAN: When was that?

TROTSKY: The fifth of August.

GOLDMAN: The fifth of August when the fascists attacked you in your home?

TROTSKY: Yes.

GOLDMAN: And before that were you arrested for anything at all?

TROTSKY: Never.

GOLDMAN: So that the first time you were arrested was in August, 1936, after the Zinoviev-Kamenev trial?

TROTSKY: Yes.

GOLDMAN: I submit to the Commission that you can cross-examine Mr. Trotsky after I get through. The question of whether or not the Soviet Union was behind the arrest is a question fundamentally of argument based upon logical deduction.

DEWEY: It is one o'clock and so I will consult the other members of the Commission with regard to adjournment. I will say that we will leave his testimony regarding the case of his arrest as coming from the Soviet Government in the record for the present, with the right to have it struck out later, unless some documentary evidence is presented. The Commission will resume its sittings at four o'clock in the afternoon.

End of The First Session—One o'clock P.M.

Second session

April 10, 1937, at four o'clock p.m.

DEWEY: The Commission will be in order. The first thing is that owing to the fact that Mr. Finerty, counsel of the Commission of Inquiry, has just arrived, there will be no meeting to-morrow. We thought of holding one, but there will be no meeting to-morrow, Sunday. The other announcement is that Mr. Herbert Solow will act as interpreter when Mr. Trotsky uses French or German expressions.

GOLDMAN: May I proceed then, Dr. Dewey?

DEWEY: Yes, if you will.

FINERTY: May I suggest before we proceed with the examination that all telegrams and letters to the various parties who were invited to participate in this inquiry, as well as all telegrams and letters of congratulation received by the Commission, be made a part of the record?

LAFOLLETTE: Shall we, Dr. Dewey?

DEWEY: Yes. It is understood for the purposes of a complete record, all telegrams and letters of invitation and replies will be entered in the record.

(The following telegrams were entered in the record.)

ZURICH. SCHWEIZ UEBERTRAEGT MANDAT NEW YORK. (SWITZERLAND GIVES MANDATE TO NEW YORK.)

PARIS. COMITÉ FRANÇAIS ENVOIE PLEINS POUVOIRS A COMITÉ AMERICAIN POUR MENER ENQUÊTE INTERNATIONALE ET ENVERRA DÉLÉGUÉ, NEW YORK. (FRENCH COMMITTEE GIVES FULL POWER TO AMERICAN COMMITTEE TO CONDUCT INTERNATIONAL INQUIRY AND WILL SEND DELEGATE TO NEW YORK.)

2 MATAMOROS, PUE 4 DE ABRIL DE 1937
JOHN DEWEY.
CASA DIEGO RIVERA
COYOACÁN D.F.

SU ATENTO MENSAJE NEW YORK YA GIRARONSE ÓRDENES PUEDEN CRUZAR FRONTERA MÉXICO SEÑORES REFIÉRESE.—ATENTAMENTE

PRESIDENTE REPÚBLICA
L. CARDENAS
12.32 EL 12 ABRIL

NOTA RETRANSMITIDO A COYOACÁN D.F., POR NO HABER SIDO ENTREGADO EN LAREDO, TEXAS.

PHILADELPHIA, PA.
PROFESSOR, JOHN DEWEY,
CARE MRS. GEORGE, AMBERES 65, MEXICO

CONGRATULATIONS ON YOUR EFFORTS TO SECURE FOR LEON TROTSKY THE RIGHT OF ASYLUM AND IMPARTIAL COMMISSION OF INQUIRY.

JOSEPH DAVIDSON, EXECUTIVE CHAIRMAN CHAPTER TEN, AMERICAN FEDERATION OF STATE, COUNTY, AND MUNICIPAL EMPLOYEES.

SAN FRANCISCO, CALIF.
JOHN DEWEY, AMBERES 65, MEXICO CITY

GREETINGS. THE COMMISSION IS AN HEROIC STEP FORWARD IN STRUGGLE FOR TRUTH AND FREEDOM.

CRARY TRIMBLE, STATE SECRETARY SOCIALIST PARTY OF CALIFORNIA

LOS ANGELES, CALIF.
PROF. JOHN DEWEY,
CARE MRS. GEORGE, AMBERES 65, MEXICO CITY

WE THE UNDERSIGNED MEMBERS OF ORGANIZED LABOR SALUTE YOUR UNBIASED EFFORTS TO ESTABLISH THE TRUE FACTS SURROUNDING THE CHARGES MADE AGAINST LEON TROTSKY BY THE SOVIET GOVERNMENT DURING THE LAST MOSCOW TRIAL. WE FEEL CONFIDENT THAT THOUSANDS OF AMERICAN WORKERS AWAIT WITH INTEREST YOUR FINDINGS. WE CONDEMN THE ORGANIZED CAMPAIGN AIMED TO DERAIL YOU FROM YOUR PURPOSE.

HENRY J. VINCENT, PATROLMAN SAILORS UNION OF THE PACIFIC, SAN PEDRO; JOE VOLTARO, DISPATCHER SEMP SAN PEDRO; ELMER BRUCE, DELEGATE I.L.A. 38-82, AND PRESIDENT DISTRICT COUNCIL NO. 4, MARITIME FEDERATION PACIFIC COAST.

MINNEAPOLIS, MINN.
PROF. JOHN DEWEY,
CARE MRS. GEORGE, AMBERES 65, MEXICO CITY

PROGRESSIVE TRADE UNIONISTS ARE UNANIMOUS IN THEIR APPROVAL OF YOUR COMMISSION'S SPLENDID ACTION IN CARRYING OUT WORKING CLASS JUSTICE BY GIVING LEON TROTSKY A FAIR AND IMPARTIAL HEARING ON THE CHARGES PLACED AGAINST HIM IN THE MOSCOW TRIALS. WE CONSIDER THE TASK OF YOUR COMMISSION VITAL TO THE FUTURE WELFARE OF THE WORLD WORKING CLASS AND PLEDGE ASSISTANCE IN EVERY POSSIBLE MANNER.

M.B. DUNNE, EDITOR NORTHWEST ORGANIZER; H.A. SCHULTZ, BUSINESS AGENT ELECTRICAL WORKERS UNION LOCAL NO.

292; FARRELL DOBBS, SEC. GENERAL DRIVERS UNION LOCAL 544; WILLIAM S. BROWN, PRES. LOCAL 544, MINNEAPOLIS, MINN.; JAMES BARTELL, PRESIDENT WAREHOUSE AND INSIDE WORKERS UNION LOCAL 20136; JOHN JANOSCOB, AGENT FURNITURE WORKERS 1859.

WITNESS: LEON TROTSKY DIRECT EXAMINATION (CONTINUED) BY MR. GOLDMAN

GOLDMAN: When did you leave the town near Oslo, where you first lived in Norway—do you remember, Mr. Trotsky?

TROTSKY: Yes: It was the 28th of August.

GOLDMAN: Of what year?

TROTSKY: Of 1936, after the Moscow trial. I was arrested.

GOLDMAN: You were taken from there by the police, were you?

TROTSKY: Yes. For a week I remained in my old home under the control of the police. Then they transported myself and my wife to a new house, a country house, and we remained there some months under the control of thirteen policemen.

GOLDMAN: What happened to your secretaries?

TROTSKY: My two secretaries, the Czech, Erwin Wolff, and the Frenchman, Van Heijenoort, were deported without any reason.

GOLDMAN: Describe the conditions in which you lived at the time you were interned. By the way, what is the name of the town where you were interned?

TROTSKY: It is not a town, it is a village. Norwegian villages do not exist genuinely. They are farms a certain distance one from another. It was the farm Sundby, and the district is Hurum.

GOLDMAN: Now, describe the conditions under which you lived.

TROTSKY: It was a prison in every respect. We could not leave the house and the courtyard. We could not correspond, and we could not have visitors. It was worse than the Tsarist prison because in the Tsarist prisons we had visits from friends and from my relatives. Here, I had no visits at all. All correspondence passed through the police. They, for example, held back, held up the manuscript of my book, "The Revolution Betrayed," for two months.

GOLDMAN: When did you leave Norway?

TROTSKY: The 19th of December, 1936.

GOLDMAN: And what were the conditions of your leaving Norway?

TROTSKY: My friends, especially in France, were very disquieted because the Norwegian Government declared that it was not inclined to continue the visa for another six months. The only possibility was an expulsion or arrest by the G.P.U. They began, my lawyer in France and my friends, they began to ask for a visa in various countries. On the 9th of December we received for the first time an answer that the Mexican Government generously agreed to give us a visa. But in the situation in which I found myself, it was—I was not very confident about this answer. I believe it was a subject of worry on the part of the Norwegian Government and the G.P.U. I demanded a meeting with my friends who were members of the Party of the Government—Knudsen and others—to consult with them, but the Government refused. I waited—I do not know until today by what means we received the visa from the Mexican Government. Then they put us, my wife and myself, on a cargo boat or tanker, and with that tanker brought us to Mexico, to Tampico.

GOLDMAN: When did you arrive in Mexico?

TROTSKY: It was, I believe, the ninth of January, 1937.

GOLDMAN: What have you been doing in Mexico since your arrival?

TROTSKY: I received a very friendly reception from the Mexican authorities. It was a totally striking thing after the last months in Norway. Until today, I can be only thankful to all the Mexican authorities with whom I had to meet and to do anything. I had no difficulties. I promised upon my arrival in the country not to intervene in any Mexican politics, and, in spite of some slanders in the Mexican press, I am absolutely faithful to my obligation.

GOLDMAN: Of what country are you a citizen, Mr. Trotsky?

TROTSKY: I am deprived of my citizenship in the Soviet Union. I am not a citizen of any country.

GOLDMAN: How long is it since you have been without citizenship of any country?

TROTSKY: Since the 20th of February, 1932.

GOLDMAN: Can you furnish the Commission with a copy of the decree?

TROTSKY: It was published in *Pravda* and *Isvestia* when—the Soviet papers published it.

GOLDMAN: Have you a copy with you?

TROTSKY: Not at the moment, but it is easy to find the issue. I have only my article in the *Bulletin of the Opposition,* with quotations from this decree.

GOLDMAN: Will you have your secretaries make a copy of the decree depriving you of citizenship, and hand it to the Commission, please? Is that satisfactory to the Commissioners? A copy will be made and handed to the Commission.

TROTSKY: We can cable to New York and receive it after tomorrow by air mail—a copy of *Pravda* and *Isvestia,* I believe, with the decree.

FINERTY: I suggest, Mr. Chairman, it be received subject to confirmation.

DEWEY: It will be received subject to confirmation.

GOLDMAN: What, if anything, did you do when you were informed of the deprivation of your citizenship?

TROTSKY: I wrote an article about it. Fortunately, I am a man armed with a pen. To this article, I gave the form of an appeal to the Executive Committee of the Soviet Union.

GOLDMAN: Have you a copy of the article?

TROTSKY: Yes, the article was published in the *Bulletin.*

GOLDMAN: In Russian?

TROTSKY: In Russian. It was reproduced in many languages. You can find it in the *Militant* and other papers.

GOLDMAN: The Commission will be furnished with the copy of this article, which was, I believe, in the nature of an open letter to the Central Committee of the Soviet Union.

TROTSKY: Yes, it was an open letter to the Central Executive Committee.

FINERTY: May I ask Mr. Trotsky whether it was a request for a hearing, for the reasons of your deprivation of citizenship?

TROTSKY: It was more of a letter of a political nature, in the sense that I predicted certain conclusions to the Soviet Government from the policy held by Stalin. I gave in this letter the advice to remove him from his post as General Secretary of the Communist Party. More concretely, I repeated the advice given by Lenin in his article or testament. He recommended to the Party to remove Stalin. I repeated or referred to his advice.

GOLDMAN: Was that letter quoted by Vyshinsky in the last trial?

TROTSKY: It was quoted in the trial of Zinoviev, Kamenev and others. It was quoted by the defendants Olberg and Holtzman and by the prosecutor Vyshinsky in the first trial. It is mentioned now by Vyshinsky in the last trial of Pyatakov-Radek.

GOLDMAN: We shall furnish the Commission with a copy of that letter. It is all-important because it was quoted by

Vyshinsky, partly quoted and distorted.

TROTSKY: It is supposed to be my article on terrorism.

GOLDMAN: Your wife is living here with you, Mr. Trotsky?

TROTSKY: Yes.

GOLDMAN: How many children have you, and where are they?

TROTSKY: We have now two sons.

GOLDMAN: Where are they?

TROTSKY: One is in Paris. It is Leon Sedov, who is accused together with me. The other, I don't know exactly where he is, but he is in the Soviet Union.

GOLDMAN: What is his name?

TROTSKY: Sergei.

GOLDMAN: And is that the son who was arrested because he was supposed to have organized the mass poisoning of workers?

TROTSKY: Yes, he is the "poisoner."

GOLDMAN: I show you a photograph, and ask you whether this is the photograph of that son?

TROTSKY: Yes, it is my son.

GOLDMAN: I want to introduce this into evidence as a sample of a "poisoner" of many, many thousands of workers, of a "mass poisoner."

(The said photograph of Sergei Sedov was introduced into evidence as Exhibit No. 3.)

FINERTY: I take it the record ought to show that Mr. Goldman is speaking satirically.

GOLDMAN: I think that is correct. I understand that you had two daughters, Mr. Trotsky. Will you kindly tell us what happened to them?

TROTSKY: The younger, Nina, she died in 1928 during my deportation to Siberia. Her husband was also arrested together with me, and deported. I don't have any news from him. He remained about eight years in prison. She became very sick at that time, and she died in Moscow. The letter she wrote to me I received, I believe, seventy days after her death.

GOLDMAN: What happened to your other daughter?

TROTSKY: She committed suicide.

GOLDMAN: Can you tell us anything about the conditions under which she committed suicide?

TROTSKY: She came to Berlin, Germany, for medical treatment, with the authorization of the Soviet Government. She did not participate in any political action abroad. She was sick. But she was deprived of citizenship together with me by the same Government decree, and this fact deprived her also of the possibility of going back to the Soviet Union. She was separated from her husband and children, and she committed suicide in Berlin.

GOLDMAN: Going back to your son, Sergei—was he interested in politics?

TROTSKY: Never. My daughter Zina was interested, not abroad, but in Russia. All the children, three, were interested in politics, with the exception of Sergei.

GOLDMAN: What was he interested in, then?

TROTSKY: As a boy he was a sportsman and athlete, then he became interested in mathematics and technical subjects. In his twenty-sixth year he became a teacher in a technical school, of mathematics.

GOLDMAN: Did he remain in Russia after you were deported?

TROTSKY: Yes. The reason why he remained in Russia—he was absolutely sure that his political neutrality, if I can so speak—he could never be persecuted by the Government. In the first year, he was a very esteemed young professor in a technical school.

GOLDMAN: Can you tell us, Mr. Trotsky, whether, under the Soviet law, treason or alleged treason in one member of the family, especially the father, is attributed to the children? What is the rule?

TROTSKY: Formally, not.

GOLDMAN: What is the practice?

TROTSKY: All the criminal proceedings, all the trials, and all the confessions are based upon the persecution of the members of the family.

DEWEY: Will that be verified by documentary evidence?

GOLDMAN: This is simply an opinion. It is an opinion of the witness. I will ask him whether there is any documentary evidence—

TROTSKY: Excuse me, it is not an opinion. It is my personal experience.

GOLDMAN: In what way?

TROTSKY: I paid for the experience with my two children.

GOLDMAN: Can you produce any further evidence outside of your own experience?

TROTSKY: I know that the wife of Pyatakov was arrested eight months before him, and you can find in his last declaration that he lost everything, "my family and everything." By personal experience and by the persecution of the Opposition, I know. Pankratov, a former militant member of the Party during the Civil War, was deported. Then he came into prison in Siberia, and his wife was arrested only because she refused to separate from her husband. The authorities declared: It is a proof that you are connected with him ideologically, because physically you are separated from him, and the fact that you will not separate from him legally is a proof of your ideological connection with him.

GOLDMAN: One last question, and I am through. I would like to get an idea from you as to the role of some of your accusers in the October Revolution, especially Troyanovsky and Vyshinsky. Just for the purpose of information—do you know anything about their roles?

TROTSKY: Yes, they played a certain role in the October Revolution, in the sense that they were on the other side of the barricades, as a great majority of the ruling stratum of the Soviet Union.

GOLDMAN: Where was Troyanovsky, for instance, Mr. Trotsky?

TROTSKY: Troyanovsky was a member of the Central Committee of the Menshevik Party, a very militant one against us.

GOLDMAN: When did he join the Bolshevik Party?

TROTSKY: He attacked me in the Constituent Assembly, he attacked my speech. He wrote, before the October Revolution, he wrote a very sharp pamphlet against Lenin. During the first year of the Civil War he was an enemy. He became a friend only after our victory, a frequent thing after the Revolution.

GOLDMAN: How about Vyshinsky?

TROTSKY: Vyshinsky was not so prominent a figure as Troyanovsky, and there are not very many things I can say about him. The Mensheviks, in the paper they published in Paris, named him "our renegade." He is a former Menshevik, but not a militant Menshevik. He adhered to the Mensheviks during the revolutionary period, when it became impossible to remain aside. Maisky was a minister of the White Government in Siberia under Kolchak. He is ambassador in London. With few exceptions, all the bureaucracy is of such a kind.

GOLDMAN: Do you want to say anything further?

TROTSKY: I wish to say it is a certain irony when they say I betrayed—

GOLDMAN: This closes the questioning on the biographical section. I turn the witness over to the Commission first, since Mr. Finerty was not present this morning. Is that satisfactory, Mr. Finerty?

FINERTY: That is satisfactory, if it is satisfactory to the

Chairman of the Commission. I would prefer to defer any questions until I get the record. I would like to have Mr. Goldman file with the Commission the statutes of the Lenin Government making the penalty of treason applicable—

GOLDMAN: You mean Stalin.

FINERTY: Stalin, making the penalty of treason applicable to all members of the family.

DEWEY: It was the thought I had in mind, whether or not there is a statute to that effect.

FINERTY: I am informed it is a statutory decree.

GOLDMAN: We shall make an investigation and, if this is so, we shall attempt to get a copy of such statute.

TROTSKY: Permit me a remark on this question. I propose as a witness Victor Serge, the famous French writer, and a member of a famous Russian revolutionary family, one of its members having participated in the assassination of Alexander the Second. He came a year ago from Russia. He passed five or six years in the prisons of Stalin, and he is a man absolutely uncorrupted. This is the best witness the Commission could have, and his own experience is very tragic. His wife became insane. She was arrested, and the sister of his wife is now in deportation in Siberia.

DEWEY: I think we will make a record of the name. I think that will be enough, thank you.

TROTSKY: There is Ciliga, a Yugoslav, who also passed five years in prison. Due to the fact that he is an Italian citizen, because he is from a province inhabited by Serbians belonging to Italy, he was released, and he can be a very good witness.

GOLDMAN: Let the record show, then, that Mr. Trotsky suggests that the Commission, not this particular sub-commission, but that the sub-commission in Paris summon Victor Serge and Dr. Ciliga to testify on the conditions in the Russian prisons and the situation of the families of the victims.

DEWEY: These names will be enough, I believe, for the record.

CROSS-EXAMINATION BY THE COMMISSION

DEWEY: I want to ask a minor question. By what route did you proceed from Halifax to Russia?

TROTSKY: Through the Scandanavias, with a Norwegian ship to Christiania (now it is Oslo), through Sweden, Finland, and then to Petrograd.

DEWEY: You had no contact with the Germans on the way?

TROTSKY: No. It was the case with Lenin. Lenin came from Switzerland through Germany. With Lenin and Zinoviev, among others, was Radek. I came from the United States, and I did not need to go through Germany. But the accusations after my arrest—not the accusation in the indictment—were also that I came through Germany. But it was only the lack of geographical knowledge by the examining magistrate.

DEWEY: I understand from your remarks this morning that the whole question of the relationships of the factions, of the Opposition, will be taken up later. Is that correct?

GOLDMAN: That depends on what year you refer to. The question, for instance, of the relationship of the Opposition to the Party will be taken up under the section of the relationship of Trotsky to Radek and to Zinoviev and Kamenev. But in general, questions that you might want to ask with reference to the political struggle of the Left Opposition and the Party, you can ask now.

DEWEY: I don't want to anticipate points that will naturally come up later, so as to avoid going over much of the same matters twice.

GOLDMAN: If I could know the general nature of your questions, I could inform you better.

DEWEY: In your remarks this morning you spoke of the political principles and objectives in which the Opposition—you asked Mr. Trotsky other points about the political and theoretical differences and their objectives and methods.

GOLDMAN: I will not go into the detailed theory such as "socialism in one country" as against international revolution.

DEWEY: I am somewhat embarrassed, but the Commission does want to know something about the methods and tactics pursued by the Opposition, say up to 1927.

GOLDMAN: Yes, I shall go into that later, in the section on the attitude of the Opposition to the defense of the Soviet Union. That will include the question of the attitude of the Opposition to the Party in the Soviet Union.

FINERTY: I want to suggest, Mr. Chairman, in view of the statement made by Vyshinsky in his closing of the case, it might be of interest to get a statement of his actual relations with Lenin.

DEWEY: That will come up. Mr. Stolberg will ask some questions on that.

LAFOLLETTE: As I remember, this morning Mr. Trotsky corrected Mr. Goldman on the date of his beginning his revolutionary experience. He said 1902 was the date when he wrote on terror. Did I understand that correctly?

GOLDMAN: Yes.

LAFOLLETTE: I think it is pertinent what he wrote on terror at that time—that is, Mr. Trotsky.

TROTSKY: Our country has the greatest experience in the matter of terror. I believe only the Irish people would have a certain competition with us. We had two great parties, the "Narodnaya Volya," "Will of the People" Party, and the Social Revolutionaries, which based their tactics upon individual terror. All Marxists in Russia began in the historic fight against individual terror. It was not a mystical or religious principle with the Marxists. It was a question of organizing the soul against the monster, of organizing the masses and educating them. Because the terrorist fight was a very glorious page in our revolutionary history, with great sacrifices of the best youth of our people, the Marxists made a terrible fight, ideological fight, against the ideology of terrorism, in order to turn the best elements of the youth to the workers. In this fight between Marxism and terrorism it is the action of the masses versus individual terror, the school which differentiated the strategy of individual terror and the organized movement. It penetrated our action, our psychology and our literature for decades. When I came in 1902 to London to the home of Lenin and met Lenin, there was a movement in Russia beginning, a mass movement of the students and workers, with the first sacrifices resulting from conflict in the streets. Now, the first reaction of the youth was revenge, the assassination of Ministers, and we told them: "Not that is our revenge, not the assassination of Ministers, but the assassination of Tsarism, the order of tyranny."

This was the sense of our fight. During my first exile, from 1902 to 1905, I held dozens and dozens of lectures, wrote dozens of articles against individual terrorism in favor of mass action. During my second exile, which was after 1907—after the defeat of the first revolution of 1905, and when the wave of terrorism became very important because the reaction was terrible; after the defeat of the revolution the desire of revenge became imperative with the youth—my second exile was filled with lectures and written articles against individual terrorism. I will present all these articles. I have them here in one of my books, published by the State publishing house of the Soviet Union before my exile.

GOLDMAN: There is a separate section that will deal particularly with terrorism—just for the information of the Commission.

STOLBERG: Mr. Trotsky, I would like to have you tell us as briefly as possible your essential differences from both the Bolsheviks and the Mensheviks. In the Social Democratic Party split in 1903 between the Bolsheviks and Mensheviks you were between the two groups, trying to bring about some plan of collaboration between them. Will you tell us, in other words, as briefly as you can, your personal, your own history with reference to the two wings of the Party and your own organizational work from then until you joined the Bolshevik Party?

TROTSKY: It is totally correct that from 1904 until 1917 I remained aside from both factions. I hoped that the unification could give us possible—push the majority of Mensheviks on the revolutionary road. Lenin was absolutely against the unification with the Mensheviks. Lenin was totally right against me in this important historical question. I recognized my error during the war, when the opportunism became chauvinism, became imperialism.

After my return to Petrograd there were no more differences between me and Lenin. Permit me to quote a remark of Lenin concerning our differences. When I came to Petrograd, I found among the Bolsheviks conciliatory tendencies toward the Mensheviks, for a unification with the Mensheviks. Stalin was one of the prominent protagonists of unification in March, 1917. It is in the official minutes of the Party. Lenin fought against this tendency. He said—I will find the quotation; I will find it in a minute. The quotation literally said: "As for a coalition, I cannot even speak about that seriously. Trotsky long ago said that a union is impossible. Trotsky understood this, and from that time on there has been no better Bolshevik." I think I referred to this in the first session as Exhibit No. 1. I published all the minutes of the Committee abroad.

GOLDMAN: Where are these minutes that you refer to? Where did you publish them?

TROTSKY: I published them in different languages. They are published here in facsimile. The minutes of the Petrograd Party Committee were published in 1926, but this session of the Committee was not in the least mentioned but destroyed by order from Moscow, by a telegraphic order to eliminate the minutes of this session.

GOLDMAN: What is the book you are holding?

TROTSKY: The Russian edition of "The Stalin School of Falsification."

GOLDMAN: That is written by you?

TROTSKY: It is written by Stalin; they are documents. It is written by me, but the contents are documents.

GOLDMAN: Have you the page where these minutes you refer to are contained?

TROTSKY: It was also published in English and all the foreign languages.

STOLBERG: Now, in these ideological differences between yourself and Lenin, certain practical issues constantly rose in the terms of these differences, from 1903 to 1917. Now, during the war, wherein did you differ with Lenin with reference to the Zimmerwald and Kienthal Conferences?

TROTSKY: The differences in Zimmerwald did not extend to the most important ideological questions. The differences in Zimmerwald were absolutely of a secondary nature. They could have a psychological importance in the moment of the fight, but no historical perspective. They appeared as pure incidents. The fact is that the Comintern published my articles during the war. What I wrote during the war, the Comintern published after the Revolution.

STOLBERG: What were your differences with him after you came into power with reference to the defense of Petrograd, the Polish war, and Brest-Litovsk?

TROTSKY: You know, I worked with Lenin hand in hand from 1917 to the moment of his illness and then his death. The questions of difference were varied and very complicated, because we were the first Workers' Government, and we had different questions which from time to time divided us—separated us. I recognized the authority of Lenin every time, but I was sufficiently independent to explain my opinion openly—openly, even when not good for me. I believe my relations with Lenin during the Soviet period were the best. He himself testified to that in his last letter, in his testament. He wrote me a letter and I published it in my autobiography, on the art—if it can be named art—in the last period, the art of distortion of the nature of the living relationship between Lenin and myself.

GOLDMAN: Pardon me, I want to ask a question. You referred to Lenin's testament. Has that been published anywhere?

TROTSKY: It was published the first time, I remember, by Max Eastman. In Russia, it is published only in the stenographic report of the Central Committee devoted only to the functionaries of the Party. Stalin read it at our insistence. He read it in August, 1927, at a session of the Central Committee—Plenum, as we call it. It is in the stenographic report published—

GOLDMAN: Has Stalin ever denied the existence of such a testament?

TROTSKY: Yes.

GOLDMAN: When?

TROTSKY: Many times.

GOLDMAN: Has he ever said anything in public which would indicate that there was such a testament in existence?

TROTSKY: I doubt if he did.

GOLDMAN: Referring to the minutes of that session—

TROTSKY: The first of November, 1917, of the Petrograd Committee—the Party Committee.

GOLDMAN: That is, wherein Lenin declared: "Since Trotsky understood that there could be no union between the Bolsheviks and Mensheviks, there has been no better Bolshevik," these minutes are contained in the book by Trotsky called "The Stalin School of Falsification." I am referring to the Russian edition, beginning with page 116. Then there is a photostatic copy of the minutes between page 116 and page 117, inclusive.

TROTSKY: Excuse me, it is a facsimile of the destroyed proofs. It was ordered destroyed in type. But workers friendly to me made a proof of that and sent that to me.

GOLDMAN: And this is a photostatic copy of that proof. This book, if I am correct, will appear in English very soon and will contain an English translation.

STOLBERG: May I ask just one more question? It is of a more historical and philosophical interest. Your theory of the permanent revolution, as I understand it from your writings, was very similar to Lenin's own. I also gather from your writings that there were some differences of a very, as far as I can see, minor nature. What, in your opinion, were the differences?

TROTSKY: I believe in this question I was right against Lenin. I had elaborated from the end of 1904 the theoretical conception and conviction that the Russian Revolution could not be victorious except through the dictatorship of the proletariat.

STOLBERG: Only through?

TROTSKY: Only through. It could not be victorious as a simple bourgeois revolution. The perspective of a proletarian dictatorship for a backward Tsarist Russia appeared as a very fantastic perspective. The Mensheviks and also the Bolsheviks named "Trotskyism" the perspective of a dictatorship of the proletariat in Russia.

STOLBERG: If I understand you correctly, Trotskyism from 1904 to 1917 meant the possibility of skipping bourgeois democracy in Russia.

TROTSKY: Trotskyism meant the perspective of proletarian dictatorship in Russia.

STOLBERG: So, in your opinion, both views cannot be discussed in terms of a clash in personality at all. Each of you took something from the other, and that became merged in the revolution.

TROTSKY: I think the part of Lenin was immeasurably greater than mine.

STOLBERG: Because it was strategic?

TROTSKY: It is too great a matter to go into now. He was the teacher. I was the pupil. If you permit me, I shall introduce the testimony of Joffe, the former diplomat. It is in "My Life," page 535 in the English edition. In his testament, in his letter before his suicide, he wrote that Lenin said to him that Trotsky "proved to be right" in this question of the revolutionary perspective.

DEWEY: We will now take a brief recess.

DEWEY: Since some may have come in since I made the announcement earlier, I will state again that contrary to the previous statement given to the press, there will be no hearing tomorrow. The next Commission hearing will be Monday morning at ten o'clock. I wish also to make, for the purpose of the record, another statement. Since some question has been raised as to why the hearings are held in the limited locality of Coyoacan, the Commission wishes to state that it is because we did not think it fitting to put the Mexican Government to the additional effort of precaution which would have been necessary if the hearings were held elsewhere, especially as definite threats of violence have been made by certain elements. The Commission's are public hearings in every sense of the word, as evidenced by the unrestricted presence of the press. Moreover, during the hearings this place serves for the purpose of the Commission and not as Mr. Trotsky's home. I will ask Mr. Beals to repeat this statement in Spanish.

(Mr. Beals translates the above statement into Spanish.)

DEWEY: Mr. Stolberg will proceed with his questions.

STOLBERG: I have three specific questions, Mr. Trotsky, which I would like to have you answer specifically. The first question is: Wherein did you and Lenin differ in reference to the problem of the defense of Petrograd?

TROTSKY: It was a strategical question. Lenin, as myself, was not a military man. But we tried to resolve military questions by our good Marxist education, by our living experience, and by common sense, if you permit me. Lenin's opinion was, at a certain moment, that we could not help Petrograd, and that we must abandon Petrograd and concentrate the defense on Moscow or on a line between Moscow and Petrograd. I had a different appreciation—that we could save Petrograd, that it was very important because Petrograd was for us the source of the best proletarian people, the most educated; and also from a military point of view, it was necessary, in my opinion, to protect and save Petrograd. We had heated discussions on this, and the Central Committee sustained my opinion. Lenin said: "Good, try to do it and I will help you." I went to Petrograd and we succeeded in saving Petrograd.

STOLBERG: The next question is: Wherein and to what degree, if any, did you and he differ in reference to the Polish war?

TROTSKY: In this question the roles were the contrary. Lenin was aggressive and I was skeptical about the attack on Warsaw. I opposed it in the Central Committee, but Lenin had won the majority. The experience confirmed my opinion in that question.

STOLBERG: And then will you discuss—

TROTSKY: Permit me to say that they were not considered as questions of principle. The next day we forgot the difference totally. It was a practical question.

STOLBERG: The third question I pose is a more political one and would enter into your differences on Brest-Litovsk. Will you explain your differences in reference to Brest-Litovsk?

TROTSKY: The differences concerning Brest-Litovsk are extremely exaggerated now by the Comintern. Every new year brings a new exaggeration. They were absolutely of a transitory and conjunctural character—the differences. I found it necessary to say to world public opinion and to the world toiling masses that we wished to fight against Prussianism, but that we could not do it. I tried to demonstrate by action the falsehood of the accusation that we had a secret agreement with German militarism. Lenin said in answer that it was of certain importance to show and to educate the masses by action, but if we perished in this demonstration—the group that was to take its message to them—how could they get their lesson? It was a question by what line we could continue the fight against German militarism in order not to perish ourselves. In the determination of this line, I had some practical and empirical differences with Lenin—no more.

BEALS: Mr. Trotsky, I would like to ask some very elementary questions. I believe, before these hearings were held, that you made the statement to the press that your archives would be open to an impartial investigation by the Commission. Is that true?

TROTSKY: Absolutely true.

BEALS: May I ask whether all of your archives are here in Mexico?

TROTSKY: I must answer this question with reservations, if the Chairman permits me. My archives were two times the object of night attacks, in Norway by the Nazis on the fifth of August, 1936, and in Paris by the agents of the G.P.U. on the seventh of November, 1936. The seventh of November is the anniversary of the Russian Revolution. The agents of the G.P.U. succeeded a bit more than the Norwegian Nazis. They stole a part of my archives, but I have copies. I know very well that through their agents, correspondents, friends, and so on, they ask me directly and indirectly, where are my archives? The G.P.U. is professionally interested in this matter. That is why I declared that my archives are completely at the disposal of the Commission; that I am ready to communicate immediately to the Chairman of the Commission or to the Commission as a whole in a secret session where they are, where the originals are and where the copies are. I am ready to present to the Commission legal copies as well as originals, and I beg the Chairman not to compel me or make me say where all my archives are.

BEALS: A further question that I wish to ask along that line is this: In bringing in your evidence, what was the basis of your selection of material which you thought would be of interest to this Commission?

TROTSKY: What was the basis of the selection?

BEALS: Yes, in coming to Mexico, what was the basis of the selection of the evidence which you brought with you which you thought would be most valuable to this Commission?

TROTSKY: I have all the necessary documents, but most of them are in copies, not in originals. The originals are at the disposal of the Commission, but not in my home. The selection is adapted to the indictment and to the political basis of the indictment. By my documents, I can prove, first, that the concrete premises of proofs and evidence are false, are frame-ups; and secondly, that politically they are impossible. There is a certain gradation of my proofs from the political to the philosophical.

BEALS: The final question I would like to ask along this line needs a certain preliminary. I believe that in the courts of the United States a defendant is considered innocent until found guilty. At least, that is the theory. Whereas, the courts of Russia proceed a little differently. A defendant is considered guilty until he proves himself innocent. For the purpose of this line of questioning, I am considering you guilty, and therefore I would like to ask you what assurance the Commission would have in examining your archives that you have not destroyed that which was unfavorable to yourself.

TROTSKY: That is an absolutely natural question. But my aim is not to convince the Commission by the documents which I have allegedly destroyed, but by the documents which remain in my archives. I will prove to the Commission that the man who wrote from year to year those thousands of letters, those hundreds of articles, and those dozens of books and had those friends and those enemies, that this man could not commit the crimes of the indictment. It is the most genuine evidence I have.

BEALS: Answering the question I have—

TROTSKY: If you will permit me a supplement. It is impossible to introduce allegedly destroyed documents. They could not find place in these archives. If you suppose, if you have the hypothesis of criminal documents to the German Minister Hess, to Hitler or the military of the Mikado, then you must find in my archives a place for them. Such a duplicity of character is impossible. But all the accused are people without psychology. They are robots of the G.P.U.

DEWEY: I think the last two sentences had better be stricken from the record.

BEALS: I still have several questions. In connection with the charges made against you at the time you were concentrated, or in the concentration camp, in Canada, that you were a German agent, you present as evidence of refutation of that the edition of *Pravda,* No. 34, in which Lenin declared that a person of your long revolutionary standing would be incapable of being an agent of the German Government. Does that constitute in itself proof, that is to say—was Lenin himself charged with being a German agent, and was he not of the same party as yourself?

TROTSKY: That is also absolutely a natural question. My

proof is not an absolute proof for people who suspect Lenin of having been an agent of Germany. But my accusers, my prosecutors, are sure Lenin was not an agent of Germany. But Vyshinsky was, for some years, absolutely sure Lenin was a German agent. Now he has repeated this accusation while officially he has rejected it. My proof is that Lenin affirmed that I could not have been a German agent in 1917, before the October Revolution, before the Civil War, before the creation of the Communist International. Now, I think it is an argument in my favor against Prosecutor Vyshinsky and his superior, Stalin. It is only one of my arguments.

BEALS: My second question in connection with this matter—and I shall not press this very much because I imagine this will be further taken up later on—is, of course, the Brest-Litovsk matter. Is it not a further charge, so far as many people in the outside world were concerned, that you were also acting in favor of Germany when you ceded Russian territory to the Germans as part of the preliminary measure to gain power, a preliminary agreement by which you were enabled to gain power? I mention this because in the present trials which we are considering, I believe that one of the charges against you is that you have entered into secret relations with Germany and Japan for the cession of Soviet territory in return for support in returning to power. This is an involved question, but the crux of the question is: To what extent was your signing of the Brest-Litovsk treaty an indication that you were a German agent?

TROTSKY: When, during our conversations at Brest-Litovsk—

DEWEY: As relates to the cession of territory?

TROTSKY: Yes. We had power in a certain territory. It was a question, if we could save the workers' power by a territorial concession, by paying a certain price. Lenin was of the opinion that we must make this concession, pay this price, in order to save the more narrow basis of the proletarian power. I was absolutely of the same opinion in principle. There were concrete differences. But now it is a totally different situation. The first thing: How can I give territorial concessions of territory which I do not have to the Japanese or to the fascists? We must also verify if it is reasonable for them—an agreement of such a kind—for the Mikado and for Hitler. The second question: Lenin did not betray his program and ideas by territorial concessions. Now the Prosecutor insinuates our aim and objective is to make territorial concessions in order to replace socialism by capitalism in the Soviet Union. The first concession during Brest-Litovsk was in order to save socialism from the attack of capitalism. It was an empirical proposition imposed by the situation. We must make the concession in order to save socialism. Now it would be a concession in order to betray socialism in favor of capitalism—the contrary.

BEALS: That I cannot distinguish very clearly. I would just like to follow it up.

LAFOLLETTE: The same thing?

BEALS: Yes. In other words, the signing of the Brest-Litovsk treaty, the question of the triumph of socialism, was considered more important than the question of the territorial integrity of Russia. Now, of course, at the present time you are opposed to the Stalin Government in Moscow. You feel that your own concept of socialism is more valid than that which today rules in Soviet Russia. Would not then your attitude be the same, that regardless whether they say that you are trying to bring back capitalism, would not your attitude be the same, that you would sacrifice Soviet territory if it enhances the return of your group to power to implant the socialism which you believe more correct?

TROTSKY: I believe that the only way possible to materialize the ideas of socialism is to win the masses and educate the masses, win them to the vanguard and to create a new régime by their will, their conscience, their devotion to their ideals. That is the only possibility. I have no others. The other means, which contradicts this education of the masses, is doomed beforehand. If I enter into relations with fascists and the Mikado, I am not a socialist, not a revolutionary, but a miserable adventurist. And if this accusation is proved to be true and correct, then I lose all. What can I have, except the power of my ideals for socialism? I compromise my aim, my ideal, myself. It is so contrary to all my Marxist education, to all my past—forty years' work in the masses and through the masses—if I can conceive of the possibility of such an indictment. When I read this book [The Verbatim Report of the Moscow Trial—A.M.G.] for the hundredth and first time, I have the impression of reading Dostoyevsky.

LAFOLLETTE: I would like to ask a factual question bearing on Brest-Litovsk. Did the Soviet Government, at any time before the signing of the Brest-Litovsk treaty, make any attempt to get the support of the Allied Governments against Germany in order that they might not have to sign the treaty?

TROTSKY: Yes.

LAFOLLETTE: Tell us about it.

TROTSKY: I conducted the conversations myself with the French General Lavergne and others and General Niessel, a French officer, in order to have their aid against Germany. But I must say openly, the difference between German militarism and French militarism was not for us a question of principle. It was only a question of a certain equilibrium of certain antagonistic forces in order to save the Soviet power. I tried to do it. They refused—the French Government refused to do so. Clemenceau proclaimed a holy war against the Bolsheviks, and then we had to conclude the peace of Brest-Litovsk.

DEWEY: Dr. Ruehle will ask a question in German which Mr. Solow will read in English. We will ask Mr. Trotsky to reply in German, and Mr. Solow will translate the reply.

RUEHLE (through interpreter): Were there in the Central Committee, or in the Communist International, differences over the question of the differentiation of bureaucracy and administration in the proletarian dictatorship? Was the danger of Bonapartism foreseen, and what position did you take on these questions?

TROTSKY (answers in German and translates into English his own answer): These questions played the greatest role in the discussions in the Central Committee, and in personal discussions between Lenin and myself. Lenin had the finest sensitivity on this question, and he was the teacher of the future Left Opposition. He affirmed many times that the greatest danger for us was that we, as a backward country, isolated—that we could see our state, the proletarian state, degenerate into a bureaucratic, Bonapartist state. He proposed certain organizational measures, as, for example, his Control Commission of genuine workers from the shops, in order to control the bureaucrats and show the bureaucrats that they are only transitory workers of the state. I want to say that the Control Commission itself degenerated and became a worse instrument in the proletarian dictatorship. Lenin understood, however, that it was impossible to preserve the Soviet dictatorship only by organizational measures. It depended upon the world situation, the historic factors in the world arena. If the German proletariat, the most developed in Europe, if it had accomplished a victorious revolution—and we hope that it will do so yet—the combination of the Soviet state with the proletarian German state would have given us the possibility to avoid the degeneration of the Soviet state in Russia. Our isolation was the most important factor in our degeneration.

RUEHLE (through interpreter): What position did you personally take in the Central Committee of the Communist International on the question of the practical liquidation of the Soviets and their replacement by the bureaucratic administration and sovereignty which betrayed the slogans of the Revolution?

DEWEY: Excuse me, one moment. Ask him what date that covers.

RUEHLE (through interpreter): In the period in which Trotsky was in the Central Committee of the Communist Party.

DEWEY: The only reason for asking that question was whether it would not go into the factional struggle.

TROTSKY: It is not dissociated from the factional struggle.

GOLDMAN: During Lenin's time?

TROTSKY: During Lenin's time? Yes, I can only repeat what I said. I believe we did what we could to avoid the degeneration. During the Civil War the militarization of the Soviets and the Party was almost inevitable. But even during the Civil War I myself tried in the army—even in the army on the field—to give a full possibility to the Communists to discuss all the military measures. I discussed these measures even with the soldiers and, as I explained in my autobiography, even with the deserters. After the Civil War was finished, we hoped that the possibility for democracy would be greater. But two factors, two different but connected factors, hindered the development of Soviet democracy. The first general factor was the backwardness and misery of the country. From that basis emanated the bureaucracy, and the bureaucracy did not wish to be abolished, to be annihilated. The bureaucracy became an independent factor. Then the fight became to a certain degree a struggle of classes. That was the beginning of the Opposition. For a certain time the question was an internal question in the Central Committee. We discussed by what means we should begin the fight on the degeneration and the bureaucratization of the state. Then it became not a question of discussions in the Central Committee, but a question of the fight, the struggle between the Opposition and the bureaucracy. That was the second stage—

DEWEY: That comes in later, I think.

GOLDMAN: Yes, that will come in later.

RUEHLE (through interpreter): Were you of the opinion that the specific methods of the Russian Revolution must be schematically and compulsorily carried by the Comintern into the rest of the world, and there become the ruling form of the class struggle?

TROTSKY: No. It was not the opinion of Lenin and myself. You can find in Lenin's speeches in the Congresses of the C.I. many severe and forceful characterizations of the idea that we Russians could impose our methods and our form of organization on other nations. In his last speech, in the Fourth Congress of the Communist International, Lenin devoted a certain part to this question. It was also my opinion that it is absolutely impossible to command the workers' movement from Moscow by telegraphic orders to sixty nations. This impossibility became more and more evident and the method of command was supplemented by the method of corruption and of bribery. One of the important differences—it was one of the important questions—of the fight since 1924 between Stalin and myself was where we protested against the bribery of the leaders of the workers' movement in the foreign countries.

RUEHLE: (through interpreter): What is your attitude towards the tendency to convert the Communist parties in the rest of the world, outside of Russia, into mere auxiliaries of Soviet foreign policy, or the manner in which they destroyed all democracy in these parties?

DEWEY: Will you tell Dr. Ruehle, I think for the present we had better confine the questioning more to matters of fact. Possibly at the end there will be an opportunity for these questions on his opinions.

LAFOLLETTE: I would like to ask Mr. Trotsky whether

there was in the reports of the Moscow trials any quotation by the prosecution from the testament of Lenin concerning any of the differences, for example? Are there any quotations actually from the testament of Lenin?

TROTSKY: I don't remember.

GOLDMAN: There is a reference to the testament of Lenin.

LAFOLLETTE: Who makes that?

GOLDMAN: Vyshinsky. But what that testament is, is not told by him.

LAFOLLETTE: But they did refer to it?

GOLDMAN: In this connection—I would like permission from the Chairman to ask one question, or rather two questions of Mr. Trotsky. You told us, when I asked you about the testament of Lenin, that Stalin never admitted the existence of such a testament. Would you like to change your answer on this question?

TROTSKY: I answered you, as far as I remember, he never mentioned it openly in public discussions. But in the afternoon, during the intermission, I found a quotation which is totally correct, of his speech in the *International Press Correspondence* of November 17, 1927. Stalin says:

> It is said that in the "testament" in question Lenin suggested to the Party Congress that it should deliberate on the question of replacing Stalin and appointing another comrade in his place as General Secretary of the Party. This is perfectly true. . . . Yes, comrades, I am rude towards those who are rudely and disloyally destroying and disintegrating the Party. I have never made a secret of it, and shall not do so now.

Now, it is clear that Stalin confirmed that proposition of Lenin to dismiss him.

GOLDMAN: Who publishes the *International Press Correspondence*?

TROTSKY: The Comintern.

GOLDMAN: Now, with the permission of the Chairman, I wish to inform the Commission that the Open Letter to the Central Committee of the Soviet Union which Mr. Trotsky wrote at the time of his deprivation of his citizenship is found in the *Militant*, published in New York, dated April 2, 1932. The Commission can examine this Open Letter at its leisure.

DEWEY: I would like to return to the matter of the relations with Lenin, because on pages 466 to 468 of the English translation of the January trial the prosecuting attorney, Mr. Vyshinsky, says that the accusations which they regard as proved and which are now brought against you: ". . . merely crown the struggle Trotskyism has been waging against the working class and the Party, against Lenin and Leninism, for decades." I don't wish to ask you about that, but I do wish to ask you about some special points that he raises in support of this speech, that the recent conduct they charged you with is merely a crowning of the struggle against Lenin and Leninism that you have been carrying on for decades. He goes on to say,

> . . . in 1904 Trotsky came out with a most despicable pamphlet entitled "Our Political Tasks." This pamphlet was packed full of filthy insinuations against our great teacher, the leader of the international proletariat, Lenin, against the great Leninist teaching regarding the paths of the Bolshevik victory, the victory of the toilers, the victory of Socialism. In this pamphlet Trotsky squirts venomous saliva at the great ideas of Marxism-Leninism.

What was the content of your pamphlet of 1904, "Our Political Tasks"?

TROTSKY: The first thing I must say is, the Prosecutor never read the pamphlet and never saw it, because he says it is a little pamphlet. It is a book. It is illegal—was illegally introduced in Russia—and that was the reason why it was in very small characters, small print. But it is even in small print in the legal printing. It is 150 pages or so. In the American general form of books, it would be three hundred pages. It is not a little pamphlet, as he represented it.

DEWEY: In the English translation, it says nothing about being a little book. It says "despicable."

TROTSKY: I will find it immediately. In the different translations there are corrections. We will see.

DEWEY: The size of the pamphlet is not at issue. We want to know what basis there is in the pamphlet of 1904 for his charges that you were attacking Lenin at that time.

FINERTY: Mr. Chairman, may I suggest that if a copy of this pamphlet is available, we should have it here? It is the sole documentary evidence Vyshinsky refers to.

TROTSKY: In the French record, it says: "A little abominable pamphlet." [Trotsky here refers to the French edition of the Verbatim Report of the Moscow Trials—Ed.] It is a theoretical and political pamphlet, and it is not objectionable. I believe it has many errors in it.

GOLDMAN: How old were you when you wrote that?

TROTSKY: Twenty-three years. I can find in this book chapters which are not so bad. There are chapters which are wrong. You know, as a young man I characterized Lenin in a certain spirit, a spirit absolutely not found in the real relations between him and myself. But I corrected, by my subsequent attitude—I corrected the error. But it is not objectionable and nothing abominable.

DEWEY: Is this book available?

TROTSKY: Yes, I believe I have it in my library. We will find it.

DEWEY: It can be entered into the record?

TROTSKY: Yes.

DEWEY: Solely in Russian?

TROTSKY: I believe only in Russian, if the Comintern did not publish it in a foreign language.

DEWEY: You say you corrected it in your subsequent writings and behavior. About what time would you put the time of your subsequent correction?

TROTSKY: It depends on the question. The book speaks on various questions; on general perspectives of the Russian Revolution, and I have a comparison between the Jacobins and the Russian Social Democrats; the political slogans of the period of 1904; and the organizational efforts of the Party; the illegal literature of the Party, and so on, and so on. It is very difficult to say when I corrected every error.

DEWEY: The next accusation which he makes on your next attack on Lenin is in connection with the August Bloc which you organized in 1911 and 1912. Then he quotes—he quotes Stalin. That is enough. What have you to say about this August Bloc that he says was directed against Lenin's ideas?

TROTSKY: Yes, the August Bloc was an emanation of my conciliatory tendency. I tried to bring together the Bolsheviks and Mensheviks. That was the idea of the August Bloc. Lenin refused to participate. I developed a certain agitation somewhat broad within Russia itself. It was a period of the darkest reaction. We had very few connections with Russia. Some months later the situation changed, but in the moment of the August Bloc there were bad working relations with Russia. They were almost totally interrupted. All the work was done by émigrés. I tried to bring them together—the Bolsheviks and Mensheviks—but Lenin refused. He was absolutely right in this question, as subsequent developments showed. I remained at the conference with the Mensheviks. Immediately, I began to fight against the Mensheviks at the conference, and the Bloc was destroyed. Nothing came from this attempt.

DEWEY: Lenin is quoted in this connection. He wrote that

this Bloc was built up on lack of principle, on hypocrisy, on empty phrases.

TROTSKY: Yes, I believe the style is absolutely Lenin's. He was right. The Bloc was a sterile attempt, and Lenin did not play with the thing. He gave serious blows to his adversaries.

DEWEY: Mr. Vyshinsky—

TROTSKY: But this is not criminal evidence.

DEWEY: He also states that this Bloc was made up of lackeys of imperialism, of Mensheviks, of those who have been expelled from the ranks of the Bolshevik Party, and refuse of the working-class parties. Of course, you have said they were Mensheviks. Were there lackeys of capital in it?

TROTSKY: Well, it is a designation for reformists. Lenin designated all reformists as lackeys of capitalism, and he named in such a manner the Mensheviks who participated in the conference. It is a question of a political appreciation and not of criminal thought.

DEWEY: Were there those in it who were expelled from the Bolshevik Party?

TROTSKY: Yes.

DEWEY: Were there members in this Bloc who did not split from the Bolshevik Party?

TROTSKY: The Bolshevik organization at this time was in a state of split. For example, Lunacharsky, who was Minister of Education under the Soviet régime, Petrovsky, the eminent professor of history who died two years ago—they were not with Lenin. They participated in the August conference, but then they merged again with Lenin, and myself, also.

GOLDMAN: This is the pamphlet which Vyshinsky refers to, called "Our Political Tasks." (Attorney Goldman exhibits said pamphlet to the Commission.)

DEWEY: This is the pamphlet of 1904.

LAFOLLETTE: How many pages are in it?

GOLDMAN: 107 pages in extremely small type. Do you

have any of them in your archives, or can I introduce this?

TROTSKY: You can introduce it, naturally.

GOLDMAN: I will mark this Exhibit No. 4.

(The pamphlet, "Our Political Tasks," written by Trotsky in 1904, was introduced into evidence as Exhibit No. 4.)

DEWEY: That is all the questions I have on that particular matter.

GOLDMAN: One more question. Has this ever been translated into English?

TROTSKY: I am not sure. It seems to me the Comintern translated it into foreign languages.

GOLDMAN: A certain book I know contains some essays in English. I want to show the pamphlet to the Commissioners. Let them see the type and print.

DEWEY: Are there any other questions on this phase of the matter?

LAFOLLETTE: I have one question I want to ask. It may not be pertinent now. I think it is just as well to get it into the record because it concerns a thing I have heard a great many people say. I think it is a criticism that is very frequently made, a criticism or an appraisal of the situation which we are examining here. I have heard many say: "This does not concern me. If Trotsky were in power, the thing that is going on in Russia would have happened. Trotsky would have done the same thing." Would you like to answer that question now, or perhaps later when you come to discuss what you have stood for in the last ten years?

FINERTY: I think that will be covered in the legal cross-examination. It involves legal cross-examination.

STOLBERG: Why is it N. Trotsky? [Commissioner Stolberg here refers to the signature under the title of the pamphlet, "Our Political Tasks"—A.M.G.]

TROTSKY: It was during the time when it was my pseudonym. The name Trotsky became my real name later. Then I had to connect it with my first name.

STOLBERG: I just had no identification for the first name, for "N."

GOLDMAN: Let the record show that the question refers to the name of the author in the pamphlet introduced as Exhibit No. 4.

TROTSKY: If you permit me, I can say that the "N" was devoted to my wife. Her name is Natalia.

BEALS: How was the work published—by the group with whom you were connected?

TROTSKY: It was by the Party. The Party had a common printing establishment. The Bolsheviks and Mensheviks had a common printing establishment. That was in January, 1904. The split came in April, 1905, but in December, 1905, a new merger occurred between the Bolsheviks and Mensheviks, and a unified party existed until 1912. The new split, the official split, came in 1912. It is very difficult to understand what the Comintern tells us about the question—that is, its chronology. The Bolsheviks and Mensheviks were at a certain time two factions of the same party, not two totally antagonistic parties. But at the time I was a conciliator between them—conciliatory in organizational questions. But in the revolutionary perspective, I explained, I had my point of view, which is named "the permanent revolution."

FINERTY: I understood you to say that there have been two raids on your archives, that attempts were made by the Nazis and by the G.P.U.?

TROTSKY: Yes.

FINERTY: Were materials abstracted, were things taken out of your archives?

TROTSKY: The Nazis stole only one letter, and some papers of no importance. There was a trial in Norway. I appeared as a witness at the trial. I had to explain all my political activities, as here, during two hours, behind closed doors. The

Government would not permit me to explain, to give a full explanation in the presence of the press, and so forth.

FINERTY: A secret trial?

TROTSKY: Secret, but only during my testimony.

FINERTY: May I ask this—I don't want to go into this in detail: Were documents taken from you by the G.P.U.?

TROTSKY: Yes.

FINERTY: Have you copies of these documents?

TROTSKY: Yes.

FINERTY: So your archives are intact?

TROTSKY: Well, this was my correspondence with my son from 1934, 1935, and even 1936. They stole it from a scientific institute. My son has the copies of his letters to me, and I have the copies of all my letters to him. And now my wife is busy copying my copies and sending them to my son, and he does the same. In such a manner, we have both a full collection of our letters.

FINERTY: All your archives are at the disposal of the Commission for examination?

TROTSKY: Totally.

DEWEY: Before we adjourn, the Commission will be glad to receive in executive session or *in camera* the information that Mr. Trotsky has to give about the location of those portions of his archives that are not here. We will then adjourn until Monday at ten o'clock A.M.

End of the Second Session.

Third session

April 12, 1937, at ten-fifteen o'clock a.m.

DEWEY: I have an announcement or two to make, part of which will be repeated in Spanish by Mr. Beals. The following persons and organizations have been invited by the Commission to attend these hearings or send their representatives. The following have declined:

Hernan Laborde, Secretary of the Communist Party of Mexico.
Vincente Lombardo Toledano, Secretary-General of the C.T.M.
Prof. David Vilchis, President of the Association of Mexican Professors of the Federal District.

From the following the Commission received no reply, but their refusal to be present by representatives was announced through the press:

The Soviet Government, through its Ambassador in Washington.

Communist Party of the United States.
Joseph Brodsky, New York attorney, and well known member of the Communist Party.

The following person and organizations have accepted the invitation of the Commission to attend its hearings:

Liga Comunista Internacionalista.
Confederación General de Trabajadores.
Confederación Regional Obrera Méxicana.
Federación de Sindicatos Obreros del D.F.
Casa del Pueblo.
Sindicato de Obreros Panaderos Bizcocheros y Reposteros del D.F.
Liga Cultural Israelita.
Louis Sanchez Ponton, Correspondent of the Secretariat of the League of Nations.

The following organizations have also been invited, but replies from them have not as yet been received:

Partido Nacional Revolucionario.
Sindicato Unico de la Construccion.
Sindicato de Trabajadores Petroleros de la Republica Méxicana.
Federación Nacional de Trabajadores de la Industria Electrica.

Hearing yesterday that the Partido Nacional had not received their invitation, the Commission has dispatched a second invitation to the Party. Mr. Beals will now translate these remarks into Spanish.

(Mr. Beals translates Dr. Dewey's remarks into Spanish.)

DEWEY: The original letters of invitation, together with

all replies received, the acceptances and refusals, will be appended and published with the permanent record.

I wish to say that the press table was reserved exclusively for the journalists of the daily papers and the news services. Any visitors sitting at the press table will please take seats in the rear.

I wish also to announce that the Commission has made a change in the order of the procedure from that which was announced Saturday. In order to avoid duplication, the direct examination of Mr. Trotsky will be completed before the cross-examination takes place. That does not mean there may not be questions in cross-examination, but the main cross-examination will be reserved. In this connection, I wish to announce that the representatives of the Mexican labor organizations will have a full opportunity to cross-examine Mr. Trotsky during this latter period of cross-examination.

(Mr. Beals translates above remarks into Spanish.)

DEWEY: I will now ask the attorney for Mr. Trotsky to state the topics upon which he proposes to conduct his direct examination of Mr. Trotsky, and, as far as possible, the order in which these topics will probably be taken up. I have to make one more announcement, that arrangements are being made so that abstracts in Spanish will be provided for the first two sessions.

(Mr. Beals translates above remarks into Spanish.)

BEALS: Mr. President, since I am not fully aware of the regular order of proceedings to be followed in today's cross-examination, I should like, before they are instituted, to address several brief questions to the defendant which have bearing upon yesterday's hearings and also bearing upon the Commission's own statements, and perhaps to make a brief rectification of essential importance for the working of this Commission.

Mr. Trotsky, it has been stated that you have made repeated demands that the Soviet Government ask for your extradition. Is that true?

TROTSKY: Not to the Government directly, but in the press, I asked many times. The only loyal way for the Soviet Government is to ask for my extradition. I declared it for the first time during the first great trial of Zinoviev-Kamenev in August, 1936. And after that, I repeated it each time in the press and in my statements, and also in my Hippodrome speech in New York.

BEALS: You didn't make any direct, official demand to the Soviet Government to that effect?

TROTSKY: I believe the Soviet Government understand themselves what to do. I am not formally a Soviet citizen, and my declaration to the world press is surely known. I declared the same thing in my writing to the Norwegian Government: "Instead of making me a prisoner of yours, you must ask the Soviet Government for proofs before your courts." I addressed the same letter to the League of Nations, the letter saying in sense: "On the initiative of Moscow you are preparing a special court for the terrorists. I ask you, if the court is a real court, to put my case on your order of the day." I addressed the French examining judge who conducts the investigation concerning my archives, the theft of my archives, and proposed that I am ready to appear before any French court in order to prove that the accusation is false. In France there is also interest in this case, as in the Soviet Union, because it concerns my alleged alliance with Hitler against France. I am ready, together with my son, to appear before the court in France immediately. I believe I did everything I could in this respect.

BEALS: Was it ever stated by the press, to your knowledge, that the Soviet Government had sought to extradite you from Norway?

TROTSKY: The Soviet Government demanded only my expulsion, not my extradition, because expulsion is an administrative matter, and extradition must be demonstrated before the court.

BEALS: In the opening statement of the Commission delivered yesterday morning by Dr. Dewey, it was stated that such demands, had the Soviet Government acted, would have automatically brought you before a Norwegian or Mexican court. Is it not true that there is no extradition treaty between Mexico and the Soviet Union, and that in fact there are no relations between the two countries?

TROTSKY: The absence of relations between these two countries is not imputed to me even by Vyshinsky.

DEWEY: May I say that any error there was the fault of the Commission and not of Mr. Trotsky?

BEALS: Mr. Chairman, in view of the foregoing it behooves me to make here at this time, and to enter it upon the permanent record of the Commission, a statement of my own position in respect to this and certain other matters covered in your opening address yesterday which in the name of the Commission gave the scope and purpose of this inquiry. I feel that this is justified and necessary since I was in no way consulted regarding the formulation of or the contents of the statement which was issued to the press as the official position of the Commission.

I do not do this because of any lack of harmony or because of disagreement with the essential purpose and meaning of that significant document, but merely that any suggestions will be accepted by the rest of the Commission which so capably drew it up; and in any case it is essential that my own attitude with regard to the affairs of the Commission of which I am a part shall not be ignored and shall be a matter of permanent record. I do this to promote and make sounder the work of the Commission, and not in any way to hamper it. I am, let me repeat, entirely in favor of the already recorded purpose of the Commission: I believe that a man condemned for high crimes and misdemeanors without a personal trial should have every opportunity for a hearing and for a presentation of his case before the world. I am honored and glad to be a member of the Commission which furthers this just purpose. But I wish it definitely on record that I engage in the work of this Commission without any prior commitments. I do not subscribe to the doctrines of Mr. Trotsky or to any of the groups that utilize his name. I am not motivated by animosity toward any existing government involved or toward any partisan groups that favor or oppose Mr. Trotsky. I should not wish that the work of this Commission be improperly utilized by any such groups against any person or government.

Therefore, I desire above all that the Commission itself shall make no mistakes of fact, even the slightest, that it shall be stringently faithful to the accepted canons of evidence and of truth. Therefore it is necessary, so far as this Commissioner is concerned, to modify, before its incongruity is pointed out by others, the sentence referring to Mr. Trotsky's desire for extradition. This change, let me repeat, does not at all modify the lofty position of the Commission as it has been outlined by Dr. Dewey.

It is also declared in the same statement of this Preliminary Commission that our function is to give the results of our investigation obtained here to the Full Commission, of which we are a part, "so that the results obtained here, in connection with those secured by other investigating bodies, may bring to light the objective facts upon which judgment in the case of Leon Trotsky must rest."

This Commissioner would have desired, had he been previously consulted, that the nature of those auxiliary investigating bodies be precisely defined in this statement, that the nature and source of evidence—so far as it be known prior to investigation—which was not available to the Moscow courts, be indicated. This Commissioner had also been assured that the present Preliminary Commission, while fully cognizant of the fragmentary nature of its own investigations, would at the earliest possible moment give, not merely to the larger or full Commission of which we are also a part, but to the general public, a résumé of these preliminary findings, together with its own conclusions. Though our work will not be completed here, since the accused is in Mexico, the most important source of information is being tapped. This Commissioner feels that the opening statement of the Commission should have contained an assurance to this effect, and an assurance that such a résumé would be issued at the very earliest date.

The necessity for this is obvious. New trials are said to be scheduled in the Soviet Union, trials of a nature similar to those which have caused the sentencing, imprisonment and execution of large numbers of persons charged with having committed acts similar to those which have caused the official condemnation of Trotsky, whose life has not yet been taken because he has been in exile. Such a preliminary report as I have suggested is highly essential, and I feel should be previously announced, for if after our examination of the evidence garnered here there should arise any reasonable doubt as to the guilt of the accused Leon Trotsky, this would not only cast doubt upon the guilt of the defendants already executed, but might have some restraining influence which would save the lives of others soon to be in danger. If, on the other hand, this Preliminary Commission fails to raise any reasonable doubt and finds that so far as the evidence at hand is concerned the previous Moscow trials cannot be impugned, then this equally should help to free Soviet justice from unfair imputations and permit it to punish those who are properly guilty, without the disturbance of outside propaganda. The responsibility resting upon the Preliminary Commission is a heavy one, but it must be faced, and we must present our honest conclusions at the earliest date feasible.

Like the other members who drafted the opening statement by Dr. Dewey, this Commissioner now likewise goes on record as in favor of limiting the scope of our inquiry to the truth or falsity of the testimony given in so far as it implicated Mr. Trotsky. But he emphatically regrets the unfortunate statement that the Commission should go on record as not being concerned with the testimony so far as it bears upon the guilt or innocence of those who were present at the Moscow trials and had a hearing. While for obvious reasons we have no means at our disposal of so fully examining into the guilt or innocence of the other parties, and whereas the scope of the hearings has been properly limited, nevertheless Mr. Trotsky's own guilt or innocence is greatly involved in the testimony concerning the other prisoners who have been sentenced, imprisoned or executed. I merely wish to suggest that while we are obliged to limit our investigations, which must perforce be very specialized, they are, nevertheless, far more important than even the innocence or guilt, or the person, of Leon Trotsky, and cannot be thus easily dissociated from the larger problems of the trials already held, of Soviet law and justice.

Permit me to repeat that there is not, in these suggestions and in my personal reservations, the slightest hint of antagonism toward the other members of the Commission. My purpose is purely constructive and in full harmony with the statement made by the other members of the Commission. It is necessary that this be made part of the permanent record.

DEWEY: The Commission is glad to have in the permanent record Mr. Beals's statement, particularly as he was not here in time to be consulted in the preparation of the statement that was read Saturday morning. I regret the error regarding extradition to Moscow, and I assume responsibility myself for permitting that error in the statement that was made on Saturday.

FINERTY: May I have the privilege as counsel to say a

word on this? Extradition is possible in the absence of an extradition treaty. While it may be there is no extradition treaty between—I think Norway was referred to—between Russia and Mexico, it does not preclude either Government recognizing the demand of extradition.

BEALS: There are no diplomatic relations to make that demand.

FINERTY: It is not a correct legal statement.

TROTSKY: I am ready to go either to Norway or France or any other country.

BEALS: I am not raising that question—just that the statement of the Commission should be absolutely correct. I wish to say further that I wish also to get on record that I was here when this report was drawn up and was not consulted.

DEWEY: Will Mr. Goldman please state the topics upon which he will examine Mr. Trotsky, as far as the probable order of it is concerned.

GOLDMAN: Asking the Commission not to limit me very strictly to the order of the topics which I will present, now I will give you an idea of that order as I intend to present the evidence at the present moment. First, I wish to declare that the section of the evidence which I already presented was done so under the heading that I might call the biographical section of the evidence.

I wish today to attempt to present evidence with reference to the relationship, both political and personal, which Mr. Trotsky had with the defendants in the last two trials.

The next section—that is, number three—will deal with Mr. Trotsky's actual friends in the Soviet Union—that is, if he had any friends in the Soviet Union, if he had any followers, loyal followers of the Opposition.

The fourth section will deal with the very important evidence which we shall present, the aim of which will be to contradict the testimony of those defendants who actually claimed to have had contact with, seen, or corresponded with

Mr. Trotsky personally.

The next section, number five, I believe will deal in a sketchy way, because we are not in a position to introduce evidence on that point to a great extent, with the question of sabotage, "explosive acts and diversions," as they are called in the indictment and in the evidence at the Moscow trial. We shall produce some evidence to indicate that the existence of alleged acts of sabotage, "explosions and diversions" attributed to Mr. Trotsky's so-called followers in Russia can be explained on the basis of the bureaucratic leadership in industry in the Soviet Union.

The next section will deal with the question of individual terror, since Mr. Trotsky is accused of having originated a conspiracy for the purpose of assassinating the leaders in the Soviet Union. We shall present evidence to the effect, first, what Mr. Trotsky's beliefs have been on the question of individual terror, what they are now, and, second, Mr. Trotsky's attitude with reference to the possible removal of Stalin at the present time through democratic means.

The next section will deal with the question of the defense of the Soviet Union. Since Mr. Trotsky is accused in the indictment, and since testimony was produced during the trials which indicated that Trotsky was an enemy of the Soviet Union, we deem it relevant to introduce testimony showing his real attitude towards the Soviet Union.

Section eight will deal with certain international phases, since Mr. Trotsky was accused by the Prosecution in the Soviet Union of trying to get an alliance and actually making an alliance with German fascism on the one hand and Japanese militarism on the other hand. We deem it to be of sufficient importance, and quite relevant, to introduce evidence showing Mr. Trotsky's real attitude to the question of Hitler, German fascism and to the question of Japanese militarism.

In the last section, which I might term a sort of omnibus

section, I shall deal in short with the struggle between the Left Opposition led by Leon Trotsky and the majority of the Communist Party led by Stalin. I shall show the fundamental principles involved in the struggle, the methods used by both sides in the struggle, the predictions that Mr. Trotsky has made with reference to the possible methods to be used in the future, the nature of the previous trials held—that is, previous to the last two trials—and the attitude that Mr. Trotsky had to the Communist Party of the Soviet Union and the Communist International prior to 1933 and subsequent to 1933.

DEWEY: Will you proceed?

GOLDMAN: Do you want to make a statement, Mr. Trotsky?

TROTSKY: Yes. It is my bad English that puts me in error, but it seems to me that Mr. Beals named me the "accused." If Mr. Beals is insisting upon exactitude, I will also. I am not the "accused" here; I am a witness.

BEALS: I accept that qualification, Mr. Trotsky. I understand this is an investigation.

TROTSKY: Thank you.

BEALS: I was referring at that moment not to the present trial, but to the attitude of the Soviet Government which has accused you.

GOLDMAN: For the purpose of the record, I also wish to make a statement to the effect that sometimes I shall call, without thinking—I might call Mr. Trotsky the defendant, the accused, the witness, because it has always been emphasized that the real defendant in the Soviet court was Trotsky. But we consider Mr. Trotsky as a witness. Of course, as far as I am concerned, and as far as Mr. Trotsky is concerned, we accuse the Soviet court. We feel ourselves to be the accusers, and they the accused. But that is a matter for the Commission.

Now, Mr. Trotsky, I shall begin the direct examination.

DIRECT EXAMINATION
BY MR. GOLDMAN:

GOLDMAN: At the last session you stated that you were twenty-three years old when you wrote the pamphlet referred to by Vyshinsky in his argument, the pamphlet called "Our Political Tasks." Do you want to make a correction of that?

TROTSKY: It was written in the middle of the summer of 1903 and published at the beginning of 1904. During the writing I was not yet twenty-four years old, but I was almost twenty-four.

GOLDMAN: You were not twenty-four yet?

TROTSKY: Twenty-three and nine or ten months.

GOLDMAN: You want to tell us how much wiser you were nine months later?

TROTSKY: It is difficult to judge.

GOLDMAN: On the question of your relations with Lenin, I would like you to tell the Commission about something you wrote in your autobiography, namely: about a blank paper upon which Lenin wrote his name giving you complete authority to do what you deemed best while you were the leader of the Red Army. Will you tell us something about that?

TROTSKY: During the Civil War, I had to take upon myself a very heavy responsibility. I discharged these responsibilities before the whole public opinion and before the working class. Many people opposed my direction of the Civil War. Stalin guided that opposition behind the scenes. Lenin proposed to me and gave me, without any insistence from me, a paper on which, at the end, was written in red ink the following:

> Comrades: Knowing the strict character of Comrade Trotsky's orders, I am so convinced, so absolutely convinced, of the correctness, expediency, and necessity for

the success of the cause of the order given by Comrade Trotsky, that I unreservedly indorse this order.

V. ULYANOV/LENIN.

I must say it was not an official document because, as head of the Red Army, I had all the necessary right to give any orders concerning the war. On the contrary, Lenin did not have himself any possibility of giving direct orders. It was merely a document of concern to the Communists, and critics and oppositionists in the Red Army.

GOLDMAN: Where is the original of that document?

TROTSKY: I explained that there was a certain opposition in the ranks of the Party directed by Stalin.

GOLDMAN: You did not understand me. Where is the original of the document?

TROTSKY: The original of the document, as all the originals written by Lenin at any time, to anybody, are in the Institute of Lenin in Moscow. There was an order by the Central Committee that any Party member who had any document written by Lenin must transmit it to the Institute of Lenin in Moscow. But we received legal copies of all the documents transmitted to the Institute of Lenin. I have three or four legal copies of all the documents. One of the collections of these copies was given by me to the Institute of Social History in Amsterdam. The others are in my possession.

GOLDMAN: You are ready to produce these legal copies for the Commission whenever the Commission requests?

FINERTY: When you say legal copies, do you mean certified copies?

TROTSKY: It was a representative of the Institute of Lenin who visited all the Ministers of all the bureaus for them to transmit all the documents. The secretariat of the Ministry, of the respective Ministries and bureaus, with the representative of the Institute of Lenin, they accordingly testified to the copies.

FINERTY: Is the Institute of Lenin an official government body?

TROTSKY: It is a Party body. In the Soviet Union, Party bodies are connected with the Soviet bodies.

FINERTY: These documents are made for the public record?

TROTSKY: Yes, they were made public many times, and never denied by anybody.

GOLDMAN: Before proceeding to any further questions, I want to call the attention of the Commission to the fact that some questions were raised about Lenin's "last testament," during the examination on Saturday. I want to call the Commissioners' attention to the fact that Vyshinsky, on page 127 of the Report of the Court Proceedings in the Case of the Trotskyite-Zinovievite Terrorist Center, makes the following statement, in the middle of the fifth paragraph, the second sentence. Mr. Finerty, have you a copy of that?

FINERTY: Yes.

GOLDMAN (reading): "It was under their leadership, under the leadership of Comrade Stalin, that great executor and keeper of Lenin's will and testament, that the counter-revolutionary Trotskyite organization was routed." If Vyshinsky referred to the official Lenin's will and testament, I want the Commission, each one of the members of the Commission, to get a copy of Lenin's will and testament. Copies will be furnished. Read that document, and see whether Stalin was designated as the "great executor and keeper of Lenin's will and testament."

On the same page, page 127, the last paragraph beginning: "That is why the Trotskyites and Zinovievites," the second sentence reads:

> That is why, in March 1932, in a fit of counter-revolutionary fury, Trotsky burst out in an open letter with an appeal to "put Stalin out of the way" (this letter was

found between the double walls of Holtzman's suit case and figured as an exhibit in this case).

I want to read into the record a very short excerpt from the letter which Vyshinsky refers to. I read now from the *Militant* of April 9, 1932, containing the Open Letter to the Central Executive Committee of the U.S.S.R., by Leon Trotsky. I read from the third to the last paragraph:

> Read again the resolutions of the plenums of the Central Committee for the years 1926 and 1927, read again the statements of the Opposition; you have a fuller set of documents than I have. And you will be convinced again that the whole evolution of the Party, of the apparatus, of the Stalinist clique were foretold by us; all the milestones were indicated before.

I want to make a remark here that the English translation of the next sentence is not a correct translation. The English translation of this sentence has no meaning. It reads as follows: "The decomposition of the Stalinist system accuses with the exact observance of the manner indicated by the Opposition." This is not the meaning I check, but you are at liberty to check up with the original in the Russian. I continue to quote:

> Do you want to follow this road further? But there is no road further. Stalin has brought you to an impasse. You cannot come out on the road without liquidating Stalinism. You must trust to the working class, give the proletarian vanguard the possibility through free criticism from top to bottom to review the whole Soviet system and pitilessly cleanse it of the accumulated rubbish. It is time, finally, to fulfill the last urgent advice of Lenin, to *remove* Stalin.

TROTSKY: May I say that in the French edition—the English edition of the Verbatim Report says: "Put Stalin out of the way." In the French edition it says: Kill or assassinate him. The translations do not coincide.

GOLDMAN: Now, Mr. Trotsky, I am going to read to you and to the Commission the names of the defendants in the first trial, and ask you whether you recognize any of the names of the persons who at the time of the trial were followers of yours and could be correctly designated as "Trotskyites": G.E. Zinoviev, L.B. Kamenev, G.E. Evdokimov, I.N. Smirnov, I.P. Bakayev, V.A. Ter-Vaganyan, S.V. Mrachkovsky, E.A. Dreitzer, E.S. Holtzman, I.I. Reingold, R.V. Pickel, V.P. Olberg, K.B. Berman-Yurin (I am at a loss to know what the dash indicates, whether it indicates that the person had two names, an alias, or whether it was actually the name of the person), Fritz David (I.I. Kruglyansky), M. Lurye and N. Lurye. Were any of these persons, Mr. Trotsky, at the time of the trial in August, 1936, correctly to be considered your followers, or "Trotskyites?"

TROTSKY: Not one of them.

GOLDMAN: I read the names of the defendants in the second trial: Y.L. Pyatakov, K.B. Radek, G.Y. Sokolnikov, L.P. Serebryakov, N.I. Muralov, Y.A. Livshitz, Y.N. Drobnis, M.S. Boguslavsky, I.A. Knyazev, S.A. Rataichak, B.O. Norkin, A.A. Shestov, M.S. Stroilov, Y.D. Turok, I.Y. Hrasche, G.E. Pushin, V.V. Arnold.

FINERTY: Mr. Chairman. May I suggest, Mr. Goldman, this question is not of great help to the Commission. Obviously, at the time of the trial, these men were not followers of Trotsky, on their own statement. The real question is whether at any time they had been followers of Trotsky.

GOLDMAN: We shall go into that. I ask you whether immediately prior to the trial any of these defendants were followers of yours, or could correctly be designated as Trotskyites?

TROTSKY: Not one of them that I know, because there are some people whose names I learned for the first time from the reports of the court. Theoretically, it would be possible to admit that there might be *former* Trotskyites. I don't know. But the people who are known to me were my adversaries for years before the trial.

GOLDMAN: Now, we shall proceed to the individuals in these trials, Mr. Trotsky. You can tell us more in detail about that. I shall take Zinoviev and Kamenev, Mr. Trotsky, and ask you when was the first time you met them, if you remember, approximately?

TROTSKY: I met Kamenev for the first time in 1902, as a young student; Zinoviev later. I was acquainted with Kamenev during all the time after 1902. Zinoviev I saw for the first time at the Party Congress in 1907 in London. But I approached him for the first time only in 1917.

GOLDMAN: What were your political relations with Kamenev and Zinoviev up to the time of the October Revolution—that is, between the time that you came to Russia in May, 1917, up to October, 1917?

TROTSKY: No personal communication with Zinoviev; personal communication with Kamenev. He was the husband of my sister. I had personal relations with him. I did not belong to the Bolshevik organization at the time, and that is the reason our political relations reflected totally my relations to the Bolsheviks, and the attitude of the Bolshevik center to myself.

GOLDMAN: You entered the Bolshevik Party in August, 1917?

TROTSKY: Yes.

GOLDMAN: After that, what were your political relations with Zinoviev and Kamenev?

TROTSKY: They were personally friendly, and also, as before 1917, with Kamenev. But the attitude of Zinoviev and Kamenev during the period of the armed insurrection and the October Revolution hindered our good relations, because they were adversaries of the October insurrection. Lenin proposed even to expel them from the Party. I opposed this proposition, and we had a great majority in the Central Committee against the expulsion. Lenin was very satisfied, because it was for him only a matter of putting pressure on them. They became known to the entire Party during this period as oppositionists to the October Revolution.

GOLDMAN: Did you have any political quarrels with them after the October Revolution?

TROTSKY: Not immediately. I have many documents, or some documents, which are friendly, of a political and personal nature from Zinoviev and Kamenev. They are favorable characterizations of my activity after the October Revolution.

GOLDMAN: What we are mainly interested in is your relationship with them after Lenin's death and their role in the struggle between you and Stalin.

TROTSKY: They became, Zinoviev and Kamenev—with Stalin they created the so-called "Troïka," or Triumvirate, which was the directing body of the Central Committee of the Party and of the country during the period from the end of 1922 to 1925.

FINERTY: Mr. Goldman, I think the record ought to show the date of Lenin's death.

GOLDMAN: What was the date of Lenin's death?

TROTSKY: It was January, 1924.

GOLDMAN: January?

TROTSKY: The 21st of January, 1924. But before his death he was sick for a long time. He became sick in October, 1922, and he was totally eliminated from the directing work for many months. That was the time of a provisional situation. We awaited his reestablishment in Party work. He came to work for some months, I believe for three months. I will establish that more exactly. But he became sick again and definitely—it was the 5th or 6th of March, 1923. This time his illness lasted until his death. During this period the bureaucracy found its head in this Triumvirate of Zinoviev-Stalin-Kamenev. I can present here to the Commission, if you permit me, a pamphlet directed against me, written by Zinoviev, Stalin and Kamenev, in the English language, with an introduction by one of the leaders of the American Communist Party, Bittelman. He represents Zinoviev, Kamenev, and Stalin as the genuine emanation of Bolshevism against me. He is the representation, or the entire spirit—

GOLDMAN: The witness here refers to the pamphlet called "Leninism or Trotskyism," written by G.E. Zinoviev, J. Stalin, and L. Kamenev, in February, or published in February, 1925, for the Workers Party of America—at that time the Communist Party was called the Workers Party of America—by the Daily Worker Publishing Co., 1113 West Washington Boulevard, Chicago, Ill. We will introduce this pamphlet as Exhibit No. 5.

(The pamphlet "Leninism or Trotskyism," written by Zinoviev, Stalin, and Kamenev, is introduced as Exhibit No. 5.)

TROTSKY: May I quote some lines from the introduction of Bittelman?

GOLDMAN: Yes, you can quote some of the lines.

FINERTY: Before Mr. Trotsky testifies, can the record be cleared up to show whether the Triumvirate originated during Lenin's first illness or during his second illness?

TROTSKY: What?

FINERTY: Was the Triumvirate formed during Lenin's first illness or second illness?

TROTSKY: When it was built? Mr. Attorney, it is very difficult to say. We had no investigation about the organization of this bloc. I made a remark that during the first illness the situation was such that they were very cautious before the impossibility of the physical reestablishment of Lenin was confirmed by the doctors. They adopted in the beginning a fight against me, with the perspective of becoming the leaders of the Party. But during the second illness of Lenin they became even more courageous. Then it was officially an institution, the Troïka—"troïka" means three. It did not become an official institution until Lenin's second illness. During the second illness it became not official in a constitutional sense, but in the opinion of the Communist Party.

FINERTY: Definitely?

TROTSKY: Definitely.

GOLDMAN: It became an open institution during the second illness of Lenin. You want to read some excerpts?

TROTSKY: Yes, Mr. Bittelman writes: "He [Trotsky] will not make peace with the fact that the Russian Communist Party and the entire Communist International are led by the old Bolshevist guard along the road of Leninism as against Trotskyism." Zinoviev is listed as the first contributor, not in the order of the alphabet, however. It is a political order. But the same Mr. Bittelman published the following in "Trotsky, the Traitor," a new pamphlet in the last few days, and in it we read:

> Trotsky, Zinoviev, Pyatakov and Company are "Old Bolsheviks," some people say. They are the "fathers" of the Russian Revolution, it is claimed. On this false basis, the question is asked: How is it possible for these "founders" of the Soviet system to try to betray it, and to join for this purpose with the worst enemies of Socialism? Those who genuinely ask such questions apparently do not know that this gang of counter-revolutionary bandits have had a long history, that their transformation into allies of fascism is no sudden or overnight affair. They were moving in that direction for a long time. [Page 12—A.M.G.]

> For the moment, suffice it to say that just as the American Revolution had its Benedict Arnold and Aaron Burr, and just as our period of the Civil War had John Wilkes Booth, the assassin of Lincoln, so the Soviet Union is having its Trotsky, Zinoviev, Pyatakov and others. [Page 3–4—A.M.G.]

In the year 1925 Zinoviev was referred to as the genuine "Old Bolshevik Guard." Now, he is "The Booth of Russia."

GOLDMAN: The witness refers to the pamphlet written by Alexander Bittelman, the same one who wrote the introduction to Exhibit No. 5, "Leninism or Trotskyism." Alexander Bittelman is a well known member of the Communist Party. Mark this pamphlet Exhibit No. 6.

(The pamphlet, "Trotsky, the Traitor," written by Alexander Bittelman, is introduced into evidence as Exhibit No. 6.)

FINERTY: Mr. Goldman, Commissioner Stolberg thinks it would be well to show what positions in the Government the Triumvirate—what positions were held by Zinoviev and Kamenev and Stalin during the Triumvirate.

GOLDMAN: Did you understand that, Mr. Trotsky?

TROTSKY: It is not a question directly of the Government. Zinoviev was never a member of the Government; nor Kamenev. But both were members of the Politburo, which is the genuine guiding center of the Party and of the country. The Government, the official Government, submits to the orders of the Politburo, and a member of the Politburo is incomparably more important than the highest Minister. It is only a technical post, the Minister. Zinoviev, Kamenev and Stalin—they built the "Troïka," not with a Party status, nor with an official status in the country. But it was sustained by the Party apparatus, and that was absolutely sufficient for their dominant role. At the Party Congress, which was held in 1923, during the illness of Lenin—it was the Twelfth Party Congress—one member, a prominent member of the Party, Ossinsky, attacked Zinoviev, and Stalin immediately answered.

GOLDMAN: Is it a short excerpt?

TROTSKY: It is not long.

> Comrades, I cannot ignore the attack of Comrade Ossinsky against . . . Comrade Zinoviev. He praised Comrade Stalin, praised Comrade Kamenev, and struck out at Comrade Zinoviev, thinking that at first it is enough to eliminate one, and that then will come the others' turn. He has taken the course of destroying the nucleus which has been formed inside the Central Committee during years of work, in order to destroy everything later, step by step . . . If Comrade Ossinsky seriously intends to undertake such attacks against one or another member of our Central Committee, I must warn him that he will bump into a stone wall on which, I fear, he will smash his head.

It was a moment when Stalin officially represented himself before the country as a member of the "Troïka" and totally connected with Kamenev and Zinoviev—or, better, with Zinoviev and Kamenev. My name was not mentioned, but the fact that it was not mentioned was very well understood by all the bureaucrats—that it was directed against me.

FINERTY: I have one more suggestion, and that is, that it would be well for him to show the structure of the Party, what the functions of the Central Committee are, and what the function of the Politburo is. The record does not show what the constitution of the Party is, as distinct from the constitution of the Government.

DEWEY: Can that be done subsequently?

GOLDMAN: I have no objection. I think that Mr. Finerty would like to have it, and perhaps he can develop that on cross-examination.

FINERTY: It may be necessary for an intelligent determination of these questions.

GOLDMAN: Yes. I don't want to take up my time with all these matters. Have you any other short excerpt that you want to quote on the question of Stalin's relations with Zinoviev and your relations with Zinoviev?

TROTSKY: I believe it is more or less sufficient at this moment. We can present more quotations about the "Troïka." The most important thing I explained.

GOLDMAN: Now will you tell us, give us an idea of the development of the struggle, the political struggle, between you and the Triumvirate. What happened in the later years? Did this bloc, this Triumvirate, remain as a bloc or did it split up? What happened after that?

TROTSKY: It split. I must introduce, that after the split of Kamenev and Zinoviev from Stalin, all the secrets of the "Troïka" became known by me as an ally of Zinoviev and Kamenev. Zinoviev and Kamenev explained—it was an official explanation in Party meetings and Party sessions—that among the members of the Politburo it was a mutual obligation never to attack one another, but only Trotsky.

GOLDMAN: When was the split between Zinoviev and Kamenev, and Stalin?

TROTSKY: It was during the preparation, the secret preparation of the split. It was in the second half of 1925. It appeared openly at the Fourteenth Congress of the Party. That was the beginning of 1926.

GOLDMAN: With reference to your relationship with Kamenev and Zinoviev, will you tell the Commissioners what actually occurred after the split?

TROTSKY: Zinoviev and Kamenev were the most embittered adversaries of mine during the time of the alliance with Stalin. Stalin was more cautious in the fight against me. But Zinoviev was the chairman of the Petrograd Soviet. Kamenev was the chairman of the Moscow Soviet. These are very important circumstances. They were under the pressure of workers, of the best workers we had—of Petrograd and Moscow—the most developed and most educated workers. Stalin's support was in the provinces, the bureaucracy in the provinces. At first they did not themselves understand—that is, Zinoviev and Kamenev, as others also—why the split came. But it was the pressure of the workers of both capitals. The pressure of the workers pushed Zinoviev and Kamenev into contradictions with Stalin. It was the fundamentals of Socialism—the foundations of Socialism. It was not possible to explain this by personal ambitions, and so on. I am not denying the role of the factor of personal ambitions, but personal ambitions begin to play a role only through the push of social forces. Without that, they become purely personal ambitions.

GOLDMAN: Did they make a bloc with you?

TROTSKY: They did, but not immediately after the Fourteenth Congress. About two or three months after, we entered into an alliance with Zinoviev and Kamenev.

GOLDMAN: How long did that alliance last?

TROTSKY: Will you permit me to quote a declaration of Zinoviev?

GOLDMAN: Yes.

TROTSKY: It was in the Central Committee of July, 1926, Zinoviev said—it is from the report of the Central Committee:

> I have committed many mistakes. I think that the most important of my mistakes are two in number. My first mistake of 1917 is known to all of you. . . . I consider my second mistake *more dangerous* because the mistake of 1917 was committed in Lenin's presence, it was corrected

by Lenin, and also by ourselves with Lenin's help a few days later. But my mistake of 1923 consisted in this:

Ordjonikidze: That you deceived the whole Party?

Zinoviev: We say that now there can no longer be any doubt that the fundamental core of the opposition of 1923, as the evolution of the present ruling faction has demonstrated, warned with justice of the dangers of the deviation from the proletarian line and of the menacing growth of the apparatus régime. . . . Yes, in the question of the bureaucratic-apparatus oppression, Trotsky was right against us. (Verbatim Report of Central Committee, IV, P. 33.)

STOLBERG: Mr. Trotsky, the first mistake which Zinoviev there speaks of, you characterize as his opposition to the October Revolution. Wasn't it rather an opposition to the October insurrection?

TROTSKY: To the October Revolution, because without the October insurrection, it could not become the October Revolution.

GOLDMAN: How long did your bloc with Zinoviev and Kamenev last?

TROTSKY: Almost two years—nineteen months, to be exact. It began in the Spring of 1926 and finished in the Fall of 1927.

GOLDMAN: What was the occasion of the split between the forces of Zinoviev and Kamenev and your own?

TROTSKY: The reason was the repressions of the bureaucracy against the Opposition. At the beginning it was possible, it seemed possible, that Zinoviev and Kamenev, to Zinoviev and Kamenev—we had great discussion about this—that by our fight we could change in a short time the policy of the Party. The reaction in the masses and the active reaction in the bureaucracy showed that it was impossible. The bureaucracy became hardened and persecuted the Opposition.

Then the question was: Break with the bureaucracy and the apparatus, with legal existence, or go back and capitulate.

GOLDMAN: Did the break-up of your bloc with Zinoviev occur after or before your expulsion from the Party?

TROTSKY: Before, some weeks before, but not formally. It was clear to us, and we were prepared for the expulsion. It was clear that my group was totally ready to accept the expulsion; that the Zinoviev group would avoid the expulsion at any price.

GOLDMAN: Did the Zinoviev group succeed in avoiding expulsion?

TROTSKY: Not immediately by the capitulation. They remained six months expelled from the Party.

GOLDMAN: At the Congress where you were expelled, were they also expelled?

TROTSKY: Yes, all the Oppositionists were expelled, in spite of the capitulation.

FINERTY: Mr. Goldman, Commissioner Stolberg thinks it would be well also to show what was the basis of the bloc between Zinoviev and Trotsky.

STOLBERG: The agreement.

TROTSKY: The basis is formulated in our platform published also in English in a book under the title, "The Real Situation in Russia." It is an important document of 150 pages, embracing all the questions of social and political life in the Soviet Union, of its international policy and questions of the Communist International. As I explained, it was a question of democracy against bureaucracy, equality against privileges, more industrialization—at that time, the bureaucracy was against industrialization—for collectivization in villages, an international revolutionary policy as against a narrow national policy in diplomacy, a total change in the policy of the Communist International, more independence of the sections of the Comintern, and, at the same time, more of an international revolutionary policy of the sections.

DEWEY: Will that document be put into evidence?

GOLDMAN: This program Mr. Trotsky refers to, published as a book, if I am not mistaken, in 1927, with an introduction by Max Eastman, is also translated by Max Eastman, and is called "The Real Situation in Russia." They are not available here.

DEWEY: We will take a short recess now.

GOLDMAN: What happened to Zinoviev and Kamenev after they were expelled from the Party, Mr. Trotsky?

TROTSKY: After the second capitulation, the second declaration of capitulation, they were admitted to the Party, in five or six months after the expulsion.

GOLDMAN: You mean that five or six months after the expulsion they capitulated?

TROTSKY: They capitulated at the time of the Fifteenth Congress, but they remained expelled for some months.

GOLDMAN: Then I understand you to say at the Fifteenth Congress they capitulated, and they signed a second statement admitting their errors?

FINERTY: Can you give us that date?

GOLDMAN: When was this Congress held, Mr. Trotsky?

TROTSKY: It was held the end of December, 1927.

GOLDMAN: They were expelled from the Party at that Congress. Were they exiled at all after that, immediately after?

TROTSKY: Yes, they were exiled, but not too far, in Siberia—in the provincial towns of Russia.

GOLDMAN: I understood you to say that six months after that they capitulated once more.

TROTSKY: Yes, they made a second declaration, and they were admitted as Party members.

GOLDMAN: Can you give—have you a copy of that capitulation statement, or can you refer the Commission to the *Pravda*?

TROTSKY: It is very regrettable that we could not prepare all the documents of the capitulation. They are all published in the *Pravda,* and they are now in the New York Public Library. We could cable New York for a copy.

GOLDMAN: In your records, do you find the date of the *Pravda* where the capitulation statement was published?

TROTSKY: No.

FINERTY: Mr. Goldman, will you furnish for the record the date of the capitulation in the *Pravda* mentioned?

GOLDMAN: Yes, we shall give the Commission the date of the capitulation and the copy of the *Pravda.*

TROTSKY: There is a great deal of material.

GOLDMAN: When was the last time you saw Zinoviev and Kamenev?

TROTSKY: It was the end of 1927.

GOLDMAN: Did you see Kamenev at a different time?

TROTSKY: At the same time, together, both of them.

GOLDMAN: Did you have a conversation with them?

TROTSKY: Yes.

GOLDMAN:What was said at the conversation?

TROTSKY: The subject of the conversation was that they were permitted to return—they returned to political life. I said it was their political death. Capitulation is political death.

GOLDMAN: Did you have any correspondence with Zinoviev and Kamenev?

TROTSKY: The last letter I received from Zinoviev was on the 7th of November, 1927. It finishes with the words:

> I admit entirely that Stalin will tomorrow circulate the most venomous "versions." We are taking steps to inform the public. Do the same. Warm greetings, Yours, G. Zinoviev.

GOLDMAN: The witness quotes from a letter from Zinoviev dated November 7, 1927, addressed to L.B. Kamenev,

L.D. Trotsky, and Y.P. Smilga. A copy will be furnished the Commission.

FINERTY: You had better identify who these other persons were, like Smilga.

GOLDMAN: Kamenev is the same Kamenev you read about.

FINERTY: Yes.

GOLDMAN: How about Smilga?

TROTSKY: Smilga is an old member of the Party, a member of the Central Committee of the Party and a member of the Opposition, of the center of the Opposition at that time. Now he is in prison, if he is not assassinated. I am not sure.

STOLBERG: What do you mean by the center of the Opposition? The executive committee?

TROTSKY: It was an executive committee, yes, the same as a central committee.

GOLDMAN: Of the leading comrades of the Left Opposition?

TROTSKY: Yes.

BEALS: By the remark "assassination," you mean he had just been put in prison and never given a trial?

TROTSKY: Never.

GOLDMAN: You don't know whether he is alive or not?

TROTSKY: I am not sure whether he is alive. On the list of the accused are appended only the names of people who signed confessions. Of the others, I don't know. He is named as a terrorist and so on, here.

GOLDMAN: In the Verbatim Report. Did you have any correspondence with Zinoviev and Kamenev after you were exiled to Alma-Ata?

TROTSKY: No.

GOLDMAN: Did you have any correspondence with Zinoviev and Kamenev after you were deported from the Soviet Union?

TROTSKY: No.

GOLDMAN: Did you have any correspondence with them through any intermediaries?

TROTSKY: No.

GOLDMAN: Did you ever talk with anyone giving any message for the purpose of transferring that message to Zinoviev and Kamenev?

TROTSKY: Never.

GOLDMAN: Beginning with your exile up to now?

TROTSKY: Beginning with the 7th of November, 1927.

GOLDMAN: The last correspondence, then, you had with Zinoviev was November 7, 1927?

TROTSKY: Yes.

STOLBERG: Zinoviev and Kamenev?

GOLDMAN: Yes, and Kamenev, too?

TROTSKY: Yes.

GOLDMAN: Have you ever written any articles or letters in which you dealt with the role of Zinoviev after that capitulation?

TROTSKY: Dozens and dozens.

GOLDMAN: Will you give us the most important articles and letters that you wrote with reference to their capitulation and to their general role in the movement subsequent to your break-up of the bloc with them?

TROTSKY: The articles about the so-called capitulators are eighty-four.

GOLDMAN: Eighty-four articles?

TROTSKY: Eighty-four articles, in the *Bulletin of the Opposition,* in different papers of our movement. Eighty-four articles, and in twelve books and pamphlets the question is also analyzed.

GOLDMAN: Are all of those articles, to the best of your knowledge, translated into English in the *Militant*?

TROTSKY: It is—this is the list of the *Militant* only.

GOLDMAN: I introduce into evidence the list of articles, also books—

TROTSKY: Also books.

GOLDMAN: Articles and books in which Leon Trotsky dealt with the capitulators, Zinoviev and Kamenev.

TROTSKY: And in general on the question of capitulation.

GOLDMAN: And other capitulators, in which he also dealt with the question of capitulations in general. I introduce this into evidence. Let the record show that copies of this list will be furnished to the Commissioners. They are all found in the *Militant*, a former organ of the Trotskyites in the United States, and cover a period beginning December 15, 1928, to June 6, 1936. I introduce this as Exhibit No. 7.

(The list of articles appearing in the Militant *dealing with capitulations is introduced into evidence as Exhibit No. 7.)*

FINERTY: May the Commission assume that these articles are all critical of Zinoviev and Kamenev?

TROTSKY: Absolutely.

GOLDMAN: The articles speak for themselves, and we can furnish the Commission at least one copy of the bound volume of the *Militant*. They are very hostile to the capitulators. In this connection, I wish to read an excerpt from Vyshinsky's speech of January 28. It is found on Page 464 of the Verbatim Report of the trial:

> The Trotskyites went underground, they donned the mask of repentance and pretended that they had disarmed. Obeying the instruction of Trotsky, Pyatakov and the other leaders of this gang of criminals, pursuing a policy of duplicity, camouflaging themselves, they again penetrated into the Party, again penetrated into Soviet offices, here and there they even managed to creep into responsible positions of the state, concealing for a time, as has now been established beyond a shadow of doubt,

their old Trotskyite, anti-Soviet wares in their secret apartments, together with arms, codes, passwords, connections and cadres.

FINERTY: Commissioner Stolberg suggests that it would aid the Commission to tell us what other leading members of the Opposition bloc did not capitulate.

GOLDMAN: You mean the Zinoviev faction?

STOLBERG: Here was a bloc of Zinoviev, Kamenev and Trotsky. Of the leading personalities, who capitulated and who did not capitulate?

GOLDMAN: We can ask Mr. Trotsky the names, but we are going through all the defendants.

STOLBERG: I think it will clarify it.

GOLDMAN: Will you tell us, Mr. Trotsky, the names of the leading members of the bloc who, after the expulsion from the Party at the Fifteenth Congress, did not capitulate?

TROTSKY: I can name only two members, who capitulated in the last years. They were firm until 1934. I am referring to Rakovsky and Sosnovsky. Rakovsky is the former ambassador, and Sosnovsky is a very well known author in Russia, a journalist, and one of the best of our country. The others capitulated one after another.

GOLDMAN: Did you ever discuss with anyone the possibility of organizing a united center between your political followers and the followers of Zinoviev and Kamenev in the Soviet Union, after the break-up of your bloc with Zinoviev and Kamenev?

TROTSKY: Never. My articles show that it is absolutely impossible. My appreciation of them, my total contempt after the capitulation, my hostility to them and their hostility to me, excluded that absolutely.

GOLDMAN: Have you read the testimony of Zinoviev and Kamenev and the other defendants in the first Moscow trial?

TROTSKY: Yes.

GOLDMAN: Wherein these defendants claimed that you instructed several of them to establish a united center between your political followers and their political followers? Have you read such testimonies?

TROTSKY: Yes.

GOLDMAN: What have you to say about that?

TROTSKY: It is a falsehood organized by the G.P.U. and supported by Stalin.

GOLDMAN: Now, proceeding to the other defendants in the first trial, I ask you whether or not you know or knew I.N. Smirnov?

TROTSKY: Yes.

GOLDMAN: How long did you know him?

TROTSKY: Beginning with the Civil War. He was one of the prominent figures in the Civil War.

GOLDMAN: And what role did he play in the Civil War?

TROTSKY: An important one. He was with me in the Fifth Army. He led the forces in Siberia. He organized and insured the victory against Admiral Kolchak.

GOLDMAN: In the struggle between you and Stalin, what position did he take?

TROTSKY: He was with me against Stalin all the time until 1929.

GOLDMAN: Was he expelled at the Fifteenth Congress?

TROTSKY: Yes.

GOLDMAN: What happened to him—was he exiled?

TROTSKY: He was exiled, yes. He capitulated later, a bit later than Radek.

GOLDMAN: Capitulated?

TROTSKY: Yes.

GOLDMAN: Somewhat later than Radek?

TROTSKY: Yes.

GOLDMAN: When?

TROTSKY: At the end of 1929, November, 1929.

GOLDMAN: Do you happen to have in your archives a copy of the statement of his capitulation?

TROTSKY: A part of it only is reproduced in the *Bulletin*.

GOLDMAN: You mean the *Bulletin of the Opposition*?

TROTSKY: If you permit me, I will show you the quotation: "November 3rd, there was printed in *Pravda* a miserable document of Smirnov and Boguslavsky."

GOLDMAN: What are you reading from now?

TROTSKY: I am reading the article of mine in the Russian *Bulletin*, which is No. 7, November–December, 1929.

GOLDMAN: No. 7 of the *Bulletin*?

TROTSKY: Of November 3rd. It was printed in *Pravda*, "a miserable document of Smirnov and Boguslavsky." It is contained in the *Bulletin*, and differs little from the cowardly declaration of Radek. And this was Smirnov, who was one of my best friends in comparison to Radek and Pyatakov.

GOLDMAN: After his capitulation in November, 1929, did you have any connection with Smirnov?

TROTSKY: I, directly, not. My son met him in Berlin in 1931, in the street.

GOLDMAN: Did your son give you any information?

TROTSKY: Yes, he told us that the man is absolutely unhappy and disoriented, without any political orientation, that he gave him some information about old friends, capitulators and non-capitulators, and that he was very friendly in conversations with him—he knew my son as a boy, and then as a young lad—contrary to Pyatakov, who met my son also on the street, but turned his head away. My son called him traitor. That was on Unter den Linden.

GOLDMAN: I want to state before the Commission that I am not going into the testimony of the defendants now—that is, the testimony that is contained in the Report—but simply to set down the attitude of Leon Trotsky towards the defendants now and what it was at that time, just for that purpose, and I am notifying the Commission that I am not going into a detailed analysis of the testimony. Do you know E.A. Dreitzer, Mr. Trotsky?

TROTSKY: Yes, he was of the younger generation. Dreitzer was an officer of the Red Army. During and after my expulsion from the Party he had, together with ten or twelve officers, organized a guard around my home. He was among them. I totally forgot his name. My wife reminded me that it was Dreitzer.

GOLDMAN: Was he a member of the guard?

TROTSKY: Yes.

GOLDMAN: A member of the Left Opposition?

TROTSKY: Yes.

GOLDMAN: Was he expelled from the Party at the Fifteenth Congress?

TROTSKY: Yes, and also capitulated in 1928.

GOLDMAN: Was he exiled, do you know?

TROTSKY: I am not sure; I don't know.

GOLDMAN: When did he capitulate?

TROTSKY: I believe in 1928.

GOLDMAN: Do you have in your records a statement of the capitulation that he made at that time?

TROTSKY: I am not even sure it was published. He was not so prominent.

GOLDMAN: Have you had any communication with him since 1928?

TROTSKY: Never; I forgot his name.

GOLDMAN: Will you please wait until I finish the question?

TROTSKY: Yes. (Laughter)

GOLDMAN: Have you ever had any communications with him in any way through third parties?

TROTSKY: Never.

GOLDMAN: Tell us your relationship with S.V. Mrachkovsky?

DEWEY: Mr. Goldman, might I interrupt for a moment? On Page 22 of the official report of the August trial, it is stated by the Prosecutor that Dreitzer was "one of the people most devoted to him and at one time was chief of his personal bodyguard." Was Dreitzer ever your bodyguard?

TROTSKY: I explained that after I left the Kremlin, after my expulsion, I occupied a private house. Some of the officers of the Red Army organized this bodyguard. He was among them. They were young people, not prominent people. I forgot even the name of Dreitzer. My wife reminded me of that. But he was never close to me—a friend of mine.

GOLDMAN: Is that all, Dr. Dewey?

DEWEY: That is all.

GOLDMAN: Now, will you tell us your relationship with S.V. Mrachkovsky?

TROTSKY: Mrachkovsky was also a so-called "Trotskyite." He was one of the proven heroes of the Civil War in the Urals. He was the commanding general of the Military Ural District. In so far as he was connected with me, it was only in our military activity. As an Oppositionist, he was very active until 1929 or the end of 1928. He capitulated, also.

GOLDMAN: Have you any record of his statement of capitulation in your archives?

TROTSKY: We will find all the records. It was published in all the papers.

GOLDMAN: You haven't got that at the present time?

TROTSKY: We will get all of them to the Commission.

GOLDMAN: Did you have any communication with him since the capitulation?

TROTSKY: Never.

GOLDMAN: Either direct or indirect?

TROTSKY: Never.

GOLDMAN: Either by word of mouth or by writing?

TROTSKY: Never.

GOLDMAN: Now, I ask you whether you knew E.S. Holtzman?

TROTSKY: Yes, I suppose that I knew him. I am not sure, because in the Party there were several Holtzmans. I am not sure that is the Holtzman whom I have in my mind. Before our deportation to Siberia, one Holtzman came to our house with greetings and good wishes. I knew him at that time, that he was a sympathizer for a certain time of the Opposition, in 1926; but he separated himself from the Opposition in 1927, before the Fifteenth Congress—before the expulsions—he separated himself from the Opposition.

DEWEY: Is there any documentary evidence on this?

TROTSKY: It is mentioned in the Verbatim Report, but the prosecutor believes it was a hypocrisy. That is another question.

GOLDMAN: Have you in any way had any communications with any Holtzman since you left Russia?

TROTSKY: Never.

GOLDMAN: Directly or indirectly?

TROTSKY: Never.

GOLDMAN: Have you ever seen anyone whom you recall as Holtzman?

TROTSKY: No.

GOLDMAN: Can you tell us anything about G.E. Evdokimov?

TROTSKY: He is also an old Party member, a Zinovievist, a worker from Leningrad and a member of the Central Committee and a friend of Zinoviev.

GOLDMAN: He was not a member of the Trotskyite Left Opposition?

TROTSKY: Never.

GOLDMAN: Have you ever had any correspondence with him since you were in exile?

TROTSKY: Never.

GOLDMAN: Directly or indirectly?

TROTSKY: Never.

GOLDMAN: Now, tell us something about V.A. Ter-Vaganyan.

TROTSKY: Ter-Vaganyan was a younger scholar, a Marxist scholar, an editor of a Marxist review. I had connections with him because I wrote from time to time articles for his review. I remember very well that he was an Oppositionist, not active because he was an abstract man, not a political man—a theoretical man. He never belonged to the leading center of the Opposition, and he capitulated officially with the others after the Fifteenth Congress.

GOLDMAN: How long after?

TROTSKY: I am not sure, but I believe during the year 1928.

GOLDMAN: When was the last time you saw him?

TROTSKY: It is possible that it was during 1927.

GOLDMAN: Did you see him since you were expelled from Moscow?

TROTSKY: Never.

GOLDMAN: You had no communication with him?

TROTSKY: Never.

GOLDMAN: Oral or written communication?

TROTSKY: Nothing.

GOLDMAN: Do you know the defendant I.I. Reingold?

TROTSKY: Reingold? Yes.

GOLDMAN: Who was he?

TROTSKY: He was connected with Sokolnikov in work in the Ministry of Defense. He was connected politically, more or less, with Kamenev. In this manner he belonged, more or less, to the bloc, the working bloc with Zinoviev, but had no active role at all.

GOLDMAN: When was the last time you saw him?

TROTSKY: It is difficult to say. It was more by chance that I saw him. I believe it was during 1927.

GOLDMAN: Did you see him since your exile?

TROTSKY: Never.

GOLDMAN: Did you write to him since your exile?

TROTSKY: Never.

GOLDMAN: Have you received any communications from him since your exile?

TROTSKY: Never.

GOLDMAN: Do you know I.P. Bakayev?

TROTSKY: Yes.

GOLDMAN: Who is he?

TROTSKY: He was also a worker from Leningrad; he was a member of the Central Control Commission and a Zinovievist. He belonged to the bloc. He belonged to the central group of the bloc with Zinoviev and Evdokimov.

GOLDMAN: Do you know whether he capitulated?

TROTSKY: At the same time with Zinoviev.

GOLDMAN: Some time in 1928?

FINERTY: When you say "capitulated," you don't always state that they were expelled. May we assume that they were expelled prior to capitulation?

GOLDMAN: All those who belonged to the bloc with Zinoviev were expelled at the Fifteenth Congress?

TROTSKY: Yes.

GOLDMAN: That is, the leading members, I presume—not all the Communists who adhered.

TROTSKY: We had our platform, our program, and everybody who signed it was automatically expelled.

GOLDMAN: And that program refers to the program contained in "The Real Situation in Russia"?

TROTSKY: Yes. The condition for readmission into the Party was to resign from the platform, to renounce the platform, and to declare the platform false.

GOLDMAN: Do you remember the name of R.V. Pickel?

TROTSKY: Yes.

GOLDMAN: What can you tell us about him?

TROTSKY: He was a certain time, I believe, working in the Military Inspection. Then he was a secretary of Zinoviev, and, I believe, head of his secretariat.

GOLDMAN: Was he a member of the bloc?

TROTSKY: I suppose he was, but not a leading member. I never met him as an Oppositionist.

GOLDMAN: By the way, I forgot to ask you whether you had any communication at all, while in exile, with I.P. Bakayev?

TROTSKY: No.

GOLDMAN: Oral or written?

TROTSKY: No.

GOLDMAN: Do you know whether Pickel was expelled from the Party at the Fifteenth Congress?

TROTSKY: I didn't pay any attention to his fate—I suppose with all the Zinovievists who capitulated. He was connected with Zinoviev, as well, personally.

GOLDMAN: During the period after you left Russia, have you heard of him, written to him, or communicated with him in any way?

TROTSKY: Never.

GOLDMAN: Do you know the name of Fritz David, also named I.I. Kruglyansky?

TROTSKY: Never have before the trial.

GOLDMAN: The first time you saw his name was when you read the reports of the trial; is that right?

TROTSKY: Yes. The first cables about the trial.

GOLDMAN: Do you know the name of M. Lurye?

TROTSKY: No.

GOLDMAN: N. Lurye?

TROTSKY: No.

GOLDMAN: When was the first time you ever saw their names?

TROTSKY: In the cable, the Moscow cable, the Tass cable, concerning the trial.

GOLDMAN: Before that you never knew the people by such names?

TROTSKY: No.

GOLDMAN: Never had any relationship with them?

TROTSKY: Never.

GOLDMAN: Do you remember the name of K.B. Berman-Yurin?

TROTSKY: The same as the others—never have before the trial.

GOLDMAN: Do you recall the name of V.P. Olberg?

TROTSKY: Yes.

GOLDMAN: Will you tell us something about him? What do you know about him?

TROTSKY: He wrote me from Berlin—it was in 1929, I believe, or the beginning of 1930—as many other young people from different countries, asking me information about the situation in Germany; and about the situation in Russia he also wrote. I answered the more or less serious letters I received. We had a correspondence over some months. All his letters are in my possession. I have copies of my answers also. During the sojourn of my son in Berlin—Leon Sedov—he came in relations with him and furnished me from time to time quotations from Russian books, Russian books from the libraries, and some services. Then he wished to enter into collaboration with me as my Russian secretary. I needed a Russian secretary. I asked my friends in Berlin, Franz Pfemfert, the editor, and his wife, who is my translator in German, Alexandra Ramm, what was their opinion about the young man. They notified him to come and see them, and on that occasion, he made an absolutely negative impression. I have in my possession both letters. They describe him as a very doubtful young man, and maybe an agent of the G.P.U.

GOLDMAN: Did you ever see Olberg personally?

TROTSKY: Never.

GOLDMAN: All your relations with him were through correspondence?

TROTSKY: From political and theoretical correspondence.

GOLDMAN: With the permission of the Commission, I want to read into the record an excerpt from the letter of Franz Pfemfert dated April 1, 1930. The letter, I presume, is to you, Mr. Trotsky?

TROTSKY: Yes.

GOLDMAN: These are only quotations from the letter: "Olberg produces the most unfavorable and the most untrustworthy impression." I want to inform the Commission that this letter is a translation, I presume from the German, and you will see by the language that it is a translation. Perhaps a better translation will be made.

TROTSKY: It is written in good German.

FINERTY: I understand, Mr. Goldman, that all these letters will be at the disposal of the Commission in originals.

TROTSKY: The originals are in my possession.

FINERTY: And will be in our possession.

GOLDMAN (reading):

> He had hardly taken a seat in my study . . . when he put a couple of questions so tactless that I answered with counter-questions: When did you come to Germany? Answer: I have been living here a long time. What is your profession? Answer: Journalist. Where do you work? Answer: Until January I was on the *Inprecorr* editorial staff.

The *Inprecorr* is a magazine published weekly by the Communist International for the benefit of the Communist Parties and distributed to all the organizations of the Communist Parties in the world.

RUEHLE: The press correspondence.

STOLBERG: It is an official organ?

GOLDMAN: Yes. I am continuing Franz Pfemfert's letter:

> I really had enough at that point . . . it was painfully clear to me . . . that he had so suddenly been transformed and now . . . was attempting to find out internal matters about T. [referring to Trotsky] and the Opposition in general. . . .
>
> . . . I observed that he . . . was already chattering (to Naville and Shachtman, who were present) about his trip to L.T. as secretary, and that he was molesting the comrades with insistent questions: How strong is the group of the *Vérité*? [*Vérité* was the French Trotskyite newspaper.] . . . How strong in the United States? What will he have to do at L.D.'s? etc. . . . Sch. had the same impression as A. and I. . . .
>
> . . . We should not underestimate Stalin's gang. They will attempt by every means to introduce spies into our ranks, at least in order to obtain our list of addresses and to know our illegal work.
>
> . . . Perhaps Olberg is only a journalist and not yet a direct agent of Stalin. But he has not yet been tested. . . . I consider it my duty as your comrade and as a revolutionary to state how I view the matter.
>
> . . . Olberg has no place in your house, because in twenty-four hours he would be an insupportable burden to you and—possibly . . . fabricate reports for the G.P.U.

FINERTY: What is the date of that letter?

GOLDMAN: April 1, 1930.

TROTSKY: Permit me to communicate to you that Franz Pfemfert did not belong to the organization. He is a personal friend of mine, an editor, but he is not a Trotskyite.

GOLDMAN: Now, I have in my possession many documents referring to the correspondence between Trotsky and

Olberg, and either a copy or an original of the letter I just quoted. These will be made available to the Commission. I simply introduce these as the "Olberg Exhibit." Such as are possible, we will translate for the Commission before the Commission leaves.

(The Olberg file was introduced into evidence as Exhibit No. 8.)

GOLDMAN: I presume that our technical equipment is not of such a nature as to do that, so that all of the exhibits referring to Trotsky's relations with Olberg, and that which will be brought out later referring to the passport of Olberg, will be made available to the Commission either here or more probably in New York.

FINERTY: Does that exhibit include correspondence between Trotsky and Olberg?

GOLDMAN: These contain correspondence between you and Olberg? There are a lot of Russian letters.

TROTSKY: Yes, they are the original letters of Olberg and the copies of my answers to him.

GOLDMAN: Did you hear that, Mr. Finerty?

FINERTY: Yes.

TROTSKY: It is the originals of the letters of Olberg and the copies of mine answering him, and also the originals of letters of Olberg to my son, but not the copies of his answers to him.

GOLDMAN: There is a supplementary sub-exhibit entitled, "Who is Olberg and What is Olberg's Passport?" all about the question dealing with the Honduran passport. That is one of the exhibits here.

FINERTY: Mr. Trotsky, is your complete correspondence with Mr. Olberg present?

TROTSKY: Absolutely complete. After the letters of Pfemfert, it was very difficult for me to enter into any more intimate correspondence with him.

GOLDMAN: The entire list of exhibits deals with copies of letters and originals of letters from friends of Trotsky, and Trotsky dealing with Olberg; this information which they gave him about Olberg containing especially the original letter of Franz Pfemfert to Trotsky.

TROTSKY: Franz Pfemfert and his wife.

BEALS: Pardon me, in this question did you use the name of Vladimir Romm?

TROTSKY: Alexandra Ramm. She is my translator in the German language.

GOLDMAN: There are parts of the exhibits containing some information not directly connected with Olberg, but information in reference to Nathan Lurye, one of the defendants.

TROTSKY: Excuse me, there is a great difference. There you have documents written to me after the Moscow trials by different people informing me about what they knew about Lurye and Berman-Yurin. It was after the Moscow trials. The first exhibit contains original letters belonging to the period indicated by me—preceding the trial.

GOLDMAN: A list of the documents with reference to Olberg, classifying these documents and, in short, giving you an idea of these documents, will be handed you before you leave. But, if not possible, all of these will be translated and given to the Commission some time after they leave, as soon as our technical equipment is better than now.

LAFOLLETTE: I understand that at this moment they are at the disposal of the Commission.

GOLDMAN: Yes. Now, I have other documents. One, a statement of Dr. Maria Blume, an affidavit, a sworn affidavit of the said Maria Blume, who lives in New York. She mentions something and gives information about N. Lurye, one of the defendants. I will introduce it for whatever it is worth, and the Commission can have a chance to read it, as it is in English. Second, a letter in German by Georg Jungclas, written in Copenhagen, October 30, 1936, dealing with Berman-Yurin. I also introduce it for whatever it is worth.

FINERTY: I understand the purpose of introducing these documents is to give the Commission lines of investigation which they may apply in tracing the history of the witnesses whom Mr. Trotsky says he does not know personally.

GOLDMAN: Also to give the Commission every authority and source existing to cross-examine other than here, and to give the Commission an idea of the character of these defendants as far as revealed through these sources by further investigation.

BEALS: Is there an indication of the whereabouts of these various people?

GOLDMAN: In the Maria Blume affidavit it states: "I, Maria Blume, resident . . . ," giving you an idea as to where she is. She can be investigated further if you so desire.

DEWEY: She can be cross-examined in New York?

GOLDMAN: She is available. I personally do not know her. We received this, and the Commission can make all efforts to see her in New York.

FINERTY: I might suggest, Mr. Goldman, you should not file with the Commission persons whose addresses you cannot give us.

GOLDMAN: Well, suppose we do this: Supposing we file with the Commission such documents, subject to be stricken from the record if we do not inform you of the addresses.

FINERTY: We do not want to receive any names or documents without—

TROTSKY: Initially, is—excuse me. We can indicate the person and get the address.

FINERTY: That is what I mean, Mr. Trotsky; we must have a means of reaching the person for investigation.

TROTSKY: Absolutely.

GOLDMAN: Here I have two documents of Maslow, a former member of the German Communist Party, expelled some time, I believe, in 1927—

TROTSKY: I am not so sure, 1927 or 1928.

GOLDMAN: 1927 or 1928. He is now residing in Paris, and his address we shall furnish to the Commission. These are documents dealing, one with Moses Lurye, one of the defendants, and the other with Berman-Yurin. Here he is referred to as Alexander Stauer. Evidently, he had another name beside Berman-Yurin. [In the Report of the first Moscow trial, his alias is given as Alexander Fomich—Ed.]

And here we have a photostatic copy of the article written by Moses Lurye, under the name of Alexander Emel, in the *International Press Correspondence*. This is the official organ of the Communist International and is No. 96, written in German.

THE REPORTER: What is the date?

GOLDMAN: It does not appear from the appended document. We shall, however, furnish—oh, yes, the 13th of November, 1932.

FINERTY: How do you identify him with the pseudonym?

GOLDMAN: Maslow's statement declares that Alexander Emel is the same as Moses Lurye—subject, of course, to being cross-examined in Paris, where Maslow is residing. [Moses Lurye is referred to as Alexander Emel on page 175 of the Report of the Court Proceedings of the first Moscow trial—Ed.]

TROTSKY: Maslow is a former member of the Executive Committee of the Communist International.

GOLDMAN: So, I repeat, I am introducing documents with reference to Olberg.

STOLBERG: Is Maslow now in the Left Opposition?

TROTSKY: More or less.

GOLDMAN: I am introducing documents with reference to Moses Lurye, Berman-Yurin, and also one document with reference to Nathan Lurye.

FINERTY: You are marking them as separate exhibit numbers?

GOLDMAN: Yes. The Olberg Exhibit, containing numerous documents, was marked Exhibit No. 8. The documents with reference to Moses Lurye, Berman-Yurin and Nathan Lurye will be bound in one exhibit and identified as Exhibit No. 9, A, B and C.

(The documents with reference to Moses Lurye, Berman-Yurin and Nathan Lurye were introduced into evidence as Exhibit No. 9, A, B, and C, respectively.)

GOLDMAN: These, I repeat, are available for the Commission's inspection. That finishes, as far as I recall, the defendants involved in the first trial, the Zinoviev trial, held in August, 1936. When did you first meet Karl Radek?

TROTSKY: I believe it was in 1909 or 1910, during one of the international congresses.

GOLDMAN: What political relationship did you have with him before October, 1917?

TROTSKY: No political relationship, in the strict sense of the word. From time to time we exchanged a letter about a book, or we met at international congresses. He belonged at that time to the German party, not the Russian party. He was working in Leipzig or Berlin.

GOLDMAN: What group was he connected with in the German party?

TROTSKY: He was connected with Rosa Luxemburg and Leo Jogisches—with the left wing. Then he separated from Rosa Luxemburg, but he remained to the right of the left wing of the Social Democratic Party.

GOLDMAN: When did you first see him—in Moscow, when you returned, or Leningrad, at that time Petrograd, when you returned from the United States?

TROTSKY: It was, I believe, during 1918. He came with Lenin through Germany to the Scandinavias, but he remained in Stockholm. He could not go to Russia at that time. It was the work largely of Germany and Austria. He was an Austrian citizen, and he remained in Stockholm as the literary representative of the Russian Bolsheviks.

GOLDMAN: He arrived in Russia when, to the best of your knowledge?

TROTSKY: It seems to me at the end of 1918.

GOLDMAN: Of 1918?

STOLBERG: I didn't hear your question.

GOLDMAN: When did Radek arrive in Russia? To the best of your knowledge, when did he become a member of the Bolshevik Party?

TROTSKY: Immediately.

GOLDMAN: Upon his arrival in Russia?

TROTSKY: Yes.

GOLDMAN: What role did he play in the Russian Revolution at the time?

TROTSKY: He didn't play a role during the Revolution, in the exact sense of the word. He came later. He was active for a certain time—throughout he was active as a journalist. He is a journalist.

GOLDMAN: That is his main profession?

TROTSKY: That is his profession; that is his nature. (Laughter) He was active for a certain time in the Commissariat of Foreign Affairs, but the diplomats claimed that it was absolutely impossible to say anything in his presence, because tomorrow it was known by all the city. We removed him immediately.

He became a member of the Central Committee, and as a member of the Central Committee he had a right to assist in the sessions of the Politburo. Lenin organized our meetings, of the Politburo, somewhat secretly to avoid Radek, because we did, as you understand, discuss very delicate matters in the Politburo. His reputation in these matters is absolutely established.

FINERTY: Will you give the dates when he was a member of the Central Committee?

GOLDMAN: When was he a member of the Central Committee?

TROTSKY: I believe it was in 1921; 1920 or 1921, I am not absolutely sure.

DEWEY: Was he removed?

TROTSKY: He was not reelected.

GOLDMAN: To the best of your knowledge, do you remember any articles by you, or Lenin, or Stalin, or some other people, characterizing Radek as you have characterized him just now?

TROTSKY: Yes. During the Seventh Party Congress, in 1918, when Brest-Litovsk was being discussed, the question of Radek's words, "Lenin yields ground to gain time," Lenin remarked—the quotation is from the verbatim report: "I will return to Comrade Radek, but here I must observe that he has *accidentally* spoken a serious phrase." And again, in the same speech: "This time it has come about that Comrade Radek had an entirely serious word."

GOLDMAN: Any further quotations?

TROTSKY: Stalin, in a speech, January, 1924, at a Party Congress—it was some days before Lenin's death—said: "Most men's heads control their tongues; Radek's tongue controls his head." Excuse me, these are not my words.

GOLDMAN: That is Stalin's?

TROTSKY: Stalin, yes.

GOLDMAN: What position did he take in the struggle of the Left Opposition against the bureaucracy?

TROTSKY: Which opposition? To each opposition—not a firm one. During 1923, between 1923 and 1926, he hesitated between the so-called Trotskyites and the Right Opposition in Germany, the Brandlerites. He hesitated between them and us, but remained in good relations with me personally. At that time he wrote his very well known article, "Leon Trotsky, the Organizer of the Victory," in the *Pravda* of March 14, 1923.

GOLDMAN: This is the article written by Karl Radek in Russian, excerpts of which have been translated, appearing in *Pravda,* March 14, 1923, entitled, "Leon Trotsky, the Organizer of the Victory."(Mr. Goldman hands document to the Commission.)

I shall read a few excerpts into the record:

> The history of the proletarian revolution has shown how one can change the pen for the sword. Trotsky is one of the best writers on world socialism, and his literary qualities did not prevent him from being the first head, the first organizer of the first army of the proletariat. The Revolution changed to a sword the pen of its best publicist . . .
>
> The Marxist Trotsky did not see merely the external discipline of the army, the cannon, the technique, but he also saw the living persons who serve as instruments of war, he saw the ranks which advanced on the battlefield. Trotsky is the author of the first pamphlet which gives a broad analysis of the fall of the International . . .

Referring to the Second International, obviously.

> At the time of its worst degeneration, Trotsky did not lose confidence in the future of socialism . . .
>
> One of the most remarkable documents of his comprehension of the class structure of the army, of the spirit of the army, was his speech on the July offensive of Kerensky, pronounced, it seems, at the first Congress of the Soviet, and to the Soviet of Workers' and Soldiers' deputies in Petrograd. In this speech, Trotsky predicted the checking of the offensive; this prediction was not on

the basis of information on the state of military technique at the front, but on the basis of the analysis of the political situation of the army. You, he said, addressing himself to the Mensheviks and the S.R.'s, you ask the government to revise the ends of the war. You say to the army that the former ends in the name of which Tsarism and the bourgeoisie asked unheard-of sacrifices do not correspond to the interests of the Russian workers and peasants. You have not arrived at the point of revising the ends. In the place of Tsar and country you have set nothing, and you ask the army in the name of this nothingness to enter into a severe struggle, pour out its blood. It is impossible to fight in the name of nothing. Thus, in Trotsky's manner of posing the question, there is the whole secret of his greatness as organizer of the Red Army. . . .

Without for a moment admitting that a voluntary army could save Russia, Trotsky built it like an apparatus that was necessary for him in creating the new army. But if already in this was shown the organizing genius of Trotsky, this firmness of thought found an even clearer expression in his courageous fashion of approaching the question of utilizing the military specialists for the building of the army. . . .

But Comrade Trotsky did not only know, thanks to this energy, how to submit the old corps of officers to himself. He did more. He won the confidence of the best elements among the specialists, and changed them from enemies of Soviet Russia into its convinced partisans . . .

It needed a man, an incarnation of the summons to the struggle, who, submitting himself to the necessity of the struggle, became the bell which calls to arms, the will which exacts, from all, absolute submission to the great, bloody necessity. Only a man who works as much as Trotsky, only a man as pitiless toward himself as Trotsky, only a man who knows how to speak to the soldier as Trotsky spoke, could become the standard bearer of the armed workers. He was all these in one person. He made the advice of the specialists into a part of his mind, and knew how to integrate it with the appreciation of the social relationships of forces, the driving forces from fourteen fronts united as one coming from tens of thousands of Communists who said, What makes up an active army, how can one work with it, under what form must one's influence be exercised? He knew how to forge it under a strategic plan and an organizational scheme. And during all the enormous work, he knew how to employ, as few can, the science of the importance of moral factors in war-time . . .

If our Party goes down in history as the first party of the proletariat which knew how to build a great army, this burning page of history of the Russian Revolution will always be allied with the name of Lev Davidovitch Trotsky, a man whose work and actions will be the objects not only of love but also of the science of the study of the new generation of the working class which is preparing itself for the conquests of the whole world.

GOLDMAN: These are translations. The original is in Russian, and the excerpts were translated to show what Radek thought, in 1923, of the witness, Leon Trotsky.

TROTSKY: He wrote another article on the 21st of August, 1936, entitled: "The Fascist Band, Trotskyist-Zinovievist, and its Hetman Trotsky."

GOLDMAN: 1936?

TROTSKY: During the trial, during the Zinoviev trial, when Radek belonged to the alleged parallel Trotskyite center.

GOLDMAN: The first document, the one written by Radek March 14, 1923, I am identifying as Exhibit No. 10.

(The document, "Leon Trotsky, the Organizer of the Victory," is introduced into evidence as Exhibit No. 10.)

GOLDMAN: The second document, the article by Karl Radek, in the *Pravda,* the article which has not been translated, but which, I hope, will be for the benefit of the Commission, was published in *Pravda* on the 21st—

TROTSKY: *Isvestia.*

GOLDMAN: *Isvestia,* that is right—on the 21st of August, 1936, and is entitled, "The Fascist Band, Trotskyist-Zinovievist, and its Hetman Trotsky."

TROTSKY: Some quotations are translated.

GOLDMAN: I read a few excerpts:

> The super-bandit Trotsky was in Norway, organizer of the assassination of the best leaders of the world proletariat. . . . The thing takes place in the presence of hundreds of persons, tens of foreign correspondents, and no one who has not lost his reason believes that the accused are calumniating themselves or Trotsky.

FINERTY: Mr. Goldman, the last article which you referred to is one referred to by Vyshinsky on Page 485 of the transcript of the second trial?

GOLDMAN: That's right, where Vyshinsky mentions the article of Radek. I will introduce it as Exhibit No. 11.

(The article, "The Fascist Band, Trotskyist-Zinovievist, and its Hetman Trotsky," is introduced as Exhibit No. 11.)

TROTSKY: There is another article by Radek, of November 21, 1935, in *Pravda,* on the Red Army. He speaks of its organization, its victories and so on. In this article my name is not mentioned. That was in November 21, 1935, during the time when Radek directed the "parallel Trotskyite center."

GOLDMAN: Now, Mr. Trotsky, was Radek a member of the bloc of Trotskyites and Zinovievites in 1926 and 1927?

TROTSKY: Yes.

GOLDMAN: What happened to him at the Fifteenth Congress?

TROTSKY: The same as with the others. He was expelled and banished to Siberia. He became very hesitating in Siberia, and he capitulated in 1929.

GOLDMAN: So, he was in Siberia between the time of his expulsion from the Party and the time of his capitulation in 1929?

TROTSKY: Yes.

GOLDMAN: Did you have any correspondence with him during that time?

TROTSKY: No.

GOLDMAN: Did you write articles about his capitulation?

TROTSKY: I had an involuntary and indirect communication with him.

GOLDMAN: What connection did you have with him?

TROTSKY: Blumkin, a member of the Bolshevik Party and a former member of my military secretariat, was in Constantinople on an official mission.

GOLDMAN: When?

TROTSKY: In Constantinople, he visited me and also met my son in the street.

GOLDMAN: In Constantinople?

TROTSKY: In Constantinople. He took him to his room, to his hotel. My son saw Blumkin. Blumkin said: "I will see the old man." My son came to me and said: "He will see you." I said, "Absolutely impossible. It is too risky." He insisted so that I had to accept, but very secretly. He went to Russia, to Moscow. Radek came from Siberia as a capitulator. He had absolute confidence in Radek—an old confidence.

GOLDMAN: You mean Blumkin had?

TROTSKY: Yes, Blumkin. He was younger than Radek. He visited him, and Radek denounced Blumkin immediately to the G.P.U.

GOLDMAN: Blumkin visited Radek, and, according to your information, what did Blumkin say to Radek?

TROTSKY: He informed him about his visit to me, on his own initiative. Because, if he had asked me about telling of this visit, it would have been absolutely impossible for him to do such a stupid thing.

GOLDMAN: What did Radek do after Blumkin informed him of his visit to you?

TROTSKY: He denounced him for his visit to me.

GOLDMAN: What happened to Blumkin?

TROTSKY: He was shot.

GOLDMAN: How did you acquire that information?

TROTSKY: We had many letters about this event from Moscow. The event itself was published in the world press.

GOLDMAN: From whom did you receive these letters?

TROTSKY: From my friends, from Trotskyites.

GOLDMAN: You are ready to produce them in executive session?

TROTSKY: They are published in the *Bulletin* without the names. They are published.

GOLDMAN: In the *Opposition Bulletin*?

TROTSKY: Yes.

GOLDMAN: Have you made any translations of certain letters?

TROTSKY: Yes; I can quote that information.

GOLDMAN: Will you please first mention the date when these articles appeared in the *Bulletin*?

TROTSKY: Yes, there is also a very interesting letter about his trip from Siberia—of the highest interest. It is an original letter from an Oppositionist, on a postal card from Siberia. It would be good to submit to the Commission.

GOLDMAN: Just for the Commission to see what kind of

cards were written from Siberia to Trotsky. You could not possibly read it. (Attorney Goldman exhibits postal cards written to Trotsky in microscopic writing.) This is part of the illegal correspondence from Russia to Trotsky.

STOLBERG: Addressed to him?

GOLDMAN: Addressed to him.

TROTSKY: My address in Turkey, Constantinople.

GOLDMAN: To what name?

TROTSKY: L. Sedov.

GOLDMAN: Will you—

DEWEY: Mr. Goldman, I suppose at some time there will be an opportunity for going into the matter of the underground work and the method or technique of communication?

GOLDMAN: Yes, we shall deal with that.

TROTSKY: It is not underground, Mr. Chairman.

GOLDMAN: I think it was written—it was legal, because the card was sent out.

DEWEY: I don't mean this particular thing.

TROTSKY: It is not signed by the genuine name of the individual from whom it comes.

FINERTY: Was it written with a code?

TROTSKY: No, it was in 1929. It was a time when there were too many Oppositionists in Siberia everywhere. The G.P.U. was demoralized by the consequences of its own action. A certain democracy was established among the deported Oppositionists. They had an opportunity to send letters and discuss. But the beginning of 1931 or at the end of 1930, this beautiful era was finished.

GOLDMAN: This post card—this stamp on it contains the numbers 2/10/1929—sent to L. Sedov, Turkey, Constantinople, deals with the affair of Blumkin and Radek?

TROTSKY: No, it precedes the affair. It is about Radek. On the ride from Tomsk to Moscow he met Oppositionists. As a capitulator, under the convoy of the G.P.U., he met some Oppositionists who held a conversation with Radek. Shall I give you some translations from this letter?

GOLDMAN: Does the Commission care to hear it?

FINERTY: Yes.

TROTSKY: At one of the railroad stations in Siberia he had a conversation with the exiles which one of the participants revealed in a letter abroad. It is published in the Russian *Bulletin*, No. 6, October, 1929. It is only part of the quotation. "Question: And what is your attitude towards L.D. [Trotsky]? Radek: I have definitely broken with L.D. From now on we are political adversaries. With the collaborator of Lord Beaverbrook we have nothing in common."

I do not know what I have in common with Lord Beaverbrook, but it is so written. The next speaks of Article 58. It is the penal code on the ground of which we were all arrested and banished to Siberia. I read on: "Question: Do you demand the abolition of Article 58? Radek: Not at all! For those who come along with us it will be abolished by itself. But we will not abolish Article 58 for those who follow a path of undermining the Party, which will organize the discontent of the masses.—The agents of the G.P.U. do not let us talk . . ." And so on.

GOLDMAN: This is a translation from the post card?

TROTSKY: Yes, it is a translation.

GOLDMAN: I will mark this post card Exhibit No. 12.

(The post card dealing with Radek's capitulation sent to Trotsky from Siberia was introduced as Exhibit No. 12.)

TROTSKY: Will you permit a quotation on Blumkin?

DEWEY: All right.

TROTSKY: In the summer of 1929, Blumkin visited me in Constantinople. Here is what I find stated in the *Bulletin* on the basis of letters received from Moscow. The date is December 25, 1929. And the quotation: "Radek's nervous babbling is well known. Now he is absolutely demoralized, like the majority of the capitulators . . . Having lost the last remnants of moral equilibrium, Radek stops before no abjection." The correspondence relates how "Blumkin was betrayed after his meeting with Radek." From that time on he became the most odious figure of the Left Opposition, because he was not only a capitulator, but a traitor.

LAFOLLETTE: Do you mean, odious to the Left Opposition or of the Left Opposition?

TROTSKY: To the Left Opposition, yes.

DEWEY: Mr. Goldman, there is considerable material in this book based on the Platform of the Opposition. Will you please have it looked through, so that the passages can be identified for the record as part of the evidence?

GOLDMAN: I think the whole platform will be introduced.

DEWEY: We will adjourn until four o'clock.

End of the Third Session.

Fourth session

April 12, 1937, at four o'clock p.m.

DEWEY: There are a few things first for the record. The Platform of the Opposition has been identified as extending from page 23 through to 195 of the book that was put in evidence this morning.

GOLDMAN: Let the record show that the book, "The Real Situation in Russia," by Leon Trotsky, contains the Platform of the Opposition, beginning on page 23 to 195, and has been introduced before the Commission as Exhibit No. 13.

(The book, "The Real Situation in Russia," by Leon Trotsky, was marked as Exhibit No. 13.)

DEWEY: The next is a telegram from President Cardenas, which was sent to the border at Laredo, but was not delivered there and has been retransmitted, giving the members of the Commission leave to pass the border. As you see, we did pass, and it will be appended to the permanent record. I understand that this telegram, as well as several others I will bring attention to, have already been appended to the record by our reporter.

The next copies, two cables received from abroad. One from Zurich, Switzerland, on April 7th, gives a mandate to New York to hold a commission there. And one from Paris, of which I am reading the translation: "The French Committee gives full powers to the American Committee to conduct the international inquiry and will send delegates to New York." This was already appended to the record. These are, of course, answers to the cables of invitation to the European groups.

Several telegrams have been received from labor unions, trade unions, in congratulation of the efforts to have a fair and impartial hearing, and they also have been appended to the permanent record. They come from the Electrical Workers Union of Minneapolis, Local 292, the Drivers Union, Local 544, Minneapolis, the President of the Warehouse and Inside Workers Union, Local 20,136 of Minneapolis, and the agent of the Furniture Workers Union of Minneapolis. From Los Angeles, from the Patrolman Sailors Union of the Pacific, President of District Council No. 4, Maritime Federation of the Pacific. From Philadelphia, Chapter 10 of the American Federation of State, County and Municipal Employees.

As I said, these will be or already have been appended to the permanent record.

I wish also on my own behalf to make a brief statement: As Chairman of this Preliminary Commission of Inquiry, I am, of course, responsible for the conduct of its internal affairs. I wish first to say that Mr. Beals—that he was in the city the day of the final draft of the opening address read by me at the first session, April 10th, is entirely correct. My remark this morning that he was not here to be consulted referred to the previous days in which the other members of the Commission were conferring together about the material to be contained in the opening address. I am sure that if we had had the benefit of Mr. Beals's counsel, that address would have benefited.

Mr. Beals's statement this morning was the first knowledge I had that he had not seen the opening document. I do not say this to excuse myself, but because I accept fully the fact that it was the responsibility of the Chairman to make sure that he had seen the document and approved or disapproved its contents. I mention the fact, then, simply formally to acknowledge that responsibility and formally to record my regret that it was not satisfactorily fulfilled.

BEALS: I would just like to remark that the matter of who was to blame, if anybody, for my not having seen the statement of the Commission prior to its delivery is quite immaterial. As I stated, I feel no inharmony with the rest of the Commission. I had to mention the fact as my reason for making independent opinions—In short, my several constructive suggestions, which I still hope the Commission will accept. I repeat, I am in accord with the Commission's statement with the exception of the reservations previously made this morning.

GOLDMAN: Since we are making declarations for the record, I would like to make one myself: The Commission's counsel, Mr. Finerty, has advised the Commission that the absence of relations between the U.S.S.R. and Mexico is not necessarily a legal obstacle to the extradition of one in Mexico accused of a crime by the U.S.S.R. I have no references at hand, but if I am not in error, Mr. Finerty is supported by the possibility of the U.S.S.R. asking for such extradition through a mutually friendly power, of which there are many. Moreover, the Commission should note that the U.S.S.R. was in no way legally barred from asking Mr. Trotsky's extradition from Norway before, during or after the trial of Zinoviev et al, in August. Finally, Mr. Trotsky has stated that he is not responsible for the absence of relations between the U.S.S.R. and Mexico, and that in any case, he is now ready to proceed to the soil of any country which has an extradition treaty with the U.S.S.R., there to stand trial in response to a request from the U.S.S.R. for extradition. He has repeatedly asked through the world press that the U.S.S.R. seek his extradition; he repeats the challenge today through the world press represented here, and awaits the action of the Soviet Government.

Now, this morning, Mr. Chairman, I meant to read into the record certain excerpts which will throw light on the attitude of Mr. Trotsky to the defendants in the trial of Zinoviev and Kamenev, especially to the main defendants, Zinoviev and Kamenev. I would like the indulgence of the Commission for three or four minutes, to read into the record certain very important excerpts from letters and documents, and pamphlets written by Mr. Trotsky. Now, a letter sent by Leon Trotsky from Alma-Ata, his place of exile prior to his forced journey to Turkey, dated May 9, 1928:

> The sense of the declaration is: Speak out what is! No exaggerations, no blinking the facts of the actual official efforts to get out of the hole, but also no diplomacy, no falsehood, no lies, no rotten, petty politics in the spirit of Zinoviev-Kamenev-Pyatakov . . .
>
> It is superfluous to say that the tone of the letter must be entirely tranquil, so that what is may be seen quite clearly—namely, that the policy of narrow-mindedness of the epigones has not embittered us in the slightest—politics knows no anger—we look higher and further than that . . .

Here is a quotation from another letter sent—

TROTSKY: Excuse me, the letter concerns our declaration to the Congress of the Communist International. I explained in the letter in what manner we should make our declaration.

GOLDMAN: The first letter read now to the Commission?

TROTSKY: Yes.

FINERTY: What date?

GOLDMAN: May 19, 1928. Here is another letter Mr. Trotsky sent from Alma-Ata, on August 30, 1928:

> It is clear to every thinking man that it is not Zinoviev-Kamenev-Pyatakov and Co. who are inside the Party, but we and you. We participate actively in the Party's life. Our documents are read by the Congress delegations. Some hundreds of signatures under our manifestoes are a great political fact. But the former chairman of the Comintern—

The former chairman is Zinoviev.

> —and all his miserable group do not exist politically. Zinoviev himself is forced to declare that now one can only keep quiet and wait. These people have reentered not the Party, but the Centrosoyus [central cooperative organization].

TROTSKY: That is because Zinoviev had the name of a functionary on this body.

GOLDMAN: Mr. Trotsky underlines to say that Zinoviev after his capitulation was named as a functionary in the central cooperative organization. In the book "My Life," by Trotsky, on page 427—

FINERTY: Published when?

GOLDMAN: 1929. On page 427, there is an excerpt which gives Mr. Trotsky's characterization of Zinoviev during the attack on Petrograd.

FINERTY: Is that the English edition?

GOLDMAN: The English edition.

TROTSKY: That is not so important.

GOLDMAN: I am not going to read it. I am just giving the

page. In a letter to Mikhael Okudzhava, dated May 26, 1928, from Alma-Ata, Mr. Trotsky says:

> The way we have progressed has convinced me beyond any doubt that we were and are right, not only against the weather-cocks and turncoats (Zinovievs, Kamenevs, Pyatakovs, etc.) but also against our dear friends on the left—the ultra-lefts (Sapronov). . . . Excerpt from "My Life," page 552.

TROTSKY: Sapronov denied the necessity for the defense of the Soviet Union. This was a distinction between our opposition and the ultra-lefts.

GOLDMAN: In "The History of the Russian Revolution," Volume No. 1, by Leon D. Trotsky, on page 300, there is a characterization of Kamenev and Zinoviev. Also on page 45 of Volume No. 2. The excerpt from Volume No. 1 was written some time in 1930, and Volume No. 2 was written some time in May, 1932. These are characterizations made by Mr. Trotsky of Kamenev and Zinoviev. In the Russian *Bulletin,* translated in the *Militant,* April 19, 1930—the *Militant* published in New York—there are excerpts from that Russian *Bulletin,* written by—

FRANKEL (Trotsky's secretary): Written under the name of "Alpha."

GOLDMAN: Written under the name of "Alpha," but actually by Mr. Trotsky. I have excerpts here which can be found in the *Militant,* entitled "Lessons on the Capitulations—Some Reflections." I have some more excerpts from the Russian *Bulletin,* from a letter from the U.S.S.R., dated November 25 and 26. It is written November 15, 1931, and published in the *Bulletin* November–December, 1931.

DEWEY: You mean the *Bulletin of the Opposition*?

GOLDMAN: The *Bulletin of the Opposition.* The excerpt reads: ". . . No news on the capitulationist front. Zinoviev is painfully writing a book on the Second International. Politically neither he nor Kamenev exists. . . ."

Another excerpt from the article "Zinoviev and Kamenev," appearing in the Russian *Bulletin of the Opposition* in July, 1933, written by Mr. Trotsky: ". . . Their personal fate is profoundly tragic. When the future historian wants to show how cruelly epochs of great shocks destroy people, he will use the example of Zinoviev and Kamenev. . . ." This was written May 23, 1933.

TROTSKY: And July, 1933, is the time of the "unified center."

GOLDMAN: You mean the alleged unified center?

TROTSKY: Yes; I said that satirically.

GOLDMAN: Here is the declaration of Kamenev and Zinoviev to the Central Committee of the Communist Party of the Soviet Union and to the Control Commission. It reads as follows:

> To the Central Committee of the C.P.S.U. and to the Control Commission: Comrades Yaroslavsky and Shkiriatov have brought to our attention a document of L. Trotsky dated January 4, 1932, which is an ignoble invention on Trotsky's part, pretending that we discussed with Comrade Stalin in 1924–25 the opportunity for a terrorist act against Trotsky, and that subsequently, when we went over to the Opposition, we told him of this discussion. All this is a perfidious lie, with the evident purpose of compromising our party. Only a diseased mentality like Trotsky's, thoroughly empoisoned with the thirst of making a sensation before bourgeois audiences and always ready to come out with the dribble and hate of the past of our party, is capable of imagining such an ignoble lie. It is beyond question that never could we have discussed such a question, nor even made an allusion to it in the Party circles, and we never said any

such a thing to Trotsky.

All this has been invented by him from beginning to end, and is one of the methods adopted in the infamous struggle that he is carrying on against the party of Lenin and its leadership, in the past as at present, for the profit and pleasure of counter-revolution. The statement from Trotsky pretending that in our Bolshevik Party one can be forced to make lying statements on this subject is the established procedure of a master blackmailer.

GOLDMAN: Have you the date of this?

VAN HEIJENOORT (Trotsky's Secretary): The 13th of February, 1932.

DEWEY: February—

GOLDMAN: February 13, 1932. That was a little while before the alleged unified center.

TROTSKY: It was the time of the preparation of the center, after the meeting with Smirnov in the Summer of 1931.

GOLDMAN: This is an excerpt from a letter of Mr. Trotsky to Albert Weisbord, published in the *Militant* September 10, 1932. The letter was written on May 24, 1932, and the following is the excerpt:

> *Zinoviev and Kamenev represent highly qualified elements. Under the régime of Lenin, they accomplished very responsible work, in spite of their insufficiency, which was well understood by Lenin. The régime of Stalin condemned Zinoviev and Kamenev to political death.* The same thing can be said of Bukharin and many others. The ideological and moral decomposition of Radek is witness not only of the fact that Radek is not made of first-class material, but also of the fact that the Stalinist régime can rely only upon impersonal "chinovniks" or morally decomposed individuals.

This letter was translated into German and French, sent to all groups and sections of the International Left Opposition, and published in the *International Bulletin*.

TROTSKY: "Chinovniks" means "functionaries" or "bureaucrats."

GOLDMAN: This is what Trotsky thought of Zinoviev and Kamenev, Bukharin and Radek.

LAFOLLETTE: What is the date of that?

GOLDMAN: May 24, 1932—that is the date of the letter. Now, will you proceed with the statement you were making with reference to Radek, Mr. Trotsky, at the time of the conclusion of the last session?

TROTSKY: I stated that in May, 1932—the same time as I wrote Weisbord—I believe, a German paper, the *Berliner Tageblatt*, published a special issue concerning the Soviet Union, and in it was an article by Radek. The article of Radek was almost, as a work, directed against me. He said in the German publication that I had lost my belief in Socialism. I answered in the Russian *Bulletin* with an article entitled, "A Light-Minded Man on a Serious Question."

GOLDMAN: That was when?

TROTSKY: It was in May, 1932. My answer is published in No. 28 of the Russian *Bulletin*, June, 1932. The article is published in a special issue of the *Berliner Tageblatt*—that is, Radek's article.

FINERTY: Will a copy of that be furnished for the record?

GOLDMAN: Yes, a copy will be furnished for the record.

TROTSKY: Yes, the whole *Bulletin* will be put in evidence. On November 21, 1935—it was three weeks before Pyatakov's flight to Oslo—

GOLDMAN: Pardon me, you mean the alleged flight to Oslo.

TROTSKY: In my answers all these references are in quotations. (Laughter.) Radek described—it is an interview about the history of the Civil War—how Stalin was the organizer of the victories, without mentioning my name. This is three weeks before the alleged flight of Pyatakov to Oslo. In January, 1935, Zinoviev, Kamenev and others were sentenced in connection with the Kirov assassination to some years in prison. During the trial they devoted themselves to proving their efforts "to reestablish capitalism." In the *Bulletin of the Opposition,* I described this accusation as a frame-up. Who came to Vyshinsky's defense? Radek! He wrote in *Pravda,* "It is not a question of knowing whether capitalism is the ideal of Messrs. Trotsky and Zinoviev, but whether the building of Socialism is impossible in our country . . ." That was January, 1935, when Radek was supposed to be a leading member of, an alleged leading member of, the alleged parallel center. In his last article, in August 21, 1936, he denounces me as having given the order to Blumkin to attack the Soviet representatives abroad for the purpose of getting money for my counter-revolutionary activity. He was not arrested at that time. He was free at that time—that is, Radek, and a member of the same center. He wrote his article about the "Hetman Trotsky," in which he says about me: "He forced Blumkin to steal money from the Soviet commercial representatives abroad to be used for counter-revolutionary activity." That was the answer to me from my "representative" in the Soviet Union.

STOLBERG: It was in *Pravda*?

TROTSKY: It was published in *Pravda* and *Isvestia.* I quoted from *Isvestia,* which I received from New York, dated the 21st of August, 1936.

GOLDMAN: This refers to a document that was introduced as an exhibit.

TROTSKY: Will you permit me one quotation more? In Spain, Maurin began to publish a paper called *Adelante,* with a list of contributors. I was named without my previous authorization. I wrote on the 3rd of October, 1933, to the editor of this Spanish paper. It is in French. I wrote it in French. Named in the list was also Karl Radek. I wrote: "The name of Radek gives to this list an absolutely fantastic and incomprehensible character. I insist that the editor cease to make misuse of my name."

GOLDMAN: Now, were you in communication with Radek, either directly or indirectly, since you left the Soviet Union, Mr. Trotsky?

TROTSKY: The only communications are represented by the quotations; no other communication.

GOLDMAN: You mean that you wrote about him, but you did not write to him?

TROTSKY: Never.

GOLDMAN: Did you receive any letters from him?

TROTSKY: Never.

GOLDMAN: Did you send letters to him through an intermediary?

TROTSKY: No.

GOLDMAN: For the purpose of the record and for the information of the Commission, I shall go into the question of Vladimir Romm, as the alleged intermediary between Mr. Trotsky and Radek, later on.

DEWEY: I was going to ask you whether the famous letter will come up later.

GOLDMAN: It will come up later. Now, Mr. Trotsky, how long have you known Pyatakov, another defendant in the last trial, the January trial of this year?

TROTSKY: Personally, I met him for the first time during the Civil War. It was in 1918 or 1919. I had some information about him before, in emigration, in exile, but for the first time I met him after the October Revolution.

GOLDMAN: What were your personal relations with him?

TROTSKY: Very good.

GOLDMAN: Was he a member of the Left Opposition?

TROTSKY: He was a member of the Left Opposition.

GOLDMAN: From the very beginning?

TROTSKY: From 1923 to the end of 1927.

GOLDMAN: What happened to him in 1927?

TROTSKY: He capitulated.

GOLDMAN: Was he expelled at the Fifteenth Congress?

TROTSKY: Yes.

GOLDMAN: That was in November, 1927?

TROTSKY: In December.

GOLDMAN: December of 1927?

TROTSKY: Yes.

GOLDMAN: When did he capitulate?

TROTSKY: He capitulated openly, publicly; he capitulated in February, 1928. He was the first "Trotskyite" who capitulated publicly.

GOLDMAN: And after that did you have any correspondence with him at all?

TROTSKY: None.

GOLDMAN: Either when you were in the Soviet Union or outside of the Soviet Union?

TROTSKY: Exactly.

GOLDMAN: Have you written any letters or any articles which would give an idea of what you thought of Pyatakov?

TROTSKY: Yes, many articles and letters.

GOLDMAN: Will you cite some of these articles and letters for the benefit of the Commission?

TROTSKY: Here is a letter about two conciliatory Oppositionists who began to capitulate. It is from Alma-Ata, and 1928 is the date. It must have been the first half of 1928:

> . . . The essence of the platform written by you is only this: "It would be well to return to the Party and to restore the world to harmony." But to return by what door? There are two doors: The Zinovievist-capitulationist one

> and the Bolshevik one, through the continuation and extension of the ideological struggle. There is not any third door; there has not been and there will not be. Pyatakov looked for it, Safarov looked for it, Sarkis looked for it. Who are they? Political corpses. Who believes in them? Nobody. They don't even believe in themselves. They opened the door for Pyatakov, not only into the party but into the State bank.

He was named the chief of the State Bank after the capitulation—that is, Pyatakov. But a more important letter is written by me on March 17, 1928, to Byeleborodov.

GOLDMAN: Who is Byeleborodov?

TROTSKY: Byeleborodov was a very prominent member of the Bolshevik Party and a former member of the Central Committee.

GOLDMAN: Was he a Left Oppositionist?

TROTSKY: Yes. He was also arrested and deported to Siberia and then capitulated. I wrote:

> Dear Alexandre Gavrilovitch! . . . You speak in your letter, on the basis of *Pravda,* of Pyatakov's little letter of confession. We received the copy of *Pravda* with this letter only today. You speak of Pyatakov's deceitful and stupid document with indignation. I can fully understand that, but I must acknowledge that I myself do not harbor this sentiment, since for a long time I have considered Pyatakov to be a man politically finished. In moments of frankness he told me more than once, in a tired and skeptical tone, that politics did not interest him, and that he wants to return to the position of "spetz." More than once I told him, half smiling, half-seriously, that if, one fine morning, he found himself under Bonaparte, he would take his portfolio and would go to his office, inventing on the way some miserable pseudo-Marxist

"theory" in order to justify himself . . . When we entered into sharp but transitory discussions with you, what distressed me most was the fact that some comrades do not want, so to speak, to see that Pyatakov is a political corpse, who pretends to be alive and hastily invents all sorts of sophisms to give himself the appearance of a revolutionary politician. Evidently, some great European or world revolutionary wave can revive Pyatakov: Lazarus was revived, although he was dead . . . In such a case Pyatakov, left to himself, will inevitably make *leftist* errors. Lenin's word was also correct at the time when he said that it is impossible to rely on Pyatakov in great questions.

. . . I have had occasion to speak with Pyatakov hundreds of times, in company as well as *tête à tête*. This fact alone testifies that I was never indifferent to the question of knowing whether Pyatakov would be with us or against us. But it is precisely these numerous meetings and discussions which have convinced me that Pyatakov's thinking, with all his capacities, is absolutely devoid of dialectic force, and that in his character there is much more insolence than will power. For me it was clear a long time ago that at the first test of "split" this material would not hold. . . .

FINERTY: What is the date of that?

TROTSKY: March 17, 1928.

GOLDMAN: Subsequent to that, did you—

TROTSKY: It was subsequent to his first declaration of capitulation.

GOLDMAN: Subsequent to that date, did you write anything against Pyatakov?

TROTSKY: He is named in almost each article devoted to the capitulators.

GOLDMAN: The Commission will note that his name

was included in the excerpt that I read this afternoon with particular reference to Zinoviev and Kamenev. His name is included with Zinoviev and Kamenev. Is there anything else that you would like to read to us which would throw light on your attitude toward Pyatakov?

TROTSKY: If you permit me, I will quote three or four lines from a letter from prison concerning the capitulators.

GOLDMAN: What prison?

TROTSKY: From the isolator. It is not indicated here for conspirative purposes.

GOLDMAN: A prison in what country?

TROTSKY: In the Soviet Union.

GOLDMAN: When did you receive this letter?

TROTSKY: This letter was sent October 12, 1930, and published in the *Bulletin of the Opposition*, November–December, 1930.

GOLDMAN: And at that time, could letters be sent from prison?

TROTSKY: Yes; not in a legal way. I will show you letters which we received from prisons at that time. The prisons had very many people in them. They were very crowded, and that is the reason why the order was not severe. We had at that time a possibility to communicate with some comrades in prison by letters sent through intermediaries. They sent to us their programmatic declarations, which I will submit in original form to the Commission. They had very important declarations. They had their magazine in prison. I will later explain the reason for this liberalism by the bureaucracy, which tried to introduce a split in our ranks. I quote: "We do not discuss with the capitulators. We merely exclude them from our ranks and keep them out of the argument." From Siberia, at that time, I received a collective photograph, with a capitulator who capitulated after the photo was taken, and he is indicated in there with a cross.

GOLDMAN: I introduce the photo which the witness refers

to, showing the picture of thirteen men and a woman.

TROTSKY: There are the names on the back.

GOLDMAN: And the names of the persons whose photos were taken are on the back, with one face marked by a cross, indicating a capitulator. I introduce that as Exhibit No. 14.

(The photograph received by Trotsky from Siberia of a group of banished Left Oppositionists was introduced into evidence as Exhibit No. 14.)

DEWEY: That cross might have been made at any time since.

GOLDMAN: When you received this photo, Mr. Trotsky, did you take a look at it immediately?

TROTSKY: Yes.

GOLDMAN: You took it out from an envelope?

TROTSKY: If you took a chemical analysis of it, I am sure it would prove the ink is at least five—five or six years old.

GOLDMAN: Did you take the photo out of an envelope?

TROTSKY: I am not sure that it was in an envelope.

GOLDMAN: You took it out?

TROTSKY: Yes.

GOLDMAN: At the time you took it out, did you see the cross on the face?

TROTSKY: It was made especially for me. At the same time, if you permit two lines that Rakovsky wrote—it was published by me in November–December, 1930—in a letter—

GOLDMAN: Who is Rakovsky?

TROTSKY: Rakovsky is my old friend, my genuine old friend, the former Chairman of the Council of the People's Commissariat of Ukraine. He was later the ambassador to London and Paris, a member of the Central Committee, and a member of the Left Opposition. He resisted until 1934. We had news—I am not sure it is correct—that he tried to escape from Siberia and that he was wounded; that he remained for some time in the hospital in the Kremlin, and only after that he capitulated. The only thing I am sure about is that he capitulated in 1934. He wrote in 1930 about relations in deportation, the isolator, and about the capitulations.

GOLDMAN: Have you anything, letters or other material, to indicate your relationship with Rakovsky, and what you thought of him?

TROTSKY: My relationship with him?

GOLDMAN: What you thought of him?

TROTSKY: I have now in my hands—the Commission asked me to be as brief as possible, but I can present two or three quotations.

GOLDMAN: Well, we will come to them.

FINERTY: Mr. Goldman, I suggest that Mr. Trotsky state the period over which he published articles hostile to Pyatakov.

GOLDMAN: Will you state the dates between which you published articles and wrote letters characterizing Pyatakov?

TROTSKY: Yes.

GOLDMAN: From what date to what date?

TROTSKY: That I will present tomorrow.

GOLDMAN: In general, give us the dates, the time when you began writing articles against Pyatakov and the time you finished.

TROTSKY: I must say that Pyatakov was not a journalist. He was an administrator. Radek reminded me of his existence every month, by his articles, and I answered in the *Bulletin of the Opposition.* Pyatakov I forgot for months and years. He was a quiet and calm administrator and forgotten by the whole world. But I believe in every article I mentioned among the foremost prominent capitulators—I named Pyatakov. Those were in the first year of the capitulations; then he lost his importance for me.

FINERTY: Did you during the period of 1931 to 1936—do

you have anything in which you wrote something about Pyatakov?

TROTSKY: I must try to find it out.

GOLDMAN: Do you know G.Y. Sokolnikov?

TROTSKY: I knew him very well.

GOLDMAN: When did you first meet him?

TROTSKY: I was in correspondence with him during the war. He was a contributor to the Russian paper edited by me in Paris, called *Nashe Slovo*.

GOLDMAN: When was that, in what year?

TROTSKY: It was from 1914 to 1916. I edited the paper during two and a half years and he contributed, from Switzerland, articles.

GOLDMAN: Did you see him in Moscow or Petrograd upon your return from the United States?

TROTSKY: Yes, he was a member of the Central Committee during the October Revolution, with Stalin. They were both editors of the central organ of the Party, *Pravda*—Stalin and Sokolnikov.

GOLDMAN: When was that?

TROTSKY: It was 1917.

GOLDMAN: Was he a member of the Left Opposition?

TROTSKY: Never.

STOLBERG: Was he a member of the Bolshevik Party before 1914?

TROTSKY: 1914?

STOLBERG: Was he a member of the Bolshevik Party before 1914?

TROTSKY: He was a member of the Bolshevik Party, but I believe he belonged at that time to a certain opposition in the Bolshevik Party. But I am not very well acquainted with his past.

GOLDMAN: What group did he belong to in the years when the Left Opposition was waging its political struggle against the majority of the Party?

TROTSKY: To the right wing of the Party.

GOLDMAN: To the Bukharin group?

TROTSKY: Not Bukharin. He had a more individual position. The best characterization is by a statement of Radek in 1927. In August, 1927—in the beginning of September, 1927, immediately after the session of the Central Committee in August, 1927—Radek wrote:

> The tendency toward Thermidorian degeneration of the Party and its leading institutions is expressed in the following points: . . . (d) in the line of augmenting the weight of the Party apparatus as against the organizations at the base of the Party, which finds its classic expression in the declaration of Stalin to the Plenum (August, 1927): "These cadres can be removed only by civil war"—in the declaration which is . . . the classic formula of the Bonapartist *coup d'état;* (e) in the foreign policy projected by Sokolnikov. It is necessary to name these tendencies openly as Thermidorianism . . . and to say openly that they find their complete expression in the Central Committee in its right wing (Rykov, Kalinin, Vorishilov, Sokolnikov) and partly in the center (Stalin). It is necessary to say openly that the Thermidorian tendencies are growing . . .

GOLDMAN: For the benefit of those who might not be so well acquainted with the theoretical terms, would you mind explaining what "Thermidor" means?

TROTSKY: "Thermidor" is the reaction after the revolution, but a reaction which does not succeed in changing the social basis of the new order.

GOLDMAN: It refers—

TROTSKY: It is an analogy cited from the French Revolution. The French Revolution destroyed the feudal property rights in favor of the bourgeoisie, but in the Bonapartist régime, the order of reaction, the new form of property remained, the bourgeois form of property remained. The same idea is—

GOLDMAN: To the best of your information, when was Sokolnikov expelled from the Party?

TROTSKY: Sokolnikov was not expelled from the Party.

GOLDMAN: Sokolnikov was not expelled from the Party?

TROTSKY: No, he was a sympathizer of the Right. He was a friend of Kamenev; he was suspected of being an Oppositionist. But at the Fifteenth Congress he declared that he had no differences with the Party. His words were met with applause, and he was elected a member of the Central Committee at the same Congress which expelled us.

DEWEY: Would he give the date of the Fifteenth Congress for those of us who are not so familiar with it?

GOLDMAN: December, 1927. Was Sokolnikov ever in disfavor with the ruling, bureaucratic apparatus, as far as you know—before the trials, I mean?

TROTSKY: Sokolnikov has original ideas. He has a very inventive mind, and that is the reason why he is not fit, he does not fit into the bureaucratic régime.

GOLDMAN: Did you ever have any communication from him when you left Russia?

TROTSKY: Never.

GOLDMAN: Did you in any way communicate with him since you left Russia?

TROTSKY: No.

GOLDMAN: Either directly or indirectly?

TROTSKY: No.

GOLDMAN: Do you know L.P. Serebryakov, one of the defendants?

TROTSKY: Yes; he is a real old member of the Bolshevik Party, one of the builders of the Bolshevik Party, the same as Smirnov. He was a member of the Central Committee for a certain time, and secretary of the Central Committee. He took part in the Civil War—a friend of mine, a good friend, and a member of the Left Opposition from 1923 to 1929, or the end of 1928. He capitulated.

GOLDMAN: Since his capitulation, have you had any communication with him?

TROTSKY: Never.

GOLDMAN: Did you write any letters to him?

TROTSKY: No.

GOLDMAN: Receive any letters from him?

TROTSKY: No.

GOLDMAN: Did you give any messages to anybody to transmit to him?

TROTSKY: To nobody.

GOLDMAN: Now tell us what you know of N.I. Muralov, one of the defendants in the last trial.

TROTSKY: Muralov was a member of the Central Control Commission, one of the heroes of the Civil War, and commander-in-chief of the Moscow Military District, my friend, and my companion in hunting. We were in the best relations with him. He is not a political man. He is a soldier, a revolutionary soldier, and very honest, an exceptionally honest man. He abandoned the Opposition without any declaration, a written declaration. But he abandoned politics. He became a "spetz," just as Pyatakov, and stayed in Siberia. He is an agronomist by profession. ["Spetz" is an abbreviation for "specialist."—A.M.G.]

GOLDMAN: When did you hear from him last?

TROTSKY: I had some information about him, I believe, in 1929 or 1930. It is possible that I have a postal card from him, but a personal card. I am referring—I am not sure about that either.

GOLDMAN: Did you ever send him any letters on political matters?

TROTSKY: On political matters? The mail communications with the Oppositionists were interrupted from 1930, 1931, and 1932, absolutely.

GOLDMAN: You mean you could not get any communications?

TROTSKY: We tried many times to reach Rakovsky and Muralov and others.

GOLDMAN: In what years?

TROTSKY: 1931 and 1932. But we must absolutely abandon every attempt in this respect, because the control became very severe. All letters were confiscated. Beginning from 1930, the G.P.U. began to accuse people in relations with me of espionage. It was a very dangerous thing to send letters to me.

GOLDMAN: Since that time, you did not have any letters from Muralov?

TROTSKY: No.

GOLDMAN: Send any?

TROTSKY: No.

GOLDMAN: Did you know anyone by the name of Y.A. Livshitz?

TROTSKY: Only from the reports about the trial.

GOLDMAN: You don't know him personally?

TROTSKY: No.

GOLDMAN: You had no communications from him or sent any communications to him?

TROTSKY: Never.

GOLDMAN: Do you know Y.N. Drobnis?

TROTSKY: Yes.

GOLDMAN: What were your relations with him?

TROTSKY: Our relations were of a friendly nature. He worked in the Ukraine. He was an old worker and member of the Party, two times condemned to death by the Whites during the Civil War. One time he was fusillated [shot—A.M.G.] by the Whites, but only wounded. When the Whites must abandon the town, the Reds found him among the corpses. He belonged to the Opposition, but not to my group. He belonged to the group of Sapronov.

It was named an ultra-left group. But he was in sympathy personally with me. Before my deportation he came to me and gave me a gift.

GOLDMAN: Where, in Alma-Ata or Moscow?

TROTSKY: No, in Moscow. He gave me a pencil and fountain pen.

GOLDMAN: Was he expelled from the Party, to the best of your knowledge?

TROTSKY: Yes.

GOLDMAN: Did he capitulate?

TROTSKY: Yes, in 1928 or 1929.

GOLDMAN: He was expelled at the Fifteenth Congress, was he?

TROTSKY: Yes, with all the others.

GOLDMAN: Since then, have you heard from him?

TROTSKY: Never.

GOLDMAN: Have you written to him?

TROTSKY: Never.

GOLDMAN: Do you know M.S. Boguslavsky?

TROTSKY: Yes.

GOLDMAN: What do you know about him; what were your relations with him?

TROTSKY: He was connected with Drobnis and Sapronov, and had been for a long time in the same group.

GOLDMAN: The ultra-left group?

TROTSKY: The ultra-left group. He was in that group, he belonged to them, but he did not have any animosity to me. We were personally friendly. He was for a certain time the chairman of an important commission of the Council of the People's Commissariat. I met him there and got to know him personally.

GOLDMAN: Was he expelled at the Fifteenth Congress?

TROTSKY: In the same manner as the others.

GOLDMAN: When did he return to the Party—when did he capitulate?

TROTSKY: It was together with Smirnov in November of 1929.

GOLDMAN: Did you have any communication with him prior to his capitulation, before his capitulation?

TROTSKY: Possibly, in the time I was in Alma-Ata, he wrote me a letter before his capitulation.

GOLDMAN: You don't remember?

TROTSKY: I don't remember.

GOLDMAN: After his capitulation, did you communicate with him?

TROTSKY: Never.

GOLDMAN: You received no letters from him?

TROTSKY: Never.

GOLDMAN: You sent him no messages?

TROTSKY: Never.

GOLDMAN: Do you know I.A. Knyazev?

TROTSKY: No.

GOLDMAN: When did you first see the name?

TROTSKY: Only from the reports of the trial.

GOLDMAN: Do you know S.A. Rataichak?

TROTSKY: No.

GOLDMAN: When did you first see the name?

TROTSKY: From the records of the trial.

GOLDMAN: Do you know B.O. Norkin?

TROTSKY: No.

GOLDMAN: When did you first see the name?

TROTSKY: From the trial report.

GOLDMAN: Do you know A.A. Shestov?

TROTSKY: No.

GOLDMAN: You first saw the name from the reports of the trial?

TROTSKY: Yes.

GOLDMAN: Is the same true of M.S. Stroilov?

TROTSKY: The same, absolutely.

GOLDMAN: You never knew him?

TROTSKY: Never.

GOLDMAN: You first saw the name in the reports of the trial?

TROTSKY: Yes.

GOLDMAN: What about Y.D. Turok?

TROTSKY: The same.

GOLDMAN: And I.Y. Hrasche?

TROTSKY: The same.

GOLDMAN: You never knew him, and the first time you saw the name was in the reports of the trial?

TROTSKY: Yes.

GOLDMAN: What about G.E. Pushin?

TROTSKY: The same.

GOLDMAN: And the first time you saw the name was in the reports of the trial?

TROTSKY: Yes.

GOLDMAN: How about V.V. Arnold?

TROTSKY: The same.

GOLDMAN: You never knew him?

TROTSKY: No.

DEWEY: We will take a short recess now.

GOLDMAN: Now, Mr. Trotsky, you have given us a short biography of the principal defendants in the two trials, and you have mentioned certain defendants whom you have identified as not knowing at all. You have told us that the main defendants were either never Trotskyites or, if they were at one time, were capitulators. Can you give us an idea briefly as to the followers of yours who actually remained loyal to the Left Opposition up to the present time, the recent period?

TROTSKY: I name two. Rakovsky and Sosnovsky.

GOLDMAN: When did Rakovsky capitulate?

TROTSKY: In 1934.

GOLDMAN: When did Sosnovsky capitulate?

TROTSKY: After Rakovsky, immediately.

GOLDMAN: After Rakovsky?

TROTSKY: Immediately, yes.

GOLDMAN: What other friends of yours remained with you?

TROTSKY: The Elzins, father and son.

GOLDMAN: Elzin?

TROTSKY: E-l-z-i-n. Dr. Elzin and son, the editor of my works in the Soviet Union, the former editor of my works. Another brother of his died in deportation. Then there is the name of Dinglestedt, who is eight years in prison; Solnzev, who died a year and a half ago on the way from one prison to another; Yakovin, a brilliant scholar, who was an exceptionally brilliant man, who is in prison for eight years. I can name Victor Serge, who succeeded in finding the possibility to go abroad, thanks to the intervention of the French authors and artists. Victor Serge is a very gifted author. He is half Russian and half French. I can name Alexandra Sokolovskaya, my first wife, who is in Siberia, separated from my grandchildren. I don't know anything about their fate. And I could name many others not so known.

GOLDMAN: Now, during the period of your exile did you communicate with some of these people to whom—whose names you mentioned?

TROTSKY: I communicated with our comrades in the prisons in the first years, but, as I said, the communications were later interrupted by the more severe control.

DEWEY: Might we identify the date when the severe control came into effect?

GOLDMAN: Up to what time, up to what date were you able to communicate with your friends in the Soviet Union?

TROTSKY: It is difficult to name the exact date, because the régime became from time to time more efficient. We tried to send letters, and one of ten letters succeeded in reaching the person in some way. It was, for example, the same with our son.

GOLDMAN: You are referring now to the son who remained in Russia, Sergei?

TROTSKY: Sergei. We sent five—my wife. I abstained from writing in order not to compromise him, but my wife wrote him five or six letters, and then she received one time an answer. Then she tried to send him money through the bank, to have assurance that he was living. But the money came back one time and a second time, and then we lost all communication with him. In the same way it was with our friends in Siberia.

GOLDMAN: Will your record show when was the last time you actually received some communications from your friends in Russia?

TROTSKY: I believe, maybe later there were one or two or three times we had letters, but 1931 is the critical year.

GOLDMAN: After 1931, you say you might have had one or two or three communications?

TROTSKY: Yes.

GOLDMAN: You had no regular communications?

TROTSKY: They were abandoned at the time. Our systematic work to sustain or to have regular communications with them was abandoned. You know, we had three or four Russian comrades abroad who helped us to write postal cards to our friends in Siberia, with general news. From time to time, I wrote also my political opinions on some questions to our friends, young friends, and put them on postal cards and sent out to trusts and known businesses. From time to time, we received answers. It was our method of communication.

GOLDMAN: Have you in your possession some of the things you received?

TROTSKY: Yes.

GOLDMAN: Can you show us samples of one or two of these

answers or replies? These came from Russia? (indicating).

TROTSKY: These came from Russia.

GOLDMAN: When is that dated?

TROTSKY: It is not dated at all.

GOLDMAN: Have you any idea when you received it?

TROTSKY: Here is one of 1929, and here is one—

GOLDMAN: At any rate, I want to show the Commission a sample of a document received from Russia. If the Commissioners can read it, they are welcome to read it.

TROTSKY: Will you show the Commission the theoretical work written in prison?

GOLDMAN: Showing the Commission the letter written in such handwriting that it would require a magnifying glass.

BEALS: Was this letter sent through ordinary mails?

TROTSKY: Yes.

GOLDMAN: It would require a magnifying glass to read this. I show it to the Commission without introducing it into evidence—a theoretical work, I believe.

TROTSKY: It is by the comrades named by me before—the younger comrades like Yakovin and those others. It is an analysis of the economic and political situation in the Soviet Union.

GOLDMAN: Received by Mr. Trotsky in a small box, a little larger than a match box. How many pages of the *Bulletin of the Opposition* does this work take up?

TROTSKY: Our *Bulletin* was not so rich as to publish the work as a whole. We published only the more important parts of this work.

GOLDMAN: How many pages of the *Opposition Bulletin* did you take up?

TROTSKY: I don't know; it was in many issues. I can't say offhand.

FINERTY: What is the date of that?

GOLDMAN: When did you receive that, if you remember?

TROTSKY: You can find it out in the *Bulletin.* I believe it was 1930 or 1931. It was sent in by the mail, sent by a foreigner who visited the Soviet Union, a sympathizer who had connections with the relatives of the people in prison. And I assure the Commission that it is a very serious work, in spite of the extraordinary—

DEWEY: Can you tell us the date of the *Opposition Bulletin* in which this material was utilized?

TROTSKY: If you will permit me, I will get it in ten minutes.

DEWEY: Any time will do.

GOLDMAN: I am not introducing this into evidence.

BEALS: Up to what date was the *Opposition Bulletin* printed?

TROTSKY: I will find out.

BEALS: Up to what date was the *Bulletin* printed?

GOLDMAN: Are you still printing that now?

TROTSKY: Yes; the last issue is devoted to the last Moscow trial. I received it from Paris five days ago.

BEALS: You get correspondence for the *Bulletin* from Russia?

TROTSKY: Unfortunately, in the last times we have no correspondence. The people became absolutely afraid of the idea to be in communication with the *Bulletin,* and the news we have is mostly from foreigners, sympathizers who visited as tourists the Soviet Union.

BEALS: Up to what time have you correspondence from the Soviet Union published in the *Bulletin*?

TROTSKY: The last correspondence is from 1931. Then it was more constantly correspondence from letters and communications, such as the meeting of Smirnov in the street with my son. In London one of our English friends met a Russian sympathizer, and he writes his impressions on the news he received from him. We have information, but no regular communication, in spite of certain experience that we have established in illegal communication, because at no time, I believe, in the human history, can you find such a régime as is now in the Soviet Union—a police régime, such a totalitarian police régime.

GOLDMAN: Did you ever make any efforts to get the Russian *Bulletin* into Russia?

TROTSKY: Yes, we published it in photo form. It is the same, in similar format, by photo. We succeeded in the first years to send this into Russia. For the last years, we abandoned this because it was totally in vain.

GOLDMAN: Did you have any information with reference to those followers or friends of yours who are still in the prisons of the Soviet Union?

TROTSKY: In recent times, we had very good information through Victor Serge. He came in 1936—he came abroad due to a certain international campaign in his favor. He came abroad directly from Siberia. He was in Siberia with Elzin, one of the most prominent Oppositionists.

GOLDMAN: Did anyone ever escape from the Russian exile—succeed in escaping?

TROTSKY: He didn't escape.

GOLDMAN: I don't mean Serge, but any Left Oppositionist.

TROTSKY: Yes, one worker escaped through Persia.

GOLDMAN: In what year?

TROTSKY: In 1935.

GOLDMAN: What is his name?

TROTSKY: His name now is Tarov. But he has another name. He is trying to get to France. I am not sure if it is advisable to give his genuine name. But I can name it in an executive session, because if he succeeds in getting to Europe, we will have one of the best witnesses for the Commission.

GOLDMAN: How about Dr. Ciliga?

TROTSKY: He is a Yugoslavian.

GOLDMAN: Did he belong to the Left Opposition?

TROTSKY: He came to the Soviet Union as a Stalinist. In 1929 he became an Oppositionist, he and his four comrades from the Communist Party of Yugoslavia. He was a member of the Politburo of the Yugoslavian Communist Party.

GOLDMAN: He is available as a witness for the Commission?

TROTSKY: Yes, a very important witness. Politically, he is not with us, he is more between the Marxists and the Anarchists, politically. But it is not a question of his political opinions, but the sincerity of his deposition.

GOLDMAN: You gave us an idea of the relationship that existed between the loyal followers of the Left Opposition and the capitulators. Can you give us any more information that you have at your disposal showing the relationship between these two groups, outside of the photograph you introduced into evidence, and the letters?

TROTSKY: I can only refer to the eighty-four articles written by me, and the books, and my correspondence, because I presented only a few quotations.

GOLDMAN: I think that you misunderstand me. I don't mean what you wrote about them. I mean the relationship that existed between the persons who remained loyal to the Left Opposition in the Soviet Union, and the capitulators.

TROTSKY: I could quote a letter from an Oppositionist who denounces Radek. He asked him for money for a sick Oppositionist in Siberia. Radek answered—I will quote what this Oppositionist writes: "In response to a request to help a deported Bolshevik who is gravely ill, Radek refused, adding: 'He will return more rapidly.' He measures with his disgusting little standard!" When friends are split, the antagonism is more bitter than between the ruling group and the Opposition as a whole. It is a historical and political law that the relationship between the Oppositionists and the capitulators was all these years more bitter than the relationship between the Oppositionists and the Stalinists.

GOLDMAN: Among the defendants, then, of the last two trials, there is not a single former Oppositionist who did not capitulate before the trials—is that right?

TROTSKY: With the exception only of Muralov; he did not capitulate officially, but abandoned politics. He declared to the bureaucracy that he was not an Oppositionist, only a "spetz." All of the others capitulated officially, and became my bitterest enemies.

GOLDMAN: Can you give us any opinion as to whether or not Zinoviev had a family?

TROTSKY: Yes. Victor Serge gives us information that after the Kirov assassination there were from 60,000 to 100,000 deportations from Leningrad to Siberia of the families—I ask you to note this number—from 60,000 to 100,000. He pictured the situation of the families at the railroad stations in Siberia, the mothers, the children, and the old fathers, and so on.

GOLDMAN: You mean the families of the Oppositionists?

TROTSKY: The former Oppositionists, the relatives of the Oppositionists.

GOLDMAN: Who were deported?

TROTSKY: To Siberia.

GOLDMAN: And from your personal knowledge, do you know whether Zinoviev had a family, wife and children?

TROTSKY: His son was arrested and his brother-in-law, who is not accused of being with the terrorist group. His brother was met by Victor Serge and Dr. Ciliga in Siberia.

GOLDMAN: How about Muralov—has he a family?

TROTSKY: Yes, but I don't know anything about him.

GOLDMAN: And Kamenev?

TROTSKY: Also, children and a wife. His first wife is my sister. The first papers announced her deportation to Siberia. She is an old woman, absolutely not a member of our political group, and never took part in our political activity.

GOLDMAN: How about Radek? Do you know whether he has a family?

TROTSKY: I have no information about his family. He has a wife and son-in-law, but I don't know their fate.

GOLDMAN: This ends the examination with reference to the relationship to the defendants, and I wish now to proceed to the question of the evidence produced at the last two trials.

FINERTY: It was suggested that perhaps the record should show more information as to who Blumkin was.

TROTSKY: This political work was published in November–December, 1931, in the *Bulletin of the Opposition.*

GOLDMAN: Referring to the—

TROTSKY: Here is only a dozen pages in this issue, but later in articles—

GOLDMAN: Let the record show that the witness is referring to a document received from the Soviet Union some time in 1930 in a match box, written on very small cards in small characters, exceedingly small.

LAFOLLETTE: Microscopic, I would say.

GOLDMAN: Microscopic is still better. Mr. Trotsky, can you give us any information about Blumkin? Some Commissioners are anxious to know what you know about Blumkin.

DEWEY: What is his position, or was his position, in the Party?

GOLDMAN: What his position was in the struggle between the factions.

TROTSKY: He belonged to the Left Opposition. He was a member of my military secretariat during the War, and personally connected with me. Then he was separated from me by the authorities and sent abroad to Constantinople in Turkey. His past—he had a very extraordinary past. He was a member of the Left Social Revolutionary Party and he participated in the insurrection against the Bolsheviks. He was the man who killed the German ambassador, Mirbach, and the Bolsheviks officially had to prosecute him. He disappeared, and then he came back, and he declared after the revolution in Germany and after the denunciation of the Brest-Litovsk peace—he appeared again before us and said: "I am now a Bolshevik; you can test me." He was sent to the front, where he was a very good fighter and a very courageous man. I employed him in my military secretariat and throughout, when I needed a courageous man, Blumkin was at my disposal.

GOLDMAN: Did he belong to the Left Opposition?

TROTSKY: He belonged to the Left Opposition.

GOLDMAN: Did he capitulate?

TROTSKY: In a very modest manner.

GOLDMAN: Was he expelled from the Party?

TROTSKY: I believe he was cautious not to compromise the Left Opposition by his past.

GOLDMAN: Do you know whether he was expelled from the Party?

TROTSKY: No, not even expelled, because of his cautious attitude.

GOLDMAN: What was his official position in the Soviet Union? I mean, what did he do there, in what Ministry was he?

TROTSKY: He was in the service, the last time, of the Foreign Affairs, the Ministry of Foreign Affairs.

GOLDMAN: That is how he happened to be in Constantinople?

TROTSKY: Yes.

GOLDMAN: He was an employee of the Ministry of Foreign Affairs?

TROTSKY: Yes.

GOLDMAN: Any other questions?

DEWEY: I have difficulty in pronouncing the name of Mrachkovsky. It says in the August trials, the English report, on page 43, that from 1923 to 1927 all correspondence passed through his hands—that all of Trotsky's correspondence passed through his hands. Is that a correct statement?

TROTSKY: No, he was from 1923 to 1927—he was a member in the Urals and not in Moscow. I was in Moscow and had my own secretariat. It is absolutely an exaggeration to present him as a closest collaborator of mine; it is an absolute falsehood.

DEWEY: It is also stated that he was one of your closest and most devoted followers.

TROTSKY: Yes, he was in the Red Army, one of the chiefs, a general of the Army. I had in the Red Army many others. He was one of them, a very good soldier, a very good fighter. He had sympathy for me personally. I can say Rakovsky was my friend for thirty-five years. I can't say the same for Mrachkovsky, a much younger comrade, with whom I worked together in the Civil War as with many others.

GOLDMAN: Any other questions on this? If none, I shall proceed now to examine Mr. Trotsky on the evidence produced by Holtzman, Berman-Yurin and Fritz David to the effect, as they claim, they met Mr. Trotsky personally in Copenhagen and received instructions from him for the purpose of committing terroristic acts against some of the leaders of the Soviet Union. When did you leave Turkey for Copenhagen?

TROTSKY: It was November 14, 1932.

GOLDMAN: Who were with you at that time?

TROTSKY: In Copenhagen or on the trip?

GOLDMAN: Who were with you when you started from Constantinople?

TROTSKY: There was a French friend, Comrade P. Frank, a German friend—I will name him only Oscar—I can notify the Commission who he is. He is a real person.

FINERTY: I would suggest that Mr. Trotsky give an initial.

GOLDMAN: Oscar.

TROTSKY: Jan Frankel, who is at my left. That is all.

GOLDMAN: Was your wife with you?

TROTSKY: Yes.

GOLDMAN: So there were four people who started out from Constantinople?

TROTSKY: An American, Field, an American couple, Field and his wife—they give a deposition about the trip, and the Commission can notify him—

GOLDMAN: We will come to that.

TROTSKY: But, you know, it was the first trip and with certain danger. The Fields were not officially with us. They were on the same boat, but as independent travelers.

GOLDMAN: That was on the first trip out of Turkey, after your exile?

TROTSKY: Yes.

GOLDMAN: What route did you take to Copenhagen; do you remember?

TROTSKY: Yes, it was through France, from Marseilles to Dunkerque by the ship "Ejsberg" to Denmark, and then by railroad to Copenhagen.

GOLDMAN: Did any other people join you on the trip?

TROTSKY: We had few friends at that time in Denmark, but on the trip friends from France joined us.

GOLDMAN: Mr. Trotsky, I am going to ask Mr. Frankel questions later on, so if you don't remember, we'll just pass it up.

TROTSKY: I must say, I made this trip two times, one time for Copenhagen and the other time for Marseilles. I think my fellow-travelers—I don't remember quite who was there the first time and who was there the second time.

GOLDMAN: Do you remember when you arrived in Copenhagen?

TROTSKY: It was, I believe, on November 23d.

GOLDMAN: 1932?

TROTSKY: 1932.

GOLDMAN: Where was your son Leon Sedov at the time you made your trip?

TROTSKY: In Berlin.

GOLDMAN: Did he join you on the way to Copenhagen?

TROTSKY: No.

GOLDMAN: Do you know of any efforts that were made either by you or your wife or by any other member of the party to get him to join you in Copenhagen?

TROTSKY: It was agreed between us that he would come to Copenhagen. But all his efforts—it was the time of—

GOLDMAN: I will ask you that later.

TROTSKY: Good.

GOLDMAN: Where did you live when you were in Copenhagen?

TROTSKY: I don't remember the address. It was a small villa of a dancer.

GOLDMAN: You occupied the whole villa?

TROTSKY: Yes.

GOLDMAN: How many rooms were there?

TROTSKY: I believe five or six rooms and two stories.

GOLDMAN: Who lived there with you?

TROTSKY: We lived, my wife, my collaborators, and I in the house. The house was occupied not only by the inhabitants, but our friends who came from France, from England, from Holland, from Germany—and I believe we had visitors, about three visitors.

GOLDMAN: Did these visitors live there in Copenhagen?

TROTSKY: Yes.

GOLDMAN: You mean stayed there overnight?

TROTSKY: Pardon?

GOLDMAN: Actually remained there overnight?

TROTSKY: They organized a guard for day and night. There was a relief of five or six persons who remained on the first story and we, my wife and myself, were on the second story.

GOLDMAN: Do you have a record of the names of the people who were there while you were in Copenhagen?

TROTSKY: Yes.

GOLDMAN: Would you give us the list of names? I am talking to Mr. Frankel, the secretary of Mr. Trotsky. I am looking at a list of names, and I see that you are the one who enumerates these names in your statement.

FRANKEL: Yes.

GOLDMAN: We shall wait until you testify before putting the list of names into evidence.

FINERTY: Mr. Goldman, would it not be well to refresh his recollection so that he could testify to that according to his recollection?

GOLDMAN: Will you look at this list of names, Mr. Trotsky, and see whether you can say whether this list has the correct names?

TROTSKY: Pierre Frank, a French friend, I remember him very well. Oscar, a German; Jan Frankel; Gérard Rosenthal, my French lawyer; Denise Naville, the wife of P. Naville, both are our best friends; Jeanne Martin des Pallières, the wife of my son; Julien, an Italian émigré. This is his pseudonym. Grylewicz, a German émigré. He is the former German official editor of the Russian *Bulletin*. Before Hitler's victory, we edited the *Bulletin* in Germany, and, after that, we transferred it to France. He was in Germany the responsible editor. Lucienne Tedeschi is the wife of Julien, also an Italian comrade. R. Molinier, a French comrade; Feroci, an Italian comrade; Jungclas, a German comrade in Copenhagen; Sneevliet, a deputy of the Parliament in Holland and a friend of mine. Bruno is a German émigré, Field and his wife, the Americans, were named before. Lesoil, a Belgian from Charleroi, a very well known militant in the workers' movement. Hippe, a German worker, who is now in prison.

FRANKEL: He was in prison.

TROTSKY: He is now out of prison. He was for two years

in prison. Schneeweiss, also a German worker who is now in emigration. The engineer Sch—— I knew him very well. He is abroad.

FRANKEL: He is in prison now.

TROTSKY: There were three or four young students from Hamburg, who came in with their bicycles. Attorney Cohn from Berlin, he was attorney for my son and he made all the efforts to secure him the possibility to come to Copenhagen. He didn't succeed. He asked me by telephone if he could help me to remain in Denmark—he would address the Prime Minister. I answered with positive gratitude. He came especially for that purpose to Copenhagen. He was a friend of Karl Liebknecht. Perhaps Mr. Otto Ruehle knows him—I am sure very well. He was a very well known man. Then, the German émigré in Paris, Bauer, and Senin, who is a Russian—I believe a Lithuanian citizen. He was the only one of the visitors who knew the Russian language, the only one.

GOLDMAN: Now, Mr. Trotsky, were there other visitors who visited you in Copenhagen outside of the people whose names you have just read to us?

TROTSKY: There was Wicks from England.

GOLDMAN: Any other names that you remember?

TROTSKY: In any case, Mr. Goldman, it was not Berman-Yurin, not Holtzman, and not Fritz David. (Laughter)

GOLDMAN: I wanted to ask you that, but you took that out of my mouth.

TROTSKY: There were two weeks in Norway when I was absolutely sure that Senin must be Berman-Yurin or Fritz David, because it was there stated, in the *Pravda,* about a visit from a man who knew the Russian language. That was some weeks after his visit.

GOLDMAN: How did he appear there to you?

TROTSKY: He came as a friend.

GOLDMAN: You are talking now about Senin, the one you knew as Senin?

TROTSKY: They were two brothers in Germany, Senin and Well. Senin is a pseudonym. Their genuine name is Sobolevitzius. I had the suspicion, as other friends who worked in the German organization, that the so-called Trotskyite was more or less an agent of the Stalinists. He came to assure me that it was not true—that is, Senin came, and we had a conversation for one hour or a bit more. And then he and his brother organized a split in our organization. They published a paper. We were absolutely sure it was paid for by the G.P.U. On another occasion, I was sure, in Norway—

GOLDMAN: In where?

TROTSKY: What?

GOLDMAN: You were sure where?

TROTSKY: In August, 1936, in Norway, during the first trial, when I had the first information concerning Berman-Yurin, I searched in my memory and asked: "Who could it be?" I concluded it was Senin; I was sure it was Senin. I wrote to my son, asking if it was not Senin. Then I received letters that Senin is abroad. I was convinced Berman-Yurin is a person absolutely unknown to me after that.

GOLDMAN: Well, for the purpose of making the record clear, I shall ask you these questions you already answered. Did you meet anyone by the name of Fritz David while you were in Copenhagen?

TROTSKY: Never.

GOLDMAN: Did you ever have any conversations with him while you were there?

TROTSKY: No.

GOLDMAN: By the way, who rented the house for you?

TROTSKY: Molinier, the French comrade.

GOLDMAN: Did he publish anything about where you lived?

TROTSKY: No; it was an absolute secret.

GOLDMAN: And when anyone wanted to see you, could he walk into your room?

TROTSKY: It was more difficult than here, because here there is only a guard. There, there was a guard, and we were incognito. Nobody knew where I was.

GOLDMAN: The fact was that you were incognito?

DEWEY: Mr. Goldman, these guards he refers to were his friends?

GOLDMAN: When you say guards, do you mean regular police officers or your friends?

TROTSKY: There were two policemen at the entrance, but they did not control officially. They were only there to assure order and quietness for the Government. The guard, the official guard who controlled all visitors, were my friends.

GOLDMAN: Did you meet anyone by the name of Holtzman while you were in Copenhagen?

TROTSKY: No.

GOLDMAN: Did you have any conversations with him at the house where you lived?

TROTSKY: No.

GOLDMAN: You say Senin was the only one who spoke with you in Russian.

TROTSKY: Not about terrorism. (Laughter)

GOLDMAN: I didn't ask you that question. I will later on. Now, you didn't see any other visitors?

TROTSKY: Yes, I remember one more—excuse me. It was the Norwegian Falk. He is a Norwegian Marxist who came in order to propose to me that I go to Norway for a lecture also.

GOLDMAN: Anybody else that you can remember now?

TROTSKY: The Danes. There was one Boeggild, the organizer of my lecture, who visited us in this house. But only at the last evening before our departure, when we had no more reason for secrecy, we admitted the visit of the delegation of Danish students, and we had a general discussion with them on Socialism.

GOLDMAN: What did you do when you were in Copenhagen?

TROTSKY: I gave a lecture to the students, and then a radio message for the United States, in my English which was not better than it is now.

GOLDMAN: Will you furnish the Commission copies of the speech?

TROTSKY: Yes.

GOLDMAN: When did you leave Copenhagen?

TROTSKY: We left Copenhagen the 2nd of December.

GOLDMAN: And who left with you?

TROTSKY: Ten or twelve, I believe, of the people named before, my collaborators. Then, the French friends named before—on the same ship.

GOLDMAN: When did you first meet your son?

TROTSKY: I met him in Paris in the Gare du Nord.

GOLDMAN: On what date?

TROTSKY: It was the 5th of December.

GOLDMAN: And that was the first time you met your son since when?

TROTSKY: Since he departed from Turkey in 1931.

GOLDMAN: When did he depart from Turkey?

TROTSKY: In February.

GOLDMAN: Where did he go to?

TROTSKY: What?

GOLDMAN: What city did he go to?

TROTSKY: To Berlin.

GOLDMAN: What was he doing in Berlin?

TROTSKY: He was studying.

GOLDMAN: Was your son's wife, Jeanne des Pallières, Leon Sedov's wife, in Copenhagen?

TROTSKY: Yes.

GOLDMAN: When did she arrive there?

TROTSKY: She had the possibility to be there because she is a French citizen. She has her passport.

GOLDMAN: She—

TROTSKY: She could leave Berlin freely for Copenhagen.

GOLDMAN: When did she come to Copenhagen?

TROTSKY: It was the 26th, or the 25th, I believe, of December.

GOLDMAN: December?

TROTSKY: November.

GOLDMAN: And how long did she stay there?

TROTSKY: As long as we—my wife and I.

GOLDMAN: Did she go with you to Paris?

TROTSKY: On the same ship to France.

GOLDMAN: She didn't go back to Berlin?

TROTSKY: What?

GOLDMAN: She didn't go back to Berlin?

TROTSKY: No, she went back to Paris for a sojourn. She has her mother in Paris.

GOLDMAN: From Copenhagen, did your daughter-in-law go direct to France or first to Berlin?

TROTSKY: She went with us together to Paris.

GOLDMAN: And the first time you met your son since 1931, when he departed for Berlin, was in Paris on December 5th?

TROTSKY: Yes.

GOLDMAN: 1932?

TROTSKY: Yes.

GOLDMAN: And while you were in Copenhagen, did you see your son at all?

TROTSKY: No, he was in Berlin at the time.

GOLDMAN: Did you have contact with your son?

TROTSKY: Yes, by telephone, two times a day. We asked every day if he could come, what was the situation with his visa, and so on.

DEWEY: Well, there are records of those telephone calls in Copenhagen. They will have to find out there, I suppose.

GOLDMAN: The Commission will have to find out in Copenhagen whether there were records of those telephone conversations.

TROTSKY: There were efforts made to ask for them, but the central telephone exchange refuses. They must have an order from the superiors. It is a delicate matter for private sources to get that information. But we have many other proofs.

GOLDMAN: Now, I have many documents dealing with Sedov's presence in Berlin at the time that Holtzman, according to his testimony at the trial, at the time that Holtzman says that he met Sedov at the Bristol Hotel in Copenhagen. I wish to enumerate for the benefit of the Commission these documents. Some of them are in foreign languages and have not as yet been translated. A list of these documents in general and the contents of these documents has been made, including the contents of the documents. I wish to read them for the benefit of the Commission, read them all into the record.

We have first the statement or depositions of various people describing the trip and the arrangement for the residence where Mr. Trotsky and his secretaries and his wife lived while in Copenhagen, and the measures taken to guard him, showing the impossibility of unobserved visitors. We have statements from people who knew Sedov and did not see him. We have statements from people who knew Sedov and lived in Berlin, and they saw him there in Berlin, and we have an additional list of visitors. The first is a statement by Mr. Frankel, who is sitting here with Mr. Trotsky. Now, I will ask the Commission whether it is their desire for me to put Mr. Frankel on the witness stand and cross-examine him, or whether you will be satisfied with the statement of his. I think it is best to put him on the stand to testify as long as he is here, so he will be subject to cross-examination by the Commission. So, I will prefer to put him on the stand.

FINERTY: It will be after Mr. Trotsky's testimony?

GOLDMAN: After Mr. Trotsky completes all his testimony, but when I am dealing with this particular subject. We have a statement from Pierre Naville, whose name was read before, testifying in general to the character of the house, and so forth. We have a statement by Oscar in a similar connection which shows that Holtzman, Berman-Yurin and Fritz David could not have been present without their knowledge. And a statement by Anton Grylewicz—

TROTSKY: And his wife.

GOLDMAN: Anton Grylewicz testifies to the fact that:

> Trotsky's son was not in Copenhagen, as I can testify under oath. (1) I was in Trotsky's house every day. (2) I know that Com. Trotsky, his wife, and Sedov's wife telephoned Sedov every day. *I also used this means of communication to Sedov twice. Again, my wife, who personally or telephonically spoke with Sedov in Berlin every day of my absence, reported to me in some letters to Copenhagen her conversations with Sedov.*

TROTSKY: Permit me, Mr. Goldman, a remark, that to our friends this trip to Copenhagen was a very important event. They were all our friends, and were more or less implicated in our family story. They knew in Copenhagen that we waited for our son, and they knew him in Berlin. They knew that our son was very busy trying to get a visa.

FINERTY: Mr. Goldman, Mr. Trotsky's secretary might have the telephone bills.

GOLDMAN: Have you any records of your telephone bills?

FRANKEL: I don't believe it, because there was an arrangement with the owner of the house about telephone calls. Only Molinier can say.

TROTSKY: It is possible.

GOLDMAN: Grylewicz further states that letters were given

him by Sedov for his father, two letters of introduction.

TROTSKY: I have the letters in my possession now.

GOLDMAN: It reads as follows: "If Sedov had himself gone to Copenhagen, he would certainly have brought the letters with him." There is a statement from Jungclas to the effect that he repeatedly heard phone calls put in for Berlin. A statement by Oscar Cohn, who confirms that Sedov was not present and that he, Cohn, was in Trotsky's villa daily. The same thing by Feroci, and the same type of declaration by Pierre Frank, and also by Leon Lesoil. There is one from E. Falk, from Oslo, a letter to Attorney Puntervold, who represented Trotsky in Norway. He is not a member of the organization, and he is a political opponent. He writes as follows:

> None of my acquaintances knew where Trotsky resided, and I remember quite well that this secrecy gave rise to some discussion. The reason given for this was an endeavor to prevent demonstrations or other disagreeable incidents. It is certain that a stranger could not have obtained the address unaided. . . . I assume that I waited in these rooms [in Trotsky's house] about an hour. Then I was taken upstairs to a little room which appeared to serve as Trotsky's office. Trotsky did not pace the floor during our conversation . . .

This refers to the testimony of one of the defendants to the effect that Trotsky was pacing the floor.

TROTSKY: That I was what?

GOLDMAN: You were walking up and down.

TROTSKY: The room was very small; it was absolutely impossible. (Laughter)

GOLDMAN: I have a statement by Gérard Rosenthal similar in character to the former statements, and he also recalls Natalia Trotsky's impatience to see Sedov again, as well as her telegram to Herriot, the Minister of Foreign Affairs of France at that time. I have a statement of one Bruno, who requests his name be kept secret, in general similar to the others, and to the effect that he never heard the names of Holtzman, Berman-Yurin or David. He gives the plan of the house. He also testifies that he knew Sedov personally, and did not see him in Copenhagen. He saw him shortly before his departure, November, 1932, from Berlin, and didn't see him again until after his return. Here is another statement to a similar effect, a statement by Moelle and his sister. These were Danish people who make a formal statement that they did not see Sedov in Copenhagen. Then there is a statement by Julien, who was present during several telephone conversations that Natalia Trotsky had with her son, and since Mrs. Trotsky did not know German, a friend had to make the connections for her.

TROTSKY: Julien's wife, she is an Italian, but she is from Austria—an Austrian section belonging to Italy.

GOLDMAN: We have also a statement from Lucienne Tedeschi to the same effect, and we have a letter of Mr. Trotsky of October 12, 1936, from his Norwegian internment to his son, giving him memories and facts about the trip to Copenhagen. We have a statement by Esther and B.J. Field similar to the other declarations on many points, also adding material on the Grand Hotel in Copenhagen referring to the Konditori Bristol, the Bristol Confectionery, showing the connection between the so-called Hotel Bristol and this confectionery. We would probably call it, in the States, an ice-cream parlor. We have a statement of Jeanne Martin similar to the others, and three documents demonstrating the strictness of the control over the visits: a) Signed requests of journalists asking interviews with Trotsky; b) List of students who visited Trotsky compiled for control; and c) The plan of seating arrangements for reception to the intellectuals. We have an affidavit by Oluf Boeggild—I presume a Danish citizen—and also by Karen Boeggild, stating that they also saw Trotsky and never saw Sedov and heard nothing about his presence there. And we have here documents and depositions concerning Sedov's presence in Berlin during Trotsky's presence in Copenhagen. First and most important is a photostatic copy of Sedov's passport, with an explanation of this photostatic copy showing that Sedov was in Berlin, and that the passport is free from anything indicating that he went to Denmark; showing further that he did go to France at the time indicated by the witness.

TROTSKY: The passport is in the possession of our son, who sent us this from Paris.

GOLDMAN: Of course, the Commission in Paris can make an examination of Sedov on that matter, and the original of the passport will be produced. I have a copy of the telegram sent by Natalia Sedov, Mr. Trotsky's wife, to Herriot, the Minister of Foreign Affairs in France.

TROTSKY: He was Prime Minister and Minister of Foreign Affairs.

GOLDMAN: This telegram asks for a visa for Sedov to permit him to come from Berlin to France. I have the copy of the telegram.

TROTSKY: During our trip back from Denmark, we crossed France to Turkey. My wife sent a telegram with the help of our French lawyer Rosenthal, who wrote the text of the telegram, to the Prime Minister, Herriot, asking him to permit our son to come to France from Berlin. This telegram of my wife and the telegraphic order of Herriot to the French Consul in Berlin, telling him to give a visa to Leon Sedov for five days in France, is here. He came to France for five days and met us at the Gare du Nord.

GOLDMAN: Here is the copy of the telegram which Herriot sent to the French Consul in Berlin authorizing a visa for Sedov. Then there are documents concerning Sedov's residence in Berlin during the time Trotsky and his wife were in

Copenhagen. There is a certificate of police registration—

DEWEY: Mr. Goldman, might I interrupt one minute? You have not identified the meetings of the mother and Sedov.

GOLDMAN: As soon as I am through. The statement of Anna Grylewicz to the effect that during her husband's absence she saw Leon Sedov daily in Berlin. Her husband was the editor of the Russian *Bulletin*. She says as follows: "My husband and I were in daily contact with L. Sedov personally or by telephone. During the time my husband was in Copenhagen, Leon Trotsky's son, L. Sedov, called me up every day, and I spoke to him about all incoming mail, etc."

TROTSKY: Her address was the address of the Russian *Bulletin*.

GOLDMAN: Then we have the statement of Alfred Schoeler, who between November 20th and December 3rd saw Sedov daily in Berlin. We have the letter of Franz and Alexandra Pfemfert to Trotsky, proving the same thing. And then a statement by Olberg, one of the defendants in the trial, in the first trial, who in his testimony makes this statement, on page 87 of the official report of the proceedings:

> Before my departure for the Soviet Union, I intended to go to Copenhagen with Sedov to see Trotsky. Our trip did not materialize, but Suzanna, Sedov's wife, went there. On her return, she brought a letter from Trotsky, addressed to Sedov, in which Trotsky agreed to my going to the U.S.S.R., and expressed the hope that I would succeed in carrying out the mission entrusted to me. Sedov showed me this letter.

Thus we use his testimony on our behalf to show that Sedov never went to Copenhagen.

TROTSKY: Can I make a remark? I communicate to the Commission that Olberg was really in communication with my son in Berlin. He was one of the defendants who really knew the situation of my son, that he could not go to Copenhagen and that his wife went to Copenhagen, and he gave this explanation before the court. It is a certain discrepancy Mr. Vyshinsky did not remark.

GOLDMAN: Well, you don't expect him to catch everything. In the matter of the Bristol Hotel, concerning which a good deal of controversy has been raging in the press, we offer a statement in the Social Democratic press of September 1, 1936, cited also in the *New York Post* by Ludwig Lore, writing in a column called "Behind the Cables," to the effect that no such hotel existed in Copenhagen at the time that Mr. Trotsky was there. The question of the existence of that hotel has been taken up. The Communists have now a new version with reference to that incident. We give the Communist version, and in addition we offer a statement by Mr. Trotsky replying to the Communist explanation of the existence of the Hotel Bristol. In short, their explanation, as the Commissioners probably know, is that there was a Grand Hotel, but there was a café, known as the Bristol Café, therefore intimating that the witness was legitimately mistaken, when he said he met Sedov in the Hotel Bristol.

TROTSKY: In the vestibule.

GOLDMAN: I therefore offer a photograph from a not very favorable source, as far as we are concerned, from *Soviet Russia Today*. We offer the photograph from the March, 1937, issue. It attempts to show that there is a Hotel Bristol. We offer this for the examination of the Commissioners, and in addition we offer an explanation which is part of the affidavit made by Esther and B.J. Field. And, further, we offer many documents. There is an explanation of B.J. and Esther Field with reference to this photograph, and also with reference to this confectionery of Bristol, its location, its distance from the hotel, and other relevant matters. Then, we have a list of speeches, press statements, film addresses, and interviews, showing what Mr. Trotsky said at the time, the tone of the conversations, his attitude towards the defense of the Soviet Union, all contradicting the testimony of Berman-Yurin, Fritz David and Holtzman to the effect that what Mr. Trotsky was actually interested in was the organization of terroristic acts against Stalin and his loyal followers.

There was there a report at that time to the effect that Zinoviev died in Russia. This is of interest because Holtzman, David and the others did not mention a single thing about that report.

TROTSKY: It was in the world press and an important event—the news about the death of Zinoviev. I received at that time cables from London asking me for a necrological article about Zinoviev. We talked about this many times, because it was to us very important news. The terrorists who came to me for instructions to go back to work with the terroristic center guided by Zinoviev did not mention this news at all, according to the reports of the Moscow trial. I should say, alleged terrorists.

GOLDMAN: I will quote some excerpts from the Copenhagen *Sozialdemokraten* cited by *Dagbladet* August 20, 1936, and also from the statement made by Karen Boeggild. The *Dagbladet* says:

> "Trotsky and five or six others were in my home," Boeggild relates, "when suddenly I had a telephone call from a friend who told me that a newspaper had just come out with a telegram from Moscow that Zinoviev had died. Trotsky arose, deeply moved, and spoke about as follows: 'I have fought against Zinoviev politically for many years. In some matters, I was also united with him. I know all Zinoviev's mistakes, but in this moment I will not think about them, I will only think about the fact that throughout his life he tried to work for the labor movement,' and then Trotsky continued for a bit to honor the memory of his dead adversary and co-fighter with

> eloquent phrases." It was, Boeggild says, very moving to hear Trotsky's solemn speech in this little group. This experience, inspired, as it was later to appear, by a false report, in no way indicated [the paper says] that Trotsky was planning assassinations in union with Zinoviev. The news about the Copenhagen conspiracy seems to us, if possible, more fantastic than all the other charges.

Now I quote from the affidavit of Karen Boeggild:

> I further remember that Mr. Trotsky held a brief memorial speech for Zinoviev at a little gathering in my home, when the false news of Zinoviev's death arrived. He portrayed him as a former friend who in recent years has become his adversary.

At the time of the report of the death of Zinoviev, Trotsky was supposed to have been plotting with Zinoviev the assassination of Stalin. The excerpt of the affidavit by, in German, by—

DEWEY: Excuse me, how long will you take?

GOLDMAN: Three or four more minutes. Then there are other excerpts from the Danish press, showing what Trotsky's attitude was. Now, I introduce all these documents under a general heading of "Copenhagen," with reference to the claim made by Holtzman, Fritz David, and Berman-Yurin—or, rather, made specifically by Holtzman—that he met and made arrangements with Sedov in Berlin to meet Sedov in the Hotel Bristol in Copenhagen and that they actually met there, and was taken by him to see Trotsky, with whom he had a conversation, and in which conversation Trotsky was supposed to have given him instructions to commit terroristic acts in the Soviet Union.

What I want to show to the Commission from all of these documents is that Sedov was never in Copenhagen;

that the first time he met Mr. and Mrs. Trotsky, his father and mother, was in Paris; that he made every effort to meet them in Copenhagen, with no success; that his wife reached Copenhagen, but not Sedov; and that conversations that Mr. and Mrs. Trotsky had with Sedov were only by telephone from Copenhagen to Berlin. That is the purpose of the introduction of all these documents. Mr. Trotsky will argue about the relevancy and about the conclusiveness of all this testimony that Sedov was not in Copenhagen, in his final argument. Are there any questions which the Commission would like to ask at this time?

DEWEY: You are introducing this for no other purpose, are you not, relative to getting this message—

GOLDMAN: These proofs, these exhibits, will show that it was impossible for anybody to visit Trotsky without the knowledge of the secretaries who were there, and that they testified that no one by the name of Fritz David, or Berman-Yurin, or Holtzman was present at Mr. Trotsky's house. That is the only purpose. I am producing this testimony further to show that Sedov never met Holtzman in Copenhagen, and that he never left Berlin. Pardon me, I want to ask one question. To your knowledge, was your son Sedov ever in Copenhagen?

TROTSKY: No.

GOLDMAN: That Sedov was never in Copenhagen. That is the purpose of the introduction of my testimony.

TROTSKY: For one purpose more, if you permit. From the testimony and the documents, it is absolutely clear that it was of no purpose for my son to come to Copenhagen and to deny it afterwards. Because I was in Copenhagen, it is clear from these documents that my son was not in Copenhagen. That is, there would be no reason for him to deny it. It is absolutely clear from the depositions of Holtzman, Berman-Yurin, and the others. Because Berman-Yurin and David, who were sent by my son to Copenhagen, allegedly sent—they did not mention his presence in Copenhagen.

GOLDMAN: That is the conclusion that you draw from that. And one incidental purpose of the introduction of these exhibits is this: That it proves that in Copenhagen, where Mr. Trotsky was supposed to have plotted the death of many leaders, he was discussing and talking about questions such as the defense of the Soviet Union and the organization of groups belonging to his tendency. Nevertheless—

DEWEY: I want to know what the object of the introduction of the testimony about the telegrams of Herriot is.

GOLDMAN: The object is to show the efforts made by both Mr. and Mrs. Trotsky in order to get their son to see them in France.

TROTSKY: It was the 3rd of December, and the telegram of my wife was sent the 3rd of December, after we left Copenhagen, Denmark. The order of Herriot was given the 3rd or 4th of December, and my son came on the 5th of December.

GOLDMAN: Now, I introduce all of these documents which will be translated—some of them, as I see, are in foreign languages; they will be translated. Many of them are in English. The Commissioners are free to look over them. They are available here. They will at all times be available for the Commission.

FINERTY: And available later, I assume, for the whole Commission.

GOLDMAN: Yes, by that time they will be translated. I introduce them under the general term "Copenhagen Exhibits." I also introduce this list showing what the documents actually contain.

DEWEY: Is there any connection in these documents about how long the persons were staying in Copenhagen? I don't mean every one of them; whether they were there a day or two?

GOLDMAN: The statements of the particular persons will

indicate how long they were in Copenhagen. The list will be marked Exhibit No. 15, and the documents will be Exhibit No. 16.

(The list indicating the documents concerning "Copenhagen" was introduced into evidence as Exhibit No. 15, and the documents concerning "Copenhagen" were introduced as a whole as Exhibit No. 16.)

DEWEY: We will now adjourn this session.

End of Fourth Session—Seven o'clock P.M.

Fifth session

April 13, 1937, at ten o'clock a.m.

DEWEY: I regret that because of indisposition, Mr. Finerty, the lawyer for the Commission, will not be able to be here this morning. We hope he will be able to be here this afternoon. We think, however, in view of the shortness of time, it would not be well to postpone the hearing. So, we regret his absence very much this morning.

GOLDMAN: I ask leave of the Commission to place Mr. Jan Frankel on the witness stand for about ten minutes or so, to testify concerning matters which Mr. Trotsky has already testified to.

DEWEY: All right.

JAN FRANKEL

was called as a witness in behalf of Mr. Trotsky, and testified as follows:

DIRECT EXAMINATION
BY GOLDMAN

Q: What is your name?
A: Jan Frankel.

Q: Where do you live?
A: Where did I live?
Q: Where do you live?
A: Coyoacan, Mexico.
Q: What is your profession?
A: I am a translator.

GOLDMAN: What connection have you with Mr. Trotsky?

FRANKEL: I am his political follower, a member of the international organization, the Fourth International, and occupied here as secretary and collaborator.

GOLDMAN: You are then his chief secretary, or just one of the secretaries?

FRANKEL: We have no hierarchy.

GOLDMAN: You are one of the secretaries?

FRANKEL: Yes.

GOLDMAN: Since when have you been a secretary for Trotsky?

FRANKEL: I was with Trotsky from April, 1930, to January, 1932, in Turkey.

GOLDMAN: And then?

FRANKEL: Then I was—from then I am connected with Trotsky even when I am out of his house.

GOLDMAN: I want to know when you served as secretary.

FRANKEL: From April, 1930, to January, 1932, and then in Norway, from June, 1935, until the end of October, 1935, and here in Mexico from February 18th, beginning February 18th.

GOLDMAN: You were connected with Trotsky as his secretary at the time he made the trip from Turkey to Copenhagen?

FRANKEL: Yes, I had the direct responsibility for all the technical arrangements of his trip.

GOLDMAN: You said you were his secretary to 1932.

FRANKEL: That is a mistake—1933.

GOLDMAN: You want to correct yourself, then?

FRANKEL: Yes.

GOLDMAN: Did you take the trip to Copenhagen with Mr. Trotsky?

FRANKEL: Yes.

GOLDMAN: Who else was on the trip beside you and Mr. Trotsky?

FRANKEL: From Copenhagen?

GOLDMAN: From Turkey.

FRANKEL: From Turkey until Marseilles were three: Pierre Frank, a French friend, Oscar, a German friend, and myself.

GOLDMAN: And from Marseilles?

FRANKEL: From Marseilles we went by car to Lyon, together with Henri Molinier.

GOLDMAN: At Marseilles a friend of Mr. Trotsky by the name of Molinier joined you?

FRANKEL: And two Americans; the American Field and his wife were on the ship. They were more or less—

GOLDMAN: Wasn't Mr. Trotsky's wife on the ship?

FRANKEL: Yes.

GOLDMAN: When you left the boat at Marseilles, where did you go?

FRANKEL: We stopped. We did not leave the boat in the port of Marseilles. We stopped before Marseilles, and we went out in a motor boat. In this motor boat were Henri Molinier and a commissioner of *Sûreté Générale.*

GOLDMAN: You mean an officer of the *Sûreté Générale?*

FRANKEL: At the time it was *Sûreté Générale;* now it is *Sûreté Nationale.*

GOLDMAN: From Marseilles, where did you go?

FRANKEL: We went to an isolated place near Marseilles, and there one friend Deshin and one named Buren were waiting for us.

GOLDMAN: Where did you go?

FRANKEL: We were going to Lyon to join friends.

GOLDMAN: And from there?

FRANKEL: From there we went by railroad to Paris, in the company of a director of the *Sûreté Générale.*

GOLDMAN: When was that? During what month of the year?

FRANKEL: It was in November, the 21st.

GOLDMAN: Of what year?

FRANKEL: Of 1932.

GOLDMAN: And then, from Paris, for Copenhagen?

FRANKEL: Yes. We arrived in the Gare de Lyon and were conducted directly, in the company of many detectives, to the Gare du Nord, and there Trotsky was waiting in a room with police, for his departure by train to Dunkerque. In France we had good service. We organized a very strong service of safety, even with a little opposition by Trotsky.

GOLDMAN: Will you kindly answer my question. From Dunkerque you went to Copenhagen?

FRANKEL: Yes.

GOLDMAN: Do you know Mr. Trotsky's son, Leon Sedov?

FRANKEL: I lived with him from April, 1930, until February, 1931, in the same house.

GOLDMAN: You mean from April, 1930, to February, 1931?

FRANKEL: In the same house.

GOLDMAN: Where?

FRANKEL: In Prinkipo.

GOLDMAN: At the time that you were either on the boat from Turkey to Marseilles or in the car from Marseilles to that small town, or in the railroad from that small town to Paris, and from Paris to Dunkerque, or from Dunkerque to Copenhagen, did you see Sedov?

FRANKEL: Never.

GOLDMAN: When did you arrive in Copenhagen?

FRANKEL: We arrived in Copenhagen in the evening, at night, of November 23rd.

GOLDMAN: Of what year?

FRANKEL: Of 1932.

GOLDMAN: Where did you go to when you arrived in Copenhagen?

FRANKEL: We left the train near Copenhagen and went together with Boeggild, the representative of the Danish students, and with Pierre Naville, who was waiting for us, and Mr. Trotsky and his wife—together we went to Copenhagen to the Rathaus Place, Raymond Molinier had at the same time prepared the place where we stayed in Copenhagen.

GOLDMAN: Molinier, then, prepared the place where you stayed in Copenhagen?

FRANKEL: Yes.

GOLDMAN: Did you go to the place at that time?

FRANKEL: We went directly from the City Hall Place to this little villa. The address was Dalgas Boulevard, I believe No. 16.

GOLDMAN: How many rooms were there in that villa?

FRANKEL: On the ground floor there were two rooms, a kitchen, and a little vestibule. In this vestibule was the telephone.

GOLDMAN: Where was Mr. Trotsky staying?

FRANKEL: Mr. Trotsky was staying on the first floor.

GOLDMAN: That is, the first floor on top of the ground floor?

FRANKEL: Yes.

GOLDMAN: That is what you mean by the first floor?

FRANKEL: Yes.

GOLDMAN: How many rooms were there?

FRANKEL: Three rooms. One bedroom for Trotsky and his wife, one bedroom for, I believe, two women friends of his. One was Jeanne Martin des Pallières, and the other—

the wife of Sedov. The other, I think, was Julien's wife, the Italian friend. He was all the time in the house or around the house. The third room was a very small room, with a table and divan.

GOLDMAN: How large were the rooms?

FRANKEL: I don't remember the two bedrooms, because I believe I was never in the rooms.

GOLDMAN: Were you ever in the room that Mr. Trotsky was working in?

FRANKEL: Yes.

GOLDMAN: How large was that room?

FRANKEL: I believe, almost three or four meters.

GOLDMAN: Three or four meters wide, and long?

FRANKEL: Wide and long.

GOLDMAN: Approximately the same width as the length?

FRANKEL: Yes, I believe so.

GOLDMAN: Three or four meters would be, approximately?

FRANKEL: I cannot give you the mathematical precision.

GOLDMAN: I am not asking for mathematical precision. I am asking you to translate meters into feet.

BEALS: It will be about four yards.

GOLDMAN: From your knowledge, what can you say with reference to the public knowledge of the whereabouts of this place where you were living?

FRANKEL: The place I lived in, or Mr. Trotsky lived in, was known only to Mr. Boeggild.

GOLDMAN: Who is Mr. Boeggild?

FRANKEL: Mr. Boeggild was a Social Democrat of Denmark, about forty or forty-five years old. He was at the same time a student and a business man. He has very good connections—had very good connections with the Soviet Ambassador. He was a personal friend of Kopensky.

GOLDMAN: How did he happen to be in touch with Mr. Trotsky and you?

FRANKEL: He was the representative of the organization which invited Trotsky to give the lecture.

GOLDMAN: That organization was some student body?

FRANKEL: Yes.

GOLDMAN: He was the representative of that student body?

FRANKEL: The leader, or the second one.

GOLDMAN: Did you say he was about forty years old?

FRANKEL: I believe about forty years old, or forty-five.

GOLDMAN: But he was a student, anyway?

TROTSKY: He was a former student, a former theology student at the university.

GOLDMAN: We will assume that even a man of forty years can study. Now, you have a list—

FRANKEL: If you permit me, I didn't finish the answer to your question.

GOLDMAN: Then finish.

FRANKEL: Our address only went out to our closest friends. I gave their names in my affidavit. I had the task to assure the guard in the house of Mr. Trotsky.

GOLDMAN: There was a guard, then, in the house? Composed of what people?

FRANKEL: We concentrated about twenty-five or thirty friends from different countries, in order to assure a guard in the house and also a guard during the lecture of Mr. Trotsky.

GOLDMAN: Now, when you get into—

FRANKEL: Excuse me; I didn't finish.

GOLDMAN: I see. I am not in a hurry.

FRANKEL: This is the second part, the people who knew the address of Trotsky. Then, the director of the Danish police had knowledge of this place.

TROTSKY: The chief.

FRANKEL: The chief; but nobody else. The first time no police were in the house, in order to avoid any attention.

GOLDMAN: Where did these guards stay?

FRANKEL: Some of them in different hotels, and about five or six were every day and night in the house of Mr. Trotsky.

GOLDMAN: You mean, they lived there?

FRANKEL: There was a relief.

GOLDMAN: Then you mean that these friends of Trotsky who constituted the guard for him lived in different places and came there during the day for a certain number of hours and during the night, to stand guard?

FRANKEL: Yes.

GOLDMAN: Then I will ask you this, was any visitor, outside of the friends of Trotsky whom you enumerated in your statement, such as Mr. Boeggild—did any visitors come to see Mr. Trotsky?

FRANKEL: Yes. First I must say that my list is not complete. I see by the affidavits that I forgot one name, Erik Kohn, from Hamburg, and the Englishman, Wicks.

GOLDMAN: I am referring now to the list which was introduced into evidence and marked Exhibits Nos. 15 and 16. You say you forgot some names?

FRANKEL: Yes, I gave in this list only the names I had in my memory during the writing of this affidavit.

GOLDMAN: You want to add names to this list?

FRANKEL: No; these names are listed by other friends, the affidavits of other friends.

GOLDMAN: You know now there were others?

FRANKEL: One named Erik Kohn and one named Wicks, an Englishman. Then, Mr. Falk—no, I quoted him in my affidavit.

GOLDMAN: Now, to the best of your knowledge or recollection, can you say whether there were any other people who came to visit Trotsky, outside of the people whose names you gave in the affidavit and whose names you just now added?

FRANKEL: I believe it was on November 25th, Mr. Trotsky received a delegation from the organization of the students.

GOLDMAN: The student body?

FRANKEL: Yes. It was Mr. Boeggild, and then Mr. Jensen. I believe he was formerly the chairman of this union. I don't remember if there was a third one. But I will remark that Mr. Trotsky was forced to receive these people on the ground floor because the room on the first floor was too little to receive more than two or three—two people. Then I remember a visit of a delegation of students, I believe after the lecture of Mr. Trotsky. The list is joined on the document. The list was elaborated by Mr. Boeggild, together with me and Mr. Molinier.

GOLDMAN: Would it be possible for anyone to see Mr. Trotsky without your knowledge?

FRANKEL: Absolutely impossible.

GOLDMAN: Everyone who came to see Mr. Trotsky was first presented to you?

FRANKEL: The decision about any visit was submitted for a collective decision of Mr. Trotsky, myself and Mr. Molinier. And only after such a decision, we gave the address to the people.

GOLDMAN: Now, how long did you stay in Copenhagen?

FRANKEL: We were in Copenhagen from November 23rd until the morning of December 2nd.

GOLDMAN: During that time do you remember ever permitting anyone by the name of Holtzman to enter, or to visit Mr. Trotsky?

FRANKEL: No.

GOLDMAN: Do you remember seeing a man by the name of Holtzman?

FRANKEL: No.

GOLDMAN: In Copenhagen, at Mr. Trotsky's villa?

FRANKEL: No.

GOLDMAN: Do you remember seeing at the villa where Mr. Trotsky was staying anyone by the name of Fritz David?

FRANKEL: No.

GOLDMAN: Did any such man ask permission to visit Mr. Trotsky?

FRANKEL: Never.

GOLDMAN: Did Holtzman ask permission to visit Trotsky?

FRANKEL: No.

GOLDMAN: Did anyone by the name of Berman-Yurin ask to visit Trotsky?

FRANKEL: No.

GOLDMAN: Do you remember seeing such a man? Do you remember seeing anyone by the name of Berman-Yurin at the villa?

FRANKEL: No.

GOLDMAN: Now, did you see L. Sedov at Mr. Trotsky's villa, at the villa where you were staying?

STOLBERG: Did Berman-Yurin claim to have seen Trotsky?

FRANKEL: Yes.

GOLDMAN: Berman-Yurin, David and Holtzman—these three claim to have been there and talked to him. Do you remember seeing Leon Sedov at the place where you were staying with Mr. Trotsky?

FRANKEL: Never.

GOLDMAN: Was Mrs. Sedov with them there?

FRANKEL: Yes.

GOLDMAN: When did she arrive, do you remember?

FRANKEL: I am not sure, I believe she arrived one or two days later than we. But I am not absolutely sure.

GOLDMAN: Did she live with you?

FRANKEL: Yes, she lived on the first floor.

GOLDMAN: She lived with you in that house?

FRANKEL: Yes.

GOLDMAN: Did you talk to Sedov at all?

FRANKEL: Yes.

GOLDMAN: How did you conduct your conversation?

FRANKEL: Sedov was naturally very anxious about the whole situation, and for that reason I had many telephone calls with him to Berlin.

GOLDMAN: You had many telephone conversations? You personally had?

FRANKEL: I personally, yes.

GOLDMAN: Did you recognize his voice over the phone?

FRANKEL: Yes.

GOLDMAN: How many telephone conversations did you have with him?

FRANKEL: I believe that I had, until the lecture of Mr. Trotsky, about four conversations, three or four conversations.

GOLDMAN: All the time that you were in Copenhagen from November 26th to December 2nd?

FRANKEL: November 23rd.

GOLDMAN: From November 23rd to December 2nd, you didn't see Sedov there?

FRANKEL: No, I heard only his voice over the telephone.

GOLDMAN: When did you first see Sedov, Trotsky's son?

FRANKEL: I first saw him on December 5th in Paris in the Gare du Nord.

GOLDMAN: That is a railroad station?

FRANKEL: Yes, in Paris.

GOLDMAN: That is a railroad station?

FRANKEL: The station we arrived at from Dunkerque.

GOLDMAN: He was waiting there?

FRANKEL: Yes.

GOLDMAN: Did you have a chance to talk with him there?

FRANKEL: Yes.

GOLDMAN: What did he say with reference to his attempts

to see his father and mother in Copenhagen?

FRANKEL: I believe we had no conversation about it, because it was generally known to us.

GOLDMAN: Did you have any conversation—

FRANKEL: I had conversations about this in Copenhagen.

GOLDMAN: With whom did you have these conversations?

FRANKEL: Principally with him.

GOLDMAN: With him when you were talking over the phone?

FRANKEL: Yes.

GOLDMAN: About when? Tell us about that.

FRANKEL: Denmark gave a visa to Mr. and Mrs. Trotsky. I did not need any visa.

GOLDMAN: You are now referring to Leon Trotsky and Natalia Trotsky?

FRANKEL: Yes. Then we received in Stamboul a visa for the little boy Syeva Wolkov.

TROTSKY: My grandson.

GOLDMAN: Also for Mr. Trotsky's grandson?

FRANKEL: He left a couple of days after we. He remained in France and did not go to Copenhagen. We received permission for him to stay in France.

GOLDMAN: Are you referring to Sedov's son?

FRANKEL: No, it is the son of the daughter of Trotsky.

GOLDMAN: Sedov has no children?

FRANKEL: He has children, but in Russia.

TROTSKY: A son.

GOLDMAN: Trotsky's son has a son in Russia?

FRANKEL: Yes.

GOLDMAN: We have got to make it clear. You are now referring to the son of one of Trotsky's daughters?

FRANKEL: Yes.

GOLDMAN: You received a visa for him to go to Copenhagen?

FRANKEL: In Stamboul.

GOLDMAN: Now, please tell me the conversation you had with Sedov over the phone with reference to Sedov's attempts to get to Copenhagen. Confine yourself to that.

FRANKEL: We had in principal an agreement with the Danish Government to allow the visit of Leon Sedov for eight days, like Mr. Trotsky. They asked, as they asked from Trotsky, a guarantee to return. So we were forced to ask the Turkish Government for a visa for a return trip.

GOLDMAN: For whom?

FRANKEL: For Mr. Trotsky. That we received. But Sedov was unable to receive this permission.

GOLDMAN: From whom?

FRANKEL: From the German police.

GOLDMAN: The German Government? Did Sedov tell you that he tried to go to Copenhagen?

FRANKEL: That was the matter of our conversation every day.

GOLDMAN: Did he also tell you that he could not get a visa?

FRANKEL: He could not get a visa because at that time he lived formally in Germany without permission.

GOLDMAN: How did that happen?

FRANKEL: The permission—the police gave every couple of months the permission to stay in Germany. In the last months he had difficulties to receive a renewal of the permission.

GOLDMAN: Have you the paper explaining that?

FRANKEL: He received a renewal only to January 2nd, so on this moment he would be able to go to Denmark, if the Danish Government would be—

GOLDMAN: Let me ask you this: Sedov's permission to remain in Germany expired when?

FRANKEL: Expired November 1st.

GOLDMAN: Sedov's permission to remain in Germany

expired November 1st, 1932?

FRANKEL: Yes.

GOLDMAN: Look at this document (referring to the document explaining the nature of the photostatic copy of the passport) and tell us when Sedov received permission from the German Government to remain in Germany subsequent to November 1, 1932, at the time when the permission to remain expired.

FRANKEL: Would you mind if I correct something? He received permission not on January 2nd, but December 3rd until January 2nd.

GOLDMAN: Now listen carefully. He received permission on December 3rd?

FRANKEL: The right to stay in Germany was granted December 3, 1932, good until January 2nd.

GOLDMAN: So, between November 1, 1932, to December 3, 1932, he had no permission to remain in Germany?

FRANKEL: Yes, and for that reason, no permission to go back to Germany.

GOLDMAN: So that he needed permission to return to Germany?

FRANKEL: Yes.

GOLDMAN: When did he receive permission to return to Germany?

FRANKEL: December 3rd.

GOLDMAN: Now, do you know the circumstances under which he received permission to return to Germany?

FRANKEL: I believe it was the work of his lawyer, Mr. Cohn. He was also in Copenhagen in order to meet Mr. Trotsky.

GOLDMAN: Did he have anything to do with the telegrams to Herriot, the Minister of Foreign Affairs at that time?

FRANKEL: I believe—I don't remember exactly—I believe it was done by Pierre Naville and Gérard Rosenthal, French friends.

GOLDMAN: Now, do you remember Natalia, Mr. Trotsky's

wife, sending a telegram to Herriot requesting permission for her son to enter France?

FRANKEL: In the moment when we had knowledge that Sedov received the permission to stay in Germany and also to go back to Germany.

GOLDMAN: Will you look in your file and give us copies of the telegrams that Natalia Trotsky sent to Herriot and the telegram Herriot sent to the French Consul in Berlin?

FRANKEL: Yes. (Hands telegrams to Attorney Goldman.)

GOLDMAN: These are the documents, these are the copies of the telegrams, one sent by Natalia Sedov Trotsky to Herriot—is the date there?

FRANKEL: No, but this is the original copy from the Minister. We received the copy from the Office of Foreign Affairs.

TROTSKY: It is the specific manner of the French Office to indicate it.

GOLDMAN: There are numbers here, but you don't know exactly what these numbers refer to?

FRANKEL: No.

GOLDMAN: And then the date of the telegram from Herriot to the Minister, or the French Consul in Berlin, is December 3, 1932.

DEWEY: Where will the original of this be verified?

GOLDMAN: Mr. Dewey, the chairman of the Commission, asks where the originals of these telegrams are.

FRANKEL: The originals are in the Foreign Office in Paris. These copies were received by the intervention of Mr. Trotsky's lawyer, Gérard Rosenthal, in Paris.

GOLDMAN: The sub-commission in Paris will be able to investigate the originals in Paris.

BEALS: These are not certified.

GOLDMAN: Now, you first saw Sedov then, at the time, in the railroad station in Paris?

FRANKEL: Yes.

BEALS: What date was that?

GOLDMAN: Yes.

FRANKEL: It was, I believe, December 5th, right after our arrival from Dunkerque.

GOLDMAN: And Sedov's passport contains no allusion at all, no visa granted him to go to Copenhagen?

FRANKEL: No.

GOLDMAN: But it does have a visa permitting him to go to Paris?

FRANKEL: Yes. I must add, I was together with Mr. Boeggild to the Danish Minister of Justice, who also has a right to give visas, in order to get a prolongation of the stay of Mr. Trotsky, but I did not even ask for or mention Sedov because we saw that it was not possible for him to come.

GOLDMAN: Then I repeat this question: During the time that you were in Copenhagen, you at no time saw Sedov, but you talked with him over the phone in Berlin?

FRANKEL: Yes.

GOLDMAN: And the first time you saw him was December 5th or thereabouts, in Paris?

FRANKEL: Yes.

GOLDMAN: If the Commissioners would like to cross-examine Mr. Frankel at this time it will be best, because I don't want to put him on the stand any more after Mr. Trotsky resumes.

DEWEY: I have one question. Can you recall whether Mr. Trotsky saw visitors alone, or was it in the presence of someone else?

FRANKEL: If visitors were alone with him?

DEWEY: Did he see them alone, or was somebody else with him?

FRANKEL: Some visitors had conversations with Mr. Trotsky alone, but before they entered the room of Mr. Trotsky they were forced to pass by the guard of five or six people on the ground floor. After they entered their person was identified, then somebody of us near the first-floor entrance to Mr. Trotsky announced that such and such a man arrived. After that he entered.

BEALS: Did Mr. Trotsky leave the house at all in Copenhagen, while he was there?

FRANKEL: Yes. Never alone. He was by some friends. I remember the first conference of some—

TROTSKY: The lecture.

FRANKEL: No.

TROTSKY: The meeting.

FRANKEL: A meeting with some intellectuals in the house of Mr. Boeggild. We have a list here. This meeting was also prepared in a very detailed manner between Mr. Boeggild and me. They consisted of students. (Witness hands list to the Commission.) That was the last meeting of Mr. Trotsky in the house of Boeggild. Then I remember—

BEALS: Were these made in Copenhagen at the time, or made—

FRANKEL: Yes, it is written by Mr. Boeggild.

TROTSKY: He is dead now.

FRANKEL: He is dead, but his wife can verify it, Mr. Beals.

TROTSKY: May I say something?

GOLDMAN: Just one moment.

FRANKEL: Then I remember once or twice Mr. Trotsky was on a trip to see the town, only in a car. He did not leave the car. The driver was once Mr. Molinier. The second time, I believe, it was to a relative of Mr. Boeggild. I remember also a visit to the movies, after his—after Mr. Trotsky's lecture, in the news-reels. We went to see the speech of Mr. Trotsky. We were about fifteen people, I believe, on this visit.

Then, naturally, his visit, his lecture before the students, was organized in a very scientific manner.

STOLBERG: Where did the lecture take place?

FRANKEL: In a public hall. Mr. Trotsky entered from another side. He was forced to walk about ten minutes through a stadium in the night. People were waiting for Mr. Trotsky at the entrance, and we entered through the other side. He was accompanied by five people. Before this lecture Mr. Trotsky was in the Telephone Center in order to speak to New York, in order to have his radio speech to New York. There he met only one stranger. He was the agent of the broadcasting company from London.

And, then, Mr. Trotsky made a short speech for the newsreel, for the Fox Movietone. And, also, a short propaganda speech, about ten minutes in French and ten minutes in German, which took place in the apartment of Mr. Boeggild's brother-in-law, Mr. Lemberg Moelle.

One day, Mr. Trotsky—or one night, I believe—was out of the house because we had the impression that some journalists found our address. He was taken to a little *pension.* He was not alone. He was conducted by Mr. Molinier, one German, Oscar, and his French lawyer, Gérard Rosenthal. That is all I remember. But he was never out alone.

BEALS: Are these people you have mentioned—you know them all well? None of them could have been Holtzman, Berman-Yurin or Fritz David under another name?

FRANKEL: Absolutely not.

BEALS: If, for instance, Mr. Trotsky had seen Holtzman, would your loyalty to Mr. Trotsky prevent you from telling the Commission that fact?

FRANKEL: I can say one thing: The basis of my collaboration with Mr. Trotsky is my political solidarity with his conceptions. His conceptions are Marxist conceptions. Employing individual terror as a method of the class struggle was never a matter of discussion, and if Mr. Trotsky would propose to do it, I can say, and I believe also not only myself, I would become his most natural enemy.

BEALS: My question is: If, for instance, Mr. Holtzman had seen him—I am not saying he did. I said, if he had seen Trotsky and you knew of that, would your loyalty to Mr. Trotsky prevent you from telling about that fact?

FRANKEL: No. I can say I also had the impression first that Holtzman was the same as Senin. May I refer to some friends who were in Copenhagen and say exactly the conversation they had with Senin? I believe we had no reason to hide the presence of these people.

BEALS: I have just a very short question. The passport of Sedov which you have shown us, is that a German passport?

FRANKEL: Yes, a German passport. It is a passport without—

TROTSKY: A foreigner's.

FRANKEL: A *"Fremden"* passport. A passport for strangers.

BEALS: Does it contain a photostatic visa for France, I mean, and an entry stamp for France?

FRANKEL: Yes, here it is. (Indicating it to Beals.)

BEALS: Would it have been possible for Mr. Sedov to have traveled to Copenhagen under another passport and under another name?

FRANKEL: Theoretically it would not be impossible, but practically he had no reason. Practically he had no possibility to prepare this, because Trotsky received a visa. Now, every student, in order—and I believe that was also the reason that he could not come to Copenhagen—to have his renewal to stay in Germany, he would need more time.

BEALS: Could he not more easily, more quickly, under some other name beside Sedov, go to Copenhagen?

FRANKEL: I believe that such a question could never be a matter of testimony, because we never tried to compromise Mr. Trotsky in any country by such methods. We are not using such methods.

GOLDMAN: Who issued that passport? What government?

FRANKEL: The German police in Berlin; the German Government.

GOLDMAN: When?

TROTSKY: It was before Hitler.

FRANKEL: It was August, 1931, to 1932.

GOLDMAN: Of 1931 to August, 1932? That was before Hitler came to power?

FRANKEL: Yes. I met Sedov in that time when Hitler was in power in Germany. I knew he was forced, more or less, to flee.

GOLDMAN: When did he leave Germany for France?

FRANKEL: He left Germany for France.

GOLDMAN: I don't mean, to visit Trotsky, but to go away from Germany altogether.

FRANKEL: I remember it was March, 1933, after he received the French order to stay. I can't say the exact date—the 23rd of March, 1933.

GOLDMAN: I am through with this witness, if the Commission is through with the witness.

STOLBERG: He was in Germany about a month during the Hitler régime?

FRANKEL: Who?

STOLBERG: Sedov?

FRANKEL: Yes, he was in Germany from February, 1931, until the end of March, 1933.

STOLBERG: Did the German Government molest him?

FRANKEL: No, but there was a danger he would be molested. For instance, the editor of the Russian *Bulletin* had to flee. His apartment was destroyed by the Nazis. They came to arrest him, saying, "We have arrived!" (At this point the witness spoke in French.—A.M.G.)

LAFOLLETTE: They destroyed his apartment.

FRANKEL: He was in the street returning to his apartment.

GOLDMAN: Are you referring to Sedov?

FRANKEL: Grylewicz. In order to show the relation of the editor of the Russian *Bulletin*, we have also a quotation from a letter—

STOLBERG: What were the difficulties, the troubles, in the relations between Sedov during that month, and the régime?

FRANKEL: I don't know exactly. I believe he was not living in his apartment. He had an official address, but he lived in some other apartments in order to avoid being arrested.

STOLBERG: Did he leave Germany openly?

FRANKEL: Yes, openly. He had a French visa.

GOLDMAN: This concludes this witness. Now, yesterday at the conclusion of the session, I touched very lightly on the question of the Hotel Bristol.

TROTSKY: Can you permit me some remarks?

GOLDMAN: Yes. Mr. Trotsky wants to make a remark.

TROTSKY: My meeting with the intellectuals—they were professors, in the university, lawyers and authors. I did not know them personally, and I asked Boeggild to give me beforehand a list with the names and places, so I should not be disorientated in my conversation with unknown people. But I did not commit mistakes in politics during the discussion. (Laughter) It is the origin of the list. Then, the second remark is that this list is an enumeration of the students who came to me.

Another remark is, that the difficulties for my son came during the Papen or Shleicher régime. You remember, between the democratic régime and the fascist régime, there was an intermediary régime of Papen and Schleicher.

BEALS: We know about Papen in Mexico.

TROTSKY: Yes, you knew him well—Papen and Schleicher. Papen became again Vice Chancellor to Hitler. During this time, my son had difficulties. Then, the first period of the Hitler régime, the régime of Hitler and Papen—it was not totally a Hitler régime—the foreigners became very disquieted. There was not a direct persecution, but the danger of persecution. My son hid himself for a month with a doctor, with an old doctor. Also, with old friends, friends who were living in legality. During that time he gave everything to obtain a visa for France. Then he left Germany for France.

GOLDMAN: On the question of the Hotel Bristol, on page 100 of the official report of Court Proceedings, published by the People's Commissariat of Justice of the U.S.S.R., dealing with the question of the Trotskyite-Zinovievite terrorist center, Holtzman testifies and says:

> I agreed, but I told him that we could not go together, for reasons of secrecy. I arranged with Sedov to be in Copenhagen within two or three days, to put up at the Hotel Bristol and meet him there. I went to the hotel straight from the station, and in the lounge met Sedov.

Now, he says here—and we want to call the Commissioners' attention to that fact—in testifying as to what the arrangements were in Berlin, that he arranged with Sedov to meet him in Copenhagen at the Hotel Bristol. The inference would be that he knew in Berlin that there was a Hotel Bristol in Copenhagen, and made arrangements to meet at the Hotel Bristol. Now, immediately after the trial and during the trial, when the statement, which the Commissioners can check up on, was made by him, a report came from the Social-Democratic press in Denmark that there was no such hotel as the Hotel Bristol in Copenhagen; that there was at one time a hotel by the name of Hotel Bristol, but that was burned down in 1917. The guide "Baedeker" of 1917, includes the name of Hotel Bristol. That was the report of the Social-Democratic press of Denmark which went the rounds throughout the world press.

About five or six months thereafter, the Communist press

issued a statement to the effect that whereas there actually was no Hotel Bristol, right next to Hotel Bristol Café—

DEWEY: Next to the Hotel Bristol?

GOLDMAN: Pardon me. Whereas there was no Hotel Bristol, there was a hotel by the name of Grand, and right next to the Grand Hotel there was a café called the Bristol Café. The photograph appears in a magazine *Soviet Russia Today,* of March, 1937. The magazine is the official organ of the Friends of the Soviet Union, if I am not mistaken. At any rate, the Commission can look through the magazine and satisfy itself that it is very, very hostile to Trotsky and exceedingly friendly to the Stalin Government in the Soviet Union. This photograph, which I now hand to the Commission, is a photograph allegedly showing that there is some connection with the name Bristol and the word "hotel." I show you this photograph, a radio photograph, especially cabled for by *Soviet Russia Today* and received from *Nordpress* of Denmark through the Radio Corporation of America on February 22nd. I show the photograph to the Commissioners and ask them to examine this photograph first. I also show the Commissioners a sketch purporting to show the exact location of the Grand Hotel and the Café Bristol. This sketch is from the magazine called *Rundschau,* a German magazine which is also very friendly—

TROTSKY: It is a publication of the Comintern and it is in German.

GOLDMAN: After the *Inprecorr* ceased publication, the *Rundschau* took its place as the official organ of the Comintern.

TROTSKY: *Rundschau* is published in Switzerland.

GOLDMAN: This sketch allegedly shows the connection between the Grand Hotel and the Café Bristol, showing that the Bristol Café is supposed to be right next to the Grand Hotel, and, if I am not mistaken, with an entrance leading from the hotel, the Grand Hotel, directly into the Café Bristol.

TROTSKY: Not an entrance, if you permit me. It is a cross—

STOLBERG: It looks like a door there.

TROTSKY: I am not sure.

GOLDMAN: Let the Commissioners investigate for themselves. Mr. Ruehle reads German, and can tell the Commissioners exactly what this is supposed to identify.

LAFOLLETTE: This is Scandinavian.

STOLBERG: The story is in German.

(Attorney Goldman hands document to the Commission.)

GOLDMAN: The Commissioners will see that the photograph published in *Soviet Russia Today* has the word "hotel." The word "Grand" does not appear on the photograph. At least, I cannot make it out. Whether it is cut off, or whether actually the fact is that it is not there, I am unable to state from an observation of the photograph itself. The word "Bristol" appearing on the extreme right of the photograph appears in very clear letters, and the word "Konditori" appearing to the left of the word "Bristol" is hardly visible, although it is visible. I mention this fact to indicate that evidently the photograph was touched up for the purpose of indicating that there is such a hotel as Hotel Bristol. Will the press take a look at that?

Now, I have an affidavit of B.J. Field and Esther Field, who are in New York and subject to be cross-examined by the full Commission after this preliminary Commission, or by another sub-commission, and in this affidavit B.J. Field and Esther Field make the following statement. Referring to the photo in *Soviet Russia Today*, they say:

> Directly next to the entrance to the hotel, and what appears as a big black splotch in the photo, is actually the location of the café next to the Grand Hotel; *and it is not the Konditori Bristol! The Konditori Bristol is not*

> *next door, but actually several doors away, at quite a distance from the hotel, and was not a part of it in any way, and there was no door connecting the Konditori ("candy store" it would be called here) and the Grand Hotel! Although there was such an entrance to the café which is blackened out in the photo, and which was not the Bristol.*

In other words, between the Grand Hotel and the Konditori Bristol there was a café and between the hotel and the café there was an entrance, but there was no entrance at all connecting the hotel and the Bristol Konditori. B.J. Field and Esther Field were actually in that café and they were also in the hotel, so they are speaking from personal knowledge. They say further:

> As a matter of fact, we bought some candy once at the Konditori Bristol, and we can state definitely that it had no vestibule, lobby, or lounge in common with the Grand Hotel or any hotel, and it could not have been mistaken for a hotel in any way, and entrance to the hotel could not be obtained through it. At the time of this trip to Copenhagen, we knew of no Danish Trotskyites and we do not believe—

Here I want to emphasize the statement that in the Communist press the statement was made that the Café Bristol was the "hang out" for Danish Trotskyites.

> At the time of this trip to Copenhagen, we knew of no Danish Trotskyites, and we do not believe that there were any. One of the German comrades, in spite of the language barrier, was sent to the headquarters of the Copenhagen Stalinists to invite them to Trotsky's lecture . . .

I think we have proved, on the basis of all the documents, first, that Sedov was never in Copenhagen, and second, there was no such hotel as Hotel Bristol where Holtzman claims that he allegedly met Sedov in Copenhagen.

Now, just one additional entry into the record, and I am through with the whole Copenhagen matter. In view of the fact that Holtzman, David, and Berman-Yurin claim that in their conversations with Mr. Trotsky, Mr. Trotsky gave them definite directions with reference to terrorist acts, I think it is very relevant to cite two quotations from the speeches that Mr. Trotsky made at that time. They are also relevant, of course, in another section of the evidence dealing with individual terrorism and the question of the defense of the Soviet Union. But, at this time, I think it might be best to enter them into the record. From a sound-film address for Communist Opposition propaganda, Mr. Trotsky—I cite from this address which Mr. Trotsky made and it concludes as follows—

TROTSKY: Made to the Left Oppositionists.

GOLDMAN: He is now speaking to the followers of the Left Opposition, a speech not generally published. I quote:

> We, Left Oppositionists, remain *devotedly faithful* to the Soviet Union and to the Communist International, with another fidelity than that of the centrist bureaucracy. . . . The Soviet Union is our country. We will defend it to the end. The ideas and the methods of Marx and Lenin will become the ideas and methods of the Communist International.

This was at the time, in 1932, when Trotsky was supposed to have given terrorist directions to Holtzman, David, and Berman-Yurin.

One more statement, a press statement of L.D. Trotsky dictated to Gérard Rosenthal, his French attorney, is as follows:

> My connections with friends in the Soviet Union and my information enable me to declare with certainty: The prevailing opinion in the Bolshevik Party demands the establishment of unity in the ranks and the replacement of individual leadership which has in no wise justified itself, by collective leadership.
>
> You ask if I am ready to collaborate with Stalin and his closest collaborators? I have never repudiated such collaboration, and now, before the serious difficulties within and without the country, I am less disposed than ever to repudiate it.
>
> Politics knows no personal resentment nor the spirit of revenge. Politics knows only effectiveness. For myself, as well as my companions, it comes back to the question of the *program* of the collaboration.

This ends my evidence on the question of Holtzman's, David's and Berman-Yurin's presence in Copenhagen, of the impossibility of their being present there, and the fact that Sedov was never in Copenhagen, the fact that there was no Hotel Bristol, and the fact that Trotsky in his open declaration stated that he would collaborate with Stalin, or the prosecution, to defend the Soviet Union to the utmost.

LAFOLLETTE: Was the sound film from which you quoted made and published?

TROTSKY: It was devoted exclusively for the inner propaganda of the Left Opposition, not published propaganda. The matter itself is for inner use.

LAFOLLETTE: Then, I would like to ask one more question: Is that film available anywhere?

TROTSKY: Yes, it is now in France. It was produced in France for a short time.

LAFOLLETTE: Then, the French sub-commission would have access to that film?

TROTSKY: Yes; it can be sent immediately to New York.

STOLBERG: There is a Konditori Bristol?

GOLDMAN: There is a Konditori Bristol.

STOLBERG: Between the Konditori Bristol and the Grand Hotel there is a café by the name of what?

GOLDMAN: For that, I am sorry, you will have to request Mr. Field to come before the Commission and question him personally. Unless I omitted that in his affidavit, I am not sure what the name of the café is.

STOLBERG: What I mean—is it your contention now that there is a Grand Hotel, next to it a café and next to it, the café, a Konditori?

GOLDMAN: That is right.

STOLBERG: Then, it would seem—maybe I had better exclude the latter—it would seem from your point of view that in the photograph from *Soviet Russia Today* the signs had been changed.

GOLDMAN: It would seem that the photograph was taken for the purpose of giving the impression that there is a Hotel Bristol.

STOLBERG: That there is a Café Bristol.

GOLDMAN: No, that there is even a Hotel Bristol. But assuming that I am going too far in my inferences, the photograph was taken to show only that there was a hotel. The name "Grand" does not appear in the white space underneath the word "Hotel." Then it would appear from the photograph that the Konditori was right next to the hotel, to the Grand Hotel. That is what would appear to the casual observer of the photograph. And, that, I assume, was the purpose of these people who took the photograph.

TROTSKY: I will at the conclusion of the statement of my lawyer add briefly four points. Nobody, neither Holtzman, Berman-Yurin, nor David, named my address, the address of the meeting place. Secondly, no one says a word about my apartment. It was a peculiar one, the apartment of a dancer. The furnishings were absolutely peculiar. A genuine visitor in such a house must absolutely with necessity say something about this house. Nobody said anything. Third, Berman-Yurin and David did not name Sedov. Berman-Yurin and David said they were sent by Sedov to Copenhagen, but they did not mention that Sedov was in Copenhagen. Fourth, nothing was said about Zinoviev, who allegedly died at this time.

GOLDMAN: Of course, I don't know whether I mentioned it. I think I did mention it yesterday, but one of the defendants—

TROTSKY: Olberg.

GOLDMAN: Olberg testified on behalf of our side without intending to do so, when he said, on page 87:

> Before my departure for the Soviet Union, I intended to go to Copenhagen with Sedov to see Trotsky. Our trip did not materialize, but Suzanna, Sedov's wife, went there. On her return she brought a letter from Trotsky addressed to Sedov, in which Trotsky agreed to my going to the U.S.S.R. and expressed the hope that I would succeed in carrying out the mission entrusted to me. Sedov showed me this letter.

Evidently, Olberg knew that Sedov never was in Copenhagen.

DEWEY: We will now take a short recess.

GOLDMAN: The next section of our evidence will deal with the very important testimony of Vladimir Romm, a witness, not a defendant but a witness, in the trial of Radek, Pyatakov, *et al*, of January, 1937. Upon the testimony of this witness rests the strength of the case for the prosecution. Half of the case, one would say. I shall read his testimony, and then with my testimony show that it was utterly false. On page 141 of the official Report of Court Proceedings published by the People's Commissariat of Justice of the U.S.S.R., dated

Moscow, 1937, in the Case of the Anti-Soviet Trotskyite Center. I read Romm's testimony on page 141:

> *Romm:* In Paris. I had arrived from Geneva, and a few days after Sedov telephoned me and made an appointment to meet me in a café on the Boulevard Montparnasse. Sedov said he wanted to arrange for me to meet Trotsky. A few days after he telephoned me and made an appointment to meet me in the same café. From there we went to the Bois de Boulogne, where I met Trotsky.
>
> *Vyshinsky:* When was that?
>
> *Romm:* At the end of July, 1933.
>
> *Vyshinsky:* How long did that meeting with Trotsky last?
>
> *Romm:* Twenty to twenty-five minutes.
>
> *Vyshinsky:* For what purpose did Trotsky meet you?
>
> *Romm:* As far as I could understand, in order verbally to confirm the instructions contained in the letter I was taking to Moscow. He started the conversation with the question of creating the parallel center. He said there was a danger in the predominance of the Zinovievites, but that the danger would be great only if the Trotskyites were not sufficiently active.

I did not read the rest of the paragraph, dealing with the nature of the conversation, because my testimony will show conclusively, without fear of being contradicted in any way, that Trotsky never met Romm, and that the whole testimony was simply an invention for the purpose of making some connection between Trotsky and Radek. Mr. Trotsky—

TROTSKY: Yes.

GOLDMAN: When did you leave Turkey to begin your residence in France?

TROTSKY: It was the 17th of July, 1933. We came by the

Italian ship, "Bulgaria," to Marseilles.

GOLDMAN: By the way, was the "Bulgaria" also the ship you used to go to Copenhagen?

TROTSKY: No, it was of the same Italian line, but the name was "Praga."

GOLDMAN: Who were with you on the "Bulgaria"?

TROTSKY: The "Bulgaria"? My wife, Natalia, our comrades Van Heijenoort, who sits here, then two Americans, Max Shachtman, who is my editor also, and Sara Weber. They are both of New York. And a German, Adolphe, who is now in Europe. He is also available, but I named him by his pseudonym, but I am ready to give his genuine name.

GOLDMAN: Your wife was with you?

TROTSKY: I named her first.

GOLDMAN: How long did it take you to go from Constantinople to France?

TROTSKY: We started on the 17th and we arrived—

GOLDMAN: Did you say the seventh or the seventeenth?

TROTSKY: The seventeenth—and on the 24th we were in Marseilles.

GOLDMAN: Did you land in Marseilles?

TROTSKY: No.

GOLDMAN: Where did you land?

TROTSKY: We landed on the sea. (Laughter) In a motor boat, sent especially for that purpose, we were informed by a radio cable to the captain of the ship.

GOLDMAN: Who sent the cable?

TROTSKY: The cable was sent by the maritime society. It was agreed with my son and Molinier, who paid for that a certain sum of money.

GOLDMAN: What did the cable say?

TROTSKY: With an approach of a motor boat you must stop the ship. Max Shachtman, the American, was on the way our intermediary with the ship authorities. I had on this question a conversation with the captain. I must say, I was not satisfied immediately with that. The small event was related by the press of the whole world. In the *New York Times* it was recalled after the last Moscow trials. All the correspondence, all the cables of its French correspondent, confirm my first statement. The *New York Times,* on its own initiative, stated that we landed not at Marseilles, but on the sea in a motor boat, and after leaving the ship we disappeared totally from the press. (Laughter)

GOLDMAN: Who were with you on the motor boat?

TROTSKY: On the motor boat, only my wife and myself, because my son, Leon Sedov, was on board. (It was promised me that Mr. Solow would help me with my English. But he is seated so far away, he cannot help.) It was organized, I must say, very well, our reception. My son, on board the ship, gave a letter to Van Heijenoort, with all the instructions in the letter. It was impossible to oblige the ship to remain too long a time. Then, all the four, Max Shachtman, Sara Weber, Van Heijenoort and Adolphe, remained aboard. We were on the motor boat and we went to Cassis. It is a small town not far from Marseilles. In Cassis, in a hidden place—it was a place not good for the public—a secluded place, there were two autos, two cars. In one of the cars there were Leprince, not a political, not my political, follower, but a neutral, an impartial, we will say—this Raymond Leprince, and then Laste, another Frenchman. He was my political companion-in-arms. He is now my *political adversary*—I underline. He has his own paper, and he gave us testimony on this. He is a very bitter adversary of mine. Then, my son—I forgot to say that in the motor boat was Raymond Molinier, a Frenchman who was also my political friend, but became a political adversary, a very bitter political adversary. And then two sailors and a representative of the *Sûreté Nationale,* of the French police. All this story was many times told by the French press. With these two cars, we immediately started, not in the direction of Paris—it was the 24th of July—not in the direction of Paris, as supposed in the depositions in the Moscow trial, but in the direction of Montpellier, Albi, Montauban, Bordeaux, to a small village called St. Palais, a town, I believe, a few kilometers from Royan, to a villa in St. Palais named "Les Embruns."

GOLDMAN: When did you arrive in St. Palais?

TROTSKY: On the 25th. We passed a night in Tonneins, in a hotel. The reason why I must rest in Tonneins was my illness. The first plan was to go directly if it was possible. But I suffered from lumbago, and the movement of the auto was intolerable to me. That is the reason we had to pass the night at Tonneins. We arrived in St. Palais the 25th, three o'clock in the afternoon, or two o'clock in the afternoon. I must immediately rest in bed, because I was sick. After one or two—one hour of rest, the atmosphere became—I don't know—but it was intolerable, and directly I fell from the bed onto the floor. The reason was a fire around our villa. It was very dry in July, and the sparks from a locomotive caused the fire. The plants, the hedges, were on fire. It is a little event, but plays a very great role in my testimony in this question, as the Commission will see.

Our four collaborators, Max Shachtman, Sara Weber, Van Heijenoort and Adolphe, they landed in Marseilles. The instruction was for Van Heijenoort—we landed without any baggage, without any baggage, to be more mobile. The instruction for Van Heijenoort was to go in the direction of Paris, but only until Lyon, and to see that he was not persecuted by the messieurs of the press.

INTERPRETER: Pursued.

TROTSKY: Pursued, yes. (Laughter) Then, if he was sure that he could continue his travel unknown, he must also go to the west, directly to the west from Lyon to Royan. He arrived the next day, on the 26th of July. Max Shachtman remained in Marseilles to arrange the matter of our big baggage—it was my library—with the company of transportation. He remained for four days, I believe, in Marseilles, to arrange the matter. Adolphe and Sara Weber, they started the same day, or in the evening, for Paris. Max Shachtman, four or five days later. I must emphasize that the arrangement was unexpected for us. We were sure that we would go together, Van Heijenoort and all the others, in the motor boat. We could not say adieu to Max Shachtman, because he left from Paris to New York in the beginning of August without having the possibility to say good-bye. I have a letter from him which confirms this. I remained—shall I continue, or will you put questions?

GOLDMAN: You proceed until I stop you.

TROTSKY: I remained in St. Palais more than two months, until the beginning of October.

GOLDMAN: Let me interrupt just a moment. I want to know what arrangements you had with the French Government about your stay in France.

TROTSKY: The cause of our going to France was the change of the French policy after the election, the new election of 1932, in May. The Radical Government came into office and the Prime Minister was M. Daladier. One of my friends, a French author and translator of all my writings in France, Parijanine, he proposed to me that I ask the Government if it would not be possible for me to come to France. I answered that I was absolutely sure that I would not be allowed. But in spite of my skepticism and doubt, I received a visa, with certain restrictions. The Government was a bit disquieted about the—

GOLDMAN: Disturbed.

TROTSKY: —the possibility of attacks, assassinations, demonstrations and manifestations on the part of the fascists and Stalinists. But the restrictions of the Government coincided with my own purposes—with my own plans. It was agreed that I reside in Corsica, but the first time, my friends—I have here all the testimony—one of them, my literary representative and the engineer, Molinier, another Molinier, not the Molinier in the motor boat, the engineer Molinier—he was in connection, or in relation with the summits of the officials. He conducted conversations, and insisted that the Government give me the possibility to live a certain time, not in Corsica, but in France itself, to have medical aid for my wife and myself. And he succeeded. They permitted me to remain in one of the Southern departments. I have a letter permitting this from the Home Minister.

GOLDMAN: Well, how long—at the time that you arrived in Royan, you say soon after there was a fire on the same day?

TROTSKY: On the same day, one hour or a bit more after our arrival in St. Palais.

GOLDMAN: What burned down, the whole building?

TROTSKY: No. Only—it was the change of the wind, an east wind, and the fire turned from the house. What burned was a small summer hut in the garden, some dry trees, and the surroundings of the house.

GOLDMAN: What did you do during the fire?

TROTSKY: During the fire we were very disquieted, not so much from the fire as the curiosity that the fire—we were afraid to be recognized by the public. Immediately, I went out and took a place in the auto. Our auto was out on the road, and I took a place in the auto in a very discreet manner. In spite of that fact, many people saw me on the road. There was a multitude around the house. They were interested in the old man, the old gentleman in the car.

GOLDMAN: How many people, approximately?

TROTSKY: I mention it because it plays a role in many testimonies.

GOLDMAN: Approximately how many people were there around the fire, around your car?

TROTSKY: I believe it lasted—I remained in the car, I believe, one hour. The fire company arrived, and the police arrived, and all the neighbors. There must have been fifty persons in the crowd.

GOLDMAN: Was that reported in the press?

TROTSKY: Yes, it was reported in the local press and later, or on another occasion, it was reproduced in the Paris press.

GOLDMAN: Did they mention your name in the local press?

TROTSKY: In the local press they didn't recognize me. We presented ourselves as Americans, in spite of my English. (Laughter) And later, when I was recognized in another place, the papers were full of publicity. All these people affirmed that it was Trotsky at the fire.

GOLDMAN: Did the press mention that?

TROTSKY: Yes, the press mentioned that, the local correspondent and the others mentioned that.

GOLDMAN: How long after the fire?

TROTSKY: It was, I believe, some months, seven or eight months. It was another story in Barbizon. I was discovered, and there was a big press comment. The press caused a certain investigation of me.

GOLDMAN: Now, after the fire, what did you do?

TROTSKY: I remained all the time in St. Palais—for more than two months. Half of the time I spent in bed, and half of the time slowly walking a bit in the garden, and a bit in the house, in the company of friends who visited me.

GOLDMAN: During the time after you arrived in St. Palais, for two months you remained there?

TROTSKY: I remained in St. Palais.

GOLDMAN: You were sick at that time?

TROTSKY: All the time.

GOLDMAN: Who were with you?

TROTSKY: My wife, Van Heijenoort, Sara Weber, an American—Max Shachtman, as I told you, left for New York from Paris. The first time, I forgot to say that the villa was prepared—rented on the 18th of July, beforehand, by the man, the engineer Molinier, who was in connection with the French officials.

GOLDMAN: Who were living with you right in the place?

TROTSKY: I will, only if you permit me a remark in parenthesis. If we could have the testimony of the French police about the investigation, all this would be unnecessary, because Monsieur Thome and Monsieur Cado, the general secretary of the police and the préfecture of the Department of Charente Inférieure—all the summits [Trotsky here refers to the highest officials—Ed.] of the police were very well acquainted with my situation. It was the secret agent of the police who was informed of every step of mine. If this would be an official state court we would have in ten minutes all the confirmation.

GOLDMAN: Were the police informed of the house where you lived?

TROTSKY: Officially, not to compromise me before public opinion, the police were very discreet. But, for example, the local chief of the customs house was, I suppose, an agent also of the secret police, and in his daily work of observation he observed also our house. He verbally deposed to two French friends who accomplished the investigation now about this matter, but he refused to give a written deposition because he is a functionary.

GOLDMAN: I don't know whether you answered this question that I asked before. In the house where you lived while you were sick, who were living with you?

TROTSKY: Living with me? The house was prepared for us by two people. They were Vera Lanis, the wife of Molinier, who met us on the motor boat. She came to keep house because we avoided to have a strange person for this purpose, in order to preserve our incognito. Then Segal, who was an associate of Molinier in his affairs—his business. We met them immediately on the 25th, when we came to St. Palais in the house. Vera Lanis remained as the cook all the time, with a small interruption. She became a bit tired for some days. In August, the end of July or the beginning of August, she again remained with us. Segal remained until the end of July. Van Heijenoort came on the 26th of July, and the young French comrade, Baussier, came especially because he was at that time a member of the Communist Party. We needed a man who could orientate us about the disposition of the Stalinists in Royan, in that district—to avoid manifestations and other things if they learned that this alleged American is Trotsky. It was the 28th of July when he came to us, and he remained, I believe, more than a month, but not in our house. For the purpose of observing in Royan the Communist organizations, he could not live in our house, but every day he came with a bicycle. He came every day in the evening with papers from Paris. He came from Royan every day with papers to us, and gave us a report. He entered into relations with the secretary of the organization in Royan.

GOLDMAN: May I—

TROTSKY: Excuse me, I forgot the name of another, the name of Laste, who accompanied us in the two cars to St. Palais. He remained also with us all the time, I believe, for more than a month.

GOLDMAN: You then lived with your wife, Sara Weber, Van Heijenoort, Laste, Segal, and the cook Vera Lanis. Baussier did not live with you, but visited you every day.

TROTSKY: He came to us in the evening.

GOLDMAN: Anyone else live with you?

TROTSKY: I believe not.

GOLDMAN: Did you have any visitors coming to Royan?

TROTSKY: We have already named them, no less than fifty persons.

GOLDMAN: During the two months?

TROTSKY: During the two months.

GOLDMAN: Then you left St. Palais?

TROTSKY: Yes.

GOLDMAN: You say there were fifty visitors?

TROTSKY: Fifty.

GOLDMAN: From St. Palais, where did you go to?

TROTSKY: To the Pyrenees, to Bagnères-de-Bigorre.

GOLDMAN: When was that?

TROTSKY: It was the 9th of October.

GOLDMAN: October 9, 1933?

TROTSKY: 1933.

GOLDMAN: You went—

TROTSKY: To Bagnères-de-Bigorre. My wife and I.

GOLDMAN: Who went with you?

TROTSKY: The engineer Molinier and then Meichler, a Frenchman, as the driver.

GOLDMAN: And who else?

TROTSKY: My wife, myself; and our daughter-in-law came also to Bagnères.

GOLDMAN: Your daughter-in-law?

TROTSKY: The wife of our son Sedov; she is named by Olberg as Suzanne. That is one mistake on that question in that deposition.

GOLDMAN: How long did you remain in that town?

TROTSKY: Three weeks.

GOLDMAN: Did the press know about it?

TROTSKY: No.

GOLDMAN: When did you leave that town, approximately?

TROTSKY: It was the beginning of November.

GOLDMAN: Where did you go to?

TROTSKY: What?

GOLDMAN: Where did you go to?

TROTSKY: To Barbizon, near Paris, in Seine-et-Marne.

GOLDMAN: That was when?

TROTSKY: In the beginning of November.

GOLDMAN: Now, when you transferred—

TROTSKY: Will you permit me to explain that the authorities permitted us to come near Paris because our attitude was loyal when we came to St. Palais and Bagnères. Our incognito was strictly observed by all members of the family. Therefore the authorities changed their minds—they said, You can approach Paris for—

GOLDMAN: Did you receive permission from the authorities to move?

TROTSKY: Yes.

GOLDMAN: The French police knew of your movements all the time?

TROTSKY: It was agreed that we telephone during our travels. We telephoned our night passed in Tonneins.

GOLDMAN: When did you arrive at Barbizon?

TROTSKY: It was the beginning of November, the 2nd or the 3rd, or the first.

GOLDMAN: How long did you remain in Barbizon?

TROTSKY: It was until April or May of 1934—April, 1934.

GOLDMAN: During the time you lived in Barbizon, did you ever visit Paris?

TROTSKY: Yes.

GOLDMAN: When was the first time you came to Paris?

TROTSKY: I believe in December—December, 1933.

GOLDMAN: What was the occasion?

TROTSKY: December, 1933, or the beginning of January, 1934.

GOLDMAN: What was the occasion of your going to Paris?

TROTSKY: To visit some friends and to see Paris again after an interruption of seventeen years.

GOLDMAN: How many times did you visit Paris while you were living in Barbizon?

TROTSKY: Not more than three or four times.

GOLDMAN: Who were with you when you visited Paris?

TROTSKY: Every time it was at least two of my collaborators. We can indicate all the apartments where I stayed and met my friends. It was for meeting some friends.

GOLDMAN: Where did you go to from Barbizon?

TROTSKY: I was discovered in Barbizon by a small accident, by the local authorities, who were not aware of my identity. All the local authorities did not know, and when they learned that I was there they were a bit angry against the summits, and that was the reason they provoked a bit of a scandal in the local opinion. A reactionary campaign began in the press, a terrible campaign against me by the reaction.

GOLDMAN: Was that after February, 1934?

TROTSKY: April, 1934.

GOLDMAN: February, 1934, was the time of the fascist movement?

TROTSKY: It was a few weeks after the insurrection of Colonel de La Rocque.

GOLDMAN: Where did you go from Barbizon?

TROTSKY: If you permit me—at that time the German fascist press published every day articles accusing me of having prepared an insurrection in France.

GOLDMAN: By the way, what did the Communist press say with reference to your being revealed as living in France?

TROTSKY: *L'Humanité,* the French paper, the official organ of the Communist Party, wrote manifestoes that I came to help the Radical Socialist Party, which was the Government. This was the terminology: that the Socialist Party was social-fascist, and the Radical Socialists, fascists. They said that I came to help Daladier to organize an invasion against Russia.

GOLDMAN: At that time, according to the testimony, you were in league with the fascists?

TROTSKY: Yes, I gave my fascist instructions to the semi-fascist Romm for the fascist Radek.

GOLDMAN: You were supposed to have given these supposed instructions?

TROTSKY: Yes.

GOLDMAN: Where did you go from Barbizon?

TROTSKY: To a small suburb near Paris, for some days. Our son had a small apartment in a suburb by Paris. We must escape from Barbizon. It was terrible to live surrounded by publicity and projectors. [Cameras—Ed.] We went to Seine-et-Marne. It is not the Department of the Seine, but Seine-et-Marne. I did not have a permit to live in the Department of the Seine, but in the next Department, the Department of Seine-et-Marne.

GOLDMAN: How long did you live in that Department?

TROTSKY: Four or five days, or a week.

GOLDMAN: Then where did you go?

TROTSKY: Then I became nomadic for a certain time. My friends looked for a more or less adequate house, as in St. Palais. But I must change and go south, I must change every time my place because I was recognized on the road. It was a hunt by the fascist press and the fascist journalists, a real hunt—

INTERPRETER: You mean a man-hunt?

TROTSKY: Yes, a man-hunt. When an Englishman in a French *Kurort* [health resort—Ed.] was identified as Trotsky, he must leave the cure. It was reported by the whole French press.

GOLDMAN: Finally, where did you go?

TROTSKY: To the Département de l'Isère, near Grenoble, near the village of Domêne.

GOLDMAN: Then you left France?

TROTSKY: From this place, the Département de l'Isère.

GOLDMAN: You left for Oslo, Norway?

TROTSKY: For Oslo, Norway.

GOLDMAN: Do you know anyone by the name of Vladimir Romm?

TROTSKY: Now, I know very well his name.

GOLDMAN: You know his name now. Did you know his name before the trial?

TROTSKY: Never.

GOLDMAN: You don't remember ever having met anyone in Russia, while you were in the Soviet Union, by the name of Vladimir Romm?

TROTSKY: No.

GOLDMAN: You might have met him, but you do not remember the name?

TROTSKY: No.

GOLDMAN: Do you read *Isvestia*?

TROTSKY: Only the foreign people think *Isvestia* is a readable paper.

GOLDMAN: What do you mean by that?

TROTSKY: I must recognize that the Soviet press is not now, in this period, the most interesting press in the world. But when I have necessity of learning any political things, I read *Pravda* or economic things, special papers. But the *Isvestia* is only the bureaucratic shadow of the *Pravda,* which is also sufficiently bureaucratic.

GOLDMAN: What is the nature of the contents of the *Isvestia,* generally?

TROTSKY: *Isvestia* prints administrative opinion and also political articles, but nobody reads them—not to speak of the foreign correspondence. When I need to know anything about the United States, I am not reading *Isvestia.* I can read the *New York Times* and other papers, or the correspondence in the French papers, but not the correspondence of Vladimir Romm. I know in advance everything he will say.

GOLDMAN: Did you in the last year read the *Isvestia,* and if so, how frequently?

TROTSKY: From time to time, an issue suddenly falls into my hands. But when I need information, I ask one of my collaborators to find *Isvestia* and to find out the date when this and that event took place.

GOLDMAN: Did you read it?

TROTSKY: Never.

GOLDMAN: You didn't read it, and when you needed information contained in the *Isvestia* your collaborators found it for you?

TROTSKY: Yes.

GOLDMAN: Did you read *Pravda*?

TROTSKY: Permanently.

INTERPRETER: Regularly.

TROTSKY: Yes, regularly. And especially economic papers, also.

GOLDMAN: You never, according to your recollection, came across the name, Vladimir Romm?

TROTSKY: Never. I must say even in *Pravda* I never read the foreign correspondence.

GOLDMAN: When you need information on foreign countries you read the press of the particular country?

TROTSKY: Yes, and the C.I. [Communist International—Ed.] press, when I need it, like *l'Humanité* in the worst case. Then also the *Daily Worker*.

STOLBERG: In your opinion, the foreign correspondence of *Pravda* and *Isvestia* was useless for information. Would it not be interesting for the peculiar opinions it reveals at the moment?

TROTSKY: Mr. Commissioner, the situation is such: I read a speech of Litvinov and a speech of Stalin, and then I know what the correspondence from Washington will convey for a month or two. It is only the confirmation of the last slogan, or the latest slogan.

GOLDMAN: Did you ever meet anyone by the name of Vladimir Romm in Paris?

TROTSKY: Never.

GOLDMAN: Did you ever give any letters to Vladimir Romm for the purpose of conveying them afterwards to Radek?

TROTSKY: Never.

GOLDMAN: Did you ever receive any letters through

Vladimir Romm from Radek?

TROTSKY: Never.

GOLDMAN: You have read, have you, the testimony of Radek and Romm about that?

TROTSKY: Yes, absolutely false, both of them.

GOLDMAN: Now, Mr. Trotsky, will you produce whatever documentary evidence is at your disposal to corroborate the statements you have made with reference to your trip to Marseilles, Royan, and with reference to your other statements?

TROTSKY: I have a letter from Parijanine proposing to me to apply for admission to France. I have a letter, my letter to the Parliamentary Deputy Guernut, who became later a Minister in the Government. He was very kind, and intervened in my favor.

GOLDMAN: Have you anything to show what the conditions of your stay should be, or would be?

TROTSKY: Yes, it is a letter of the Minister, Chautemps. It is a copy of the letter of the Minister, Chautemps, to the Deputy, Guernut, and a cable from Henri. Henri is the first name of the engineer, Molinier. He says—I am reading in French and translating: "Provisional sojourn in the South definite soujourn in Corsica for you per request. Henri."

GOLDMAN: That is a copy?

TROTSKY: No, it is in the primitive manner in Prinkipo of writing cables.

GOLDMAN: This is the original telegram received by Mr. Trotsky when he was in Prinkipo, from his friend, Henri Molinier. This is a part of the general exhibit which I designated as the "Royan-Romm Exhibit," for the purpose of identifying the documents and for the purpose of proving that Mr. Trotsky never met Romm in Paris. Here I give the Commissioners a copy of the telegram.

TROTSKY: And a letter.

GOLDMAN: And a letter signed by C. Chautemps, the

Minister of the Interior, to the Deputy Guernut.

TROTSKY: Guernut. He says (Trotsky reading in French and translated by interpreter):

> You have had the kindness to call my attention to Mr. Leon Trotsky, exile of Russian origin, who has asked, for reasons of health, authorization to live in the Departments of the South and later to settle in Corsica. I have the honor to inform you that the decree of expulsion which concerns this foreigner has been withdrawn—

My expulsion of 1916, during the war, and reported yesterday to the Commission. I continue to read: ". . . and that the interested party will obtain without difficulty, when he makes the request, a passport visa for France."

GOLDMAN: A copy of that letter. Now, Mr. Trotsky, have you any statement from the innkeeper of Tonneins which shows that you stayed there about the 24th of July or the 25th of July?

TROTSKY: It is not very precise. We did not give our names in Tonneins, but with the professional memory of the owners of hotels and with the help of his books—it was not a frequent case, because we had five or six rooms at once—he said: "I affirm that on the night of the 24th–25th of July—

INTERPRETER: I will translate it. It says:

> The undersigned declares that on the night of the 24th–25th of July, 1933, he rented rooms 13 and 14 in his hotel and room 3 in the annex to five travelers who arrived late at night, in connection with whom one was an elderly couple—ANDRÉ COURET.

TROTSKY: We were six, not five, but my son in a letter explains the mistake. (Mr. Trotsky hands letter to the Commission.) My son explains the mistake in the following manner: Laste, the Frenchman, and he, they roomed together and they changed. They remained on guard during the night, they replaced one another. That was one room for both. That explains why the hotel-keeper, in his memory—it was not persons to him, but rooms.

GOLDMAN: We have at our disposal other documents which I simply mention, such as the fact that at the Café Labrède, in La Réole, Leon Trotsky and Natalia Trotsky, accompanied by the four comrades mentioned above—that is, accompanied them for breakfast in the morning of July 25th at about nine-thirty in the morning. That is in the deposition of the one who is named Laste. Another deposition to the effect that Henri Molinier has among his papers a receipt, No. 170, of the agency, made out to the said Molinier, in the sum of four thousand five hundred francs. The receipt is actually here, and the date is July 18th, when Sedov and Molinier engaged the rental of the villa at Royan with the agency.

Then, we have the important testimony of the adjutant of the fire brigade of St. Palais, Mr. Soulard, the Corporal-in-Chief. I suppose their official titles in France are Corporal-in-Chief. We have the deposition of Albert Bardon, the reporter who gave the local press the notice of the fire, the date and circumstances of the fire. Both recall perfectly that the fire coincided with the arrival of the tenants at the villa "Les Embruns." They noted the elderly gentleman who had gone out to the automobile, and later they became certain this was Trotsky. Mr. Soulard is, incidentally, a Captain of the Reserves. The Commissioners will note that they—by the way, on July 23rd you arrived at Cassis and July 25th—

TROTSKY: July 24th–25th.

GOLDMAN: The night of the 24th–25th, they stayed at the hotel at Tonneins.

STOLBERG: The 23rd?

TROTSKY: No, we arrived on the 24th.

GOLDMAN: Mr. Trotsky arrived July 24th, and was in Tonneins on the night of the 24th–25th and stayed there. That accounts for that time. You arrived at St. Palais and had breakfast on the morning of the 25th, according to the deposition, in the Café Labrède, at La Réole, near Bordeaux. And you arrived in Royan—

TROTSKY: The afternoon at two o'clock.

GOLDMAN: The afternoon of the 25th?

TROTSKY: Yes, at two o'clock.

GOLDMAN: And the fire was on the 25th?

TROTSKY: Around three o'clock.

GOLDMAN: And the testimony of the fire chief corroborates that the fire was on the 25th.

TROTSKY: Permit me—I gave the press a statement about the fire and named the date. All of the affirmations came only four or five days ago during the sojourn of the Commission here.

STOLBERG: During the last four or five days?

TROTSKY: Yes.

GOLDMAN: Do you have amongst your documents all these people who were present with you?

TROTSKY: Yes.

GOLDMAN: Who of their own knowledge give testimony, and they say so in their statements, that you were in the villa in St. Palais continuously from July 25th until you left two months later?

TROTSKY: If you will permit me, I will give you testimony of how Mr. Leprince, our driver, found the villa here. They must make a long trip along the coast. Leprince is fortunately a very attentive husband, and he wrote to his wife every day a postal card. We have now the route of my son, Leon Sedov, Leprince and Molinier—we have now the geographical exactitude as characterized by the postal cards. It precedes, these postal cards precede our arrival. It precedes the renting of the villa. My son, I believe, had left Paris five or six days before. He could not have had a meeting with Vladimir Romm or arranged a meeting with Vladimir Romm because he was not in Paris, as this postal card shows. Then, I named Mr. Baussier, our young comrade who had the mission to observe the Royan Stalinists' maneuvers. We have another deposition, from the hotel in which Baussier stayed in Royan, the first night, on the 29th. He came on the 28th, and the first night he passed in the hotel was the 29th. Then, we have the testimony of Baussier himself. We have the testimony of Vera Lanis, who is the woman who functioned as our cook during our sojourn.

GOLDMAN: Here is the declaration of Vera Lanis, who arrived—

TROTSKY: She arrived before us.

GOLDMAN: She departed from Paris about the 23rd, she left Paris the 23rd or the 24th of July. I wish to ask Mr. Solow to translate this letter.

STOLBERG: Mr. Trotsky, Vera Lanis is the wife of Molinier, now your political enemy. In spite of that, she made this deposition?

TROTSKY: Yes, a bitter political enemy, not only of mine, but of the organization.

STOLBERG: Does he refuse to make any deposition?

TROTSKY: Who?

STOLBERG: Molinier.

TROTSKY: He refused for a long time to make a deposition, but my son writes now, definitely, he will make a deposition.

STOLBERG: And his wife was willing all the time?

TROTSKY: I don't know. I received all the documents in the last few days. I am not sure. I cannot say what is her attitude toward us. I like her personally very much, but politics change very often even homes.

GOLDMAN: Will Mr. Solow read that letter?

INTERPRETER (reading):

> I was assigned to prepare the residence of Trotsky at Royan. I left Paris about the 22nd or 23rd of July to put the villa in shape, and assisted Mr. Segal on the last day. I recall very well the arrival of Trotsky and his friends. I was present at the fire of part of the house, which took place on the day of his arrival. I saw the inhabitants and the friends turn everything upside down in the kitchen, in order to put out the fire. I remained to do the cooking and to help with the household until about the end of August, at which time I took several days' rest at the hotel Saint Germain, near Royan. I was very tired. I came back to Royan again, and I remained in this villa until he departed to Bagnères. I returned to Paris afterwards. I saw Trotsky every day several times. It is altogether a fable to say that he left Royan, where he arrived on the 25th of July, during the entire months of July and August. I can declare that I always remained at the house, and that he hardly went out of doors at all. If Mr. Trotsky had gone away, I, who did the cooking and served at the table, two or three times a day, would certainly have noticed it. The 14th of March, 1937, VERA LANIS.

There is the signature. They are certified and signed by Alfred Rosmer.

TROTSKY: Rosmer is a very well known militant in the labor movement.

GOLDMAN: That does have the original of the signature of Vera Lanis.

DEWEY: Mr. Trotsky, did you have a physician while you were in St. Palais?

TROTSKY: Pardon?

DEWEY: You say you were ill. Did you have a physician?

TROTSKY: Yes; it was the great difficulty for us to get a French doctor unknown to us in this locality, because a doctor would become familiar with us. We notified a friend from another country. I cannot name him publicly. The name I will give you is the name in the deposition of this physician. He is an old friend from a semi-fascist country. He came and remained in our house three weeks.

DEWEY: We will get that in private, then?

TROTSKY: Yes.

DEWEY: Did you receive police permission to leave St. Palais for the Pyrenees?

TROTSKY: Yes, it was the function of Molinier, the engineer Molinier, who was in connection with the chief of *Sûreté Générale,* Cado. I have the testimony here of Henri Molinier.

DEWEY: The last question. Did you carry on and receive correspondence while you were in St. Palais?

TROTSKY: The correspondence was through friends, such as Molinier, and my son in Paris. It was the official address, and from time to time they came to me and submitted to me that correspondence.

DEWEY: Is that correspondence during the month of July and the first part of August?

TROTSKY: Totally, and many letters.

DEWEY: I will now declare a short recess.

DEWEY: I am going to ask you this question, Mr. Trotsky. Have the French police refused to give data on your case?

TROTSKY: Yes. I wrote to the engineer Molinier, but he answered that it cannot be given in general, and especially in my case because it is against the Soviet Government—that no official can give any answer. Even in Denmark, we tried to have the official information about the telephonic connections with Berlin. They refused. I have here a very important deposition of the customs official in Royan, who gave this deposition only orally. He refused to give it in writing, but his oral answer is sufficient.

STOLBERG: Mr. Trotsky, I would like to be clearer than I am on one point I asked you before. The Molinier who was with you near Marseilles in the boat has since become a political enemy of yours? Has he since gone into another faction or has he become a Stalinist? That is part of my question.

TROTSKY: He has his own organization and his own paper, and his organization and his paper are bitterly attacked by our organization.

STOLBERG: What dealings have you had—may I ask these questions later?

GOLDMAN: It does not matter.

STOLBERG: What dealings have you had with him, or what is his attitude toward you in your effort to get him as a witness?

TROTSKY: I don't have any personal relations directly. He visited me for the last time in Oslo.

STOLBERG: I don't mean that—excuse me. Does he collaborate with your friends in this matter?

TROTSKY: Not he; his brother, the engineer, Molinier—to say something about the facts.

STOLBERG: And his wife is also helping?

TROTSKY: Vera Lanis is the wife not of the engineer but of Raymond Molinier. She wrote the deposition I received yesterday and read to you just now.

End of Fifth Session—One o'clock P.M.

Sixth session

April 13, 1937, at four o'clock p.m.

WITNESS: LEON TROTSKY
DIRECT EXAMINATION
BY MR. GOLDMAN

GOLDMAN: Mr. Trotsky, I would like to ask you one question I forgot to ask you this morning. But before that I want to introduce an exhibit with reference to the incident of Copenhagen on the question of the Hotel Bristol. We have just received a letter which we would like to introduce into evidence, and the Commission can suggest to any other sub-commission that it examine the writer of this letter, who is in Copenhagen. It is dated March 23, 1937, and it reads as follows:

> Having lived in Copenhagen without interruption since 1931, and having taken part in the Socialist movement all the time, I can attest:
>
> 1. In the year 1932 there did not exist any Trotskyists in Denmark.

2. The first Trotskyist organization in Denmark came up in the autumn of 1934, as a Social-Democratic opposition group passed over to Trotskyism. This organization has existed ever since, and I have been the chairman all the time, and I attest that all the time the organization has existed we have not held a single meeting or conference in the coffee-house "Bristol." I myself have never been there, and the very existence of the coffee-house was quite unknown to me until I read the article in *Arbeiderbladet.*

As an explanation, I want to remark that the Communist press claimed that the Café Bristol was a Trotskyist "hangout." The letter is signed by Poul Moth, chairman of the Trotskyist organization, "Leninistisk Arbejdsgruppe" in Copenhagen. I introduce it into evidence, and ask the Commission, if it wishes, to investigate this further. I introduce this as Exhibit No. 17.

(The said letter from Poul Moth was introduced into evidence as Exhibit No. 17.)

I want to say this, that all documents that I introduce into evidence, coming from strangers and others referring to the incidents that happened some time ago—we do not vouch for the absolute correctness of these documents. We think they are correct. We hope that the Commission will find means of investigating these facts. Mistakes in memory are very possible. This refers, for instance, to the document I introduced this morning by B.J. Field and his wife, referring to events in 1932. It may be mistaken as to details.

I want to read into the record a statement by Jan Frankel. He says:

"1. I fear that the language handicap hindered me from expressing my complete thoughts in answering Mr. Beals's question regarding whether or not I might conceal the presence of Holtzman out of loyalty to Trotsky. I tried to explain that the basis of my collaboration with Trotsky is my political solidarity with his conceptions, which are Marxist ones. These Marxist conceptions made it superfluous for Trotsky and his political friends even to discuss whether or not we must employ individual terrorism in the fight against the Stalinist bureaucracy.

"In this way, Mr. Beals's question answers itself. My loyalty to Trotsky could not be maintained on a basis diametrically opposed to all my thoughts and convictions. If Holtzman had actually visited Trotsky but had not received instructions of a terrorist nature, there would be no reason whatsoever for me to conceal the visit. On the other hand, had Holtzman come and received such instructions, the political solidarity upon which my collaboration with Trotsky is based would no longer exist. I would break with Trotsky and become his political adversary. Thus, in either case, I would have no motive for remaining silent about such a visit, had it actually materialized.

"Furthermore, I must state that the visits neither of Sedov nor of Holtzman could have been kept hidden, even by Trotsky's 'closest' and 'most loyal' friends, since many of these friends have since become his most bitter enemies.

"2. It seems to me that Raymond Molinier and I had one or more telephone conversations with Leon Sedov in Berlin from Molinier's hotel, in Copenhagen Palace, in addition to my calls from the house. The period concerned is from Nov. 24th to Dec. 1st, 1932. May I take the liberty to suggest to the Commission that an investigation in this connection might be possible and fruitful?"

For the benefit of the press, I want to spell out the name of the writer of this letter I introduced before, from Copenhagen. It is a letter from Poul Moth. The first name is spelled P-o-u-l. It may be a different way of spelling "Paul" in Denmark.

Now, Mr. Trotsky, I would like to ask you the question why all the precautions were taken on your trip from Marseilles to Royan—why some persons in your party went to Royan by a different route, and why others went to Paris? Will you explain to us the necessity of all this caution?

TROTSKY: We tried in this manner to hide our future address from the adversary. Van Heijenoort, with a small baggage, went to Lyon. He gave the impression to the journalists—I will not in any case offend the journalists; I, in a manner, adhere to the same profession. But it was not against the journalists; it was a political measure of self-defense. He gave the impression that he went to Paris and that Shachtman, with the big baggage and boxes, went to Paris. And Sara Weber also went to Paris. So, everybody in Marseilles thought that my wife and myself were also going to Paris by other means, by car or airplane. All our baggage was directed to Paris. That was our purpose—to betray the adversaries, to disorientate them. That we succeeded—we succeeded very well. The deposition of Vladimir Romm shows that we succeeded in betraying the G.P.U.

GOLDMAN: You mean "confuse"?

TROTSKY: Confuse.

BEALS: What evidence do you have that the G.P.U. was following you there?

TROTSKY: You know, this question makes me a bit perplexed. Excuse me, Mr. Commissioner. You see, all the trials are directed against me. The G.P.U. wants to give me a vital blow. It is the aim of all the trials. It signifies that before the trials the G.P.U. must collect material against me.

BEALS: The point is whether you did that because you were followed by the G.P.U., feared the G.P.U., or whether you knew they were following you.

TROTSKY: I was absolutely sure they had threatened to follow me, absolutely sure. They have a sufficient number of agents, because every functionary of the Comintern, of the French Communist Party, is an agent of the G.P.U. And in the United States, the same. The Politburos of the Communist Parties all consist of paid agents of the G.P.U.

BEALS: Well, I was just asking if you had definite evidence—

TROTSKY: If the Commission will appoint an investigation of the Comintern—

BEALS: I was just asking for evidence of your statement. You made a statement, and I was wondering whether you could prove it.

TROTSKY: I made the affirmation based upon my fight and experience.

BEALS: You used a very definite phrase, Mr. Trotsky. You said the G.P.U. was following you, and you did that because the G.P.U. was following you back and forth from there. I said, how did you know, in that stretch of country, how did you know that they were following you?

TROTSKY: It is my conclusion, not my evidence. The conclusion I will make in my final speech, if you wish.

BEALS: I might have the same conclusion, but I have not the proof.

TROTSKY: I will develop my position on that question immediately. I preferred to do it at the end. The proof is that Romm affirmed twice that he met me at the end of July, 1935. You must ask yourself: Why at the end of July, 1935? Why, especially, at the moment when I was in St. Palais? Why do they choose that moment? I explained why very clearly; that we tried to confuse them by some measures. We directed our collaborators to Paris, our baggage to Paris, Van Heijenoort to Lyon. It was an expense of money and time, and more important, of forces, of people, of friends. For what purpose? It was more simple to go directly with the baggage and with my friends, my young friends, my collaborators, to St. Palais. What was the reason we sent people to Paris? What was the reason? Only one: That I am a man persecuted by the perfidious organization, the G.P.U.

DEWEY: Mr. Trotsky, you said "1935."

GOLDMAN: You mean 1933?

TROTSKY: 1933—in the same period, yes. If you read the Communist Party press of Marseilles, if you read the Communist Party press of every town in France, you will see that it is a device of the G.P.U. They will not discuss with me as I discuss with them. I say: Your policy is bad. They denounce me as an agent of the French military staff or an agent of the German military staff. It depends exclusively on the fact of Moscow's friendship with either Germany or France.

DEWEY: I think we will hear that at the end, Mr. Trotsky. Mr. Beals wishes to ask another question.

BEALS: I do want to ask about some other documents. One was the telegram which you received in Constantinople. I presume the Commission will look into it. I would like to clarify a point in my mind. I could not tell to whom that telegram was addressed.

TROTSKY: Sedov, wasn't it?

BEALS: I think it was from the French authorities.

TROTSKY: Sedov. It was the name of my wife and my legal Soviet name. The passport was given me in the name of Sedov for my trip to Europe, and for my exile they gave me a passport with the name of my wife. The Russian laws permit it. It was done not to expose us to the curiosity of the public.

BEALS: Can I see the telegram? (Mr. Trotsky hands telegram to Commissioner Beals.) It is here addressed, but what I don't understand is "Buyukada."

VAN HEIJENOORT: It is the Turkish name for Prinkipo. Buyukada signifies "Greek island."

BEALS: I want also to ask you: You travel under the passport given under the name of Sedov by the French Government?

TROTSKY: From where?

BEALS: Turkey.

TROTSKY: From the Turkish Government. After I was deprived of Soviet citizenship, I left my passport from the Soviet Government. They delivered to me a Turkish passport for foreigners.

BEALS: That was the passport you traveled on, to France?

TROTSKY: Yes.

BEALS: Will you present that as evidence?

TROTSKY: Yes, I can present it.

GOLDMAN: Will you make a notation of that?

BEALS: Also, for instance, I noticed in this letter from the hotel in the town of Tonneins that it mentioned a party of five which stopped on that day. Does not that hotel keep a record of its guests' names?

TROTSKY: There is a letter here stating that we had reason to avoid giving our names.

BEALS: My understanding is that in all hotels in France you are required to give your names and passports.

VAN HEIJENOORT: (Speaking in French.)

LAFOLLETTE: He says he wants to make a statement in French.

VAN HEIJENOORT (through interpreter): The village is located in the summer resort region. This was the season of the summer vacation, and it is very common in such districts during the vacation season, that when people come only for one night, they do not bother to fill out the usual form of staying over-night in a hotel. When I arrived the next day, after landing at St. Palais, I discussed with Molinier their experiences on the trip, having come different ways. Molinier explained that when they arrived late at the hotel, they went to bed right away, intending to fill out the forms the following morning. But when the morning came they were anxious to go away as rapidly as they could. Molinier, who hurried the departure, left without filling out the forms.

TROTSKY: We did not foresee that we would not give our

signatures, Mr. Commissioner. We tried giving our names to the hotel keeper.

GOLDMAN: Perhaps Mr. Trotsky did not quite understand Mr. Beals's question about his proof of the G.P.U. Mr. Beals's question is a very legitimate one. We have no direct evidence that Mr. Trotsky saw a certain man who was an agent of the G.P.U. We have no direct proofs to offer. But his whole life-story since his exile, all the trials, all his tribulations, the stealing of his archives, the fact that Romm made such a statement that he met him in July, 1933—all this, as far as Mr. Trotsky and as far as I am concerned, is conclusive proof that the G.P.U. had been following him. Otherwise, there would be no explanation whatever.

BEALS: The only thing I wished to bring out was to keep the testimony on the basis of proof rather than opinion.

GOLDMAN: That is perfectly correct. But there are certain things that happened, and you draw deductions that another thing is true. Now, are there any other documents that you have in your files which would corroborate your testimony that you spent two months in St. Palais and from there left for Southern France? Have you any other documents that you want to present?

TROTSKY: My letters to friends and visits to me. I have had, as I mentioned—I had about fifty visits of people coming from Paris, England, from Holland, Belgium, and so on. Among these people we find my best friends for years, such as Naville, for example, and Sneevliet from Holland. If I should be in Paris to meet him, an unknown man—Vladimir Romm—a young man whom I met for the first time, as he explained, I would meet other people, my old friends.

GOLDMAN: Mr. Trotsky, may I interrupt just a moment? Would you not save the argument, your conclusions, for the final closing of the case? And now, simply to the facts.

TROTSKY: We will come to that.

GOLDMAN: Have you the affidavit of Sara Weber?

TROTSKY: Yes, and Max Shachtman's. I believe on a box—we have a box with the initials of Max Shachtman on the box. The box can testify in our favor. (Laughter) His initials are on the box.

GOLDMAN: The Commissioners can get the box later. It is right here.

TROTSKY: And all the boxes with the initials of Max Shachtman.

GOLDMAN (Pointing to a large trunk on which are the initials "M.S.")

TROTSKY: We had, I believe, ten or twelve boxes with the same marks. It remains from the year 1933, and our trip from France coincides with the testimony of Max Shachtman, the legal testimony of Max Shachtman.

GOLDMAN: We have a series of depositions—

TROTSKY: Of Van Heijenoort.

GOLDMAN: —of people who were with Mr. Trotsky at Royan, and a statement from his French collaborator, Mr. Van Heijenoort, sitting to the right of Mr. Trotsky. I want to make this statement to the Commission. The time is getting very short. I don't want to put Mr. Heijenoort on the stand as a witness unless the Commission is absolutely anxious to have him. I suggest that I finish with my examination of Mr. Trotsky first. If there is time available, I would be more than glad to put Mr. Heijenoort on the stand for cross-examination. But you can read his statement. And at the end of the—you will read the statement before—then, at the end, if you have questions to put to Mr. Heijenoort, you can put it at the end of my examination of Mr. Trotsky. Is that suitable?

DEWEY: Any questions at the present time?

GOLDMAN: From Mr. Heijenoort. (No questions were asked.)

GOLDMAN: We have here a deposition—the statement, rather—of Natalia Sedov Trotsky, Mr. Trotsky's wife, and again because of the pressure of time, I suggest that you read this statement. It is in English, and if you have any questions of Mrs. Trotsky, you can save them until the end of the direct examination of Mr. Trotsky.

The Commission can at this time—if they want me to put Mrs. Trotsky on the witness stand, I shall be more than glad to do so. Perhaps, if you have time, I shall favor that, because I want to put them on the stand in order to have them testify in the same manner that Mr. Frankel testified this morning, as a witness, giving the Commissioners an opportunity to cross-examine on my direct examination.

We have other documents here, a document by J. Laste to the same general effect—as to his presence with Mr. Trotsky in Royan, that Mr. Trotsky was ill and did not leave the house where he lived at St. Palais. I don't think it is necessary for us to put into the record all of the depositions. They are cumulative evidence. I simply mention them. I believe that tonight, tomorrow night and every night, the Commission will have time to come here and do this—all of the Commissioners can go through all of these documents and acquaint themselves with the nature of these documents.

Mr. Chairman, the press would like to see the statement of Mrs. Trotsky. With your permission, I can give the press the statement of Mrs. Trotsky now. Then you can take all these statements along with you, and look them over at your leisure tonight. I want to save time.

DEWEY: I certainly have no objection, personally.

GOLDMAN: If any Commissioner has any objection to that—

BEALS: You are going to introduce that as evidence?

GOLDMAN: We are introducing now all of the documents, all of the statements with reference to Royan. It is my opinion that we have introduced sufficient evidence now, conclusive proof, that Mr. Trotsky was not in Paris and could not have been in Paris at the end of July, 1933, when Vladimir

Romm claims to have talked to him. Now, to save time, I don't want to go through all of the documents. They are cumulative evidence. I am going to introduce them into evidence to give the Commissioners an opportunity to examine them at their leisure, and then put questions to the witnesses who are present. Or suggest further examination of the witnesses who are not present.

BEALS: Personally, I think any person, any serious person, should see any of the evidence we have.

GOLDMAN: I shall, then, since there is no objection, give the statement of Mrs. Trotsky to the press.

DEWEY: As far as I am concerned, it is more of a matter for Mrs. Trotsky than for the Commission.

GOLDMAN: I think that since she made the statement for the purpose of making public the record, that I will not assume to ask her this. I will hand it to the press.

LAFOLLETTE: Is this to be handed around to the press, or what is to happen? Will it come back?

GOLDMAN: It will come back here, I am sure. I'm sure of that. We have here a series of depositions of all kinds, of persons who came to visit Mr. Trotsky. I introduce the whole file of what I call the "Royan-Romm incident." We introduce documents referring to the location of the villa in St. Palais, giving a picture of the whole situation, for whatever they are worth, and documents dealing with the fire in the villa at St. Palais.

Here are very important documents dealing with the political discussions held, I assume, between you and your visitors in 1933, giving the Commissioners an idea of what the actual discussions were that Mr. Trotsky was interested in.

TROTSKY: Yes.

GOLDMAN: Here, I want to quote some excerpts.

DEWEY: I don't understand. Is this in the form of a deposition?

GOLDMAN: No, the political discussions come from the

archives of Mr. Trotsky. I gather that they are excerpts from your archives?

TROTSKY: Yes, if you show them to me I can tell you better.

DEWEY: They are introduced as parts of his archives?

GOLDMAN: Yes.

TROTSKY: The document in German is the report of a German Socialist who visited me. He was my adversary—he became my enemy. I will not name him, but I believe his name is known by one member of the Commission, and that the Commission can have more information about this personality. It is a report—I don't name him only because he does not want it—but it is a general report concerning our discussion. He is an old member of the workers' movement in Germany, and I could not hide from him the ideas which I had been concealing from Vladimir Romm. (Laughter)

GOLDMAN: Here is a sub-file. We titled the letters "Romm-Royan file."

TROTSKY: This letter is not written for the Commission. It was written immediately after our discussion for his own organization.

DEWEY: That is what I wanted to find out. It was prepared by this man, not by you?

TROTSKY: It is prepared by this man, the German Socialist, not for my handing to the Commission, but at the time of his visit, to his followers—for the S.A.P.

DEWEY: You will give us the name in private session?

GOLDMAN: This was written August 23, 1933. Now, here is an interesting sub-file.

INTERPRETER: What Mr. Trotsky said in German was "S.A.P.," the Socialist Workers Party of Germany.

GOLDMAN: At the time Mr. Trotsky arrived in France, in July, 1933, the Communist press wrote many articles about him. We deem it to be relevant to show what the Communist press said at that time concerning Mr. Trotsky. Whereas now they claim—the Communists claim—that Mr. Trotsky called on Romm for terroristic acts against the leaders of the Soviet Union, caused sabotage, and even attempted the organization of a foreign alliance with Hitler and Japan, at that particular time the Communist press—we have excerpts from *l'Humanité,* the French Communist paper—accused him of being in league with the French Social-Fascists and the French Radical-Fascists against the Soviet Union. [Mr. Goldman here refers to the French Socialist Party and the Radical Socialist Party of France—Ed.] We deem them as being relevant and important, and we add these in the general file of "Royan-Romm."

I introduce all of these documents into evidence for the purpose of having the Commission examine them—put questions to Mr. Trotsky in case they so see fit. I will mark this as Exhibit No. 18.

(The "Royan-Romm" file was introduced into evidence as Exhibit No. 18.)

BEALS: May I make just a statement in regard to my previous question to Mr. Trotsky? I state my interest was not in the G.P.U. I have a hearty contempt for all secret services of all nations; but it was merely a question of evidence.

GOLDMAN: We understood that.

TROTSKY: And the form of my answer was directed not at all against the Commissioner, but against the G.P.U.

GOLDMAN: That ends the matter of the alleged visit of Mr. Trotsky to Paris for the purpose of having a conference with Vladimir Romm. Are there any other questions that you want to take up with reference to that matter?

TROTSKY: Yes, two things. The first thing, Vladimir Romm said that he met my son twice before meeting with me. Now, I repeat that the documents delivered by me prove that my son was out of Paris weeks preceding the alleged meeting with Mr. Romm.

GOLDMAN: That will also be subject to the investigation by the Commission in Paris of Sedov.

TROTSKY: The Preliminary Commission on the basis of the documents, significantly, can judge the dates itself. We can suppose it is a mistake. Or, as our famous British lawyer, Mr. Pritt, would say, "a slip of the pen." But the date is represented two times in the verbal report, in such a manner that the first time Romm said it was in July, 1933. At the end of his deposition about the meeting with me, Vyshinsky asked him again about the date. He repeated: At the end of July, 1933. Two times he repeated that, and the second time with more precision.

GOLDMAN: Will you bring that out in detail in the final conclusion? Will you have that section dealt with in the final argument on Romm?

TROTSKY: Yes.

GOLDMAN: You will bring that out. In American procedure, that will constitute argument, not facts.

TROTSKY: I wanted only to stress the date. It is not a mistake. Because to-morrow we can read—

STOLBERG: In New York, a bit before your article on the Romm incident appeared in the *New York Times,* I had lunch with a man, Louis Fischer. He had just come to help Spain in this country. And then, the next day, he read your statement in the *Times* about the Romm incident. In the afternoon he called me up and he said that in *Pravda,* since the trials, there appeared a statement that Trotsky did not see Romm only in 1933, but also five or six times in 1934, and so on. That he saw you several times. According to Louis Fischer, that statement appeared in *Pravda.* Do you understand?

TROTSKY: Yes, I understand. Vladimir Romm is an official witness, not only a witness, but a defendant in another trial. He was arrested, and brought under convoy to the court to give his deposition. If Louis Fischer would be arrested in Moscow and would be presented as a witness, I would analyze his testimony. But now when he writes and tells stories, very confused, it can be nothing I don't know the dates, the facts, the places.

STOLBERG: I mean, did such a story appear in *Pravda?*

TROTSKY: I never noticed it. I must say at this question that it is a gift of heaven that I have the possibility to refute his deposition by positive proofs—a negative fact by positive proof. It is a pure accident. If they had named other dates, I would be disarmed—it is possible. But this time I am very well armed.

DEWEY: You have already testified that you never met him.

TROTSKY: Never, never heard his name.

GOLDMAN: Of course, it is very easy; if you don't meet a man in October, you can meet him in December.

TROTSKY: That is the reason why I insisted upon the date. If you will permit me, I will quote the *New York Times* about the matter. In the *New York Times* of February 17, 1937—that is, a month after the trial—it was the verification of the investigation of the *New York Times* editorial board itself. I quote:

> The ship that brought Mr. Trotsky from Turkey to Marseilles in 1933 docked after he slipped secretly ashore, according to a Marseilles dispatch to the *New York Times* of July 25, 1933. He had been taken aboard a tugboat three miles outside of the harbor and landed at Cassis, where an automobile was waiting [I explained there were two automobiles, not one]. At that time, Mr. Trotsky was variously reported at Corsica, in Royat, in the center of France, in Vichy.

It signifies that I disappeared from the people, even the press, and the adversary.

DEWEY: I just have one slight question. You say you were visited by about fifty friends?

TROTSKY: Yes.

DEWEY: How did they know you were there?

TROTSKY: They were friends who knew my friends in Paris. The fact that I was in France was known by my friends. For example, the Dutch Parliamentary Deputy Sneevliet, who is an old friend—I wrote him immediately to Amsterdam and I gave him an invitation to come to me, and to meet in Paris Molinier, and Naville, and my son—they would indicate my address. The same to the former secretary of the Independent Labor Party of Great Britain. He was in Paris for a certain conference. He met my son, who indicated to him the possibility of visiting me. The French author Malraux, who visited just now the United States—he visited me also in the same manner.

DEWEY: That is all they knew, whether from your friends or whether they had your direct invitation?

TROTSKY: Yes.

GOLDMAN: Any further questions? (No further questions were asked on this point.)

GOLDMAN: The next matter that I will take up is the question of the trip that Pyatakov is alleged to have made to Oslo in December of 1935. We shall introduce evidence in the same way we have introduced it in the case of the alleged visit of Holtzman to the Hotel Bristol in Copenhagen and in the case of the conversation, or the alleged conversation, which Romm had with Mr. Trotsky, to prove that Pyatakov never did visit Oslo in December, 1935, and never did speak with Mr. Trotsky in December, 1935. I will first read the testimony of Pyatakov, given in the official Report of the Court Proceedings published by the People's Commissariat of Justice of the U.S.S.R., Moscow, 1937. I am reading from page 59—no, I shall begin with the last paragraph on page 58. I quote:

Pyatakov: It was on December 10, in the first half of December. That same day, or the next, I met Bukhartsev, who, taking advantage of a moment when nobody was about, told me that he had heard of my arrival a few days before, had informed Trotsky of it and was awaiting news from Trotsky on the matter. The next day Trotsky sent a messenger, with whom Bukhartsev brought me together in the Tiergarten, in one of the lanes, literally for a couple of minutes. He showed me a brief note from Trotsky, which contained a few words: "Y.L., the bearer of this note can be fully trusted." The word "fully" was underlined, from which I gathered that the person Trotsky had sent was an agent of his.

I do not know the name of this man. I can't say exactly now what he called himself, either Heinrich or Gustav—I think it was Gustav, that may have been a nickname, or Heinrich. He had received instructions from Lev Davidovich . . .

Lev Davidovich refers to Trotsky.

. . . to arrange a meeting for me, to go and visit Trotsky, as Trotsky strongly insisted on having a talk with me.

As it transpired later, this particular insistence was caused by the last letter Radek had sent to Trotsky.

He asked me whether I was prepared to travel by airplane. I said that I was prepared, although I realized how risky such an operation was; but since I had had such a conversation with Radek and, generally speaking, the problems confronting us were extremely serious and acute, I thought it was better to take the risk of flying and meeting Trotsky than to shirk the risk and remain in the state of perplexity we were in.

In short, I decided to go, although, I repeat, for me it meant taking a very great risk of discovery, exposure, and anything you like; nevertheless, I decided to make the journey.

Vyshinsky: Did your conversation with him end there?

TROTSKY: What was the name of the passport?

GOLDMAN: It does not say. He says with his own name, Pyatakov.

TROTSKY: The passport was a German passport. What name? It must be another name. I ask you if you can indicate from the Verbatim Report the name.

GOLDMAN: I read again: "The passport was a German one. He saw to all the customs formalities himself, so that all I had to do was to sign my name."

TROTSKY: Not a word about his conversations with his companion!

GOLDMAN: Then Pyatakov goes on to say what Mr. Trotsky told him with reference to killing all the leaders of the Soviet Union, and destroying factories, and reintroducing capitalism. I quote from page 442 with reference to the question of Pyatakov's trip to Oslo. I made a remark to the Commission that immediately after the report of Pyatakov's alleged trip to Oslo, there was made public in the press, the press of Oslo, an open statement to the effect that no foreign airplane came to Oslo.

TROTSKY: During December.

GOLDMAN: During December, 1935. At the end of the examination of the witness at the trial, Vyshinsky questions Pyatakov on this matter: "Vyshinsky: I have a question to put to Pyatakov. . . ."

STOLBERG: What page is that on?

GOLDMAN: 442, the last paragraph. I continue to quote:

> I have a question to put to Pyatakov. Accused Pyatakov, please tell me, you traveled in an airplane to Nor-

way to meet Trotsky. Do you know in which airdrome you landed?

Pyatakov: Near Oslo.

And on page 60 he says, "In Oslo."

Vyshinsky: Did you have any difficulties about the landing or admission of the airplane to the airdrome?

Pyatakov: I was so excited by the unusual nature of the journey that I did not pay attention.

Vyshinsky: Have you heard of a place called Kjeller or Kjellere?

Pyatakov: No.

Vyshinsky: You confirm that you landed in an airdrome near Oslo?

Pyatakov: Near Oslo, that I remember.

Vyshinsky: I have no more questions. I have an application to the court. I interested myself in this matter and asked the People's Commissariat of Foreign Affairs to make an inquiry, for I wanted to verify Pyatakov's evidence from this side too. I have received an official communication which I ask to have put in the records. (Reads)

GOLDMAN: This is from the People's Commissariat of Foreign Affairs:

"The consular Department of the People's Commissariat of Foreign Affairs hereby informs the Procurator of the U.S.S.R. that according to information received by the Embassy of the U.S.S.R. in Norway the Kjellere Airdrome near Oslo receives all the year round, in accordance with international regulations, airplanes of other countries, and that the arrival and departure of airplanes is possible also in winter months."

(To Pyatakov.) It was in December?

Pyatakov: Exactly.

Vyshinsky: I ask that this be placed in the records. Now a question to accused Radek.

LAFOLLETTE: Mr. Goldman, I think that document was submitted for the Commissioners, the information that has—

GOLDMAN: It cannot be read?

LAFOLLETTE: That I don't know. It was handed in by someone who came to the Commission and said that he would like to make a certain statement, but without a name. Let the Commission read it, and if it deems it necessary and advisable to make it public, I will read it into the record.

GOLDMAN: What was the name of the place where you were living in Oslo before you were interned?

TROTSKY: It was Weksal, a village, near the small town of Hoenefoss. The distance from Oslo is about two hours by railroad or car.

GOLDMAN: How many miles, do you know?

TROTSKY: It was about fifty-five or sixty kilometers. But you know, it is not a question only of kilometers, but of the road itself. It is a very hilly road, a very difficult road. In winter it is necessary to put chains on the wheels.

STOLBERG: On the tires?

TROTSKY: On the tires, because the road is covered by snow. In the winter it is two hours to two and a half hours.

GOLDMAN: Whom did the house belong to where you lived?

TROTSKY: A rich farmer, but it was occupied by Konrad Knudsen.

GOLDMAN: Who is Konrad Knudsen?

TROTSKY: He is a prominent member of the Norwegian Workers Party, and now he is a Deputy of the Storting, the Norwegian Parliament.

GOLDMAN: Knudsen is spelled K-n-u-d-s-e-n. And Mr. Knudsen was living there in the house?

TROTSKY: Yes, his family. They gave us two rooms in their apartment.

GOLDMAN: You occupied rooms with him in his house?

TROTSKY: In the house there were six rooms. One on the first floor—on the ground floor there were five rooms. They occupied three, and we, two. The dinner room was common, and the entrance was through the dining room. The entrance was common, then the vestibule and then the dining room. It was absolutely impossible—

GOLDMAN: How many members were there in the Knudsen family?

TROTSKY: Four members: Knudsen, his wife, Hilda Knudsen, the daughter, Hjordis Knudsen, and Borgar Knudsen. And then the woman who served in the kitchen, the cook, a Norwegian woman.

GOLDMAN: She lived there in the house?

TROTSKY: Yes, in the house.

GOLDMAN: How many were there in your group?

TROTSKY: We were my wife and myself, and during a sojourn, Jan Frankel, who lived also in the house of Knudsen. Then he left us and he was replaced by Erwin Wolff. Erwin Wolff lived in a neighbor's house.

GOLDMAN: You came to Oslo, if I remember correctly, in June?

TROTSKY: June, 1935.

GOLDMAN: 1935. You lived in that house with the Knudsens ever since you came to Oslo, from the very beginning?

TROTSKY: For a couple of days we were in a hotel before we found this place.

GOLDMAN: And Mr. Frankel was collaborating with you during 1935, was he?

TROTSKY: Until November.

FRANKEL: Until the end of October.

GOLDMAN: Then Mr. Erwin Wolff came in?

TROTSKY: Yes.

GOLDMAN: You received many visitors in that house, Mr. Trotsky?

TROTSKY: I believe the sum total of ten or twelve.

GOLDMAN: During what period?

TROTSKY: During more than a year.

GOLDMAN: Your visitors there were not as many as in France?

TROTSKY: Not so many. It was too far. Maybe there were a few more, fifteen or twelve. I can't say the exact total.

GOLDMAN: With reference to the entrance to the house, where was your working room, where you received visitors, where you worked?

TROTSKY: It was by the entrance, in the dining room. To the right was the room of Knudsen, and to the left was my working room. Then there was a bedroom.

GOLDMAN: And people who came in, in order to get to your working room, had to go into the dining room?

TROTSKY: The first thing, the vestibule. The vestibule connects with the kitchen and the dining room.

GOLDMAN: Were you ever alone in that house?

TROTSKY: Pardon?

GOLDMAN: Were you ever alone in that house?

TROTSKY: Never.

GOLDMAN: You had no guard at that time around the house?

TROTSKY: No, no guard. But, a guard in the very friendly family of Knudsen. It was for us very important to have such a friendly family. In spite of our differences in political views, they personally had sympathies for my wife and myself and my secretaries also. They were occupied with the question of my safety. But all the communications were with Hoenefoss—were organized by the family. They had a car, and so on.

GOLDMAN: And when any visitor came to see you, how did he arrive from Hoenefoss?

TROTSKY: The first thing: In Hoenefoss, the daughter of Knudsen had a small shop of books. Everybody who came to us received a communication to visit this shop and to have subsequent communications—there was the shop of Knudsen in the same house. Her father had his bureau, had his working room of his paper there, and his auto. It was a working-class paper. She instructed all people: You can wait one hour or a half hour, and then you can go with my father in his car to Weksal.

GOLDMAN: Did visitors ever come without having gone first to the daughter of Knudsen? Had any visitor come to you—

TROTSKY: In so far as I remember, it was the rule to visit the shop of the daughter of Knudsen and Knudsen himself, in his bureau, in his working room.

GOLDMAN: Let me ask you this: The house that you lived in, was that the house into which some Norwegian fascists broke at one time?

TROTSKY: Yes.

GOLDMAN: When was that?

TROTSKY: It was the 5th of August, 1936, during our summer trip with the family of Knudsen.

GOLDMAN: Once in a while you took a trip with the Knudsen family? For how many days?

TROTSKY: It was a long trip of twelve days, I believe.

GOLDMAN: Did you ever take any shorter trips with them?

TROTSKY: To Oslo, three or four times, for a day.

GOLDMAN: Did you ever take any trips without anybody at all?

TROTSKY: Never.

GOLDMAN: All alone?

TROTSKY: Never. It is impossible, Mr. Attorney, because

if I am on the street and recognized by the people I am absolutely helpless. I am surrounded by people, and especially in Norway—I don't speak Norwegian—I must have some Norwegian people who can defend me.

GOLDMAN: Didn't you learn Norwegian while you were there?

TROTSKY: Not sufficiently to speak.

GOLDMAN: Was the door leading into the house closed or open?

TROTSKY: The door leading into the house—during the day it was open.

GOLDMAN: It was winter time.

TROTSKY: Because the kitchen—the door of the kitchen was open into the vestibule. Nobody could come without—it was the entrance, then the vestibule to the kitchen and the dining room. During the daytime the door—

GOLDMAN: It was closed?

TROTSKY: What do you mean, closed? With a key?

GOLDMAN: No.

TROTSKY: Naturally, it was closed. I didn't understand. But not with a key.

GOLDMAN: It wasn't locked, but it was closed?

TROTSKY: Yes, especially in the winter time. Norway is very cold.

GOLDMAN: There was a door-bell?

TROTSKY: Pardon?

GOLDMAN: There was a door-bell? Anybody would ring, or would they announce when they wanted to come in?

TROTSKY: I believe they only had to knock.

GOLDMAN: Mr. Frankel wants to say something.

FRANKEL: Generally, we saw everybody who approached the house.

GOLDMAN: I just wanted to know one thing, whether there was any door-bell.

FRANKEL: Yes. Anybody who arrived at the door—before

they arrived at the door, we were there waiting for them.

TROTSKY: I forgot to say that from our windows you saw the street totally. Whoever approached our courtyard, from both sides. My friends and my secretary were all the time very vigilant.

GOLDMAN: At the time that the Norwegian fascists raided the house, was anybody in the house?

TROTSKY: The daughter Hjordis and the son Borgar. Thanks to the courage of the daughter of Knudsen, my archives were saved, because she fought with them and called the neighbors.

GOLDMAN: Now, you knew Pyatakov, didn't you?

TROTSKY: Yes.

GOLDMAN: When was the last time you saw him?

TROTSKY: 1927. He said in the deposition 1928, but it is a small mistake in a great falsehood.

GOLDMAN: Now, did you see him—did you see Pyatakov when you were living in Weksal? That is, the village of Weksal?

TROTSKY: Never.

GOLDMAN: You didn't see him and you didn't talk with him?

TROTSKY: Never.

GOLDMAN: Did you ever send a message with someone by the name of Bukhartsev for the purpose of inviting Pyatakov to Oslo?

TROTSKY: I must repeat that in spite of the fact that Bukhartsev is a correspondent of *Isvestia* I have never heard his name before the publication of the report of the trial.

GOLDMAN: So, you state you never saw Pyatakov in Oslo in December of 1935, or at any other place, and that you never saw him since 1927 or thereabouts?

TROTSKY: Never.

GOLDMAN: Never had any communication with him?

TROTSKY: Never.

GOLDMAN: Either with him directly or through some intermediary?

TROTSKY: Never. I never heard the name of Bukhartsev before the trial.

DEWEY: We will take a short recess now.

GOLDMAN: I forgot to ask you one question, Mr. Trotsky. Amongst your visitors in Weksal, were there any Russians at all?

TROTSKY: No, none at all. We had Frenchmen, Americans, Canadians, British people and Czechs.

GOLDMAN: No Russians?

TROTSKY: No Russians. I must repeat that every one of the visitors was presented to the family of Knudsen and ate together with us at the same time, I believe.

GOLDMAN: I turn to the Oslo-Pyatakov exhibits. They are the following documents: The affidavit by Konrad Knudsen, who housed Mr. Trotsky, Hilda Knudsen and Hjordis Knudsen, his daughter, who testified to these facts:

> Trotsky and his wife had a bedroom and a workroom for themselves, and the dining room and the rest of the apartment was used by all the inhabitants of the house in common. It follows that we were excellently informed about all the visitors whom Trotsky received in this time. Visitors could not even enter the house without announcing themselves to the people in the house. Trotsky presented us to his visitors. This holds good for all the visitors. Thus we had exact knowledge about all of Trotsky's guests . . . Phone calls were always answered by people in the house, and never by Trotsky and his wife . . . The few times when Trotsky left my house for short trips, he was generally in my car and in my company . . . Trotsky's visitors were Czechoslovakians, German émigrés, Englishmen, Frenchmen and Americans, but no Russians.

The second is an affidavit by Jan Frankel describing Trotsky's conditions of life. I quote:

> Trotsky's conditions of life, such that it was impossible to approach him without being observed and introduced, were not different from the conditions which prevailed in Turkey and France. . . . For this reason I can affirm even the powerful G.P.U. could not organize a visit for Pyatakov or anybody else without being remarked by the other inhabitants of the house.
>
> Moreover, I can state that in the period of 1935 Trotsky was occupied with the Russian question only on a purely scientific basis (writing his book, "The Revolution Betrayed") and that no organizational questions regarding the work of the Russian Opposition were touched upon.

GOLDMAN: Mr. Frankel is here, and, if time permits, we shall put him on the stand, and the Commission can cross-examine him. We have an affidavit of Walter Held, who confirms the above statement. Held visited Trotsky between the end of June, 1935, and the end of August, 1936, about ten times. He notes that Weksal is not a country resort, and that it is not a half hour, but two hours from Oslo. There are the affidavits of Harold Isaacs and Viola Robinson. They visited Trotsky in August, 1935, and state that in order to meet Trotsky they were obliged to wire Knudsen and to meet Jan Frankel first at the bus. They confirm the general information already given. I have the original affidavit which the Commission should look into at its leisure. Then there is the affidavit of Earle Birney, who visited Trotsky in 1935. He says he was obliged to meet Trotsky's secretary—at that time, Erwin Braun—and Knudsen's daughter, Hjordis. He confirms the above information. The same thing from Max Sterling, who makes an affidavit in general on the same things and the same conditions.

On the question of Pyatakov's flight to Oslo, on January 29, 1937, a few days after the trial commenced, Konrad Knudsen sent a telegram to Vyshinsky. The telegram was published in the *Arbeiderbladet* of January 29, 1937, to this effect:

> To State's Attorney Vyshinsky, Supreme Military Court, Moscow: I inform you that today officially verified that in December, 1935, no foreign or private airplanes landed at the airport near Oslo stop as Leon Trotsky's host I also confirm that in December, 1935, no conversation can have taken place in Norway between Trotsky and Pyatakov.

In my opinion, it was this telegram that caused the Prosecutor Vyshinsky to ask for some kind of statement from the embassy of the U.S.S.R. in Norway.

TROTSKY: It is not, I believe. Here is the chronology. The first initiative in this case belongs, as I am informed, to the conservative, the very conservative, Norwegian paper *Aftenposten*. It began an independent investigation on the 24th of January, and its statement on the 24th or 25th states that it is impossible that that deposition is correct.

GOLDMAN: It is impossible that airplanes should be there?

TROTSKY: They investigated at the airport, and the authorities assured them that not one foreign airplane landed at the airport at Oslo. It was the statement of the *Aftenposten*, and it was, I think now, the 23rd or the 24th of January. The speech of the Prosecutor was on the 28th and the cable is dated the 29th.

GOLDMAN: So that the speech of the Prosecutor resulted—questions with reference to the possibility of an airplane landing at Oslo on the part of the Prosecutor Vyshinsky resulted from the report in the *Aftenposten* of January 23rd or 24th.

TROTSKY: And repeated by all other papers.

GOLDMAN: Then we have the affidavit of Konrad Knudsen, who states that Trotsky was at home the whole month of December save for his visit to Knudsen's cabin, that no foreign visitors came in the month of December, and that "Pyatakov was not able to visit Trotsky without my knowledge, neither in my home nor in the cabin where my son and maid were together with him."

By the way, Mr. Trotsky, when was it that you left the house to go to Mr. Knudsen's cabin?

TROTSKY: It was the 20th of December, and until the 22nd.

GOLDMAN: You lived there three days?

TROTSKY: For three days.

GOLDMAN: Were you with Knudsen at that time?

TROTSKY: I was with the son of Knudsen, with the cook, a woman, and with my wife.

GOLDMAN: How large a cabin was it?

TROTSKY: It was a cabin, nine square meters. It is on a mountain and used for hunting and fishing.

GOLDMAN: How far away from Knudsen's home?

TROTSKY: It is more than one hour.

GOLDMAN: On the way to Oslo or from Oslo?

TROTSKY: No, from Oslo.

GOLDMAN: It has only one room and a kitchen?

TROTSKY: One room, and then on a separate structure is a floor, a second floor.

GOLDMAN: An attic? Do you know what an attic is?

TROTSKY: Yes, possibly for sleeping.

GOLDMAN: On top for a second floor?

TROTSKY: Yes.

GOLDMAN: So there is one room downstairs and one upstairs?

TROTSKY: They were not separate rooms, but connected with one another.

STOLBERG: A balcony?

GOLDMAN: Was that a balcony?

TROTSKY: Yes.

GOLDMAN: There is an article in the *Arbeiderbladet* of Oslo of January 29, 1937, where the director of the airport, Director Gulliksen, says: "No foreign aeroplane at Kjeller." I will read from *Arbeiderbladet* as follows:

> Director Gulliksen has examined the customs register, which is kept daily, before he gives us this information, and in answer to our questions he adds that there is no question of any aeroplane being able to land at Kjeller without being observed.
>
> "When was the last time a foreign aeroplane landed at Kjeller before December, 1935?" our representative asked Director Gulliksen.
>
> "On the 19th of September . . ."
>
> "And after December, 1935, when did a foreign aeroplane come to Kjeller for the first time?"
>
> "On the first of May, 1936."
>
> "In other words, from the books of the aviation ground it is thus established that no foreign aeroplane landed there between September, 1935, and May 1st, 1936?"
>
> "Yes."

GOLDMAN: We also have correspondence between Trotsky's lawyer, Stoeylen, of Oslo, to the director of the Kjeller Airport, Gulliksen. Gulliksen's letter of February 14, 1937, says: "I beg to state that my statement published in *Arbeiderbladet* is correct, as no foreign aeroplane landed here in December, 1935."

Then I have a letter from Stoeylen to Trotsky, dated March 16, 1937. It says: "I have also written to the Minister for Foreign Affairs, Mr. Koth, and asked him for the result of the Government's step to find out all about Mr. Pyatakov's travel to Norway in December, 1935."

We have a statement by Erwin Wolff, printed in part in the *Manchester Guardian* of January 25, 1937, and his letter to Trotsky, February 8, 1937. He states that Trotsky received no visitor in December, 1935, and I quote: "Furthermore, the first foreigner who came to us in Weksal after November, 1935, was my friend W., who visited me personally, and came on January 28, 1936."

Erwin Wolff was the secretary of Trotsky—is that right?

TROTSKY: Yes.

GOLDMAN: And the affidavit of Borgar Knudsen.

TROTSKY: That is his son.

GOLDMAN: The son of Konrad Knudsen.

TROTSKY: He is fifteen or sixteen years old.

GOLDMAN: He states that he was with Trotsky, Trotsky's wife, and Erwin Wolff in the cabin from December 20th to December 22nd. Trotsky, he says, "was not out of the cabin in these days. I can furthermore confirm that in these days no visitors came to Trotsky, and that nobody could have visited him without my knowledge."

TROTSKY: Excuse me, I forgot to say that Erwin Wolff was with us in the cabin.

GOLDMAN: And then there are general documents concerning the whole matter. We offer the important document, Trotsky's statement of January 27, 1937, entitled "My Concrete Proposition to the Moscow Court," a statement in which he enumerates questions, I believe, to be transmitted to Pyatakov. Have you that statement there?

TROTSKY: Yes, I have the statement, but I have another statement from the 24th. It was the second day of the trials, immediately after the deposition of Pyatakov. The statement was given to the press and published by the press. It was from the 24th. The prosecutor had the full possibility to investigate in the direction indicated by me. Here is the statement:

> If Pyatakov had traveled under his own name, all the Norwegian press would have carried this information. Consequently, he must have traveled under another name. What name? All Soviet functionaries abroad are in constant telephonic and telegraphic communication with their embassies, commercial missions, and do not find themselves beyond the watch of the G.P.U. for a single hour. How could Pyatakov have achieved his trip without the knowledge of the Soviet representatives either in Germany or Norway? Let him describe the internal arrangement of my room. Did he see my wife? Did I have a beard or not? How was I dressed? The entrance to my study was through the Knudsen apartment, and all our visitors without exception became acquainted with the family of our hosts. Did Pyatakov see them? Did they see Pyatakov? Here is a series of precise questions by the aid of which it would be easy for any honest court to show that Pyatakov is repeating the inventions of the G.P.U.

These are the questions of the 24th of January.

GOLDMAN: Then, on January 27th, you had other questions?

TROTSKY: On the 27th, I gave some questions of a more precise form. If you permit me, I will read the introduction to the questions. We are here concerned with the confession of Pyatakov. It was the 27th, before the prosecution speech of Vyshinsky. The prosecution speech was held on the 28th. I will quote now:

> We are concerned here with the confession of Pyatakov. He testified that he visited me in Norway in December, 1935, for the purpose of conspiratorial plotting. Pyatakov alleged that he came from Berlin to Oslo by airplane. The enormous importance of this testimony is evident. I declared many times, and I repeat again, that Pyatakov,

> like Radek, has been during the last nine years not my friend but my bitterest and most perfidious enemy, and that there could be no question of negotiations between us. If it should be proved that Pyatakov actually visited me, my position would be hopelessly compromised. If, on the contrary, I can prove that the story of the visit is false from beginning to end, the entire system of "voluntary" confessions would be thoroughly discredited. Even if we should admit that the Moscow trial is beyond all suspicion, the defendant Pyatakov remains suspect. His testimony must be verified immediately, before he is shot . . .

It was the 27th. ". . . by putting to him the following series of questions." Then follow thirteen questions. I repeat the questions. I can read them because my first request did not find any answer from the court. I read the questions:

> 1. On what day did Pyatakov come from Moscow to Berlin, in December, 1935? What was his official mission? Pyatakov is too important an administrative figure to make the trip in such a manner that it would not be known to the Soviet Government. The day of his departure must be known in his Commissariat. The German press must have announced his arrival.
>
> 2. Did Pyatakov visit the Soviet Embassy in Berlin? Whom did he meet?
>
> 3. When and how did he fly from Berlin to Oslo? If he came to Berlin openly, he must have left secretly; it is impossible to conceive of the Soviet Government sending Pyatakov to plot with Trotsky.
>
> 4. What kind of passport did Pyatakov use when he left Berlin? How did he obtain this false passport? Did he also obtain a Norwegian visa?

We know how he obtained it.

5. If we admit for a moment that Pyatakov embarked upon this trip legally and openly, his arrival must have been announced in the Norwegian press. In that case, who were the Norwegian authorities whom he must have visited officially?

6. If Pyatakov came to Oslo illegally, with a false passport, how did he succeed in disappearing from the keen eyes of the Soviet officials in Berlin and Oslo? (Every Soviet administrator abroad remains in permanent telegraphic and telephonic communication with the embassies and commercial agencies of the U.S.S.R.) How did he explain his disappearance upon his return to Russia?

7. At what time did Pyatakov arrive in Oslo? Did he pass the night in the town, and if so, in what hotel? (We hope it was not in the Hotel Bristol.) The well known Norwegian paper *Aftenposten* affirms that at the time mentioned by Pyatakov no foreign plane landed in Oslo. This must be verified.

8. Did Pyatakov inform me beforehand of his contemplated visit by the regular telegraphic channels of communication? This can easily be verified in the telegraphic offices of Oslo and Hoenefoss.

9. How did Pyatakov locate me in the village of Weksal? What means of transportation did he use?

10. The trip from Oslo to my village required at least two hours; the conversation, according to Pyatakov's affirmations, took three hours; and the return trip required two more hours. December days are short; Pyatakov must inevitably have passed one night in Norway. Again: Where? In what hotel? How did he depart from Oslo—by train, ship, or airplane? For what destination?

Bukhartsev said in the same airplane.

11. All of my visitors will confirm that it was possible to come in contact with me only through the members of the family of our host, Knudsen, or through my secretaries, who remained on permanent guard duty before my room. With whom did Pyatakov meet?

12. In what way did Pyatakov make the trip in the evening from Weksal to the station of Hoenefoss—in the automobile of our host Knudsen, or by taxi summoned by telephone from Hoenefoss? In either case, the departure, like the arrival, could not have been accomplished without witnesses.

13. Did Pyatakov also meet my wife? Was she at home on the day in question? (My wife's trips to her doctor and dentist in Oslo can easily be established.)

It is necessary to add that the appearance of Pyatakov is striking and easily remembered—tall, blond, with tinges of red in his hair and beard, very regular features, high forehead, glasses, and very lean. (In 1927, when I saw him for the last time, he was exceedingly thin.)

Not only a lawyer, but every thinking man as well, will understand the decisive importance of these questions for the purpose of the verification of Pyatakov's confessions. The Soviet Government has the full possibility to utilize the services of Norwegian justice. (It was obliged to do this even before the trial.)

These were the questions by me to the world press on the 27th of January.

GOLDMAN: In a letter from Trotsky during his internment, to his lawyer on September 5th, 1936, before the trial, Trotsky wrote:

The last note of the Soviet Government says that the Norwegian Government "bears the full responsibility for the future stay of Trotsky in Norway." This phrase

> might easily be considered a diplomatic formula in order to cover the retreat. In my mind this would be light-minded and false . . . After the fiasco of the Zinoviev trial the G.P.U. must intend to transfer my "terroristic" basis of operation from Copenhagen to Oslo. A new chapter in the book of amalgams begins. . . . The art of the G.P.U. will consist in finding new Olbergs, Berman-Yurins, etc., pretending to have received their instructions directly from Oslo.

In the same letter Trotsky warns Puntervold of the possibility of visits from provocateurs of the G.P.U. In other words, this simply introduces this communication of September 15th. Trotsky predicted that a new trial would be held, and that somebody would testify that he visited him in Norway.

TROTSKY: Excuse me, I must read four lines, the last lines of my thirteen questions:

> Are the president of the court and the prosecutor ready to put these cogent questions to Pyatakov? Their attitude in this connection should be decisive for the trial in the eyes of all honest people throughout the world.
>
> I hope that all the papers interested in the truth will publish this statement in full.

It was largely published.

GOLDMAN: During the only time that Trotsky was out of Knudsen's house in Weksal, in the latter's cabin, from December 20th to the 22nd—I want to quote from the commercial section of the *Berliner Tageblatt,* which stated:

> At present there is in Berlin the first Vice Commissar of Heavy Industry of the Soviet Union, Mr. Pyatakov, and also the chief of the Department of Imports of the

> Commissariat of Foreign Commerce of the Soviet Union, Mr. Smolensky.

The same report appeared in the economic review, *Die Ostwirtschaft,* in Berlin, December, 1935, No. 12, page 185.

Concerning the alleged meeting between Pyatakov and Leon Sedov in Berlin, we have a letter from Leon Trotsky, during his internment in Norway, a letter of November 26, 1936, in which he relates the reminiscences of Natalia Sedov on a letter from Leon Sedov which arrived from Berlin to Kadikoy during 1931–32. I quote:

> Do you know whom I saw on Unter den Linden? The redhead. (This was the name the young people gave Pyatakov because of the color of his hair.) I looked him squarely in the eye, but he turned his face away as though he didn't recognize me. What a miserable fellow!

Kadikoy is another name of Turkey?

TROTSKY: After the fire in our house in Prinkipo we had to change our place of residence for a year. We moved to a town called Kadikoy.

GOLDMAN: Leon Sedov wrote this. This fact is confirmed by two letters on December 3rd and 11th, 1936, from Leon Sedov to Puntervold. And also in a statement in the *Manchester Guardian* of February 9th, 1937. Then there are clippings and excerpts from Norwegian newspapers concerning the different versions of Pyatakov's flight to Oslo.

TROTSKY: Permit me to give a short explanation. It was very difficult to prove a positive fact by a negative fact—that my son did not meet Pyatakov. I tried to use our internment—we could not communicate with our son without the police, the Norwegian police, censorship. I wrote through the intermediary of the police to Puntervold, my lawyer, to ask my son if my son—my wife remembered that he met him on the street under such and such conditions. Pyatakov turned his back to him. My son cried, "Traitor!" Puntervold sent my son a question: "What was your meeting with Pyatakov?" Our son confirmed to Puntervold what I have stated. We were separated by the Norwegian police. This coincides with what he wrote my wife. This is a positive proof of a negative fact.

GOLDMAN: I will introduce all of these documents into evidence as Exhibit No. 19, called the "Oslo-Pyatakov Exhibit." These exhibits all refer to this incident of Pyatakov's alleged visit to Oslo. They are available for the Commission whenever the Commission wants them.

DEWEY: What is the exhibit labelled?

GOLDMAN: "Oslo-Pyatakov."

DEWEY: Number?

GOLDMAN: We have not numbered these exhibits because of the fact that there are so many documents in them. However it might be best to give them a number in addition to a name.

DEWEY: Well, it does not matter.

(The "Oslo-Pyatakov" file of documents was introduced into evidence as Exhibit No. 19.)

DEWEY: I understand that these questions which you addressed to the Prosecutor were written, of course, before you had seen a printed testimony. The papers had not stated at that time, and the news from Moscow had not stated, the dates and time.

TROTSKY: Yes. My questions can be divided in two parts. One part is based upon the lack of information of the *Times,* and all of the American agencies. This part lost its importance. It is available in the Verbatim Report. The second part—

DEWEY: But the testimony itself—according to the testimony, Mr. Pyatakov arrived there at three p.m. of December 11th.

TROTSKY: He arrived in Berlin—as I remember, he arrived in Berlin the 10th of December. In any case, the first half of December. It is officially formulated. I asked for an exact date.

LAFOLLETTE: It says December 10th in the official report. It was on December 10th or the first half of December.

TROTSKY: Pyatakov claims the trip itself—the trip in the first half of December. But it is a trip which begins on the 9th of December. But at what hour? Because he must on order of his Commissariat transfer his power to another. The secretary must know his departure, and a chauffeur must know the hour or minute of his train, when he starts. He is too prominent a figure to travel without the dates of his trip being known more exactly than "the first half of December."

DEWEY: On page 58, it was on December 10th, the first half of December. That is the official record—and that he got there the next day, approximately at three p.m. I only raise that to ask if you have any special information of your whereabouts on December 11th.

TROTSKY: Only about three or four days ago we received a quotation from the *Berliner Tageblatt* which confirms the fact that Pyatakov in December, 1935, visited Berlin. And it is confirmed by the German press, and only one day is indicated, the 20th day of December—indicated that Pyatakov is in Berlin. I made the question not only when he came to Berlin, but when he started from Berlin to Oslo. He could not forget such a date, when he came back to Berlin. How did he explain to the authorities in Berlin his disappearance for two days?

DEWEY: According to the official report, it was December 11th.

TROTSKY: No.

DEWEY: That he went to Berlin. He says, the next day.

TROTSKY: It is possible there is a contradiction. The French edition: "It was on December 10th. In the first half of December."

FRANKEL: In the French edition there is a period; but here is a comma.

DEWEY: It actually says: "*Vyshinsky:* Did your conversation with him end there? *Pyatakov:* He arranged to meet me the next morning at Tempelhof Airport." It would make it the 11th.

BEALS: He says he met with Bukhartsev that day or the next.

DEWEY: Then it would be the 11th or the 12th. I was merely asking if you have any special recollection or information of your whereabouts on the 11th and 12th, similar to that which you have on the 20th and 22nd.

TROTSKY: No. My question was based on the supposition that Pyatakov really visited Oslo. I say there it was impossible.

DEWEY: Do you keep a diary?

TROTSKY: Pardon?

DEWEY: A diary?

TROTSKY: Myself?

DEWEY: Yes.

TROTSKY: Not a diary. My letters are noted, letters sent and letters which arrive. In that manner, I can more or less establish my real diary.

DEWEY: Do you have any information, even from your letters, bearing on these two dates? You will submit it to the Commission?

GOLDMAN: From your recollection did you leave Mr. Knudsen's in December, outside of the time that you visited the cabin on the 20th to the 22nd?

TROTSKY: No.

GOLDMAN: You were, all the time in December, outside

of those two days, in Knudsen's home?

TROTSKY: The month of December was the worst month of my life. I was all the time in bed. I tried to escape from the illness by this trip in the cabin. It was not successful.

GOLDMAN: Mr. Chairman, I am of the opinion that the Communists raised the question of the Pyatakov visit somewhat later, when Mr. Trotsky was outside of the Knudsen home. I am not sure about it. I am merely suggesting it as a hypothesis. Therefore, it is necessary to cover all possible eventualities. They may claim that Pyatakov visited Trotsky on the 20th, the 21st and the 22nd, and consequently it is important to state that the *Berliner Tageblatt* made a statement to the effect that Pyatakov was in Berlin on the 22nd.

DEWEY: I was not objecting to that part of the evidence, but asked whether there was any special testimony regarding the 11th and 12th.

BEALS: May I suggest that it would be rather difficult for us to go beyond the Verbatim Record of the trial?

GOLDMAN: I agree with that one hundred per cent, that we ought to stick to the verbatim evidence of the trial—just as in the case when Commissioner Stolberg made some other statements appearing in *Pravda*. But the evidence in the trial is for us authoritative, upon which we base our testimony. Are there any more questions?

LAFOLLETTE: I want to refer to the quotations of the *Berliner Tageblatt*. Does that announce his arrival or simply that he is in Berlin?

TROTSKY: That he is in Berlin.

STOLBERG: The Tempelhof is an airdrome for land planes. Still I heard somewhere—and I wonder if anyone can answer—that the official airdrome near Oslo is for seaplanes.

TROTSKY: What?

STOLBERG: For seaplanes.

TROTSKY: No, it is not correct. The Kjeller Airport is for ordinary airplanes. But the Comintern press later invented the hypothesis that he landed not in the airport, but on a frozen fjord. But to land on a frozen fjord it is necessary to have skis. To start from Tempelhof, it is necessary to have wheels. The hypothesis is contradictory. Then, from a frozen fjord a trip cannot be made in an automobile. Pyatakov informed them that he used an automobile. On a frozen fjord he must use skis—a horse with a sled. He could not approach my cabin with an automobile, especially in the mountains.

BEALS: Mr. Trotsky, do you have any information of the flying time, the ordinary flying time between Berlin and Oslo?

TROTSKY: There is no regular communication at all during the winter period. It is theoretically—from a meteorological point of view, it is possible, as informed by Prosecutor Vyshinsky, but there is no communication during the winter. It is too dangerous.

BEALS: I don't think you quite understand my question. My question is: Do you have any information as to how long it takes a plane to go from Berlin to Oslo?

TROTSKY: I am not sure, but I think the time indicated by Pyatakov is theoretically right. They show it in the schedule, the time-table of flying. He started in the morning and he landed at three o'clock. It must correspond more or less to the distance. It is theoretically correct. I don't know what airplane he received from the German authorities.

STOLBERG: We have heard testimony of Mr. Gulliksen and other authorities in Norway, to the effect that no plane landed. I am asking this question, and anybody might answer it. I heard that afterwards the Norwegian Government stated that, purely theoretically, a plane might have landed without their knowledge.

TROTSKY: I never heard of it from the Norwegian Government.

GOLDMAN: The Russian Consul made that statement.

TROTSKY: Even Vyshinsky dare not affirm that. Vyshinsky said only, the meteorological conditions did not exclude the possibility of the flight.

STOLBERG: The Norwegian Government never made that statement?

TROTSKY: I can't say; I never heard it.

GOLDMAN: Any more questions from the Commissioners? (No questions were asked.)

GOLDMAN: By the way, before I forget it—I want to introduce the map that is hung on the wall, the map of France, into evidence. If possible, a small map can be made—in smaller proportions, and if not, the map as is. I want to introduce it into evidence for the Commissioners so that they can have it when they discuss this particular question.

(The map of France was introduced into evidence as Exhibit No. 20.)

GOLDMAN: Now, before going on to a different section of the evidence, I want to clear up some matters with reference to the evidence of the prosecution in the Soviet Union, statements that were made by some witnesses.

Mr. Trotsky, Dreitzer, one of the defendants in the first trial, the Zinoviev trial, on page 51 of the report, claims to have received instructions from you to resort to terrorism. Did you send him any such instructions?

TROTSKY: Did I what?

GOLDMAN: Did you send him any instructions?

TROTSKY: No.

GOLDMAN: You never sent him such instructions?

TROTSKY: No.

GOLDMAN: He also claims he established contact with you in Berlin in 1931. Did your son Sedov ever write you anything referring to Dreitzer?

TROTSKY: Never; nothing.

GOLDMAN: On page 52 of the report, he testifies that he received a message from Trotsky in October, 1934, written with invisible ink, and containing instructions on terrorism; that he passed this letter on to Mrachkovsky, and that Mrachkovsky burned it. Did you ever send him a letter in invisible ink?

TROTSKY: No; the entire thing is very invisible.

GOLDMAN: You mean you never sent him such a letter?

TROTSKY: No.

GOLDMAN: Smirnov, in his testimony, refers to a man by the name of Putna, who was supposed to be in communication with you personally and to organize terrorism. Who is Putna?

TROTSKY: I think I explained that. Is it not for the second time?

GOLDMAN: Perhaps it would be better two times than not at all.

TROTSKY: Putna is an officer of the General Staff, a military scholar and a good officer of the Red Army during the Civil War. He belonged to the Left Opposition. In view of the fact that he was a subordinate, I never spoke with him on the question of the Opposition.

GOLDMAN: Did you ever discuss—did you ever have any communication with him since your exile?

TROTSKY: Never.

GOLDMAN: In the testimony of M. Lurye there is an observation to the effect that he received instructions in Berlin on March 4th, 1933, from Ruth Fischer and Maslow, but actually these were instructions of Trotsky. Who are Ruth Fischer and Maslow?

TROTSKY: Fischer and Maslow are former leaders of the German Communist Party, and were my bitter adversaries. Then they became Oppositionists, Zinovievists. They capitulated after Zinoviev, and in the time indicated in these depositions they were absolutely antagonistic to me.

GOLDMAN: Did they ever belong to the Left Opposition?

TROTSKY: They belonged to Zinoviev.

GOLDMAN: After your expulsion from the Soviet Union, did they belong to the Left Opposition in Germany?

TROTSKY: No, they adhered to the Fourth International at the end of 1934 and the beginning of 1935, during my sojourn in Barbizon.

LAFOLLETTE: Which International?

TROTSKY: To the so-called Trotskyite International.

LAFOLLETTE: The Fourth International?

TROTSKY: Yes.

GOLDMAN: Did you ever hear of a man by the name of Gaven?

TROTSKY: Yes.

GOLDMAN: Who is he?

TROTSKY: He is a Latvian Bolshevik. He, if I remember, gave all his sympathies at a certain time to the Opposition. As Holtzman, for example. In 1926 or 1927, he was connected for a time with Smilga, a member of the Central Committee. But he disappeared from my eyes absolutely after 1926.

GOLDMAN: In the testimony of Mrachkovsky, and also Smirnov, there is a reference that you sent communications through Gaven to Smirnov about the necessity of killing Stalin.

TROTSKY: I don't know anything about it. No, it is an absolute falsehood. He is not among the defendants.

GOLDMAN: No, he is not. He is a witness.

TROTSKY: Not even a witness.

GOLDMAN: That's right.

TROTSKY: He disappeared.

GOLDMAN: It is simply mentioned by Mrachkovsky, by the defendant Mrachkovsky. Now, it is a quarter of seven. If you want me to start on the next section for fifteen minutes, I will be glad to do so.

DEWEY: What is the next section?

GOLDMAN: The next section deals with the sabotage in the Soviet Union.

DEWEY: I think, we all think, it would be better to have it tomorrow.

GOLDMAN: All right; we can reserve that for tomorrow.

End of Sixth Session—Six Forty-five o'clock P.M.

Seventh session

April 14, 1937, at ten o'clock a.m.

DEWEY: I will ask Mr. Beals first to read the telegrams from workers' organizations that have been received, in Spanish.

(Commissioner Beals reads the following telegrams in Spanish:)

MEXICO D.F. 13 ABRIL D 14.40
JOHN DEWEY
AMBERES 65 SEIS CINCO CIUDAD

SINDICATO DE CAMPESINOS DISTRITO FEDERAL ADHERIDO CENTRAL CASA DEL PUEBLO, BOLIVAR 238 DIRIGESE SEÑOR JOHN DEWEY PRESIDENTE Y DELEGACION COMISION INTERNACIONAL INVESTIGA SOBRE CARGOS LANZADOS A LEON TROTZKY EN PROCESOS MOSCU ESPERANDO SUS TRABAJOS SEAN UN ESFUERZO GARANTIAS VERDAD Y JUSTICIA ASUNTOS COMPETEN EN ABSOLUTO PROLETARIADO REVOLUCIONARIO MUNDIAL. RECIBAN DELEGACION NUESTRA BIENVENIDA. SRIO GENERAL. MACEDONIO FUENTES, BOLIVAR 238.

MEXICO D.F. ABRIL D 14.40
JOHN DEWEY
AMBERES 65 SEIS CINCO CIUDAD

SINDICATO UNICO TRABAJADORES INDUSTRIA ACEITES VEGELATES SIMILARES DISTRITO FEDERAL MIEMBRO CASA DEL PUEBLO BOLIVAR 238 COMUNICA A USTED ESTIMACION DE ESFUERZOS HACE COMISION INTERNACIONAL INVESTIGA CARGOS ATRIBUIDOS LEON TROTZKY EN PROCESOS MOSCU YA QUE VERDAD Y JUSTICIA INTERESAN VIVAMENTE PROLETARIADO REVOLUCIONARIO MUNDIAL. DAMOS BIENVENIDA ESTA DELEGACION POR ACUERDO NUESTROS, REPRESENTADOS SRIO GENERAL. ALEJO GARCIA.

MEXICO D.F. 13 ABRIL D 14.40
JOHN DEWEY
AMBERES 65 SEIS CINCO CIUDAD

SINDICATO DE VAQUEROS TRABAJADORES DE ESTABLOS DEL DISTRITO FEDERAL DE CENTRAL OBRERA CASA DEL PUEBLO BOLIVAR 238. ENVIA BIENVENIDA AL PROFESOR JOHN DEWEY Y DELEGACION INTERNACIONAL JUZGA CARGOS IMPUTADOS LEON TROTZKY EN PROCESOS MOSCU. ESPERAMOS SUS ESFUERZOS HAGAN LUZ EN BENEFICIO PROLETARIADO REVOLUCIONARIOS MUNDIAL. PRO SECRETARIO. MANUEL GARCIA.

MEXICO D.F. 13 ABRIL D 14.40
JOHN DEWEY
AMBERES 65 SEIS CINCO CIUDAD

SINDICATO DE OBREROS PANADEROS, BIZCOCHEROS Y REPOSTEROS DEL DISTRITO FEDERAL MIEMBRO CASA DEL PUEBLO BOLIVAR 238, SALUDA EN SU PRESIDENTE SEÑOR JOHN DEWEY A LA DELEGACION DE LA COMISION INTERNACIONAL DE ENCUESTA SOBRE LOS CARGOS HECHOS A LEON TROTZKY EN LOS PROCESOS DE MOSCU. ESTA AGRUPACION VE EN LA

COMISION UN ESFUERZO PARA GARANTIZAR LA VERDAD Y LA JUSTICA EN ASUNTOS QUE ATAÑEN DIRECTAMENTE AL PROLETARIADO REVOLUCIONARIO MUNDIAL. POR ESO DAMOS LA BIENVENIDA A DICHA DELEGACION. SRIO GENERAL. VICTORIO MUÑOZ.

GOLDMAN: For the purpose of the record, Mr. Chairman, I want to read a telegram which we received yesterday. It deals with the question that Mr. Finerty raised a few days ago with reference to the new treason law in the Soviet Union. We inquired about it from New York, and we received a telegram giving us some information. The Commission will check up on the information we received, by an examination of the original documents in New York. It is addressed to Bernard Wolfe, one of Mr. Trotsky's secretaries.

49 NEW YORK, N.Y. 13 DE ABRIL DE 1937
BERNARD WOLFE
LONDRES, 127
COYOACAN D.F.

TREASON LAW AMENDED JUNE EIGHTH THIRTY FOUR PRESCRIBING DEATH PENALTY FOR TREASONABLE CRIMES INCLUDING FLIGHT FROM COUNTRY AND PROCEEDING AS FOLLOWS QUOTE ARTICLE ONE PARAGRAPH THREE COLON IN EVENT ESCAPE OR FLIGHT ABROAD OF MAN IN MILITARY SERVICE (VOYENNO SLOOZHASCHEGO) IF MEMBERS OF FAMILY OF LEGAL AGE ASSISTED IN ANY WAY IN PREPARATION OR COMMISSION TREASON OR EVEN IF THEY ONLY KNEW OF CRIME BUT UNBROUGHT TO ATTENTION AUTHORITIES ARE PUNISHABLE IMPRISONMENT FIVE TO TEN YEARS WITH CONFISCATION PROPERTY STOP OTHER MEMBERS HIS FAMILY OF AGE WHO LIVED WITH HIM OR AT HIS EXPENSE WHEN CRIME WAS COMMITTED ARE SUBJECT TO DEPRIVATION VOTING RIGHTS AND EXILE SIBERIA FOR FIVE YEARS STOP PARAGRAPH THREE FAILURE BY MAN IN MILITARY SERVICE

TO INFORM AUTHORITIES PREPARATION OR ACCOMPLISHMENT OF TREASON IS LIABLE TEN YEARS IMPRISONMENT STOP FAILURE BY ALL OTHER CITIZENS (NOT IN MILITARY SERVICE) PUNISHABLE ACCORDANCE WITH ARTICLE TWELVE THIS STATUTE UNQUOTE FROM PRAVDA JUNE NINTH THIRTY FOUR STOP ARTICLE TWELVE DATING FROM FEBRUARY TWENTY SEVENTH NINETEEN TWENTY SEVEN PRESCRIBES NOT LESS THAN SIX MONTHS SOLITARY CONFINEMENT FOR FAILURE REPORT PREPARATION OR ACCOMPLISHMENT OF COUNTER-REVOLUTIONARY CRIME. WRIGHT.

GOLDMAN: With reference to the question of Pyatakov's alleged presence in Oslo, I wish to introduce into evidence the original copy of the paper *Aftenposten,* a paper published in Oslo, containing an article dealing with that question. It is merely a news item where the director of the air field in Oslo makes a statement to the reporter of this paper. I read a translation of the article:

> According to telegrams from Moscow regarding the new "Trotsky Trial," the defendant, Pyatakov, is said to have confessed that he visited Oslo in December, 1935, and while there had a conference with Trotsky somewhere near that city—probably at Hoenefoss. According to his own statement, Pyatakov arrived by plane from Tempelhofer Feld, and was traveling on a false passport. He entered Norway under the pretence that he was going to have a conference with the leaders of the Norwegian cooperation.
>
> The mere fact that the journey was made by plane—in December, when all regular air traffic is cancelled—makes his statement doubtful. He is supposed to have arrived in a monoplane at the Kjeller airfield. Information obtained at that field, however, states that no civil airplane landed there during December, 1935. The same information was

given us at the Gressholmen station.

All Russian subjects entering the country must have a visa, and are placed under very careful observation. In the event that Pyatakov was provided with a false passport there is, of course, no reason why he should not have been here. "But I consider it entirely improbable," says Mr. Konstad, Chief of the Central Office of Passports.

We have also interviewed Konrad Knudsen, member of Parliament and editor, who at that time was Trotsky's host.

"Pyatakov's confession is utterly unfounded," he says. "In any event it is absolutely impossible that he could have had a conference with Trotsky at that time. Trotsky arrived from Ulleval at the end of October, 1935, and did not leave my house until the last week before Christmas, because he was still ill. He received no visitors at all, or telephone messages. Either one of the members of my family or I received his telephone calls, and I have asked everyone in the household if any telephone call to him could in any way be connected with the above statement. They are all perfectly certain that nothing of the sort happened.

"The first time Trotsky left my house after his stay at Ulleval was the week before Christmas, as already stated, when he went with me to my cottage on Oiiangen near Ringkollen, where he spent a few days. He lived entirely secluded from the world here, and I doubt that Pyatakov or anybody else could have found him."

GOLDMAN: The article is entitled: "Pyatakov's Conference with Trotsky at Oslo Quite Improbable. No Civil Airplane landed at Kjeller or Gressholmen during December, 1935." There is a reference note in the article which reads as follows: "Kjeller is a military air field 25 kilometers east of Oslo. Gressholmen is a small island near Oslo used as a station for hydro-airplanes."

I will introduce the original of this article into evidence as Exhibit No. 21.

(The article entitled "Pyatakov's Conference with Trotsky at Oslo Quite Improbable," from the newspaper Aftenposten, *was introduced into evidence as Exhibit No. 21.)*

TROTSKY: May I point out that the paper is a conservative paper?

GOLDMAN: The *Aftenposten* is a right-wing paper of Norway. I understand it is an organ of the Right-Wing Party.

Now, I have finished with that part of the testimony produced at the last two trials in Moscow which deals with matters allegedly transpiring outside of Russia, such as Pyatakov's visit to Oslo, Romm's alleged conversation with Trotsky in Paris, and Holtzman's alleged visit in Copenhagen, matters which we are in a position to refute with our own evidence. As for the testimony which was given with reference to matters transpiring exclusively within Russia, we are, of course, unable to deal with these matters as effectively as we have done with the matters I have indicated as allegedly transpiring outside of Russia. We are in a position to offer some evidence, evidence which in our opinion is worthy of consideration by the Commission, indicating that the testimony of the defendants in the last two trials in Moscow, with reference to such things as wrecking and sabotage—that such testimony is false.

Especially will I deal with the defendant Grasche or Hrasche, who was a defendant in the last trial of January, 1937. His testimony is contained in the Verbatim Report on pages 421–433. In that testimony he states that he was a Czech by birth, that he came to Russia, was interned in Russia during the World War as an Austrian citizen, took out Russian citizenship in November, 1917, left for Czechoslovakia in

1919, and returned to Russia in 1920 or 1921 in the guise of a former prisoner of war.

The prosecutor, Vyshinsky, attempted to bring out all these matters to show that Hrasche, because of the fact that he changed citizenship several times, or because he had documents showing different citizenships, was a very suspicious character. And Hrasche testified that he came in contact with Trotskyism on the basis of espionage and wrecking activities, that he was connected with the German Intelligence Service, and as well with the Czechoslovakian Intelligence Service. Then, too, when he was working for the Communist International, he further testified, he had connections with three Danish Trotskyites, one engineer Wienfeld, another Lund, and a third, Nielsen, and that the engineer Wienfeld made use of his flat as a rendezvous for the purpose of making their conspiracies in order to complete the destruction of Soviet property.

We have statements from former leaders of the Czechoslovakian Communist Party—their names I cannot reveal in the open, but they will be communicated to the subcommission in private session and give these statements—and from these statements, I quote as follows:

> Jan Hrasche was not the only Bolshevik who traveled at that time (1920–1921) from Russia to Czechoslovakia in order to return again as a war prisoner to Russia. This was a general method employed for courier service between the Moscow Center and the Czechoslovakian Party. At that time it was practically impossible to procure a passport and visa for couriers in order to travel from Russia to Prague and back. In this difficult situation—it is no longer an indiscretion to speak about it—they made use of the transports of war prisoners between both countries. The respective person must know Czechoslovakian and Russian.

In the following, the concrete method of using this is shown. Hrasche "left Moscow after a direct order of the Czechoslovakian delegates at the Second Congress of the Comintern (among them were, for example, Milosch, Vanjek, Antonin Zapotecky, J. Handlirsch). . . ."

Mr. Handlirsch gave to the authors of the statement a written declaration in which he mentions that in 1921 he "met Hrasche in the Lubianka (the name of the building of the G.P.U. in Moscow) where he intervened for the liberation of some Czechoslovakians arrested by the Cheka."

The documents I refer to contain other information of Hrasche's activities in the question of his accusation of these three Danish engineers. Hrasche accused these three Danes, during the trial, of being his accomplices. In that, I must say, he expressly involves Wienfeld, and only by inference involves Lund and Nielsen. We have quotations, excerpts from the Danish newspapers collected in a statement written by a political émigré living in Copenhagen, whose name is written as Friedrich. His real name will be communicated to the Commission in private session. I shall communicate to you the contents of these newspaper articles.

This declaration, given by the engineer Windfeld-Hansen—Windfeld-Hansen is really Wienfeld, the same one indicated by Hrasche in the testimony. He says:

> Since my name has been mentioned in connection with the Moscow trial, I consider it necessary in my own interest to give a brief report regarding my connections with the accused Grasche and regarding my activity as adviser to the Commissariat of heavy industry in 1932–1934.
>
> The said Grasche during these years held the position of head of the foreign bureau of the Russian nitrogen industry. In this capacity he was in charge of concluding contracts with foreign suppliers of machines for the

Russian nitrogen factories, of arranging furthermore the conditions of work and of life of the foreign engineers and technicians who worked in the Russian nitrogen industry. In 1933 their number still amounted to about 200, of various nationalities. When I arrived in Moscow for the first time, in May, 1932, to work as adviser, my conditions of work were similarly arranged in Grasche's office. Since during the first year I had no apartment of my own, I lived in an apartment of the nitrogen trust's building. In the same apartment Grasche lived in a poor room. In this way I knew him very closely, and held him in high esteem, since he was a very cultured and intelligent man. I never observed anything which might lead one to believe that he was engaged in sabotage or espionage; quite on the contrary. So far as I can remember, he did a great deal of work, concerned himself much with foreign engineers, and did everything to utilize their experience in the best way.

I noticed that this sometimes provoked dissatisfaction among the Russian engineers. Grasche was an old member of the Party and lived in an extremely modest manner, with a low salary, and I never saw him in possession of important pecuniary means. In the last period of my activity I had at my disposal a three-room apartment and had my own household. Grasche was frequently my guest and at my house met the other Danes whose names have been mentioned along with mine during the trial, but I never noticed that he had a suspicious connection with them. When my work in the service of the Government was ended, I again visited Moscow in the summer of 1935 to attempt, with Grasche's support, to interest the competent authorities in the chemical center in some inventions concerning calcium phosphate which, in my opinion, could be of great interest for the chemical industry of the Soviet Union. My plan failed due to the resistance of certain professors and engineers, and moreover I was refused permission of sojourn, so that the negotiations could not be continued.

Rataichak, who directed the principal chemical center, I saw only twice in my life, when he presided at sessions of the Commissariat. I know nothing more about him. I have never seen Pyatakov and I never sent him letters or packages.

It is self-evident that I carried out neither espionage nor sabotage, nor any anti-Soviet activity, but on the contrary, I placed all my experience and ability to work at the service of the institutions in which I worked; I did everything to avoid the mistakes which were committed, often of great proportions, and on these occasions I often had to fight vigorously with the Russian specialists. In these controversies I was often supported by Grasche or his staff, and especially by Kjaerulf-Nielsen who, being a member of the Russian Party, felt himself obliged to aid me with all his power. I am evidently convinced that none of the Danes mentioned did anything of which they are accused. We were all sympathetic to the cause and loved to help in the work of enlightenment wherever we could. I can not venture an opinion as to the motives which led Grasche to launch his accusations, baseless from every point of view. In so far as I myself am concerned, I wish only to add that I am neither Communist nor Trotskyite nor a member of any political party or group. I do not regret the two years and the work that I devoted to the chemical industry of the U.S.S.R.; I regret only that my experience could not have been better utilized.

Another personal interview with Windfeld-Hansen by the liberal daily newspaper, *Politiken*, and in this interview he said:

> Mr. Winfeld-Hansen ended his report with some fine words about the accused Grasche who accomplished great work and who—although millions and millions of German marks for the erection of nitrogen factories passed through his hands—received a very small salary, not more than 400 rubles per month. This high Soviet functionary, a Marxist of a high level and an extraordinary dialectician, really lived in entirely undeserved conditions.

The second Danish citizen mentioned in the trial, S. Lund, author of a novel "Bread and Steel," stated on January 29, 1937:

> Sigvard Lund, who was named as one of the Trotskyites with whom the accused Grasche, according to his "confessions," was in connection, yesterday addressed himself to *Socialdemokraten* with a denial. Mr. Lund declares that he is affiliated to no party, including the Trotskyites. His trip to Russia, he says, had the sole purpose of orientation for his literary activity, and he did not return suddenly and deceived.

Then there is a quotation from one of the leaders of the Danish Communist Party which says:

> We asked Thoeger Thoegersen, who returned last autumn from a sojourn of several years in Russia, his opinion on this question and he replied:
>
> *I think that everything Grasche said in the cross examination is invented.* But on the other hand it evidently is not excluded that the Danes participated in the Trotskyite plot. I know in any case that the engineer Winfeld-Hansen was employed in the chemical industry, with which Pyatakov had dealings as Vice-Commissar of Heavy Industry,

and that Strandgaard is in Russia each summer. In 1932 he had some connection with Intourist.

We have a letter from someone whose name we do not care to mention in public. We will refer to him as "W." In this letter "W" states that he visited Copenhagen in March, 1937. He was sent especially, by the way, to find out all about the activity of these Danish engineers.

DEWEY: Sent by whom?

GOLDMAN: Sent by the American Committee for the Defense of Leon Trotsky. He tells us in this letter that he has interviewed Windfeld-Hansen, and that Windfeld-Hansen will send very important documents to the Commission containing his analysis of the testimony of Hrasche, and containing also his analysis of what actually occurred in the years 1932 and 1933, when he was there with reference to the management of the chemical industry. We will give you this letter as an indication of what the latter actually felt.

In this letter, or another letter by the same person, dated April 1st, 1937, reporting conversations that the writer of the letter had with Windfeld-Hansen—this letter gives the conversation. We simply give it to the Commission for whatever it is worth, and we state that the documents which Windfeld-Hansen is preparing for the Commission will appear later—some very interesting documents by a man who was actually in Russia, an engineer working with Hrasche.

FINERTY: Mr. Goldman, you stated that you would furnish the Commission the correct names of some of the people identified with pseudonyms?

GOLDMAN: Yes.

FINERTY: Are you keeping a copy of that? Perhaps the transcript will not be written up before we leave. We should have these names communicated to us before we leave.

GOLDMAN: Yes. When we take the names out of the exhibits, we shall know what names we have concealed from the public. We shall give these names to the Commission.

FINERTY: Before?

GOLDMAN: Before the Commission leaves, that will be done. I call the Commission's attention to an article written by Dr. Ciliga, a Yugoslavian, or rather an Italian citizen but actually a Yugoslavian, who was a member of the Yugoslavian Communist Party.

TROTSKY: A member of the Politburo of the Communist Party.

GOLDMAN: A member of the Politburo of the Communist Party. He came to Russia as a Stalinist, but later on became a sympathizer of the Left Opposition. He was arrested, but finally succeeded in getting out of the Soviet Union. We call the Commissioners' attention to the article published in the *International Review,* Volume II, Number 2, where he describes the conditions, from personal observation, under which the engineers are forced to confess to sabotage while they are in the presence of the G.P.U. I will merely read some of that article. I will read certain excerpts: "Among the engineers there were some who had 'confessed' their participation in sabotage. We were in the period of the monstrous 'sabotage' trials."

In referring to the trials of Ramzin, the trials of certain engineers that took place some years ago, he says: "Little by little, with some difficulty, I learned the story of their troubles: their connection with 'sabotage.'" Then follows the story of how the engineers confessed.

FINERTY: Mr. Goldman, I think the record should identify these sabotage trials. Was it 1930?

TROTSKY: 1931.

GOLDMAN: 1931.

FINERTY: How were they officially known?

GOLDMAN: They were officially known, I think, as the Industrial Trials.

TROTSKY: The Trials of the Industrial Party.

GOLDMAN: The engineer who confessed says as follows:

> They kept me for five months in isolation without newspapers, without anything to read, without mail, without any contact with the outside, without a visit from my family. I was hungry. I suffered from solitude. They insisted I should confess to an act of sabotage that had never taken place. I refused to assume the guilt for crimes that had not even been committed. But I was told that if I was really for the Soviet power, as I said I was, I should confess to the charge, as the Soviet power needed my confession; I was assured that I should have no fear of the consequences. The Soviet power would take into consideration my open-hearted confession and give me the chance to work and repair my mistakes with work. *As soon as I confessed, I'd have visits from my family, correspondence, walks, newspapers.* But if I remained obstinate and persisted in saying nothing, I should have to bear pitiless repression. Not only I, but my wife and my children . . . For months I resisted. But the situation became unbearable. Nothing, it seemed to me, could be worse. At any rate, I actually became indifferent to what people might say. I signed every statement offered by the examining judge.
>
> After this engineer "confessed," the G.P.U. really gave him all they had promised. That way, no less than by terror, the G.P.U. buy human beings, leading them little by little on the road to lying declarations. But morally the engineer was completely crushed by his conduct. He walked about the cell like a man with a broken heart. And that is the crisis that must have been suffered by many accused who had saved themselves by falsely confessing to "sabotage." Sometimes this moral crisis ended in

suicide, but that is another topic. That belongs under the heading of "consequences."

GOLDMAN: And here he goes on and gives his conclusions. I need not read it, but it has been suggested before that the general Commission invite Dr. Ciliga to the United States for the hearing, or else send a sub-commission to France, where I believe he is now.

TROTSKY: Permit me to add that Ciliga passed about five years in Soviet prisons.

GOLDMAN: Here I produce an important document which will throw—

FINERTY: Mr. Goldman, before you go ahead, did you intend to suggest by something you said prior that Hrasche was a member of the G.P.U.?

GOLDMAN: I didn't say anything of the kind. I simply stated that in accordance with his testimony, or, rather, if you will read the testimony, in accordance with what Vyshinsky puts in his mouth—under the American system it would be unbearable, a leading question—he was a spy of the Czechoslovakian Intelligence Service in 1922, and later of the German Intelligence Service.

FINERTY: You mean the same person who had served the G.P.U.?

GOLDMAN: It is just a statement. I see nothing relevant in it except that he was in Moscow, a trusted member of the Party, that he went to the G.P.U. house for the purpose of intervening for some Czechoslovakians who had been arrested by the G.P.U.

FINERTY: You have no evidence directly connecting him with membership in the G.P.U.?

GOLDMAN: No evidence.

TROTSKY: It is absolutely excluded that a foreigner would be sent abroad on a special mission without authorization or without a special commission from the G.P.U.

FINERTY: In that sense—

TROTSKY: In that sense I am absolutely sure that Hrasche, in the periods referred to—I don't know Hrasche personally—but from my general experience in these matters, he was an agent of the G.P.U.

FRANKEL: The document from the former Czech Party leaders indicates this hypothesis, that he was a member of the G.P.U.

GOLDMAN: Now, I refer to an opinion given by members, by prominent members, of the French trade unions, the miners' trade unions, who were present in Russia at the time of the trial involving the engineers of Kemerovo last November, and other so-called Trotskyites who were accused of causing an explosion in a certain mine in the Kuznets Basin.

FINERTY: Are you speaking of the second Moscow trial?

GOLDMAN: No.

FINERTY: Are you speaking of the sabotage trials?

GOLDMAN: I was going to say, this trial was held in November, 1936—Novosibirsk trial in Novosibirsk.

TROTSKY: It plays a role in the last trial.

GOLDMAN: The same testimony that was presented at the Novosibirsk trial was adduced in the last trial.

TROTSKY: Drobnis and Muralov.

GOLDMAN: Drobnis and Muralov. I refer to the testimony of Drobnis beginning on page 212 of the Reports. Beginning with the second sentence from the top of page 212, Drobnis testified:

> The second task was to reduce the output of coal, and, in addition, to damage the ventilation system, fill the pits with gas and cause explosions. In July, 1935, Noskov reported to me that he had completed preparations for the explosion of the "Tsentralnaya" Mine, which was in his charge. I approved of this.
>
> *Vyshinsky:* When did he say that he had completed

preparations for the explosion at the "Tsentralnaya" Mine?

Drobnis: This conversation took place in the beginning or the middle of July, 1936.

Vyshinsky: And did you discuss with him under what conditions this explosion was to take place?

Drobnis: Noskov said that such a wrecking measure as allowing gas to accumulate in the mine would result in explosion and would cause loss of life. I replied: well, then, we must be ready for this, too. It would even be a good thing, because it would arouse the resentment of the workers which will enable us to win their sympathies.

Vyshinsky: That is to say, you not only approved of Noskov's plan for an explosion in the mine, but even gave your sanction to the explosion taking place under conditions which would directly involve the death of workers?

Drobnis: Yes.

Vyshinsky: With all the consequences?

Drobnis: Yes.

Vyshinsky: You said that workers were bound to be killed?

Drobnis: I asked Noskov whether such a wrecking act could be performed without loss of life. He told me that it was out of the question. Thereupon I said that there was no use being finicky and that we must be ready for this.

Vyshinsky: How did you explain that?

Drobnis: I said that . . . that we must . . . I already explained that we must be prepared for this, too, that it would even . . . and even if it did cause loss of life it would also arouse the resentment of the workers, and that would be in our favor.

Vyshinsky: But this is not what you tried to assert here. You just said that you asked Noskov whether the sacrifice of life could not be avoided. But it follows from what you said that, far from being opposed to sacrifice of life, you thought, to the contrary, that the more lives lost the better for you.

Drobnis: Well, yes, that's so, more or less. . . .

Vyshinsky: Well, I realize that it is of course somewhat inconvenient for you to speak of such things here in public. But there is nothing to be done about it. Did you say that there was nothing to shrink from?

Drobnis: I did.

Vyshinsky: And that meant that if workers were to perish, as a result, well, let them perish. Did you encourage Noskov?

Drobnis: Yes.

Vyshinsky: You encouraged him with regard to the killing of workers, and even said that the more there were killed the better. Did I understand you to say that?

Drobnis: Yes.

Vyshinsky: That is, I am exaggerating nothing?

Drobnis: You are exaggerating a little.

Vyshinsky: Let us make this clear, let us recall the facts. Did you say to Noskov that the more victims the better?

Drobnis: Yes.

Vyshinsky: What, then, am I exaggerating?

Drobnis: I did not mean by this that he should kill more.

Vyshinsky: Did you think that if you said "more" he would understand you to mean "less," that he would understand you to mean that you wanted to reduce the loss of life?

Drobnis: I wanted to reduce. . . .

Vyshinsky: Yet you said, let there be more, and even explained why more deaths were necessary. You said, let there be more victims, since that would arouse the resentment of the workers. The greater the number of victims, the less the resentment?

Drobnis: No, on the contrary.

Vyshinsky: The greater the number of victims, the greater the resentment?

Drobnis: Yes.

Vyshinsky: Is that what you wanted?

Drobnis: Yes, in effect, that is what I wanted.

Vyshinsky: In effect—or did you want it? Speak plainly.

Drobnis: I fully and completely confirm the testimony I gave at the preliminary investigation.

Vyshinsky: Why confirm? You are now in court, and you can give testimony without confirming the old testimony.

Drobnis: I am not quibbling; I fully and completely confirm my earlier testimony.

Vyshinsky: Did you speak to Noskov about preparations for an explosion in the "Tsentralnaya" Mine?

Drobnis: Yes.

Vyshinsky: Did Noskov ask you, or did you ask him, what about the people? Who asked the question?

Drobnis: Noskov.

Vyshinsky: He asked you what about the workers? Is that true?

Drobnis: Yes.

Vyshinsky: And you first said that you asked whether loss of life could not be avoided. What did you answer?

Drobnis: I said that we must be prepared for this.

Vyshinsky: "For this," for what?

Drobnis: For the sacrifice of workers.

Vyshinsky: What does "sacrifice" mean?

Drobnis: It means murder.

Vyshinsky: And how did you justify it?

Drobnis: The more victims the better.

Vyshinsky: For whom?

Drobnis: For the wrecking work.

Vyshinsky: For the Trotskyites?

Drobnis: Yes.

Vyshinsky: Why?

Drobnis: Because this might arouse the resentment of the workers against the Soviet government.

Vyshinsky: Arouse the resentment of the workers against the Soviet government—was that your aim?

Drobnis: Yes.

Vyshinsky: And it was for this that you were willing to resort to any means, even the murder of workers?

Drobnis: Yes.

Vyshinsky: What, then, am I exaggerating?

Drobnis: Nothing.

Vyshinsky: Then this explosion was effected?

Drobnis: I was arrested on August 6, and the explosion took place on September 23.

Vyshinsky: But you sanctioned the explosion?

Drobnis: I sanctioned it at the end or in the middle of July.

Vyshinsky: Consequently, your arrest did not prevent the explosion from being effected, because Noskov remained at the mine?

Drobnis: Yes.

Vyshinsky: And could it have been prevented?

Drobnis: Prevented? Of course it could.

Vyshinsky: Who could have prevented it?

Drobnis: I could have prevented it.

Vyshinsky: You did not prevent it?

Drobnis: I did not prevent it.

Vyshinsky: The explosion was effected?

Drobnis: Yes.

Vyshinsky: I have no more questions.

TROTSKY: Permit me to add that Drobnis was an old member of the revolutionary movement, the Bolshevik Party. He was twice condemned to death by the Whites, and once fusillated.

INTERPRETER: Shot.

TROTSKY: Shot by the Whites without the necessary efficiency, and then found among the corpses, living. Now, he was shot with all the necessary efficiency.

GOLDMAN: Now, I want to read just a few lines of the President of the court, instead of Vyshinsky.

> *The President:* Accused Drobnis, did you advise Noskov, in case everything came out and he was questioned, on whom he was to lay the blame for these diversive and wrecking acts?
>
> *Drobnis:* Yes.
>
> *The President:* What instructions did you give Noskov if he should be called to account?
>
> *Drobnis:* To lay all the blame on the non-Party specialists.
>
> *The President:* Even on those who were in no way involved?
>
> *Drobnis:* Well, of course.

GOLDMAN: Now, I read an opinion of French trade unionists with reference to the explosion of the "Tsentralnaya" Mine.

TROTSKY: Will you say who they are?

GOLDMAN: I think it is mentioned here. "At the time of the trial of the 'sabotaging' engineers of Kemerovo last November, there was in the U.S.S.R. a delegation of the National Federation of Miners of the C.G.T. of France." This is the federation of labor in France. The letter goes on to say:

> . . . It included, among others, the national secretary, Vigne, and the associate secretary, Kléber Legay. The ac-

cusations were communicated to them. As professional men, they refused to believe it, and on their return to France Kléber Legay sent a letter to Magdeleine Paz in which he showed, from the technical point of view, the absurdity of the official accusations against the engineers who "had kept the mine pits in a permanent explosive state."

K. Legay wrote:

> There were five of us: Vigne, secretary of the National Federation of French Miners; Sinot, secretary of the Carmaux Miners; Planque, miners' delegate to Vermelles (Pas de Calais), and Quinet, Communist deputy, who went to hear the lecture and the explanations of the interpreter Smerling.
>
> I can still see my friend Vigne indignantly saying to Smerling, "It is singular to note how all your accused not only recognize their guilt, but mutually accuse each other of the most unbelievable things."
>
> We did not and never will believe, we told Smerling, the accusations they bear, and this is why:
>
> Responsible unions (of the U.S.S.R.) told us that a very stringent service for the inspection of the mines existed.
>
> It functioned in the following manner:
>
> 1. An engineer, designated by the People's Commissar;
>
> 2. Local and inter-local presidents of the workers' unions, designated by the workers themselves;
>
> 3. Delegates of the pits, of sections of the mines, also designated by the workers.
>
> These delegates, it seems, have full power. They can stop a mine, a section of a mine, or the yards, if they think there is some danger or even the threat of danger.

We cannot understand how, with such an apparatus for the inspection and safety of the mines, it could be possible for the engineers to operate under complete secrecy for the preparations of such crimes, and above all over a period of years.

As a miner, and knowing perfectly the difficulty of mining, and having worked more than 30 years, during 12 of them as a delegate for the security of the workers in one of the most gaseous mines in France, I defy any technician, no matter how competent, systematically to put a mine in an explosive state without the inspectors, even if they were complete idiots, perceiving it within the hour.

If the inspector of the security of the Kemerovo mines was not aware of it, he was either an accomplice or he did not exist.

If he did exist, he is even more guilty than the others accused, and since it is the mode in Moscow to shoot, he should have been the first to be shot.

If he did not exist, we were lied to about the protection of the worker's safety. In that case, what can one think of the men in power if they lie, even to their guests, on the gravest questions?

Even if the service for the inspection of safety did not exist, I still say it is impossible to place a mine in an explosive state without its being remarked.

There were the superintendence, inspection, thousands of workers at work in these mines, who should have seen it, he said.

Is one to admit that all, even though they knew their lives were in danger, would have kept quiet, only for the purpose of establishing with greater certainty the proof of the guilt of the accused, even though at one moment or another all might have perished if the condition existed?

No; technically, by the assent of everyone, it is im-

> possible to keep a mine in a permanent explosive state by the accumulation of fire-damp.
>
> The least informed person on mining affairs would say as we do: One could never believe in such a possibility.

FINERTY: Mr. Goldman, is that part of the testimony of the experts of the prosecution?

STOLBERG: In the Novosibirsk trial?

FINERTY: Mr. Goldman says it is the same explosion as that with which the Moscow trial is concerned. Does this information of the French trade unionists apply to the testimony of the experts for the prosecution in the second Moscow trial, on pages 451–456?

GOLDMAN: I am inclined to believe that this information refers to the testimony of the experts in the Novosibirsk trial.

TROTSKY: Yes.

GOLDMAN: I am not positive from a reading of the pages of the Verbatim Report whether the testimony in the Novosibirsk trial was the same as the testimony of the experts in the last trial. Drobnis, in giving the reason—I read the testimony of Drobnis. He mentions on page 212 that, "the second task was to reduce the output of coal and, in addition, to damage the ventilation system, fill the pits with gas, and cause explosions." That is why I assume that the testimony—and I believe Drobnis was involved in Novosibirsk—

TROTSKY: As a witness.

GOLDMAN: As a witness. That this testimony is the same information. The French trade unionists refer to this particular explosion. Obviously, as far as information is concerned, it deals with these experts who might have testified that it resulted from an accumulation of gas. But whether or not the experts testified in the last trial about this particular thing, I don't know. From a reading of the experts' testimony I am not sure that the "Tsentralnaya" mentioned was identified.

FINERTY: It is not identified here. But the technique seems to be the same—the technique attributed to the saboteurs seems to be the same.

GOLDMAN: Except in the Report, the technique involves false construction, which this information does not in any way deal with.

TROTSKY: Mr. Chairman, permit me to add some remarks. The Federation of Miners in France has now about a million members. Both secretaries are reformists and adversaries of the Trotskyites. The federation includes Stalinists and reformists. They were invited to Russia as friends.

FINERTY: Friends of Stalin?

TROTSKY: Friends of the bureaucracy. They made the trip in the company of a Stalinist deputy, a parliamentary deputy. He was the fifth in the group. They are all my terrible adversaries.

FINERTY: May I also ask if you have the transcript of the Novosibirsk trial? Is it available?

GOLDMAN: As far as I know, the transcript of the Novosibirsk trial was not written up.

TROTSKY: Only in Russian in the *Pravda* in fragments.

GOLDMAN: Now, the last of my exhibits in the question of "sabotage" I wish to introduce after I put some questions to Mr. Trotsky.

Mr. Trotsky, with reference to the industrialization of the Soviet Union, what was your attitude prior to your expulsion from the Soviet Union?

TROTSKY: During the period from 1922 until 1929 I fought for the necessity of an accelerated industrialization. I wrote in the beginning of 1925 a book in which I tried to prove that by planning and direction of industry it was possible to have a yearly coefficient of industrialization up to twenty. I was denounced at that time as a fantastic man, a super-industrializer. It was the official name for the Trotskyites at that time: Super-industrializers.

GOLDMAN: What was the name of the book that you wrote?

TROTSKY: "Whither Russia, Toward Capitalism or Socialism?"

GOLDMAN: In English it was published, I am quite sure, under the title, "Whither Russia, Towards Capitalism or Socialism?"

TROTSKY: The march of events showed that I was too cautious in my appreciation of the possibility of planned economy, not too courageous. It was my fight between 1922 and 1925, and also the fight for the Five-Year Plan. It begins with the year 1923, when the Left Opposition began to fight for the necessity of using the Five-Year Plan.

GOLDMAN: And Stalin at that time called you a "super-industrialist"?

TROTSKY: Yes.

GOLDMAN: He was opposed to the rapid industrialization of the country?

TROTSKY: Permit me to say that in 1927, when I was chairman of the commission at Dnieprostroy for a hydro-electric station, a power station, I insisted in the session of the Central Committee on the necessity of building up this station. Stalin answered, and it is published: "For us to build up the Dnieprostroy station is the same as for a peasant to buy a gramophone instead of a cow."

GOLDMAN: When the plans for the first Five-Year Plan first came out, what criticisms did you make of them?

TROTSKY: What?

FINERTY: Mr. Goldman, may I suggest that you ask when the first Five-Year Plan came out? You mean the official Five-Year Plan?

GOLDMAN: Can you give us the time when the first Five-Year Plan was officially placed before the Soviet Union and the world?

TROTSKY: I believe October, 1928, towards the end of 1932, because—

GOLDMAN: You mean the Five-Year Plan was started in 1928?

TROTSKY: Yes, and finished in 1932. The plan was transformed into a Four-Year Plan. They changed the beginning of the economic year from October to January.

GOLDMAN: At first it was a Five-Year Plan and then subsequently it was changed to be completed into a Four-Year Plan?

FINERTY: What I would like to know is when the Government of Stalin, the Government first promulgated the Five-Year Plan, not when it first started, but when it first announced it.

GOLDMAN: When the Soviet Government first announced the plan?

TROTSKY: The Five-Year Plan had a long pre-history. It was elaborated, I believe—the beginning of the elaboration was 1926 or even 1925. The first plan was not announced publicly, but presented only to the Politburo. It was a plan in which the first year had a coefficient of nine, the second eight or seven, the last year only four—a declining line of growth. That was the beginning of a terrible fight. I named this plan "The Sabotage of Industry," not in the criminal sense as here charged, but in the sense that it was an absolutely cowardly conception of the possibilities created by the October Revolution. The second plan, elaborated in 1926, had a general coefficient of nine for all the five years. The Commissioners can find that in the book, "The Real Situation in Russia," in our platform. That was the second plan. At that time I fought for the possibility, and I tried to prove the possibility of having a coefficient of twenty—until twenty.

INTERPRETER: As high as.

TROTSKY: As high as twenty, or to be more correct, eighteen. Because I showed that the growth of bourgeois or capitalist industry was six under the Tsar, and I tried to prove that it was possible to double and triple it.

DEWEY: Mr. Trotsky, both—or what you call the first and second plans—were promulgated by the Left Opposition?

TROTSKY: We began the fight for the Five-Year Plan in 1922 or 1923.

DEWEY: And all of these were by the Opposition—all of these plans were presented by the Opposition?

TROTSKY: By the State Planning Commission, by the official State Planning Commission as the incarnation of the spirit of cowardice, economic cowardice. We accused them of "sabotaging" in this sense, as I explained.

DEWEY: How was that "sabotaging"—

TROTSKY: It was not bad will by the authors of the plan. I used the word "sabotage" here in quotations, in a polemical sense, in a journalistic sense.

DEWEY: Mr. Trotsky, both were presented by the State Planning Commission. Who refused to put them into effect? That is all I want to know.

TROTSKY: That was the first. After our criticism, the first plan was rejected by the Politburo. The second, with the coefficient of nine, was confirmed by the Politburo, was adopted by the Politburo with nine the first average.

FINERTY: A constant coefficient, you said.

TROTSKY: Yes, constant for the five years. We gave the criticism in our platform. The results of the first year showed that we were right. Then they changed the plan. That is the genuine history of the first Five-Year Plan.

GOLDMAN: That is, after the completion of the first year of the Five-Year Plan, they changed the plan. The Soviet authorities changed the plan to coincide more with the plans of the original—

TROTSKY: With the reality, or the prognosis of the Opposition coincided with the realities.

FINERTY: You mean the actual coefficient of the first year was nearer eighteen than nine?

TROTSKY: It was more than twenty.

GOLDMAN: During the progress of the Five-Year Plan, did you express any opinions in writing with reference to the methods used by the Soviet authorities in completing the Five-Year Plan?

TROTSKY: During the second year the bureaucracy proposed to accomplish the Five-Year Plan in four years. In the *Bulletin* I protested vehemently. All impractical men—it is very characteristic of impractical men that before they began, they did not foresee the correct possibilities, but that when the possibilities were realized against themselves they were very frightened by the possibilities, and then saw no limits. They began, under the whip of the bureaucracy, to raise the coefficients without paying any attention to the living conditions of the workers. They built up factories, but no houses for the workers. It was necessary now to have a coefficient of 30 per cent and 35 per cent.

GOLDMAN: What was there to the contention that it was necessary to make haste in order to defend—prepare the Soviet Union for defense against a possible attack?

TROTSKY: I wrote, and it was published and translated in several languages, that this hasty bureaucratic industrialization signified the inevitable accumulation of inner contradictions in industry itself. In the capitalist system, the necessary proportions are reached by competition between different capitalists, capitalist industries and enterprises. But in a planned economy it is necessary to foresee all the necessary proportions. It is not possible to foresee by abstractions. It is necessary to foresee, correct and perfect the plan by the opinion of the people, by the experience of the people, by the degree of satisfaction of its needs, by the proportion between the different industries, the different factories, and even the different sections of the same factories. Nobody built up Socialist economy before us. It is the first experience and the greatest in history. And then I warned more cautiously: "It is not possible to run away with yourselves. You will land in a crisis."

GOLDMAN: Now, from your information derived from a reading of the Soviet press, what can you tell us now about the successes of industrialization or the defects of industrialization, if anything?

DEWEY: We will take a short recess now.

GOLDMAN: Read the last question. (Previous question read by the reporter.)

TROTSKY: My attitude toward the economic development of the Soviet Union can be characterized as follows: I defend the Soviet economy against the capitalist critics and the Social Democratic reformist critics, and I criticize the bureaucratic methods of the leadership. The deductions were very simple. They were based on the Soviet press itself. We have a certain freedom from the bureaucratic hypnosis. It was absolutely possible to see all of the dangers on the basis of the Soviet press itself.

GOLDMAN: Can you give us an idea, very generally, of the successes of the industrialization in the Soviet Union?

TROTSKY: The successes are very important, and I affirmed it every time. They are due to the abolition of private property and to the possibilities inherent in planned economy. But, they are—I cannot say exactly—but I will say two or three times less than they could be under a régime of Soviet democracy.

GOLDMAN: So the advances are due, in spite of the bureaucratic control and methods?

TROTSKY: They are due to the possibilities inherent in the socialization of the productive forces.

GOLDMAN: Before I go any further, Mr. Chairman, will you permit me to make a statement for the record? In one of the Mexican papers this morning there is an affirmation that Mr. Trotsky has refused to present his documents to the Commission, and the reason for the refusal is given as his lack of confidence in the Commission. Mr. Trotsky profoundly regrets this extremely unkind affirmation about people who enjoy world-wide confidence. He has never refused to present any document to the Commission. Entirely on the contrary, he places at the disposal of the Commission all his archives without the slightest exception. He has only requested of the President of the Commission authorization (a) not to name in public session the places where the different parts of his archives are located, (b) not to cite in public session names and circumstances which might hurt a third person in fascist countries or in the U.S.S.R.

The Commission was unanimous in authorizing Mr. Trotsky to present supplementary explanations about the archives, etc. (explanations of a purely technical and nonpolitical nature), in a private administrative session of the Commission.

Mr. Trotsky has a too great consideration for the Mexican press and for the paper in question to admit for a single moment that there is involved a spiteful interpretation of his words. There can only be a question of a deplorable misunderstanding. Mr. Trotsky hopes that this declaration will be printed in the paper in question, and that the incident will in this way be closed. Mexican public opinion will only gain by that.

I will ask Mr. Beals to translate that.

BEALS: May I ask you to give the name of the paper, or if you don't wish to, communicate it to the Commission privately?

(Commissioner Beals translates Attorney Goldman's statement into Spanish.)

DEWEY: May I state that the Commission clearly understands that Mr. Trotsky has offered to submit, and will submit, to the Commission, all documents relative to the inquiry, and that the Commission has already agreed that certain names should be presented in administrative or executive session.

GOLDMAN: Mr. Trotsky, can you tell us—

FINERTY: Mr. Goldman, I think it should be understood, in your interest, that the Commission has agreed that certain of these names be communicated to us privately, so that these witnesses may not be apprehended by the fascist Governments or the Soviet Government.

DEWEY: That is correct.

GOLDMAN: Will you briefly tell us your attitude to the collectivization of 1928?

TROTSKY: It was parallel to my attitude toward industrialization, with a certain delay. Our fight for collectivization began a year or eighteen months later than our fight for industrialization. Our fight against the hasty collectivization also a year later than our fight against the hasty industrialization. In the Five-Year Plan adopted by the Politburo, not in the second version but in the third version with the high coefficient for industry—it was adopted that at the end of the Five-Year Plan the Soviet Union would have 20 to 22 per cent of the peasants in collective farms. But in the third year it was more than 60 per cent—in the third year of the plan. It was decided that all peasants must be collectivized during the first plan.

We protested that this was not possible: "You do not have the necessary agricultural machinery—tractors, and so on; and, what is more important, the necessary level of culture in the country, no roads, no cultivated technicians, and so forth."

GOLDMAN: What is your opinion at the present time on the successes of the collectivization in the Soviet Union?

TROTSKY: It is more difficult than with industry. I must say that the Soviet statistics—and I say it with great regret—are almost as false as the indictments. I know by my own experience that honest statisticians, who tried to present the situation as it is, were imprisoned and sent to Siberia, because their expositions were in contradiction with the conjunctural plans of the bureaucracy. In the names of the chiefs of the statistical bureau, the most important collaborators, you can find the different phases of the development of the ideas of the Politburo. The statistics are totalitarianized. That is why even people who are educated and proceed theoretically must proceed empirically here, by some isolated facts in the Soviet press.

Concerning industry it is easier, because industry is concentrated. Agriculture is dispersed, and that is why a general appreciation is more difficult. But I never denied the successes of collectivization. On the contrary, I defended the collectivization against the bourgeois critics and the reformist critics. But at the same time I tried to defend the collectivization against the Soviet bureaucracy. This complete collectivization during five years did not give the economic, the necessary economic results, but it gave—I don't know the figures, but it is hundreds, thousands and millions of exterminated peasants.

GOLDMAN: You were opposed to the administrative measures of collectivization?

TROTSKY: That is a totally correct expression. I insisted that the collectivization, which supposes a more—or, rather, the highest—level of activity or dependence on the peasants, their capacity for collective social work, that the advance towards collectivization must be accomplished with the conscious agreement of the peasants themselves. That it was necessary to explain to them, to teach them, to win them—not to kill the kulak. I am not afraid of the kulak. The kulaks are peasants who exploit the other peasants. But the actions of the bureaucracy were to kill the kulaks and to push, by these methods, the other peasants into the camp of the hostile elements, by fear.

DEWEY: Mr. Goldman, I understood Mr. Trotsky to say that certain statisticians were imprisoned and exiled because they preferred to proceed honestly.

TROTSKY: Yes.

DEWEY: Where did you derive that information?

TROTSKY: I can name a very scientific man, the authority, Bazarov. He was in his youth a Bolshevik, but he was essentially a scientist. He worked on the Planning Commission and during the trial of the Mensheviks and during the trial mentioned here, of the Industrial Party—there were two members of the Industrial Party and two Mensheviks. The trial of the Industrial Party had as its aim to accuse the specialists and the engineers on the Planning Commission of too cowardly plans. They became the scapegoats of the first Five-Year Plan.

Then came the second trial against the Mensheviks, two Mensheviks, the well known Sukhanov, the historian, and Groman, the economist. They confessed. Now, nobody knows where they are. The third, Bazarov, connected with them, refused to confess. He disappeared, and nobody knows where he is. It was a question of their work on the Planning Commission. Bazarov was one of our best statisticians and mathematicians.

Another was Popov, who was also a chief of the state Statistical Bureau. He was dismissed, and then prosecuted. I don't know his fate, whether he is in prison or in Siberia. But I know very well the reason for it. The man who accomplished this action was Yakovlev, who afterwards was People's Commissar of Agriculture. He presented absolutely false statistics.

GOLDMAN: Did I understand you to mean that the engineers who were placed on trial during this trial of the Industrial Party were responsible for the first version of the original Five-Year Plan?

TROTSKY: Yes.

GOLDMAN: And that the Soviet authorities made them the scapegoats for the slow tempo?

TROTSKY: They minimalized the Socialist possibilities.

GOLDMAN: You mean "minimized."

TROTSKY: Yes, minimized. The pair of engineers did not have their own answers. They showed what they conveyed to the Politburo. Then, with their pencils they showed the figures they gave in the tables and documents. Then, when the situation changed, the Politburo said, "Their documents are bad, the figures are bad. We must shoot them."

BEALS: I just want to ask Mr. Trotsky: The Five-Year Plan, you mentioned, had certain defects due to the bureaucratic conditions. You have also stated that the statistics of the Five-Year Plan are open to doubt because the chairman of the statisticians and others are not allowed to give proper statistics. Third, you have been out of the Soviet Union since before the Five-Year Plan went into effect. What are these—can you state briefly the general sources of information about the Soviet Union if the statistics are false? On what do you base your own statistics?

TROTSKY: The systematic falsification of the statistics began with the year 1926. We had not very good statistics, because statistics correspond to the general level of culture of the country. But we had inherited from Tsarism many bad things and also some good things. The statistics of the "zemstvos," the self-governing bodies in the provinces, gave honest reflections of the situation in the country. There were in the "zemstvos" régime liberals, Socialists, and so on. They were in opposition to the Tsar. Many of them became revolutionists. Then they began to fight, to oppose the tendentious information about the Soviet Union. They had the same fate. That began as a rule at the beginning, or rather, the end of 1925, during the split, on the one side of Zinoviev and Kamenev, and Stalin on the other side. It was during the preparation of the Fourteenth Congress of the Party when all the statistics, the most important statistics, were changed. Yakovlev named the new statistics as statistics.

GOLDMAN: Mr. Trotsky, Mr. Beals wants to know—

TROTSKY: I will answer the question. When one says the truth it is a very simple matter. But when the bureaucracy begins to lie about the whole situation, the different elements of the bureaucracy contradict themselves. It is only possible for an honest man to find the truth by a comparison of the lies. That is a simple exposition of my method. I will give you an example: Stalin presents the results of the Five-Year Plan as a complete success. Molotov, in a speech after Stalin's speech, some weeks after, said in passing that the last year of the Five-Year Plan had a coefficient of only eight, not twenty or more than twenty, as was announced, but only eight. I ask: How was it possible to accomplish the Five-Year Plan in four years if the coefficient of the last year was only eight? Why only eight? Because the contradictions accumulating during the first three years by the bureaucratic whip were so terrible they totally handicapped industry in the last year.

GOLDMAN: In what papers did you read that?

TROTSKY: In *Pravda*. I quoted it officially. I asked them, as I asked Pyatakov, I asked them in my paper: What does the contradiction signify?

GOLDMAN: Where did you get your statistics, from the Soviet Union?

TROTSKY: Yes. You know, you have generalized statistics, a general report of Stalin and of Molotov, and you have the detailed statistics in the papers. It is not possible to oblige or force everybody to say a falsehood. The director of a factory, the director of a branch of industry, in their reports, tell the truth. And his truth on the second floor, or their truths, become falsehoods. I can compare both. I cannot contend that my evaluation is mathematically exact, but it has the privilege of being more honest. Yet mine is nearer to the truth.

GOLDMAN: Is it understood that all your statistics upon which you based your conclusions you derived from the press in the Soviet Union?

TROTSKY: Exclusively.

STOLBERG: From separate statistical reports?

TROTSKY: Yes, from general reports, and those of a scientific character, as far as I can use them, and so on.

GOLDMAN: Does that answer your question?

DEWEY: Does that last statement of yours exclude your having received private or secret information?

TROTSKY: Of economists?

DEWEY: Yes.

TROTSKY: It was absolutely unnecessary. In the past we had general correspondence, but it was all published in the *Bulletin*. The correspondence about the fact that they built up a very good factory, a genuine American factory, and great dams, bigger than in the United States. But the roads remain impracticable—that is, roads leading to factories. There are new houses for the workers. But the houses exist, and no sanitary conditions are prepared. Then the workers, after two or three months of work, become sick with epidemics, and after the second epidemic they go away illegally. The director becomes the scapegoat and is removed from the factory.

GOLDMAN: Did I understand that your answer to Dr. Dewey's question is, that you have no secret information?

TROTSKY: No; everybody who is interested knows it. It is not a military secret.

GOLDMAN: From a reading of the Soviet press?

TROTSKY: From a reading of the Soviet press.

FINERTY: Mr. Trotsky, did I understand you to say that the coefficient was in the last year of the first Five-Year Plan—that is, in 1932—was eight?

TROTSKY: Eight, yes, according to the information of Mr. Molotov.

FINERTY: According to Molotov it was eight, and that was before they charged you with any act of sabotage?

TROTSKY: Yes.

FINERTY: None of these acts of sabotage go beyond 1932?

TROTSKY: I tried to find out the dates when my alleged sabotaging action began. It is very difficult.

FINERTY: They claim the instructions for sabotage were given Radek in 1932.

TROTSKY: Yes, but in the same report you find the affirmation that what was new in 1934 was my instructions about general sabotage actions. After I gave Mr. Goldman all the material I found in my archives a quotation from *Pravda,* from a speech, which says that in 1929 the Trotskyites were saboteurs. But if it was to be understood with quotations or without quotations, is unclear. It is emphatically stated in the first accusation: "You are a Super-industrialist." Then how, by being a Super-industrialist, can you be a saboteur of industry? Trotsky, from his exile, from his powerful exile, disorganized industry in the Soviet Union, in spite of the leadership. It is genuine infallibility. That is the situation today.

GOLDMAN: Now, to substantiate what Mr. Trotsky has testified to with reference to his ideas on industrialization in his criticism of the methods of industrialization and collectivization by the bureaucracy, I offer excerpts from his writings. I thought of reading them, but Mr. Trotsky's analysis, in my opinion, has been sufficient. I shall refer the Commission to the sources, where they can actually read the whole articles referred to by Mr. Trotsky.

The article that was of interest was written by Rakovsky at the time that he was still in Siberia—an article on the Five-Year Plan—published in the *Militant,* New York, 1932, beginning with March 5th and ending March 26th. In short, the article states that

> . . . the growth in quantity was produced, in a decisive measure, not at the cost of an increase in investment capital and not at the cost of an improvement of the tech-

> nical basis, but at the most of a more intensive exploitation of the investment capital that was at hand, with the increase in the number of workers on the one hand and the rise in the intensity of labor on the other.

He speaks here of the quality of production as being very bad, which should be taken into consideration where the question of quantity is concerned.

In the *Militant* of July 23d, 1932, there is an article signed by—there is a letter from Moscow signed "M.M.," that gives an idea of the feelings of the workers toward the hasty and rapid tempo of industrialization. Also, in the *Militant* there are letters from Moscow, October 3d–8th, 1932.

Mr. Trotsky wrote a pamphlet called, "Soviet Economy in Danger." The pamphlet is now out of print, but the contents of the pamphlet were republished in the *Militant* November 12th, 1932, to January 7th, 1933, inclusive. There he speaks about the matters he has referred to in his oral testimony. I just want to read one or two quotations from that pamphlet:

> Every attempt to influence from below the economic management is immediately assigned to a deviation either to the Right or Left; i.e., it is practically made a capital offense. The bureaucratic upper crust, when all is said and done, has pronounced itself infallible in the sphere of Socialist planning (disregarding the fact that its collaborators and inspirers turned out often to be inimical machinators and sabotagers). Thus was liquidated the basic mechanic of Socialist construction—the pliant and elastic system of Soviet Democracy.

In the article on the "Danger of Thermidor," published in the *Militant*, February 4th, 1933, I quote: ". . . Only such reciprocal economic relation between the city and country—

what Lenin called *smytchka*—

TROTSKY: Meaning "connection," or "joined."

GOLDMAN (reading):

> . . . can free the workers' state from the necessity of taking forcible measures against the village to compel the exchange. Only from the moment when the voluntary exchange is assured will the proletarian dictatorship be unshakable. The *smytchka* thus secured, means the closest political alliance of the poor peasantry with the urban workers, the firm support of the decisive masses of the middle peasantry, and, consequently, the political isolation of the kulaks and of all capitalist elements in the country in general. The *smytchka* thus secured means the unshakable loyalty of the Red Army to the proletarian dictatorship, which in view of the successful industrialization and the unlimited human, largely peasant, reserves, will make it possible for the Soviet state to repulse any imperialist intervention . . . The hungry workers are dissatisfied with the policies of the party. The party is dissatisfied with the leadership. The peasantry is dissatisfied with industrialization, with collectivization, with the city. Part of the peasantry is dissatisfied with the régime. What part? We cannot know, but it is clear that under present circumstances it can only grow.

In the *Militant,* of March 18th, 1933, Trotsky wrote a series of articles which were called: "Alarm Signal! Danger Draws Closer in U.S.S.R." In the *Militant,* from May 27th, to June 3d, 1933, Trotsky wrote a series of articles called, "Problems of the Soviet Régime."

In the book or pamphlet, "What Next?" by Trotsky, on pages 134–5, there are matters dealing with Soviet economy.

DEWEY: What year was that?

GOLDMAN: "What Next?" was published in 1932.

TROTSKY: It is directed against German fascism.

GOLDMAN: The book deals with the problems of Germany in that period, with German fascism and the German proletariat, also including some questions dealing with the Soviet Union.

LAFOLLETTE: Isn't that called "Germany, What Next?" in the English edition?

GOLDMAN: The exact title is: "What Next? Vital Questions for the German Proletariat."

This closes the section dealing with the alleged acts of sabotage and acts of diversion. I shall next take up the question of individual terror, the question of the attitude which Mr. Trotsky now has towards the possibility of changing the Stalin régime in the Soviet Union, and towards what means must be used to change the Stalin régime in the Soviet Union.

On the question of Mr. Trotsky's attitude towards individual terror, I refer the Commission to a series of excerpts, and, what is more important, a volume from the collected works of Trotsky, volume IV, in Russian. Excerpts have been translated. I shall read them. The first excerpt on terrorism is not by Trotsky, but from a statement by Zinoviev, in 1911, in Zinoviev's works, published by the State Publishing House in Leningrad in 1924. It is entitled: "The Provocateurs of Nicholas II and the Trial of the Social-Democratic Deputies in the Second Duma." I read:

> In order to give the affair a "polished appearance," they composed a provocative fable saying that our workers' deputies of the Second Duma have carried out a special plot to kill the Tsar. It is not even necessary to mention that it was a complete lie. Our workers' deputies had too much real revolutionary work to do to be occupied with stupid "plots." With Nicholas the Bloody and his whole gang, the insurrectionary people will themselves

finish in due time—this is what the Social-Democracy teaches. Precisely for that reason it *refuses* to undertake any "plot," and devotes all its forces to the organization of the working class, to the cause of the preparation of the mass revolutionary fight. That the fable of the "plot" is the basest provocative invention was known to everybody. This was very well known to the majority of the Second Duma, composed of members of the Cadet Party—

TROTSKY: The Cadets were a bourgeois party.

GOLDMAN (reading):

> . . . although they have been silent about it until the present. The Cadets themselves now recognize this, after four years. Our Social-Democratic deputies of the second Duma tried to unmask this provocation from the tribune of the Duma. But the Cadets kept their mouths shut.

That was from Zinoviev. In 1902 Trotsky wrote: "Not for personal but for a revolutionary vengeance. Not for the execution of Ministers but for the execution of autocracy." In 1909, Trotsky wrote:

> Terrorist work, in its very essence, demands such a concentration of energy upon the "supreme moment," such an overestimation of personal heroism, and, lastly, such an hermetically concealed conspiracy as . . . excluded completely any agitational and organizational activity among the masses. . . . Struggling against terrorism, the Marxian intelligentsia defended their right or their duty not to withdraw from the working-class districts for the sake of tunneling mines underneath the Grand Ducal and Tsarist palaces.

Again in 1909:

> In so far as terror introduces disorganization and demoralization in the ranks of the Government (at the price of disorganizing and demoralizing the ranks of the revolutionists), to that extent it plays into the hands of none other than the liberals themselves.

TROTSKY: Excuse me. Permit me to say that the word "liberal" has in America another sense. It was the possessing classes in Russia, the liberal nobles and bourgeois capitalists.

GOLDMAN: I read again:

> Terrorism in Russia is dead. . . . Terror has migrated far to the East . . . to the provinces of Punjab and Bengal. . .It may be that in other countries of the Orient terrorism is still destined to pass through an epoch of flowering. But in Russia it is already a part of the heritage of history.

Again in January, 1910, Trotsky wrote: "In the blind alley of terrorism, the hand of provocation rules with assurance."

Again in 1910:

> The irreconcilable attitude of the Russian Social Democracy toward the bureaucratized terror of the revolution as a means of struggle against the terrorist bureaucracy of Tsarism has met with bewilderment and condemnation not only among the Russian liberals but also among the European Socialists.

Once more, in 1910, Trotsky wrote:

> Whoever stalks a Ministerial portfolio . . . as well as they who, clasping an infernal machine beneath a cloak,

> stalk the Minister himself, must equally overestimate the Minister—his personality and his post. For them the *system* itself disappears or recedes far away, and there remains only the *individual* invested with power.

The translation here must be very bad.

TROTSKY: Not for the Minister, for the terrorists.

GOLDMAN: We shall get a new translation of this section. In 1911, Trotsky wrote in *Der Kampf*, the theoretical organ of the Austrian Social Democracy:

> Whether or not a terrorist attempt, even if "successful" introduces confusion in the ruling circles, depends upon the concrete political circumstances. In any case, this confusion can only be of short duration. The capitalist state does not rest upon Ministers, and cannot be destroyed together with them. The classes whom the state serves will always find new men—the mechanism remains intact and continues to function. But much deeper is that confusion which the terrorist attempts introduce into the ranks of the working masses. If it is enough to arm oneself with a revolver to reach the goal, then to what end are the endeavors of the class struggle? If a pinch of powder and a slug of lead are ample to shoot the enemy through the neck, where is the need of a class organization? If there is any rhyme or reason in scaring titled personages with the noise of an explosion, what need is there for a party? What is the need of meetings, mass agitation, elections, when it is so easy to take aim at the Ministerial bench from the Parliamentary gallery? Individual terrorism in our eyes is inadmissible precisely for the reason that *it lowers the masses in their own consciousness*, reconciles them to impotence, and directs their glances and hopes toward the great avenger and emancipator who will some day come and accomplish his mission.

On the 28th of December, 1934, four weeks after the Kirov assassination, Trotsky wrote in the *Bulletin of the Opposition:*

> . . . If Marxists have categorically condemned individual terrorism . . . even when the shots were directed against the agents of the Tsarist government and of capitalist exploitation, then all the more relentlessly will they condemn and reject the criminal adventurism of terrorist acts directed against the bureaucratic representatives of the first workers' state in history. The subjective motivations of Nikolayev and his associates are a matter of indifference to us. So long as the Soviet bureaucracy has not been removed by the proletariat, a task which will eventually be accomplished, it fulfills a necessary function in the defense of the workers' state. Should terrorism of the Nikolayev type spread, it could, given other unfavorable circumstances, render service only to the fascist counter-revolution.
>
> Only political fakers who bank on imbeciles would endeavor to lay Nikolayev at the door of the Left Opposition, even if only in the guise of the Zinoviev group as it existed in 1926–1927. The terrorist organization of the Communist youth is fostered not by the Left Opposition but by the bureaucracy, by its internal decomposition. *Individual terrorism, in very essence, is bureaucratism turned inside out.* For Marxists this law was not discovered yesterday. Bureaucratism has no confidence in the masses and endeavors to substitute itself for the masses.

It was published in January, 1935, in No. 41, of the *Bulletin of the Opposition.*

Now, Mr. Trotsky, can you give us your opinion about the Nikolayev assassination of Kirov, the causes, the background of that?

TROTSKY: The general causes are present, more or less, in the last quotations. It is the dissatisfaction of a certain part, if I can say it, the most critical part of the youth—there is a certain historical and political *impasse* for the youth. Every youth can develop only in the atmosphere of a certain liberty of criticism. The youth must oppose the older generation and break the way for themselves. It is almost a physiological law. When all possibilities are hermetically closed, explosions are inevitable. But the reasons, the individual reasons, for the individual Nikolayev have remained absolutely enigmatic up to the present time. You cannot find in the Soviet press under what conditions Nikolayev assassinated Kirov. Had he access to Kirov every day as a secretary? I don't know. Nobody tells about the concrete circumstances. Who was Nikolayev? He remains unknown. In the Soviet press, after the assassination of Kirov, you cannot find any description of this event, of this very important event in the life of society.

My first hypothesis was that it was individual revenge. Maybe certain conflicts about a woman, concerning a woman question, and so on—a situation which could compromise Kirov if it would be published. It was for me the only one explanation for this secrecy.

GOLDMAN: Have you ever written any articles as an appeal to the youth of the Soviet Union to avoid terror?

TROTSKY: Naturally—before the Kirov assassination, in that sense: That certain terroristic tendencies appeared in the youth. We mentioned it as a symptom—that it was not a method of fighting, but as a symptom—to prevent decomposition.

GOLDMAN: You said before, correspondence, you had certain correspondence. What do you mean?

TROTSKY: Letters from Russia?

GOLDMAN: That is what I mean.

TROTSKY: Yes.

GOLDMAN: You received letters from Russia?

TROTSKY: They were published in the *Bulletin*. It was

about liberal bureaucrats, a certain stratum of liberal bureaucrats, who in the family circles criticize the bureaucrats, and refer to Stalin as "him." Then they go about doing their ordinary duties. But the son and daughter develop terrorist tendencies. They hear their father say: "It is a falsehood, it is a frame-up against the family." The son and daughter hear it and say: "We must kill them!" Because they have no other means, no public means of expression. This is the reason for terrorism. It is possible, also, that it was a political act by Nikolayev. I don't know.

GOLDMAN: Did you write a second article, an open letter, warning against these tendencies?

TROTSKY: Yes; it was in my articles concerning the Kirov assassination, or before it, I believe. It is a thing which understands from itself—it is self-explanatory. Our whole tradition of Marxism is directed against it. On every occasion we repeated it. That was an axiom with us.

GOLDMAN: I want to call the Commissioners' attention to a pamphlet written by Trotsky, called "The Kirov Assassination," published in 1935 by the Pioneer publishers. It can be readily obtained in New York. In this pamphlet, Trotsky deals with the general question of terrorism.

LAFOLLETTE: I would like to ask one question. You spoke of letters from Russia in the *Bulletin*. What were the dates of these letters from Russia?

TROTSKY: I am not very sure. I believe it was from 1931–1933. In that period we had some information about the terroristic tendencies among the youth. We published it in the *Bulletin*. I will find it for the Commission and I will present it for translation.

FINERTY: On that occasion, Mr. Trotsky, how do you explain the ability to correspond, to communicate with the *Bulletin*, not having direct communication yourself, with Russia?

TROTSKY: I say, we did not have a systematic—after 1931,

a systematic communication with our friends in Russia. But from time to time we had correspondence in the persons of liberal bureaucrats coming from Russia to Berlin and Paris, who had conversations with our friends; and some even sent letters. They communicated on very interesting things. Then, we used every foreigner sympathizing with us who went as tourist or guest to the Soviet anniversaries. We followed them up and asked them that they report to us when they got back.

FINERTY: Did you also give them written communications for that purpose?

TROTSKY: No; it was too dangerous for them and for our friends. I never proposed it, because it was unnecessary. What could I say to them? I could not say anything to them that I could not say in my writings. You know, I cannot invite an intermediary or a foreigner and say: "Please kill Stalin; please kill Voroshilov." It is not my system of action. I can only say: "Please communicate to me what is the mood of the workers, if you meet them in the factory. Or, if you are in there, tell me if the American technique is really used by the Russians." Because that is a greater historical perspective than the present duel with Stalin. But that is not the way the narrow bureaucracy looks at it.

FINERTY: Did you at any time subsequent to 1931 succeed in sending written communications into Russia?

TROTSKY: Yes; I explained, we sent systematically, postal cards, with my personal point of view, my appreciations. Postal cards are not so severely controlled as letters. And we succeeded from time to time in 1930–1931 or 1929–1930. Very often we reached our friends by these cards. We received answers because it was the time when thousands and thousands of Oppositionists were simultaneously thrown into prisons and deportations. The G.P.U. was not, or did not control so strictly.

FINERTY: I am speaking after that period.

TROTSKY: After that period it became more and more difficult to have communications. They began to accuse everybody who was in communication with me by writing. I can present hundreds of postal cards from Russia. Then they began to accuse them of espionage. The political and psychological factors, the victories of fascism in one country after another—the Oppositionist isolated in Siberia says: "What can I do? I have only the choice between Hitler and Stalin. The ideas of Trotsky might be good. But he is isolated and in exile. If I continue to correspond with him, I can only be shot and my family will suffer. That is all."

It is the psychology of reaction. I passed through such periods two times between the revolutions of 1905 and 1917. We had two or three years of a hermetically—rather, a hermetical isolation from Russia. My revolutionary fathers of the 'eighties were in the same position. Plekhanov and Zasulich and the other Russian Marxists were in the same position in the 1880's. It is the same repetition, three times.

BEALS: During the Tsarist period you did have underground communications, I presume?

TROTSKY: Yes.

BEALS: How was that carried on?

TROTSKY: It was after the revolution. Before the revolution we were very rich in our methods of communication because all the opinion, with the exception of the bureaucracy and the summits, were against the Tsar and the rich landlords. The liberals who came abroad visited Plekhanov and Lenin, but Lenin less than Plekhanov. We received money from them. We used to pack their valises with literature, and so on. Even bureaucrats, liberal bureaucrats, were radicals and Socialists abroad. After the revolution of 1905, after the defeat, the bourgeoisie became conservative, and our communications with Russia relied only upon a number of radical intelligentsia, the highest stratum of the working class. The blows of the Tsarist reaction of 1906–1907 succeeded in isolating us. It was the first time that we were isolated—in 1908–1909, and even 1910—almost totally isolated. It was the exception to see anybody from Russia to speak to, and to have correspondence. I was at that time the editor of a Russian paper in Vienna—an illegal paper—and I had the greatest difficulty. But in 1910–1911 a new wave arose. You saw new correspondence and new publications. The intelligentsia became more radical, and the workers more active. You know, there is a law, not created by any one of us, a historical law, in the ebb and flow in the development of the revolution. Now, I am waiting for a new flow.

BEALS: You are a member of the Fourth International, are you not?

TROTSKY: Yes.

BEALS: Does the Fourth International have any organization at all in the Soviet Union?

TROTSKY: In the formal sense of a working organization? I believe I can say that we have a section, but not in the formal sense of an organization. But as sympathizers, I believe we have many. It is very difficult to answer that, Mr. Commissioner.

BEALS: You don't have—you don't know how communication is maintained with the Fourth International to friends in the Soviet Union?

TROTSKY: Unfortunately, all the communications were through Ciliga and Victor Serge, who came out in the last few years. In the last two years, no communications at all. Tarov was a correspondent; he was a worker who escaped through Persia. I told you about him yesterday.

GOLDMAN: Now, I want to get this point cleared up for the record: After 1931, did you receive letters from your friends or send letters to your friends in Russia, and did they receive them, as far as you know?

TROTSKY: After 1931?

GOLDMAN: After 1931.

TROTSKY: Yes; we tried to do it after 1931. We sent postal cards, but they did not receive them.

GOLDMAN: Now, did you receive any letters after 1931?

TROTSKY: It is possible. I must look again. It is possible I received some communications. I believe that we received two or three, but they were personal communications: "I am transported from one place in Siberia to another."

FINERTY: Will such communications be in your archives?

TROTSKY: I believe so.

FINERTY: If you have them—you will find it?

TROTSKY: It was a postal card. Before 1931, manuscripts and books in the form of letters came. In your absence, Mr. Attorney, we showed them around.

FINERTY: They are in evidence?

BEALS: In the period right after 1905, did you ever, in your communications, use codes and secret ink?

TROTSKY: Yes, naturally.

BEALS: Why do you not do that in this more recent period?

TROTSKY: Pardon?

BEALS: Since you knew how to do this, why have you not done this in the recent period?

TROTSKY: In order to write such a letter, it is necessary to have two persons, one who writes and one who receives, who is ready to receive it and carry all the risk. The reaction exists even in the fact that our friends in Russia, who are so many, will not do it. You can see the same now in Germany and Italy. Ask, please, the Communist Party and other radical parties, if they are in communication with these countries. Why? Because the defeat was so terrible, after the great possibilities of the Italian and German proletariat, the greatest historical possibilities, and the defeats so terrible, that the workers say: "Now, I will wait and see. It is unnecessary to communicate with them abroad. They are bankrupt." I believe the workers can say the same about me: "Trotsky was one of the organizers of the October Revolution. Now he is in exile. Possibly he is more honest than the others. I believe the latter have degenerated. But what is the necessity for me to correspond with him?" That is the opinion of the worker in a reactionary period. That is the mood.

DEWEY: May I ask one question? Mr. Trotsky, did I understand that the correspondence you did have was purely on matters and conditions—deals with personal matters, to the exclusion of all conspiratorial material?

TROTSKY: All correspondence we had until 1931 was collected and sent to them with *Bulletins.* We tried to publish the same *Bulletin* in photographic form, and in very small copies, to send to them. But it was also difficult. We tried then to copy some articles, the most important articles, from the *Bulletin,* or extract excerpts from the articles and send them to different comrades in Siberia and Russia itself. We succeeded. I never said to my friends anything I did not say in the *Bulletin.* I have no panacea for them. All I can say to my followers is: "You must understand your mission to organize the new cadres of the new generation and continue our work when a new situation comes, when the reaction is finished, when a new wave comes." What I say before the Commission, I can say before the whole world. Excuse me; I have no other ideas, Mr. Commissioner.

DEWEY: Then you deny that you did have conspiratorial communications?

TROTSKY: What is now conspiratorial, Dr. Dewey? These very simple lines written on postal cards are also conspiratorial communications in the sense that the censorship does not approve them and confiscates them—it is also conspiratorial work. If I can have the possibility to send anybody the *Bulletin,* to introduce it into the valises—one or two copies of the *Bulletin*—I will do it. It is conspiratorial work, but it is subordinate to my ideas. It is the technical method of presenting my ideas to Russian public opinion.

FINERTY: What Dr. Dewey means, Mr. Trotsky, is, did you have any correspondence with any friends, any organization of your sympathizers in Russia, giving directions as to the method of bringing about a reaction against the Stalin government?

TROTSKY: Yes, in every postal card, in every message I gave to any foreigner who went to Russia, I said: "Now, the greatest danger is this hasty collectivization. It is absolutely necessary not to fear to say openly that it is a danger. With the hasty industrialization, we are against it. They will say: 'You are now a reactionary.' Do not fear it. Say it openly." That is my instruction. The other instruction: "The youth are in an impasse. Terroristic methods can only mean the extermination of the best elements in the youth. You must say to the young people: 'Create groups of self-education; study the history of the Party; and prepare yourselves for the future.'"

FINERTY: I think we are really going into a question we will have to go into later.

GOLDMAN: You didn't, in your letters or post cards, advise anybody to kill Stalin or Kirov and to destroy any factories?

TROTSKY: No.

GOLDMAN: You merely dealt with political problems?

TROTSKY: The same as in my books and articles.

DEWEY: We will adjourn until four o'clock this afternoon.

End of Seventh Session—One o'clock P.M.

Eighth session

April 14, 1937, at four o'clock p.m.

GOLDMAN: Mr. Chairman, this morning the question came up—a question how Mr. Trotsky—or whether he knew that there were terroristic tendencies amongst the youth in the Soviet Union. I want to read two excerpts that were found this noon which will indicate that Mr. Trotsky did know of these terroristic tendencies, and how he replied to them and how he forewarned the youth against them. In the *Bulletin of the Opposition*, No. 33, March, 1933, Mr. Trotsky wrote—this, for example, is an indication—

TROTSKY: It is correspondence from Moscow, not my article.

GOLDMAN: A letter that was received from Moscow. Is it in the form of a letter?

TROTSKY: I don't remember—if it was an oral communication from a man coming from the Soviet Union we changed it into the form of correspondence in order to conceal the evidence that we were in communication with a foreigner who—but if it was really correspondence, I am not sure.

GOLDMAN: At any rate, this is from a communication.
TROTSKY: A direct communication from a certain—
GOLDMAN: Received from Moscow. I quote:

> Thus, for example, in connection with the arrest of the group of the militant Syndicalist Nemchenko. We communicate the following: First a group of Komsomols were arrested, among whom was the son of Nemchenko, accused of preparing terrorist acts (!), and they were asked in an urgent manner how they, the youth, arrived at such thoughts. The son of Nemchenko might have replied: "At our house it was repeated incessantly that the leader was causing the loss of the country."

TROTSKY: Excuse me, it is not Syndicalist, it should be trade unionist. "Syndicalist" is French.

GOLDMAN: "Syndicalist" in English means something altogether different from "trade unionist." Then in the article published in the *Militant* on March 25th, 1933, by Trotsky, this is continued:

> As far back as 1926 Stalin was told that he was clearly grooming himself as a candidate for the post of undertaker to the Party and the Revolution. For the past six years, Stalin has come very close to the fulfillment of this role. Throughout the Party, and outside of it, there is spreading ever wider the slogan, "Down with Stalin!" The causes for the origin and the growing popularity of this "proverb" require no explanations. But, nevertheless, we consider this slogan incorrect. The question touches not Stalin personally, but his faction. It is true that for the last two years it has become extremely constricted in its scope. But it still includes many thousands of apparatus functionaries. Other thousands and tens of thousands, whose eyes have been opened as regards Sta-

lin, continue to support him, nevertheless, from fear of the unknown. The slogan "Down with Stalin!" may be understood, and could inevitably be understood, as the slogan for the overthrow of the faction now in power, and even more—the overthrow of the apparatus. But we do not want to overthrow the system, but to reform it by the efforts of the best proletarian elements.

It is self-evident that an end must and will be put to the Bonapartist régime of a single leader and of the pack compelled to revere him, because that is the most shameful perversion of the idea of the revolutionary Party. But the matter touches not the expulsion of individuals, but the changing of a system.

It is precisely the Stalinist clique that indefatigably circulates rumors to the effect that the Left Opposition will return to the Party not otherwise than with a sword in its hand, and that it will immediately begin merciless reprisals against its factional opponents. This poisonous lie must be refuted, repudiated, and exposed. There is no feeling for revenge in politics. Bolshevik-Leninists—

By that is meant the Left Oppositionist faction

—never were motivated by it in the past, and least of all do they intend to be motivated by it in the future . . . We are ready to work hand in hand with every one who seeks to prevent catastrophe through the restoration of the Party.

Now, Mr. Trotsky—

TROTSKY: Permit me a statement.

GOLDMAN: You want to make a statement on the question of conspiracy?

TROTSKY: The Chairman asked me about my conspiratorial work. In view of the great importance of this question, I will supplement my oral answers by this brief statement:

Under a more or less normal Party and state régime, such as prevailed during the first period after the October Revolution (1917–1922), the tendency I represent would be able to find normal and legal channels of expression within the framework of Party and Soviet Democracy. Only the fact that democracy has been abolished by the bureaucracy imposes upon every criticism and form of opposition an illegal character. In this sense, everybody who does not believe in the infallibility of the leadership, and who expresses, even behind closed doors, his nonconformist ideas, is inevitably accused of doing "conspiratorial work." The Stalin régime transforms the most elementary functions of human thought into "conspiratorial work."

It is true that I and my friends use conspiratorial methods to introduce our views within the borders of the U.S.S.R., as well as within the borders of Germany and Italy, because the political régimes of those countries prevent any other method of introducing those views. But the views themselves are no different from those we express elsewhere publicly and without any conspiratorial methods. The object of the frame-up system is to inject into the conspiratorial form a terrorist content which is utterly alien to it.

With respect to Germany, I desire to clarify a statement made by me this morning. I did not want to give the impression that the Communist or Socialist Parties are utterly without contacts in Germany. I desired only to state that, like ourselves, the number of their contacts has catastrophically declined since the consolidation of the Hitler police régime.

GOLDMAN: Now, Mr. Trotsky—

BEALS: May I ask a question? Mr. Trotsky did make this comparison between the Soviet Union and Germany at this time as an indication of certain ties, conspiratorial work, underground work, illegal work or whatever you wish to call it, as virtually impossible of maintaining contacts abroad. Yet, even in the worst part of the Nazi terror there were a great many contacts and communications going back and forth between the various revolutionary groups of Germany. Why is it so utterly impossible in the case of the Soviet Union?

TROTSKY: If you compare Germany with Italy, you will see that the communications in Italy are less than in Germany, as a comparison. In Germany the reaction is on the bottom. The new régime is too new, and the great wave of the masses which preceded the victory of Hitler continues, and it gives the possibility to revolutionary parties to have some contact and do some work. I had great polemics with the Comintern concerning this question. After the victory of Hitler, Stalin and all the others affirmed that it was only an episode, that "tomorrow we will have power in Germany." I declared: "This is the greatest stupidity you can say; it is the greatest defeat in the history of the German proletariat." If you compare the situation in 1933 and 1934 to the situation of today, you will see that the Communist Party and the Socialist Party have now less connection than two years ago. And it is possible they will have less in the next years than today. When a new wave begins, and I hope to see it—but today we have in Germany a declining line. In the Soviet Union the reaction began in 1923. From 1923 we have open reaction, organized for thirteen years. The fact that Zinoviev, Kamenev, Rakovsky and myself—the people who were more or less the guiding line in the Party—were expelled from the Party, deported, and so on, produced in the masses the profoundest impression. It was the beginning of the reaction in the masses—not only in the bureaucracy. In the bureaucracy it is an active reaction to insure its privileges. In the masses it is a passive reaction, a spirit of: Nothing to do. It is the mood of the masses. This wave of reaction lasts now thirteen years, and that is the reason why it is profound—the reaction—why we have no regular communication with

Russia. In Italy, it is more or less similar.

GOLDMAN: Now, Mr. Trotsky, you proved that you are against individual terrorism, and your followers are against individual terror. You have also stated, and proof is perhaps not necessary, that there is no democracy in the Soviet Union. Do you expect that there will be a change, that the Stalin régime will at one time or another be removed?

TROTSKY: I am sure that it can be removed under the threat of workers' democracy or under the threat of a fascist reaction.

GOLDMAN: If it should be removed in the form of workers' democracy, what will be the method that will be used in order to remove the Stalin apparatus?

TROTSKY: The force of workers to establish workers' democracy. Only the workers are capable of doing that. It is the force of the mass. It cannot be replaced by individual threats or chemical preparations.

GOLDMAN: When you say the force of the workers, will you explain that a little more fully? What do you mean by that? You don't mean individual workers are going to shoot Stalin and other leaders and followers?

TROTSKY: I defend myself against this idea. I believed that in time it would be possible to change the régime by reform, by peaceful means, and our slogan was: "Reform, not revolution, in the Soviet Union." That was until the second half of 1933. After the victory of Hitler and the recent change of policy by Stalin and the Comintern, and after we became convinced that the C.I. [Communist International—Ed.] is absolutely incapable of drawing the necessary conclusions from the greatest defeat—that is, the defeat of the German proletariat and the victory of Hitler—we said: "The Comintern is no more a revolutionary organization, and the leading party of the Comintern, the old Bolshevik Party, is no longer considered as a revolutionary party." The Party was, in our mind, the lever, the instrument, for the peaceful reform of the Soviet state. There must now be a revolutionary lever, a new instrument. It was the slogan of the Fourth International to build a new revolutionary party in the Soviet Union. Stalin declared in August, 1927, in a session of the Central Committee—I quoted that when we discussed Radek, the Radek question—he declared, in opposition to me, that "these cadres can be removed only by civil war." The cadres are the bureaucracy. Radek answered—this he wrote in September, 1927—"This is virtual Bonapartism." We answered, "Stalin is of the opinion that it is impossible to remove him by the strength of the Party." We were of another opinion. We were sure that it was possible for the vanguard of the proletariat by an active movement to change totally the staff of the Party and state, and we were ready in the Party to guide this movement of the vanguard to change the Party, the Party structure and the state structure.

GOLDMAN: Peacefully?

TROTSKY: Peacefully. At that time it was a policy of reform. It lasted until the second half of 1933. But shortly after the victory of Hitler we declared: "In this respect, Stalin was right. The cadres, the bureaucracy, can be removed only by a new political revolution."

GOLDMAN: Why do you say a political revolution?

TROTSKY: Because in the past we knew social revolutions which were also political. We can take as an example the great French Revolution, which was social and political. It changed the feudal forms of property into the bourgeois forms of property. After the great French Revolution, the French people had the revolutions of 1830, 1848, and 1870. They were political revolutions. A bourgeois state, on the basis of its own form of property, created by the great French Revolution, the great social revolution, changed its political state. We see now in Russia to a certain degree how the proletariat can repeat these experiences. By the great October Revolution, the proletariat created new forms of property.

These forms remain today in spite of the bureaucracy and its privileges. But the bureaucracy itself menaces the new form of property, menaces the political and moral life of the proletariat. It makes inevitable a conflict between the proletariat and the bureaucracy. The overthrow of the bureaucracy is only a political revolution, because the proletariat will not be obliged to change the form of property. It will adjust that to the genuine interests of the masses and not the bureaucracy.

GOLDMAN: Did you deal with this question in your latest book, "The Revolution Betrayed"?

TROTSKY: Yes. If you permit me, we had a conference of the Fourth International—it was in July, 1936. It was a conference without my participation. It was not in Norway. Merely theoretically, I participated in the preparation of that conference. It adopted a motion entitled: "The Fourth International and the Soviet Union." The fifteenth paragraph says:

> 15. *The working class of the U.S.S.R. has been robbed of the last possibility of a legal reformation of the state. The struggle against the bureaucracy necessarily becomes a revolutionary struggle.* True to the traditions of Marxism, the Fourth International *decisively rejects individual terror,* as it does all other means of political adventurism. The bureaucracy can be smashed only by means of the goal-conscious movement of the masses against the usurpers, parasites and oppressors.

I will only emphasize what we have to say when we say we are for a revolution in the Soviet Union. We are not afraid to say it. If we were to be for terror, if we were to be of the opinion that by individual terror we could help the working class in its movement forward, I would proclaim it and appeal to the best elements of the working class to resort to individual terror. Say what is, what is necessary;

that is the first rule of my thoughts and my actions. If I say I am against terror, it is not because I am afraid of Stalin's police or any other police; it is only because I am a Marxist, for mass action and not individual terror.

BEALS: Mr. Trotsky, how many workers of the Soviet Union support your doctrines?

TROTSKY: If I could establish the statistics in this question, you know I must have meetings with them, and votes. I must have, to answer your question, Soviet democracy.

BEALS: How are you going to reach them if the means of communication do not exist?

TROTSKY: Pardon?

BEALS: How are you going to reach them to establish your ideas?

TROTSKY: I never said communications did not exist. I said we have no regular, organized communication. It is absolutely different. You know, from the Soviet Union came every year hundreds and some years thousands of engineers and students and workers, to America and France, to Germany before Hitler, to study industry and to study technique. All these people read the *Bulletin*. We searched for them, and we gave them the *Bulletin* through our German friends, our American friends and French friends. They go back, and as the German poet, Heinrich Heine, said to the functionary on the border: "You look at my valise, but the contraband is in my head." There are hundreds and thousands going back with contraband in their heads.

BEALS: How many copies of the *Bulletin* do you ordinarily print?

TROTSKY: From two to three thousand, but it is only the beginning. We will print in the future more.

DEWEY: Was this change of attitude on your part first announced in the *Bulletin of the Opposition* of October, 1933, which was referred to on page 507?

TROTSKY: My "violence"—the quotation of Vyshinsky.

DEWEY: Was that the time you first announced your change of attitude?

TROTSKY: I believe it was in the second half of 1933. We can find immediately the exact date. In August, 1933.

DEWEY: It is not very important. It says here October.

BEALS: I think it makes a direct reference to terrorism.

DEWEY: I didn't get the characterization against the document.

FINERTY: I think it would be well if the document were produced now.

TROTSKY: Wait. It is the first of October, 1933, that quotation.

FINERTY: Mr. Goldman gave a direct reference to it as No. 36–37, October, 1933.

TROTSKY: Even the prosecutor of the Tsar never committed such miserable falsifications.

GOLDMAN: In the *Bulletin.* I think Vyshinsky quoted from the *Opposition Bulletin,* No. 36–37, October, 1933. Is that right?

FINERTY: That's right.

GOLDMAN: The subject of the article from which Vyshinsky quoted is, if I am correct, "The Class Nature of the Soviet State."

DEWEY: Mr. Finerty, I take it that the whole matter will be gone into definitely at this time. I just wanted to identify the article on the change from evolution to revolution.

GOLDMAN: The article is in Russian. There is, I believe, an English translation printed in the *Militant.* The exact date I don't know, but we shall furnish it to the Commission either today or tomorrow. Let the record show that we referred to it now, and we shall introduce it later. Is that where Vyshinsky says: "I will not continue to quote because of the terrible things in it?"

TROTSKY: May I introduce another "conspiratorial" document? I forgot totally this thing. I received this letter, written by me in Copenhagen in November, 1932, and given by me to the English friend, Wicks, who visited me in Copenhagen. Now, before the Commission came here, all my friends began to look for any documents of mine and sent them to me. Every day we receive here documents from all countries of Europe. Wicks said to me: "I have connections with Russians in London and they have connections in the Soviet Union, but they do not have the necessary confidence in me"—That is, Wicks—"I know they sympathize with the Opposition. Can you give me a letter to them?" The letter is written in pencil. I am not sure whether you can by chemical means establish the date of the letter, but it was written in November, 1932, in Copenhagen. The letter is not so important, but it characterizes what we tried to do by conspiratorial methods. I wrote to unknown sympathizers of the Left Opposition the following:

> Dear Comrade: I am not sure whether you know my handwriting. If not, you will probably find someone else who does. I am profiting by this fortunate occasion to write a few words to you. The comrades who sympathize with the Left Opposition *are obliged* to come out of their passive state at this time, maintaining, of course, all *precautions*. To communicate with me *directly* is not always easy. But it is possible to find an absolutely sure way, of course, not direct; for example, through my son in Berlin. You can find him through Pfemfert (I am inclosing his address) through Grylewicz—

Pfemfert is the German editor. I gave you the letters of Pfemfert and his wife. Grylewicz is the editor, or was the editor of the Russian *Bulletin*

> —through personal acquaintances, etc. Keeping all precautionary measures, it is necessary to establish com-

munications for: *Information*, to distribute the *Bulletin*, aid with money, etc., etc. I am definitely expecting that the menacing situation in which the Party finds itself will force all the comrades devoted to the revolution to gather actively about the Left Opposition.

I will wait for a written (typewritten) affirmation that this letter has been received. It can be written to:

M. Pierre Frank, Poste Restante, Pera, Istambul.

I clasp your hand firmly. Yours, L. TROTSKY.

This is one of my conspiratorial letters.

GOLDMAN: This letter you wrote in Copenhagen?

TROTSKY: Copenhagen.

GOLDMAN: In 19—

TROTSKY: November, 1932, during my sojourn in Copenhagen. I gave this to the British citizen, Wicks.

GOLDMAN: For him to give to some Russians?

TROTSKY: Russian sympathizers of the Opposition.

STOLBERG: Where? In the Soviet Union?

GOLDMAN: In England.

TROTSKY: I had the possibility of getting it to Russia through London. He is connected with the sympathizers in Moscow. All the official Russians who are for a certain time in London and in Moscow, they have the possibility—

GOLDMAN: I introduce the original into evidence and mark it Exhibit No. 22.

(The letter of November, 1932, given to Wicks was introduced into evidence as Exhibit No. 22.)

FINERTY: You ought to show that the letter was delivered to the person in London or the Russian sympathizer.

GOLDMAN: Do you know, Mr. Trotsky—by the way, when did you get this letter back?

TROTSKY: I believe it was three or four days ago.

VAN HEIJENOORT: Three days.

GOLDMAN: Did you get a letter with this letter explaining the return?

TROTSKY: "Maybe you need it for the Commission inquiry." The letter remained in his hands. If he did anything, if he showed it to the Russians, I don't know. But I can ask him. He is in London, and I can write him or I can cable him.

FINERTY: We can subsequently determine that.

GOLDMAN: At any rate, this letter can be introduced even if we assume it wasn't turned over to any Russian sympathizers. It can be introduced to indicate the nature of the conspiratorial work that Mr. Trotsky engaged in.

FINERTY: I would just warn Mr. Goldman—you had better use the word "alleged" for your own purpose, because this record will want to show these things.

GOLDMAN: Yes, the alleged conspiratorial work.

TROTSKY: It is for the purpose of showing to one Russian, then he copied it for a second occasion. It was in his hands. It was as a legitimation.

INTERPRETER: You mean "credential."

TROTSKY: Yes, credential.

GOLDMAN: That is in your handwriting, Mr. Trotsky? That letter is in your handwriting?

TROTSKY: Yes.

STOLBERG: When you say there is needed a political revolution in Russia, not a social revolution, does that imply that in your belief there are no class differences in Russia? When you say that from your point of view it is necessary in the Soviet Union to have a political revolution, does that imply you believe that because there is no class struggle going on in Russia?

TROTSKY: I would say that the class struggle is of an embryonic nature. At this stage, the new ruling caste has not changed the forms of property. The forms of property were created by the proletariat, and the new ruling caste tries to use them in its own behalf and not in the interest of the proletariat. In this present situation, it is possible to eliminate the ruling caste by a political revolution, not a social revolution. But it is not for eternity. If the political revolution comes too late, the ruling caste will change the social forms of society.

FINERTY: Mr. Trotsky, when you say "eliminate," do you mean "exterminate"?

TROTSKY: No.

FINERTY: In other words, when you say "eliminate," you mean to eliminate politically?

TROTSKY: Yes, to deprive them of the apparatus of the dictatorship and replace them by democracy.

FINERTY: When you said "Remove Stalin," you used it in the same political sense?

TROTSKY: Not only that; I am astonished to what degree I was cautious in my article. I wrote a second time to the Central Committee: "You must remove Stalin." But as a slogan, "Down with Stalin!" I repudiated it in my article. Because in the Central Committee everybody understands that it is in a legal way I proposed to remove him; to change the secretary. When it becomes a slogan of the masses, it cannot mean assassination. I repudiate it.

FINERTY: When you use the word "revolution," you do imply violence, but organized violence?

TROTSKY: It depends entirely on the bureaucracy. If the bureaucrats are inclined to concede to the politically organized expression of the masses, everything will be very satisfactory. If they will oppose the masses, the masses will use violence. It is legitimate.

FINERTY: What you really mean is, that if the bureaucracy uses violence to resist their removal, the masses will use violence to remove them?

TROTSKY: Absolutely correct.

GOLDMAN: I don't know whether you answered the question of Commissioner Beals, put to you before. Mr. Beals asked you how you hoped or expected the masses of the Soviet Union to be won over to your ideas.

TROTSKY: Yes?

GOLDMAN: Now, isn't it a fact that if the reaction should remain for a long period of time, no matter how many letters you will send, no matter how many people you will talk to, the masses will not be won over? Explain the relationship between the change in the reaction and the effect your ideas will have upon the masses.

TROTSKY: My opinion is that now the key to the situation in the Soviet Union is not in the Soviet Union, but in Europe. If the people in Spain are victorious against the fascists, if the working class in France will assure its movement to Socialism, then the situation in the Soviet Union will change immediately, because the workers are very dissatisfied with the dictatorship of the bureaucracy. They, as I say, are in an impasse. They say, "Given choice only between Hitler and Stalin, we prefer Stalin." They are right, Stalin is preferable to Hitler. And at the moment when they see a new perspective in Europe, a revolutionary movement toward the victory of Socialism, they will—

GOLDMAN: Raise their heads?

TROTSKY: Raise their heads. Then, I believe the only program which they can accept is our program, because it is based upon their own experience, their own past, and, I am sure, their own future. That is why I do not despair of the fact that in the last two or three years we have lost almost all our direct communications, our connections with the Soviet Union. I understand that it is a period of the most terrific reaction and the first step, the beginning of a new wave, will begin our opportunity, and then we will see.

I have patience. Three revolutions have made me patient. It is absolutely necessary for a revolutionist to be patient.

It is a false idea that a revolutionary must be impatient. Adventurists are impatient, but a revolutionary is patient. [Trotsky here pronounced the word "patient" as "passion," and "patience" as "passions"—A.M.G.]

INTERPRETER: You mean "patience."

TROTSKY: Yes; a revolutionary must know English and with the help of patience I will learn English. (Laughter)

It is on this false idea of a revolutionary that all the frame-ups are based: "Trotsky wants power. He is impatient. He will kill everybody to take power." This is absolutely stupid. I am not hungering for power personally. I am more satisfied with my literary work. Power is a burden, but it is necessary and an inevitable evil. When your ideas are victorious, you must accept it. But the mechanics of power is a miserable thing. If you permit me this personal observation: During the time I was in office, the best time was the vacations when I wrote my books. I consider this time a longer vacation. I write my books. It is giving me full satisfaction. I am patient and await a new wave, a revolutionary wave, and then, if I can serve the interests of the proletariat, I will do anything I can.

FINERTY: I take it that you do not think, from what you say, that it will help the cause for the proletariat to overthrow Stalin by using Hitler as a means.

TROTSKY: This accusation is so absurd! Every time I repeat it, it makes—I am so perplexed that I cannot find arguments against this absurdity—thinking I can use Hitler against Stalin. For what purpose? What can I win by this? Vyshinsky did not explain to me what I can win by this procedure. I must sacrifice all my past, all my friends and all my future, and what can I win? I cannot understand it.

FINERTY: As you see the situation now, Hitler must first be overthrown before Stalin will be overthrown?

TROTSKY: I hope it will be so. All the articles I wrote about this—and I repeat it in dozens of interviews and articles—

if a war comes, the first revolution will be in Japan, because Japan is like the old Tsarist Russia, with a most brutally organized authority; and the contradictions of the social body of Japan will burst out. The first revolution will occur in Japan. The second, I hope, in Germany, because Germany, hermetically sealed, will during the war inevitably explode, as during the imperialist war with the Hohenzollerns, because now all of the contradictions, the social contradictions and the economic, remain in more sharp form in Germany. I repeated this simple idea dozens and dozens of times and then, unexpectedly, I tied my fate with the two doomed régimes. (Laughter) Two doomed régimes, Japan in the East and Germany in Europe.

GOLDMAN: The article that I referred to before, and from which Vyshinsky quoted, from the *Russian Opposition Bulletin,* was translated in the *Militant* on January 6th, 1934. A pamphlet was made out of that article, and if they are available, they will be given to the Commission. I am fairly certain that they are available in New York. The pamphlet was headed, "The Soviet Union and the Fourth International," with a sub-title "The Class Nature of the Soviet State," by Leon Trotsky.

DEWEY: Mr. Goldman, I would like to ask Mr. Trotsky the date of the formation of the Fourth International.

TROTSKY: If you permit, Mr. Chairman, I will present a statement with all the necessary dates. There are different stages—we proclaimed the necessity of the Fourth International only—we will present you with all the dates.

GOLDMAN: Now, that finishes that section of the evidence which deals with individual terror.

TROTSKY: Permit me to say a word about the list of victims. I will now establish only simple facts necessary for my conclusions later. I will prove to the Commission that the list of the alleged victims of the future terrorist attempts is established by Stalin, by the Politburo of Stalin, and not by the alleged terrorists. I will prove by the fact that in the trial of Zinoviev and Kamenev you will find a list, a full list, of the future victims of the future terrorist attempts, including Stalin, Voroshilov, Zhdanov, Kaganovich, Kossior, Ordjonikidze and Postyshev. My instructions, my alleged terrorist instructions, were to kill Stalin and Voroshilov—and I believe that there was a third, Kaganovich, but no matter—Kaganovich was held for the future. (Laughter) You will find more than that, you will find a dialogue between Vyshinsky and Zinoviev in the trial of Zinoviev in August, 1936. Vyshinsky asks Zinoviev, as regards the prepared terrorist acts, "Against whom?"

> *Zinoviev:* Against the leaders.
>
> *Vyshinsky:* That is against Comrade Stalin, Voroshilov and Kaganovich?
>
> *Zinoviev:* Yes.

"Yes"—that is the general answer. (Laughter)

Zinoviev says against the leaders; and Vyshinsky answers very well which are the leaders. That is, Stalin, Voroshilov and Kaganovich. He omits Molotov. Molotov is the second personality in the Soviet Union. He is a member of the Politburo, an old Bolshevik, and President of the Council of People's Commissars. He is omitted. There are five or six depositions of the defendants who were supposedly under my instruction. And in the sentence of Vyshinsky, as well as everybody else, Molotov is omitted.

In the second trial you will find Molotov in the second place, not only for the future, but also for the past. I will explain it, will expose it. The explanation of this exists only in the relationship between Stalin and Molotov, a relationship which is revealed in the Soviet press and the Russian *Bulletin*. There was a conflict between Stalin and Molotov. Molotov was in a discreet opposition to Stalin for two years or more. And Stalin did not permit him to be elevated to the height of a victim of Trotsky's terror. He introduced new leaders, and the names of these leaders are for me nothing. Kirov was not so important. You know the name of Kirov only because he was killed. Before his assassination nobody knew who Kirov was. Postyshev and Kossior are of the same kind, but they sustained Stalin against Molotov. He introduces them as a monarch would introduce a colonel or a marshal. He named them victims of Trotsky, and he excluded Molotov. I will try to show it with exact quotations and dates in my conclusion.

GOLDMAN: This concludes the section on individual terror and the opinion of Mr. Trotsky as to the methods of removing the Stalinist bureaucracy.

DEWEY: What point comes next?

GOLDMAN: The next question is on the attitude of Mr. Trotsky on the defense of the U.S.S.R. against Japan and Germany.

FINERTY: May I ask Mr. Trotsky one question before we finish this? As I understand you, Mr. Trotsky, your position on individual terror, leaving aside any moral question, is a question of—a programmatic question. It is not an effective method.

TROTSKY: Not an effective method, as we learned through experience. The whole of the Russian revolutionary movement is filled with divisions on this question. Our revolutionary parties were divided into two camps, for individual terror and against individual terror. It is not the procedure, the mode of procedure, the conception—it is a fundamental thing for me what my action is.

FINERTY: You don't think it is an effective political method?

TROTSKY: Politically, economically, and strategically, it is absolutely contrary to the best interests of the working masses.

FINERTY: Without any question of, or any moral point of

view one way or another? Excluding the moral question, it is not effective?

TROTSKY: If you permit me to say my opinion: When the oppression of the masses is so terrible, especially in certain countries, then every method is morally justified if the masses can be liberated. It is only a question, if this method is capable of liberating the masses or not.

FINERTY: Your opposition to individual terror, while it may be morally justified, is that it is not an effective political movement?

TROTSKY: Absolutely so.

GOLDMAN: I want to mention to the Commission that in the book of Trotsky that I mentioned—that is, volume four of the collected works in Russian—there are not only quotations with reference to individual terror. There are dozens of other quotations, and if the Commission will get the book and translate it for itself, they will convince themselves of that fact.

DEWEY: We will now take a short recess.

GOLDMAN: In the next section of the evidence, I shall attempt to disprove the idea that Leon Trotsky was at any time or is now an enemy of the Soviet Union. The evidence will show that at all times—before he was expelled from the Soviet Union and after, and at the present time—he stands for one thing as far as the Soviet Union is concerned, and that is, to defend the Soviet Union against all enemies.

Mr. Trotsky, will you very briefly give us your idea on the nature of the Soviet Union from the point of view of economy and the point of view of the state.

TROTSKY: The Soviet state was created by the proletarian revolution which set up the proletarian dictatorship. The proletarian dictatorship has as its objective to defend the new forms of property, the collective property. And the proletarian dictatorship signifies politically the proletarian democracy. But the factors of the backwardness of the country, the isolated position of the Soviet Union, and the defeats of the proletariat in other countries, changed the situation in this sense, that the state became a bureaucratic one, and this state has now a dubious function.

GOLDMAN: You mean "dual"?

TROTSKY: Yes, a dual function. It defends the new form of property against the capitalist class and the capitalist enemies, and it applies the new form of property in the interest of the bureaucracy. With the Left Opposition, we declared many times we will sustain Stalin and his bureaucracy, and we repeat it now. We will sustain Stalin and his bureaucracy in every effort it makes to defend the new form of property against imperialist attacks. At the same time we try to defend the new forms of property against Stalin and the bureaucracy, against inner attacks against the new form of property. That is our position.

GOLDMAN: Then, the Soviet Union is still a workers' state; is that your position?

TROTSKY: A deformed workers' state, a degenerated workers' state.

GOLDMAN: What is the nature of its economy?

TROTSKY: Its economy is a proletarian economy, a deformed Socialist economy.

GOLDMAN: A transition economy, would you call it, between capitalism and Socialism?

TROTSKY: Yes. From the political point of view it is a necessary condition for the Socialist future. But, materially, the Soviet society today is nearer to the capitalist than the Socialist. The new forms of property permit the development of society towards Socialism without a new social revolution.

GOLDMAN: What distinction do you make between the Stalin bureaucratic régime and the Soviet Union?

TROTSKY: We defend the Soviet Union—I will say, we defend the acquisitions of the October Revolution, in spite of Stalin's bureaucracy.

GOLDMAN: In other words, in attacking the Stalin bureaucracy, you are not attacking the Soviet Union; you are attacking something that is like a cancer, as you call it, upon the Soviet Union?

TROTSKY: Yes.

GOLDMAN: In your opinion, what effect does the struggle against the ideas and practices of Stalin have in so far as defending the Soviet Union against its internal and external enemies is concerned?

TROTSKY: I don't get you.

GOLDMAN: There are those who claim that in attacking Stalin you are weakening the Soviet Union against both the external and internal enemies. What have you to say to that?

TROTSKY: Every reaction repeats the same objection against the critics. In this connection, I quote the example of Clemenceau, who plays a great role in the indictment.

GOLDMAN: Yes, and the next question is with reference to the Clemenceau thesis.

TROTSKY: Yes; it is connected. I will answer both questions. Beginning with the year 1926, Stalin and Molotov and others affirmed on every occasion that it was impermissible to tolerate any critics because the war danger approached us. Every Bonapartist régime uses the war danger as a means of stifling any critic. It is an old exaggeration. I answered, "Even if the war comes, we must have—for the defense—we must have the possibility of free criticism in the country," and I gave in one of my speeches the example of, and I quoted Clemenceau. I said even in the bourgeois state in France, where the bourgeoisie during the war was very afraid of the discontent of the masses, it, the bourgeoisie, did not dare to stifle at any time the criticism of Clemenceau. During the third year of the war, he had an uncompromising attitude towards all the Governments, the war Governments. He criticized them verbally, and he convinced the Parliament in 1917. He took power and assured the victory. I quoted this example to show the necessity of a certain elasticity even during a war—not only before the war—even for a bourgeois régime. The more so for a proletarian régime. We have no fear of the masses during war, because our war would only be imposed on us. It is not a provocation, it is a genuine defense of our revolution. My thesis was denounced as the thesis of Clemenceau, the terrible thesis of Clemenceau. If you will see the statement of the Prosecutor, Vyshinsky, he says Trotsky wishes to organize an insurrection as Clemenceau did when the Germans were eighty kilometers from Paris. I never heard that Clemenceau was the organizer of an insurrection in France. I believe the French will be very astonished on reading the French translation of the Verbatim Report. Clemenceau was not a defeatist. The French people name him the father of the victory. That is his popular name.

You see in what a brutal and dishonest way they deform and distort every idea of Opposition critique. It is not only in articles in the *Pravda,* but in the indictment. Vyshinsky did not quote me: "Trotsky said this and that." He has only assumed that Clemenceau was a defeatist and the organizer of an insurrection during the war.

GOLDMAN: Now, subsequent to your expulsion from the Soviet Union, did the Left Opposition formulate any program which contains sections dealing with the defense of the Soviet Union?

TROTSKY: Yes; it is "The War and the Fourth International," an official document. This is the official program of the Fourth International.

GOLDMAN: This Fourth International was at that time not formed?

TROTSKY: No; it is not formed today.

GOLDMAN: It is in the process?

TROTSKY: It is the preparation, the programmatic preparation for the Fourth International.

GOLDMAN: Will you mark this Exhibit No. 23?

This exhibit is the programmatic pamphlet entitled "The War and the Fourth International." I quote now from the pamphlet, the official program on war adopted by the International Secretariat of the International Communist League. I believe, if I am not mistaken, that you wrote this program?

TROTSKY: Yes.

GOLDMAN: On page 9, I quote the following:

> The indubitable and deep-going bureaucratic degeneration of the Soviet state as well as the national-conservative character of its foreign policy do not change the social nature of the Soviet Union as that of the first workers' state. All kinds of democratic, idealistic, ultra-Left, anarchistic theories, ignoring the character of Soviet property relations which is Socialistic in its tendencies and denying or glossing over the class contradiction between the U.S.S.R. and the bourgeois state, must lead inevitably, and especially in case of war, to counter-revolutionary political conclusions.
>
> *Defense of the Soviet Union* from the blows of the capitalist enemies, irrespective of the circumstances and immediate causes of the conflict, is the elementary and imperative duty of every honest labor organization.

This was published in July, 1934, and was adopted some time in May—

TROTSKY: It was written in 1933.

VAN HEIJENOORT: 1934.

TROTSKY: That's right, 1934.

GOLDMAN: It was written in May, 1934?

LAFOLLETTE: Adopted when?

GOLDMAN: Adopted June 10, 1934, by the International Secretariat.

TROTSKY: It was discussed between the moment it was written—it was discussed internationally, and then it was adopted. Will you please put in my article on Clemenceau, appearing in the *New International*?

GOLDMAN: The question of the Clemenceau thesis referred to in the indictment and in the argument of Vyshinsky was dealt with in an article by Mr. Trotsky dated September 24th, 1927, Moscow, and published in the *New International* of July, 1934. The *New International* was a publication published in New York. I refer to it without introducing it into evidence. The Commission can readily obtain that.

FINERTY: Can you give me a reference as to where in the indictment that reference is made?

TROTSKY: It is not in the indictment, it is in the accusation on page 497.

GOLDMAN: Not in the indictment, but in the speech of the Prosecutor. I have the pamphlet entitled "In Defense of the Soviet Union," a compilation of articles and excerpts from Leon Trotsky's works beginning with 1927 and ending with 1937, published by the Pioneer Publishers of New York, this year—I think, the last month. The pamphlet has an introduction by Max Shachtman. I introduce that into evidence as Exhibit No. 24.

(The pamphlets "War and the Fourth International" and "In Defense of the Soviet Union," by Leon Trotsky were introduced into evidence as Exhibits Nos. 23 and 24, respectively.)

DEWEY: May I interrupt for a moment? On page 497, they have it in quotation marks as coming from Mr. Trotsky: "We must restore the tactics of Clemenceau, who, as is well known, rose against the French Government at a time when the Germans were eighty kilometers from Paris."

GOLDMAN: That is what Mr. Trotsky refers to as Vyshinsky's own interpretation.

TROTSKY: It is a little literary falsification in a great frame-up.

GOLDMAN: Now, Mr. Trotsky, did you ever have any controversy with members of the Left Opposition, or with persons belonging to other groups, on the question dealing with the defense of the Soviet Union?

TROTSKY: Very often. I can say it was all the time. My exile is full of such discussions and conflicts, and even now, especially now, after the Moscow trials. We received from France, from young friends in France—I received accusations that even now I do not renounce the idea of the necessity of the defense of the Soviet Union. Psychologically, it is absolutely explainable for young people, not sufficiently politically educated and not experienced sufficiently politically—it is Don—

STOLBERG: Quixotic.

TROTSKY: Exotic? No, not exotic.

INTERPRETER: Quixotic.

TROTSKY: Yes, Don Quixotic. All right, we will omit the word. (Laughter) They say: "He insists on the defense of the Soviet Union when such terrible acts are possible." But we defend the Soviet Union not for either Stalin or Vyshinsky. We defend it as an inheritance of the October Revolution, as an open door to a better future, in spite of Stalin and Vyshinsky.

GOLDMAN: Can you name some of the members who used to belong to the Left Opposition with whom you split on the question of that issue?

TROTSKY: It was not only members but organizations. There was in Germany the "Leninbund," an organization connected with us; but we separated ourselves 1929, the beginning of 1929, over this question. Then we have in

France a paper of a group which divided from us. One of the editors is Laste, who is our witness, a very important witness. He is my adversary, and he attacks me especially on this question.

GOLDMAN: This article in this paper is by whom?

TROTSKY: I don't know if it is signed or an editorial. It is an editorial.

GOLDMAN: Who is the editor?

TROTSKY: Here is the editor. It is signed "Laste."

GOLDMAN: He is the one who gave a statement in your favor in this case with reference to Royan, isn't he?

TROTSKY: Yes.

GOLDMAN: He takes a position contrary to yours with reference to the defense of the Soviet Union?

TROTSKY: Yes.

GOLDMAN: I introduce this paper into evidence as Exhibit No. 25.

(The paper, l'Internationale, *containing editorial on defense of the Soviet Union was introduced into evidence as Exhibit No. 25.)*

TROTSKY: In Belgium we had an organizer of the Communist Party who became an Oppositionist. Then he separated himself from us, especially on the question of the defense of the Soviet Union. His name is Van Overstraeten. In every other country we can find such people.

GOLDMAN: Does that article against the defense of the U.S.S.R. contain any references to your views?

TROTSKY: Yes, I believe so. In every issue you can find it.

GOLDMAN: I introduce this magazine entitled *l'Internationale* dated the 23rd of May, 1936, for two purposes: One, to show by this, by the editorial in this magazine, that Trotsky is for the defense of the Soviet Union, and that the editorial writer criticizes him for being for the defense of the Soviet

Union. Two, to show that his adversaries—that the deposition by Laste is a deposition made not by one who is politically friendly with Mr. Trotsky or in the same organization, but by one who is in a different organization hostile to Trotsky. I will have this magazine marked—that's right, I have already introduced it.

STOLBERG: Mr. Trotsky, on these questions, like the defense of the U.S.S.R., how do those revolutionists in France, like Souvarine, stand?

TROTSKY: They say: "We will see, we will remain neutral." They say that there is a different question; for example, of state capitalism. Their position is: "We will see; we will have a neutral position on that and fight against all of them."

GOLDMAN: You want to continue?

TROTSKY: I will say only that the forms of confusion are barriers to every organized defense of the Soviet Union.

GOLDMAN: I take it that your present attitude is the same?

TROTSKY: The same.

GOLDMAN: For the defense of the Soviet Union?

TROTSKY: For the defense of the Soviet Union.

GOLDMAN: In case of an attack on the Soviet Union by Germany, Japan or any other country, in what way would your attitude for the defense of the Soviet Union express itself? How would you show that you are for the defense of the Soviet Union? Can you give us an idea of the concrete attempts that you would make to help the Soviet Union?

TROTSKY: Yes. I believe that in the next war the Communist Parties of all countries will sustain their own countries as the Social Democracy did in the last war. I believe the Fourth International will fight the imperialist countries, the imperialist classes and will defend the Soviet Union. I believe, now, when the truth about the inner situation in the Soviet Union becomes more and more known by the workers, a certain disappointment and dissatisfaction will be very widespread, with a danger that the workers will say: "The Communists have fooled us. They have—"

GOLDMAN: Deceived.

TROTSKY: "They have only deceived us. We will have nothing to do with the Soviet state." We will say: "We never deceived you. We told you the truth all the time. Despite everything, there is a difference between the Soviet Union, the workers' state, and Japan and Germany. You must help the Soviet Union, in spite of all its weaknesses and its social illnesses. You must defend it against Japan and Germany." I believe in an hour of great danger the workers will with more confidence listen to us than to the official Stalinist-Communists who betray them every day.

STOLBERG: Mr. Trotsky, suppose the Soviet Union in case of war has an alliance with—of a kind which you could not defend. What would you do then?

TROTSKY: First—I must give an answer to that, but I must have more concrete data on the situation. It is too concrete a question with too abstract elements. It is not possible to answer it.

GOLDMAN: Well?

FINERTY: Suppose an alliance between France, England and Russia.

TROTSKY: Pardon?

FINERTY: An alliance against Germany, Italy and Japan. That is a possible alliance. What would your attitude be? In support of Russia?

STOLBERG: Surely Russia in the next war will have an alliance.

TROTSKY: It is a very complicated question. I believe that during the war the allies can impose on the Soviet Union such concessions, social and economic concessions, that the Soviet state can become a bourgeois state. It is, in connection with bourgeois states, all alone. At the end of the war, it is possible we will have a capitalist Soviet Union. If the

Soviet Union will oppose the pressure of its allies, then I believe that the allies will come together with its enemies to stifle the Soviet Union at the end of the war. Because it is the allies who believe that the combinations of powers will be the same at the beginning of the war, during the war and the end of the war. And we, as a revolutionary party, we must prepare ourselves not for a certain conjuncture, not for a moment, but for a period. I will say, for my part, that I would not support the French bourgeois government, I would not support the British bourgeois government during a war. But in the Soviet Union, I would support the Soviet Union, the Red Army, the Soviet state against all its enemies. Because—

FINERTY: One way you would try to sustain or support the Soviet government would be by fomenting revolutions in Germany and Japan?

TROTSKY: By both means. In the Soviet Union, I would try to be a good soldier, win the sympathy of the soldiers, and fight well. Then, at a good moment, when victory is assured, I would say: "Now we must finish with the bureaucracy."

FINERTY: I understand. But if you were in Germany, how would you go about your work?

TROTSKY: I said if I am personally in the Soviet Union, I will be a soldier. If I am in Japan or Germany, I will do everything I can to develop the revolutionary movement.

FINERTY: What would you do if you were in France or England?

TROTSKY: In France or England I would prepare also the overthrow of the bourgeois régime.

STOLBERG: You are a responsible revolutionary figure. Russia and France already have a military alliance. Suppose an international war breaks out. I am not interested in what you say about the Russian working class at this time. I know that. What would you say to the French working class in reference to the defense of the Soviet Union? "Change the

French bourgeois government," would you say?

TROTSKY: This question is more or less answered in the thesis, "The War and the Fourth International," in this sense: In France I would remain in opposition to the Government and would develop systematically this opposition. In Germany I would do anything I could to sabotage the war machinery. They are two different things. In Germany and in Japan, I would apply military methods as far as I am able to fight, oppose, and injure the machinery, the military machinery of Japan, to disorganize it, both in Germany and Japan. In France, it is political opposition against the bourgeoisie, and the preparation of the proletarian revolution. Both are revolutionary methods. But in Germany and Japan I have as my immediate aim the disorganization of the whole machinery. In France, I have the aim of the proletarian revolution.

FINERTY: If you succeeded in disorganizing the Hitler régime in Germany and the feudal régime in Japan, have a successful revolution in these two countries, the Soviets and these two proletarian states could resist the aggression of French and English capitalism; but would you want to offer as a price for war—it might be that the Soviet Union would be forced to give such a concession as would turn it into a capitalist state.

TROTSKY: That is the reason why, during the alliance between France and Russia, it is necessary to have the proletariat in France in active opposition to its bourgeoisie in order to have the possibility of hindering its bourgeoisie from imposing on the Soviet Union at the end of the war a bourgeois régime or capitalist régime.

GOLDMAN: Suppose you have the chance to take power during a war, in France, would you advocate it if you had the majority of the proletariat?

TROTSKY: Naturally.

GOLDMAN: In that way, would that not hinder the war against Japan and Hitler?

TROTSKY: No. I am absolutely sure that the only way to help and preserve, to save and develop the Soviet Union, is to develop and provoke the revolution in Japan and Germany. For success in this direction, it is necessary to destroy the German national ideology, the idea that everybody is against Germany. During the war it is sufficient to advise in Germany what was advised by Liebknecht and in France by Monatte: "Overthrow your own bourgeois government." If in France we have an opposition to the war, it will provoke in Germany a ten times more powerful movement of the proletariat, because in Germany, in the hermetically closed state, the contradictions are very explosive. It is necessary to have in France a revolutionary movement. If we declare that all the people, the proletariat and the bourgeoisie, must fight fascist Germany, then Hitler will say: "You see all humanity is against the German nation." It is the best cement, national cement, Hitler has. He has nourishment from this. It is necessary to continue the revolutionary opposition against the government in France in order to give the possibility for the revolution to develop in Germany.

GOLDMAN: In other words, you don't trust the French or English bourgeoisie to defend the Soviet Union?

TROTSKY: No.

FINERTY: As you stated, allies at the beginning of the war are not always allies at the end of the war. With the help of the bourgeoisie of England and France, you might defeat Germany and Japan and then ally yourself with the proletariat of Japan and Germany.

TROTSKY: Mr. Attorney, France and Great Britain are not my allies. They can be the allies of the Soviet state. My allies are the workers of all countries, and the only allies I recognize are the workers of all the other countries. My politics are established not for the purpose of diplomatic conventions, but for the development of the international revolutionary movement of the working class. I cannot put any hopes in the allies of the Soviet Union, in France and England. They can betray one another. They can separate from one another. But I am sure that ten workers who understand very well the situation—they will be free and they will win one hundred workers, and the hundred workers a thousand soldiers. They will be victorious at the end of the war. It seems to me very simple, but I believe it is a good idea.

RUEHLE (In German, through interpreter): The defense of the Soviet Union can lead to a point where you have to collaborate with Stalin. What would your position be then?

TROTSKY: You know, I am opposed to the reformists. I am opposed to Jouhaux in France, the leader of the trade-union organization. But when the fascists will attack Jouhaux, I am ready to come into an alliance with Jouhaux for the practical purpose of creating companies—

GOLDMAN: Defense?

TROTSKY: Defense organizations to fight jointly against the fascists with Jouhaux, who is my bitterest adversary. The same with Stalin. There was in the Russian Revolution a known example. Kerensky put me in prison on the accusation that I was an agent of Germany. Then Kornilov attacked Kerensky. Kerensky was obliged to give me my freedom. I went from the prison to a session of the Defense Committee with representatives of Kerensky and Company. The Bolsheviks were the best fighters against Kornilov. It is not a sentimental consideration or a personal consideration. The only consideration is the interest of the masses, what is necessary for the safety of the masses.

GOLDMAN: Then your answer is that you are willing to collaborate with Stalin in defending the Soviet Union against the capitalist enemies?

TROTSKY: Absolutely. I declared it in Copenhagen in my statement, and I gave that statement—

GOLDMAN: Yes, the statement is now in evidence. You declared before the press.

TROTSKY: Yes.

DEWEY: May I ask a hypothetical question? Suppose the bourgeoisie of England and France, in alliance with the Soviet Union, defeated fascist Germany and feudal Japan, might not the result be to make the Soviet Union a bourgeois country?

TROTSKY: Yes, a victory. A victory of France, of Great Britain and the Soviet Union. A victory over Germany and Japan could signify first a transformation of the Soviet Union into a bourgeois state and the transformation of France into a fascist state, because for a victory against Hitler it is necessary to have a monstrous military machine, and the fascist tendencies in France are powerful now. A victory can signify the destruction of fascism in Germany and the establishment of fascism in France. That is the reason why I cannot carry any responsibility for any of these gentlemen who are in office in these states. The only guarantee against fascism and reaction is the consciousness of the revolutionary masses, and their organizations.

GOLDMAN: Now, what effect, in your opinion, can the defeat of the Soviet Union have with reference to the fulfillment of your hopes and ideas?

TROTSKY: The defeat of the Soviet Union is inevitable in case the new war shall not provoke a new revolution. I believe it is impossible, it is incredible, that a new war will permit capitalism, decadent capitalism, to remain as it is. The revolution is inevitable. But if we theoretically admit war without revolution, then the defeat of the Soviet Union is inevitable.

LAFOLLETTE: Mr. Trotsky, the revolution in Russia or outside of Russia?

TROTSKY: Outside of Russia, the social revolution outside of Russia, and in the first line, Germany and Japan.

LAFOLLETTE: I would like to ask one more question since all other possibilities have been discussed. What would be your attitude assuming there was a war in which the Soviet Union found itself allied with Mr. Hitler?

TROTSKY: I will wait and see. (Laughter) It is not excluded. I believe that the accusation against me is directed against a certain part of the bureaucracy. In the Soviet Union—it is my hypothesis—is recurring a tendency to make peace with Hitler at any price, because war is a great danger, not only for the Soviet Union, but especially for the bureaucracy. The bureaucracy is frightened, from its point of view. But there must be a tendency for peace with Hitler. You know, in the beginning of 1933 Stalin declared that "we never opposed his movement." That is, referring to Hitler. I attacked him and I criticized him. He declared openly: "We never opposed the movement which is victorious in Germany, and we are ready to remain in the same relations with the new Germany as with the Weimar Germany."

LAFOLLETTE: He declared that Russia did not oppose that movement?

TROTSKY: Stalin in the first six months of 1933 hoped to keep in good relations with the fascists in Germany. I can introduce articles, my articles against him on that occasion. I quote from *Isvestia* about the 15th of March, 1933: "The U.S.S.R. is the only state which is not nourished on hostile sentiments towards Germany and that, independent of the form and the composition of the government of the Reich." It was Hitler who repulsed it, not he. Then only did he begin to look in the direction of France, and so on. The first half of 1933, I was an agent of France, the United States and Great Britain. I changed my profession only after the crushing of Stalin's hopes to remain in friendship with Hitler. I can prove it. It was in the *Pravda*. I am represented as "Mr." Trotsky. I am "Mr." Trotsky in spite of my English. (Laughter) The article is entitled: "Mr. Trotsky in the Service of Lord Beaverbrook." I am represented by Radek as an ally of Lord Beaverbrook. I don't know why especially Beaverbrook.

Yaroslavsky names me an ally of Winston Churchill. It is in the same issue, the same copy of *Pravda.*

FINERTY: I think we would like to have that paper in evidence.

LAFOLLETTE: Yes.

GOLDMAN: I will introduce it in evidence.

TROTSKY: Yes; I can give you the quotation. You see, I am only impressed by the multitude of the press evidence. I have a series of quotations from the official press where I am represented as the ally of Poland, as the defender of the Versailles Peace—and Stalin was against the Versailles Peace. Only now he is for it and I am against it. (Laughter)

FINERTY: Mr. Goldman, I think that it would help the Commission if we would appraise all the differences in the charges made by the Stalin Government against Mr. Trotsky.

GOLDMAN: Yes.

BEALS: I would like to ask one question along these lines, since we are talking about it. I would like to ask one question since we are talking about the world war: the most imminent danger of war in Spain. Are you responsible for the Trotskyites in Spain?

TROTSKY: What is "Trotskyites in Spain"?

BEALS: Are you responsible for the various factions in Spain who use the name of "Trotskyites"?

TROTSKY: There are no Trotskyites. The situation is such that everybody who opposes the politics of the Comintern is named by the Comintern "Trotskyite." Because Trotskyite means fascism in the Comintern propaganda. It is a simple argument. The Trotskyites in Spain are not numerous—the genuine Trotskyites. I regret it, but I must confess, they are not numerous. There is a powerful party, the POUM, the Workers' Party of Marxist Unification. That party alone recognizes that I am not a fascist. The youth of that party has sympathy with our ideas. But the policy of that party is very opportunistic, and I openly criticize it.

BEALS: Who is the head of it?

TROTSKY: Nin. He is my friend. I know him very well. But I criticize him very sharply.

BEALS: One reason I bring this out is that the charge has been made that the faction of Trotskyites sabotage the loyalist movement in Spain.

TROTSKY: That we allegedly sabotage the loyalist movement. I believe that I have expressed it in many interviews and articles: The only way possible to assure victory in Spain is to say to the peasants: "The Spanish soil is your soil." To say to the workers: "The Spanish factories are your factories." That is the only possibility to assure victory. Stalin, in order not to frighten the French bourgeoisie, has become the guard of private property in Spain. The Spanish peasant is not very interested in fine definitions. He says: "With Franco and with Caballero, it is the same thing." Because the peasant is very realistic. During our Civil War—I do not believe that we were victorious principally because of our military science. It is false. We were victorious because of our revolutionary program. We said to the peasant: "It is your soil." And the peasant, who at one time went away and then went to the Whites, compared the Bolsheviks with the White Guards and said, "The Bolsheviks are better." Then when the peasantry, the hundreds and millions of Russian peasantry, were of the conviction that the Bolsheviks were better, we were victorious.

BEALS: Would you expand a little further the statement that Stalin is guarding private property in Spain?

TROTSKY: He says, and the Comintern declared with regard to Spain, that the social reforms will come after the victory. "Now, it is war. Our job now is war. Social reforms will come after the victory." The peasant becomes indifferent. "It is not my war; I am not interested in the victory of the generals. The generals are fighting one another." That is his opinion. You know, in his primitive way, he is right.

I am with this primitive Spanish peasant against the fine diplomats.

BEALS: Then you don't think it is of great importance which side wins the war in Spain? It does not make a great deal of difference which side wins the war?

TROTSKY: No, the workers must win the war. It is necessary that the workers win. But I assure you that by the policy of the Comintern and Stalin you have the surest way of losing the revolution. They lost the revolution in China, they lost the revolution in Germany, and now they are preparing the defeat in France and in Spain. We had only one victory of the proletarian revolution. That was the October Revolution, and it was made directly in opposition to the method of Stalin.

BEALS: Now, what steps would you take in the case of Spain today, if you were in Stalin's place?

TROTSKY: I could not be in his place.

BEALS: Say, if you were in Stalin's place—if you had the destiny of the Soviet Union in your hands, what would be your action in Spain?

TROTSKY: It is not a question of the Soviet Union. It is a question of the revolutionary parties of the Comintern, it is a question of the parties. Naturally, I would remain in opposition to all the bourgeois parties.

STOLBERG: Mr. Trotsky, may I ask a question which relates to Carleton Beals's question? If you had been in power from 1923 on, in that case, from your point of view, the Chinese Revolution would have been either saved or would have gained additionally. There would have been no German fascism. I mean, if your position had been victorious back in 1923. There would have been the situation in Spain, but it could not have occurred exactly that way. But you lost. The Comintern politics in China and Germany brought about a defeat. Now we have the Spanish situation. I am merely presenting what I think is your position. Then I will ask the question. We have the Spanish situation on top of the mistakes made in the last fourteen years. We have a civil war in Spain. Surely a purely orthodox or puristic position does not answer the problem. With whom would you side at the present time in Spain?

TROTSKY: I gave the answer in many interviews and articles. Every Trotskyite in Spain must be a good soldier, on the side of the Left. Naturally, it is so elementary a question—you know it is not worth discussing. A leader or any other member in the Government of Caballero is a traitor. A leader of the working class cannot enter the bourgeois government. We did not enter the Government of Kerensky in Russia. While we defended Kerensky against Kornilov, we did not enter his Government. As I declared that I am ready to enter into an alliance with Stalin against the fascists, or an alliance with Jouhaux against the French fascists. It is an elementary question.

FINERTY: Mr. Trotsky, if you were in power in Russia today and your help was asked by the loyalists in Spain, you would condition your help on the basis that the land was given to the peasants and the factories to the workers?

TROTSKY: Not on the condition—not this question. The first question would be the attitude of the Spanish revolutionary party. I would say, "No political alliance with the bourgeoisie," as the first condition. The second, "You must be the best soldiers against the fascists." Third, "You must say to the soldiers, to the other soldiers and the peasants: 'We must transform our country into a people's country. Then, when we win the masses, we will throw the bourgeoisie out of office, and then we will be in power and we will make the social revolution.'"

FINERTY: Then, to make effective any help, you will have to have an alliance with the Marxist party in Spain?

TROTSKY: Naturally, I would help Caballero with all the material means against fascism, but at the same time I would give the advice to the Communist Party not to enter into the Government, but to remain in a critical position against Caballero and to prepare the second chapter of the workers' revolution.

BEALS: Isn't that one of the reasons that the Azaña Government, when first in office, brought in the reaction, precisely because of that policy?

TROTSKY: Because of a conservative bourgeois policy: because he tried to make half a revolution, a third of a revolution. My opinion is that the revolution must be—better not begin that way. If you begin the revolution, do it to the end. To the end signifies the social revolution.

BEALS: This would mean, by the policy you follow, the probable victory of Franco, would it not?

TROTSKY: The victory of Franco is assured by the present policy of the Comintern. The Spanish revolution, the Spanish proletariat and peasantry, by their efforts and energy and devotion during the past six years, could have assured five victories or six victories—every year a victory. But the ruling stratum of the working class did everything to hinder, sabotage and betray the revolutionary power of the masses. The revolution is based upon the elementary forces of the proletariat, and on the political direction of its leaders. It is a very important problem, and the leadership in Spain was miserable all the time. The Spanish proletariat shows that it is of the best material, the best revolutionary force we have seen for the last decade. In spite of that, it is not victorious. I accuse the C.I. and the Second International of hindering the victory by their perfidious policy, which is based on cowardice before the bourgeoisie, the bourgeoisie and Franco. They remain in a Government with the bourgeoisie, which is the symbol of private property. And Caballero himself bows before the symbol of private property. The masses, however, do not see the difference between the two régimes.

GOLDMAN: Do you exclude the possibility of a victory, of

a military victory of Caballero over Franco?

TROTSKY: It is very difficult to say—a military victory. It is possible that even by a military victory, the victorious régime can in a very short time be transformed into a fascist régime, if the masses remain dissatisfied and indifferent and the new military organization created by the victory is not a Socialist organization.

GOLDMAN: But the masses in Spain might be under the illusion that they are actually in the struggle against Franco and the fascists—they are actually struggling for their own proletarian interests.

TROTSKY: Unfortunately, the majority of the masses have lost all their illusions. And this explains the dragging character of the civil war, because the People's Front Government prepared an army for Franco. The new Government issued from the People's Front, from the victory, and protected the army and Franco, so that under the Government of the People's Front the army was prepared for the insurrection. Then began the civil war, and the bourgeoisie said to the people: "You must await victory. Then we will be very generous, but after the victory."

GOLDMAN: Now, you didn't answer the question asked a half hour ago.

BEALS: I didn't quite finish. I don't yet see, Mr. Trotsky, how you or Mr. Stalin is going to save the situation in Spain. It seems to me that both of the policies you have indicated will have the most immediate results of winning the war for Franco. I can't see, personally, anything in favor of Franco at all. I don't quite clearly get your point. It seems to me that in the meantime Mr. Franco will have won the war.

TROTSKY: I can only repeat that I gave the key, a little key to my friends and everybody who is of the same conviction, and my first advice is to be the best soldiers now in the camp of Caballero. That is the first thing. You know there is a group of the Fourth International, a company of our comrades in the trenches. It is so elementary that I will not dwell on it. It is necessary to fight. But, you know, it is not sufficient to fight with a gun. It is necessary to have ideas and give these same ideas to others, to prepare for the future. I can fight with the simple peasant, but he understands very little in the situation. I must give him an explanation. I must say: "You are right in fighting Franco. We must exterminate the fascists, but not in order to have the same Spain as before the civil war, because Franco issued from this Spain. We must exterminate the foundation of Franco, the social foundation of Franco, which is the social system of capitalism. Are you satisfied with my ideas?" you ask the peasant. He will say: "Yes, I believe so." Then explain the same thing to the workers.

BEALS: Why would you send the soldier to fight Franco and yet refuse to enter the Government of Caballero to assist in the same purpose?

TROTSKY: I explained it. We refused categorically to enter the Kerensky Government, but the Bolsheviks were the best fighters against Kornilov. Not only that, the best soldiers and sailors were Bolsheviks. During the insurrection of Kornilov, Kerensky must go to the sailors of the Baltic fleet and demand of them to defend them in the Winter Palace. I was at that time in prison. They took him to the guard, and sent a delegation to me to ask me what must be done: To arrest Kerensky or defend him? That is a historical fact. I said: "Yes, you must guard him very well now; tomorrow we will arrest him." (Laughter)

GOLDMAN: Are you through?

BEALS: Yes.

GOLDMAN: Now, Mr. Trotsky, your accusers say that you want the defeat of the Soviet Union. I ask you this: What effect would the defeat of the Soviet Union have upon the possibility of realizing the ideas of Socialism that you stand for?

TROTSKY: It would signify a tremendous historical retreat,

because the overthrow of the present Government would signify economic chaos for years, possibly for decades, if it is not overthrown by the proletarian revolution. But a defeat and the restoration of capitalism would signify a historical retreat.

GOLDMAN: This finishes the section of the evidence dealing with the defense of the Soviet Union. I think we have some time in which to deal with the next section, so we can be sure to finish tomorrow.

TROTSKY: Mr. Chairman, I would like to quote only five or six lines to prove that the accusation that the Opposition is for defeat is not an invention of yesterday. Stalin advanced this accusation in 1927 in the session of the Central Committee. He accused us of not being in favor of victory. Here is a quotation from a section of the report of the session of the Central Committee, and my answer.

STOLBERG: What page?

TROTSKY: It is page 9 in the pamphlet entitled "In Defense of the Soviet Union." I quote: "The Opposition is *for* the victory of the U.S.S.R.; it has proved this and will continue to prove this in action in a manner inferior to none."

DEWEY: I might announce now that if Mr. Goldman can finish by noon tomorrow, there will be no session in the evening. The Commission has to confer together on the line of questioning, Mr. Finerty's line of questioning of Mr. Trotsky. I hope very much that Mr. Goldman can finish by tomorrow afternoon.

GOLDMAN: If we adjourn now, I want to introduce these two documents of *Pravda*.

TROTSKY: Of the 8th of March, 1929.

GOLDMAN: Of the 8th of March, 1929, containing the article, "Mr. Trotsky in the Service of the English Bourgeoisie." We will make this Exhibit No. 26.

(The issue of Pravda *of March 8, 1929, was introduced into evidence as Exhibit No. 26.)*

TROTSKY: Here is a facsimile on the Pilsudski matter.

GOLDMAN: In the *Bulletin of the Opposition,* No. 23, of August, 1931, there is an article in which is included a citation showing the accusation of *Pravda* that Trotsky was allied with Pilsudski and that Mr. Trotsky published an article in the Polish Government paper.

TROTSKY: An article against the Five-Year Plan.

GOLDMAN: I will introduce this as Exhibit No. 27.

(The said facsimile on the Pilsudski matter was introduced into evidence as Exhibit No. 27.)

DEWEY: We will now adjourn this session.

End of Eighth Session—Seven o'clock P.M.

Ninth session

April 15, 1937, at ten o'clock a.m.

GOLDMAN: I want to introduce statements into the record if you will permit me, Mr. Chairman. With reference to certain of the depositions that we received from France, I wish to make the following announcement: Many of the depositions included in the folders concerning Copenhagen and Royan give their names. A great number of them were made by émigrés who are now in an illegal situation. Due to the impossibility of legalizing their depositions by official means, the French Committee for an Inquiry into the Trials has created a commission entrusted with the certification of the depositions. The members of this Commission are Alfred Rosmer, well known in the workers' movement in France, Fernand Charbit, militant syndicalist, and André Breton, author. The signers of the depositions presented themselves before the Commission which certified their depositions by the three signatures of its members and by the seal of the Committee.

Another statement I would like to make refers to the very

important question, although not so relevant, the question of Mr. Trotsky's attitude in the Spanish situation. Naturally, his English is a barrier which makes it somewhat difficult for him to explain clearly what he thinks about the situation. For the sake of complete clarity I wish to read into the record: "Answers to Certain Questions of the Representative of Havas, the French Newspaper Agency."

TROTSKY: And the date.

GOLDMAN: February 19th, 1937. It reads:

> Have I or have I not given "instructions" to aid the Republican front with volunteers? I have given "instructions" to no one. In general, I do not give "instructions." I express my *opinion* in articles. *Only cowards, traitors, or agents of fascism can renounce aid to the Spanish Republican armies.* The elementary duty of every revolutionist is to struggle against the bands of Franco, Mussolini and Hitler.
>
> On the left wing of the Spanish Governmental coalition, and partly in the opposition, is the POUM. This party is not "Trotskyite." I have criticized its policies on many occasions, despite my warm sympathy for the heroism with which the members of this party, above all the youth, struggle at the front. The POUM has committed the error of participating in the electoral combination of the "Popular" Front; under the cover of this combination, General Franco during the course of several months boldly prepared the insurrection which is now ravaging Spain. A revolutionary party did not have the right to take upon itself, either directly or indirectly, any responsibility for a policy of blindness and criminal tolerance. It was obliged to call the masses to vigilance. The leadership of the POUM committed the second error of entering the Catalonian Coalition Government; in order to fight hand in hand with the other parties at the front,

there is no need to take upon oneself any responsibility for the false governmental policies of these parties. Without weakening the military front for a moment, it is necessary to know how to rally the masses politically under the revolutionary banner.

In civil war, incomparably more than in ordinary war, *politics dominates strategy*. Robert Lee, as an army chieftain, was surely more talented than Grant, but the program of the liquidation of slavery assured victory to Grant. In our three years of civil war the superiority of military art and military technique was often enough on the side of the enemy, but at the very end it was the Bolshevik program which conquered. The worker knew very well what he was fighting for. The peasant hesitated for a long time, but, comparing the two régimes by experience, he finally supported the Bolshevik side.

In Spain the Stalinists, who lead the chorus from on high, have advanced the formula to which Caballero, president of the Cabinet, also adheres: *First* military victory, and *then* social reform. I consider this formula fatal for the Spanish revolution. Not seeing the radical differences between the two programs in reality, the toiling masses, above all the peasants, fall into indifference. In these conditions, fascism will inevitably win, because the purely military advantage is on its side. *Audacious social reforms represent the strongest weapon in the civil war and the fundamental condition for the victory over fascism.*

The policies of Stalin, who has always revealed himself as an opportunist in revolutionary situations, are dictated by a fear of frightening the French bourgeoisie, above all the "200 families" against whom the French Popular Front long ago declared war—on paper. Stalin's policies in Spain repeat not so much Kerensky's policies in 1917 as they do the policies of Ebert-Scheidemann in the German Revolution of 1918. Hitler's victory was the punishment for the policies of Ebert-Scheidemann. In Germany the punishment was delayed for fifteen years. *In Spain it can come in less than fifteen months.*

However, would not the social and political victory of the Spanish workers and peasants mean European war? Such prophecies, dictated by reactionary cowardice, are radically false. If fascism wins in Spain, France will find itself caught in a vise from which it will not be able to withdraw. *Franco's dictatorship would mean the unavoidable acceleration of European war,* in the most difficult conditions for France. It is useless to add that a new European war would *bleed the French people* to the last drop and lead it into its decline, and, by the same token, would deal a terrible blow to all humanity.

On the other hand, the victory of the Spanish workers and peasants would undoubtedly shake the régimes of Mussolini and Hitler. Thanks to their hermetic, totalitarian character, the fascist régimes produce an impression of unshakable firmness. Actually, *at the first serious test they will be the victims of internal explosions. The victorious Russian revolution sapped the strength of the Hohenzollern régime. The victorious Spanish revolution will undermine the régimes of Hitler and Mussolini. For that reason alone the victory of the Spanish workers and peasants will reveal itself at once as a powerful force for peace.*

The task of the true Spanish revolutionists consists in strengthening and reinforcing the military front, in demolishing the political tutelage of the Soviet bureaucracy, in giving a bold social program to the masses, in assuring thereby the victory of the revolution and, precisely in that way, upholding the cause of peace. Therein alone lies the salvation of Europe!

LEON TROTSKY.

TROTSKY: It was also published in the United States, if I remember correctly.

GOLDMAN: This statement was published in the French press.

TROTSKY: And in the *New York Post,* where Lore works.

STOLBERG: The *New York Post*?

GOLDMAN: The *New York Evening Post.* Now, the next point I will take up is the question of the international situation. By that I mean, what Mr. Trotsky's attitude has been on the international relations of the Soviet Union and its foreign policy, and his attitude also with reference to a possible attack by Hitler against the Soviet Union and by Japan against the Soviet Union. Necessarily, some of the questions have already been covered, but some of them are not. I want to take up more of the material under this heading.

FINERTY: I suppose this will be directed to the question of his complicity or noncomplicity in the intervention of Germany and Japan, or the alleged intervention of these two countries.

GOLDMAN: Will you state, Mr. Trotsky, what basic principles determined the foreign policy of the Soviet Union during the time when Lenin and you played leading roles in guiding the destiny of the Soviet Union?

TROTSKY: We considered the Soviet Union as a part of the world revolutionary movement of the working class. We considered it our duty to take every measure which could save and preserve the Soviet Union. We considered that the revolutionary movement in every country—that its success would best guarantee the stability of the Soviet Union. We never tried to submit the revolutionary movement in any country to the specific interests of the Soviet Union, because such a submission signifies the weakening of the workers' movement in that country—in all countries. Our doctrines, in our opinion, coincided totally with the independent revolutionary development of the proletariat across the world. I can remember—it was in 1922, in the last year of Lenin's active life—when Zinoviev and Bukharin—more Zinoviev—directed by mere organizational narrowness, tried to revise the leadership of certain countries by measures of pressure from above. Lenin wrote then—this letter is published: "By such measures you will make only a selection of docile and stupid people. That is not what we want in the C.I., docile and stupid people." I regret it very much, but I am obliged to say that this selection has since made very great progress, because the method of pressure from Moscow, of replacing all leaders in the conjunctural interests of the Moscow bureaucracy, became the rule.

GOLDMAN: In what way has the foreign policy, in your opinion, changed since Stalin has assumed control?

TROTSKY: The first thing which was proclaimed was the theory of "Socialism in one country." The posing of "Socialism in one country" signifies that all the other sections lose for a long period, an indeterminate period, their independent role. They represent now only the "guard" of the Soviet Union. "Socialism" is applied in the Soviet Union independent of the happenings in the world.

We see now the struggle with fascism in Spain, fascism in Germany, fascism in Austria and Italy, but the Socialist bureaucracy says that the revolution progresses in the Soviet Union. In our Marxist eyes, the reaction in the Soviet Union is only a part of this tremendous world-reaction. If this world-reaction continues as now, the Soviet Union as a Soviet proletarian state is doomed.

GOLDMAN: Did you ever believe that the Soviet Union should send the Red Army into other countries for the purpose of overthrowing the rule of the capitalist classes?

TROTSKY: In such an abstract form, it is difficult to answer. It is possible to imagine a situation where civil war is developing in one country. The proletariat creates one government, and the fascists another government. Then the government of the proletariat appeals to the Soviet Government for aid. Naturally, I will not refuse if I can. Imagine the situation in Spain. And Spain, imagine, is a neighboring country of the Soviet Union. Caballero appeals to us for help. It would be the elementary duty—as during a strike it is the duty of the trade unionists in every country to help the strike, the same duty it is to help by military force if it is not imposed on them and if they themselves ask for the aid.

GOLDMAN: But assuming there is no dual power in a country. Assuming that the proletariat does not attempt to take power. Did you ever believe or advocate the idea that the Red Army should be sent into other countries?

TROTSKY: A revolution by the Red Army would be the worst adventurism. To try to impose revolution on other people by the Red Army would be adventurism.

GOLDMAN: When you were one of the leading figures of the Soviet Union, did you ever advocate this idea: That the Soviet Union should have no political or economic relations with the capitalist world?

TROTSKY: Never.

GOLDMAN: What was your general conception with reference to that problem?

TROTSKY: It is unfortunately a question dealing with an objective situation we cannot escape. It would be the same as if I said I would not use a train because the owner is a capitalist. You cannot wait for the moment of the proletarian dictatorship to use the train. The same rule—from all sides we are surrounded by capitalist countries. We must buy and we must sell. We must have the possibility of sending our citizens to other countries to learn, to buy and sell. We must have relations, economic, political and diplomatic relations, with them. It is absolutely natural. I give a better example: It would be the same if the trade unions should cease or refuse any conversations with the boss. It is impossible. We were, in our opinion, a trade union which became the state. The other states are the bosses, and we must have conversations with them. It is absolutely necessary, even, to make concessions to them, as workers make concessions to their bosses after a strike has not succeeded. We are the only workers' state in the world, surrounded by hostile capitalist nations.

FINERTY: Mr. Goldman, I think it would be a help if Mr. Trotsky would define the period in which he had joint responsibility with Stalin for the Russian Government, the Soviet Government.

GOLDMAN: Did you understand the question, Mr. Trotsky?

FINERTY: With Lenin, I mean.

GOLDMAN: Will you give us the period during which you assumed joint responsibility with Lenin for determining the foreign policy of the Soviet Union?

TROTSKY: Until 1922 Government responsibility was complete. During 1922, during the illness of Lenin, it was the transitory period of the illegal "Troïka." From 1923, came the struggle of the Opposition.

GOLDMAN: And from then on you assumed no responsibility for the conduct of the Soviet Government's policy?

TROTSKY: Until 1927, I remained a member of the Politburo. I was in opposition in the Politburo, but before the world I had my part of the responsibility.

GOLDMAN: Now, what is your theory concerning the possibility of a peaceful coexistence of the Soviet Union, the only country where capitalism does not rule, with the capitalist countries?

TROTSKY: The theory is simple. We needed that the others let us alone in peace. We were not interested in war, in provoking wars. We were interested in peace. That is the reason for the great concessions we made to the capitalist countries during this time, beginning in 1918 to 1924. But in 1933 or 1934, Stalin sold to Japan the Chinese Eastern Railroad. He was attacked by many Left elements in Europe, and I believe also unnecessarily, for this concession. I defended him in 1933. I explained that if it was a question of peace and war, if we have a reason for war with Japan, if it is necessary, it would not be a question only of the railroad. If we can, by a concession of the railroad, gain one or two or three years of peace, we must make that concession. I had great discussions about this, international discussions, with my own friends.

GOLDMAN: Now, can you tell us your theory in general about the possibility of the existence of the Soviet Union, the workers' country, for a long period of time in the midst of a capitalist world?

TROTSKY: It cannot be indefinitely—such a coexistence. Because the capitalist world is not stable—excuse me, I am tired. [At this point Trotsky halted in his answer—A.M.G.] It is not a stable one, and every country is gravitating either to workers' revolution or to fascist dictatorship. In both cases, the relations between the Soviet Union and the capitalist states must change. For many years there was a certain friendship between the Soviet Union and Germany. It changed after the victory of Hitler. If the proletariat is victorious in Spain, the relations will be the best, I hope, between the Soviet Union and Spain. If it is fascist, the Soviet Union will have a mortal foe, one mortal foe more.

GOLDMAN: One more mortal foe?

TROTSKY: Yes, one more mortal foe. It is not a stable situation. And we are interested in prolonging this situation, to give the possibility to the revolutionary workers' movement to develop, not to provoke ruptures, because the Soviet Union can be abolished as a workers' state. The capitalist states are now more powerful, many times more powerful, than the Soviet state. But we must understand that this situation is not an eternal one, that the existence of the Soviet state depends in the last analysis on the development of revolution in the capitalist countries.

GOLDMAN: And I gather that your idea is that in the state of capitalism at the present time, in the state of decline, you don't think that the Soviet Union can last for a very long period as an isolated Socialist stronghold in the capitalist world?

TROTSKY: No, it is excluded. When they say in the Soviet Union I am a pessimist, I can only be astonished, because it is a question of the world proletariat. Why must I be pessimistic about the world proletariat? I am especially optimistic about their establishing international Socialism. I hope the world proletariat will win power so that humanity will not decline totally. The situation is such: Either capitalism will abolish human culture through fascism, or the working class will win power and create a new basis for the new civilization. This is the only possibility. In that situation, I am optimistic. I don't believe our civilization will perish. I believe the new development will begin, the Socialist development across the world.

In this life process, I see the fate of the Soviet Union. It is not a special paradise—the Soviet Union—for a select nation. It is part of human civilization, and no more. And I must recognize even the backward aspects in spite of the very important progress made.

GOLDMAN: Then, I take it that you believe that in order to save the Soviet Union, you have to extend the workers' revolution to capitalist countries?

TROTSKY: Yes, it is the reason also for the creation of the Fourth International.

GOLDMAN: What is your opinion about the desirability of war as furthering the interests of Socialism?

TROTSKY: It is almost the same as if the question were asked: What is your opinion of cholera and epidemics for human civilization? (Laughter) When there was cholera—there was in Russia, and is now from time to time—we revolutionists sought by illegal leaflets to help the peasants.

We denounced the régime of the Tsar. You know it is an interesting parallel. The Black Hundreds, our specific Russian reactionaries, accused us of spreading the germs of cholera. There were pogroms against the doctors, the students, the radical intelligentsia, and Jews, as a vengeance for spreading cholera. It was the measure of the reaction to reject the responsibility about sanitary conditions and to place it on the radical elements. I thank you very much for your question because I find the analogy very important. I assure you, under Tsarism we had twenty-five years of revolutionary activity, and I never asked for cholera. (Laughter) The same with war. If war comes in spite of us, we will use all the means to place the responsibility on the ruling classes and to accelerate the revolution. But to wish a war—it is absurd from every point of view. What do we need with artificial means for revolution? We have a revolution in Spain without war, but we are not capable of being victorious yet. We had in Germany two and three revolutions. There was in 1918, and in 1923 during the Ruhr occupation, a totally revolutionary situation. Before the victory of Hitler we had a totally revolutionary situation. The lack was not objective revolutionary situations, but revolutionary parties which had the necessary confidence of the masses and adequate leadership. Now, we need the creation of such parties and such leadership. For that we need time, and not to provoke artificial revolutionary situations with the purpose of losing them and so to allow millions of workers, hundreds of thousands, to perish in the defeat.

GOLDMAN: May I ask if you have always in your writings agitated against war?

TROTSKY: Yes. I believe the more a party, a workers' party, is revolutionary, the less is the danger of war, because the only handicap for the imperialists in beginning a new war is the fear of a new revolution. If the danger is real, if the working class is penetrated with a revolutionary spirit, we can postpone the war and the revolution can proceed and not only make war impossible, but the revolution can replace war.

GOLDMAN: Is it not one of your theories that a war might destroy civilization altogether?

TROTSKY: Yes. If we have now in Europe a war without revolutionary parties, the danger is very great that the war will finish with the decline of European civilization. I wrote many times that in such a case civilization will find its new fatherland in the New World. Europe will become a backward province for a long period.

GOLDMAN: What has been your attitude towards German fascism both before and after it took power?

TROTSKY: I tried—I quoted, I believe, the first or the second day of the sessions, I quoted many articles and pamphlets written by me on the question: Why we can hinder Hitler to take power.

INTERPRETER: You mean how.

TROTSKY: Yes; how we can. I have many pamphlets, brochures and articles beginning in 1930. I tried to draw the attention of the Comintern to this tremendous danger, and they accused me of being in a panic, that I overestimated the Nazis in Germany, and that the most immediate foe was the Social-Fascists.

STOLBERG: You mean the so-called Social-Fascists?

TROTSKY: The Social Democrats.

STOLBERG: You don't subscribe to that characterization?

TROTSKY: No. I was also a Left Social-Fascist, not a genuine fascist, but a Left Social-Fascist. The reason was, I insisted upon the necessity of the united front between the Communist Party and the Social Democratic Party, the united front against Hitler. But you know that in Germany the Communist Party concluded a united front with Hitler in Prussia against the Social-Democratic Government on the 9th of August, 1931. It was the famous Prussian plebiscite initiated by Hitler and supported by the Communists. During all this time, I wrote those many pamphlets, and they are named in the list I presented to the Commission.

GOLDMAN: You wrote at that time the famous pamphlet, "Germany, the Key to the International Situation"?

TROTSKY: It was published in part by von Ossietzky. He is now the winner of the Nobel Prize, and was in a concentration camp in Germany. He published my first pamphlet in his magazine, with a favorable introduction. He tried to interest the Communist Party and the Social Democratic Party in the question.

GOLDMAN: You also wrote "What Next? Vital Questions for the German Proletariat"?

TROTSKY: Yes; it is a pamphlet of one hundred and fifty pages, where I accuse the Soviet bureaucracy of preparing the victory of Hitler by its policy.

GOLDMAN: Now, after Hitler—

TROTSKY: Excuse me; I named Hitler at that time the future super-Wrangel. Wrangel was the last General-in-chief of the White Guards in Russia. He was a great danger for us. I said: "By your policy, you prepare a new Wrangel, a super-Wrangel on a worldwide scale. He will be Hitler."

GOLDMAN: After Hitler took power, what was your attitude towards the relationship between Hitler and the Soviet Union?

TROTSKY: I didn't try to provoke a war. But I showed in my writings how the Soviet bureaucracy in their hopes to remain in good relations with Hitler were absolutely wrong. Then I wrote in the French press in 1933 or 1934—I wrote a series of articles in the bourgeois press denouncing the genuine plans of Hitler. You know, Mr. Chairman, I had a very peculiar manner of serving my allies, Hitler and the Mikado.

GOLDMAN: You mean your alleged allies.

TROTSKY: Yes, my alleged allies. (Laughter)

GOLDMAN: I introduce into evidence a pamphlet by Leon Trotsky entitled: "What Hitler Wants," one of the John Day pamphlets, which is a translation of the articles written by Trotsky in the French press in 1933.

TROTSKY: Permit me to show a quotation in this connection—it is an official paper of the Soviet Union. It is about the 15th of March, 1933. I have not the exact date, but we will find it. It is a quotation, not indicating the exact date, about the 15th of March, 1933. I quote: "The U.S.S.R. is the only state which is not nourished on hostile sentiments towards Germany and that, independent of the form and the composition of the government of the Reich." [*Isvestia*, March 4, 1933.—Ed.] That was the official line.

GOLDMAN: At that time, just immediately after Hitler took power, the rulers of the Soviet Union attempted to continue their relations with Germany as they were before—is that right?

TROTSKY: Yes; Stalin declared and it was repeated in the press, that "we never opposed the movement in Germany."

GOLDMAN: Where did you first point out in a series of articles the danger to the Soviet Union after Hitler came into power?

TROTSKY: I wrote an article about the Red Army. It was published in March, 1934, in ten languages. I wrote it especially also for the United States. It was published in the *Saturday Noon Post*, a large weekly.

FRANKEL: *Evening Post.*

TROTSKY: Yes, the *Saturday Evening Post;* I believe it is one of the important conservative weeklies in the country. A long article about the Red Army with the purpose—everybody knows that I am an exile. On one side, they can suppose that I am more critical than the officials. On the other side, I took part in the organization of the Red Army, and am acquainted with the question. By my article, I tried to give the Red Army more authority in the eyes of world opinion. I repeat, the article was printed in ten languages. It says: "To appreciate the strength of the Red Army, there is no necessity to idealize it." It is the final paragraph.

> To speak of the prosperity of the people of the Soviet Union is, at least, premature. There is still too much misery, suffering, injustice, and, consequently, discontent. But the idea that the Soviet masses are inclined to await aid from the armies of the Mikado or Hitler cannot be appreciated except as delirium. In spite of all the difficulties of the transitional régime, the political and moral cohesion of the peoples of the U.S.S.R. is sufficiently strong, in any case stronger than that of their possible adversaries. What has just been said does not at all mean that a war, even if victorious, will correspond to the interests of the Soviet Union. On the contrary, it will thrust her backward. But maintenance of peace depends at least on two parties. The facts must be taken as they are; not only is war not excluded, but rather it is almost inevitable. He who knows how and reads the book of history, he will understand in advance that if the Russian Revolution, which has lasted with ebb and flow for almost thirty years (since 1905!), is forced to direct its course in the channel of war, it will unroll a formidable and destructive force.

GOLDMAN: Where was that article written in the United States?

TROTSKY: Pardon?

GOLDMAN: In what magazine did it appear in the United States?

TROTSKY: It was published in the *Saturday Evening Post*.

GOLDMAN: Will you furnish the Commission with the date?

TROTSKY: I will furnish a copy. It was published in my *Bulletin* on March 13th, 1934. It was during my alliance with the Mikado and Germany—my alleged alliance. (Laughter) It was published in the French paper, *l'Instransigeant*. In German, it was published in Czechoslovakia. It was published in ten languages.

GOLDMAN: Now, I forgot to number the exhibit I introduced just a while ago. The pamphlet "What Hitler Wants" I introduce into evidence as Exhibit No. 28.

(The pamphlet by Leon Trotsky, "What Hitler Wants," was introduced into evidence as Exhibit No. 28.)

GOLDMAN: Now, did you write any articles—

RUEHLE (LaFollette translating from the German): I would like to know your opinion of the policy of the German Communist Party, and why it did not struggle at the time Hitler took power, why it did not struggle in opposition to Hitler.

TROTSKY: It is a very important question. The Communist Party conceded all the positions to Hitler without a blow. I declared—it was my crime in the eyes of the C.I.—that it was one of the greatest treasons of a revolutionary party in all history. With the bitterest enemies seizing power, the leaders had their passports for abroad, and the story was finished. It was a miserable attitude, and I accused the Comintern openly of betrayal of the German working class. It is not our position to provoke an artificial revolution; but it is a situation where I am in my home, in a worker's home, the enemy enters by violence, and I sit in my place or go abroad. It was one of the most miserable treasons in history, and I accused them openly of it. I can say that they were objectively the allies of Hitler in that situation, and not myself.

RUEHLE (LaFollette translating from the German): One more question. What was the official Comintern position to Hitler's seizure of power, and what was your reaction?

TROTSKY: The Communist Party and the Comintern, in order to justify their position, declared: "It is very good that Hitler comes into power now. He will last two or three weeks or two or three months, and then we will be the bosses in the house." It was the current formula. I mentioned it yesterday in my writings presented to the Commission. I affirmed, "It is the greatest defeat, and the consequences will become more and more profound for years, and maybe for a decade."

GOLDMAN: Have you ever written any articles dealing with the situation of Japan and the possibility of war between Japan and the Soviet Union?

TROTSKY: Yes; I wrote an article also in 1934. It was written in the beginning of 1934 and it was published—it was written July, 1933, and published in the *Bulletin* in February, 1934, under these two dates, July 12th, 1933, and February, 1934. It was published in several foreign languages. It was published in the United States, in France, and I believe also in Czechoslovakia and in Denmark—in different countries. The title of the article is, "Japan Advances Toward Catastrophe." I will give you a quotation. It begins:

> Without doubt, the ruling classes of Japan have had their heads turned. . . . Economically Japan is weaker than any of her possible adversaries in a great war. Japanese industry is incapable of assuring, to an army of many millions of men, arms and military equipment over a period of many years. The Japanese financial system, which does not support the weight of militarism in time of peace, will undergo a complete retrenchment at the very beginning of the war. The Japanese soldier, in the mass, does not respond to the needs of the new technique and the new tactics. The population is profoundly hostile to the régime. The ends of the conquest will be incapable of welding together a divided nation. With the

> mobilization there will enter into the army hundreds of thousands of revolutionists or candidates for the title of revolutionists. Korea, Manchuria, and, behind them, China, will disclose, in fact, an implacable hostility for the Japanese yoke. The social thread of the country is broken, the lines are distended. In the steel frame of the military dictatorship, the Japanese official seems powerful, but war will pitilessly unveil this myth.
>
> We have said nothing on the qualities compared with the Red Army; this question must be submitted to an independent examination. But even if, manifestly violating the proportions in favor of Japan, one admits the equality of material conditions in the two countries, there will remain the profound difference of moral factors. History tells us how military defeats give birth to revolution; but it will teach us how victorious revolutions, arousing the people and uniting its spirit, will give it an enormous dynamic force on the field of battle . . .
>
> In the interests of the two peoples and in that of the entire human civilization, we hope that Japanese militarism will not tempt fate.

I understand very well that history is not made by articles. But in so far as an article can have influence, I tried to make the Japanese general staff understand that it is not facing the Tsarist army. The whole article is constructed with the idea that the Japanese army as now compared with the Soviet Army is the same as the old Tsarist army compared with the Japanese army, and that Japan can meet on the fields of Siberia the same fate as the Tsarist army in the fields of Manchuria. That was the general idea of the article.

GOLDMAN: Do you know a man by the name of Hess?

TROTSKY: Yes; I learned his name from the papers and from the Verbatim Report.

GOLDMAN: He is connected with the fascists in Germany.

TROTSKY: Rudolf Hess is one of the Ministers of Hitler.

GOLDMAN: Did you ever see him?

TROTSKY: Only in the photos.

GOLDMAN: Did you have connections with him?

TROTSKY: No; I only heard his voice on the radio.

GOLDMAN: Did you ever communicate with any official of the fascist régime of Hitler?

TROTSKY: Never.

GOLDMAN: Did you ever come to any agreement with them with reference to the surrender of Soviet territory?

TROTSKY: No.

GOLDMAN: I ask the same questions about the Japanese militarists.

TROTSKY: I give you the same answers.

GOLDMAN: This next section is on the international situation. Mr. Glotzer is very anxious to rest his hand now.

DEWEY: We will take a short recess.

GOLDMAN: There are several questions that I want to ask you, Mr. Trotsky, before we proceed to the next section. When you played a leading role in the Soviet Union, did you express yourself in any way as against making any alliance between the Soviet Union and the capitalist countries?

TROTSKY: Never.

GOLDMAN: What is your general attitude towards making alliances for war purposes or other purposes between the Soviet Union and a capitalist country?

TROTSKY: In so far as it can serve to preserve the Soviet Union, an alliance becomes a necessity. It is only a question of not hindering by this alliance the workers' movement abroad. But in principle I admit it—the necessity of an alliance to preserve the Soviet Union.

GOLDMAN: In other words, in principle you admit that

under certain circumstances it is necessary to make an alliance with a capitalist country?

TROTSKY: Under the condition that the Communist Party of the allied country is not obliged to support its Government, and that the Communist Party remains free in its opposition against the Government.

GOLDMAN: Concretely speaking, you have no objection to the Soviet Union making an alliance with France, a military alliance, but at the same time you object to the Communist Party voting in favor of the war budget of the French militarists?

TROTSKY: Yes.

GOLDMAN: Now, a question has been asked many times in reference to this point. I would like to have you clear it up. Lenin accepted aid from the German Kaiser in the sense that he accepted permission of the Kaiser to go through Germany to Russia. Would you accept that aid?

TROTSKY: To go to Russia? Hitler would help me with pleasure in this direction—to go to Russia.

GOLDMAN: For the purpose of getting rid of you?

TROTSKY: Yes; I understand your question.

GOLDMAN: Another question that is raised in the Communist press and by some well meaning people is to this effect: That in order to achieve your motives you would even be willing to make an alliance with Hitler. I think you answered it once before.

TROTSKY: I will answer it again. This argument is made often by intellectuals friendly to the Soviet Union. The accusation against me seems so absurd to them, even when they are my adversaries. The accusations are politically and psychologically unexplainable, and they must try to help themselves in finding some precedent. They say, "Lenin used a German car during the war and why cannot Pyatakov use a German airplane?" It is almost a transportation question, and no more! But I find there is an important difference between the two cases. Lenin was in Switzerland during the war. He tried to go through England to Russia, but England did not permit it. The only way to Russia was across Germany. Lenin proclaimed it clearly and openly to everybody. He convoked a conference in Switzerland of the German internationalists and the French internationalists and others, and said: "Ludendorff hopes that Russia will break apart through internal fights. He hopes to have help in that way from the radical and revolutionary elements. That is his hope. My hope is another one; but I will use his help. Are you in agreement with me?" They discussed it and said, "Yes, it is totally permissible in this connection." And they signed a statement, all of them, the Germans and the Frenchmen, as a sort of international commission. Then he entered into the car and closed the door. There were twenty persons in the car. Nobody could enter the car during its trip across Germany. He came to Russia with the statement signed by the conference, and he explained openly to the workers, the first Soviet in Petrograd; "My situation was such and such. The only way possible was to go across Germany. The hopes of Ludendorff are his hopes, and mine are totally different. We will see who will be victorious." He explained everything. He concealed nothing. He said it before the whole world. He was an honest revolutionist. Naturally, the chauvinists and patriots accused him of being a German spy, but in his relationship with the working class he was absolutely impeccable.

I ask where is the relationship, the analogy? I write articles and letters absolutely hostile to Hitler, to fascism and to the Japanese militarists. But, in secret, I enter into relations with Hess. My work, however, according to that opinion, signifies that ninety-nine, or more, nine hundred and ninety-nine thousandths of my time is devoted to camouflage. My whole life is a camouflage, but my real work and action take only one or two hours. I find Hess—or, rather, I am alleged to have found Hess and discussed with him the manner of the dismemberment of the Soviet Union. After the discussion, I write a new article, in effect contrary to my supposed real work. Do you see here any similarity with Lenin's trip across Germany? "Similar," that is the word—yes?

GOLDMAN: Yes.

TROTSKY: It was the contrary. Lenin's attitude was honest. The attitude which they attribute to me characterizes these people as absolutely demoralized people, demoralized by irresponsibility and an arbitrary régime—that is, a totalitarian régime which forces everybody to lie in a manner approved by the bureaucracy.

BEALS: Can I ask one question, Mr. Trotsky? When you were in charge of the Red Army, the Soviet Army during the war—

TROTSKY: Yes?

BEALS: During the war with Poland, did you not feel that as you advanced into Poland the Polish proletariat would rise to support you, would rise and throw off the Polish military régime?

TROTSKY: Repeat that.

BEALS: Did you think that the Polish proletariat would rise and throw off the Polish military régime?

TROTSKY: I explained before to the Commission that we had some differences with Lenin on this question. Lenin considered it simply under the influence, and from the information on Poland given through the Polish émigrés. The Polish émigrés, like all émigrés, were very optimistic about the possibility of revolution in their country. They made very optimistic observations. I was in the military train. I had no time to speak with the Polish émigrés, and I considered the situation more from a military point of view and the situation of the army. I was opposed to the war. The war was imposed by Pilsudski. We did not begin the war. Pilsudski began the war. We did our best to defend ourselves.

Then it was a question of prolonging the war, the defensive war. Our discussions began. I was skeptical concerning the possibility of an upheaval of the Polish proletariat. But I recognized the superiority of Lenin in this respect, that he was better informed. I fought against it, and Rykov fought with me. I believe we had two or three votes against it, or four votes.

BEALS: Do the Communists now charge you with being responsible for that advance?

TROTSKY: Pardon?

BEALS: Don't the Communists blame you for this advance?

TROTSKY: No. If they do, it is absolutely false. It is known in Russia by everybody, our discussions are known. Lenin said at a Congress that he had made a great mistake. Lenin was a very honest adversary.

BEALS: How about the idea of imposing Bolshevism in Poland?

TROTSKY: In that case, I was personally opposed to that idea. I repeat, it was not a war which we began for the purpose of imposing the revolution. It was only a question to what limits the defense should continue. It was a war of defense which, by the logic of the struggle, transformed itself into a war of aggression against Warsaw. The question was whether we would be supported or not by the Polish proletariat. In that case I was opposed. It is known, it is written about, and articles were printed on this question. And also discussions held in our Congresses.

BEALS: May I ask one other question along the same line? I believe following the World War the American forces occupied a part of Soviet soil in various places. There was a charge that these forces supported, either directly or indirectly, the White Army. That was evidently for the purpose of spreading American democracy in the Soviet Union. Now, how would you go about spreading your ideas in the United States?

TROTSKY: At the moment, I have not at my disposition any armed force, nor use of them. (Laughter) I believe the danger for the United States from my side is not so tremendous for a long period. But I tried to explain that it is absolutely an absurd idea to try to impose on another country revolution against its own will, because we know that Napoleon tried to do it in Spain. Spain was a weak country. But there was a great defeat for Napoleon in Spain. He had only to fight against guerillas with his well organized army, but he was defeated. Even Robespierre said that people did not like missionaries with bayonets. Robespierre was right in this question.

GOLDMAN: Any other questions the Commissioners would like to put?

FINERTY: No.

GOLDMAN: The next section—the general section that deals with the struggle between the Left Opposition and the Stalinist majority in the Communist Party of the Soviet Union, the methods of that struggle and the developments in that struggle. In order to give us a picture of that general political situation—

FINERTY: Will you read that, Mr. Reporter? (Last remark read by reporter.)

GOLDMAN: Describe briefly the struggle between the Left Opposition and the Stalinists.

TROTSKY: I have already testified in part on this question. Because of the two attacks of illness of Lenin—Lenin was afraid of the development of the bureaucracy. It was a correct impression he had for some months during the interruption of his work. He proposed, and I described that in "My Life"—he proposed that I create a sub-commission for the purpose of fighting against bureaucracy, bureaucratism in the state apparatus. I answered: "It is not sufficient, because the origin—because it is connected with the Party." He answered me: "You mean the Orgburo and the

Central Control Commission?" It was his manner of making it precise. The Orgburo was a fortress of Stalin. The Political Bureau was the body—Lenin, Zinoviev and myself and others were on it—where all important questions were decided. The Orgburo was a subordinate body. Stalin was the general secretary of the Organizational Bureau. After Lenin's illness and my illness, and under the "Troïka," the Orgburo became the genuine center. The apparatus was in the hands of the Orgburo. When I answered Lenin that the fight against bureaucratism of the state was impossible without a fight against the bureaucracy in the Party, he said: "You mean the Orgburo and the Central Control Commission." It is the organizational bureau of the Central Committee. He said: "I propose to you a bloc." I answered, "A good bloc with a good man is a good thing." He said, "In a few days we will make plans for the fight." It was our last discussion.

Then, after his second illness, they became bolder. It would be very interesting to give that procedure from a psychological point of view. Stalin never dared to believe that it would be possible to advance in such a manner, but when he began to speak against the international revolution and the permanent revolution he found immediately from all sides sympathy and support. Then the bureaucracy said: "We are in office, we are resolving our social questions. They, the adventurists, they want permanent revolution and the international revolution." Stalin found immediately a tremendous echo. Then he began to feel he was the man in power. And then the bureaucracy began to elaborate its new ideas. The transformation of the revolutionary formulae of the proletarian revolution began. To the conservative bureaucracy, the formulae were just that. It is interesting from a theoretical, political and psychological point of view. It is not the personal falsification of one man, but the falsification of a whole caste of parvenus. They became totally satisfied, and they had to teach the people that they must also be satisfied. That was the mentality of the bureaucracy. It proceeded to do this in a short time. It was necessary to be more hasty than in the plans for collectivization and industrialization, and to elaborate new formulae to replace the old; all the old formulae of Bolshevism were named "Trotskyist." That was the trick. What was the genuine thing in Bolshevism is opposed to every privilege, to the oppression of the majority by the minority. It was named "the program of Trotskyism." That was the beginning of the frame-up.

When you have only the Verbatim Report and read it, it seems to me absolutely incredible that one man or two men, Stalin and Vyshinsky, could elaborate such a dialogue as we heard yesterday, the dialogue between Drobnis and Vyshinsky. That was only a small part. Altogether, it is a libretto, a libretto by two or three or four people. It is absolutely impossible to understand how they could dare to do it. I want you to consider it not as a thing in itself, but as a part of a thing long prepared, beginning with the camouflage of the privileges of the bureaucracy. Then it is absolutely a natural thing. You can see the coefficient of the lie, the coefficient of the calumny, the coefficient of slander and the coefficient of falsification. When you establish this movement and the elements of its coefficient, you can predict what will be next time, next year. We predicted, without having the gift of prophecy, but only with simple observation and analysis.

GOLDMAN: The struggle between you and the Stalin majority began with the struggle by you against the bureaucratic tendencies of that majority—is that right?

TROTSKY: Yes; it began at first as an empirical difference. We asked them for more loyal preparation of the Party Congresses; to give more possibility to the members to express their opinions; not to forget that the functionary is himself connected with the Party secretary, and that it is necessary to be more severe with the bureaucracy.

I myself, for example, was afraid at the end of 1924, when they began to pay the leaders of the workers' movement in Great Britain. I will not give here the names. I will communicate the names. They gave to the wives of the leaders—they dared not give money—they gave jewelry to the wives who visited Russia, to win their sympathy. The Irish-English author, O'Flaherty, describes that in his book in a very cynical manner. He himself took a thousand rubles. He said, "In every country it is the custom to buy some authors, but nowhere is it done with such cynicism as in the Soviet Union." That was in 1925 or 1926.

GOLDMAN: The Left Opposition fought for greater democracy?

TROTSKY: Yes, greater democracy and greater honesty, also.

GOLDMAN: Will you give us an idea of the development of the struggle and the issues that came up, up to the time of the expulsion?

TROTSKY: We tried not to lose our Party. We thought we could reestablish the Party with a Marxist program, without splits and without danger to the Soviet state. In 1926, the struggle was very acute. Then we tried to find some compromise between us and the apparatus, to introduce the struggle into more statutory channels. But then came the Chinese Revolution. The attitude of the Stalinists in the Chinese Revolution was as dangerous as now in Spain. It was in 1927, in October, when the Central Committee, behind our backs, sent a telegram—it is also published—to the Chinese Central Committee to stop the agrarian movement because it was the time of an alliance between Stalin and Chiang Kai-Shek.

GOLDMAN: You mean the Central Committee of the Chinese Communist Party?

TROTSKY: The Central Committee of the Chinese Communist Party—to stop the agrarian movement because the

Generals and officers of the National Armies were in their majority landlords and rich farmers. The agrarian movement of the poorer peasants, which was the genuine Chinese revolutionary movement, was dangerous to the higher stratum of the officers. Stalin was afraid to lose his alliance, as now with France. He sent a cable. He has assured the French bourgeoisie not to be afraid of a revolutionary policy in Spain. He reflects the French bourgeoisie. The same thing in China. Then the struggle became very acute for many months on the basis of our differences concerning the Chinese revolution.

GOLDMAN: In the previous sessions, during the former direct examination, you mentioned among the differences the question of democracy, Soviet democracy, trade-union democracy, and party democracy. You also mentioned the question of industrialization as being one of the issues between you and Stalin.

TROTSKY: It was the first question. It began with the question of industrialization, and at that time it was not a question of two principles. We began new economic orientations. We were all pupils of history. The question of industrialization was a new one. We looked for a good road. I proposed a more courageous policy in this respect. Stalin was very timid, but at the beginning this question took on a venomous character and connected fully with the question of democracy and the bribery of our functionaries. Then we had this feeling, that it was not incidental differences, but that there were two minds, two methods, two moods, and two moralities, if you wish. Then it became a factional struggle.

GOLDMAN: And the fundamental theory upon which the whole struggle revolved was the question or the theory of "Socialism in one country"?

TROTSKY: Yes.

GOLDMAN: That was adopted by Stalin?

TROTSKY: That was adopted by Stalin. In the Spring of

1924, he rejected the theory.

GOLDMAN: In the Spring of 1924, he rejected this theory?

TROTSKY: Yes.

GOLDMAN: When did he adopt it?

TROTSKY: In the Fall he adopted it for the first time. All the dates are established. You know, everybody in Russia who has the quotation of Stalin back from the Spring, 1924—if the G.P.U. finds this quotation and Lenin's testament on a student, it is a sign that he is an Oppositionist. Then he is accused of having conspiratorial counter-revolutionary literature—that is, Lenin's testament and Stalin's statement of the Spring of 1924. It is not an exaggeration. I affirm that with full responsibility.

GOLDMAN: Some of these questions—

TROTSKY: Why he adopted it? Because the bureaucracy had a feeling that we had accomplished our work with the revolution, and now we must enjoy the fruits of this work. The theory that our revolution was connected with the revolutions abroad was a menace to a calm situation. It was necessary to give assurance to the bureaucracy that the revolution was finished. It was our national revolution and we were now in peace. That is why Stalin, to satisfy his own apparatus, must adopt the theory he rejected six months before.

GOLDMAN: And all of these issues culminated in the expulsion of the Left Opposition at the Fifteenth Congress; is that right?

TROTSKY: The beginning of the discussion was at the Thirteenth Congress, before the Thirteenth Congress.

GOLDMAN: When did the Thirteenth Congress take place?

TROTSKY: The Thirteenth Congress took place in 1925.

GOLDMAN: And the Fourteenth Congress?

TROTSKY: In 1926. It was the Congress where Zinoviev and Kamenev for the first time appeared as Oppositionists.

GOLDMAN: At the Fourteenth Congress, you had already made a bloc with Zinoviev and Kamenev?

TROTSKY: No. You know, the explosion was absolutely unexpected by me. I was in the Politburo. They had there—

GOLDMAN: A caucus?

TROTSKY: A caucus, but a secret caucus, unpenetrable by me. The expectation of a struggle between Stalin and Zinoviev and Kamenev was unsuspected at the Congress. During the Congress I waited in uncertainty, because the whole situation changed. It appeared absolutely unclear to me. It characterized in what manner the apparatus was separated from the masses when I, a member of the Politburo, was absolutely ignorant of the doings in their caucus. At the Congress, I pronounced only one word, a characterization of Zinoviev's speech. He said Stalin accused him, Zinoviev, of being too sharp against me. Zinoviev answered, "After all the accusations were launched against Trotsky, I believed it was impossible to have him in the Politburo." I cried, "Totally correct!"

But only after the Congress did Zinoviev and Kamenev look for a new orientation in their depreciation before the workers of Leningrad and Moscow. They were chairmen of the two Soviets. Then they could find no other way than the program of the Left Opposition. Zinoviev declared three months after the Party Congress that Trotsky was right in his accusations.

GOLDMAN: And after that Congress, the Fourteenth Congress, you made a bloc with Zinoviev and Kamenev?

TROTSKY: Yes.

GOLDMAN: That bloc lasted until when?

TROTSKY: Until the Fall of 1927.

GOLDMAN: And when was the Opposition expelled?

TROTSKY: It was December, 1927.

GOLDMAN: At the Fifteenth Congress. Now, you have already answered this question, but I want you to answer it again. What was the attitude of the Left Opposition to the Party and Communist International after your expulsion?

TROTSKY: We regarded ourselves, in spite of our expulsion, as part of the Party and part of the Communist International. Among the leaders, I can state, Zinoviev gave his capitulation the formula: "To enter the Party." But he must keep quiet. We were expelled, but we could openly proclaim our opinions and, in that way, discuss with the Party. We were actually members of the Party.

GOLDMAN: I believe you told us before, your attitude on this matter changed after Hitler took power.

TROTSKY: Then we declared that the historical event was the defeat of the German proletariat. We said, "By the attitude of Stalin's Politburo and the C.I., they are a hindrance to the understanding of the lessons of this defeat. We cannot wait for a long time for historical miracles. The Comintern as a revolutionary organization is dead. We must create a new organization."

GOLDMAN: Can you tell us briefly if there were any new questions that arose after your expulsion from the Party, upon which there were differences of opinion between the Left Opposition and the Stalinist majority?

TROTSKY: New events in the Party?

GOLDMAN: Between 1927 and 1933, were there any new questions that arose upon which there were differences between you and Stalin?

TROTSKY: Yes; there was the question of the Five-Year Plan, of collectivization and industrialization, and then the question also concerning the Right Wing. The Right-Wing question was an important question. During the Fourteenth Congress, Zinoviev accused Bukharin and Rykov of a right deviation. And Stalin took their defense. He proclaimed, "You call for the blood of Bukharin." He cried: "Zinoviev, you want the blood of Bukharin. We will not give you the blood of Bukharin." Zinoviev answered: "It is not a question of blood, it is a question of a political tendency. We will condemn some ideas of Bukharin at this Congress and remain good friends."

GOLDMAN: Where is Bukharin?

TROTSKY: Bukharin is now awaiting the moment when Stalin will take his blood.

GOLDMAN: Were there any questions with regard to Germany where there was a difference of opinion?

TROTSKY: Yes, in 1923. Back in 1924, or the end of 1923.

GOLDMAN: I mean between 1927 and 1933.

TROTSKY: It was the beginning of the fight against fascism.

GOLDMAN: On the united front?

TROTSKY: The united front with the Social Democracy.

GOLDMAN: Stalin was against the united front with the Social Democracy?

TROTSKY: At that time he gave the famous slogan that the Social Democracy and fascism were not antipodes, but—what is the word?

STOLBERG: Twins?

TROTSKY: Twins, and not antipodes. That is why, when I asked or when I demanded an exact formula—I demanded the united front—he declared I was a Social-Fascist.

GOLDMAN: Now, describe briefly the methods of the struggle.

TROTSKY: I must say, it is a tragic situation that in the Politburo no one—they direct not only Russian politics, but the politics of the Comintern—not one of them knows any foreign language. It is not a reproach; it is not the duty of everybody to know a foreign language. How can they in such a despotic manner guide sixty sections of the Comintern without knowing any foreign language?

GOLDMAN: You mean Stalin does not know any language outside of Russian?

TROTSKY: Yes.

GOLDMAN: He knows Georgian? (Laughter)

TROTSKY: Yes; it is a very important language for the Georgian people.

GOLDMAN: Now tell us briefly the methods which the Left Opposition used, beginning with 1923 or 1922, to get the majority of the Party to adopt its ideas. What methods were used by the Left Opposition?

TROTSKY: The methods were the common methods of Party life. We made speeches and we wrote articles.

GOLDMAN: Were these articles printed?

TROTSKY: In 1923 and 1924, part of the articles were printed from time to time. But in every case, where the article was very persuasive and important, there was a special decision of the Central Committee not to print it. It was—for example, there was for our discussions in the Central Committee a stenographer.

GOLDMAN: Taken down by a stenographer?

TROTSKY: Yes. But after the defeat of the Chinese Revolution we had all the documents in order to answer—all documents concerning Stalin's cable to stop the agrarian revolution, and then the story about submitting the Communist Party to the dictates of the bourgeoisie in China. The decision was that this question was very dangerous from the international point of view. That is why the discussion must be held without a stenographer and behind closed doors. It was the ordinary procedure. Then they refused to print our articles at all.

GOLDMAN: And what did you do when they refused?

TROTSKY: We typed them on a machine and then gave them to friends. They typed them again, and so we had some primitive method of printing.

GOLDMAN: Was that done—

TROTSKY: The young comrades, they were more impatient. They secured a mimeograph machine. They were discovered. That was the case when the G.P.U. agent, the former Wrangel officer, proposed to get them connections for paper and so on. The G.P.U. accused them of being in an alliance with a White Guard officer.

GOLDMAN: When was the first time that violence was used against the Left Opposition?

TROTSKY: In 1927 were the first arrests officially.

GOLDMAN: Who was arrested?

TROTSKY: I believe it was Mrachkovsky. It was a question of a "conspiracy." Another agent of the G.P.U., Tverskoi, was involved. I have all the documents, and I would be glad if the Commission would create a sub-commission to study them. They reveal the embryo of the present frame-up. There was a young man by the name of Shtsherbakov. He had in his room a "printshop," that is, a hectograph. Another was Stroilov of the G.P.U., the former officer of Wrangel. This same Stroilov allegedly discovered a military plot of the White officers in Siberia through a man named Tverskoi. There was the former officer of Wrangel, the agent of the G.P.U. who proposed to get paper for the young Oppositionist. This same former officer of Wrangel was connected with Tverskoi. He had nothing to do with the Opposition. Both were agents of the G.P.U. Then the G.P.U. and Stalin affirmed that this printing job, through a Wrangel officer and Mrachkovsky, was connected with a military plot in Siberia. At the session of the Central Committee Menzhinsky, chief of the G.P.U., read some papers and documents on the "conspiracy." That was in 1927. The overwhelming majority of the Central Committee were absolutely perplexed. Komensky was there. He was a member of the Central Committee and is now Minister of Health. He was close to Stalin, a friend of his group. He became pale as the wall. Everybody was so shaken by the falsehood that the chairman had to interrupt the session. Stalin was too impatient in this question. It was not prepared well. It was necessary to implicate everybody and demoralize them by specific methods. He began too early. The embryo of the frame-up was totally abandoned, as a painter abandons a sketch which is not good. They began another—a bigger sketch. Here is a map of the sketches for the frame-up in Moscow. (Trotsky indicates a number of files.) It was necessary to educate not only the prosecutor, for example—because Vyshinsky was not born as he is now. It was necessary for Stalin to educate himself as well as all the others. Ulrich, the chairman of the Military Court, was named by me. I knew him when he was a boy of ten.

STOLBERG: He was appointed?

TROTSKY: He was appointed as a military judge by me. He was an honest young man. I knew his father in Siberia. He was of German Baltic origin, but totally Russianized. His father and mother, I knew them in Siberia. When I visited them, Ulrich was a boy of ten years. He had a hole in his trousers. I remember well how he covered this hole with his hand. He was at that time a boy of ten years. I had sympathy for this boy. Then he became a jurist and was recommended to me by one of my close collaborators as a good young man. He produced on me the best impression, and I named him a military judge. Stalin must have educated him during the ten years to become what he is now. With the others it is the same. It is a system of demoralizing good people. Stalin also was not born a master of frame-ups. He was a good learner. If he could have had more imagination, historical imagination for ten years, he would never have begun his plots. It was only his lack of historical imagination and the shortness of his vision, which is penetrating, but very short and for empirical things. By and by, he became an instrument of the bureaucracy himself, its leader only because he follows it. He became demoralized himself. Such is the ultimate logic of the bureaucratic system.

GOLDMAN: In 1927, November 7th, during the celebration of the October Revolution—was there any incident at that time between the Left Opposition and the Stalinist majority?

TROTSKY: Yes. It was the incident which is presented now by the official historians and by Mr. Louis Fischer, for instance, in the last copy of *The Nation*. But it is impossible to read his article, because it is better to read the official documents. He gives only a mechanical interpretation of the last official documents of the Soviet Union. I prefer the original to a belletristic copy. It is a semiofficial, novelistic copy. He affirms that it was an insurrection—not the beginning of an insurrection. We participated in the official anniversary manifestation with our slogans. In the past, it was the right of every Party section to have some slogans, some specific slogans, and so on. Our slogans were: "Fight against the kulak, and against the Nepman [the "Nepman" was the new speculator] and against the bureaucrats. We will accomplish the testament of Lenin."

GOLDMAN: Fulfill?

TROTSKY: Fulfill the testament of Lenin—something of that kind. You know it was pretty difficult to accuse them officially about the testament of Lenin in the Soviet Union at that time. In spite of that, the G.P.U. squads—they took the manifestoes and they annihilated—

GOLDMAN: Destroyed?

TROTSKY: Destroyed, rather, the placards, and they arrested some people. Then I visited my friend Smilga in his room. I believe Zinoviev was in Leningrad. I read you a letter of Zinoviev from Leningrad at that time. The letter ends with the words: "I admit entirely that Stalin will tomorrow circulate the most venomous 'versions.' We are taking steps to inform the public. Do the same. Warm greetings, Yours, Zinoviev." They had in Leningrad the same experiences as we in Moscow.

FINERTY: You mean they had street demonstrations in Leningrad?

TROTSKY: It was called officially a street demonstration. Radek and Zinoviev were pushed into a closed room and arrested for hours by the G.P.U. in advance, and accused of preparation of an insurrection. It was our first insurrection.

GOLDMAN: Alleged.

TROTSKY: Yes, alleged.

FINERTY: Mr. Goldman, Mr. Trotsky referred to a file with sketches of the frame-ups. Are you introducing that into evidence?

GOLDMAN: Yes; it is a folder for introduction.

TROTSKY: It is not quite ready. If the Commission this afternoon is not working with us, why, during this afternoon I will prepare it better.

DEWEY: May I ask just one question: Was there any popular response or reaction to the attack on the demonstration?

TROTSKY: There was. You know, the official demonstration, Mr. Chairman, was this time prepared in an absolutely military and G.P.U. manner. You had, at the head of every column—you have a squad of the G.P.U., only in civil clothes. The bureaucratic elements, as a nucleus, are incorporated in the demonstration. All the preparation is minute. There is the director of the factory, the secretary of the factory, and a section of the factory. They know everybody, and everybody follows them, under the control of his superiors. It is a question of the existence of his family, because in the hands of the rulers are the means which they can employ to eliminate him from the factory. Then he must die, because all the means of production are concentrated in the same hands. In 1936—I will ask for the introduction of this document—in 1936, before the trial, before the Zinoviev-Kamenev trial, during the purge of the Party—"purge," not?

GOLDMAN: Yes.

TROTSKY: There was an order in *Pravda* saying: "When it is a man who is not politically dangerous, but only corrupt"—

it was expressed in other words—"we can use him at another job. Only if he is a political adversary, that is, an Oppositionist, then nobody has a right to give him work." What does it mean in the Soviet Union not to get work? He cannot go to a private capitalist. He supports himself by material means. The wife of Joffe, the famous Soviet diplomat who committed suicide as an Oppositionist in 1927, his wife is in Siberia, or was in Siberia, and the last news was that she committed suicide also. She was sent to Siberia because of her activity and help to people who were deprived of any means of existence.

DEWEY: I suppose there was a danger created by this celebration. There must have been a great many people.

TROTSKY: Yes, a half a million, or even a million.

DEWEY: Now, I was simply asking whether there was any reaction on the part of this guard against the inferences of the banners or placards, and the spectators—from the spectators?

TROTSKY: There were no spectators. All the people were marching in a military manner. There was no place for spectators.

DEWEY: I mean the guard.

TROTSKY: The guard is a military organization. The attitude of the guard was simply the attitude of the members of the Central Committee.

DEWEY: There was no reaction?

TROTSKY: No active reaction.

DEWEY: That is all I wanted to know.

GOLDMAN: It was after the expulsion that wholesale arrests began of the Left Opposition, after the expulsion at the Fifteenth Congress?

TROTSKY: After the expulsion, immediately.

FINERTY: May I ask one question, Mr. Trotsky? How many of that half a million or million people would you say were sympathetic to you?

TROTSKY: It is very difficult to say, because there was a change in the structure of the Party. It is not the people, it is the Party organization which decides, even the attitude of the guard. In the beginning—in 1924, the Party changed totally its composition—the Party was composed of revolutionaries who participated in the October Revolution. But in 1924, the best qualification of a new member of the Party was to be a worker who had been twenty or twenty-five years in the same factory. In Russia, who could be in the same factory twenty or twenty-five years? In every strike, every progressive worker was arrested and sent to Siberia, and only the pious, religious people, the docile people, could have remained twenty to twenty-five years in the same factory. Now, these people, hearing new authorities, say, "Now we must have the same attitude, whoever are the new authorities." The new composition was a minority of the proletariat—the minority of the politically active proletariat. Then there was an intermediary stratum, and they formed the reactionary element. The reactionary elements became the best supporters of the majority after they entered the Party.

FINERTY: What I mean is this: The implication is that you organized street demonstrations of large proportions in Moscow. Is that the fact, or did you plant in this general Party celebration—did you plant banners and slogans at certain points?

TROTSKY: It was a silent manifestation with placards. In the guard, in the organized guard, were comrades who belonged to a factory and who participated with their own factory. It is very important. When they left the factory with their slogans, the workers did not protest. They came with the factory workers in a general column.

DEWEY: Procession?

TROTSKY: Yes, procession. Then when the G.P.U. squads took them—

GOLDMAN: Did the masses know the differences that divided the Left Opposition from the Stalinist majority?

TROTSKY: It depends. In the more progressive factories, the greater part of the workers understood it, but many workers were more backward. The old workers, the old reactionary workers—or, rather, the conservative workers—

FINERTY: What I would like to find out is whether your demonstration, such as it was, was accomplished by means of a few sympathizing sectors of the various units in this parade, or whether you had a large mass of the parade organized by you?

TROTSKY: We had, in Moscow, active members of the Opposition, I believe twenty thousand or thirty thousand workers. They were among their factories; in the factories, where we had support, they entered into the manifestations with their placards. They were tolerated and even passively and actively supported by the other workers. I believe—I can say, not in an active manner, the sympathy of the workers was on our side. But it was not a spirit of fight. The masses said: "We will see what we can do. We will see." It was a moment when the Opposition had been banned two or three times.

FINERTY: Was this an attempted organization of a *coup d'état?*

TROTSKY: No; absolutely no. We did not overestimate our forces. We had an absolutely clear reckoning on the forces. It was only to show to the Party that we were calumniated in the press and that we said not to fire against the progressive worker but against the speculator, and to fulfill the testament of Lenin, and so on. It was our defense against calumnies, against the frame-up, against the first amalgam.

FINERTY: I was going to ask: Did Stalin understand it at that time and approve this removal?

TROTSKY: Yes, I believe so. What we proposed was to the Party by legal Party means.

DEWEY: I just wanted to ask whether there was documentary evidence of what was on these placards. Is there a record of the actual content?

TROTSKY: The text of them?

DEWEY: Yes, the text.

TROTSKY: I believe there were seven slogans. I believe I can find them in my archives.

DEWEY: I think that should be in the record at the disposal of the Commission.

GOLDMAN: All right.

DEWEY: We will take a short recess now.

GOLDMAN: Now, Mr. Trotsky, you told us during the previous sessions what the methods were that were used by the Left Opposition after the expulsion. Will you repeat that answer briefly so that we can get it into the record at this time?

TROTSKY: During my sojourn in Siberia, the Left Opposition was permitted correspondence in Siberia. It was proposed to give to the G.P.U. the possibility to follow our inner life, and to see which one was inclined to capitulate, which one was opposed, et cetera. During the first eight or nine months our activity consisted of writing the principal political and theoretical theses, and so forth.

GOLDMAN: Have you any idea, approximately, how many Left Oppositionists were arrested and deported to Siberia at that time?

TROTSKY: At that time our appraisal was that there were about eleven thousand.

INTERPRETER: You mean estimate.

TROTSKY: We estimated about eleven thousand.

GOLDMAN: Subsequent to that, did you get any information—

TROTSKY: Excuse me, it was immediately after the Fifteenth Congress.

GOLDMAN: Eleven thousand were arrested in that short period after the Fifteenth Congress?

TROTSKY: During the same weeks.

GOLDMAN: From Moscow only or from the whole country?

TROTSKY: From the whole country.

GOLDMAN: Did you receive any information which would enable you to make an estimate as to how many Oppositionists were arrested after that?

TROTSKY: It is difficult to say. I quoted Victor Serge, who affirms in his very serious and cautious appreciation that from Leningrad alone in the last time, before the Zinoviev-Kamenev trial, they banished to Siberia between 60,000 and 100,000 women and children, families of people under suspicion. He had seen them at the railroad station, absolutely helpless, in crowded wagons.

GOLDMAN: Meaning trains.

DEWEY: What date?

TROTSKY: That was 1935 or 1936. Ciliga affirms the same.

GOLDMAN: From 1927, the end of 1927, when you were expelled, up to the present, did the Left Opposition ever use any other methods outside of education and propaganda to win over the masses?

TROTSKY: Not in the slightest degree. We warned in letters and conversations that we must be prepared to have provocations from certain elements to use violence. I warned them against that.

GOLDMAN: Will you prepare for the benefit of the Commission a list of those letters, articles, and documents wherein you predicted that violence would be used against the Left Opposition? Will you prepare such a list?

TROTSKY: Yes; it is only a question of translation. I hope we will succeed in translating it—all the quotations are in my hands. Only it is necessary to translate them into English. I hope to translate them before the Commission leaves for New York.

GOLDMAN: Do you claim that you anticipated the use of violence, the use of frame-ups by Stalin against you?

TROTSKY: I cannot say anticipation, because it was anticipation supported by some sketches from the bureaucracy, and I could appreciate the direction of the bureaucracy. I was sure that—in the session of the Central Committee in the Fall of 1927, I tried to picture it—I was absolutely sure that the next step would be better prepared by Stalin. That was my prediction. It would not be the last attempt. It was only a fiasco, but that fiasco predicted a new attempt, better prepared.

GOLDMAN: Do you refer to that session of the Central Committee in which Stalin came out with the accusation about the Wrangel officer printing the Left Opposition program?

TROTSKY: Yes.

GOLDMAN: Now, will you briefly enumerate the trials that have been held in the Soviet Union since the Kirov assassination, involving you directly or indirectly? Give us in very summary form an idea of the accusations and the results.

TROTSKY: The first trial—before the trial, there were one hundred and four shot according to the Soviet press; they were supposed to be White Guards.

GOLDMAN: After the Kirov assassination?

TROTSKY: After the Kirov assassination.

GOLDMAN: And before the first trial?

TROTSKY: During the first sixteen days of December. They communicated themselves that there were one hundred and four shot without trial; that they came from abroad as agents of foreign powers, agents of diversion and terrorism and so on. Without appreciation—

GOLDMAN: Without what?

TROTSKY: Without appreciation. (Trotsky here spoke in French.)

FINERTY: Without defining the charges?

TROTSKY: Have you the word precise? They did not precise what connection there was between the people shot and the murder.

GOLDMAN: They did not give any definite charges?

TROTSKY: They were in a general formula connected with the murder of Kirov. Then, the first trial was the trial of Nikolayev, the genuine murderer of Kirov, and of his alleged accomplices, on the 28th and 29th of December, 1934; with fourteen condemned to be shot.

GOLDMAN: You are taking your reports from the Soviet press?

TROTSKY: Exclusively from the Soviet press. The indictment in the Nikolayev trial was published, and in this indictment my name appeared for the first time in such a question—that Nikolayev after twenty days of arrest confessed that a foreign consul in Leningrad gave him five thousand rubles for terroristic acts; that the same consul asked if he did not wish to send a letter to Trotsky, because, he, the consul, could possibly transmit the letter. In the indictment there is not a word about the answer of Nikolayev about the letter, only about the proposition of the consul, who gave him five thousand rubles and asked for a letter to me. I abstain from making any comment.

GOLDMAN: You will comment on that in your argument; is that right?

TROTSKY: Yes. I have here the official statement in the press.

GOLDMAN: The witness refers to an edition of the *Pravda*, the 27th of November, 1934. If a translation can be made, it will be made and put into the record.

FINERTY: And the original filed with the record?

GOLDMAN: The original filed with the record.

TROTSKY: I must add that the diplomatic corps asked for the name of the consul because everybody was compromised, all the consuls. Then, after many days, the Soviet Government declared it was a Latvian consul, Bisseneks. His name was Bisseneks. He left Russia for Finland. I believe he was helped on his trip to Finland by some Moscow authorities. He, the consul, said to Nikolayev that he could establish communication with Trotsky if Nikolayev transmitted some letters from his group to Trotsky.

GOLDMAN: When was the next trial?

FINERTY: Will you show for the record whether any proceedings of the Kirov trial were published, or whether they were secret?

GOLDMAN: Were there any proceedings reported and published with reference to this trial?

TROTSKY: Never. In all the following trials, the name of this consul is never even mentioned.

GOLDMAN: What was the verdict in that trial? What happened to the defendants?

TROTSKY: All fourteen were shot.

GOLDMAN: That was for the murder of Kirov?

FINERTY: Was the trial published?

TROTSKY: No; the genuine Kirov trial was secret.

GOLDMAN: When was the next trial?

TROTSKY: The next trial was the trial of Zinoviev and Kamenev on the charge of moral responsibility for the assassination of Kirov, held on the 15th and 16th of January, 1935. After the assassination of the fourteen, only after, they opened a new trial against Zinoviev and Kamenev.

GOLDMAN: How many were involved in that trial?

TROTSKY: In that trial, I believe, nineteen. It is not mentioned here.

GOLDMAN: And the indictment charged they were morally responsible?

TROTSKY: The indictment was ambiguous in this sense: It was supposed that there was more than a moral responsibility, but they did not have proof, and that is why the moral responsibility was used.

GOLDMAN: What was the result of that trial?

TROTSKY: Prison, from five to ten years, for all the accused.

GOLDMAN: When was the next trial involving the Kirov assassination?

TROTSKY: It was the trial of the head of the Leningrad section of the G.P.U., Medved, and also of his associates, on the charge that they "had at their command information on the plot against Kirov," but "had not taken measures to discover and put an end" to the activity of the terrorist organization.

GOLDMAN: You are quoting from what?

TROTSKY: I quoted from the official statement of the Government in the Soviet press.

GOLDMAN: In the *Pravda*?

TROTSKY: Yes.

GOLDMAN: Have you a copy of the *Pravda* that contains that?

TROTSKY: It is not mentioned here.

GOLDMAN: You will furnish the Commission with the original and translation?

TROTSKY: Yes.

GOLDMAN: How many defendants were there during that trial?

TROTSKY: Twelve, all condemned to prison from one to ten years.

GOLDMAN: And Medved?

TROTSKY: And Medved; yes.

GOLDMAN: What did you say the verdict was, condemned to prison for what?

TROTSKY: From two to ten years. I must add that in spite of the fact that all were accused that they knew of the preparation of the Kirov assassination but did not take measures, none of them was quoted as witness in the subsequent trials. Officially it is stated that they knew, but none of them gave testimony in the trial of Kamenev and Zinoviev and others.

GOLDMAN: By the way, were there any official reports issued on that trial?

TROTSKY: Yes; I believe, not the full indictment, but an official communiqué.

GOLDMAN: With the evidence included?

TROTSKY: No; only the general formula that the accused knew of the preparations.

GOLDMAN: But no official report of the evidence?

TROTSKY: No.

STOLBERG: Did they all confess?

TROTSKY: Naturally. (Laughter) Nobody appears at the trial unless he is prepared to confess.

FINERTY: In the Kirov trial, did they all confess?

TROTSKY: We know nothing. I believe—it was not made known—it was not the case. Before, they did not publish anything. It was behind closed doors.

FINERTY: How about the Zinoviev-Kamenev trial? Did they all confess moral responsibility?

TROTSKY: There was a trial of Zinoviev and Kamenev in July, 1935—

FINERTY: The one in January, 1935, I mean.

GOLDMAN: Did they confess?

TROTSKY: It was the first sketch of confessions of this kind. It was not perfect. Zinoviev confessed that he made criticisms against the Government, and these criticisms provoked dissatisfaction. This dissatisfaction provoked terroristic inspiration. Kamenev confessed only that he did not break off his relations with Zinoviev. It was the confession of Evdokimov, Bakayev, and the other defendants of the next trial—they confessed in the same way.

GOLDMAN: After the Medved trial, when was the next trial?

TROTSKY: The next trial was that of Kamenev and others, held in July, 1935, on the charge of preparing a plot against

Stalin. Kamenev received five additional years in prison. He had five years already. There was no report, no communiqué, concerning this trial. I can learn about this only from the verdict of the August, 1936, trial, where it is mentioned in the enumeration of the defendants, that Kamenev was condemned to five additional years in July, 1935.

GOLDMAN: You are reading from what now?

TROTSKY: It is page 174.

GOLDMAN: Of the official report?

TROTSKY: Of the official report of Court Proceedings in the case of the Trotskyite-Zinovievite Terrorist Center.

FINERTY: What was he convicted on?

TROTSKY: Only one thing we know. I repeat it is official that he received five additional years in prison. But we know from Ciliga and Victor Serge that the trial was especially organized in order to educate Kamenev for the next trial and to break his backbone, especially when he was denounced by his own brother, a demoralized artist.

GOLDMAN: Bankrupt?

TROTSKY: Bankrupt and totally demoralized. He was the most important witness against Kamenev, and Kamenev told Ciliga and others in prison that he knew only two persons, his own brother and another. Of the thirty defendants, he knew only one. Two were shot. I believe one officer of the Red Army of the Kremlin Garrison and another—I don't know who the other is.

FINERTY: As a result of this trial?

TROTSKY: It is not official. It is what he knew in private, arising from various other serious sources.

GOLDMAN: After that trial, when was the next trial?

TROTSKY: The next trial was the Zinoviev-Kamenev trial in August, 1936. Sixteen defendants were shot.

GOLDMAN: And then the last trial was the one—

TROTSKY: The Novosibirsk trial on the charge of sabotage and terrorism was held the 19th to the 22nd of November,

1936. Six of the nine accused were shot. It is my explanation, but it is based on the situation, that the Novosibirsk trial was organized especially for Pyatakov, as the trial of July, 1935, for Kamenev. In the Novosibirsk trial Drobnis appeared for the first time as a witness against Pyatakov. The nine defendants were presented as the instruments of Pyatakov. Six of them were shot. It seems to me that Pyatakov confessed only after that trial. I believe he confessed only in December, and the trial was held in November. I must verify my affirmation, but I believe it is correct.

GOLDMAN: And after Novosibirsk?

TROTSKY: It was the Pyatakov-Radek trial of January, 1937. Thirteen of the seventeen accused were shot.

GOLDMAN: Now, since then, has anything happened in Soviet Russia which was attributed to you or to your followers, that you knew, reported in the press?

TROTSKY: Yes; there was reported the news concerning our son. But it was not so concrete. There was a fire in a school, and the school was demolished. Three Trotskyites were shot because they knew and permitted it in order to set the school on fire with the purpose of the assassination of children, and to provoke dissatisfaction of the population.

GOLDMAN: When you say three Trotskyites, you mean three people alleged to be Trotskyites?

TROTSKY: Yes, yes.

GOLDMAN: Anything else that happened since then attributed to you or your followers, or your alleged followers?

TROTSKY: Yes, I read in a cable that the Government issued a manifesto to the population in which are enumerated acts of sabotage and other crimes. Then are enumerated the factories where Trotskyites, alleged Trotskyites, were saboteurs, and so on. It seems that there can be only the purpose of preparing a new trial; I don't know.

GOLDMAN: Do you care to give us any opinion about any future trial involving Bukharin and others?

TROTSKY: I heard from private sources that Rykov refused to confess, and that is the reason why the promised trial cannot be materialized. Vyshinsky can accuse only people who confess.

GOLDMAN: Do you expect that Bukharin and Rykov also will be connected with you?

TROTSKY: Everything is possible. It is a witch's play, a very terrible one, but it is a combination of gunfire and what is necessary for Stalin. I could indicate that he eliminates for the moment Molotov as a national hero, from the list of victims. I could explain it because I knew the material. I can say now what it is about. It is the preparation for a new trial. I don't know the concrete circumstances. I know only that Bukharin was sent abroad in 1936, the beginning of 1936, for the factories. He was their agent. He was in Prague, a tourist. Now, I ask myself if it was not with the purpose of preparing with him a new combination. He gave a lecture in Prague, totally in the official spirit. But it is possible they sent him in order to have the possibility to affirm that abroad he entered into communications with Trotskyites and German agents. I don't know, but it is quite possible. The same with Rakovsky. Immediately, he was sent to Japan. I was a bit astonished. What was the meaning of it? It was at the end of 1934, and the British friends of the Soviet Union—the friends of the Soviet Union are everywhere—they are directed by the agents of the G.P.U., without their knowing; the genuine direction is everywhere in the hands of the G.P.U. The friends in London declared: "You see, the repentance of Rakovsky is totally sincere. The Government sent him abroad." But his family remained in Moscow, the family of Rakovsky. At that time I was of the opinion that he was sent for demonstrative purposes in order to show the whole world that he was free, his repentance was sincere. Now, I ask myself if it did not have a second purpose, to frame him afterwards—that he was connected with the Japanese military chiefs in the Government, and so forth.

GOLDMAN: Your archives were stolen in France?

TROTSKY: Yes.

GOLDMAN: When?

TROTSKY: On the anniversary of the October Revolution, the 7th of November, 1936.

GOLDMAN: Have you any documents, reports, such as you want to give the Commission as to the possible perpetrators of the crime?

TROTSKY: Yes, I have the report of the French police, the testimony of my son to the examining judge, and my own testimony.

GOLDMAN: I will introduce it into evidence.

TROTSKY: It was sent to me by my French lawyer.

GOLDMAN: What is your opinion as to the possible perpetrators of the crime?

TROTSKY: It is not an opinion, it is a certainty. It is the work of the G.P.U. You know in this institute—it is a scientific institute—they have thousands of manuscripts, and they had eighty-five kilograms of my archives, but the greater part of them was clippings of papers bearing a scientific interest for me, but of no interest to the masters of the frame-up. Another part of it was letters. The people penetrated in there by burning up the door.

INTERPRETER: You mean blowing?

TROTSKY: Burning up the door with such a magnificent technique that the police declared: "Our people are not so educated—the French gangsters." It was the highest technique in the world. Then they took only the eighty-five kilograms of my archives. There was money—the manager forgot one hundred francs. They did not touch it. Then there were very interesting manuscripts. But they only took my eighty-five kilograms.

GOLDMAN: There were only two parties interested in your documents, you and the G.P.U.?

TROTSKY: Yes.

GOLDMAN: You didn't steal your own documents?

TROTSKY: No. There were three persons—the Nazis; they tried in Norway in the summer of 1936. It is absolutely parallel, but the G.P.U. was more skilled and more successful.

GOLDMAN: I introduce into evidence the report of the French police with respect to the theft of the documents. It is in French, and I hope it will be translated. I also introduce into evidence—

TROTSKY: My deposition to the examining judge.

GOLDMAN: The deposition of Mr. Trotsky to the Presiding Magistrate. I will have these two exhibits marked Nos. 29 and 30, respectively.

(The report of the French police regarding the theft of Trotsky's archives, and the deposition of Trotsky to the Presiding Magistrate on this matter, were introduced into evidence as Exhibits Nos. 29 and 30, respectively.)

TROTSKY: If you permit me, I will add that in this deposition I declared that because the matter concerns also the Soviet Union and France, and my alleged conspiracy with Hitler, I am ready to appear before the French Judge of Instruction or any other authority to respond and answer all questions before the court.

GOLDMAN: And this is a copy of the report you sent in?

TROTSKY: Yes.

GOLDMAN: The report of the police is the original you received from the police?

TROTSKY: Yes.

GOLDMAN: When did you receive it?

TROTSKY: About two or three weeks ago.

GOLDMAN: When did you send the original of the report to the Magistrate?

TROTSKY: The date is indicated. I received a letter from

my lawyer—I was in Mexico—that I must send my deposition also.

GOLDMAN: It is dated March 10th, 1937. You have not as yet been accused of any other crimes in the Soviet Union outside of the—

TROTSKY: What other? Where do the others begin?

GOLDMAN: Let us say, crucifying Jesus Christ.

TROTSKY: I have not at this moment.

GOLDMAN: Now, I want to introduce into evidence a list of the defendants in both of the last two trials, giving the dates of their capitulations, their arrest, when they were arrested, when they were released. It will help the Commission in arriving at a conclusion as to the possibility of these defendants having participated in a conspiracy, especially some of the defendants. I will mark this Exhibit No. 31.

(The list of the defendants in the last two Moscow trials was introduced into evidence as Exhibit No. 31.)

TROTSKY: Zinoviev and Kamenev were arrested one year or half a year before the assassination, and Smirnov more than two years before the assassination of Kirov. They were all accused of the assassination of Kirov. Vyshinsky says—I am sure that you know this.

GOLDMAN: There are some matters I want to clear up before closing. There was a man by the name of Bukhartsev, the man in the evidence—the man who was supposed to have made the arrangements for the flight of Pyatakov. Will you give me an idea of who he is?

TROTSKY: I depose, absolutely the same as with Vladimir Romm—I regret very much, but I do not know the second correspondent in Berlin, Bukhartsev. I don't know him, as I didn't know Vladimir Romm in Washington. I never saw him and never spoke with him, and had no communications with him.

GOLDMAN: You testified at one time that Muralov was a good friend of yours and a very honest man.

TROTSKY: Yes.

GOLDMAN: When he testified at the trial that he received a letter from Sedov about terroristic instructions, was he honest at that time?

TROTSKY: His deposition was false, but I am absolutely sure that it was the false deposition of a simple soldier, to whom they stated after the assassination of all the others: "You are a friend of Trotsky. Now, you understand you cannot have Trotsky here. He is in exile." They were threatening him: "Stalin is the chief of the state. We have Japan from one side, and Germany from the other. The activity of Trotsky is dangerous. Trotsky completely recognizes Zinoviev and Kamenev. You must confess. You will be shot." He, as a soldier, confessed.

GOLDMAN: Now, Pyatakov testified to the fact that he gave, at the request of your son—he gave orders, Government orders to several firms in Germany, and that the arrangement was to have a good part of the profits for himself, which he was to turn over to you for counter-revolutionary purposes. Will you furnish the Commission an account of the moneys that you received since you left Russia, how you spent these moneys?

TROTSKY: Yes.

GOLDMAN: Just for the purpose of the record, I am going to enumerate—

TROTSKY: I have the privilege, that the management of my finances is also organized more or less collectively. I never myself manage the money, but can present witnesses with testimony on the accounts, very exact.

GOLDMAN: You have read all the charges leveled against you in both of the indictments, the indictment involving Zinoviev and Kamenev and the indictment of Pyatakov and Radek, have you?

TROTSKY: Yes.

GOLDMAN: You know all the charges that are made against you in these indictments?

TROTSKY: Yes.

GOLDMAN: What have you to say on each and every allegation in these indictments?

TROTSKY: False; they are completely false from beginning to end.

GOLDMAN: On behalf of Leon Trotsky, we close the case, with permission of the Commission to introduce any other evidence which might turn up between now and the close of the case before this Commission.

FINERTY: Before we adjourn, Mr. Chairman, I would like to know if the correspondent of *El Nacional* is here. (There was no response from the reporter of *El Nacional.*)

FINERTY: I would like to correct a statement made in that paper that I am an attorney and friend of Trotsky, in that I am not an attorney or friend of Trotsky. My only previous connection with a Russian matter, if it was a Russian matter, was to represent Mr. Browder in the Supreme Court of the United States just before the last Presidential election in order to have his name restored on the ballot of Illinois. My representation of Browder and association with the Commission in this instance, are entirely in the interests of civil liberties. I will represent Browder or anyone else. I want to make clear, I had no previous connection with Mr. Trotsky or any connection with the Russian question before.

DEWEY: Wait a minute; I would like to announce that there will be no session this afternoon. The next session will be at ten o'clock tomorrow morning. (Beals translated the Chairman's remarks into Spanish.)

End of Ninth Session—One o'clock P.M.

Tenth session

April 16, 1937, at ten o'clock a.m.

GOLDMAN: Mr. Chairman, will the Commission permit the introduction of a document which I think will be very helpful? It is an article written by Trotsky and published in the *New York Times,* May 8th, 1932. It will be very helpful to the Commission, because in résumé form it gives a history of the Left Opposition and the causes of the conflict and the possible outcome. I will mark the Exhibit No. 32.

(An article by Trotsky in the New York Times *of May 8th, 1932, was introduced into evidence as Exhibit No. 32.)*

DEWEY: Before Mr. Finerty begins his inquiry, I wish to refer to an error appearing in the *Nacional* paper this morning, doubtless due to the ignorance of what has been said in the previous hearings—namely, that it was not known to whom this Commission would report. In the very first press release, the members of the larger Commission to which this sub-commission would report was stated, and the names given.

FINERTY: I would like to supplement that with a statement that *El Nacional* names me as Trotsky's attorney. I was assured by them it was a typographical error. It also follows a statement made a day or two before to the effect that I am a friend of Trotsky's. I have asked the paper to withdraw that false statement.

DEWEY: Will you begin, Mr. Finerty?

FINERTY: I think, Mr. Chairman, it will clarify my examination, both for Mr. Trotsky and for the public, if I state the intent and purpose of it. I believe, and I think the Commission agrees with me, that the Commission must reach its ultimate conclusions on the basis of the published record made by it and on the basis of the facts developed in that record or the impossibility of developing the facts.

Therefore, my examination will develop facts that in my opinion are necessary for an intelligent conclusion by the Commission on the questions here involved. Mr. Trotsky is not to be treated as a hostile witness in my cross-examination to the extent that he agrees that I may ask any question I think pertinent, and that he will give any information which is in his power to give and which I ask for.

I may say that some of my questions will seem elementary. But that is of interest to the case, as I see it. I believe that the Commission must act within the record, which means to take the mass of facts which it develops. It is therefore necessary, as a preliminary, to develop certain elemental facts which the record now lacks.

I also think it proper to say that certain of the documentary evidence introduced by Mr. Trotsky, certain of the factual evidence introduced by him, is not properly subject to cross-examination but to subsequent investigation; that is, to determine its authenticity, and therefore, if I do not examine on all the facts testified to by Mr. Trotsky, it is not because either I or the Commission accept these facts as true or question their truth, but we believe a more efficient method of determining their truth is not by cross-examination, but by investigation of the sources of these facts.

Mr. Trotsky, may I presume to ask you to make your answers to me as concise as possible? When was the Communist Party organized?

TROTSKY: In Russia?

FINERTY: In Russia.

TROTSKY: The Communist Party proper had the name "Bolshevik," the Russian Social Democratic Labor Party. The Party was organized officially as a party in 1903. But the first manifesto proclaiming the Party was issued in 1898.

FINERTY: 1908?

TROTSKY: 1898. The real organization of the party begins in 1903.

FINERTY: What was the basis of membership in the Party?

TROTSKY: To recognize the program; the recognition of Party discipline; and active work in the Party organization.

FINERTY: Was anyone admitted to the Party who undertook to carry out the program, or expressed agreement with the Party program, and undertook the work of the Party?

TROTSKY: Yes.

FINERTY: There was no selection of people and no exclusion of people?

TROTSKY: At that time not, because illegal conditions made it not so attractive for careerists to adhere to the Party.

FINERTY: At that time, what were the governing bodies of the Communist Party or the Bolshevik Party?

TROTSKY: The governing persons?

FINERTY: Governing committees and bodies.

TROTSKY: The Central Committee, and the editorial board of the central organ of the Party. The Central Committee acted inside the borders of Russia and the editorial board abroad, in emigration. We had two centers. The most important leaders remained abroad in exile. They were the political and theoretical leadership. The Central Committee in Russia was the direct practical leadership.

FINERTY: How were these committees selected?

TROTSKY: They were elected by the Party Congresses.

FINERTY: They were elected annually?

TROTSKY: It was not annually. In the illegal conditions, it was very difficult to convoke a Party Congress. We had the second Party Congress in 1903. Then, a Party Congress and split in 1905, a new Congress in 1906, and then in 1907. After the Revolution in 1905, it was easier to convoke a Party Congress.

FINERTY: Were these Party Congresses held in Russia or abroad?

TROTSKY: The first Party Congress was simply a Party Congress which issued only the manifesto in 1898. It was in Russia. The second took place in Brussels—partly in Brussels and partly in London. We were expelled from Brussels and compelled to go to London. The third in Stockholm, and the fourth again in London in 1907. Then we had a long interruption until the next Congress. It was only in April, 1917, a conference which played the role of a Congress, in Petrograd.

FINERTY: In April, 1917?

TROTSKY: 1917, at the beginning of the Revolution.

FINERTY: Now, during the early Party Congresses, were all members of the Party permitted to attend Congresses and vote?

TROTSKY: Not the Congresses; the meetings which elected the delegates. The Party organization as an organization was small at that time. It was also a selection of the best elements for the purpose of avoiding *agents provocateurs*. But all the members would participate in the elections.

FINERTY: There was permitted a regular election of delegates, was there?

TROTSKY: In so far as it was possible under the régime of the Tsar.

STOLBERG: Mr. Trotsky, you said in 1905 the Bolshevik Party split?

TROTSKY: In 1903, it split.

STOLBERG: That is why I didn't quite understand. You said in 1905 there was a split.

TROTSKY: In 1903 there was the first ideological split, not even a political one. Organizationally, the Party remained formally as a unified Party. The organizational split occurred in May—April or May—1905. At the end of 1905, new efforts were made to unify and merge both fractions. They merged in the Congress of 1906, in Stockholm.

STOLBERG: In Stockholm, the Bolshevik split went back in the Social Democratic Party as one section of the Party?

TROTSKY: Yes. At Stockholm, they were a minority of the Party. The Mensheviks had a majority. At that time I was not present, and personally I did not participate in that Congress.

FINERTY: At that time, the Party was composed of what elements? Mensheviks, Bolsheviks, and Social Democrats?

TROTSKY: They were both named Social Democrats. That was the name of the Party, the Russian Workers Social Democratic Party. It divided into Bolsheviks and Mensheviks and the so-called conciliatory elements. Part of the conciliators were Trotskyites.

FINERTY: I think you testified in your direct examination that you tried to bring about harmony between the Bolsheviks and Mensheviks, and that you were mistaken in that effort.

TROTSKY: As a general political line it was false.

FINERTY: Then, the first Congress of importance held in Russia was in 1917?

TROTSKY: It was a conference in April. Then, we had the same year a Party Congress—at the end of July or the beginning of August, 1917. It was the Party Congress.

FINERTY: About what was the membership of the Party at the time of the Party Congress in 1917?

TROTSKY: It was in principle the same, practically.

FINERTY: I mean numerically.

TROTSKY: Pardon?

FINERTY: Numerically.

TROTSKY: I believe before the October Revolution, before the October insurrection, we had some three hundred thousand members.

FINERTY: Even prior to the October Revolution?

TROTSKY: Yes.

FINERTY: What was your membership succeeding the Revolution? Was it increased?

TROTSKY: Yes; there were two or three waves. At the beginning we had new members, many new members. Then during the July manifestation, which they called an insurrection—that is, the Government—many new members left the Party because they were afraid of the consequences which arose. Lenin had to go underground. After the insurrection of Kornilov, during the period of August, September and October, we had thousands of new members again.

FINERTY: At that time were there any restrictions of membership other than the basis you have given?

TROTSKY: We were a persecuted party, terribly persecuted by the Government, the Provisional Government, and we had no reason for an artificial selection.

FINERTY: Did the Congress of 1917 precede or follow the October Revolution?

TROTSKY: Preceded it. It finished in the first days of August, 1917. It was the official merger between the Bolsheviks and the smaller revolutionary organizations, among them an organization to which I belonged myself.

FINERTY: As a result of the Revolution, were the Mensheviks subsequently split from the Party?

TROTSKY: No; at that time they were a totally independent party. Officially, it began in 1912. I forgot to say that the Bolshevik fraction at that time had not a Party Congress, but a Party conference in Prague, Czechoslovakia, in 1912, and declared that from that time it would become an independent party. It was the formal and definite split with the Mensheviks, in the year 1912.

FINERTY: What was the name of the Communist Party?

TROTSKY: After the October Revolution—it was in 1919—Lenin proposed at the April Conference, but the majority—I believe all with the exception of Lenin—rejected the name of Communist Party. They wanted to abide by the old name. Lenin said, "We must change the name of Social Democrats as we must change a dark shirt."

GOLDMAN: You mean dirty?

TROTSKY: Yes, a dirty shirt. Because the Social Democracy during the war had a miserable attitude.

FINERTY: In 1919, did the official name of it become Communist Party?

TROTSKY: Yes.

FINERTY: In 1919, what, approximately, was the membership of the Communist Party numerically?

TROTSKY: Pardon?

FINERTY: Numerically?

TROTSKY: It is difficult to say. I am not prepared to say, but all our efforts were directed not to allow the Party to grow too rapidly. We had at that time possibly a half a million members; I am not sure.

FINERTY: In other words, in 1919 during the increase of the Communist Party membership, you began to make it a selective party?

TROTSKY: Yes.

FINERTY: What was the theory upon which it was determined to make the Communist Party a selective party rather than a popular party?

TROTSKY: We tried to have workers, the first thing. The worker, the average worker who thinks, does not think of making a career. He comes into the Party only when he is convinced that it is a good thing. But the bureaucrats, and some of the intellectual people who were Mensheviks yesterday, they all wished to enter into the Party. There was a great danger that the Party might become a party of bureaucrats and careerists.

We tried to eliminate these elements by an examination of the past of everyone and of their activities, having guarantees or recommendations of old Party members, old revolutionaries who knew them before, and could say that his or her genuine attitude is sincere. That was only in the case of a bourgeois or intellectual. But for the workers the door of the Party was open.

FINERTY: Then your selection in 1919 was really an effort to make the membership of the Party workers?

TROTSKY: It was the class guardian.

FINERTY: And not to have merely intellectuals and bureaucrats?

TROTSKY: Yes.

FINERTY: In 1919, what were the governing committees of the Communist Party?

TROTSKY: The Central Committee and the Politburo. The Central Committee and the Politburo were permanent institutions. The Central Committee was convoked once a month, and later once in two months. But in the first year it was once a month.

FINERTY: And there was a committee on organization as well at that time, or was that later?

TROTSKY: Pardon? The organizational bureau was created, I believe, in 1918.

FINERTY: In 1918?

TROTSKY: Yes.

FINERTY: Who were the members in 1919 of the Central

Committee? Can you name them?

TROTSKY: Of the organizational?

FINERTY: The Central Committee.

TROTSKY: The Central Committee, yes. It is difficult to say that from memory only. In 1919?

FINERTY: Yes.

TROTSKY: Serebryakov played a role as one of the defendants in the Moscow trial. He was secretary and a member of the organizational bureau. Krestinsky, who was later ambassador in Germany, then a Commissar of Foreign Affairs, in the Commissariat of Foreign Affairs; now he is removed because for a certain time he belonged also to the Trotskyites.

FINERTY: Mr. Trotsky, I think that you should give the names without giving their history. Just give the names.

TROTSKY: Good.

FINERTY: Particularly the names of those who were defendants in the first and second Moscow trials.

TROTSKY: Zinoviev was a member of the Central Committee and the Politburo. Kamenev was a member of the Central Committee and the Politburo.

FINERTY: Mr. Trotsky, will you name the Central Committee first? I will ask you about the Politburo.

TROTSKY: Zinoviev, Kamenev, Radek—I believe he was there at that time—Sokolnikov and Serebryakov. From the defendants, I believe they are all.

FINERTY: You and Lenin were both members of the Central Committee?

TROTSKY: Yes.

FINERTY: Was Stalin?

TROTSKY: Stalin also.

FINERTY: Now, who were the members of the Politburo? Strike that out a minute. How many members were there on the Central Committee at that time?

TROTSKY: There were at the time of the October Revolution only five and then seven.

GOLDMAN: The Central Committee?

TROTSKY: The Central Committee?

FINERTY: Yes.

TROTSKY: In the first year, 1917, there were about thirteen or so, then eighteen—about eighteen. I am not sure if that was in 1919. I regret very much not to have the membership. I don't know—you can ask me these special questions again and I can give you the precise figures after recess.

FINERTY: I think it would be well if on any of these details you cannot give us, you can subsequently furnish the Commission the information. How was the Central Committee selected in 1919?

TROTSKY: By the yearly Congresses of the Party.

FINERTY: As in the past?

TROTSKY: Yes, but more democratically, because we had full freedom. Under the Tsar it was restricted; the democracy was restricted.

FINERTY: All the members were free to vote for delegates to the Congress?

TROTSKY: Yes; naturally.

FINERTY: And the delegates selected the Central Committee?

TROTSKY: Yes. A period of six to eight weeks preceding every Congress was set aside for discussion. Also, a discussion of the composition of the Central Committee, openly in every organization of the Party, in the basic organization of the Party.

FINERTY: Who were the members of the Politburo in 1919?

TROTSKY: Lenin, Zinoviev, Stalin, Kamenev, and myself.

FINERTY: What were the relative functions of the Central Committee and the Politburo?

TROTSKY: The Politburo was subordinated to the Central

Committee. It was an executive committee, the most important executive organ of the Central Committee.

FINERTY: It was a sub-executive committee of the Central Committee?

TROTSKY: Yes, but the organizational decisions were submitted to the organizational bureau.

FINERTY: The organizational bureau was subordinated?

TROTSKY: To the Political Committee, the Politburo.

FINERTY: Who was at that time the head of the organizational bureau?

TROTSKY: Krestinsky, Serebryakov, and I don't remember who was the third.

FINERTY: And were both the Politburo and the organizational bureau selected by the Central Committee?

TROTSKY: Yes.

FINERTY: When was the Soviet Union officially constituted? What date?

TROTSKY: It was officially proclaimed the next day after our victory. It was the 27th of October, the old style, or the 8th of November, European and American style.

FINERTY: Now, what were the governing bodies of the Soviet Union, the official governing bodies?

TROTSKY: The insurrection took place during the session of all the soviets. In this Congress, all the Russian soviets selected the executive committee, the Executive Soviet Committee of all soviets, and selected the Council of People's Commissars.

FINERTY: The soviets selected the—

TROTSKY: The delegates. The local soviet delegates to the Congress.

FINERTY: And the Congress appointed the executive?

TROTSKY: Maybe of 150 members, and they appointed the Council of People's Commissars.

FINERTY: All the Commissars?

TROTSKY: Yes.

FINERTY: And the Commissars were over various departments of Government?

TROTSKY: Pardon?

FINERTY: The various Commissars were over various departments of Government? I mean, such as war, foreign affairs, and so on?

TROTSKY: Yes. It was, more or less, simply a division of the work as in every government and in every ministry.

FINERTY: Now, who were the members, in 1919, of the Government? Who were the Commissars of the Soviet Government in 1919?

TROTSKY: Lenin was the chairman, Chicherin was for Foreign Affairs, Rykov was for economy, for agriculture Serebryakov, and Shliapnikov—he is now in prison, if he is alive—was for labor organizations, and myself for army and navy. For finances—I am not sure who was at that time for finances. Maybe Sokolnikov—no, Sokolnikov was a bit later.

FINERTY: Those were the principal Commissars that you named?

TROTSKY: Pardon?

FINERTY: Those were the principal Commissars that you named?

TROTSKY: Yes.

FINERTY: In that form—

TROTSKY: Excuse me, Stalin was for national questions, for the different nationalities in the Soviet Union.

FINERTY: Now, what were the relations between the Communist Party organizations, such as the Central Committee, or the Politburo, and the Commissars? Did they have any official relationship, so that one official had no authority over the other?

TROTSKY: It is very difficult to present clearly the relationship. After the split with the Left Social Revolutionaries in 1918—they also participated in the Council of People's Commissars, but after the insurrection against the Brest-Litovsk peace which they organized, a military insurrection, only the Bolshevik Party remained in office. All the Commissars were Bolsheviks, and they recognized the authority of the Politburo. If they had a difference concerning an important question in the Council of People's Commissars, they addressed themselves to Lenin with the demand to convoke the Central Committee. They would discuss the question and consult with the Central Committee. As I remember, every decision of the Central Committee had for them absolute authority.

FINERTY: So that, in fact, whether in theory or not, the Party was supreme over the Commissars?

TROTSKY: Yes.

FINERTY: As I understand you, the Commissars were directly and indirectly, through the Congress and through the Executive Committee, elected by the soviets?

TROTSKY: Yes.

FINERTY: What was the basis of membership in the soviets?

TROTSKY: In the soviets, all toiling people, excepting the exploiters. We had at that time small bosses and "kulaks," rich farmers, and so on. All the toiling people had a right to participate in the soviet elections.

FINERTY: There were both workers' soviets and agricultural soviets?

TROTSKY: Yes; at that time there were peasants, also intellectuals and also functionaries. Only exploiters and moral compromisers were excluded.

FINERTY: So that, democratically speaking, the soviets were a more democratic body than the Party?

TROTSKY: Naturally, yes.

FINERTY: And even in the early days of the Soviet Union, the Commissars who were directly and indirectly elected by the soviets were subordinated to the least democratic organization of the Party?

TROTSKY: Yes, but it is—excuse me—it is too formalistic a formula. The relationship between the Party and the Commissars was known throughout the country.

FINERTY: I am not questioning that. I am trying to get as a basis for your testimony that the change from democratic control of the Soviet Union as originally constituted, to the bureaucratic control that you now allege—that it is under the control of Stalin. How far was the control democratic from the start?

TROTSKY: When the people in Belgium—their Ministers are Catholic; they address the Holy Father in Rome who gives them advice. It is not a challenge of democratic rights. The people know they are Catholics.

FINERTY: It would be a challenge to democratic rights if the Pope exercised temporal authority?

TROTSKY: Then the people have the opportunity not to elect a second time the Ministers, if universal suffrage, universal democracy, remains intact.

FINERTY: Suppose there had been a difference of opinion between the Commissars and the Central Committee or the Politburo. Under your organization, as I understand it, the policies of the Central Committee or the Politburo would have controlled the action of the Commissars?

TROTSKY: Yes.

FINERTY: If the soviets had elected new Commissars, the new Commissars would have been just as subject to the control of the Central Committee and the Politburo?

TROTSKY: It was a question—a more provisional question, depending on the relationship between the Party and the working class—if they had confidence in the Party. Only formally, the Party was less democratic than the soviets. One time the people had the fullest confidence in the Party which guided the people during the October insurrection and which gave to the peasants the soil.

FINERTY: I want to ask: Whether or not they had the fullest confidence in the Party, short of a revolution there was no way they could prevent the Party from controlling the Commissars, was there?

TROTSKY: It is not correct.

FINERTY: Now, understand, I am asking for information. I am not expressing an opinion.

TROTSKY: Because every Congress of the Party and every Congress of the Soviets was preceded by a discussion by all the people. Everybody had the possibility of expressing his criticism, to oppose comrades to the Central Committee and elect to the Central Committee of the Party.

FINERTY: I understand that there was a full opportunity for discussion and a full opportunity for criticism. What I am asking is: What were the means of popular control, not through the Party, but through the people as a whole, through the people of the Soviet Union as a whole? What would be the means of popular control, or were there any?

RUEHLE: Was the voting by secret ballot or open ballot?

FINERTY: Commissioner Ruehle wants to know if the voting was by secret or open ballot?

TROTSKY: Open ballot. At that time it was a measure not against the people but against the old tradition of fear before the more intelligent people, and so on. In order not to give the possibility to the agents of the bourgeoisie, and so on, to exercise influence, we insisted upon open votes. Later it was transformed into an instrument of oppression against the people. At the beginning, to give the possibility to the majority to say to the exploiters and their agents: "We are the majority; you must be cautious."

FINERTY: The majority could elect the Commissars?

TROTSKY: The majority elected the delegates to the Congress of Soviets.

FINERTY: And they in turn, elected the Commissars?

TROTSKY: Yes.

FINERTY: But these Commissars were still subordinated

to the selected workers' party, the Communist Party?

TROTSKY: Not subordinated. They were elected on the basis of their program. It was the Bolshevik program. They, at their election, declared: "I am a Bolshevik, a member of the Bolshevik Party. You know my program. It is my program, the guide of which is my Central Committee. It is for me the highest authority." Everybody knew it.

DEWEY: Might I repeat the question in a little different form? Was there any method outside of discussions and criticism by which the people could control the Party?

TROTSKY: Elections.

FINERTY: Nonmembers of the Party could control it?

DEWEY: Limit it to the worker. Was there any organized, recognized method by which, aside from criticism and discussion, the worker could control the committees, the different branches of the Party?

TROTSKY: Of the Party or of the Soviet?

DEWEY: Of the Party.

TROTSKY: It was the right only of Party members to change the Party and to control the Party. In the soviets, it was the right also of non-Party members—the Constitution assured to the workers and peasants the right to remove at any time their representatives to the soviets and to elect new ones.

DEWEY: I was not referring to the soviets. I was referring to the governing bodies of the Party.

TROTSKY: The bodies of the Party were elected only by the Party members and submitted only to the Party Congress.

DEWEY: Under these circumstances, how can you say that it was democratic?

STOLBERG: May I interrupt, Dr. Dewey?

TROTSKY: I didn't say it was democratic in the absolute sense. I consider democracy not as a mathematical abstraction, but as a living experience of the people. It was a great step to democracy from the old régime, but this democracy in its formal expression was limited by the necessities of the revolutionary dictatorship.

FINERTY: That was what I was leading up to, Mr. Trotsky.

TROTSKY: When you speak of democratic control in Russia, you mean such democratic control as is—

FINERTY: Consistent with the interest, as you conceive it, of the dictatorship of the proletariat?

TROTSKY: You mean, Mr. Attorney, the present or the past?

FINERTY: At that time.

TROTSKY: Now?

FINERTY: At that time. When you spoke of democratic control at that time, you meant such democratic control as was consistent with the dictatorship of the proletariat?

TROTSKY: Yes; absolutely correct.

STOLBERG: Mr. Trotsky, I think possibly this thing can be clarified in my own mind if you explain what you mean by democratic centralism—would that not have answered the questions raised?

TROTSKY: Yes, to a certain extent. Our party was throughout organizationally based upon the principle of democratic centralism. It signified that everybody has the same right of discussion, control and election of the leadership of the Party. The leadership of the Party had the right to direct the Party and later, also the country.

FINERTY: We will—I am coming to this later. But in connection with this question, when you speak of democratic control in Russia, or the Soviet Union, you are still speaking now—I mean in the terms of the present. You are still speaking of the democratic control of the Party rather than of the democratic control by the people as a whole of the government?

TROTSKY: No. We, as the Opposition, asked for Party democracy, soviet democracy and trade-union democracy. There were three principles. Even in 1924 and 1925 we used to insist on the secret vote because the people were terrorized by the bureaucracy.

FINERTY: I am anticipating, so I will go back. Now, will you define for the record, Mr. Trotsky, what you mean by the dictatorship of the proletariat?

TROTSKY: The dictatorship of the proletariat signifies that all the exploiters are eliminated from the right of determining the fate of the country, and all the elements who support them are automatically eliminated. Only the revolutionary class of the proletariat and all the exploited masses which support the proletariat have the right to determine the fate of the country.

FINERTY: What I want to know is, if within that definition is included the meaning of a dictatorial government?

TROTSKY: Yes; of a dictatorial government. It is a government which represents the dictatorship of the proletariat. The class cannot be the government. The class—

FINERTY: What I really want to ask you, is, if the more correct designation would be the dictatorship for the proletariat, rather than the dictatorship of the proletariat?

TROTSKY: The question is of the relationship between the Party and the class and between the Central Committee and the Party. If the Party has the full confidence of the workers and the elections are free, then these two formulae coincide, because it is impossible for a class directly to form the government. The whole class cannot do it. There is the trade union with secretaries and directing bodies. If the secretaries are elected freely—if a G.P.U. does not have the means of oppression—it is a democratic means of election in the trade unions.

FINERTY: It is a democratic method of selecting the dictatorship?

TROTSKY: We named that the dictatorship of the proletariat as the first experience of genuine proletarian democracy.

FINERTY: But the government in essence is a dictatorial government?

TROTSKY: Dictatorial government? You must make it precise. The question is, if its dictatorial power is directed against the people—if the G.P.U., if the function of the G.P.U.—is to oppress the masses, or if the G.P.U. and the newly acquired rights of the masses are against the exploiters. It is a simple definition.

FINERTY: Well, the dictatorship, whether for better or worse, is a dictatorship?

TROTSKY: Formally, yes. But my opinion is, that in Norway, where the Government is Socialist, we have a genuine dictatorship of the shipowners. The state is governed exclusively by the shipowners. The Socialist Government is a decorative ornament in this instance.

FINERTY: Now, I understand that your belief is that even such a democratic organization of the Communist Party and of the Soviet government as was possible within the limits of the theory of dictatorship has been set aside by Stalin through the means of the bureaucracy.

TROTSKY: Transformed into its contrary; not only changed, but transformed into its contrary.

FINERTY: Into its contrary?

TROTSKY: Yes.

FINERTY: In other words, it has become a purely bureaucratic government?

TROTSKY: Defending the privileges of the new caste, not the interests of the masses. Because, for me the most important criterion is the material and moral interests of the masses, and not only constitutional amendments. It is important, but it is subordinated in my conceptions to the real material and moral interests of the masses.

DEWEY: Might I ask one question? Just on what you said, did I understand that you hold that these privileges have reached a point where there are class divisions in the Soviet Union?

TROTSKY: It is difficult to get a strict social formula for

this stage of development, because we have it for the first time in history, such a social structure. We must develop our own terminology, new social terms. But I am inclined to affirm that it is not a genuine class division.

DEWEY: Yet it is a real class. That is the reason why I asked the question.

INTERPRETER: A caste.

TROTSKY: I said a caste.

DEWEY: I beg your pardon.

FINERTY: In the Socialist state, Mr. Trotsky, the state controls the forms of production, does it not?

TROTSKY: Yes.

FINERTY: The sources of production and the methods of production?

TROTSKY: Yes.

FINERTY: And in order to have an effective control, the state itself must employ technicians. Isn't it then inevitable in a Socialist state that the bureaucracy will grow up automatically?

TROTSKY: What do you name a Socialist state? The Socialist state is a transitory form which is necessary to prepare to build up the future Socialist society. The Socialist society will not have any state.

FINERTY: I understand that. But in the intermediate form of the Socialist state, you have an inevitable bureaucracy.

TROTSKY: It depends on two factors which are connected with one another: The productive forces and the power of the country. It is the function of the new régime to satisfy the material and moral needs of the population. Secondly, and what is connected with it, the cultural level of the population. The more the population is educated, the easier it is that everyone can realize the simple functions of an intermediary regulation of distribution. The bureaucrat in a cultivated, civilized country has not the possibility of becoming a half-god.

FINERTY: Demi-god.

TROTSKY: Demi-god, yes.

FINERTY: What I mean is this: It is obviously impossible in a Socialist state, as an intermediary organization, to have a democratic control of industry. I mean, a truly democratic control. It must be a bureaucratic control.

TROTSKY: I repeat, the relationship between the bureaucracy and the democracy depends—the elements of bureaucracy are inevitable at the beginning, especially because we inherited all the past, the oppression and misery of the people, and so on. We cannot transform it in twenty-four hours, this relationship. Here the quantity is transformed into quality. The relationship between them depends upon the material prosperity and the cultural level of the population.

FINERTY: I understand, but we cannot now discuss what the relationship should be between the democracy and bureaucracy. But it is the inevitable result of a Socialist state?

TROTSKY: Not only a Socialist state. Bureaucracy—

FINERTY: Just confine it, if you will, to the Socialist state. Whatever may be good in the Socialist state, the bureaucracy is inevitable from the start?

TROTSKY: I cannot accept that formula, as a Marxist. The first period of the Socialist state is the victory over the bourgeois state. That is the formula of the Marxist—until the time we have reached a state to satisfy freely, as with a *table d'hôte*. The rich people have a *table d'hôte*, wines and jewels. It is not necessary to have a dictatorship when you have *table d'hôte*. On the contrary, everybody gets the same things, especially the ladies. When the table is very poor, everybody forgets whether it is a lady or a man. He will take all he can. Then it is necessary to have a dictatorship. The reason for the existence of gendarmes is the misery of the people. In other words, the economic condition has a basic influence on this question.

FINERTY: Limit it this way: When the revolutionary Socialist state takes the place of the former capitalist state, the bureaucracy is inevitable at the start.

TROTSKY: It is an inheritance, just as misery is an inheritance.

FINERTY: Inherited or not, it is inevitable?

DEWEY: May I, before we adjourn for recess, ask one question along the same line? On page 44 of the English translation of "The Revolution Betrayed," I find this statement:

> If the state does not die away, but grows more and more despotic, if the plenipotentiaries of the working class become bureaucratized, and the bureaucracy rises above the new society, this is not for some secondary reasons like the psychological relics of the past, etc., but it is a result of the iron necessity to give birth to and support a privileged minority, so long as it is impossible to guarantee genuine equality.

I would like to correct the page. It is on page 55. Isn't that a statement that this dictatorship in the early stage is a matter of iron necessity?

TROTSKY: In a poor, backward and isolated workers' state, yes. To a certain degree, not an absolute measure, but to a certain degree it is an historical necessity.

DEWEY: We will now take a short recess.

DEWEY: Dr. Ruehle wants to ask some questions.

RUEHLE: I would like Trotsky to express himself on the basic differences between administration and democracy—

TROTSKY: In two words: It is the difference between—

RUEHLE (through interpreter): Rather, bureaucracy.

TROTSKY: —servant and collectivity. A cooperative, a workers' cooperative organization has also administrators, but they are not demi-gods, simply functionaries. The chief of the G.P.U. is not a simple functionary. He is somewhat of a demi-god, or three-quarters god. (Laughter) It depends upon the quality of the members and upon their general cultural level.

FINERTY: Then, Mr. Trotsky, whether or not it is an inevitable incident of a Socialist state, or a variant of a Socialist state that there be a bureaucracy, there is a tendency, unless it is controlled, that the bureaucracy will grow up.

TROTSKY: The growth of bureaucracy in the Soviet Union is the reason of the backwardness of the Soviet Union and its isolation.

GOLDMAN: The result.

TROTSKY: Result, yes. If the workers of Germany had won power in 1918 during their revolution, the economic combination of Soviet Germany and Soviet Russia would have given formidable results on the economic and cultural basis of these two countries. This terrible bureaucracy could not have a place in the Soviet Union. It is not a Soviet Union of an abstract principle. The material factors and the ideological factors are determinant. I am sure that the proletarian dictatorship in a more cultivated and civilized country would have an absolutely different appearance; and the notion of the dictatorship would have a different sound to our ears, in a more cultivated country.

DEWEY: And Russia, the Soviet Union, was a backward and undeveloped country, historically?

TROTSKY: Yes.

DEWEY: Then, in the Soviet Union, it was necessary that the bureaucracy grow up?

TROTSKY: Yes, in so far as the Soviet Union remained isolated. With the help of more advanced peoples it could have—or could shorten the period of bureaucracy and attenuate it.

FINERTY: Now, Mr. Trotsky, that leads to my question, if you can answer it briefly: What has Stalin done to perpetuate the bureaucracy instead of shortening it, and what would you have done to shorten it?

TROTSKY: He declared in 1927, openly, "You cannot remove these cadres except by civil war." That is, the bureaucracy cannot be removed, except by civil war. He proclaimed officially that the bureaucracy is independent of the people, of the Party and non-Party people.

FINERTY: If you can, will you refer to that declaration?

TROTSKY: Yes, in August, 1927. I quoted it in Radek's statement. Radek named it in December, 1927, as the formula of the Bonapartist régime.

FINERTY: Can you briefly state how you would have shortened its dominion, or controlled the power of the bureaucracy?

TROTSKY: You will, Mr. Attorney, place me in a very difficult situation. You will place me in a régime which is created by the bureaucracy, and you will ask of me that I conduct myself as an angel. It is impossible. It is necessary to smash up the bureaucracy. I cannot do it. Only a new political revolution can do it.

FINERTY: Let me put it this way, Mr. Trotsky: Had the Left Opposition been successful and had it not been expelled in 1927, what measures would the Left Opposition have taken to prevent the growth of the bureaucracy?

TROTSKY: First, the Left Opposition was not expelled accidentally. It was the defeat of the German proletariat, the defeat in China and the defeat in Austria. We were also defeated with the world proletariat. It explains why we are not in office. Secondly, in our platform we gave measures which were not a panacea, but which we considered necessary measures to attenuate the oppression of the bureaucracy. It was the secret vote in the Party, in the soviets, in the trade unions and the different enterprises.

FINERTY: You advocated the secret vote beginning with, I believe, 1926–1927?

TROTSKY: Then, freedom of speech, discussion and criticism against the bureaucracy. Then, the abolition of the civil paragraph in the penal code, by which the bureaucracy tries to stifle the workers, the more critical workers. That is the gradation of measures which we proposed in our platform.

FINERTY: The recent Constitution does purport to accord the secret vote. Now, do you think that will not operate to control the bureaucracy?

TROTSKY: It will have the same consequence as the secret vote in Germany. Hitler did not touch the Weimar Constitution, the democratic Constitution. It was an astonishment for everybody. Everybody believed that Hitler would change the Constitution, but the Constitution remains. But he broke the backbone of the Constitution. That is all he did, and even the secret vote gave him the majority.

FINERTY: In other words, you don't believe the new Constitution affords any means of controlling the bureaucracy? The only possibility is a revolution against the bureaucracy?

TROTSKY: Yes.

FINERTY: You gave, as one of the reasons for the bureaucracy and its strength, the isolation of the Soviets as the only Socialist state, and you believe that if the Socialist revolutions had succeeded in Germany, in China and Italy, there would be less of a chance for the bureaucratic control in Russia?

TROTSKY: Yes.

FINERTY: I also have understood from your direct testimony that an opportunity for the Socialist revolution is afforded by war between the capitalist states; is that correct? In the event of war between capitalist states, it gives an opportunity for Socialist revolutions?

TROTSKY: No; for a Socialist revolution, it—war sharpens social contradictions and augments the dissatisfaction of the masses.

FINERTY: Yes.

TROTSKY: It creates conditions for uprisings and so on. But

it is absolutely not sufficient for the Socialist revolution.

FINERTY: There must be the basis of the Socialist revolution at the time?

TROTSKY: Yes. For the Socialist revolution, it is necessary that the proletariat wishes to take power, and that it has at its head a party capable of conducting that revolution.

FINERTY: The proletariat must be educated to want the Socialist revolution, and must have some organization to effect it if the opportunity is present?

TROTSKY: Yes.

FINERTY: Where there is such education and such organization, would it not be in the interest of the Soviet Union to foment war in such capitalist states?

TROTSKY: I don't see any reason for that, because we have had, in these twenty years after the war, many revolutionary situations across the world. We have now a revolution in Spain. Why must we look for war? There is a revolution in Spain. It is a question of making this revolution victorious. We have now in France a situation which I characterized for two years as pre-revolutionary.

GOLDMAN: Pre?

TROTSKY: Pre-revolutionary. It means, turning either to fascism or to a proletarian state. It is only a question of who will win, the fascists or the proletariat. We have not the necessity for a war. A war can only destroy this pre-revolutionary situation.

FINERTY: Would a war now between France and Germany provide an opportunity for the Socialist revolution in both countries?

TROTSKY: It depends—I repeat, revolution is not an automatic machine. The revolution is made by living people, conducted by certain organizations under certain slogans, and so on. If the party of the proletariat is not on a level corresponding to the necessities of the revolution, then the war between Germany and France will finish with the victory of fascism in France and the material destruction of Germany for twenty or thirty years, without any perspective for Socialism.

FINERTY: Has it then ever been within your philosophy to foment war and revolution in other countries?

TROTSKY: War and revolution?

FINERTY: To foment war in other countries as an opportunity for a Socialist revolution?

TROTSKY: I can only repeat what I answered my lawyer; it is the same as if in my political revolution I was favorable to cholera and other epidemics. Never.

FINERTY: I understood you yesterday to say that one reason it was not in your political philosophy is because you don't believe in artificial revolutions.

TROTSKY: Yes. To provoke an artificial revolution is impossible. Revolution is an historical event which must be produced by the development of society. War can accelerate the revolution, but this acceleration can be disfavorable—

INTERPRETER: Unfavorable.

TROTSKY: —to the proletariat if it is not prepared for revolution. Now, in this situation—we will be concrete—war in Europe will be fatal.

FINERTY: Have you ever, while in power in Russia, when you, Stalin and Lenin were jointly in power, or since, advocated fomenting war in any country?

TROTSKY: Never.

FINERTY: Are you in favor of propaganda in foreign countries as a means of educating the proletariat for revolution?

TROTSKY: Naturally. It is the task of the Fourth International.

FINERTY: And that means that you would be in favor of propaganda in every capitalist country to educate the masses in that country for the social revolution?

TROTSKY: Yes. It is not my invention, Mr. Attorney.

FINERTY: I understand that.

TROTSKY: It is in the tradition of Marxism, beginning with the Communist Manifesto of 1847. I remain in the same tradition. It does not mean or signify that I am personally in every country occupied with propaganda.

FINERTY: But as a political measure, it is one you advocate?

TROTSKY: Yes, the revolutionary education of the masses.

FINERTY: Now, you referred, in your direct examination, to your knowledge that the government of Stalin, the present Soviet Government, had used bribery in foreign countries?

TROTSKY: Yes.

FINERTY: You instanced the case of England. I want to ask you if you know whether that Government has used bribery in the United States?

TROTSKY: I must make the question precise. I am in favor of mutual aid of different workers' organizations across the whole world. During strikes it is necessary to aid the workers of a country where the strike occurs. In the past, we had the greatest aid from the United States, material and financial aid, in order to fight against Tsarism. It is not bribery; it is solidarity. If the Russian Communist Party aids another party abroad, it is not bribery.

FINERTY: I understand.

TROTSKY: But it is another thing when the Soviet bureaucracy—or better, the summits of the Soviet bureaucracy—when they use money in order to win friends to the Soviet Union, so-called friends and lawyers—lawyers in the juridical sense of the word—authors, artists and from time to time, also lawyers who defend the G.P.U. You can be sure from the start that they will defend not me—they will defend the G.P.U. I say they are corrupted people, corrupted by the Russian bureaucracy. I would be ready to establish a list of such people internationally corrupted by the Soviet bureaucracy. They name them "Friends of the Soviet Union." Not all friends are corrupted. But between the friends—

INTERPRETER: Among.

TROTSKY: —among the friends, the directing elements are in the hands of such people. It is the system of the Soviet bureaucracy to demoralize them by direct bribery and indirect bribery. Then people say that he or she is personally impartial in the Soviet trial. "Is he a friend of Trotsky's or not?" No, that is not the question. To everybody who defends the Soviet trial, "Have you a contract with the publishing house of the Soviet state, or not?" Because it is one of the more important means of corruption of journalists and authors abroad. The Soviet state has not a literary convention with other countries, and for "good" authors, it has good contracts.

FINERTY: I understood you to refer to the bribery of labor leaders in Great Britain.

TROTSKY: Also. It was in 1924 and 1925. Please do not forget that I am separated from the scene since the beginning of 1927. I don't have direct observation.

FINERTY: During that time have you had knowledge of any similar bribery among United States labor?

TROTSKY: At that time it did not exist, because the question—the American labor movement did not play such a great role for the Soviet Union. It was too far—the question of recognition was not so acute. No; I am not sure. I am sure that the leading elements of the Communist Party have every privilege described in the Constitution of the Soviet Union. I am absolutely sure of the leading Communists. I suppose that many authors are also very privileged. The *Masses*—I believe the paper, the *Masses*—

STOLBERG: The *New Masses.*

TROTSKY: It also is a semi-official paper of the G.P.U., and has every privilege from the Soviet state.

FINERTY: When you speak of privilege, do you mean subsidies?

TROTSKY: Also, directly and indirectly.

FINERTY: Did you ever believe that the Soviet government as such has a right to support revolutionary movements in other countries by financial aid?

TROTSKY: Mr. Attorney, it is not the support of revolutionary movements, it is the support of counter-revolutionary movements.

FINERTY: I am not speaking of the present Soviet Government. You might strike out that question. What I want to ask you is this: As a political matter, you think that the government of a Socialist state has a right to support revolutionary bodies in foreign capitalist states?

TROTSKY: I declared yesterday that I considered the Soviet State as a big trade union which has become the state, a big trade union organized as the state after the political victory. Now, the big trade union has the duty to help the weaker trade unions in other countries.

FINERTY: Do you know whether the Soviet Union permits capitalist propaganda in the Soviet state?

TROTSKY: I believe that now the propaganda of Stalin is an unconscious but very effective preparation for the victory of capitalism in the Soviet state.

FINERTY: Does it permit capitalist propaganda?

TROTSKY: No.

FINERTY: It does not. Would you as head—were you the head of a Socialist state, would you permit open capitalist propaganda?

TROTSKY: It depends on the concrete situation, upon the strength of the state. If it is a rich state with a civilized population, which became a Socialist state, capitalist propaganda would be so ridiculous that it would be ten times more ridiculous to forbid it. It would not be necessary to have a one-party dictatorship. It would permit everybody to create a party to advocate the return back to feudalism, capitalism and even to can—

LAFOLLETTE: Cannibalism?

TROTSKY: Cannibalism. In this sense, I would give the advice to be totally liberal in a civilized country. If you permit me, I can present an article written about this, for *Liberty,* a very reactionary paper, in which I presented my ideas on a Socialist state in the United States. I wrote that article about two or three years ago. I expressed—

GOLDMAN: You were against chewing gum in that article.

TROTSKY: Yes; sure.

DEWEY: You did not state under what conditions you would forbid capitalist propaganda. Under what conditions would you forbid the propagation of capitalist propaganda?

TROTSKY: Where, in the Soviet Union?

DEWEY: In any Socialist state.

TROTSKY: I don't forbid at all. We have now the Soviet Union. If we had two or three states more with the proletarian state, then the danger of capitalist restoration would disappear totally, and it would not be necessary to prohibit capitalist propaganda. We would perhaps create a museum in every paper. It would be—in this sense—it would be a museum for the remainders of all the old culture.

FINERTY: You take in their right—you recognize the government right of a capitalist state to prevent Socialist—

TROTSKY: I am not an adviser of a capitalist Government, but I can only remark—

FINERTY: In other words, if you had the Government you would permit advocating criticism of the Government, freedom of speech?

TROTSKY: What state, what time, and under what conditions? It depends. I work not with abstractions, only with realities.

FINERTY: I understood you, on direct examination, to testify that your opposition to individual terror as a political means was, that it was an ineffective political means, while it might be morally justified under certain conditions.

TROTSKY: Totally right.

FINERTY: It was not suitable as a political measure?

TROTSKY: Totally right. If I can give an example—many examples. We are for William Tell, not for Gessler, in Switzerland. We are for the glorious heroes of the Irish people, not for their oppressors.

FINERTY: Does Engels recognize their moral position?

TROTSKY: Yes, not only recognized, but clarified it.

FINERTY: But as a political measure, would have thought them mistaken?

TROTSKY: Yes, especially when the working class begins mass activity. Because it preceded working-class mass activity; it was, in fact, without mass support. It was an individual measure. In our history, the terrorist Narodnaya came before the appearance of the proletariat.

FINERTY: I also understand you believe that individual acts of terror are inevitable in the reaction of oppressed people against their oppressors. That is, under an oppressive government, individuals will react and express their reaction by assassination, individual assassination.

TROTSKY: We have the fact of the assassination of Kirov by Nikolayev. It is not accidental. This act, in a so-called Socialist country, is the symptom of an insupportable oppression from the bureaucracy. In that case, I say to any other Nikolayev: "You are opposed to the bureaucracy. You are ready to sacrifice yourself. It is not the way, to kill Kirov. That means nothing. You must explain to the masses the necessity to change the political régime."

FINERTY: And the only result of such an individual assassination is to give the Government in power the chance to exterminate the opposition?

TROTSKY: Absolutely correct.

FINERTY: So that, as a political measure, you would be against the measure of terror, individual terror, because it gave an opportunity for exactly what the Soviet Government did today?

TROTSKY: Yes.

FINERTY: Do you recognize mass terror as an effective political means of obtaining power?

TROTSKY: Yes. We have that now in Spain. What is the civil war? It is mass terror against the oppressors.

FINERTY: I don't mean merely revolutionary war. I mean mass executions.

TROTSKY: Permit me to answer more concretely. We began our revolution, our October insurrection. It was successful without victims. We had the great majority for us. Then the first insurrection was by General Krasnov, a Cossack general. We arrested him, and we set him free. It was stupid of us. He then organized the White Army in the South, and he assassinated thousands and thousands of workers and peasants. When began the Red Terror? After the intervention of the foreign capitalist powers. We were absolutely surrounded from all sides. They organized in Yaroslav an insurrection paid for by the French Generals and by British agents. Then the people remarked about the great danger of the restoration of the old régime. The historical responsibility for the severe terror of our revolution we must reject on the capitalist interventionists.

GOLDMAN: You mean, "place on the capitalist interventionists."

TROTSKY: Yes, place.

FINERTY: That is, the only effective political means to remove that opposition under those circumstances was mass execution?

TROTSKY: Yes; if they try to execute me, I must defend myself. When the masses begin to defend themselves against the dirty hangmen, the masses become severe. It was absolutely revolutionary. It was not possible to say, "Please observe the form of a judicial discussion," against the hangmen armed to the death.

LAFOLLETTE: Mr. Trotsky—

TROTSKY: Excuse me. I am not advocating severity, but I am ready to carry all the responsibility for all the terroristic acts committed by the Russian people against their oppressors.

FINERTY: Does that include the executions of the bourgeoisie, the Russian bourgeoisie?

TROTSKY: It included them in so far as the Russian bourgeoisie participated in the insurrection in the White Armies, and so on. The Russian bourgeoisie found courage for this intervention only when supported by foreign armies.

FINERTY: But, as a political measure, you believe it is within the right, the political right of a government to protect itself by mass executions?

TROTSKY: It is not an abstract right. I hope that after one or two victories in other countries the revolutions will become absolutely friendly revolutions.

FINERTY: Bloodless revolutions?

TROTSKY: Bloodless revolutions; yes. But the pioneers were everywhere severe people, on the road of revolution. I believe the Americans know that better than myself. It is the character of the pioneers, your pioneers, on the road of the revolution.

LAFOLLETTE: I have here a pamphlet by a man by the name of P. Lang, published by the Workers Library Publishers in New York.

STOLBERG: It is a Communist organization.

LAFOLLETTE: It is a Communist Party organization. It is entitled, "Trotskyism and Fascism." I quote from page 44:

> Only a few months before the publication of the indictment, in the recent case of the terrorist center, Trotsky published an article in the New York *New Militant* of May 9th, 1936, entitled "The New Constitution of the

> U.S.S.R.," in which, with exceptional cynicism, he extolled the employment of individual terror in the Soviet Union. In this article he wrote: ". . . At the dawn of the Soviet power the terrorist acts were perpetrated by S.R.'s and the Whites in the atmosphere of the still unfinished civil war. When the former ruling classes abandoned all their hopes, terrorism disappeared as well. Kulak terror, traces of which are observable even now, was always local in character, and was an accompaniment of the partisan war against the Soviet régime. This is not what Molotov had in mind. *The new terror does not lean upon either the old ruling classes or the Kulak. The terrorists of recent years are recruited exclusively from among the Soviet youth, from the ranks of the Y.C.L. and of the Party.* While utterly impotent to solve those tasks which it sets itself, *individual terror is, however, of the greatest symptomatic importance, because it characterizes the sharpness of the antagonism between the bureaucracy and the wide masses of the people, especially the younger generation. Terrorism is the tragic accompaniment of Bonapartism.* [Our italics.]"

Does that not sound a little like a justification of terror under the bureaucracy?

TROTSKY: I show that some basis—

GOLDMAN: Some causes.

TROTSKY: The bases are the consequences of bad nourishment, but it is not a justification of the bases. I gave the reason for the bases only. The terrorist acts in the Soviet Union are a terrible thing, which compromise, in the eyes of large masses the ideal of the Soviet state. I must explain why terrorist acts occur in the Soviet state. It is an explanation.

FINERTY: I understand that statement you have read as exactly what Mr. Trotsky has testified: That he recognizes that under an oppressive bureaucracy there will be individual acts of terror as one phenomenon of that oppression; that it is important—terrorist acts are important as indicating the existence of oppression.

TROTSKY: Yes.

FINERTY: Of a great oppression.

TROTSKY: I will show from the other side the same thing, but on a lower plane—the fact that stealing is very large—

GOLDMAN: Very extensive.

TROTSKY: —very extensive in the Soviet Union. It is for the Socialist state very compromising that they must punish stealings by civil means. What does it signify? I would say a miserable economic basis leads to stealings. And the bureaucracy punishes them. It is an explanation. It is a very symptomatic fact, this stealing.

FINERTY: Incidentally, Mr. Trotsky, the Soviet state has lately enacted a law, has it not, to punish by death, thefts by children as young as twelve years?

TROTSKY: I am not sure if it is not now abolished.

STOLBERG: Repealed?

TROTSKY: But it was a law.

FINERTY: When was that law passed?

TROTSKY: It was in 1932. I believe in 1932; yes. Precisely at a moment when they proclaimed that Socialism was totally reached in the Soviet Union. It coincided.

LAFOLLETTE: If you permit me, I will continue the quotation:

> "Each individual bureaucrat is afraid of the terror; but the bureaucracy as a whole successfully exploits it for the justification of its political monopoly. Stalin and Molotov did not discover any gunpowder in this field, either."

TROTSKY: It must be a Stalinist pamphlet in your hand.

LAFOLLETTE: Yes.

TROTSKY: They now commit a small frame-up, because

the quotation eliminates my conclusion, and is given only for the purpose of introducing an error in the minds of the readers.

LAFOLLETTE: There is one more question I would like to put: I want to ask you what your opinion is of the idea that the revolutionary terror must almost necessarily lead to the Thermidorian terror.

TROTSKY: Also, in such a general form I cannot accept it and cannot deny it. Terror in a revolution is an indication, a symptom of weaknesses, not of strength.

LAFOLLETTE: Of weakness?

TROTSKY: Of weakness—such terrible means. The revolution on a low basis must have more terror than a revolution on a higher basis. In a revolution on a low basis you incur more danger of counter-revolution.

LAFOLLETTE: But was not France at the time of its revolution a pretty highly developed country?

TROTSKY: No.

STOLBERG: Of its day?

TROTSKY: Yes, of its day, but it is not a criterion. The people were poor and uncultured, and must crush all the foes from all other countries.

DEWEY: We will take a short recess now.

DEWEY: Miss LaFollette wishes to ask further questions.

LAFOLLETTE: I want to go back to the French Revolution, and the Thermidor, for a moment. As I understand it, the pressure of the Civil War on seven fronts—the soviets, I take it, were surrounded by many forces, so that there was in the Soviet Union, if my understanding is correct, produced a consolidation of power and a militarization, as you said the other day, of the Party and the soviets. It immensely increased, did it not, the power, the concentrated power in the hands of the Party and the Government organizations of the Party? In other words, the Party was forced, as I understand it, more or less to strengthen the bureaucracy during that period because it was a period of emergency. Isn't it true, that after that had happened, after it had been thoroughly militarized and the power concentrated in the hands of the governing party, it was extremely difficult and perhaps impossible to go back to a democratic basis? In other words, wasn't the germ of the bureaucracy contained in that situation and did not therefore, that situation lead to the Thermidorian reaction and the Thermidorian terror? Isn't it political more than economic?

TROTSKY: It is political and economic, because if Russia had been richer and a more cultured country at the time of the Civil War, our victory would have been assured in three to six months and not in three years. The prolongation of the Civil War created the centralization and militarization of the Party and the state power. The political reasons coincided with the economic reasons here. Of course, I will not deny that the germs of the bureaucracy were given in that situation. It is a historical fact. It is only a question, as we say in the Hegelian terminology, of transforming the quantity into quality. Everybody has some cruel instincts, but not everybody is an assassin. We had the germs in our régime at the beginning—the bureaucracy. We tried to attenuate the bureaucracy, not to give them the possibility to win power. Then came a certain change, and that change had a personification, a personified expression.

All the leaders of the Revolution were removed and banished, and new leaders came into power. The same transformation, the same change, took place in the composition and in the organization of the state and other places, not only in the summits but in all the layers of the state. The best fighters, the rank-and-file fighters, were removed and imprisoned, and new elements, more conservative, without revolutionary traditions, without political education, came into power.

FINERTY: If I understand your direct testimony yesterday,

Mr. Trotsky, you think that, whether or not Stalin was the instigator of the powerful bureaucracy, he is now in part at least, a victim of it?

TROTSKY: That is my opinion. I repeat, he is simply a man who will still his *soif*—

LAFOLLETTE: Thirst.

TROTSKY: —thirst with salt water.

FINERTY: You know our allegorical character, Frankenstein? You mean, he has created a Frankenstein?

TROTSKY: Yes.

FINERTY: You mean, in your belief, he is partly a victim of the bureaucracy he has created?

TROTSKY: Yes, and that is why terrorism in this connection is absolutely stupid. Because the bureaucracy can replace Stalin and Molotov. That is why individual terrorism is stupid.

FINERTY: That is, if the bureaucracy now determines that Stalin is a danger, that bureaucracy can frame a trial against him as anyone else?

TROTSKY: I don't think it is so near, but it is possible. Yagoda prepared the trials—the chief of the G.P.U. prepared the trials. The famous chief of the G.P.U. was Yagoda, who had ten years to prepare all the trials. Now he has been in prison for two months. Yezhov, the new chief of the G.P.U., will put to him the same questions as Vyshinsky put to Drobnis, "You are preparing the poisoning of Stalin, or not?" Similar questions. He will answer, "Yes."

FINERTY: Perhaps I had better take precaution and say, alleged to have framed trials.

TROTSKY: Pardon?

FINERTY: I spoke of the present Government framing trials. I had better use alleged—alleged to have framed trials.

TROTSKY: It is for me.

FINERTY: I want to ask you, Mr. Trotsky, to assume for a moment that the confessions of Zinoviev and Kamenev, Radek and Pyatakov, the leaders, the alleged leaders, were true to this extent: That they had at one time been members of the Party; that they had then gone in opposition to the Party; that they had then capitulated and, after their capitulations, according to their confessions, had gone and betrayed the Party. I am asking you, for a moment, to consider that it is true they did it. As a political measure, would you consider the Soviet Union justified in accusing these men?

TROTSKY: No, if they were not in connection—if they were to be in connection with Germany and Japan, yes. If you ask me if they betrayed Stalin in the sense that they began to criticize him again, it is another thing.

FINERTY: In other words, would you not think their executions justified as a political measure to remove the Party opposition?

TROTSKY: We didn't even execute the terrorist, the Social Revolutionary terrorist who put two bullets into Lenin's body or those who killed Uritsky and Volodarsky. There was a famous trial in 1921. We admitted Vandervelde, the leader of the Socialist International, as a lawyer for the defendants—Vandervelde and Kurt Rosenfeld, one a German and one a Belgian, two prominent members of the Second International. They visited them in prison, without any control—also friends of the terrorists. Our verdict was death, but the Central Executive commuted it under the condition that the Party abandon terror against us. They are living now.

FINERTY: Assume for a moment—I understand from your answer that you don't believe, even as a political measure, that mass executions are justified merely to remove political opponents?

TROTSKY: It is suicide. It is a form of political suicide. That is why I affirm that Stalin's policy now is the beginning of his end, a terrible end.

LAFOLLETTE: I want to ask a question about the Social Revolutionaries.

FINERTY: May I follow that up just a moment? Assume, however, that the Government of the Soviet Union believes that the defendants whom they executed were actually counter-revolutionaries attempting to restore a capitalist state. Under these circumstances, would you think the executions justified?

TROTSKY: I must then ask, what action they committed, what were their means? If they genuinely wished, only by propaganda, to prepare to restore capitalism, it would be absolutely sufficient to give the evidence to the masses and kill them morally. It would be better to give that evidence than to kill them physically.

FINERTY: You mean, discredit them morally?

TROTSKY: Morally, in the eyes of the masses.

FINERTY: Then, unless the allegations made against all these defendants were actually proved, sufficiently legally proved, you would not think, as a political measure, their executions justified?

TROTSKY: If they killed Kirov, if they were in connection with the German Gestapo and so on, I would be for the—

GOLDMAN: Executions?

TROTSKY: —executions.

FINERTY: If they actually sabotaged?

TROTSKY: Killing workers, poisoning workers? I proclaimed before the world that if the impartial Commission finds myself guilty of these crimes, I will be ready—I will do it—to give myself into the hands of the executioners of the G.P.U.

BEALS: Mr. Trotsky, you were saying that terrorism is an ulcer, an abscess on the body politic, which you do not advocate. Evidently these abscesses are a natural thing in the Soviet Union. You are now telling us of terroristic trials when you were part of the Soviet State. Will you distinguish for us why these abscesses existed in your régime and why they still seem to exist today?

TROTSKY: It is expressed, I believe, in the quotation read here by Miss LaFollette. The terroristic acts in the first period were the continuation of the Civil War, the remainders of the vanquished privileged class. The most fighting elements, the most militant elements, wished not to recognize the defeat. They tried to have their revenge by individual terror. They were terrorist people coming from the other camp, against us. Now, the new terrorists come from the camp of the Communist Party—new people, young people like Nikolayev and his accomplices, or alleged accomplices. They are all educated by the Communist Party. They are incensed at the Soviet bureaucrats, and that is the form of their protest. It is a totally new chapter. The one chapter is closed and the new chapter begins. That is the difference.

FINERTY: In other words, the bourgeois survivors were terrorists during the early part of the Soviet régime, and now the terrorists are coming from the ranks of the Communist Party itself?

TROTSKY: Yes.

FINERTY: Let me ask you this: In the event of a political revolution overthrowing the Stalin Government and the bureaucracy, would it, in your opinion, be a necessary political measure, a defensive political measure, to execute the bureaucracy?

TROTSKY: No, I don't believe it. I presented yesterday a quotation of 1933. Stalin's bureaucracy did not accuse me of terrorism openly or of a systematic terroristic plot. But they affirmed that in case Trotsky came into office, he would persecute the whole bureaucracy, he would remove them from their posts. I repeat the article I presented yesterday, and I say, I understand it is not a question of my coming now into office. It is not a practical question. But, in principle, this is not the question. I quoted yesterday Ulrich, who was an honest person and who is caught by the machine. He commits this most dishonest action. It is a question of the régime.

FINERTY: In other words, even in the political revolution and the overthrow of the bureaucracy, you would not contemplate as a necessary, even a defensive means, the personal destruction of the bureaucracy, or their personal extermination?

TROTSKY: I am sure that when the hour of the revolution comes, the political revolution, in Russia, it will be such a powerful uprising of the masses that the bureaucracy will become immediately disoriented and disorganized, just as the Tsarist régime in the February revolution.

FINERTY: So, Mr. Trotsky, it does not lie within your political philosophy either to exercise individual acts of terror against the bureaucracy or mass terror against it?

TROTSKY: Mass terror depends upon the circumstances of the bureaucracy itself. I repeat, I hope, even in the critical moment, this powerful and terrible bureaucracy would be absolutely pitiful, and then even the revolution could be more bloodless than the February Revolution in our country and also the October Revolution. But I cannot carry any responsibility for that. If the bureaucracy will oppose the masses, they will naturally take severe measures. But individual extermination, no. It is not a revolutionary perspective.

FINERTY: And not a political necessity?

TROTSKY: Not a political necessity.

LAFOLLETTE: Mr. Trotsky, I have here a pamphlet by Earl Browder, the secretary of the American Communist Party, published by the Workers Library Publishers, Incorporated. It is a speech which he made in Madison Square Garden on February 5, 1937. It is a Communist publishing company. Mr. Browder says—he quotes from your article on the bureaucracy:

> To come to power through the might of foreign armies, however, demanded from the Trotskyists an inner program acceptable to the capitalist powers. Trotsky formu-

lated such a program in April, 1930, printed in his *Opposition Bulletin* No. 10. This called for the restoration of capitalism in Russian economy. I quote:

"Retreat is, nevertheless, inevitable. It is necessary to bring it about at the earliest possible time . . . To discontinue mass collectivization . . . discontinue jumps in industrialization . . . to revise the question of the tempo of industrialization in the light of experience . . . to abandon 'ideals' of a self-contained economy . . . to work out a new, alternative plan calculated on the widest possible interaction with the world market . . . It is impossible to emerge from the present contradiction without crises and struggle."

There are a great many omissions here.

TROTSKY: It is quoted from the prosecution speech of Vyshinsky, with the same falsifications.

LAFOLLETTE: I can leave that out.

TROTSKY: Mr. Browder is not so attentive to my writings as to quote them originally. He has to repeat Mr. Vyshinsky.

LAFOLLETTE: May I go on from that? Mr. Browder says:

That last-quoted thought of Trotsky was further concretized by him in his book, "The Soviet Union and the Fourth International," published in the United States in February, 1934, in these words:

"No normal, 'constitutional' ways remain to remove the ruling clique. The bureaucracy (the Soviet power) can be compelled to yield power into the hands of the proletarian vanguard (the Trotskyists) only by FORCE."

TROTSKY: Also from Vyshinsky.

GOLDMAN: Also Vyshinsky?

LAFOLLETTE (reading):

> From Mexico, Trotsky sent a signed statement to the Hearst newspapers: "Inside the [Communist] Party, Stalin has put himself above all criticism and above the State—"

TROTSKY: This is from Troyanovsky, it sounds to me. I know very well the quotations.

LAFOLLETTE: The quotation goes on: "'It is impossible to displace him except by assassination.'"

TROTSKY: I am not the most—what is the word? I am not the most ardent reader of the Hearst press; I must confess it. I never saw this issue and the possible deformation of my statement. I said in my statement what I say here. Permit me in two words to explain this misuse, not only by Browder, but by Troyanovsky. I made statements, and in all my writings, I declare it is a falsehood: I am not a terrorist. It is contrary to my ideas. Then Troyanovsky takes one copy of the Hearst press, and says: "But Trotsky confesses he is a terrorist." This is contrary to all my statements and all my speeches. I make a separate statement for Hearst and for Troyanovsky. In this statement I am supposed to confess myself as a terrorist. Troyanovsky presents himself to me as an absolutely stupid man. I see no other explanation. Because to them I am a terrorist who conceals his terrorism. That is the accusation. What was the reason for me to confess it especially in the Hearst press? I cannot understand it. The quotation, the fragmentary quotation of Mr. Browder, is only a repetition of the fragmentary quotation of Mr. Troyanovsky. Permit me to put a rhetorical question:

If Mr. Troyanovsky, in the United States, in a great civilized and advanced country, with liberty can make such an affirmation before the forum of public opinion, can you imagine what exaggerations the chiefs of the G.P.U. permit today during their investigations in the cellars and behind the scenes? It is a form of frame-up. He connected me with Hearst. In the same way, Troyanovsky openly brought up my connection with Hearst, and affirmed that Trotsky confessed. It is a confession like Zinoviev's and the others. You have here a new embryo of the Moscow trials.

BEALS: Mr. Trotsky, may I ask why you do not like this connection with Mr. Hearst now? Have you not published many articles in the Hearst press?

TROTSKY: Nothing; not one article. There is here a gentleman representing him as a journalist. I notified at the beginning of the trial—I declared I cannot accept here a representative of the Hearst press. I give my statements to everybody, to the representatives of all the papers, all the agencies, even the conservative, but who are relatively honest. It is not my appreciation of the Hearst press. I refused systematically any statement for the Hearst press.

LAFOLLETTE: Then, you don't make statements to the Hearst press?

TROTSKY: Not only the Hearst press, but the agency connected with the Hearst press. What is the name?

STOLBERG: The Universal Press.

TROTSKY: I have refused it categorically during my sojourn.

BEALS: You have never had your articles published in the Hearst press?

TROTSKY: No; it is only the slander of the Communist Party.

DEWEY: You mean, none of your things has ever been printed?

TROTSKY: Yes; they steal many things. What can I do against them? From the Russian *Bulletin* I received clippings of the Hearst press quoting articles of the Russian *Bulletin,* from my articles. What can I do?

STOLBERG: About a month ago I saw a long article by you in the Hearst paper in New York.

FINERTY: Purported?

STOLBERG: Well, I want to describe how it appeared. Following the heading, it said, "By Leon Trotsky." Do you mean to say they stole your article?

TROTSKY: I mean, stole.

STOLBERG: Did you ever actually give your by-line, "By Leon Trotsky"?

TROTSKY: I asked my friends whether I could make a complaint before the American court.

STOLBERG: If you could sue them?

TROTSKY: Yes. Because this "By Leon Trotsky," by me, was not for the Hearst press. It was written for the other press, and given to the correspondents. In what way Hearst got it in his hands, I don't know.

DEWEY: Mr. Trotsky, since this statement appeared in one of the Mexican papers this morning, for the sake of the record I would like to ask you if you ever received, directly or indirectly, any money from the Hearst papers, or any agency associated with them?

TROTSKY: Never.

DEWEY: This statement is made this morning, that is the reason why I asked you that.

GOLDMAN: Mr. Trotsky, during the years 1929–1930–1931, while you were in Prinkipo, did you ever write directly or indirectly for the Hearst press?

TROTSKY: I never wrote direct for the Hearst press. I am not sure my literary agents in the United States did not make agreements to give one interview and an article at that time. I am not sure. I never heard they did agree, but it is possible. I was absolutely not orientated on the American press. I had a literary agent who published where he wished. But since the time I know what is the Hearst press—it is some years since my exile—I have never directly had connection with them. Since I know what it is, I have not even indirect connection with them.

DEWEY: Now to come to a really important other matter—

BEALS: May I suggest that the remarks of Mr. Trotsky arc not the opinions of the Commission? We have not gone on record.

DEWEY: Did you, in January, somewhere around the 25th, of this year, make any statement that was published in the newspapers, as you recall?

TROTSKY: January 25th?

DEWEY: Of this year.

TROTSKY: I don't remember, but we can immediately find all my statements, copies of my statements, and clarify it.

DEWEY: I think the more important thing is, if you did make any statements at that time, we should have it on record.

TROTSKY: Yes; immediately we shall find it.

DEWEY: May I state that this little sidelight regarding the connections, the alleged connections rather, of Mr. Trotsky and the Hearst press, will not appear on record? It is not really relevant to the charges.

TROTSKY: I regret it very much, for my part.

LAFOLLETTE: May I suggest that it go on record, if it does not refer to the Commission? I think it is pertinent to the record.

BEALS: I made the statement. I feel that it should definitely appear in the record, this statement of Mr. Trotsky. But the Commission took no side on the matter of the press.

DEWEY: I correct the statement I made. The record will appear, as Mr. Beals stated.

TROTSKY: I have it only in Russian. It was translated in English and given to the Mexican press here, then taken over by the Hearst press from the Mexican press. All the statements I gave on the 25th of January, 1937. They are in the papers associated with the press organizations in the United States, but not Hearst; Havas in France, and one more agency which received this statement—the statement of the 25th of January, in Russian. We can present it in an English translation.

DEWEY: If you please. We will now adjourn this session.

End of Tenth Session—One o'clock P.M.

Eleventh session

April 16th, 1937, at four o'clock p.m.

LAFOLLETTE: This morning I asked some questions based on the assumption that the Thermidorean reaction does exist in the Soviet Union. I would like to follow up that line of questioning. In your recent book, you stated the Soviet Union had made great progress in building socialism. Isn't it true that they have made great advances?

TROTSKY: Yes.

LAFOLLETTE: And in your previous testimony you stated that the revolutionary terror in 1918 and 1919 was necessitated by the fact that Soviet Russia was surrounded by hostile powers, and that it was necessary to kill off the opposition in order to defend such socialism as had been created—is that right? I take that as having been your statement this morning.

TROTSKY: I wish now to clear up the question. I cannot say. I cannot say whether it is correct or not. It is your formula.

LAFOLLETTE: I was wondering if I got the correct quotation.

TROTSKY: It is difficult for me to answer such a fragmentary question. I would prefer to have the question as a whole.

LAFOLLETTE: Perhaps I could just go on and ask my last question, which is this: Is it not possible that at least in the opinion of the bureaucracy—of course, the bureaucracy does not think there is a Thermidor—is it not possible that there is no Thermidor, but since Russia is still surrounded by hostile capitalist states, some fascist, Stalin feels it necessary to save the gains of the revolution? Is it not possible that the bureaucracy feels itself still a revolutionary power?

TROTSKY: It is not my opinion. If the society is Socialist, or near-socialist, as society is built up the solidarity—the fascist surrounding cannot change the inner relationships, because the solidarity of the Socialist society is the best weapon against fascism. Where the militarization and the bureaucratization is a product not of a surrounding fascism, but of inner contradictions—when a society is solidified, it is not necessary to have a G.P.U. in order to fight fascism; the G.P.U. is not against Hitler; the G.P.U. is against the enemies in the country—then, I ask, who are the enemies? In a certain period, they were the representatives of the former ruling class. Now, they are the more progressive proletariat, the worker oppositionists, and members of the Party and of the Youth. The fascist surroundings don't explain anything in this connection. Only the inner contradictions can explain the role of the G.P.U.

LAFOLLETTE: Then I have one more question, which bears on something you suggested yesterday. I asked you what your stand would be if Russia were allied with Hitler. You said that possibility was not excluded; that there was a certain section of the bureaucracy which was in favor of a rapprochement with the fascists. Is it not possible that Stalin is fighting against the bureaucracy, that section of the bureaucracy, using you, really accusing you of that ambition in order to create a sentiment against such an alliance?

TROTSKY: Yes, it is very possible. Many symptoms indicate that Stalin has to fight a certain part of the bureaucracy which will assure its position at any price, even at the price of an alliance or friendship with Hitler. Stalin is, I suppose, not inclined now to go along in this way, but will expose this tendency by the specter of Trotskyism: "It is Trotsky's policy; we will execute everybody who is of the same opinion." This is not an opinion on my part, only a supposition.

STOLBERG: Is it your opinion—

TROTSKY: It is very difficult to say. I don't know of anybody in the Politburo or the Central Committee who is of this opinion, but it is very probable that large strata of the bureaucracy, in the higher bureaucracy and in the middle bureaucracy, are of this opinion, that "if the fascist régimes do not threaten us, we will be quiet, have peace to do our work, and we can be in very good friendship with the fascist countries."

LAFOLLETTE: How would it stand in relation to your theory that Stalin used this method of mobilizing the masses against a rapprochement with the fascist states by making Trotsky and Trotskyism—accusing you and your followers—accusing that part of the bureaucracy through you and arousing the masses through accusing you?

TROTSKY: I do not understand.

LAFOLLETTE: You don't understand?

TROTSKY: No.

LAFOLLETTE: Would it be in accord with your own theory for Stalin to use such methods if he wanted to arouse the masses against a rapprochement with fascist countries?

TROTSKY: I believe that the Marxist, the revolutionary, policy in general is a very simple policy: "Speak out what is! Don't lie! Tell the truth!" It is a very simple policy. If Stalin has an adversary who is for an alliance with Hitler he must speak out openly before the masses, attack him, engage him in a discussion. Then, with the help of the masses, reduce him to nothing, politically, not by assassination, but politically. That would be the only way, the sound policy. I feel sure that the Russian workers in their great majority would support him in this way.

DEWEY: One more question—

INTERPRETER: Mr. Ruehle has a point on this.

RUEHLE (through interpreter): I would like to know whether Trotsky is aware of the statement in the *Prague Press*, the Government organ in Czechoslovakia, of March 5th, 1937, in which the possibility of a secret understanding between Germany and Russia is discussed; whether he sees any connection between the information in that dispatch and the trials.

STOLBERG: About the whole thing.

INTERPRETER: The citation is from the *Prague Press* and is reprinted in the magazine, *Sozialistische Wahrheit*, printed in Paris. The citation is as follows:

> It is true that England is now looking toward the East, but they are there trying to solve quite another puzzle than that which stands in the foreground of conversations and reflections of specialists. Right now a great deal is being said here about secrets between Berlin and Moscow, by which is meant the seriousness of German-Russian enmity is no longer altogether believed, and even that it would not be surprising if the whole tremendous propaganda from both sides were merely the slickest of political bluffs to obscure a great political reorientation. That Germany could decide on a thorough change in her conception of foreign policy is at least a possibility or even a probability, when one considers that a 180-degree change in German policy—to an understanding with Russia—would open to her what is almost the sole escape from the present blind alley. The facts underlying these political considerations are: The tripling of Germany's

> exports to Russia in 1936, including a large item of munitions from the Krupp-Gruson Works in Magdeburg, and the visit, kept a secret in Berlin, of German General Staff members to Moscow.

TROTSKY: Yes, I know it. It is an affirmation of my hypothetical opinion, a partial affirmation. Whether it is serious or is only a bluff, a diplomatic bluff against France, to force her to come into closer connection with the Soviet Union, I don't know. But every bluff can become serious.

DEWEY: Can I ask you a question on terrorism? In the appeal of the Russian Opposition to the Communist International, made after your expulsion from the Party, you state that it is still possible without new revolutionary disturbances to put in order and reenforce the system of the proletarian dictatorship. When I say you, I mean the leaders of the Opposition. Before that it says:

> Terror can play a great affirmative role if it is based on a correct political line and promotes the dissolution of reactionary groups. As Bolsheviks we fully understand the role of the revolutionary terror. We applied it to the bourgeoisie and their agents, the Social Revolutionaries and Mensheviks, and not for one moment do we intend in the future to renounce the revolutionary terror as against enemies of the proletariat. We well remember, however, that the terror of the parties hostile to the Bolsheviks was powerless.

That is on page 356 of the English "The Real Situation in Russia." Part of it runs over on the top of 357. I am merely asking you whether there is anything inconsistent in that with what you stated this morning, whether it is in the same line with the remarks you made this morning?

TROTSKY: I don't remember all this document, but it was

not signed by me. It is after my expulsion.

DEWEY: Yours is the first name there.

TROTSKY: Oh, yes, it is signed. My exposition in the first session today was in a larger historical line. I say if the society becomes genuinely Socialist, if solidarity is the cement of the society, then terroristic methods would be dying out, the method of dictatorship abandoned and the line of dictatorship, and that the status of terrorism must be declining. The fact that this line is rising is an argument against the Socialist character of the society and state. I repeat again that I can see that in every situation of an isolated workers' state, it is not possible—you see it now in Spain. The workers must fight for their existence and their power. When they want power, they must defend by violence their power against violence. In that sense we say that if the former ruling class and the Mensheviks and Social Revolutionaries attack the Soviet state, we will attack them with all our vigor and defend Stalin in that respect. It is a representation of our fidelity to the Soviet state. If we will appreciate the Soviet state in its development, if we forget the classless society, we must ask ourselves if the depreciations are on a declining line and not on a rising line. The rising line is the line of temperature, of sickness, a sign that the body is sick. We say the alleged Socialist body of the U.S.S.R. is sick and that the sickness is provoked by the bureaucracy.

FINERTY: Mr. Trotsky, there are a few miscellaneous matters, more properly belonging in the earlier part of my examination. I want to ask them before I forget them. Will you define the difference between the united front and the popular front? It is not shown in the record.

TROTSKY: Yes, we may make concrete the difference between the two notions. During 1917, all the politics of the Bolsheviks consisted in fighting against the popular front—not so called—-in favor of the united front. The Russian bourgeois party, the Kadets—it is from the words Constitutional

Democrats which became abbreviated to Kadets—remained as the only bourgeois party. All the bourgeois parties merged with the Kadets in 1917. The Kadets were in an alliance with the Social Revolutionarics and the Mensheviks. It was named at that time the coalition, not popular front as now, but coalition. We addressed the workers, and said to them: "You must ask of your leaders, the Mensheviks and Social Revolutionaries, that they abandon their alliance with the bourgeoisie and that they enter into an alliance with us, and the Bolshevik workers are ready to fight with them together in a united front." It was our policy. Every worker by and by understood our policy. They abandoned the Mensheviks and the Social Revolutionaries, and we became a genuine party of the masses at the turning point.

FINERTY: Will you also identify for the record the meaning of the word, "Comintern"?

TROTSKY: The "Comintern" is now defending the positions and the principles of the Mensheviks and Social Revolutionaries of 1917.

GOLDMAN: No; what does the word "Comintern" stand for?

FINERTY: What organization, what body?

GOLDMAN: The word "Comintern" stands for the Communist International.

FINERTY: It is the Communist International as distinct from the Russian Communist Party?

TROTSKY: The Russian Communist Party is the leading party in the Communist International.

FINERTY: The Communist International consists of many sections, does it not?

TROTSKY: Yes, and the sections are known as the Comintern, the aggregate.

FINERTY: A reference was made this morning also about the selectivity of the Communist Party; that the basis after 1919 was the effort to confine it actually to workers. Let me ask you what methods are now used or have since been used to restrict the membership in the Party, to change the basis of membership? Purges, I refer to purges.

TROTSKY: Now the genuine Party is only the higher stratum of the bureaucracy. The rank and file, they are not invited into the Party, but pushed out of the Party. There is now a purge from 2,000,000 to 2,500,000. There remain in the Party only one million and a half. The expulsions, most of the expulsions, are organized on orders from above. The bureaucracy now submits demands to the Party for the Stakhanovites, for example.

FINERTY: Do these purges result in removing from the Party the majority of the old Bolsheviks, the Party—

TROTSKY: The purges depend upon the dictates of the bureaucracy. If today the bureaucracy gave a concession to the rich peasants and the workers were discontented, then the bureaucracy expelled 100,000 to 500,000 workers. When the bureaucracy changed the policy and began to expropriate the "kulaks," the rich farmers and peasants, the great part of the peasants became discontented and dissatisfied. Then the bureaucracy began to expel the peasants from the Party.

FINERTY: What are the mechanics of expulsion? Is there some provision for a yearly membership? Does it take an active expulsion, or is it by means of revising and renewing Party membership?

TROTSKY: You see, Mr. Attorney, they expelled the whole Politburo, the old Politburo of Lenin. They expelled it by a summary decision. With the rank and file they have no more concern.

FINERTY: How is that accomplished?

TROTSKY: They have a Control Commission, also made up of the same bureaucrats. The Control Commission invited the defendants, and examined them briefly. Then they declared them expelled. They even expelled them without examination.

FINERTY: I want now to refer to the question of sabotage. I want to ask you if in your opinion sabotage of the Five-Year Plan by the Opposition would have been a practical political measure for discrediting and overthrowing the Stalin bureaucracy?

TROTSKY: No. From my Marxian point of view every progress is based upon the development of the productive forces of mankind, and of the nation in that case. Now, the overthrow of the bureaucracy by the people is possible only on a higher political and cultural level of the people. It is necessary to raise the people, and not push them into the depths. By the disorganization of economy, we could create only the basis for social reaction. How can we hope then to vanquish the bureaucracy?

FINERTY: Is it not conceivable that by convincing the people that the Stalin bureaucracy was incompetent to raise their economic and industrial level—as a means of convincing them, to sabotage the efforts of the Stalin bureaucracy? Isn't it possible that to do that would be a means of getting the people to overthrow the bureaucracy?

TROTSKY: It would be the same as if I said to the mechanic of a train that he was a bad mechanic, and then put myself on the railroad to provoke some accident. After that, I could not accuse the mechanic. If the Opposition—the Opposition which represents a certain ideological capital, the tradition of the leading stratum of the October Revolution—expects to educate the people, and instead of educating the workers we begin preparing catastrophes, it would signify the destruction of the best capital of the revolution, of the old generation of the revolution, the best fighters of the Civil War who were educated to represent the great tradition of history. Instead of employing them for the education of the people, we would destroy the factories, and pay for that destruction by dozens of lives. It is unimaginable, the accusation itself.

FINERTY: It is not unimagined, because it is being made.

What I want to ask you today is to consider it purely objectively.

TROTSKY: The accusation is totally conceivable from the point of view of the bureaucracy. If the bureaucracy made mistakes, it is natural. Anybody would make mistakes. The bureaucracy made more mistakes than necessary. The reason is that the bureaucracy did not allow the people to participate in the direction of the economy. If the bureaucracy is interested in rejecting responsibility for all the mistakes and errors in industry and blames the Opposition, it is totally natural. I can understand it. But that the Opposition could imagine that they, by the destruction of some factories, could take power—it seems to me absolutely absurd.

FINERTY: I can understand you, the expression of your point of view, and add that it may be the excuse of the bureaucracy for its own inefficiency. In other words, that the alleged sabotage is not sabotage at all, but was an excuse to hide the inefficiency of the bureaucracy. What I want to ask you is this: Not whether you did, not whether with your own views—let us say merely, whether from the practical point of view or from any other point of view, it would have been a practical means of overthrowing the Stalin bureaucracy if the Opposition would have sabotaged the Stalin program?

TROTSKY: I deny it. It is impossible—if I understood you—it is absolutely impossible for the Opposition. It is not necessary to provoke artificial catastrophes. There are sufficient natural catastrophes created by the bureaucracy. Mistakes. And we can sufficiently criticize the bureaucracy on the basis of these naturally negative sides of the bureaucratic economy. It is not necessary by sabotage to provoke new disasters.

FINERTY: Mr. Trotsky, assuming the condition where under the ordinary course of events the inefficiency of the bureaucracy would finally disgust the people to a point where they would overthrow the bureaucracy, would it be a possible political tactic for the Opposition, in place of waiting for that long process of overthrow by the people, to hasten the overthrow by adding to the natural inefficiency of the bureaucracy by sabotage?

TROTSKY: Mr. Attorney, you have only the experience of the class struggle in capitalist society. The anarchists propose from time to time to sabotage. We Marxists have denied it categorically every time from the beginning of our movement. How can it be possible—the new society's promise for the future. If we should begin this absurd tactic, it would be economic and cultural suicide. I deny it categorically.

FINERTY: In other words, if I understand you, while you might be willing to use any practical means to overthrow the bureaucracy, you don't think that sabotage would be a practical means of accomplishing that end.

TROTSKY: It means suicide for every political tendency.

FINERTY: In that connection, I assume that you have read the confessions, the alleged confessions, of the various defendants confessing sabotage. Do you think it within the realm of possibility that for some other motive, and under some other direction, they were actually guilty of sabotage? I understand it would be pure speculation. Have you speculated along these lines?

TROTSKY: For the defendants whom I know personally, I can affirm with absolute certitude that this hypothesis is excluded. For Drobnis, for example, absolutely excluded. The confessions are another thing. It is very possible that many or some of the defendants, who were directors in industry or economy, committed errors. What kind of errors? During Stakhanovism, the bureaucracy asked more and more productivity, more and more efficiency, and by this work under the whip they destroyed a minor factory or new machines. But the reason was the absurd policies of the higher authorities. And then the higher authorities accuse them: "You are responsible. We will shoot you for the destruction of the factories and mines," and the judge of inquiry says: "If you will recognize that you are a Trotskyite, that you committed these crimes in a premeditated manner, I hope they will save your life." That is very possible.

FINERTY: Now, Mr. Trotsky, if I am correct, in the first Moscow trial there were no charges of sabotage as such. There were charges of terror. But the defendants in the second Moscow trial, having seen all the defendants in the first Moscow trial shot in spite of any promises of clemency, would they be apt to accept promises of clemency as the basis for making a confession of acts which they had not committed?

TROTSKY: The answer is: When anybody has to choose between death at one hundred per cent, and death at ninety-nine per cent, when he is in the hands of the G.P.U., he will choose the ninety-nine per cent against the hundred per cent. We saw that in the second trial. Four of the defendants were saved. Not all were shot. In the trials before the Zinoviev-Kamenev trials, the trial of the Industrial Party for sabotage, and the Menshevik trial, nobody was shot, if I remember well. Many of them, the defendants who confessed, became again very important dignitaries in the Soviet state.

FINERTY: Did they confess in this trial about deliberate sabotage?

TROTSKY: Yes—Professor Ramzin.

FINERTY: Did they in any way impute that sabotage to you?

TROTSKY: Pardon?

FINERTY: Did they impute that sabotage to you?

TROTSKY: No; at that time, no. At that time it was connected with France; the French Government was accused of that sabotage. But in 1929, you can find in the Russian paper, only 1929—I have here, with the permission of Mr. Chairman—we prepared this sketch of the accusations. You can find in 1929 in the papers accusations against Trotskyites as saboteurs and railroad wreckers, but it was only the literary preparation of the new trial. Only the agitation of that time.

FINERTY: I want to ask you, then, if you exclude the possibility of any of the defendants of the second trial being guilty of actual acts, of deliberate acts of sabotage?

TROTSKY: In the second trial?

FINERTY: Yes.

TROTSKY: I don't know; I don't know nine or ten of them. It is possible there was a Japanese agent. I don't know Arnold, Pushin, Norkin, Rataichak, Knyazev and others. I don't know them at all. It was possible that some were genuine German and Japanese agents, and that they committed sabotage on the orders of the Japanese General Staff. It is not excluded.

FINERTY: That is what I wanted to ask you. What I then want to ask you after this, in line with Miss LaFollette's question, is your theory of the possibility of a plot participated in by the pro-Hitler branch of the bureaucracy, and that Stalin, not being ready as yet to purge the bureaucracy, preferred to throw the blame on you?

TROTSKY: I don't believe that the bureaucracy as a social category, that part of the bureaucracy, is capable of sabotaging industry in the interest of Hitler. It is absolutely improbable; it is not those corrupt individuals who received money from Hitler's agents.

FINERTY: What I am suggesting to you is, whether you have excluded the possibility. I understand that you testified that there was, or that Stalin apparently believed there was, a branch of the bureaucracy favorable to an alliance with Hitler.

TROTSKY: But not at the price of the destruction of Russian economy. A political alliance for the defense of the Soviet Union, but in order to avoid war, not to destroy the Soviet Union and Soviet economy. They are not agents of Hitler. They are only interested in peace, not interested in the fate of the world proletarian revolution, and so on. Ready for peace, even in friendship with Hitler. And if Hitler can then destroy France and stifle for twenty or thirty years the German proletariat, it does not concern them. That is their belief. But never will they consent to destroy Russian industry. They are in their way very good Russian patriots.

FINERTY: In other words, you don't even charge your enemies within the bureaucracy with being tools of Hitler?

TROTSKY: No; only individuals. It is possible that there are groups of individuals who represent their own personal interests. In every country you find them.

FINERTY: It is possible that some of these minor saboteurs and the ones you mentioned were actually Hitler and Japanese agents?

TROTSKY: Yes; it is possible.

DEWEY: May I ask a question, I think along the same lines? With reference to the range of sabotage that occurred in Siberia, about which the more secondary persons testified, there are many references to Trotsky centers in Siberia.

TROTSKY: Centers, yes.

DEWEY: That is my impression. None of these centers, however, are in any way identified. They are generally and vaguely referred to. But the question I want to ask is, when you were in exile, did you ever try to create Trotskyite centers?

TROTSKY: In Siberia?

DEWEY: In Siberia.

TROTSKY: The only ones they named here, the only ones they named as members of the center were Muralov, Boguslavsky and Drobnis. I know all three. They were expelled from the Party together with me and sent to Siberia. I know Muralov very well. Muralov confessed to be the chief of the Siberian center of saboteurs.

DEWEY: I mean the secondary people. There are vague general references to Trotskyite centers.

TROTSKY: There was Shestov. I believe, reading the Verbatim Report, that Shestov was an agent of the G.P.U., absolutely. Stroilov I don't know. About Hrasche we had some information, but he was not involved in Siberia.

DEWEY: Mr. Trotsky, you don't quite get my point. When I said Trotskyite centers, I did not mean delegates, I meant locals.

GOLDMAN: Groups.

DEWEY: Local groups. Did you have any part in forming such important blocs and centers, or groups of your followers?

TROTSKY: In Siberia?

DEWEY: In Siberia.

TROTSKY: In Siberia, the Trotskyites were in centers themselves, colonies of déportés. In the village where there are four or five déportés, they are connected one with another. They correspond with another colony or another village; that is, another colony in another village. The same situation we had under the Tsarist régime. They do not have the possibility of changing their place. They cannot take organizational measures. They are in a certain place, a village or a small town. And they are connected one with another. We can call them a center, but not an organization. It is only a colony of exiles.

DEWEY: That is all.

FINERTY: Mr. Trotsky, may I ask you this: How do you explain that Muralov, in his closing statement, in his plea, not only confessed, but stated that he told the truth in confessing active sabotage, but also called you "agent of the fascists, enemy of the working class and the Soviet Union who deserved every contempt." That man had been your friend, had been a comrade of yours in the army. Under what circumstances do you explain, or can you explain, that in open court he made these statements?

TROTSKY: If a man such as Muralov—if he cries to be shot as a German and Japanese spy, he does his work to the end. He was arrested, and remained eight months in prison without confessing. Then they show him one confession after another. On the ground of this Verbatim Report, it is not difficult to show that every one of the defendants had the same environment as himself at the Moscow trials. Radek confessed that he resisted confessing for three or four months, but they showed him one confession after another; I believe, fifteen confessions. The first confession was of his own secretary, then of his collaborator, a historian—I forget his name—and so on. They created around Radek a wall of confessors, and everybody affirmed: "Radek is guilty! Radek is guilty!" The investigators from time to time visited him in prison. Then they asked him: "Will you confess? We will begin our trial in two weeks." Radek says, "You will shoot me." And they reply, "No, we will not shoot." Radek says, "You shot Zinoviev and Kamenev." They reply, "You know yourself Zinoviev and Kamenev were adversaries. You are not an adversary. You must help us annihilate Trotsky personally, and Trotskyism. You have no other choice. You must confess." And he confessed.

BEALS: Where did you get the information that the first confession Radek saw was that of his own secretary?

TROTSKY: In the Verbatim Report. It was in the *Pravda* also. Radek says so himself.

BEALS: Can you give us the citation?

TROTSKY: I will give you this in two minutes.

FINERTY: Mr. Trotsky, I want to call your attention in this connection to the fact that Muralov does not, as Radek does, challenge the Soviets to execute him and deny any hope for clemency. What Muralov specifically says are the words: "I ask that this frank testimony be taken into account in passing sentence on me." In your opinion does it indicate that Muralov had been promised some hope of clemency?

TROTSKY: I believe so. Even a heroic personality such as Muralov asserts the will not to be assassinated, not to be executed. He had done what he promised to the end. And then in a very sober form he declared, "If you can save my life, good." The first thing—I don't have at this moment at my disposition the confessions of Vyshinsky, Yagoda, Yezhov and Stalin. If I had the confessions in my hands, I could present you with all the ties, the inquisitorial mechanics of the extortion of confessions, because these mechanics are very individual. They are, in their way, psycho—what is that word?

INTERPRETER: Psychoanalysts?

TROTSKY: Psychoanalysts. They have time. The defendants remain in prison one month, five months, ten months. They have different ways. They arrest the son and they arrest the wife. Permit me to give you a personal example. Our son is now arrested on the accusation—you know my son's accusation. If we were in Russia, the mother would be arrested, I would be arrested. They press her with the thought, "If you will save your son you must confess your man to be such and such a criminal."

INTERPRETER: Your husband.

TROTSKY: Your husband. They address the son and they say, "If you want to see your mother free, you must confess that and that." I believe it is very probable the son would confess. Then they come with the confession of the mother to me and ask me, "What will you do?" The situation is very difficult—such a situation exists with hundreds and thousands. Pyatakov's wife was arrested eight months before he was. He declared in his last words, "I lost all, my family and all."

FINERTY: Is there anything in the Bolshevik—the old Bolshevik Party—discipline, on the attitude of the members of the Bolshevik Party towards the Party, that would psychologically expose them to serve the Party at the expense of personal honor, by confessing anything that was not the truth?

TROTSKY: No. The Bolshevik discipline was very strong, very often severe. But it was a discipline of dignity, revolutionary dignity; it was discipline based on discussions, inner struggles, and then democratic decisions.

FINERTY: And nothing that would warrant a member of the Party, in the interests of the Party, degrading himself by a confession and slandering others?

TROTSKY: No, it is a measure which can only demoralize the Party. The Party exists on human beings, not robots, not automatons. The method of a revolutionary is a combination of dignity and the spirit of concession and sacrifice. It is absolutely impossible to ask from him such degrade actions as in the Moscow trials.

INTERPRETER: Degrading.

FINERTY: If these confessions were false, Mr. Trotsky, do you exclude as a motive for the confessions the desire on the part of the defendants unselfishly to serve the Party?

TROTSKY: I said, I can admit it for Muralov. They stand now in a situation—because the psychosis of war is now the most important factor in the hands of the bureaucracy. Everything is explained by the war danger. People like Muralov and others read only the Soviet papers. They don't know foreign languages. For years they read that I am abroad, acting against the Soviet Union, that I am in an alliance with Lord Beaverbrook and Winston Churchill. Everyone of them says, "It is false, but it is possible that everything is true." He is not in connection with me and he is shaky—

INTERPRETER: Shaken.

TROTSKY: —shaken in his confidence. That is from one side. From the other: "Stalin is the chief of the country. If we fight against Germany and Japan, we will fight under the leadership of Stalin. You are a friend of Trotsky, but you can't invite him to come here. In the situation his activities are prejudicial to the defense of the Soviet Union."

At the time, he merely hesitates. He hesitated for one, two, three months. He hesitated for eight months. They showed him one deposition, one confession after another. Then this man broke down. He satisfied them in every way.

FINERTY: So, he might actually have believed that you were party to a foreign—

TROTSKY: I cannot admit that he accepted the accusation as it is, because he took upon himself the same false accusation. But my oppositionist activity, my critique against the ruling caste—it is possible that it seemed to him prejudicial for the defense of the Soviet Union.

FINERTY: That was coupled with some hope of clemency?

TROTSKY: With Muralov less than with others. He was in the full sense of the word a heroic personality.

FINERTY: But his last statement indicates that he did not lie. Radek openly stated that he expected to be executed.

TROTSKY: He had a lifelong contempt for Radek, who was a dirty personality. Muralov was a pure man, an absolutely pure personality.

FINERTY: Let me ask you this: It is noticeable that the men who were executed in this trial were the men who apparently had hoped for clemency and asked for it, and that the men who were positive they had no clemency, like Radek, were not executed?

TROTSKY: I am almost sure it was convenient between Stalin and Radek for Radek to be saved.

STOLBERG: You mean arranged?

TROTSKY: Arranged before the trial. Under these conditions Radek confessed. Radek existed more or less near to Stalin.

FINERTY: But this different deduction is wrong from the fact—the fact is that men who expressed hope of clemency were shot and Radek, who expressed no hope of clemency, was not executed.

TROTSKY: Radek did not express—but the actions of Radek were an expression of—

FINERTY: What I mean is that Radek challenged the Government to execute him. Was the challenge made with some assuredness that it would not be done?

TROTSKY: I cannot be positive of that.

DEWEY: We will now take a short recess.

GOLDMAN: I want to clear up one matter which is very important. The record must be absolutely clear on it. Also the press must be absolutely clear on it, as well as the members of the Commission, who are clear on it. Mr. Trotsky, we asked you certain questions with reference to the possibility of a political revolution, and the question also came up whether or not in the Soviet Union, at the time when the masses attempt to remove Stalin, violence would be used. In the *New York Times* of April 15th, in the dispatch signed by Frank L. Kluckhohn, this following statement is made. I ask you whether it is correct or it is not correct. You can make a statement as to your position. "Mr. Trotsky insists, however, that he opposed terrorism and isolated violence, contrary to the charges made at the recent Moscow trials . . ." Now comes the statement I refer to: "He declared, 'Stalin must be eliminated, but not killed unless he . . .'"

Did you ever declare that he should be killed, if Stalin opposed the movement of the masses?

TROTSKY: Never.

GOLDMAN: What did you say—what is your position?

TROTSKY: In this connection, I spoke not about Stalin, but about the bureaucracy. The revolutionary violence can be applied against the bureaucracy—the violence of the masses—but not personally against Stalin. The connection is false. The question concerning Stalin was put in connection with terrorism. The question of the bureaucracy, the despotic régime, the bureaucracy, was connected with the question of mass violence. I say that the mass can be obliged to apply violence. For me, it is impossible to guess. If the bureaucracy will dare to oppose the mass movement with violence, then the masses will answer by violence. It is not a personal question. It is a question of the régime.

GOLDMAN: It does not necessarily follow from your statement that even if the bureaucracy uses violence and the mass of workers answer with violence, Stalin would necessarily be killed?

TROTSKY: It has nothing to do with the other.

FINERTY: I understood you to repudiate in any case, Mr. Trotsky, the assassination of Stalin, or anything along that line?

TROTSKY: Permit me to present, Commissioner Beals, from the pages in the Verbatim Report; it is on page 94, the last paragraph. Radek says as follows: "In 1935 I heard about the Zinoviev group; this was the Zaks-Gladnyev group with which my assistant, Tivel, was connected in Moscow." On page 134, the last part of the page is in connection with his relationship to Tivel.

BEALS: 134?

TROTSKY: 134.

GOLDMAN: On page 548, Radek also talks about Tivel's arrest and about fifteen confessions confronting him. On page 548, second to the last paragraph.

TROTSKY: Yes, it is most important. Thank you. It is the most important part of the deposition.

BEALS: Yes, I have that; thank you.

FINERTY: Mr. Trotsky, I want to direct your attention to the Report of the Proceedings of the first Moscow trial, the Zinoviev-Kamenev trial. I assume that you have read the alleged confessions in that trial, and the alleged last statements of the defendants.

TROTSKY: Yes.

FINERTY: As I understand it, Zinoviev, Kamenev and Smirnov were all members of the alleged center.

TROTSKY: Yes.

FINERTY: Am I correct in believing that there is no testimony or confession by any of them to implicate you in anything but directions for terror? They don't claim that you gave any instructions, in their confessions, for anything but terror.

TROTSKY: Yes.

FINERTY: They don't charge that you gave any instructions for sabotage or foreign intervention or the concession of territory—is that correct?

TROTSKY: Totally correct.

FINERTY: In reading the reports of their last statements, as well as reading their testimony, it is taken as repudiating you, the men repudiate you as totally as possible. I want to ask you if you can explain how it is that if you had given instructions for sabotage, for foreign intervention, and for the cession of Soviet territory, of territory to foreign nations, that Zinoviev, Kamenev and Smirnov could have been ignorant of it as members of the main center. If they were honestly repudiating you, why didn't they mention these charges as well as the charges of terror? Can you explain what could have motivated them in concealing these more serious charges, or at least, equally serious charges, which were subsequently made against you, if the facts existed?

TROTSKY: I tried to explain it in my speech prepared for the Hippodrome meeting in New York. Zinoviev, Kamenev and Smirnov, and all the genuine Bolsheviks in the trial of the sixteen, denied totally any connection with the German police. We find in the first trial only unknown personalities such as Berman-Yurin, David, Olberg and Lurye, who recognize or confess their connection with the German police.

It is stated that the connections were organized on my personal order or instruction. Everything is done on my instruction. Good. They were absolutely politically inconsequential people, and their connections were only with the agents of the Gestapo. One thing they succeeded in having: a

Honduran passport. Now the Honduran passport for Olberg, received from the Gestapo, was paid for by my son, allegedly, who is also another agent of the Gestapo.

FINERTY: Alleged, again.

TROTSKY: Alleged. Thus my great alliance with Germany was reduced to the passport, the Honduran passport, for an unknown young man, Olberg. And this passport was paid for allegedly by my son. Everybody, after the first trial, said: "It is too absurd that Trotsky entered into an alliance with the Gestapo, with the police, for the purpose of getting a Honduran passport. It is too stupid." Stalin anticipated too much from the first trial. He hoped that the fact that Zinoviev and the others were confessed terrorists, and that they were shot, was all that was absolutely necessary to cover everything about the trial, and that nobody would be interested in the deposition of Olberg. What will remain is that they confessed great crimes and some suspicion about the Gestapo. But world opinion was—

INTERPRETER: Distrustful.

TROTSKY: Yes; distrustful of the first trial. We have here a collection from papers all over the world—even conservative papers—to bear that out.

It was necessary to correct this trial by a new trial. I will say that at the moment of the first trial neither Stalin nor the chief of the G.P.U. had an idea about my alleged alliance and sabotage. It was only the idea of terror, and then to arouse some suspicions concerning the relations between Trotsky and the Gestapo. But the critics obliged them to organize a new trial on a more solid basis. But, unfortunately, the most important defendants were shot before the new trial. He needed for the alliance with Hitler and Japan, for those plans, Zinoviev, Kamenev and Smirnov. But they were shot. Stalin must look for other more important defendants to impose that, the most important criminal activity on an international scale.

That is why the G.P.U., during the first trial, did not demand from Zinoviev a confession of sabotage or a confession of an alliance with Hitler. The G.P.U. was, during the preparations for the first trial, modest, because a terroristic confession was sufficient. Then the G.P.U. asked, "Can you say anything about the Gestapo?" Zinoviev said, "No; it is impossible for me." You see that in the dialogue with Vyshinsky: I can say "terrorism." It is enough, but it is not so degrading as a world alliance, let us say, or that I am in connection with the Gestapo. Kamenev also and Smirnov also. Good. "We will have a suspicion of the Gestapo from Olberg, our own agent." Because he is very probably an agent of the G.P.U.

FINERTY: Mr. Trotsky, what I want to ask you is, assuming that Zinoviev, Kamenev and Smirnov were making an honest confession of what they knew, and assuming that they honestly believed you to be an enemy of the Soviet Union, was there any reason if they knew that you had given instructions for sabotage and for foreign intervention, that they should not have disclosed it then?

TROTSKY: It would be absolutely absurd. In a sincere confession in the interest of the state and of the Revolution, naturally they should have confessed the most important thing and the most important crime. It is absolutely clear.

FINERTY: Incidentally, if Vyshinsky and the Soviet Government had thought up the idea at that time that you had given instructions for sabotage to the parallel center, and had given instructions for foreign intervention, in your opinion would they then shoot their most important witnesses—Zinoviev, Kamenev and Smirnov—to such instructions?

TROTSKY: Excuse me, will you rephrase that question?

FINERTY: If the Soviet Union at that time, the first Moscow trial, knew that you had given instructions for sabotage and for foreign intervention, foreign intrigue, and that Zinoviev, Kamenev and Smirnov knew of such instructions as members of the center, would they have shot their principal witnesses?

TROTSKY: Yes?

FINERTY: Would there have been any reason for shooting them?

TROTSKY: Now I understand your question. That coincides absolutely with what I said about the second trial, that they missed the most important personalities for the second trial, where they treat of the most important crime. Naturally, it proves that the preparation of the second amalgam began only after the political fiasco of the first. It was my opinion from the beginning. My second proof is that the parallel center did not exist in the first trial. There is only the reserve center, in case of the arrest of the unified center. It was the reserve center. It was necessary to have a reserve center, not an active center, not for the future, but for the past, to have the possibility for the organization of a second trial.

FINERTY: Let me ask you this: About when were Kamenev, Zinoviev and Smirnov arrested?

TROTSKY: It was a mistake on my part—excuse me. Before the Commission I affirmed yesterday that Zinoviev and Kamenev were arrested before the assassination of Kirov. It was only the case with Smirnov, who was arrested almost two years before the assassination of Kirov. Zinoviev and Kamenev were arrested after the assassination of Kirov. In the first trial, Zinoviev says on the request of the Prosecutor that his activity lasted almost to the end of 1936. Until 1936! Including one year and a half of his prison confinement.

FINERTY: At any rate, Zinoviev, Kamenev and Smirnov were alive at that time and members of the alleged center, at the very time you were supposed to be giving Radek and Pyatakov instructions for sabotage and foreign intervention?

TROTSKY: Totally correct.

FINERTY: And must have known of such instructions if they were active?

TROTSKY: Absolutely.

FINERTY: You mean, on the theory of the Soviet Government.

TROTSKY: Vladimir Romm, the young man unknown to me—according to his own words he saw me only one time—he knew beginning from 1932 about the existence of the parallel center. He was informed by me in 1932 that the parallel center was then constructed for such purposes. But Zinoviev and Kamenev did not know anything about this.

FINERTY: In other words, under the testimony of the first trial there is no testimony of the existence of a parallel center?

TROTSKY: No; only the reserve center in case of arrest.

FINERTY: Now, I want to ask you—

LAFOLLETTE: You want to finish? I just wanted to ask—

FINERTY: I have not finished. I want to refer now to the testimony with relation to Putna—

LAFOLLETTE: May I interrupt? I want to ask, for the purpose of the record, concerning a point of Soviet law. I understand the British lawyer, Pritt, writing on this question, said it was impossible legally for the prosecutor to corroborate confessions by documentary evidence, or words to that effect. Is there to your knowledge anything in the court procedure of the Soviet Union which precludes documents corroborating evidence in the case of confessions?

TROTSKY: I am not very learned in the Soviet Union penal code, but my son published in the last issue of our *Bulletin* a quotation from a book by Vyshinsky on Soviet law. In that book he affirms that confessions are not sufficient to prove—that it is necessary for objective evidence to verify subjective confessions. It must correspond to Soviet law.

LAFOLLETTE: I would like the title of that book.

TROTSKY: Vyshinsky's book?

LAFOLLETTE: Yes.

TROTSKY: It is—I believe he must be some professor of

law in the university, a professor of law, not of frame-ups.

FINERTY: It is not the same Vyshinsky?

TROTSKY: Vyshinsky, the Prosecutor. We will see immediately. I saw it only in passing.

FINERTY: Just while we are waiting, I want to ask a question that has been suggested. This is referring to the question of terror. Was the execution of the Tsar and his family part of the revolutionary terror by the revolutionary party?

TROTSKY: It was done in Sverdlovsk, during the Civil War, by local authorities, when the White Guards wished to have Ekaterinburg in order to make free the Tsarist family.

FINERTY: In order to rescue them?

TROTSKY: Yes.

FINERTY: It was done in order to prevent the rescue? Was the execution in order to prevent their rescue?

GOLDMAN: In order to prevent freeing them?

TROTSKY: Yes. Not only that, but the aim to take Ekaterinburg by military measures was motivated especially by the presence of the Tsarist family. And they were sure that the White Guards in Ekaterinburg would exterminate thousands and thousands of workers. It was then.

FINERTY: It was, then, concretely speaking, an act of revolutionary terror, rather than a military measure?

TROTSKY: It was a military measure of a local type or character.

FINERTY: Referring to the Pyatakov visit to Oslo, I want to ask you, have you the text of the statement issued by the Norwegian Government as to the possibility of a plane having landed at the airport at Oslo at the time of Pyatakov's alleged visit?

TROTSKY: Not by the Government. It is by the airdrome authorities.

FINERTY: Have you that there? May I glance at it?

TROTSKY: Can I give now the answer to Miss LaFollette concerning the book? This book is by another professor, edited—under the editorship of Vyshinsky. It is on criminal procedure. The title is: "Criminal Procedure." It is published in 1936.

LAFOLLETTE: Is that translated, do you know?

TROTSKY: I don't know. We find here, "False witnesses who learn their work by heart can make very persuasive depositions." It is the quotation. He affirms it is necessary to have objective proof for a deposition, and so on.

LAFOLLETTE: Thank you.

FINERTY: I see by the statement of the director of the airport that it is stated that no foreign plane had landed at the airport.

TROTSKY: From the 19th of September.

FINERTY: Between the 19th of September—

TROTSKY: And the first of May.

FINERTY: May 1st, 1936, and identified the last foreign plane landing there as a British plane.

TROTSKY: A British plane.

FINERTY: Now I want to ask you, assuming for the purpose of argument that the charges of the Soviet Government were true on an alliance with Hitler or an attempted alliance with Hitler, and Pyatakov was party to the conspiracy, would it not have been possible for Pyatakov, in connection with Hitler, to have obtained a German plane, and in connection with the fascists in Norway, to have landed in an airport and have prevented a report by the manager of the airport of the fact that such a plane had landed? I am asking you if this is not in the realm of possibility.

TROTSKY: I believe, the first thing, that it was impossible for Pyatakov to disappear from the Soviet staff in Berlin. I know from my experience that every member of the Central Committee and member of the Government who goes abroad presents immediately—he is met at the railroad station by the Soviet representative and he remains all the time in connection by telephone or telegraph with Moscow, because he may receive, as a member of the Central Committee and of the Government, important communications and maybe missions. It is absolutely impossible for such a person as Pyatakov to disappear for twenty-four hours. But it was necessary for at least forty-eight hours. The second thing: If he would have from Hitler a passport he must give his own name. He must communicate his name. He said, "I had only to sign." Everything was organized by the mystical personality Gustav Heinrich. He had only to sign. To sign, he must have had a name. He didn't communicate the name. But the Prosecutor Vyshinsky had the obligation to ask the name on the passport. The fact that the Prosecutor Vyshinsky did not ask him a question concerning the passport is the greatest and most direct evidence of Vyshinsky as the organizer of the frame-up. Pyatakov says that he visited me in a not badly furnished house. That is all—he visited me in a not badly furnished house. It is a neutral phrase, however, not an appreciation. Did he meet my wife in the house? Was it memorized or not? Pyatakov's glance at my desk was sufficient for him to see my Russian texts, papers and manuscripts. If it was a Norwegian—the room or the apartment of a Norwegian? He was constantly in this room, he said nothing. He came for three hours.

DEWEY: Until three o'clock.

FINERTY: You mean he left at three o'clock?

TROTSKY: The discussion lasted two hours—until five o'clock. At that time, it is night in Norway, in December. He left to go where? To the ship, to the airplane, or to a hotel? What hotel? In a hotel he must show his passport and sign his name. The Prosecutor did not ask him about the hotel, about the night. He has not the slightest interest in handicapping his very delicate exposition.

FINERTY: Mr. Trotsky, admitting the force of all the arguments you make, what I want to ask you is this: The fact that the director of the airport reports that no foreign plane landed there is not necessarily conclusive evidence or evidence that a foreign airplane did not land there?

TROTSKY: I think it is very conclusive in the present situation.

FINERTY: Let me ask you before you go on: Might it not be in the interests of the director of the airport, had such a plane landed there and he had made no record of it, to deny that it landed, to excuse his failure to make a record?

TROTSKY: That question is very complicated—more complicated. The director of the airdrome affirmed that there is a military patrol day and night, for customs reasons. Now, is it a lie or is it true? If he is a fascist, the Government is Socialist in Norway. There are different parties. Their papers sent their correspondents to the airdrome, and the papers gave their impressions. Pyatakov came at three o'clock to the airdrome.

FINERTY: Alleged that he came.

TROTSKY: He could start only the next day in the morning. The airplane must remain on the place twelve or fifteen hours, and take new provisions of gasoline. Where? An auto waited at the airdrome. I am not entering into the question whether it was possible in the winter on an airdrome to use an auto, because the snow is, I believe, or was too deep. But I am not entering into this technical question. But the fact is that the airplane must have remained from twelve to fifteen hours and there might have been other people at the airdrome.

FINERTY: Now, Mr. Trotsky, admitting the force of your argument, I want to ask you this: Is it still not possible that for diplomatic reasons, if an airplane did land, the Norwegian Government would want to deny it?

TROTSKY: I believe that the Norwegian Government would be glad to denounce me immediately, because they interned me for four months, if not longer, only for the benefit of the Soviet Government. And if they had no reason to conceal it, it would be the best justification for their civil measures against me, because the Government is severely attacked by its own parties. It is not correct. If the Government could use any evidence in my sojourn which would implicate me in such counter-revolutionary propaganda, it would be glad to present all the proofs. It is also the reason why the director of the airdrome who gave the deposition, when my Norwegian lawyer asked him for a formal deposition for the Commission, said: "I have said it already. I cannot give you that without authorization of the higher authorities. They prohibit me from giving it."

FINERTY: And that statement is the statement just shown to me in which he states he is prohibited from giving it?

TROTSKY: Yes; he confirms his deposition to the press, and he is prohibited from giving a formal deposition to us.

FINERTY: I understand, Mr. Trotsky, that part of the Commission have additional questions to ask. Maybe further questions will occur to me. I would like to ask you this one question: If you were, as Mr. Stalin charges, and Mr. Vyshinsky charges, in your intentions—if you intended to overthrow the Socialist state in the Soviet Union, in favor of a capitalist state, would you have considered the methods which they charged you used, effective methods for even that purpose?

TROTSKY: I don't know whether they would be effective. If I allegedly acted only in the interests of Hitler, if I transported myself, or rather, deported myself as an impersonal agent of Hitler in order to establish capitalism, it is very difficult for me to say in what manner I would act in this sense.

FINERTY: I was going to ask you if you could tell us how you would act.

TROTSKY: But they affirmed that at the same time I tried to take power—in order to take power I transformed myself into an agent of Japan, to begin to destroy Soviet economy. I never heard that he who is ready to take power in a country becomes an agent, a subordinate, a miserable agent of an enemy general staff. I allegedly became a police agent for a miserable purpose, with the assurance in advance that my activity must be known tomorrow, because for sabotage you must use things and people in different parts of the country. How could it remain a secret during two months, if they acted genuinely? We read now that in Siberia, Muralov and other Trotskyites were instructed by me to commit sabotage. It was absolutely sure that my activity must be discovered in a short time. Now, then, what a road to power! I cannot understand it. Assume me to be mad, assume I have become insane and I elaborate this plan. I have to ask myself: "The Trotskyites, the alleged Trotskyites, who are the alleged agents, what is their psychology, what are their objectives, and what are their aims?" Because they must sacrifice their lives immediately and not take power. The man who is shot cannot take power and give the power to Trotsky to establish capitalism in the interests of Hitler. Anyway, a man cannot give his life for a false ideal. It must be an ideal, it must be an ideal for him. It must be a religious ideal, a political ideal, or a national ideal. But what ideal could move the executors of my plan? I can't understand it. It is the weakest point. And this weakest point is not explained. It is disregarded by the bureaucracy, the small, the little people, like Vyshinsky. They do not have any interest in asking this of the executors: What was their ideal, their program, their idea?

FINERTY: In other words, what would they get out of it?

TROTSKY: Pardon?

FINERTY: In other words, what would the leading people get out of it?

TROTSKY: Yes; what?

DEWEY: We will now take a short recess.

DEWEY: Mr. Trotsky, I would like to ask you a question which we have asked you during the direct examination. It is a very special matter of fact. On page 84 of the English translation of the official proceedings, Radek refers to a group of former leaders of the Leningrad Young Communist League who later became the leaders in the assassination of Kirov. Did you have any connection either personally or politically with the Young Communist League?

TROTSKY: The Young Communist League of the Party is a legal organization. You mean the terroristic group in Leningrad?

DEWEY: Well, he says they were the leaders of the assassination of Kirov.

TROTSKY: I did not even know the names, before I read them for the first time in the report, of these young people, of the fourteen young people who were shot in Leningrad. But it is not a league, it is only a conspiratorial group, an allegedly conspiratorial group.

DEWEY: Now, I wish to ask you a question more on the line of your theoretical position, about a question involved in the struggle of the Left Opposition. Why did the question of Socialism in one country and the world revolution become such a fundamental point of division?

TROTSKY: Because the theory of Socialism in one country signifies in our eyes the repudiation of all internationalism. We consider internationalism not as an abstract idea, but as the first interest of the workers' movement of the world; not for the purpose of building an independent, isolated, Socialist state. Then the Russian worker would not have a vital interest in connection with the workers of other countries.

DEWEY: Was that a theoretical objection, based on general theory?

TROTSKY: Yes, theoretical, and at the same time practical, because the international policies of the Stalin Government are directed against the interests of the international proletariat. And, more than that, as I tried to explain, I believe yesterday, Stalin himself changed his position during one year.

DEWEY: That is in the record.

TROTSKY: Why? Because they substituted for Socialism—for the idea of Socialism, the régime of the solidarity of all the population—substituted for that idea the idea of the satisfied bureaucracy. They named that "Socialism in one country." What we named deformation of the workers' state, they named "Socialism in one country." It was the question of the essence of Socialism itself.

DEWEY: What was your attitude on the theory of the uneven capitalistic development in different countries?

TROTSKY: It is absolutely the theory of the October Revolution. The October Revolution was the emanation of this law of uneven development, because backward—

DEWEY: Did you at any time oppose this theory of the uneven capitalistic development?

TROTSKY: No; it is only a variety of the banal and trivial distortion of my discussion with Russia—I mean, discussion with Lenin—on the United States of Europe, during the war. The misinterpretation of this discussion tries to give the idea that I denied the unequal development. I believe one must be absolutely ignored to deny such a law.

DEWEY: You mean "ignorant."

TROTSKY: Yes; ignorant. I am not a very skilled historian, but I know the development of Great Britain and India are very different, had a very different tempo. The same with Russia and France, and so on. How could I deny this law?

DEWEY: Now, briefly, because it is a rather specific point—one of the accusations of your being anti-Lenin is some controversy you were alleged to have had with him about the trade unions.

TROTSKY: Just this question cannot be answered briefly. (Laughter) I can only say that it was an episodic discussion. At that time, at the moment, it had importance, but only a month later Lenin and I forgot this question totally. Later, they selected everything where we were in disagreement in discussion. It was a false discussion from both sides. It was before the introduction of the New Economic Policy. Our feelings were very bad under military communism. We wished to have a change, and the discussion began on an absolutely secondary and false point. During the discussion, we arrived at the idea of the necessity of changing the whole economic policy. And then we agreed.

FINERTY: May I interject a question here? Is there, or are there, in your archives any letters from Lenin?

TROTSKY: Yes.

FINERTY: And are there any of them in the last period of his life?

TROTSKY: Yes. The last day—I think one of the last letters he wrote to me was before his second illness. They are very short, but very characteristic of his friendship.

FINERTY: They are in your archives?

TROTSKY: And also published.

LAFOLLETTE: Apropos your relations with Lenin, I have a pamphlet here, "Trotsky, the Traitor," and it begins: "Lenin called Trotsky Judas, and cautioned the people repeatedly to beware of him." Is that true?

TROTSKY: Yes; I believe in 1911 he wrote that, but not "Judas." It is a frame-up. There is in a Russian novel the name Judushka, a personality in a Russian novel. In a polemic, he used this personality. It was not a friendly one, but it was a sharp discussion. It has nothing to do with Judas Iscariot. (Laughter) In my autobiography is published a letter of Krupskaya after the death of Lenin, which is—

GOLDMAN: Have you the original of that in the archives?

TROTSKY: Yes.

FINERTY: Is there in existence, Mr. Trotsky, some letter of Lenin's breaking off relations with Stalin?

TROTSKY: Yes; I read it. It is the last, or maybe before the last.

LAFOLLETTE: Next to the last.

TROTSKY: The last letter of Lenin—the last letter Lenin wrote in his life was the rupture with Stalin.

FINERTY: Is that available for the record?

TROTSKY: It is available. I don't have the record itself, but the discussion of this in the Central Committee was taken down by stenographic report, and republished by me—the mention that this letter by Lenin existed. They took up the defense of Stalin against me, but they recognized that such a letter was written.

FINERTY: Do I understand that you actually saw such a letter?

TROTSKY: Pardon?

FINERTY: Did I understand that you actually saw such a letter?

TROTSKY: Yes; I was a little sick myself, in bed. The stenographer of Lenin came to me—a woman—with this letter. It was a letter written to Stalin. I telephoned Kamenev—they were both against me at that time, Stalin and Kamenev. I consulted with him. I asked: "What does this signify?" Kamenev was absolutely disorientated. I consulted Krupskaya by telephone, and asked her what this was. She explained that Stalin tried to surround Lenin to hinder him from having communications with the Party, under the pretext that he was too sick; that it was not advisable to give him information. And he treated with animus Krupskaya, the wife of Lenin, at this time. Lenin gave him some warning, about two or three times, and the last time he dictated this letter. And I gave the advice either to Stalin or Kamenev, to go to Krupskaya and make some—

LAFOLLETTE: Excuse?

TROTSKY: Yes; in order to calm Lenin's nervousness. He followed my advice, but it was too late. Lenin was unconscious.

DEWEY: Is it true that as late as May, 1917, Lenin referred

to you as a vacillating petit bourgeois?

TROTSKY: 1919?

DEWEY: 1917—as late as 1917.

TROTSKY: I can't believe it. From that time I had the best relations with Lenin. Before, I believe yes. Lenin wrote very sympathetically on my attitude in July, when some of the Bolsheviks, and very important Bolsheviks, separated themselves from Lenin. It was after the manifestation. All the letters of Lenin in this time were of the best I could wish for me. I believe it is not correct. I don't know what is the source.

DEWEY: It is referring to Lenin's "Collected Works," Volume 30, the Russian edition, page 331.

TROTSKY: It is absolutely impossible. It is possible that in the beginning, from abroad—we were separated from Lenin; I was in the United States and he was in Switzerland—that he wrote some sharp letter to Kollontai. No; it was before the February Revolution, not in May. It was connected with the fact that I collaborated in the United States with Bukharin, and Lenin was very dissatisfied with Bukharin at that time. He supposed that I supported Bukharin against him.

DEWEY: What year was that?

TROTSKY: It was before the February Revolution, in 1917, during my sojourn in New York. It was January or February, 1917.

DEWEY: Now, a good deal is made of the point that you were not a member of the Central Committee—I mean of the five appointed in October to organize the uprising.

TROTSKY: I was not a member of this committee, because it never existed. It was only decided through the chairman of the Military Committee for the preparation of the insurrection, and the Party Central Committee decided that five members, Sverdlov, Stalin and others, must enter into the Military Committee, of which I was chairman. But even after they were in there, in the Military Committee, my situation could not be changed. I was chairman before they were appointed. But they did not enter. It was a chaotic period, a period of preparation, and the Central Committee made one decision, and itself forgot about it.

DEWEY: One question along the same line, but from a little different angle: It is plain that the controlling organization in the practical work of the insurrection of October was a Party center composed of Stalin and others around the Revolutionary Military Committee.

TROTSKY: That was invented only in 1924, when, in classifying the archives, anybody found in the archives a long before forgotten decision of the Central Committee concerning these five members. It was only in 1924.

STOLBERG: You mean "somebody."

TROTSKY: Yes, somebody. When you, Mr. Chairman, when you read all the memories concerning the October Revolution of an honest participant like Ovseenko, or the book of John Reed—they do not show it, nor any of the people who were in the insurrection and wrote about it. It is impossible to find the name of the alleged center. I heard the name only for the first time in 1924. It did not exist at all.

DEWEY: Are you claiming that the earlier history was falsified?

TROTSKY: Absolutely.

DEWEY: Have you any documentary evidence of that?

TROTSKY: In my history of the Russian Revolution, a chapter is dedicated to this legend. I think it is a most important chapter, with all the documents.

FINERTY: May we have reference to that chapter, for the record?

TROTSKY: I read to the Commission two appreciations of Stalin himself. In 1918, on the 7th of November, he didn't mention this center.

DEWEY: We will check that up in the documentary records.

BEALS: Mr. Trotsky, how early did the controversy in the Soviet Union begin between those who believed that the world revolution should be fomented and those who believed rather that thc Soviet state—wished that the Soviet economy itself should be built up?

TROTSKY: In the beginning of 1924, Stalin himself opposed the idea of building Socialism in one country. Here, in a new work which I received from London, there is a facsimile of Stalin's pamphlet, published April, 1924, in the Spring, denying the possibility of Socialism in one country.

BEALS: My question was: When did this controversy appear—how early, on what date?

TROTSKY: Between this statement of Stalin and his statement in the Fall of the same year.

BEALS: Was there any discussion on this change earlier?

TROTSKY: Never.

BEALS: Wasn't there a discussion as early as 1919 or 1920?

TROTSKY: In 1920? I never heard about it, that it was discussed. They affirm now that it was discussed between me and Lenin in 1915, but I must say briefly that it is only ignorance.

BEALS: What was the prominent theory prior to 1924—that the world revolution should be promoted and extended—

TROTSKY: Not that. It is not a question of promoting or fomenting. These terms provoke the impression of an artificial thing. It was a more objective statement, that our revolution was only the beginning of a series of revolutions, and that only in this historical context could it be victorious. We have here in the same work, my history—I have another chapter with all the quotations from Lenin and from all the others. I don't know if I can introduce it into evidence. All the quotations concerning this question are given in another supplementary chapter.

BEALS: We have this book in your bibliography, which you put into the record.

TROTSKY: How?

BEALS: We have this book in your bibliography, which you put into the record.

FINERTY: Can you give the reference to this?

DEWEY: Can you give us the reference?

TROTSKY: It is two chapters only of quotations.

BEALS: Do you know Mr. Borodin?

TROTSKY: Personally, no.

BEALS: He was in China.

TROTSKY: Maybe I met him one or two times, but I didn't know he was Borodin. I knew him as a political personality.

BEALS: He came secretly to Mexico toward the end of 1919 or toward the early part of 1920.

TROTSKY: Yes?

BEALS: He founded the first Communist Party in Mexico. He at that time made the statement that he was an emissary of yours.

TROTSKY: Of mine? At that time I was in my military train. I forgot all the world geography except the geography of the front.

BEALS: The reason I ask that is, that at that time he stated there was a controversy along these lines in the Soviet Union.

TROTSKY: May I ask the source of this sensational communication? It is published—no?

BEALS: It is not published.

TROTSKY: I can only give the advice to the Commissioner to say to his informant that he is a liar.

BEALS: Thank you, Mr. Trotsky. Mr. Borodin is the liar.

TROTSKY: Yes; it is very possible.

GOLDMAN: I want one question cleared up on a certain thing. Mr. Beals might be led to misunderstand. He asked about when the struggle started between those who believed in fomenting world revolution and those who believed in building up Soviet economy. That might indicate that you did not believe in building Soviet economy. Is that correct?

TROTSKY: Building Soviet economy is a tendentious Stalinist formula. I cannot believe that a member of the Commission can employ such tendentious formulae.

BEALS: I mean when the controversy, when it was decided to build up Soviet economy and attempt to live completely through compromise with the capitalist nations—

TROTSKY: Excuse me. I didn't mean to place on you the incorrect formula, which is of Stalinist origin. But the genuine formula, corresponding to fact, is not invented by the Stalinist bureaucracy and the C.I. The question was not building up Soviet economy, or not. I was among the first to propose industrialization and a five-year plan, but it was not for replacing the world movement. It was our economic duty in our borders, and at the same time also to work as a Communist International in the world arena. The question is whether it is sufficient only to remain in our borders and to turn our back upon the world movement.

BEALS: This is merely a prelude to one question, which is: To what extent, when you were part of the Soviet Government, did you attempt to promote or inspire revolutionary activities in other countries?

TROTSKY: I answered this question. The Comintern was created for the purpose. I believe that the Comintern—it is the Communist International; it is a party, a world party, in order to guide the proletariat to victory, to revolutionary victory.

BEALS: I understand that.

TROTSKY: Yes; I am absolutely sure. I was myself a participant also in the Comintern. It was not my own creation. It was the creation of the Party. The chairman of the Comintern was Zinoviev. The genuine inspirer of the Comintern was

Lenin. I was one of the collaborators with Lenin and Zinoviev at this time, concerning the work of the Comintern.

DEWEY: We will go on tomorrow morning. It is a little after seven. We will continue again tomorrow morning at ten o'clock.

End of Eleventh Session—Seven o'clock P.M.

Twelfth session

April 17, 1937, at ten o'clock a.m.

GOLDMAN: I would like to make a statement for the record, if the Commissioners will allow me: "In the afternoon session of April 16th—that is, yesterday—Commissioner Beals asked me—"

STOLBERG: That is Trotsky's statement?

GOLDMAN: It is the statement of Trotsky I am reading. "—if I knew Borodin personally. My answer was in the negative. Actually I knew him only through his activity in China. Mr. Beals asked me if I had not sent Borodin in 1919 to Mexico with the mission of fomenting revolution. Completely taken aback by this question, which, so it seems to me, does not have the slightest basis even in the official Stalinist calumny, the verification of which is one of the tasks of the Commission, I, in my turn, asked Mr. Beals from what source his information came, and whether or not it has been published. Mr. Beals replied that it was from Borodin, without mentioning the persons to whom Borodin gave the alleged information. Then I answered that my advice was to tell the informant that he was a liar. It was after that that I understood that the informant was Mr. Borodin himself. This information naturally changes nothing in my answer. Mr. Beals's informant is a liar. The falsehood which he has utilized has a definite purpose—to compromise my situation in Mexico. I am anxious to repeat in writing with the necessary precision: 1. I have never had personal relations with Borodin; 2. I knew him only through his activities in China; 3. I have attacked him openly as the most harmful man in the Chinese revolution (see my writings on China); 4. I have never concerned myself with questions of Mexican politics, and I have never sent anybody to Mexico. I do not even know if somebody was really sent to Mexico in 1919 and if it was Borodin. At that time I was entirely absorbed in the Civil War.

"Having given great importance to the question and its obvious purpose, which is not to examine the Moscow accusations but to throw upon me through other means new suspicions in the eyes of Mexican public opinion, I immediately ask the Commission to throw light on the source of Commissioner Beals's information. If he has received this information directly from Borodin, then where and when? If he received this information through a third person, through whom and when? I expect that through an investigation into these questions, which involve Mr. Beals's personal honor, a new amalgam will be discovered, a new amalgam created with the purpose of preventing me from unmasking the judicial crimes in Moscow.

"If Mr. Beals himself is not consciously and directly involved in this new intrigue, and I will hope that he is not, he must hasten to present all the necessary explanations in order to permit the Commission to unmask the true source of the intrigue."

TROTSKY: We can immediately make copies for the press.

DEWEY: With reference to Mr. Trotsky's statement just read, I simply wish to say that the Commission in private session formally expressed itself as aware of the complete impropriety of Mr. Beals's question. After I read a letter received from Mr. Beals, I hope Mr. Trotsky will realize the difficulties which the Commission is now under in conducting the inquiry of Mr. Beals, which Mr. Trotsky has very properly requested of us. The letter is as follows:

MEXICO, D.F.
APRIL 17, 1937.

Dr. John Dewey
Chairman of the Commission to Inquire into the Charges Against Leon Trotsky.
Coyoacan, D.F.

Dear Dr. Dewey:

Kindly accept my irrevocable resignation from the Commission. This step is for the best interests of Mr. Trotsky, the Commission and myself.

The important purpose, among others, for which I became a member of the Commission, namely: to give Mr. Trotsky the opportunity which every accused person should have, to present his full case to the world, has been fulfilled to the extent possible with the present arrangements. Unfortunately, I do not consider the proceedings of the Commission a truly serious investigation of the charges. For this and other reasons, my further participation in the work of the Commission, now that the sessions have been completed, would not prove fruitful.

Sincerely yours,
CARLTON BEALS.

I wish to make, on behalf of the Commission, a brief statement: In expressing the regret of the Preliminary Commission at Mr. Beals's resignation, I wish to say that

Mr. Beals has been given full opportunity to ask questions. We are especially sorry that he is not here this morning to continue his personal cross-examination.

I wish to repeat the statement made at the opening meeting, that the Commission is to be judged by the way in which it conducts its hearings and by the public record. We regret that Mr. Beals has prejudged the case, not only before the full Commission has begun its inquiries, but even before the Preliminary Commission has completed its investigations. The statement of Mr. Beals that the sessions have been completed is an obvious error.

I wish to emphasize the fact that these hearings are preliminary, and that the investigation will be continued by the full Commission. The record will be public, and this sub-commission gladly refers to public opinion the decision whether the investigation into the charges made against Mr. Trotsky is fair, serious and complete.

Incidentally, I wish to remark that it has been understood from the beginning that each member of the Commission has the right to submit an independent or minority report to the full Commission.

GOLDMAN: On behalf of Mr. Trotsky and myself, I would like to state that, of course, we are even more interested in having as members of the Commission persons who are absolutely impartial but who do not agree with Mr. Trotsky's viewpoint—more than anxious. These are the type of people we want on the Commission. Of course, we could not possibly want people on the Commission who are friends of the accusers in Moscow and accept the accusations as true. But, on our part, we would say that Mr. Beals would be perfectly welcome in his attitude or disagreements politically with Trotsky. As far as the Commission is concerned, we have nothing to do with the composition of the Commission. Here you can examine and cross-examine Mr. Trotsky in order to attempt to break down Mr. Trotsky's testimony.

There will be the full Commission and sub-commissions in other countries in which to continue such examination. Not only do we extend this invitation to Mr. Beals, but we extend this invitation to everyone who believes in the monstrous charges of Moscow.

DEWEY: All I need say on Mr. Goldman's statement is that it has already been done and is in the record that we have asked a very considerable number of official representatives of the Communist Party, both in the United States and Mexico, to be present and participate fully in the cross-examination of Mr. Trotsky.

Everybody has understood, of course, that Mr. Goldman has made the statement he has just read, on his own account.

GOLDMAN: And Mr. Trotsky's account.

DEWEY: And Mr. Trotsky's account. It is their statement, and not ours. For the purpose of the record I wish to say that as soon as possible copies of Mr. Beals's resignation and my own brief statement will be given to the press. I wish to read into the record a letter just received:

THE SOCIALIST PARTY
Of the United States of America
549 Randolph Street
Chicago, Ill.

APRIL 13, 1937.

John Dewey, Presiding Commissioner,
Avenida Amberes 65,
Mexico City, Mexico.

Dear Dr. Dewey:

In behalf of the Socialist Party of the United States of America I wish to extend to you our earnest well wishes in the pursuit of the truth in this important inquiry now being conducted under your auspices.

The Socialist Party has endorsed the work of the

American Committee for the Defense of Leon Trotsky and is very anxious that the work of this committee will bring to light the necessary information which will permit us and all other working-class forces to come to a just conclusion.

In behalf of the party we salute your efforts and hope that they will come to successful fruition.

Fraternally,
ROY E. BURT (Signed)
Executive Secretary.
FRANK N. TRAGER.

DEWEY: I have a certain number of questions to ask Mr. Trotsky. In connection with the first section of these questions, I wish to offer for the record the pamphlet of M.J. Olgin, entitled: "Trotskyism, Counter-Revolution in Disguise." I offer this so that there may appear in the record the basis for questions which I might wish to ask.

FINERTY: Mr. Chairman, before you do that may I make a correction on the record? Yesterday, in questioning Mr. Trotsky, I stated that Sokolnikov was one of the two who had not asked clemency, as the basis of a question to Mr. Trotsky. I find that I was in error. The two who had not asked clemency were Radek and Pyatakov. Pyatakov was shot and Radek not. On that basis the deductions from my questions will have to be weakened.

DEWEY: A complete answer to my questions would take up a good deal of time. To economize time, I suggest, while you cannot literally confine your replies to "yes" and "no," that you make them as brief as possible, and then submit to the Commission documentary material which you present in support of your answers. Will that be satisfactory, Mr. Trotsky?

TROTSKY: Yes.

DEWEY: Between 1923 and 1927, is it not true that you

had full opportunity to present your ideas of policies you regarded proper, to the Party organization?

TROTSKY: No; it is not true. It is false. I will prove it by many documents.

DEWEY: You referred earlier to the fact that one of the conditions of membership in the Bolshevik Party was the acceptance of disciplinary rules and regulations. Will you state the nature of these regulations?

TROTSKY: Full freedom in discussion, and discipline in the execution of decisions. That is the rule.

DEWEY: What did you commit yourself to in agreeing to submit to the disciplinary regulations?

TROTSKY: Yes?

DEWEY: What did you commit yourself to? What did your acceptance of the disciplinary regulations involve with respect to your actions?

TROTSKY: My actions were never directed against the decisions of the Central Committee of the Party.

DEWEY: I have not made my question quite clear. I want to know more specifically the nature of these disciplinary rules in controlling your action or the action of any member of the Bolshevik Party, because of your membership in it. Did you commit yourself—this is merely an example—did you commit yourself to take any course in opposition to the decisions of the Party?

TROTSKY: I can only repeat that I criticized decisions, or a number of decisions, before the decision in the Party; that I criticized them in the Central Committee after they were accepted by the majority, but I never acted practically against the decisions, and that is what I consider Party discipline.

DEWEY: Were these rules and regulations on Party discipline definitely formulated?

TROTSKY: In the sense I indicated: Freedom of discussion before a decision; practical discipline in the execution after the decision. It is the main rule of discipline.

DEWEY: Now, I would like to ask you whether you—whether the preparation and circulation of typewritten documents, mimeographed, and so forth, was not a violation of the regulations of Party discipline?

TROTSKY: No; because the prohibition of discussion in such important questions was a violation of the Party statutes which assured to the Party members the freedom of discussion. Our action was a legitimate protest against this Bonapartist violation of the Party statutes.

DEWEY: That is, Mr. Trotsky, do you accuse the other side of violating the regulations of Party discipline?

TROTSKY: Absolutely. By a *coup d'état* in the Party.

FINERTY: In that connection, can I ask a question? Did the right of criticism extend to the right of criticism after a decision as well as before, so long as you conformed to the decision?

TROTSKY: Yes; because the Central Committee is not the highest body. There is a Party Congress. Every Party member can appeal now to the Party Congress—by such means and by writings.

FINERTY: In the meantime he must conform to the decisions of the Central Committee?

TROTSKY: Totally correct.

DEWEY: I would like to ask a similar question about the seven—I think it was—banners that were carried by members of the Left Opposition in the parade, or procession, in November, 1927—the alleged insurrection or attempt at insurrection. Was that a violation of the regulations of Party discipline?

TROTSKY: No. You must excuse me—in the deposition I mentioned seven placards, but I find out there were only five. We found the texts of them, and we present them to the Commission. Only five of them. They were absolutely not in contradiction with the rules of conduct of the Party. We had the possibility every time, as I mentioned, of participating—all the Party organizations, the workers and the members, with their own placards.

DEWEY: One more question about that, or two more. Suppose the situation had been reversed, would your group not have favored the expulsion from the Party of those persons and groups that used tactics which you used?

TROTSKY: You know the first thing I would do? It is to expel from the Party all the demoralized people such as Vyshinsky, Yagoda and others who are the enemies of the working class and who are working now only for their personal material interest. Not persons with different opinions from mine. That is a different thing. Not I myself would expel them. I would convoke a conference of workers: "You may select between honest and dishonest people in the Party." I mean, workers from the factories, without ambitions for a career. I am sure they would make a good selection.

GOLDMAN: Mr. Trotsky, if I am not mistaken, Dr. Dewey referred to the time of 1926, not the present moment.

TROTSKY: So?

DEWEY: Yes.

TROTSKY: Excuse me. I am sure it would be impossible for us to exclude people with similar slogans. It depends on the slogan. If they would be slogans: "Long Live Capitalism! Down with Socialism!" we would say: "You must go from the Party, because it is a Socialist party." But our slogans: "Long live Socialism! Long live Workers' Democracy! Long live Lenin's Teachings!" In that sense, I say no. What are the slogans of my adversaries? What were the charges at that time?

FINERTY: I think it would be informative, Dr. Dewey, if we have the five slogans—if he stated what the texts of the slogans were.

DEWEY: I understand that the texts of the slogans are to be submitted to us.

TROTSKY: They are translating them, and they can be submitted immediately.

DEWEY: Perhaps you can tell us orally.

GOLDMAN: May I be permitted to formulate a question somewhat in the nature of what Dr. Dewey asked, but a little different? Let us assume, Mr. Trotsky, that in the period of 1925–1927, the Left Opposition would have been in the majority. Would the Left Opposition have expelled the Stalin faction because of their beliefs?

TROTSKY: No.

FINERTY: Would they have expelled them if they had displayed similar placards implying that you had betrayed Socialism, that you had betrayed the Socialist state, and so forth?

TROTSKY: The explanation can be given through the statement that the bureaucracy feared the echo of these slogans, not myself. We could not have these fears, because they were directed against the bureaucracy in the interest of the masses. May I read them? They were very short: 1. "Fulfill Lenin's Testament!" 2. "Turn the Fire on the Right—Against the Nepman, the Kulak and the Bureaucrat!" 3. "For Genuine Workers' Democracy!" 4. "Against Opportunism, Against Splits—For the Unity of the Party of Lenin!" 5. "For the Central Committee of Lenin!"

DEWEY: I understood these placards were seized. Did I understand you to say that these placards were seized?

TROTSKY: Yes.

DEWEY: I have forgotten whether or not I asked if the persons carrying them were arrested?

TROTSKY: Yes; many of them were arrested.

FINERTY: Take your second slogan, your second placard: "Turn the Fire on the Right—Against the Nepman, the Kulak and the Bureaucrat!" Do you think that the bureaucrats might have interpreted that as a threat of individual terror?

TROTSKY: No; it was a quotation from Stalin's speech in the last Congress. He said: "Fire against the Left," against us. There was—

FINERTY: In other words, your second placard was paraphrasing Stalin's own speech?

TROTSKY: Yes.

GOLDMAN: You mean to say, Mr. Trotsky, that the G.P.U. was against fulfilling Lenin's testament?

TROTSKY: I believe so, because they concealed the testament in spite of the insistence of Lenin's widow on publishing it. They didn't publish it.

DEWEY: You have denied that you acted against the regulations of Party discipline. If it had been true that you and your group had acted contrary to the disciplinary rules, is there any logic to the statement that that was simply the first step which led to more serious acts of disloyalty? That is hypothetical.

TROTSKY: No, Dr. Dewey. Because even in the Bolshevik Party, with its very severe discipline, Lenin first emphasized that the essence is more important than the form; that the ideas are more important than the discipline; that if it is a question of fundamental importance, we can break the vows of discipline without betraying our ideas.

STOLBERG: Mr. Trotsky, in this connection—I am rather hazy about it, but did not Zinoviev and Kamenev, in 1917, write an article in a Menshevik paper, an opposition paper, to the effect that they were against the insurrection? That was a very important issue at that time, wasn't it?

TROTSKY: Yes.

STOLBERG: Now, Lenin then called them down.

TROTSKY: Yes, as traitors.

STOLBERG: It was felt that it was a breach of discipline, yet they honestly did not believe that the insurrection was advisable. Isn't that somewhat of an analogy?

TROTSKY: It was an important question in the history of the Party. All depended on that. In that very hot moment, Lenin proposed to expel them. We, the majority, refused Lenin that expulsion. And he was, two days after the insurrection, very well satisfied with our decision.

DEWEY: I wish to ask you a few more questions on the different phases of the Party struggle. On page 193 of the Opposition Platform, contained on page 193 of "The Real Situation in Russia," English translation, I find the following: "A split in our party, a formation of two parties, would mean enormous danger to the revolution. We, the Opposition, unqualifiedly condemn every attempt whatsoever to create a second party." On page 194: "We will struggle with all our force against the formation of two parties . . ."

I am not going to question you on that, but I want to ask you whether you changed your mind upon that point at some subsequent time.

TROTSKY: Two parties in embryo were created by our expulsion, by the split committed by the bureaucracy. That is the first answer. The second answer: In spite of that, we tried to consider ourselves as a fraction of the Party, not as a second Party. Only in 1933 we changed our mind; that it is impossible to reform the old Party, that it is necessary to create a new one.

DEWEY: On page 267, of "The Revolution Betrayed," English translation, I find the following, which comes in connection with the criticism of some statements of Stalin: "In reality, classes are heterogeneous; they are torn by inner antagonisms, and arrive at the solution of common problems not otherwise than through an inner struggle of tendencies, groups and parties."

TROTSKY: What page?

DEWEY: On page 267.

TROTSKY: Yes.

DEWEY: Now, when you wrote that, then you had become convinced of the necessity of different parties?

TROTSKY: The development of the Russian proletariat consisted in the struggle among three parties, the Menshevik, the Social Revolutionary and the Bolshevik. The Bolsheviks won the overwhelming majority during the Civil War, and in spite of that we permitted the existence of other parties. Only when the Civil War began, when the most decisive elements of the Mensheviks and Social Revolutionaries took part in the Civil War on the other side of the barricades, we prohibited them. It was a military measure, not as a permanent step.

FINERTY: May I ask, in that connection, whether anything in the Constitution in the Soviet State, the Soviet Union—anything in the Constitution of the Soviet Union itself forbids more than one party?

TROTSKY: No. It is so in the new Constitution.

FINERTY: That is, before the Constitution of the Soviet Union as organized originally?

TROTSKY: Originally, yes.

FINERTY: It was possible to have more than one?

TROTSKY: We had four parties, or five. One was the Anarchists.

FINERTY: The new Constitution prohibits more than one Party?

TROTSKY: Yes.

FINERTY: Directly?

TROTSKY: Yes, directly.

STOLBERG: You mean, the other parties had a right to participate in the soviets?

TROTSKY: Yes.

STOLBERG: Did they—but they had no right of participation in the Government, in the administration?

TROTSKY: We had the Lefts, who were. Naturally, the Government must be, more or less, a homogeneous body. But we had, from the victory until July, 1918, a coalition with five or six Social Revolutionaries.

STOLBERG: You considered it was a mistake in July?

TROTSKY: There was a military insurrection, a genuine military insurrection with guns, seizing of administration houses, and bombardment of the Kremlin by cannon.

It was in July, against the Brest-Litovsk peace. They killed the German Ambassador Mirbach.

STOLBERG: You mean, the Social Revolutionaries did?

TROTSKY: Yes; all the Left members of the Government and the organizer were arrested.

STOLBERG: The July insurrection activities of the Left Social Revolutionaries were a few months after you had thrown them out of the Government. They were thrown out in March?

TROTSKY: It was seven or eight months after the creation of the Soviet Government.

STOLBERG: I mean, your Coalition Government began in November. You had two Social Revolutionary members, hadn't you, in the Council of People's Commissars?

TROTSKY: Not two. I believe six or seven, even.

STOLBERG: These members either resigned, or were thrown out in March. They didn't stay in your coalition until July?

TROTSKY: Not in March; later, I believe. I am not totally sure, now.

STOLBERG: What I want to get at is—whether the insurrection on their part—they claimed that since you would not permit them to function within the Government after they were suppressed, they had to resort to insurrectionary methods. Was there—

TROTSKY: They had their paper until the insurrection. They had meetings after their resignation from the Government.

STOLBERG: You didn't force their resignation?

TROTSKY: No.

STOLBERG: They resigned themselves?

TROTSKY: Yes, absolutely.

DEWEY: On the same page, 267, I find the following statement: "An example of only one party corresponding to one class is not to be found in the whole course of political history . . ." Isn't that statement in complete contradiction with the idea of a single-party dictatorship?

TROTSKY: Yes; as a normal status, it is a complete contradiction. We never said, Mr. Chairman, that the single party as an absolute expression of the class is a normal status. We answered to the critics: "We are in a civil war. It is not a measure of democracy, but a measure of civil war." It was our honest answer.

DEWEY: When the Party, not merely you but the Party, used the expression, "dictatorship of the proletariat," what was included in the term "proletariat"? Is it the proletariat in the very strict sense of the word?

TROTSKY: No. Our conception is, that by the abolition of private property the proletariat, as the vanguard of the toiling masses, becomes naturally the leading class of all the nation, with the exclusion of the conscious exploiters, speculators, and so on. All the petit bourgeoisie can only gain from the ruling work of the proletariat. In this sense—for the first time the proletariat won the confidence of the peasants and petit bourgeoisie and could establish its proletarian dictatorship.

DEWEY: You were charged with opposing Lenin by wishing to exclude the petit bourgeoisie, the peasantry and the intelligentsia from membership in the dictatorship, from the Party, and from the dictatorship of the proletariat. Is that a correct statement?

TROTSKY: It is a pure invention, amongst more others.

LAFOLLETTE: Many others.

TROTSKY: Many others. I proved that with quotations from writings, I hope, with absolute correctness.

DEWEY: And did you not assert that after the first stages of the revolution had been accomplished in collaboration with the petit bourgeoisie, the peasants and the intelligentsia, the proletariat would come into conflict with the great masses of peasants and petit bourgeoisie?

TROTSKY: Yes; it was my own opinion. It is in the Marxian tradition, especially concerning Russia. Lenin repeated that a hundred times: "We can accomplish with the peasants, all the peasants, the democratic revolution, but when we attempt to set up Socialism, we will have the majority, or a great part, of the peasants against us." I believe that Stalin, practically, gave that prophecy the most terrible expression during the collectivization. Under him the collectivization was accomplished with the extermination of millions of peasants.

DEWEY: You were charged with desiring to accelerate, to hasten, the collectivization of the agrarian elements by means of force.

TROTSKY: By means of what?

DEWEY: Force.

TROTSKY: It is contrary to the truth, Dr. Dewey. The contrary is true. I attacked Stalin for his policies of violence in collectivizing the peasants.

DEWEY: Many of the accused in the Moscow trials asserted in their confessions that they had no political program whatsoever. I mean, in these latter years. That they were simply desirous of obtaining power. I won't ask you what you thought of that. It is charged against you and the Left Opposition, the so-called Trotskyites, that during the Revolution, you naturally developed the attitude and habits of revolution and that therefore, psychologically and morally, you could not help but continue revolting, if I may say so, against whatever government was in power. Now, I won't ask about that. But that leads on to the accusation that since the early years your work, and that of your faction, has been purely destructive, that you have not engaged in constructive work, or shown a desire in any way to engage in constructive work.

TROTSKY: The Party considered that the creation of the Red Army was a constructive work. In 1920, when our railroads were absolutely destroyed, Lenin asked me to accept a second portfolio, of the Peoples' Commissar of Railroads. After his insistence, I accepted. I can present to the Commission the most favorable expressions from Lenin during the Party Congress on my activity as chief of transport. That is one evidence. Lenin asked me to create a Commission, to be president of the Commission. I worked in that function for some time, not without success. When our furnishing of coal became intolerable, Lenin asked me to go to the Don Basin as president of the Commission. I worked for some time in the Don Basin. Lenin declared: "After the activity of Comrade Trotsky, the situation in the Don Basin became better." Dnieprostroy—if you care, I can quote more.

LAFOLLETTE: Go ahead; it is important.

TROTSKY: The first five-year plan was introduced by me in the railroad economy. Lenin declared that it was the most brilliant example of leadership. It was his own expression. Dzerzhinsky, who was my successor as chief of the railroads, declared that the five-year plan of Trotsky in the railroads—it was in 1920–1921—was the lesson for us. And so on.

FINERTY: Mr. Trotsky, was there an official plan for the railroads, and is there a record of it?

TROTSKY: The plan was No. 1042. It became very famous. There were placards, pictures, and so on, of Plan No. 1042.

FINERTY: Have you a copy of that plan available in your files?

TROTSKY: It was the plan for the reestablishment of locomotives and wagons and roads, for five years, with proposals for every month and every line. It was elaborated in conference with engineers.

FINERTY: Is there an official report on the plan and its execution?

TROTSKY: Yes; in the Soviet Congress and the Party Congress there are quotations from Lenin and Dzerzhinsky. I will present all these things.

FINERTY: Will you file with the Commission—these reports?

TROTSKY: I will present my new book. It is an old book. But it appears now in New York. It is polemical, and is entitled "The Stalin School of Falsification." These documents are in this book and will appear in the next days, the next weeks, I hope. All the sources are indicated.

DEWEY: This is contained in the bibliography you presented?

TROTSKY: Yes.

DEWEY: So it will be in the record.

TROTSKY: I don't know.

DEWEY: It is not necessary to enter that again on the record.

TROTSKY: This book has been published in Russian for a long time. Now it appears in English.

DEWEY: In the Thirteenth Party Conference of 1924—

TROTSKY: Pardon?

DEWEY: In the Thirteenth Party Congress—

TROTSKY: In 1926, the Thirteenth.

DEWEY: Well, it is the Thirteenth, anyway.

TROTSKY: The Thirteenth was in 1925.

DEWEY: You know the date better than I do. There was a resolution passed requiring new members from workers of the bench. I suppose that means people actually laboring?

TROTSKY: Yes.

DEWEY: In the pamphlet published later, the English translation of which is "The New Course," did you not directly or by implication criticize this resolution?

TROTSKY: Not the resolution itself, but its tendency and execution. There was, I believe, at one time—there was a tendency to eliminate the revolutionary workers from the Party and to attract to the Party the old disciplined workers, the old-time workers who were very often religious and docile to the old bosses. They became now the best supports of the bureaucracy—a totally social alteration in the Party.

GOLDMAN: A social change.

DEWEY: We will now take a short recess.

DEWEY: I will ask Commissioner Stolberg to ask any questions he wishes.

STOLBERG: Mr. Trotsky, why were you silent about the Menshevik trials?

TROTSKY: I must recognize that I took the trials seriously. It was a great error. I was in Prinkipo—it was in 1931—absolutely isolated from any political milieu. I had no illusions about the justice of the Soviet Union at that time, but on the other hand I knew that the Right Wing Mensheviks, such as Maisky, the present ambassador in London, such as Vyshinsky, the prosecutor, such as Troyanovsky, the ambassador in the United States—they genuinely took part in the struggle in the Civil War against us. I admitted that it was possible to know about a plot of such a kind as was discovered. I didn't study the trial at that time. I was very busy with my history of the October Revolution, and I admitted that the trial was more or less correct. It was a great error on my part.

STOLBERG: Mr. Trotsky, didn't you once disavow Max Eastman's statement that there was such a thing as Lenin's testament.

TROTSKY: Yes.

STOLBERG: Why did you?

TROTSKY: The question was at that time not to disavow it, but his action in publishing it.

STOLBERG: Did you deny there was such a thing as a testament?

TROTSKY: Yes; officially it is not a testament. It is a letter to the Party. It is not what in a juridical—everybody who is acquainted with it calls it a testament; but in a juridical sense, a testament is another thing. Hitler can make a testament for his party, to give over the honor to another. Lenin did not have the feeling that he was the permanent chief of the Party and that he could indicate his successor. In that sense, it was only advice. But the letter—we all became acquainted with it as a testament.

STOLBERG: Did you deny the possibility of the paper?

TROTSKY: I did not deny there was a document, a letter from Lenin, but as a document which could be officially named a testament—in that sense I made a denial. Eastman published this document without consulting me and the others, and by these means he sharpened terribly the inner struggle in the Soviet Union, in the Politburo, which was the beginning of the split. We tried on our side to avoid a split. The majority of the Politburo asked me, demanded of me, to take a position toward this. It was a very diplomatic document I signed at that time, in that sense, that it was not a testament, and that I had never had any connection with Eastman and so on, at that time. Eastman, I must say, is my friend, but he is not a member of our organization, he is not a disciplined militant of the Party. He is more or less of a free lance. It is his right, but it is my right as a disciplined member of the organization to disavow him when it is necessary.

STOLBERG: I don't think, Mr. Trotsky, that the record will be clear as to whether or not you ever denied the existence of such a document, whether you called it a testament or letter.

TROTSKY: I admit that my denial had a diplomatic nature, imposed upon me by the inner situation of the Party. If you ask me, Mr. Commissioner, if it was the most clear truth I have declared in my life, I would answer "No." It was not the genuine truth. It was an equivocal document. That I must recognize. It was imposed on me. I am a political man. It was imposed upon me by the situation. It was not a lie, but it was not the full truth.

STOLBERG: In other words, you did that from the point of view of Party discipline?

TROTSKY: Yes.

STOLBERG: Now, looking back, do you think—I just want your opinion—do you think that you delayed too long, from your point of view, the organization of the Left Opposition, and that that was one of the errors made? That as a diplomat you were not very good?

TROTSKY: I am ready to discuss this question, but I am afraid it will be very difficult to discuss it here. How to stop too sharp a division—it signified provoking a definite split. The bureaucracy at that time was hesitating. Everybody was afraid of the possibility, if there was a split in the Party, of an immediate civil war at that time. Our programs were not sufficiently clear to the masses. I remained very cautious, and when I consider the whole situation I believe it was correct, because I could not have a victory even by the most courageous, by the most risky policy. I could not have a serious victory because of the situation in the world arena, the defeats after defeats of the proletariat in the various countries.

STOLBERG: The next question I did not phrase in my own mind very clearly. This is the gist of it: In your indictments of the German leaders of the Second International and of the Second International itself, there is a tone of almost personal blame. Now, the Second International in the European West was, of course, the expression of social conditions. I mean, it was not only personal deficiency on the part of the leaders, but it expressed in a certain way the whole tendency within the labor movement itself, as well as the whole economic structure of Germany; we might say, the stabilization of capitalism. In this sense, do you think that the activities of the Third International are to be blamed, with the whole situation as it is both abroad and in Russia? I don't know whether my question is clear.

TROTSKY: Yes, it seems to me that I understand it. It seems to me that this appreciation is fatalistic. Naturally, everything is caused by objective factors. Nothing falls from the heavens. It is caused by material factors. And every historical interest has two answers.

STOLBERG: Two sides?

TROTSKY: I will say two answers. One side tries to pull to one side, and the other pulls to the other side. When you say that the leaders of the Social Democracy with their politics represented historical necessity, I answer: I, with my criticism, am also a part of historical necessity.

FINERTY: May I ask a question, Dr. Dewey? Mr. Trotsky, you have just stated, in connection with the article on Lenin's testament, that in your statement on that testament you equivocated for political reasons, that you were, after all, in political life. The question will inevitably arise. Therefore, I am asking how far the present situation might require you to equivocate with the truth?

TROTSKY: I can say that never in my life did I take the interest—take the contrary of the truth. If you will, in plain words, a lie. I believe, in our society, which is very contradictory, that the conventional rules of conduct in family, society or corporation—everybody from time to time is obliged not to say the truth. I committed it sometimes. I believe the question can be decided only by comparison of the lies I was obliged to give, and the truth. I believe that in the balance my truths are more heavy than the lies. It seems to me so, in the more important questions, the decisive questions, in the questions upon which depend the actions of many people, of friends, of their fate—it seems to me that I never committed such crimes.

FINERTY: You will concede, Mr. Trotsky, that the Commission will have the right to judge, among other things—

TROTSKY: Absolutely.

FINERTY: —their judgment, among other things, on the possibility that political necessity might affect your statements.

TROTSKY: It is, gentlemen, the justification of the Commission. The Commission does not consider me an angel. The Commission must verify the testimony from my side. I am only too glad that this is possible, that you will verify it.

DEWEY: I want to ask you a few questions regarding the question of the international revolution. Taking now, for the purpose of questions, the general revolutionary position for granted, has not the idea of the world revolution, the international revolution, been proved false by the course of events?

TROTSKY: I don't believe, Mr. Chairman, that it is proved false. On the contrary, the situation in Spain, the situation in France, the international relations between the nations, the danger of war—it is the danger of the destruction of our culture, all of civilization—it seems to me to prove that the socialist revolution is inevitable, and salutary for mankind.

DEWEY: Well, somewhat in support of my first question, I want to ask whether the proletariat of different countries is sufficiently international-minded to support your thesis? Even events prove that upon the whole they are national, rather than international-minded.

TROTSKY: I am not of the opinion that the proletariat can be raised under the capitalist system, to a very high international Socialist level. That is why I condemn terrorism, that it does not give the possibility of educating the proletariat in such a sense. By its destruction, its decline, by its rottenness, at this time, capitalism pushes the workers to revolution. Even the last war—in that situation, I find the importance for the existence of a revolutionary party that can appreciate the situation and give leadership to those masses pushed by the destruction of capitalism.

DEWEY: Well, taking the position of your answer for granted, for the purpose of questioning, is there any reason to suppose that a series of proletarian revolutions are going to take place simultaneously in close connection with each other?

TROTSKY: No; it is not assured before. It depends upon the historical situation. In Europe the nations are more connected with each other. Australia is far away; America is a world by itself. I can predict the following—

LAFOLLETTE: Sequence?

TROTSKY: Sequence in insurrection. I believe that in Europe the revolution in France would immediately, if it moves on in any way, exercise or provoke a revolution in Hitler Germany. If it is the other way, the revolution in Germany will provoke one in France.

DEWEY: Naturally, you can predict, but unless you have very good reasons for anticipating simultaneous revolutions, or in entirely close connection, is not the whole theory of the world revolution without any basis?

TROTSKY: I can suppose that if in one or two important nations the revolutions are victorious, then the resistance of the ruling classes in the other nations will almost totally disappear, and we can win all the best elements of the intelligentsia and the middle classes—even the best elements of the capitalist class will see that Socialism is not destruction and that the revolution must be accomplished. For the revolution will become less and less violent, less and less bloody, after the first successes.

DEWEY: Do you think the failure of the German revolution was entirely or even chiefly the fault of the Social Democracy?

TROTSKY: Yes; it is my conviction.

DEWEY: Wasn't it in a very considerable part due to the belief of the German people that the revolution was being stimulated by foreign elements, by Russian elements?

TROTSKY: No; it was only the accusation of the reactionary elements, the bourgeois elements. We did not stimulate the German revolution. The German revolution was stimulated by the October Revolution as a historical event. But at that time we had no influence on the Social Democracy.

DEWEY: But does not the very existence of the Comintern, at least, create the impression that these revolutions are being stimulated and fomented from the outside?

TROTSKY: When you read the history of revolutions, in every revolution the world ruling class accused the revolution of being in essence from abroad.

DEWEY: I don't mean that; I mean even among the masses of the people.

TROTSKY: Not of the revolutionary masses, because they were very enthusiastic for the revolution and wished for it. But the Social Democracy stifled them by violence.

DEWEY: Do you think that there is a very good reason for believing that any revolution in any country which would create the feeling that it was being promoted by non-nationals, outside countries, whether the Third International or the Fourth, would create a very great resentment in the population of that country?

TROTSKY: Even trade unions have their international organizations. The American trade unions did not participate, but now they are split, and I believe that we can foresee that a part of them will adhere to international organizations of trade unions. For the working class of all countries, an international evaluation is totally natural. The same on a political basis. It is only a question whether the international organization will try to handle the national sections in a bureaucratic way, or only to help them by advice, by experience, good experience, and so on.

DEWEY: Mr. Trotsky, there is no analogy with an international trade-union organization, because they are not committed to proletarian revolution.

TROTSKY: But they are committed to strikes, for example. The bourgeoisie accuses everybody, even the reactionary workers, that strikes are provoked from abroad. Strikes—what is it to strike? A strike is an embryo social revolution.

FINERTY: We have had sympathetic strikes in the United States and France.

DEWEY: On page 211 of "The Revolution Betrayed" you say: "An international general staff could arise only on the basis of the national staff of *several* proletarian states; so long as that is impossible, an international staff would inevitably turn into a caricature." I am not questioning you on that. I want to know if the same principles do not apply with even greater force to the economic side of the union of the proletariat in different nations. Until you have got several proletarian states, is there any basis for assuming, even assuming, the probability of a union on the economic side, any more than there is on the military side?

TROTSKY: Yes, if I understood you well—that strikes could be provoked in any country by the leaders of another country. The strike is a natural thing in the life of the workers in any country. Trade unions arise from the strike movement. An international evaluation is possible only on the basis of international trade unions. The same with the possibility—the same for the general staff. To have an international staff, you must have international states. I believe the analogy is totally correct.

DEWEY: Perhaps I could put my meaning more clearly this way: Is there any economic basis in the different countries for a world revolution?

TROTSKY: I believe that a good economic basis is necessary for a good world revolution, and I hope that it will be created—the world economy. For the revolution it is sufficient, as the Russian example shows, to have national reasons for the revolution. We accomplished our revolution without asking all the other nations if they agreed with us or not. And then our revolution gave a certain example for the German workers, the Austrian-Hungarian workers, and they also had revolutions, but not victorious. A new situation will provoke new revolutions in other countries.

DEWEY: You do think, that for the present there is no good economic basis—for the present?

TROTSKY: For the revolution?

DEWEY: For the world revolution.

TROTSKY: I believe that the economic reasons have existed for a long time. I believe they have existed since 1913, so far as I can give dates. In 1914—because the war—the World War was an expression of the impossibility for capitalism to develop itself without bloody degeneration, violence and catastrophe. If the proletariat could have accomplished the revolution in 1913, we would have avoided the last war and the next war. It is only the weakness of the parties, the weakness of the vanguard of the proletariat—it is that which procured to humanity the last war, made possible the carrying through of the last war.

FINERTY: I just want to ask this, Mr. Trotsky: Assuming that by some means or other you could have simultaneous Socialist revolutions, successful Socialist revolutions in all the present capitalist states—has anyone worked out a world economy—that is, any harmonious commercial and economic relations between these Socialist states?

TROTSKY: I am sure. The Soviet Union gives us an example that the economy disturbed by competition is now organized in a planned economy. It gives great successes in spite of the bureaucracy. If we imagine the same possibility in the world arena—and why not?—then the scientists, engineers and the leaders of the trade unions will in a conference, in a world conference, establish what we have, what we need, the productive powers, the natural resources, and the creative forces of humanity, of mankind. Then they will begin cautiously, not by an economic catastrophe, but more and more planned change in the efforts between the different nations; by a plan, not by war which must introduce merchandise in a foreign country, but on a scientific basis.

It is absolutely possible, absolutely possible.

STOLBERG: I want to ask this question: Am I right in assuming that you believe that the Communist International should grant almost complete autonomy to the Communist Parties?

TROTSKY: The Communist International?

STOLBERG: Should grant complete autonomy to the national sections? Well, is it or is it not true that the Italian Socialist Party, when it was considering affiliation to the Third International, received from Lenin certain demands which were quite centralized, rather than permitting autonomy?

TROTSKY: Here I must again insist—

STOLBERG: I personally think the Comintern made a mistake.

TROTSKY: It is not my opinion. I must again insist upon the necessity of giving the concrete content of centralization and autonomy. If we say absolute autonomy, it is not necessary to create an international. If every section lives its own life, without consulting the others, without submitting to democratically established decisions, it is not necessary to create an international. On the other side, if the international creates a central body which commands the national sections, it is not necessary to have intelligent people. It is sufficient to have robots in the national sections. Between these two extremes is the real policy, between the two extremes. We can discuss with you, Mr. Commissioner, if in this or the other question there was too much centralization or too much autonomy, if I can speak so. It is a concrete question, a concrete analysis.

STOLBERG: Do you think that the fact that world economy is unevenly developed means that revolutions which occur will have a Thermidorian tendency because of the unevenness of development? That actually happened in Russia, in your opinion?

TROTSKY: Until today, mankind has not succeeded in rationalizing its history. That is a fact. We human beings have not succeeded in rationalizing our bodies and minds. True, psychoanalysis tries to teach us to harmonize our body and mentality, but until today without great success. But the question is not if we can reach the absolute perfection of society. The question is, for me, whether we can make great steps forward. Not to rationalize the character of our history, because after every great step forward mankind makes a small detour, even a great step backward. I regret it very much, but I am not responsible for it. (Laughter) After the revolution, after the world revolution, it is possible that mankind will become tired. For some, a part of them, a new religion can arise, and so on. But I am sure that in general it would be a very great step forward, as the French Revolution. It finished with the Bourbons, but everyone analyzes this victory by the teaching of the lessons of the French Revolution.

DEWEY: I have a very few questions along the line of the question I asked you the other day, quoting your passage about iron necessity developing the bureaucracy in Russia, considering the backwardness of the country and the lack of revolution, successful revolutions, in other countries. I want to ask you what reason there is for thinking that the dictatorship of the proletariat in any country will not degenerate into the dictatorship of the secretariat.

TROTSKY: It is a very good formula. I must answer that even the dictatorship of the secretariat now in Russia is a very important progress in comparison with the dictatorship of the Tsar. That is the first thing. It signifies that on the eve of the October Revolution, if anybody could have predicted to me the consequences, I would still have accepted it. Because Russia had only the choice between the Kornilov régime and the dictatorship of the proletariat. Secondly, just because the dictatorship of the secretariat is caused by the backwardness of the country and its isolation, the answer is that the more civilized countries, and not isolated, will have a more sound and more democratic dictatorship and for a shorter period.

LAFOLLETTE: May I interrupt? You have planned economy, and how can you avoid having a lot of bureaucrats; how can you avoid having a dictatorship of the secretariat?

TROTSKY: I must repeat the answer suggested to me by Commissioner Otto Ruehle: What is the distinction between administration and bureaucracy? The difference is fundamental. The administration has a certain function. In America you name administration also government, if I am correct. But we don't apply this name for government, as administration. I have in my mind the administration of a workers' cooperative, the administration of a good, sound trade union, or the best sometimes that we can find; but they are not bureaucrats, if it has a sound relation between the members and the leaders.

FINERTY: Mr. Trotsky, just taking your own example, is there such a good sound trade union that, in any case, the so-called administration has not degenerated into an autocracy?

TROTSKY: Yes.

FINERTY: Have you any of these in Russia?

TROTSKY: For a certain time; for some years.

FINERTY: Do you know of any in America?

TROTSKY: I proclaim that I don't intervene in American politics, if the Commission permits.

DEWEY: It is a very simple matter. My opinion is that we don't confine the word "administration" simply to the government. There is government administration, and there is administration of this and that and the other thing. It is a very minor point. It is merely regarding the use of the word "administration."

STOLBERG: In your book, "The Revolution Betrayed," you insist that a new class is developing in Russia. You called it a caste. You do not speak of the class struggle—you speak of social antagonisms, and so on. Is that because you accept the Marxian concept of the division into classes only in the sense in which they differ functionally, in reference to the means of production? Or do you believe that under Socialism there can be no valid practical basis for classes in the sense that no group can exploit another group? Because you say a caste might become a class if capitalist measures are really introduced. My question is, Can a caste become a class simply because through every means of political and cultural administration it exploits a great many people?

TROTSKY: I answered a simple question in this manner, that the social organism of the Soviet Union is unique. We don't have other examples. That is why it is very difficult to apply our notions, our sociological notions based upon the past, to the new formations. But I tried to do it with the necessary correctness. My idea is, that the ruling caste in the Soviet Union is an intermediary body—between the small bureaucracy and the new ruling caste. It depends upon the events on a national as well as an international scale, whether this intermediary body will desire also to smash away the present basis and will be transformed into a new ruling class. The tendencies exist.

STOLBERG: Yes; but your conceptions of a ruling class—

TROTSKY: It is the forms of property. When they introduce an inheritance of their privileges, it will be the new ruling class.

STOLBERG: Do you believe Socialism is inevitable?

TROTSKY: In so far as human progress in general is inevitable. By a cosmic catastrophe our basis for Socialism can be destroyed. In that general sense of world determinism, it is not inevitable. But in the sense of human progress, it is inevitable.

STOLBERG: I would like to ask one more theoretical question—or do you have other questions to ask, Doctor?

DEWEY: Go ahead.

STOLBERG: The class struggle, in the Marxian sense, is generated by the dialectic. The thesis today is capitalism; then it creates the working class—that is, the antithesis—and finally the Socialist revolution which is the synthesis. That is the Hegelian conception. Now, how will this dialectic work in the classless society in which there will be only the thesis and no antithesis?

TROTSKY: I hope, and my every hope is, that this perspective, that the course of thesis and antithesis will arise in our new Socialist society, but not on a material ground—on the appetites, the human appetites—but on the ground of our ideological interests, of the arts, the sciences, philosophy and so on. It will be an interestless—

FINERTY: You mean "disinterested"?

TROTSKY: —permanent fight of human beings on this new, very high level.

DEWEY: I want to ask another question along the same line. On page 59 of "The Revolution Betrayed" you say: "The power of the democratic Soviets proved cramping, even unendurable when the task of the day was to accommodate those privileged groups whose existence was necessary for defense, for industry, for technique and science." Now, can you confine that to a backward country, or does not that same situation arise, but even more so, in a very advanced industrial country?

TROTSKY: It depends upon the material level. I believe that the more or less educated man or woman has no desire to have two or three cutlets in a day if assured of a daily cutlet. Then I have the possibility to read, to learn to write, to speak, to discuss. In that sense, in a country, in a developed country, technicians and intellectuals would not ask for a better nourishment than the workers. It is not necessary. I hope the workers will have the best nourishment that is possible. It is possible economically, absolutely. Statistically it is so. In that sense, only in a backward country like Russia, in the first period, we were obliged to give certain privileges to the more skillful workers and intellectuals.

DEWEY: Taking it in terms of contradictions of the dialectic, aren't there many more contradictions and conflicts in an advanced country than in a backward one? Are they not in not only more, rather much more, inner conflict with each other? Isn't it pure theory that there is only one thesis and one antithesis?

TROTSKY: The contradictions in a backward country such as Russia are most terrible. Everybody is hungry, and shows that the other has more.

INTERPRETER: Sees.

TROTSKY: Yes, sees—I must follow my ideas with my English together. It is most degrading and humiliating. It is the basis of the gendarme and the bureaucrat. He distributes and never forgets himself. The best parts are for him. It is the basis of privilege. The privileged bureaucracy can become a new ruling class. That is why the reaction is possible in Russia.

DEWEY: The emphasis of my question was on the other side of the matter. In a more advanced country, where even the bourgeois democracy exists, are not the conditions such as to increase the number of conflicting tendencies instead of crystallizing them into two opposing forces? I ask that because that is the way I personally see the situation. But I would like your answer.

TROTSKY: We have now, because of the retreat of the Socialist revolution, much disappointment. But the more progressive elements among the workers and intellectuals of the different countries must not lose hope in Socialism. The situation in the capitalist countries becomes impossible and intolerable. We can say there is a certain psychosis among the most advanced elements, especially in Europe. A victory in Spain, for example, could give a new turn to the mentality of the progressive elements in France. I believe it is possible.

It is an unstable equilibrium, the mentality of the whole society, caused by the disorientation of the Socialist revolution. There is necessary a certain push—success. A success is the answer in Spain, to give a new orientation to the best elements of the toiling masses and intellectuals.

DEWEY: One more question on quite a different point. Do you think it is possible or probable that in your criticisms of the failure of the present régime to develop industry progressively, you fail to take into account the very great divergence of finance and technique into the channels for the defense of the country?

TROTSKY: Yes?

DEWEY: Is my question clear?

FINERTY: Restating what you said earlier this morning, in reply to Dr. Dewey, would you think that the two-party system in Russia, or the Soviet Union, would have a tendency to restrain the bureaucracy?

TROTSKY: The two-party system?

FINERTY: Yes; make democratic control more possible?

TROTSKY: I believe it is a bit of an abstract question in the sense that we cannot introduce two parties under the dictatorship of the Stalin oligarchy. It is necessary to prepare the arena for two parties—I don't know, maybe three or four. It is necessary to smash away the dictatorship of Stalin. It can only be done by an upheaval of the people. If this upheaval—if this new political upheaval is successful, the masses, with these experiences, will never permit the dictatorship of one party, of one bureaucracy.

FINERTY: Let me put it this way: If in 1927, either under the theory of the Communist Party itself, it had been possible to tolerate the Opposition, or there had been a provision for two parties, instead of one, would it have prevented the development of the present bureaucratic government?

TROTSKY: Now, when you consider the situation from a historical point of view, we can say that we had two parties in the cadres of the official Party. There were two parties, one to which I belonged, and the other which was guided by Stalin. We tried to continue this situation, to control them by our criticisms, and we demanded that they give us the possibility to criticize them. But they did not permit it. They abolished us. It is the situation. Our intention was to have some substitute for the two parties, and even the substitute was stifled.

DEWEY: I take it as well known that there has been a very great diversion of national finances and both quantity and quality of technical service into the military, in the need for the defense of the nation.

TROTSKY: Yes.

DEWEY: Now, in your criticism of the present régime, have you taken that fact into account?

TROTSKY: Every time, Mr. Chairman. I underline and recognize the necessity of this expense, but I underline that this is a factor which shows to us the international dependence of the Soviet Union. It is one side of the theory of Socialism in one country. It is a positive proof for a negative fact, also in this case (laughter)—the proof that it is impossible to create Socialism in one country, because the isolation of this country creates a tremendous expense.

FINERTY: I also assume it would be part of your answer that if there had been a proper support of the Chinese and German revolutions, they would not need the enormous army they now have?

TROTSKY: No; not now. I accuse Stalin that by his false policy in China he provoked the greatest military danger and the necessity to create a great army in the fight on the East.

DEWEY: I think this closes the examination of Mr. Trotsky, by both his lawyer and our lawyer.

FINERTY: May I make a reservation in that respect? I think, Mr. Trotsky—I think that it should be understood by Mr. Goldman and Mr. Trotsky, that either this sub-commission or any future Commission has the right to examine Mr. Trotsky further if need develops, in the opinion of the Commission.

TROTSKY: I have the same hope, the same wish. I consider this a preliminary investigation.

FINERTY: This is to be treated as a preliminary investigation.

DEWEY: I am very glad that Mr. Finerty brought out that point, because what we all referred to as the examination of this particular Commission at this particular time—it is quite likely that, either by this Commission or some other, it may be resumed later.

GOLDMAN: Before closing the testimony, I would like to refer the Commission to a book, I don't want to introduce it into evidence, but I simply want to refer the Commission to it. It is "The Defense of Terrorism," by Leon Trotsky, and published in London.

TROTSKY: It is not a different book from that which was written in 1919.

GOLDMAN: The date of publication does not appear. I think it is last year.

TROTSKY: It is 1935 or 1936. See the preface.

DEWEY: When was that originally written?

TROTSKY: In 1919, under the title of "Communism and Terrorism."

DEWEY: It is already in the record through the bibliography, is it not, Mr. Goldman?

GOLDMAN: I don't know.

DEWEY: If it is not, then it should be in the record.

GOLDMAN: Then I want to introduce a document which is entitled, "A Series of Amalgams," which is nothing but a series of excerpts from the writings of different Oppositionists, or different people showing the beginning of the system of amalgams up to the final conclusion—I should not say conclusion—up to the last amalgam in the January trial. I will introduce that into evidence, and also furnish the Commissioners with some copies. Mark this document Exhibit No. 33.

(The document, "A Series of Amalgams," was introduced into evidence as Exhibit No. 33.)

DEWEY: While the Commission has concluded the inquiry on this particular occasion, I wish to state that on resuming at the afternoon session there will be an opportunity for the representatives of the Mexican labor organizations to cross-examine Mr. Trotsky. I will make that statement at the opening of the afternoon meeting. But I wish to give time for preparation.

GOLDMAN: Lest there be any impression that the proceedings are concluded, I understand that the proceedings will not be concluded until Mr. Trotsky has had an opportunity to make his closing remarks. Counsel and the Chairman of the Commission will also have an opportunity, if that is necessary.

DEWEY: It is correct. My intention was simply to inquire if there were any questions from the representatives of the Mexican labor organizations. Mr. Goldman will have an opportunity to make any further closing remarks. Mr. Trotsky will have an opportunity.

GOLDMAN: The title of the book I just referred to, "The Defense of Terrorism," might be misconstrued. I have in my hand the sub-title to it. It is a defense not of individual terrorism, but the terror of the revolution, mass terror.

TROTSKY: Even the title is by the publisher. My title was "Communism and Terrorism." But Kautsky wrote a book in connection with terrorism, and to avoid mistakes or errors, I changed the title.

DEWEY: It will be on the record. The session is now ended. We will resume this afternoon.

End of Twelfth Session—One-thirty o'clock P.M.

Thirteenth Session

April 17th, 1937, at four o'clock p.m.

DEWEY: We will first repeat the statement made this morning. There will now be an opportunity for questions asked of Mr. Trotsky by the Mexican labor organizations, provided any of them wishes to ask such questions.

(The remarks of Chairman Dewey were translated into Spanish by Dr. Bach.)

ADELAIDE WALKER: They have not arrived yet.

DEWEY: We will give them an opportunity later.

FINERTY: It may be well, Mr. Dewey, to give them an opportunity after the next recess.

DEWEY: I wish now to refer to quite another matter. A considerable and quite legitimate interest has been expressed in the question of the official transcript of the testimony. I am going to ask the official stenographer if there is a statement to make on that.

GLOTZER: I have most of the record finished, and I am going to stay several days to complete the record of the last day and a half, and finish the transcript before I leave Mexico.

GOLDMAN: Before I launch into my closing speech, I am going to ask permission of the Commission to present documents just received on the Copenhagen matter, referring to the questions of Mr. Trotsky's stay in Copenhagen, and the possibility or impossibility of Holtzman, Berman-Yurin and Fritz David having seen him in Copenhagen. There is a deposition by one Kenneth Johnson of England. There is a deposition by Raymond Molinier of France, and one by Anton Grylewicz, who is now residing in Prague. Then there is a lease showing that someone on behalf of Mr. Trotsky leased a certain villa. These I ask to be considered as part of the folder introduced into evidence as the Copenhagen exhibit, if I am not mistaken.

FINERTY: I suggest, Dr. Dewey, that these be received subject to the right of the Commission to examine the documents at some future time.

DEWEY: They will be accepted under the conditions as stated.

GOLDMAN: President of the Commission, Mr. Finerty, ladies and gentlemen of the Commission: Mine is not the task of examining and analyzing the evidence which was produced at the last two Moscow trials on behalf of the Soviet Government and here on behalf of Leon Trotsky; nor shall I attempt to answer the speeches of Vyshinsky, who prosecuted the defendants in Moscow. It is a rather unenviable position for an attorney to be in, where he is compelled to state that his client will argue his own case, but I am reconciled to being in such a position because the client is none other than Leon Trotsky. Trotsky needs no attorney to analyze the evidence and answer Vyshinsky.

It is my desire simply to present before the Commissioners some aspects of the case which may be considered of a legal character, although not everything that I shall say will readily find its place under that category.

In my opening statement I asserted that if we wanted to

be technical we could readily claim that all we needed to do was to raise a reasonable doubt as to the truth of the accusations made against Trotsky. It would then become the duty of the Commission—at least under the Anglo-Saxon procedure—to find Trotsky not guilty. But I stated that we would not rely on such a technicality; that, on the contrary, we would assume the burden of proving Trotsky's innocence beyond all doubt.

Was I too rash in making such a statement? It might have seemed so before we presented our evidence. Some, perhaps, would say that my boldness was due to my failure to understand that it is impossible to prove a negative—a proposition which, taken generally, is quite correct.

If Trotsky did not plot to assassinate the leaders of the Soviet Union, if he did not enter into an agreement with the German fascists and Japanese militarists to surrender Soviet territory to these two powers, and if he did not instruct his fellow conspirators, allegedly, to commit acts of wrecking and diversion, how can he prove that by documentary evidence? There are no documents of events that never transpired or that were not even thought of.

Were it simply a question of a general accusation, without the production of any evidence by the accusers, then an accused would indeed be in a bad position. For a defendant would be unable to prove his innocence—that is, to prove a negative—if the accuser would not be required to prove his accusation by producing evidence of time, place, occasion, circumstance, etc. That is why under all forms of judicial procedure it is necessary for the prosecution to produce some evidence of the alleged guilt of the accused.

The prosecution in the Soviet Union was in a dilemma. Merely to have asserted the guilt of Leon Trotsky and his son, Leon Sedov, without producing some evidence of direct contact on the part of some of the defendants with Trotsky or his son, would have weakened its case tremendously.

On the other hand, to manufacture evidence of such direct contact would mean to risk the possibility of a grave slip-up that might compromise the whole case. A perfect frame-up is just as difficult to create as it is to commit a perfect crime. In spite of the risk involved, however, the Soviet prosecution decided to pursue the second course.

That was fortunate for us. We were thereby afforded an opportunity to prove the innocence of Leon Trotsky and his son beyond all doubt. We are now able to prove a negative, to prove the innocence of Trotsky and his son, by demolishing the chief pillars of the prosecution's evidence, by proving to the satisfaction of every person with an independent mind that the testimony of Holtzman, Berman-Yurin, Pyatakov and Romm, who claimed to have met and talked with Trotsky, was completely false. And since the testimony of all the other defendants depended directly and fully upon the testimony of those whom I have just mentioned, the whole case falls to pieces, and before us is revealed a frame-up as crude and vile as the frame-ups against Tom Mooney and Sacco and Vanzetti.

It is because we knew that we had at our disposal incontrovertible evidence of the falsity of the testimony of the key witnesses in the Moscow trials that we dared to assume the burden of proving the innocence of Trotsky and his son. We were neither bold nor rash when we assumed that burden at the opening of the hearing; we were merely confident, because we knew what we had in our possession. And we have met that burden clearly and decisively.

There are those like D.N. Pritt, the English lawyer who has rushed to the defense of the Soviet prosecution, who will claim that by proving Trotsky innocent and claiming that the prosecution in the Soviet Union was a frame-up we have placed ourselves in a "grave logical difficulty"—to quote Pritt's words in his pamphlet "At the Moscow Trial."

Because, forsooth, to use his own words, "it follows inescapably that Stalin and a substantial number of other high officials, including presumably the judges and the prosecutor, were themselves guilty of a foul conspiracy to procure the judicial murder of Zinoviev, Kamenev and a fair number of other persons."

In the first place, for the Commission to find Trotsky innocent does not necessarily mean that it also finds that the prosecution is guilty of a frame-up. In the second place, I cannot for the life of me see any logical difficulties for those who, like myself, believe in the innocence of Trotsky and in the guilt of Stalin and his henchmen as creators of a frame-up. The difficulty, logical or otherwise, exists for Stalin and his prosecutors and judges, and not for those who accept Trotsky's innocence because he is proved to be innocent.

But, then, if Trotsky is innocent, are not the defendants at the Moscow trials also innocent, and if they are innocent why did they plead guilty and why did they confess?

From a strictly logical point of view, it does not follow that to pronounce Trotsky innocent is also to assert that the defendants were innocent as well. For it may be that the defendants were guilty and dragged Trotsky in because the prosecution compelled them to do so, or because they had some personal grievance against Trotsky. But it has been our contention all through, and it is now our contention, that the defendants—at least those whose revolutionary career is known to us—were just as innocent as Trotsky is. It is true that the Commission does not have to pass on that point, just as it does not have to pass on the question of frame-up. The Commission will undoubtedly cling to its original intention of finding Trotsky and his son guilty or innocent of the charges leveled against them. That does not, however, preclude us from asserting that the inevitable conclusion of the evidence presented in the Soviet court and in this hearing is that the chief defendants of the Moscow trials are also innocent.

If innocent, why did they plead guilty? I shall not enter into a discussion of the possible reasons for their pleading guilty. We have introduced the article of Dr. Anton Ciliga, printed in the *International Review*, which gives a first-hand description of the methods used to extort confessions from Soviet prisoners by the G.P.U. We have also referred you to Victor Serge, who, like Dr. Ciliga, spent several years in prison in the Soviet Union because of his opposition to the Stalinist régime. We sincerely hope that a sub-commission will take their evidence in Paris. Here I want to stress the point, that the fact that any one of a dozen theories advanced to explain the incredible "confessions" proves to be incorrect, does not make the confessions true when, as a matter of fact, they have been proved false in every essential particular. The theory explaining the existence of a certain phenomenon may be incorrect; that does not, however, do away with the phenomenon. I hope that all of the Commissioners, as well as the rest of us, will live long enough to get a true confession by the G.P.U., explaining the methods used to compel the defendants to give false testimony against themselves and Trotsky and his son.

A legitimate question arises: Since the defendants pleaded guilty, what was the necessity for their lengthy confessions and the voluminous testimony? The answer by the Stalinist attorneys is that upon a plea of guilty it is proper for a court to hear evidence for possible mitigation of punishment. That is correct. But if that were the real reason and not simply a pretext, we would not have close to five hundred pages of testimony printed in an official report of the Radek-Pyatakov trial, and over one hundred and fifty pages of summarized testimony printed in an official report of the Zinoviev-Kamenev trial. If that were the real reason and not simply a pretext, the Commissariat of Justice of the U.S.S.R.

would not print those reports in various languages and sell and distribute them by the tens of thousands.

It is clear, both from a reading of the official reports of the two last trials and from the nature of the distribution of those reports, that the purpose for the taking of the defendants' testimony was not to determine the degree of punishment but to convince a skeptical world.

Obviously, there were far better methods that the prosecution could have used to convince an astonished and skeptical world opinion. It would be asserting that Stalin is the greatest of fools to say that he did not realize that trials involving leaders of the October Revolution in an alleged conspiracy to commit terrorist acts and to help Hitler and the Mikado would cause the greatest of excitement. Was he anxious to allay all doubts? It could have been accomplished very easily. Responsible organizations could have been invited to send their attorneys and representatives to talk privately with the accused, to cross-examine them at the trial if necessary. Doubters and cynics could have been put to rout had such a procedure been followed. It was a duty that the leader of the Soviet Government had to the workers of the Soviet Union and the workers throughout the world.

Oh, yes—advantage can be and has been taken of the technicality that the Soviet Government is a sovereign state, and it is not meet and proper for a sovereign state to have anyone interfere with its functioning. But such an attitude is false to the very roots, and only condemns those who advance it, as lacking in an attitude of responsibility to the working masses. For the sake of clearing Soviet justice of all suspicion, the Soviet Court was in duty bound to do the very thing I suggested. The Soviet Government, under Lenin and Trotsky, did this very thing when the Social Revolutionaries were on trial, and it was proof that they had nothing to hide. The failure of the Stalinist Government to do the same thing, the haste with which the defendants were tried and executed, are very powerful bits of circumstantial evidence that the accusations could not stand the light of day.

To this hearing the Commission invited our adversaries and enemies to come and cross-examine our chief witness, Leon Trotsky. I am only sorry that they did not accept the invitation of the Commission. Your invitation indicated a sincere desire to arrive at the truth; their refusal to accept indicated a feeling on the part of our enemies that they knew they could not possibly shake our testimony, which is based on absolute truth.

Oh, if we had only been invited to cross-examine the witnesses and defendants at the Moscow trials! How eagerly and gladly we would have accepted such an invitation! I understand that more Moscow trials are to come. Let the Soviet prosecution invite me to be present and cross-examine anyone testifying to the same things that the defendants of the last trials testified to. I don't claim to be among the best cross-examiners, but I can say with great confidence that had any fairly good lawyer been permitted to cross-examine the defendants at the Moscow trials, this hearing would not be necessary. Out of their own mouths it could have been proved that the principal defendants were lying against Trotsky and against themselves.

Here I want to mention something about the nature of our evidence. I raise this question because petty lawyers, anxious to defend the Soviet trials, will undoubtedly point out that some of our evidence would not be admissible under Anglo-Saxon rules of evidence. That may be true. In my opinion, however, the sub-commission acted wisely in not following the strict rules of evidence that prevail in American courts. First, because the sub-commission is not a court in the ordinary sense of the term; if anything, it is more in the nature of a Congressional investigation committee which investigates matters without following any strict rules of evidence;

and, second, because the nature of the case is such that it is necessary to permit wide latitude in the introduction of evidence, in order to get at the truth.

FINERTY: Mr. Goldman, I don't want to interrupt your speech, but the Commission had a legal adviser. We received all the evidence subject to investigation. Any evidence which would not be admitted as legal evidence in a court, ultimately will not be received—that is, evidence not verified by subsequent investigation. I understand that to be the sense of the Commission. Such evidence as has been received might very well be received in any court. The exhibits should be verified and an exhibit stricken out if not verified. I want to say for the Commission that we think—so as to make it clear—to say we received no evidence finally at this hearing. It is not received under rules of evidence permitting its proper introduction.

GOLDMAN: I am glad that Mr. Finerty explained the attitude of the Commission. However, I must say frankly that I don't agree with that attitude, for the following reasons: In the first place, the Commission is not a court in the ordinary sense of the term, and has not the powers that a legal court has. The Commission is more of an investigating body to attempt to get at the truth. I think that Mr. Finerty will agree when I say that very frequently, in American courts, the application of the strict rules of evidence under Anglo-Saxon procedure sometimes hides the truth. I think that the Commission could be more likened to an investigating committee—

FINERTY: Mr. Goldman, I stated that we are not governed by the rules of court. We will, of course, have to take the best evidence under the circumstances. We have not accepted any evidence now, except subject to subsequent verification.

GOLDMAN: The very nature of the case, Mr. Finerty—you have to agree with me that the very nature of the case is such that to attempt to apply strict rules of evidence would mean to throw out most of the evidence. But I won't raise this point. I think that Mr. Finerty will agree with me—at least I hope so.

Of course, the Soviet prosecution and its defenders should be the last to raise any question concerning the introduction of testimony which under Anglo-Saxon rules of evidence would be inadmissible. Conservatively speaking, ninety-five per cent of the testimony contained in the Soviet official reports of the trials with reference to Trotsky would be absolutely excluded in an American court.

The difference between that part of the evidence which we introduced at this hearing and the evidence admitted in the Moscow trials which would be excluded in an American court is this: Whereas our "inadmissible" evidence is subject to verification if the Commission is in the least doubtful of its truth, the "inadmissible" evidence of the Moscow trials cannot be verified either because the witnesses who testified are dead or because we are unable to enter into the Soviet Union for the purpose of verifying the testimony given at the Moscow trials.

Matters have been gone into at this hearing which might be considered irrelevant. On our part, we have not objected to a single question put by any of the Commissioners, although problems might have been involved that could not possibly throw any light on the real issue—that is, whether or not Trotsky is guilty of the charges made against him. It was evident that Trotsky was willing to discuss all questions of history and theory upon which there may be and there are legitimate differences of opinion.

Let me illustrate: It is well known that Trotsky is bitterly opposed to the theory of Socialism in one country. Is it the duty of the Commission to pass upon the correctness of that theory? Obviously not. It may be that certain members of the sub-commission agree with Stalin that Socialism can be built in one country. Would they be disqualified for that reason from serving on the Commission? Of course not—unless they would draw the very far-fetched conclusion that opposition to such a theory must inevitably lead to acts of terrorism or to plots with Hitler to surrender to him some Soviet territory.

Other questions of great theoretical importance were raised. For instance, Mr. Beals, who resigned from the Commission and whose attitude was such that we can justifiably conclude that his motives in asking some questions were not of the best, wanted to know Trotsky's attitude towards the People's Front Government in Spain. This question was not, of course, nearly so bad as the one whereby Mr. Beals attempted to find out whether it was not Trotsky who sent Borodin to Mexico in 1919 for the purpose of creating a Communist party and fomenting revolution. The latter question was obviously put with the express purpose of making Trotsky's presence in Mexico impossible. Trotsky did not even refuse to answer that impermissible question. Of course, he had nothing to conceal, for the simple reason that he never had anything to do with Borodin. On the question of Spain, I doubt whether there are any members on the full Commission who will agree fully with Trotsky. Can it possibly be, however, that the Commission will undertake to pass on the correctness of Trotsky's ideas as to the tactics to be followed in Spain? That is hardly conceivable. Much less is it conceivable that the Commission, because it disagrees with Trotsky on the Spanish situation, would find him guilty of plotting against the Soviet leaders.

Does this mean that Trotsky's theories have nothing to do with the charges made against him? Not in the least. We have contended from the beginning that Trotsky's theories, expounded for four decades, would in themselves be sufficient to disprove the accusations against him. Trotsky's theories are very relevant to the questions at issue, and we are anxious to have every member of the Commission read everything that Trotsky has written, in order to understand the absolute inconsistency between the accusations and Trotsky's conceptions. This is of exceedingly great importance, because there are those Stalinist followers and other simpletons who, with an ignorance that is colossal, have the audacity to claim that Trotsky's ideas on war and international revolution make the accusations against him highly probable—in fact, so probable that he is guilty. Vyshinsky has torn sentences out of their context to prove that Trotsky advocated terrorism. We challenge any honest man who can understand simple language to find a single idea in the works of Trotsky to justify in the slightest the allegations in the indictment of the Soviet prosecution or the evidence of the defendants in the trials.

Our answer to these Stalinists who speculate about the guilt of one who has devoted his whole life to the cause of the working class is, first: Every bit of evidence introduced against him is false; and, second: His whole life, everything he has said, written or done, is overwhelming proof of the falsity of the charges made against him.

Many who feel that the evidence of the defendants in the Moscow trials cannot be believed are at a loss to understand why these trials were staged. If there is anything that can clear up the mystery, it is the last statements of the main defendants. Read those last statements carefully, and the reason why the trials were held becomes clear as daylight. I read from Sokolnikov's last plea, on page 555 of the official report of the Radek-Pyatakov trial:

> I express the conviction—or, at any rate, the hope—that not one person will now be found in the Soviet Union who would attempt to take up the Trotskyite banner. I think that Trotskyism in other countries, too, has been exposed by this trial, and that Trotsky himself has been exposed as an ally of capitalism, as the vilest agent of

fascism, as a fomenter of world war who will be hated and execrated by the millions everywhere.

I therefore think that inasmuch as Trotskyism, as a counter-revolutionary political force, ceases to exist, has been finally smashed, that I and the other accused, all the accused, may nevertheless plead, citizen judges, for clemency.

Read Pyatakov's, and especially Radek's, last pleas, and between the lines you will read as follows: "You demanded that we degrade and stultify ourselves in order to expose Trotsky and Trotskyism. Because we are broken and demoralized individuals, because of the mental torture we have suffered, because we fear that you will torture our loved ones as you are torturing us, we have agreed to say everything that you dictated to us. Now grant us our lives, and, if not, then shoot us and save our fathers, mothers, wives and children."

Can there be any doubt that the Moscow trials are staged in order to discredit in the eyes of the Russian workers and the workers throughout the world the chief representative of the current of revolutionary Marxism, which is the greatest danger to the ideas and practices of Stalinism? Why is that necessary? Trotsky himself, in his final argument, will discuss why that is necessary.

It must be repeated over and over again that the "defendants" in the Moscow trials were not in reality defendants; they were witnesses against the real defendant, who was not present—Leon Trotsky. In passing, I might ask the Stalinist attorneys to explain how it happens that the Soviet court convicted Trotsky and his son in their absence and why, after having been convicted, they should be subject to immediate arrest and trial if they should be discovered on Soviet territory? We can expect as little logic from the Soviet court as truth.

Vyshinsky, in his closing argument in the Pyatakov-Radek trial, made a remarkable statement. "In order to distinguish truth from falsehood," he said (page 513 of the official report of the trial), "judicial experience, is, of course, sufficient; and every judge, every procurator and every counsel for defense who has taken part in scores of trials knows when an accused is speaking the truth and when he departs from the truth for some reason or other." From this statement something very peculiar follows, as far as Vyshinsky himself is concerned.

He was, I believe, the prosecutor in the Zinoviev trial of January, 1935, where the defendants assumed moral responsibility for the assassination of Kirov. According to the very penetrating Vyshinsky, the defendants departed from the truth because, indeed, they were guilty not only of moral responsibility but of actually organizing the assassination. Did Mr. Vyshinsky at that time proclaim to the world that the defendants had departed from the truth? Perhaps he did not have sufficient experience at that time.

Then came the Zinoviev-Kamenev trial of August, 1936. By that time Vyshinsky had more experience. The defendants at that time admitted that they were directly responsible for the murder of Kirov and that they plotted to murder other leaders of the Soviet Union. But they did not divulge some very important "facts"; they testified nothing at all to the alleged existence of any parallel center nor to their alleged connections with the German and Japanese Governments nor to their program for the reestablishment of capitalism. Were they lying? Vyshinsky, at the Radek trial, accused them of wholesale lying.

But why did not Vyshinsky, who has surely taken part in scores if not hundreds of trials, charge the defendants of the Kamenev-Zinoviev trial with concealing the whole truth at the time of their testimony?

The reason is obvious: Vyshinsky knew that Zinoviev,

Kamenev and the other defendants were lying, for the simple reason that he knew that the defendants were repeating the lies prepared for them by Vyshinsky with the help of the G.P.U. and at the command of the master before whom he bends his knees so frequently and humbly.

I have also had experience in scores of trials, but I claim no such penetrating powers of detecting truth from falsehood as Mr. Vyshinsky. Together with other persons of fair intelligence, I make mistakes of judgment. But there are undoubtedly many instances where all of us—and we need not be lawyers or judges or prosecutors—become possessed of a profound conviction that a certain person is or is not telling the truth.

For a week you have listened to the testimony of Leon Trotsky. Judge by the frankness of his replies, even in those instances where he knew the members of the Commission could not be in agreement with him, judge by his whole demeanor as a witness, and is it possible to conceive that Trotsky was uttering the least falsehood? In my humble opinion, only one whose mind is completely closed by ignorance, hatred and prejudice can have the least doubt about the truthfulness of the testimony presented here.

I think I am correct in saying that we all feel that we are participating in a historic event. And to me, at least, it is not historic simply because it involves Leon Trotsky, a person who has achieved a great reputation by his writings and revolutionary activities. To those of us who have devoted our lives to the struggle for a great social ideal which we believe will abolish all exploitation of man by man and which will raise mankind to an infinitely higher cultural level, the hearing which the Commission is conducting has a far greater significance than simply clearing the name of a great man who is innocent. We are anxious to clear the name of Leon Trotsky, because that will renew the faith of hundreds of thousands of workers and intellectuals in the movement which is mankind's only hope, because that will, to some extent, heal the terrible wound inflicted on the Socialist movement by the monstrous frame-up concocted by those who have dragged the word "Socialism" into the dust.

For myself, for thousands of others who have been acquainted with Trotsky's writings and activities, who have participated in a common struggle for the liberation of the working masses from all forms of degrading slavery, there was no necessity for a hearing, to convince us that Trotsky is innocent. We are not, we cannot be, "impartial." For not only Trotsky, but we ourselves were subjected to attack: from the very first moment when the accusations were made we recognized that the accusers were the criminals, and not the accused.

But it would be absurd for us to deny that there are tens of thousands, if not millions, of workers and intellectuals, believers in and sympathizers with the ideas of Socialism, who have been bewildered and whose faith has been shaken. Trotsky is innocent; we are innocent; and in spite of the smallness of our number, in spite of the powerful forces arrayed against the movement represented by Trotsky, we have a profound faith that the truth will ultimately conquer. We do not blind ourselves to the tragic fact, however, that the one who is responsible for the accusations and the bureaucracy which he represents are at the head of the first workers' state created by such huge sacrifices on the part of the Russian workers. And it is because of that, that the blow to the Socialist movement is a severe one indeed.

The Commissioners, I presume, do not see eye to eye with me on the question of the significance of this hearing for the cause of Socialism, because their ideas are not the ideas of the movement represented by Trotsky. The Commissioners may look at the whole matter simply from the point of view of affording an accused man a chance to present his case before the bar of world opinion. Very well—that is, by far, not an unimportant task. The report and verdict of the Commission will be of tremendous significance, regardless of the point of view adopted by the Commissioners as to the significance of this hearing. And the fact that your report and your verdict cannot end in a formal judgment and in a writ of execution granted by a court of law supported by all the powers of a state, does not in the slightest detract from the value of that report and verdict. On the contrary, its moral value is all the greater.

What can that report, what can that verdict be?

You have listened to the evidence; you have examined Trotsky; you can read the record. It is hardly believable that anyone, under such circumstances, should not agree with us that the innocence of Trotsky has been proved beyond the shadow of a doubt. We promised at the very beginning to destroy completely the structure of falsehoods erected at Moscow. We have fulfilled our promise. And if there will be those who will not be convinced by our evidence or by the report of the Commission, then they or their posterity will be convinced by the victory of the ideas represented by Leon Trotsky.

DEWEY: First, I want briefly to make a statement that I am not a lawyer, and the other members of the Commission are not lawyers. We cannot pass upon the technical question about evidence raised. We shall take under advisement the statement of Mr. Finerty, but, in advance of that, I want to say that while we cannot speak for the full Commission, I am confident that it is the attitude of the preliminary Commission that any testimony presented here that is not reasonably confirmed or verified by subsequent investigation will not be taken into account in any final report the Commission may make. On the other hand, whatever evidence or testimony we find that impugns or impeaches the evidence or testimony presented here will certainly be given due consideration, serious consideration. We will now take a recess. I wish to repeat that immediately after the recess representatives of the Mexican workers' organizations will have an opportunity to ask questions of Mr. Trotsky.

DEWEY: I will now ask the representatives of the Mexican labor organizations to ask such questions as they wish to put to Mr. Trotsky.

(Chairman Dewey's remarks were translated into Spanish by Dr. Bach.)

(At this point, Ramon Garibay, the representative of the Casa del Pueblo, asks the following questions: 1. Why is Stalin persecuting Mr. Trotsky in this way? What are the reasons? 2. Where would Lenin be if he would still be alive, and if Stalin would have the same power today? 3. Has Stalin made a pact with the bureaucracy of the world? 4. Is Mr. Trotsky in accord with the world proletariat? These questions were translated by Dr. Bach.)

BACH: The workers' delegates are from the Casa del Pueblo.

DEWEY: The first questions are presented to the Commission?

BACH: Yes; they are addressed to the Commission, and the last question is for Mr. Trotsky to answer.

DEWEY: Regarding the first three questions, we are unable to make any reply at this time, because we are down here simply to collect, in a preliminary gathering, any evidence and facts upon which the decision of the full Commission must be based. We have not as yet the privilege at this time of answering these questions.

(Diego Rivera translates Dr. Dewey's remarks into Spanish.)

LAFOLLETTE: Repeat the last question to Mr. Trotsky.

BACH: The first three questions are directed also to Mr. Trotsky, they say. So that Mr. Trotsky may answer all four.

Mr. Garibay says that the first three questions are for the Commission and that they are not only for the Commission, but also for you, Mr. Trotsky.

TROTSKY: I understand.

BACH: The last one only for you, and the others for the Commission.

TROTSKY: I will only suggest that my closing arguments, genuinely closing, for this Commission—that they involve also the answers to the questions put to me by the representatives of the Mexican organizations. It would be better for them to receive the answers through the translation of my closing argument. The answers can be made in my closing argument, because they are more fully presented than in the short answer that I can give orally. I believe they would consent to accept this procedure.

(Rivera translates Trotsky's remarks.)

DEWEY: Are there more questions?

GOLDMAN: I would suggest that we proceed.

BACH: They agree that Mr. Trotsky shall answer the questions in his final speech.

DEWEY: The representative of the Pueblo labor organization says they are satisfied that Mr. Trotsky shall give his answers in his final speech. Mr. Finerty, do you want to make a statement now or later?

FINERTY: I think it might be well, Mr. Chairman, in order to make clear both to Mr. Trotsky and to Mr. Goldman and perhaps to the public, that I advised the Commission that the rule of evidence that should apply in receiving evidence here is what is well known, as a fundamental rule of evidence—"the best-evidence rule." That is, that the Commission should take the best evidence adapted to the issues before it and which the circumstances permit. I think that in that connection, I pointed out that the Commission is in a somewhat difficult position. The alleged accomplices of Mr. Trotsky are dead, and their alleged confessions are not subject to cross-examination. Those who conducted the trial of the defendants, though asked to participate in this investigation and offered a full opportunity to participate in this investigation—have refused to participate, and they leave the Commission in a position where it must determine, among other things, the question of the fairness of the trials by which the Soviet Government claims to have established Mr. Trotsky's guilt. Under these circumstance, we could only take the best evidence which in the honest judgment of the Commission, is available to it. What I have stated to the Commission, is that even this situation would not excuse the Commission in accepting Mr. Trotsky's unsupported denial of his guilt—accepting unsupported statements not subject to cross-examination by the Commission. Mr. Trotsky, in this hearing, has, as far as possible, supported his denials by circumstantial evidence, and has placed at the disposal of the Commission all his archives, all the documentary evidence to bear on this question. The Commission has tentatively accepted the depositions and sworn statements of certain persons. It is expected that these depositions or sworn statements are subject to the right of the Commission to examine these persons personally—either by this sub-commission or by the full Commission. I want Mr. Goldman to understand why I have advised the Commission that all the evidence offered by Mr. Trotsky which would not ordinarily be acceptable under strict rules of evidence has been accepted only subject to final authentication by the Commission through future investigation. I just want to make it clear that we have a practical situation to face, and in that practical situation we are endeavoring to apply only such rules of evidence, as in the best authenticated opinion, will permit the Commission to obtain the best evidence within these limits. We have received his evidence under these conditions.

DEWEY: Mr. Trotsky will now sum up.

TROTSKY: I consider my closing speech as closing only for this Commission, as I mentioned. I present only a part of my arguments today. The other part I present in writing, in order to finish tonight. I will begin with the question, why the investigation is inevitable. If you permit me, I read my statement sitting.

I. WHY IS AN INVESTIGATION NECESSARY?

It is entirely beyond dispute that the trials of Zinoviev-Kamenev and Pyatakov-Radek have aroused the utmost distrust of Soviet justice, among workers' and democratic circles throughout the entire world. However, it was precisely in this affair that full clarity and unimpeachable judicial power of persuasion were absolutely necessary. The accusers, like the accused—at least the most important of them—are of world-wide renown. The aims and motives of the participants had to flow directly from their political position, from the characters of the persons involved, from their whole past. The majority of the defendants have been shot; their guilt—we assume—must have been absolutely proved! However, if one leaves aside those who can be convinced of anything, no matter what, by simple telegraphic orders from Moscow, Western public opinion has flatly refused to support the accusers and the hangmen. On the contrary, alarm and distrust have grown into horror and revulsion. Moreover, no one supposes that a judicial "mistake" has been made. The Moscow authorities could not have shot Zinoviev, Kamenev, Smirnov, Pyatakov, Serebryakov, and all the others "by mistake." To lack confidence in the justice of Vyshinsky is, in the present case, directly to suspect Stalin of a judicial frame-up, with political aims. There is no room for any other interpretation.

But perhaps sentimental public opinion has been misled

by preconceived sympathies for the accused? This argument was used more than once in the cases of Francisco Ferrer in Spain, of Sacco-Vanzetti and Mooney in the United States, etc. But so far as the Moscow defendants are concerned, there can be no question of partisan sympathies. The most informed section of world public opinion, it must be plainly said, no longer had either confidence in or respect for the principal defendants, in view of their numerous previous recantations and, above all, their conduct in court. The prosecution represented the accused, with their assistance, not as capitulators to Stalin, but as "Trotskyites" who had assumed the cloak of capitulation. Such a characterization, to the extent that it was accepted as true, could in no way increase sympathy for the accused. Finally, "Trotskyism" itself today is represented by a tiny minority in the workers' movement, which is in sharp struggle with all other parties and factions.

The accusers are in an incomparably more favorable position. Behind them is the Soviet Union, with all the hopes of progress which it represents. The rise of world reaction, especially in its most barbarous form—fascism—has turned the sympathies and hopes of democratic circles, even the very moderate ones, toward the Soviet Union. These sympathies, to be sure, are very hazy in character. But that is precisely why the official and unofficial friends of the U.S.S.R. are not inclined, as a general rule, to unravel the internal contradictions of the Soviet régime; on the contrary, they are ready in advance to consider all opposition against the ruling stratum as voluntary or involuntary cooperation with world reaction. To this it is necessary to add the diplomatic and military ties of the U.S.S.R., taken in the general context of present-day international relations. In a number of countries—France, Czechoslovakia, to some extent Great Britain and the United States—purely nationalist and patriotic sentiments predispose the democratic masses in favor of the Soviet Government, as the adversary of Germany and Japan. It is not necessary to mention that, to cap this, Moscow has at its disposal powerful levers, tangible and intangible, with which to exert pressure on public opinion in the most widely separated layers of society. The agitation about the new Constitution, "the most democratic in the world," which was made public, not accidentally, on the eve of the trials, has aroused still more sympathy for Moscow. An overwhelming preponderance of *a priori* confidence was thus assured to the Soviet Government at the outset. Despite all this, the omnipotent accusers have not convinced and have not conquered world opinion, which they tried to take unawares. On the contrary, the authority of the Soviet Government dropped sharply after the trials. Implacable adversaries of Trotskyism, allies of Moscow, and even many traditional friends of the Soviet bureaucracy, have demanded verification of the Moscow charges. It is enough to recall the steps taken by the Second International and the International Federation of Trade Unions in August, 1936. In its incredibly rude response the Kremlin, which had counted on a complete and absolute victory in advance, exposed the full depth of its disappointment. Friedrich Adler, secretary of the Second International and, consequently, an implacable foe of Trotskyism, compared the Moscow trials to the witchcraft trials of the Inquisition. The well known reformist theoretician, Otto Bauer, who considers it possible to declare in the press that Trotsky is speculating on a future war (a statement which is not only false but also absurd!), is compelled, despite all his political sympathy for the Stalinist bureaucracy, to recognize that the Moscow trials are judicial frame-ups. The *New York Times*, an extremely prudent newspaper and far from having any sympathy for Trotskyism, sums up the end of the last trial in the following words: "The burden of proof lies not on Trotsky but on Stalin." This single, crushing phrase reduces the juridical persuasiveness of Moscow's court procedure to zero.

If it were not for diplomatic, patriotic and "anti-fascist" considerations, the lack of confidence in the Moscow accusers would assume incomparably more open and vigorous forms. This can be easily demonstrated by a secondary but extremely instructive example. In October of last year my book "The Revolution Betrayed" was published in France. Several weeks ago it appeared in New York. Not one of the many critics, most of them my adversaries—among them the former French Premier Caillaux—so much as mentioned the fact that the author of the book has been "convicted" of an alliance with fascism and Japanese militarism against France and the United States. No one, absolutely no one—not even Louis Fischer—considered it necessary to compare my political conclusions with the charges of the Kremlin. It was as if there had never been either trials or executions in Moscow! This single fact, if one thinks about it, is irrefutable proof that the thinking sections of society, beginning with the most interested and most sensitive country, France, not only have not accepted the monstrous accusation but have, quite simply, cast it out with scarcely concealed disgust.

We cannot, unfortunately, say what the stifled population of the Soviet Union thinks and feels. But in all the rest of the world the toiling masses have been seized by a tragic confusion which poisons their thought and paralyzes their will. Either the entire old generation of Bolshevik leaders, with a single and sole exception, has really betrayed Socialism for fascism, or the present leadership of the U.S.S.R. has organized a judicial frame-up against the founders of the Bolshevik Party and the Soviet state. Yes, that is precisely how the question stands: *Either Lenin's Political Bureau was composed of traitors, or Stalin's Political Bureau is composed of falsifiers*. There is no third possibility! But it is precisely because there is no third possibility that progressive public opinion cannot, at the risk of its very existence, evade making this difficult and tragic choice and explaining it to the popular masses.

II. IS THE INVESTIGATION POLITICALLY ADMISSIBLE?

The oft-encountered, semi-official objection that the work of the Commission can "politically harm" the U.S.S.R. and help fascism constitutes—to put it mildly—a compound of stupidity and hypocrisy. Let us for a moment grant that the charges of the Court against the Opposition have some basis—that is, that dozens of men were not shot for nothing. In that case, it can be little trouble for a powerful government to produce the materials from the preliminary investigation, to fill in the gaps in the records of the court proceedings, explain the contradictions, and dispel doubts. In such case an examination could only increase the authority of the Soviet Government.

But what if the Commission laid bare the premeditated fraud of the Moscow charges? Would not political caution then dictate avoiding the risk of an investigation? Such a consideration, seldom expressed candidly and fully, is based on the craven notion that one can fight the forces of reaction with fictions, humbug and lies, as if the best remedy for curing a sickness consisted in refraining from calling it by name. If the present Soviet Government is capable of resorting to bloody judicial frame-ups to deceive its own people, it cannot be the ally of the world proletariat in the struggle against reaction. Its internal inadequacy must in this event reveal itself at the first major historic shock. The sooner the infection is exposed, the sooner the inevitable crisis comes, the greater the hope that it can still be overcome in time by the living forces of the organism. On the other hand, closing one's eyes to disease means only to drive it deeper internally. This would lead to a great historic catastrophe.

Stalin rendered his first great service to Hitler through the theory and practice of "social-fascism." He rendered his second service through the Moscow trials. These trials, in which the greatest moral values are crushed and violated, cannot be blotted out from the consciousness of mankind. It is possible to help the masses recover from the wound inflicted upon them by the trials only through complete clarity and the full truth.

The opposition of a certain type of "friend" to the investigation, which in itself is a crying scandal, arises from the fact that even the most zealous defenders of Moscow justice *lack inner conviction of the soundness of their case.* They cover their secret fears with completely contradictory and unworthy arguments. An investigation, they say, is "intervention in the internal affairs of the U.S.S.R."! But has not the world proletariat the right to intervene in the internal affairs of the U.S.S.R.? In the ranks of the Comintern they still repeat: "The U.S.S.R. is the fatherland of all the toilers." A strange fatherland in whose affairs nobody dares intervene! If the working masses are suspicious of the acts of their leaders, the latter are under obligation to give them full explanations and every facility for an investigation. Neither the state prosecutor, nor the judges, nor the members of the Political Bureau of the U.S.S.R. are exempt from this elementary rule. Whoever tries to raise himself above workers' democracy, by that very act betrays it.

To the above it must be added that the question is not an "internal" affair of the U.S.S.R., even when viewed purely formally. It is already five years since the Moscow bureaucracy deprived me, my wife and our elder son of Soviet citizenship. Thereby they also robbed themselves of every special right with respect to us. We have been bereft of a "fatherland" which could defend us. It is but natural that we should place ourselves under the protection of international public opinion.

III. THE OPINION OF PROFESSOR CHARLES A. BEARD

In his reply of March 19, 1937, to George Novack, the secretary of the American Committee for the Defense of Leon Trotsky, Professor Charles A. Beard motivates his refusal to take part in the Commission of Investigation with principled arguments which have great value in themselves, apart from the celebrated historian's participation or nonparticipation in the investigating commission.

First of all, we learn that Professor Beard has made "a careful study of many documents in the case, including the official report of the last Moscow trial." One understands without unnecessary comment the weight of such a statement from a scholar who knows very well what a careful study is. Professor Beard, in a very restrained but at the same time absolutely unequivocal manner, communicates "certain conclusions" to which he has been led by his study of the question. First of all, he says, the accusation against Trotsky rests *exclusively* on the confessions. "From a long study of historical problems, I know that confessions, even when voluntarily made, are not positive proof." The word "even" indicates clearly enough that the question of the voluntary character of the Moscow confessions is for this scholar, at the very least, open. As an example of false self-accusations, Professor Beard cites the classic cases of the trials of the Inquisition, along with instances of the darkest superstition. That single comparison, which coincides with the development of the thought of Friedrich Adler, secretary of the Second International, speaks for itself. Furthermore, Professor Beard deems it proper to apply a rule which governs American jurisprudence, namely: The accused must be considered innocent if there have not been brought against him objective proofs which leave no room for reasonable doubt. Finally, the historian writes that "it is almost, if not entirely, impossible to prove a negative in such a case; namely, that Mr. Trotsky did not enter into the relations of conspiracy charged against him. Naturally, as an old revolutionist, experienced in the art, he would not keep incriminating records of the operations, if he did engage in them. Furthermore, no person in the world could prove that he has not engaged in a conspiracy, unless he had a guard set over him every moment of the time covered by the charges. In my opinion it is not incumbent upon Mr. Trotsky to do the impossible—that is, prove a negative by positive evidence. It is incumbent upon his accusers to produce more than confessions, to produce corroborating evidence to specific and overt acts."

As has already been said, the conclusions reached are of the highest importance of and by themselves, since they contain an annihilating appraisal of Moscow justice. If unconfirmed confessions of a doubtfully "voluntary" character are insufficient basis for accusing me, they are also insufficient for accusing all the others. This means, in Professor Beard's opinion, that dozens of people who were innocent or whose guilt had not been demonstrated were shot in Moscow. Messrs. Executioners must reckon with this estimate, made by an exceptionally conscientious investigator on the basis of a careful study of the question.

Nevertheless, I must say that in my opinion Professor Beard's formal decision—namely, his refusal to participate in the investigation—does not at all follow from his material conclusions. Indeed, public opinion seeks above all to resolve the enigma: Is the charge proved or not? It is precisely this question which the Commission primarily wishes to resolve. Professor Beard declares that he personally has already arrived at the conclusion that the charge has not been established, and that *that is why* he does not join the Commission. It seems to me that a correct decision would be the following: "I enter the Commission in order to test the accuracy of my conclusions." It is absolutely clear that the collective decision of the Commission, in which representatives of the various branches of intellectual endeavor are found, will carry much more weight with public opinion than the conclusions of a single person, even a great authority.

Professor Beard's conclusions, with all their importance, are incomplete, however, even in their material essence. The question does not consist simply in knowing whether or not the charge against me has been established. In Moscow dozens of people have been shot. Dozens of others await execution. Hundreds and thousands are under suspicion, accused indirectly or calumniated, not only in the U.S.S.R. but also in all other parts of the world. All this on the basis of the "confessions," which Professor Beard finds himself able to compare to the confessions of the victims of the Inquisition. The fundamental question, consequently, should be formulated in this manner: Who organizes these inquisitorial trials, these crusades of calumny, why, and for what purpose? Hundreds of thousands of men throughout the entire world are firmly convinced, and millions suspect, that the trials rest on systematic falsifications, dictated by definite political aims. It is precisely this accusation against the ruling clique in Moscow that I hope to establish before the Commission. Consequently, it is a question not only of a "negative" fact—that is to say, that Trotsky has *not* participated in a plot—but also of a positive fact; namely, that Stalin *did* organize the greatest frame-up in human history.

However, even so far as the "negative facts" are involved, I cannot accept Professor Beard's over-categorical judgment. He supposes that, being such an experienced revolutionist, I would not keep documents which would compromise me. That is absolutely correct. But neither would I write letters to the conspirators in the least prudent and most compromising way. I would not heedlessly reveal the most secret plans to young people unknown to me, nor entrust them, at our first meeting, with serious terrorist missions. Since Professor Beard grants me a certain credit as a conspirator, I, basing myself on that credit, can fully discredit the "confessions," in which I am presented as a comic-opera conspirator, primarily concerned with furnishing the greatest possible number of witnesses against myself for the future prosecutor. The same holds true as far as the other defendants, especially Zinoviev and Kamenev, are concerned. Without rhyme or reason they enlarge the circle of initiates. Their lack of prudence, which cries to high heaven, has a deliberately calculated character. All this notwithstanding, there is not a shred of evidence in the hands of the prosecution. The whole affair is built on conversations—more exactly, on recollections of alleged conversations. The absence of evidence—I shall never cease repeating this—not only annihilates the charges, but also is a terrible piece of evidence against the accusers themselves.

However, I also have more direct and, moreover, quite positive proofs of the "negative fact." That is not so very unusual in jurisprudence. Naturally, it is difficult to demonstrate that in eight years of exile I had no secret meetings—with anyone, anywhere—devoted to a conspiracy against the Soviet authorities. But that is not in question. The most important witnesses for the prosecution, the defendants themselves, are forced to indicate *when* and *where* they had meetings with me. In all of these cases, thanks to the circumstances of my mode of living (police surveillance, constant presence of a guard composed of my friends, daily letters, etc.), I can with irrefutable certainty demonstrate that I was not and could not have been at the places named at the times indicated. In juridical language, such positive proof of a negative fact is called an alibi.

Furthermore, it is absolutely indisputable that I would not preserve in my archives records of my crimes had I committed any. But my archives are important for the investigation, not for what they lack, but for what they contain. Positive acquaintance with the daily development of my thought and acts over a period of nine years (one year of banishment and eight of exile) is entirely sufficient to demonstrate a "negative fact"—namely, that I could not have committed acts contrary to my convictions, to my interests, to my whole character.

IV. A 'PURELY JURIDICAL' EXAMINATION

The agents of the Moscow Government are themselves well aware that the Moscow verdicts cannot stand without the support of authoritative, expert opinion. For this purpose the English attorney Pritt was secretly invited to the first trial, and another English attorney, Dudley Collard, to the second. In Paris, three attorneys—obscure but quite devoted to the G.P.U.—tried to use for the same purpose the shingle of the International Juridical Association. By arrangement with the Soviet Embassy, the obscure French attorney Rosenmark, acting under the cover of the League for the Rights of Man, issued an expert opinion no less benevolent than ignorant. In Mexico, the "Friends of the Soviet Union" have proposed to the "Socialist Lawyers' Front"—by no means accidentally—that they undertake a juridical investigation into the Moscow trials. Similar steps are apparently being prepared at the moment in the United States.

The People's Commissariat of Justice in Moscow has published in foreign languages the "verbatim" report of the trial of the seventeen (Pyatakov, Radek, etc.), the better to obtain from authoritative jurists certification that the victims of the inquisition have been shot entirely in accordance with the rules established by the inquisitors.

In fact, a certification of a purely formal observance of external rules and the ritual of jurisprudence has an importance which is close to zero. The essence of the affair is in the material conditions of the preparation and conduct of the trial. Of course, even if one disregards for the moment the decisive factors which are to be found outside the courtroom, one cannot help recognizing that the Moscow trials are a pure and simple mockery of justice. The investigation, in the twentieth year of the Revolution, is carried on in absolute secrecy. The entire old generation of Bolsheviks is judged before a military tribunal composed of three depersonalized military functionaries. The whole trial is dominated by a Prosecutor who has been all his life, and still is, a political enemy of the accused. Defense is waived, and the procedure is deprived of any vestige of controversy. The material proofs are not presented to the court; they are talked about, but they do not exist. The witnesses mentioned by the Prosecutor or by the defendants are not questioned. A whole series of accused who form a part of the judicial inquiry are absent from the defendants' bench, for reasons unknown. Two of the principal accused who happen to be abroad are not even apprised of the trial, and, like those witnesses who are outside Russia, are deprived of the possibility of taking any steps whatsoever to bring out the truth. The judicial dialogue is wholly constructed of a prearranged game of question-and-answer. The Prosecutor does not address a single concrete question to any of the defendants which might embarrass him and expose the material inconsistencies of his confession. The presiding judge obsequiously covers up the work of the Prosecutor. It is precisely the "verbatim" character of the record which most clearly reveals the malicious sidestepping of the Prosecutor and the judges. To this it is necessary to add that one is scarcely inspired with confidence in the authenticity of the record itself.

But, however important these considerations are in themselves—opening as they do broad grounds for juridical analysis—they are nevertheless secondary and tertiary in character, since they concern the *form* of the frame-up and not its *essence*. Theoretically, one can imagine that if Stalin, Vyshinsky and Yezhov are able over a period of five or ten years to stage their trials with impunity, they will attain such a high technique that all the elements of jurisprudence will be found in formal accord with one another and the existing laws. But perfection in the juridical technique of the frame-up will not bring it one millimeter closer to the truth.

In a political trial of such exceptional importance, the jurist cannot divorce himself from the *political* conditions out of which the trial arose and in which the preliminary investigation was conducted—to put it concretely, the totalitarian oppression to which, in the final analysis, all are subjected: accused, witnesses, judges, counsel, and even the prosecution itself. Here is the nub of the question: Under an uncontrolled and despotic régime which concentrates in the same hands all the means of economic, political, physical and moral coercion, a juridical trial ceases to be a juridical trial. It is a juridical play, with the roles prepared in advance. The defendants appear on the scene only after a series of rehearsals which give the director in advance complete assurance that they will not overstep the limits of their roles. In this sense, as in all others, the judicial trials only represent a coagulation of the political régime of the U.S.S.R. as a whole. At all the hearings the orators say one and the same thing, taking their cue from the chief orator, in utter disregard of what they themselves said the day before. In the newspapers all the articles expound one and the same directive, in the same language. Following the orchestra leader's baton, the historians, the economists—even the statisticians—rearrange the past and the present without any regard for facts, documents, or the preceding editions of their own books. In the kindergartens and schools, all the children in the same words glorify Vyshinsky and curse the defendants. No one acts this way of his own volition; everyone violates his own will. The monolithic character of the judicial trial, in which the accused try to outdo each other in repeating the formulas of the Prosecutor, is thus not an exception to the rule, but only the most revolting expression of the totalitarian inquisitorial régime. It is not a court we see in action, but a play in which the chief actors play their roles at pistol point. The play can be performed well or badly; but that is a question of inquisitorial technique and not of justice. The "purely juridical" examination of the Moscow trials reduces itself essentially to the question of whether the frame-up was well or poorly executed.

To illumine the question still further—in so far as it requires illumination—let us take a fresh example from the domain of constitutional law. After Hitler took power he declared, contrary to all expectations, that he had no intention of changing the fundamental laws of the State. Most people have probably forgotten that even today in Germany the Weimar Constitution remains intact: but into its juridical framework Hitler has introduced the content of the totalitarian dictatorship. Let us imagine an expert who, adjusting his scholarly spectacles and arming himself with official documents, sets out to study the structure of the German State "from a purely juridical point of view." After several hours of intellectual effort, he will discover that Hitler's Germany is a crystal-clear democratic republic (universal suffrage, a parliament which gives full power to the "Fuehrer," independent judicial authorities, etc., etc.) Every sane man, however, will cry out that a juridical "appraisal" of this nature is at best a display of *juridical cretinism*.

Democracy is based on the unconfined struggle of classes, of parties, of programs and ideas. If this struggle be stifled, there then remains only a dead shell, well suited for cloaking a fascist dictatorship. Contemporary jurisprudence is based on the struggle between the prosecution and the defense, a struggle which is conducted in certain judicial forms. Wherever the conflict between parties is stifled by means of extra-judicial violence, the judicial forms, whatever they may be, are only a cover for the inquisition. A genuine investigation of the Moscow trials cannot avoid embracing all their aspects. It will, of course, utilize the "verbatim" reports; not, however, as things in themselves, but as a constituent part of a great historical drama, whose determining factors remain behind the scenes of the judicial play.

V. AUTOBIOGRAPHY

In his summation of January 28, Vyshinsky said: "Trotsky and the Trotskyites have always been the agents of capitalism in the working-class movement." Vyshinsky denounced "the face of real, genuine Trotskyism—this old enemy of the workers and peasants, this old enemy of Socialism, loyal servant of capitalism." He painted the history of "Trotskyism which spent the more than thirty years of its existence on preparing for its final conversion into a storm detachment of fascism, into one of the departments of the fascist police."

While the foreign publicists of the G.P.U. (in the *Daily Worker, New Masses,* etc.) spend their energy trying to explain, with the aid of fine-spun hypotheses and historical analogies, how a revolutionary Marxist can change into a fascist in the sixth decade of his life, Vyshinsky approaches the question in an entirely different manner: Trotsky has *always* been an agent of capitalism and an enemy of the workers and peasants; for thirty-odd years he has been preparing himself to become an agent of fascism. Vyshinsky is saying what the publicists of the *New Masses* will say, only later on. That is why I prefer to deal with Vyshinsky. To the categorical assertions of the Prosecutor of the U.S.S.R., I oppose the equally categorical facts of my life.

Vyshinsky errs when he speaks of my thirty years of preparation for fascism. Facts, arithmetic, chronology, as well as logic, are not, generally speaking, the strong points of this accusation. Indeed, last month marked the completion of the fortieth year of my uninterrupted participation in the working-class movement under the banner of Marxism.

At eighteen I organized illegally the "Workers' Union of Southern Russia," numbering more than 200 workers. Using a hectograph, I edited a revolutionary paper, *Nashe Delo* ("Our Cause"). At the time of my first exile to Siberia (1900–1902), I participated in the creation of the "Siberian Union of Struggle for the Emancipation of the Working Class." After my flight abroad, I joined the Social-Democratic organization "Iskra," headed by Plekhanov, Lenin and others. In 1905 I did leading work in the first Petersburg Soviet of Workers' Deputies.

I spent four and a half years in prison, was twice exiled to Siberia, where I spent about two and a half years. I escaped twice from Siberia. In two periods I spent about twelve years in exile under Tsarism. In 1915 in Germany I was sentenced in contumacy to prison for anti-war activities. I was expelled from France for the same "crime," arrested in Spain, and interned by the British Government in a Canadian concentration camp. It was in this manner that I performed my function as "an agent of capitalism."

The tale of the Stalinist historians that until 1917 I had been a Menshevik is one of their customary falsifications. From the day Bolshevism and Menshevism took form politically and organizationally (1904), I remained formally outside of both factions, but, as is shown by the three Russian revolutions, my political line, in spite of conflicts and polemics, coincided in every fundamental way with the line of Lenin.

The most important disagreement between Lenin and me

in those years was my hope that through unification with the Mensheviks the majority of them could be pushed onto the path of revolution. In this burning question, Lenin was entirely right. Nevertheless, it must be said that in 1917 the tendencies toward "unification" were very strong among the Bolsheviks. On November 1st, 1917, at the meeting of the Petrograd Party Committee, Lenin said in this connection: "Trotsky long ago said that unification is impossible. Trotsky understood this, and from that time on there has been no better Bolshevik."

From the end of 1904, I defended the view that the Russian revolution could end only in the *dictatorship of the proletariat,* which, in its turn, must lead to the Socialist transformation of society, given the victorious development of the world revolution. A minority of my present adversaries considered this perspective fantastic right up to April, 1917, and inimically labelled it "Trotskyism," opposing to it the program of the bourgeois democratic republic. As for the overwhelming majority of the present bureaucracy, they did not adhere to the Soviet power until after the victorious termination of the Civil War.

During the years of my exile I participated in the workers' movement in Austria, Switzerland, France and the United States. I think of the years of my exile with gratitude—they gave me the possibility of coming closer to the life of the world working class and of changing internationalism from an abstract concept into the driving force of the rest of my life.

During the war, first in Switzerland and then in France, I carried on propaganda against the chauvinism consuming the Second International. For more than two years I published in Paris, under the military censorship, a Russian daily newspaper, in the spirit of revolutionary internationalism. In my work I was closely connected with the internationalist elements in France and took part, together with their representatives, in the international conference of opponents of chauvinism in Zimmerwald (1915). I continued in the same work during my two months' stay in the United States.

After my arrival in Petrograd (May 5th, 1917) from the Canadian concentration camp where I taught the ideas of Liebknecht and Luxemburg to the imprisoned German sailors, I took a direct part in the preparation and organization of the October Revolution, particularly during the four decisive months when Lenin was forced to hide in Finland.

In 1918, in an article in which his task was to *limit* my role in the October Revolution, Stalin was nevertheless forced to write: "All the work of practical organization of the insurrection was carried out under the immediate leadership of the chairman of the Petrograd Soviet, Comrade Trotsky. We can say with certainty that the swift passing of the garrison to the side of the Soviet and the bold execution of the work of the Military Revolutionary Committee the Party owes principally and above all to Comrade Trotsky." (*Pravda,* No. 241, Nov. 6th, 1918.)

This did not prevent Stalin from writing six years later:

"Comrade Trotsky, a comparatively new man in our Party in the period of October, neither did nor could play a *special* part, either in the Party or in the October Revolution." (J. Stalin, "Trotskyism or Leninism," pp. 68–69.)

At the present time the Stalin school, with the aid of its own scientific methods, in which both the court and the prosecution are educated, considers it beyond dispute that I did not direct the October Revolution but was opposed to it. However, these historical falsifications do not concern *my* autobiography, but the biography of Stalin.

After the October Revolution, I was in office for about nine years. I took a direct part in the building of the Soviet state, revolutionary diplomacy, the Red Army, economic organization, and the Communist International. For three years I directly led the Civil War. In this harsh work I was obliged to resort to drastic measures. For these I bear full responsibility before the world working class and before history. The justification of rigorous measures lay in their historical necessity and progressive character, in their correspondence with the fundamental interest of the working class. To all repressive measures dictated by the conditions of civil war, I gave their real designation, and I have given a public accounting for them before the working masses. I had nothing to hide from the people, as today I have nothing to hide from the Commission.

When in certain circles of the Party, not without the behind-the-scenes participation of Stalin, opposition arose to my methods of directing the Civil War, Lenin in July, 1919, on his own initiative and in a fashion wholly unexpected by me, handed me a sheet of blank paper, on the bottom of which he had written: "Comrades, knowing the harsh character of Comrade Trotsky's orders, I am so convinced, so absolutely convinced, of the rightness, expediency and necessity, for the good of our cause, of the orders he has given, that I give them my full support."

There is no date on the paper. In case of need, the date was to be inserted by myself. Lenin's caution in everything that concerned his relations to the workers is known. Nevertheless, he considered it possible to countersign in advance an order coming from me, even though on these orders often depended the fate of great numbers of men. Lenin, did not fear that I would abuse my power. I may add that not once did I make use of this *carte blanche* given me by Lenin. But this document is testimony to the exceptional confidence of a man whom I consider to be the highest model of revolutionary morality.

I participated directly in the drafting of the programmatic documents and tactical theses of the Third International. The principal reports at the congresses on the international situation were shared by Lenin and me. The programmatic manifestoes of the first five congresses were written by me. I leave to Stalin's prosecutors to explain what place this activity occupied on my road to fascism. As far as I am concerned, I still stand firmly today by the principles which, hand in hand with Lenin, I put forward as the basis of the Communist International.

I broke with the ruling bureaucracy when, due to historical causes which cannot be adequately dealt with here, it was transformed into a conservative, privileged caste. The reasons for the break are set down and sealed at every stage in official documents, books, and articles, accessible for general verification.

I have defended Soviet democracy against bureaucratic absolutism; the raising of the living standard of the masses against excessive privileges at the top; systematic industrialization and collectivization in the interests of the toilers; finally, international policy in the spirit of revolutionary internationalism against nationalist conservatism. In my last book, "The Revolution Betrayed," I attempted to explain theoretically why the isolated Soviet state, on the basis of a backward economy, has extruded the monstrous pyramid of the bureaucracy, which has almost automatically been crowned by an uncontrolled and "infallible" leader.

Stifling the party by means of the police apparatus and crushing the opposition, the ruling clique banished me, at the beginning of 1928, to Central Asia. On my refusal to cease political activity in exile, it deported me to Turkey at the beginning of 1929. There I began to publish the *Bulletin of the Opposition,* on the basis of the same program I had defended in Russia, and entered into relations with ideological companions, still very few at that time, in all parts of the world.

On February 20th, 1932, the Soviet bureaucracy deprived me and the members of my family who were abroad, of Soviet citizenship. My daughter Zinaida, who was abroad temporarily for medical treatment, was thus deprived of the possibility of returning to the U.S.S.R. to rejoin her husband and children. She committed suicide on January 5th, 1933.

I am presenting a list of my most important books and pamphlets, which have been completely or partly written during my last period of exile and deportation. According to the calculations of my young collaborators, who in all my work have given and are giving me devoted and irreplaceable aid, I have written 5,000 printed pages while abroad, without counting my articles and letters, which together would comprise several thousand pages more. May I add that I do not write with facility? I make numerous verifications and corrections. My literary work and my correspondence, therefore, have constituted the principal content of my life in the past nine years. The political line of my books, articles and letters speaks for itself. The citations given by Vyshinsky from my works represent, as I will prove, gross falsification—that is to say, a necessary element of the whole judicial frame-up.

In the course of the years from 1923 to 1933, with respect to the Soviet state, its leading party and the Communist International, I held the view expressed in those chiseled words: *Reform, but not revolution.* This position was fed by the hope that with favorable developments in Europe, the Left Opposition could regenerate the Bolshevik Party by pacific means, democratically reform the Soviet state, and set the Communist International back on the path of Marxism. It was only the victory of Hitler, prepared by the fatal policy of the Kremlin, and the complete inability of the Comintern to draw any lessons from the tragic experience of Germany, which convinced me and my ideological companions that the old Bolshevik Party and the Third International were forever dead, as far as the cause of Socialism was concerned. Thus disappeared the only legal lever with which one could hope to effect a peaceful, democratic reform of the Soviet state.

Since the latter part of 1933, I have become more and more convinced that for the emancipation of the toiling masses of the U.S.S.R. and of the social basis established by the October Revolution from the new parasitic caste, a *political* revolution is historically inevitable. Naturally, a problem of such tremendous magnitude provoked an impassioned ideological struggle on an international scale.

The political degeneration of the Comintern, completely shackled by the Soviet bureaucracy, led to the necessity for launching the slogan of the *Fourth International* and for drafting the bases of its program. The books, articles and bulletins of discussion which relate to this are at the disposal of the Commission, and present the best proof that it is a question not of "camouflage" but of an intense, impassioned ideological struggle on the basis of the traditions of the first congresses of the Communist International. I have been continually in correspondence with dozens of old and hundreds of young friends in all parts of the world, and I can say with assurance and pride that precisely from this youth will come the firmest and most reliable proletarian fighters of the new epoch which is opening.

Renouncing the hope of *peaceful* reform of the Soviet state does not mean, however, renouncing the *defense* of the Soviet state. As is particularly demonstrated in the collection of extracts from my articles in the past ten years ("In Defense of the Soviet Union"), which recently appeared in New York, I have invariably and implacably fought against all vacillation on the question of the defense of the U.S.S.R. I have broken more than once with friends on this question. In my book, "The Revolution Betrayed," I theoretically proved the idea that war menaces not only the Soviet bureaucracy, but also the new social basis of the U.S.S.R., which represents a tremendous step forward in the development of mankind. From this flows the absolute duty of every revolutionist to defend the U.S.S.R. against imperialism, *despite* the Soviet bureaucracy.

My writings in the same period give an unequivocal picture of my attitude toward fascism. From the first period of my exile abroad, I sounded the alarm on the question of the rising fascist wave in Germany. The Comintern accused me of "over-estimating" fascism and of becoming "panicky" before it. I demanded the united front of all organizations of the working class. To this the Comintern opposed the idiotic theory of "social-fascism." I demanded the systematic organization of workers' militias. The Comintern countered with bragging about future victories. I pointed out that the U.S.S.R. would find itself greatly menaced in case of a victory for Hitler. The well known writer, Ossietzky, printed my articles in his magazine, and commented on them with great sympathy. All to no avail. The Soviet bureaucracy usurped the authority of the October Revolution only to convert it into an obstacle to the victory of the revolution in other countries. Without the policy of Stalin, we should not have had the victory of Hitler! The Moscow trials, to a considerable degree, were born of the Kremlin's need to force the world to forget its criminal policy in Germany. "If it is demonstrated that Trotsky is an agent of fascism, who will then consider the program and tactics of the Fourth International?" Such were Stalin's calculations.

It is quite well known that during the war every internationalist was declared to be an agent of the enemy government. So it was in the case of Rosa Luxemburg, Karl Liebknecht, Otto Ruehle and others in Germany, of my French friends (Monatte, Rosmer, Loriot, etc.), of Eugene Debs and others in the United States, and finally of Lenin and myself in Russia. The British Government imprisoned me in a concentration camp in March, 1917, on the charge, inspired by the Tsarist Okhrana, that in agreement with the German high command I attempted to overthrow the provisional government of Miliukov-Kerensky. Today this accusation seems a plagiarism from Stalin and Vyshinsky. In fact, it is Stalin and

Vyshinsky who are plagiarizing from the Tsarist counter-espionage system and the British Intelligence Service.

On April 16th, 1917, when I was in the concentration camp with German sailors, Lenin wrote in *Pravda:* "Can one even for a moment believe the trustworthiness of the statement . . . that Trotsky, the former chairman of the Soviet of Workers' Deputies in Petersburg in 1905—a revolutionist who has devoted decades to the disinterested service of revolution—that this man had anything to do with a scheme subsidized by the German Government? This is clearly a monstrous and unscrupulous slander against a revolutionist." (*Pravda,* No. 34).

"How fresh these words sound now," I wrote on October 21, 1927—I repeat, in 1927!—"in this epoch of contemptible slanders against the Opposition, differing in no essential from the slanders against the Bolsheviks in 1917."

Thus, ten years ago—that is, long before the creation of the "unified" and "parallel" centers and before the "flight" of Pyatakov to Oslo—Stalin was already flinging against the Opposition all the insinuations and calumnies that Vyshinsky later converted into an indictment. However, if Lenin in 1917 thought that my revolutionary past of twenty years was in itself sufficient refutation of these filthy insinuations, I make bold to think that the twenty years which have since elapsed—important enough in themselves—entitle me to cite my autobiography as one of the most important arguments against the Moscow indictment.

VI. MY 'JURIDICAL' SITUATION

The very necessity of having to "justify" oneself against the charge of being in league with Hitler and the Mikado indicates the full depth of the reaction which today is conquering a great portion of our planet, and particularly the

U.S.S.R. But none of us can leap over historically conditioned stages. I put my time and my energy at the disposal of the Commission with entire willingness. It is superfluous to remark that I have and can have no secrets from the Commission. The Commission will itself understand the necessity of being guided by caution with respect to third parties, especially subjects of fascist lands and of the Soviet Union. I am ready to answer *all* questions and to place at the disposal of the Commission all my correspondence, personal as well as political.

At the same time, I think it necessary to state in advance that I do not at all regard myself as a "defendant" before the bar of public opinion. There is not even a formal basis for such a characterization. The Moscow authorities did not indict me in a single one of the trials. And that is, of course, not accidental. To indict me they would have had to summon me before the court, or to demand my extradition. For this purpose they would have had to announce the date of the trial, and to publish the indictment at least some weeks before the opening of the court proceedings. But Moscow could not even go that far. Their whole plan was to take public opinion by surprise, and to have the Pritts and Durantys ready in advance as commentators and reporters. They could have asked my extradition only by opening the question in a French, Norwegian or Mexican court, before the eyes of the world press. But that would have meant for the Kremlin to court a cruel failure! For this very reason, the two trials were not a prosecution of myself and my son, *but only a slander against us, carried out by means of a legal process, without notification, without summons, behind our backs.*

The verdict of the latest trial states that Trotsky and Sedov "having been convicted . . . of personally directing the treacherous activities . . . in the event of their being discovered on the territory of the U.S.S.R., are liable to immediate arrest and trial." I leave aside the question of the technical means by which Stalin hopes to "discover" me and my son on Soviet territory (apparently by means of the same technique which permitted the G.P.U., on the night of November 7th, 1936, to "discover" a part of my archives in a historical institute in Paris and to transport them in substantial diplomatic valises to Moscow). The fact which, above all others, commands attention is that the verdict, after declaring us "convicted," although we have not been indicted and examined, promises to deliver us to the court for trial, in the event of our being discovered. In this way I and my son have *already* been "convicted" but *not yet* tried. The object of this nonsensical but not accidental formulation is to arm the G.P.U. with the possibility of shooting us upon "discovery," without any judicial procedure whatsoever. Stalin cannot permit himself the luxury of a public arraignment of us, even in the U.S.S.R.!

The most cynical among the agents of Moscow, including the Soviet diplomat Troyanovsky, raise the following argument: "Criminals cannot choose their own judges." In its general form, this idea is correct. It is only necessary to determine on which side of the dividing line are the criminals. If one accepts the view that the real criminals are the organizers of the Moscow trials—and that is the opinion of wide and growing circles—can one then permit them to set themselves up as judges of their own case? Just because of this the Commission of Inquiry stands above both parties.

VII. THREE CATEGORIES OF PROOFS

The territory covered by the Moscow trials is immense. If I assumed the task of refuting before you all the false accusations directed against me, if only those contained in the official reports of the two most important Moscow trials, I would be forced to take up too much time. It is sufficient to recall that my name is met on almost every page, and more than once. I hope that I shall have the opportunity to speak more fully before the entire Commission. Now I am forced to impose severe limitations upon myself. For the time being, I am compelled to leave aside a whole series of questions, each of importance for the refutation of the charges. For a series of other questions, still more important, I must confine myself to a short résumé, noting only the general outline of the conclusions which I hope to present in the future to the Commission. On the other hand, I will attempt to bring out the crucial points of the Soviet trials, principled as well as empiric in nature, and to clarify them as much as possible. These crucial points lie on three planes:

1. The foreign apologists of the G.P.U. monotonously repeat the selfsame argument: It is impossible to admit that responsible, veteran politicians accused themselves of crimes they had never committed. But these gentlemen obstinately refuse to apply the same common-sense criterion not to the confessions, but to the crimes themselves. Yet it is much more appropriate to the latter.

My point of departure is that the accused were responsible individuals—that is, normal—and consequently could not knowingly carry out absurd crimes directed against their ideas, their whole past, and their present interests.

In planning a crime, each of the accused had what from the juridical point of view can be called freedom of choice. He could commit the crime, or refrain from doing so. He considered whether the crime was expedient, whether it corresponded to his aims, whether the means employed were reasonable, etc.—in a word, he behaved as a free and responsible person.

The situation, however, changes radically when the real or pretended criminal falls into the hands of the G.P.U., for whom, because of political reasons, it is necessary at all costs to obtain certain testimony. Here the "criminal" ceases to be himself. It is not he who decides; everything is decided for him.

That is why, before I deal with the question whether or not the accused acted in the trials in accordance with the laws of common sense, another preliminary question must be posed: Could the accused have perpetrated the incredible crimes to which they confessed?

Was the assassination of Kirov advantageous to the Opposition? And if not, was it not advantageous to the bureaucracy to ascribe the assassination of Kirov to the Opposition, whatever the cost?

Was it advantageous for the Opposition to commit acts of sabotage, to cause mine explosions, and to organize railroad wrecks? And if not, was it not advantageous for the bureaucracy to place the responsibility for the mistakes and accidents in industry on the Opposition?

Was it advantageous for the Opposition to enter into an alliance with Hitler and the Mikado? And, if not, was it not advantageous for the bureaucracy to obtain from the Opposition the confession that it was in alliance with Hitler and the Mikado?

Qui prodest? It is enough to formulate this question clearly and precisely, in order to have the first outlines of the answer already apparent.

2. In the last trial, as in all the preceding ones, the only bases of the charges are the standardized monologues of the accused, who, repeating the thoughts and expressions of the Prosecutor, outdo one another in confessing, and invariably name me the principal organizer of the plot. How explain this fact?

In his summation, Vyshinsky tries this time to justify the absence of objective proofs by the considerations that the conspirators did not have membership cards, did not keep records, etc., etc. These miserable arguments appear doubly miserable on Russian soil, where plots and trials stretch out over many decades. The conspirators write pseudo-conventional letters. But these letters can be seized during raids, and then constitute serious evidence. The conspirators quite frequently have recourse to chemical ink. But the Tsarist police hundreds of times seized such letters and presented them in court. Among the plotters there are provocateurs who give the police concrete information about the progress of the plot, and make it possible to seize documents, laboratories, and even the conspirators themselves at the scene of the crime. We find nothing like that in the trials of Stalin-Vyshinsky. Despite the five-year duration of the most grandiose of all plots, with ramifications in all parts of the country and connections across the western and eastern borders, despite the innumerable raids and seizures and even thefts of archives, the G.P.U. has not been able to present to the tribunal a single piece of concrete evidence. The defendants refer only to their real or pretended conversations about the plot. The judicial inquiry is a conversation about conversations. The "plot" has no flesh and blood.

On the other hand, the history of the revolutionary and counter-revolutionary struggle alike knows of no case in which dozens of seasoned conspirators, over a period of years, committed unparalleled crimes, and, after their arrest, despite the absence of evidence, confessed without exception, betraying one another and furiously blasting their absent "leader." How do criminals who yesterday assassinated leaders, shattered industry, prepared war and the dismemberment of the country, today so docilely sing the Prosecutor's tune?

These two fundamental features of the Moscow trials—*the absence of evidence* and *the epidemic character of the confessions*—can but arouse suspicion in every thinking man. *The objective verification of the confessions,* therefore, assumes so much the more importance. Yet the court not only did not make such a verification, but, on the contrary, avoided it from every side. We must take this verification upon ourselves. To be sure, it is not possible in all the cases. But there is no need for that. It will be entirely sufficient for us, as a beginning, to show that in many extremely important instances the confessions are in complete contradiction with the objective facts. The more the confessions are standardized, the more they will be discredited by the revelation that some of them are false.

The number of instances in which the testimony of the accused—their denunciations of themselves and others—falls to pieces when confronted with the facts, is very large. That has already been made sufficiently apparent here during the inquiry. The experience of the Moscow trials shows that a frame-up on such a colossal scale is too much even for the most powerful police apparatus in the world. There are too many people and circumstances, characteristics and dates, interests and documents, which do not fit into the framework of a ready-made libretto! The calendar stubbornly maintains its prerogatives, and the seasons of Norway do not bow even before Vyshinsky. If one approaches the question in its artistic aspect, such a task—the dramatic concordance of hundreds of people and innumerable circumstances—would have been too much even for Shakespeare. But the G.P.U. does not have Shakespeares at its beck and call. In so far as it is a question of "events" in the U.S.S.R., the external semblance of concordance is maintained by inquisitorial violence. All—the defendants, the witnesses and the experts—chorus their confirmation of materially impossible facts. But the situation changes abruptly when it is necessary to extend the threads abroad. Yet, without threads abroad, leading to me, "Public Enemy Number One," the trials would lose most of their political importance. That is why the G.P.U. was forced to risk dangerous and most unfortunate combinations with Holtzman, Olberg, David, Berman-Yurin, Romm, and Pyatakov.

The choice of objects for analysis and refutation thus unfolds by itself from the "facts" which the accusation alleges against me and my son. Thus, the refutation of Holtzman's assertion about his visit to me in Copenhagen, the refutation of Romm's testimony about his meeting with me in the Bois de Boulogne, and the refutation of Pyatakov's account of his flight to Oslo, are not only important in themselves, since they pull down the main props of the charges against me and my son, but also because they permit one to peer behind the scenes of Moscow jurisprudence in its entirety and to illumine the methods which are there employed.

Such are the first two stages of my analysis. If we succeed in demonstrating that, on the one hand, the so-called "crimes" contradict the psychology and the interests of the defendants, and that, on the other hand—at least in several typical cases—the confessions contradict facts established with precision, we accomplish, by the same token, a very great task for the refutation of the indictment as a whole.

3. To be sure, even then there remain not a few questions which demand answers. Chief among them are: Why, then, did the accused, after twenty-five, thirty, or more years of revolutionary work, agree to take upon themselves such monstrous and degrading accusations? How did the G.P.U. achieve this? Why did not a single one of the accused cry out openly before the court against the frame-up? Etc., etc. In the nature of the case, I am not obliged to answer these questions. We could not here question Yagoda (he is now being questioned himself by Yezhov), or Yezhov, or Vyshinsky, or Stalin, or, above all, their victims, the majority of whom, indeed, have already been shot. That is why the Commission cannot fully uncover the inquisitorial technique of the Moscow trials. But the mainsprings are already apparent. The accused are not Trotskyites, nor Oppositionists, nor fighters, but docile capitulators. The G.P.U. had educated them for these trials for years. That is why I think it extremely important, for the understanding of the mechanics of the

confessions, to bring out the psychology of the capitulators as a political group, and to give a personal characterization of the most important defendants of the two trials. I have in mind not arbitrary psychological improvisations, constructed after the event in the interests of the defense, but objective characterizations based on unimpeachable documents which pertain to various parts of the period which interests us. I have no lack of such materials. On the contrary, my dossiers are bursting with facts and citations. That is why I choose one example—the clearest and most typical, namely: Radek.

Already on June 14th, 1929, I wrote of the influence exerted by the powerful Thermidorian tendencies on the Opposition itself: ". . . We have seen by a whole series of examples how old Bolsheviks, striving to preserve themselves and the traditions of the Party, tended with all their strength to go with the Opposition; some until 1925, others until 1927, and yet others until 1929. But in the long run, they did not hold out; their nerves gave way. Radek is now the most headlong and vociferous ideologue of the elements of this type." (*Bulletin of the Opposition,* Nos. 1–2, July, 1929.) It was none other than Radek who in the last trial provided the "philosophy" for the "criminal activities" of the "Trotskyites." According to the testimony of many foreign journalists, Radek's testimony seemed in the trial to be the least artificial, the least constructed on a model, the most deserving of confidence. All the more important is it to demonstrate by this example that on the defendants' bench sat not the real Radek, as nature and his political past made him, but a "robot" out of the laboratory of the G.P.U. If I succeed in demonstrating this with full conviction, then the role of the others accused in these trials will also be clarified to a considerable extent. That does not mean, obviously, that I discard the clarification of each separate personality. On the contrary, I hope that the Commission will give me the opportunity to carry out this task at the next stage of its work. But now, because of the limitations imposed by time, I am obliged to concentrate attention only on the most important circumstances and the most typical figures. The work of the Commission, I hope, will only gain thereby.

VIII. THE MATHEMATICAL SERIES OF FRAME-UPS

1. It can be unimpeachably established, on the basis of official sources, that the preparations for the assassination of Kirov were made with the knowledge of the G.P.U. The head of the Leningrad section of the G.P.U., Medved, and eleven other G.P.U. agents, were sentenced to prison because "they possessed information concerning the preparations for the attempt on S.M. Kirov . . . and failed to take the necessary measures." One should imagine that the police agents who "knew" ought to have figured as witnesses at all the subsequent trials. But we never hear again of Medved and his collaborators; they "knew" too much. The Kirov assassination serves as the basis of all the subsequent trials. Yet at the basis of the Kirov assassination lies a colossal provocation of the G.P.U., attested to by the verdict of the military court on December 29th, 1934. The task of the organizers of the provocation consisted in implicating the Opposition, and especially myself, in a terrorist deed (through the medium of the Latvian consul Bisseneks, an *agent provocateur* employed by the G.P.U. who has likewise vanished without leaving a trace). The bullet fired by Nikolayev was hardly part of the program, but rather one of the incidental costs of the amalgam.

This question was analyzed in my pamphlet, "The Kirov Assassination and the Stalin Bureaucracy," written at the beginning of 1935. Neither the Soviet authorities nor their foreign agents even attempted to answer my arguments, which were based exclusively on official Moscow documents.

2. As we have proved before the Commission, seven trials took place in the U.S.S.R., with the Kirov assassination as their starting point: (a) the trial of Nikolayev et al, December 28–29th, 1934; (b) the trial of Zinoviev-Kamenev, January 15–16th, 1935; (c) the trial of Medved et al, January 23d, 1935; (d) the trial of Kamenev et al, July, 1935; (e) the trial of Zinoviev-Kamenev, August, 1936; (f) the Novosibirsk trial, November 19–22nd, 1936; (g) the trial of Pyatakov-Radek, January 23–30th, 1937. These trials are seven variations played on one and the same theme. Among the different variations there is almost no discernible connection. Each contradicts the others in fundamentals and details. In each trial, different persons organize the assassination of Kirov, by different means and for different political objectives. The mere comparison of the official Soviet documents is ample proof that at least six of these seven trials must be frame-ups. In fact, all seven are frame-ups.

3. The Zinoviev-Kamenev trial (August, 1936) has already inspired a voluminous literature, which contains a number of extremely important arguments, testimonies and weighty considerations in support of the idea that the trial constitutes a malicious frame-up by the G.P.U. I mention here the following books:

Leon Sedov: "Livre Rouge sur le Procès de Moscou."
Leon Sedov: "Lettre au Comité Central de la Ligue des Droits de l'Homme et à la Ligue."
Max Shachtman: "Behind the Moscow Trial."
Francis Heisler: "The First Two Moscow Trials."
Victor Serge: "Destin d'une Révolution, U.R.S.S., 1917–1937."

Victor Serge: "16 Fusillés. Où Va la Révolution Russe?"
Friedrich Adler: "The Witchcraft Trial in Moscow."

Not one of these books, which represent the product of serious and careful study, has thus far met with a critical appraisal—leaving aside the gutter epithets of the Comintern press, which for a long time has not been taken seriously by any self-respecting person. The fundamental arguments of these books are also my arguments.

4. As far back as 1926, the Stalin clique tried to charge various oppositional groups with "anti-Soviet" propaganda, connections with White Guards, capitalist tendencies, espionage, terrorist aims, and, finally, the preparation of armed insurrection. All these attempts, which are akin to rough drafts, have left their traces in official decrees, in newspaper articles, in documents of the Opposition. If we were to arrange chronologically these rough drafts of and experiments in frame-up, we would obtain something in the nature of a *geometric progression of false accusations,* whose end terms are the indictments in the last trials. Thus we uncover the "law of frame-ups" and the mystery of the alleged Trotskyite conspiracy vanishes into thin air.

5. It is the same with the improbable declarations of the defendants, which at first sight contradict all the laws of human psychology. *Ritualistic recantations on the part of Oppositionists* date back to 1924, and especially the end of 1927. If we collate the texts of these recantations on the basis of the leading Soviet press—often consecutive recantations made by the self-same individuals—we obtain a second geometric progression, the end terms of which are the nightmarish confessions of Zinoviev, Kamenev, Pyatakov, Radek and others at the judicial trials. A political and psychological analysis of this accessible and unimpeachable material wholly and conclusively reveals the inquisitorial mechanics of the recantations.

6. To the mathematical series of frame-ups and the mathematical series of recantations, there corresponds *a third mathematical series—that of warnings and predictions.* The author of these lines and his closest co-thinkers followed attentively the intrigues and provocations of the G.P.U., and in advance, on the basis of particular facts and symptoms, warned time and again, in letters as well as in the press, against Stalin's provocative plans and against amalgams in preparation. The very expression, "Stalinist amalgam," was given currency by us almost eight years before the Kirov assassination and the spectacular trials which followed it. The relevant documentary proofs have been placed at the disposal of the Commission of Inquiry. They show with absolute incontestability that what is involved is not an underground Trotskyite conspiracy first unearthed in some startling manner in 1936, but a systematic conspiracy of the G.P.U. against the Opposition, with the aim of imputing to it sabotage, espionage, assassinations and the preparation of insurrections.

7. All the "recantations" extorted from tens of thousands of Oppositionists since 1924 contained by compulsion a barb directed at me. All who wished to reenter the Party, the exiles wrote in the *Bulletin of the Opposition* (No. 7, Nov.–Dec., 1929), were ordered to "give us Trotsky's head." In conformity with the previously indicated law of the mathematical series, the threads of all the crimes of terrorism, treason and sabotage, in the trials of 1936–1937, lead invariably to me and my son. But our entire activity during the past eight years was, as is well known, carried on abroad. Here the Commission enjoys, as we have already seen, a great advantage. The G.P.U. abroad had no approach to me, since I was always surrounded by a circle of devoted friends. On November 7th, 1936, the G.P.U. stole a *portion* of my archives in Paris, but until now they have been unable to make any use of them. The Commission has at its

disposal *all* my archives, the testimonies of my friends and acquaintances, not to speak of my own depositions. The Commission is in a position to compare my private correspondence with my articles and books, and in this way determine whether my activity bears the slightest tinge of double-dealing.

8. But that is not all. The directives of the conspiracy allegedly came from abroad (France, Copenhagen, Norway). Thanks to an unusually fortunate combination of circumstances, the Commission has full opportunity to determine whether any of the alleged conspirators—Holtzman, Berman-Yurin, Fritz David, Vladimir Romm and Pyatakov—did visit me at the specified times and places. While the Moscow court has not lifted a finger to prove (by questions regarding passports, visas, hotels, etc.) that these meetings and interviews really did take place, we are able here to solve a much more difficult problem: To prove with documents, depositions of witnesses, circumstances of time and place, that these meetings and interviews did not and could not have taken place. To employ legal terminology—I am able in all important instances, where exact dates are given, to establish an unshakable alibi.

9. If the criminal is not mentally deranged, but a responsible person and even an old and experienced politician, then his crime, however monstrous it may be, must fit in closely with his specific aims. Yet in the Moscow trials there is no such concordance of aims and methods. The state Prosecutor at different trials ascribes different aims to the very same defendants (now a naked "struggle for power" under the Soviet régime, now a struggle for the "restoration of capitalism"). In this question, likewise, defendants docilely take their cue from the prosecution. The methods to which the defendants resort are absurd from the standpoint of their supposed aims; certainly, they appear to be specially created to furnish the bureaucracy with the best possible pretext for

exterminating every kind of opposition.

The conclusions which flow from the initial stages of this investigation are, in my opinion, the following:

1. Despite long years of struggle against the Opposition, despite tens of thousands of raids, arrests, banishments, imprisonments, and hundreds of executions, the Soviet judicial authorities do not have at their disposal even a single substantial fact, not a shred of material proof, to confirm the truth of the accusations. This fact constitutes *the most damning evidence against Stalin.*

2. Even if we concede for sake of argument that all or some of the defendants really committed the monstrous crimes attributed to them, their stereotyped references to me as the principal organizer of the plot do not carry any weight. Moral degenerates capable of preparing railroad wrecks, poisoning workers, entering into relations with the Gestapo, etc., would naturally have attempted to ingratiate themselves with the bureaucracy by means of standardized slanders against its principal adversary.

3. The testimony of the defendants—at least those whose political physiognomy is well known—is, however, false also in those sections where they expose their own criminal activity. We are not dealing with bandits, or with criminal perverts, or with moral degenerates, but with the unfortunate victims of the most horrible inquisitorial system of all time.

4. The trials are a judicial comedy (hard as it is to use the word "comedy" in this connection), whose lines have been worked out over a number of years on the basis of countless experiments by the organs of the G.P.U., under the direct and personal supervision of Stalin.

5. The charges against old revolutionists ("Trotskyites") of desertion to fascism, of alliance with Hitler and the Mikado, etc., were dictated by the same political causes as the accusations of the French Thermidorians against Robespierre and

other Jacobins guillotined by them, that they had become "Royalists" and "agents of Pitt." Analogous historical causes produce analogous historical consequences.

IX. THE POLITICAL BASIS OF THE ACCUSATION: TERRORISM

If terror is feasible for one side, why should it be considered as excluded for the other? With all its seductive symmetry, this reasoning is corrupt to the core. It is altogether inadmissible to place the terror of a dictatorship against an opposition on the same plane with the terror of an opposition against a dictatorship. To the ruling clique, the preparation of murders through the medium of a court or from behind an ambush is purely and simply a question of police technique. In the event of a failure, some second-rank agents can always be sacrificed. On the part of an opposition, terror presupposes the concentration of all forces upon preparing acts of terror, with the foreknowledge that every one of such acts, whether successful or unsuccessful, will evoke in reply the destruction of scores of its best men. An opposition could by no means permit itself such an insane squandering of its forces. It is precisely for this, and for no other reason, that the Comintern does not resort to terroristic attempts in the countries of fascist dictatorships. The Opposition is as little inclined to the policy of suicide as the Comintern.

According to the indictment, which banks on ignorance and mental laziness, the "Trotskyites" resolved to destroy the ruling group in order in this way to clear for themselves the path to power. The average Philistine, especially if he wears the badge of a "Friend of the U.S.S.R.," reasons as follows: "The Oppositionists could not but strive for power, and could not but hate the ruling group. Why, then, shouldn't they really resort to terror?" In other words, for the Philistine the matter ends where in reality it only begins. The leaders of the Opposition are neither upstarts nor novices. It is not at all a question of whether they were striving for power. Every serious political tendency strives to conquer power. The question is: Could the Oppositionists, educated upon the enormous experience of the revolutionary movement, have entertained even a moment's belief that terror is capable of bringing them closer to power? Russian history, Marxist theory, political psychology reply: No, they could not!

At this point, the problem of terror requires clarification, even though briefly, from the standpoint of history and theory. In so far as I am delineated as the initiator of the "anti-Soviet terror," I am compelled to invest my exposition with an autobiographic character. In 1902, I had no sooner arrived in London from Siberia, after almost five years of prison and exile, than I had the occasion, in a memorial article devoted to the bicentennial of the fortress of Schlüsselburg, with its hard-labor prison, to enumerate the revolutionists there tortured to death. "The shades of these martyrs clamor for vengeance . . ." But immediately thereafter I added: "Not for a personal, but for a revolutionary vengeance. Not for the execution of ministers, but for the execution of the autocracy." These lines were directed wholly against individual terror. Their author was twenty-three years of age. From the earliest days of his revolutionary activity he was already an opponent of terror. From 1902 to 1905 I delivered, in various cities in Europe, before Russian students and émigrés, scores of political reports against terrorist ideology, which at the beginning of the century was once again spreading among the Russian youth.

Beginning with the 'eighties of the past century, two generations of Russian Marxists in their personal experience lived through the era of terror, learned from its tragic lessons, and organically instilled in themselves a negative attitude toward the heroic adventurism of lone individuals. Plekhanov, the founder of Russian Marxism; Lenin, the leader of Bolshevism; Martov, the most eminent representative of Menshevism; all dedicated thousands of pages and hundreds of speeches to the struggle against the tactic of terror.

The ideological inspiration emanating from these senior Marxists nourished my attitude toward the revolutionary alchemy of the shut-in intellectual circles during my adolescence. For us, the Russian revolutionists, the problem of terror was a life-and-death matter in the political as well as the personal meaning of the term. For us, a terrorist was not a character from a novel, but a living and familiar being. In exile we lived for years side by side with the terrorists of the older generation. In prisons and in police custody we met with terrorists of our own age. We tapped out messages back and forth, in the Peter and Paul fortress, with terrorists condemned to death. How many hours, how many days, were spent in passionate discussion! How many times did we break personal relationships on this most burning of all questions! The Russian literature on terrorism, nourished by and reflecting these debates, would fill a large library.

Isolated terroristic explosions are inevitable whenever political oppression transgresses certain boundaries. Such acts almost always have a symptomatic character. But politics that sanctifies terror, raising it into a system—that is a different thing. "Terrorist work," I wrote in 1909, "in its very essence demands such a concentration of energy upon 'the supreme moment,' such an over-estimation of personal heroism and, lastly, such a hermetically concealed conspiracy as . . . excludes completely any agitational and organizational activity among the masses . . . Struggling against terrorism, the Marxian intelligentsia defended their right or their duty not to withdraw from the working-class districts for the sake of tunneling mines underneath the Grand Ducal and Tsarist palaces." It is impossible to fool or outwit history.

In the long run, history puts everybody in his place. The basic property of terror as a system is to destroy that organization which by means of chemical compounds seeks to compensate for its own lack of political strength. There are, of course, historical conditions where terror can introduce confusion among the governing ranks. But in that case who is it that can reap the fruits? At all events, not the terrorist organization itself, and not the masses behind whose backs the duel takes place. Thus, the liberal Russian bourgeois, in their day, invariably sympathized with terrorism. The reason is plain. In 1909 I wrote: "In so far as terror introduces disorganization and demoralization into the ranks of the Government (at the price of disorganizing and demoralizing the ranks of the revolutionists), to that extent it plays into the hands of none other than the liberals themselves." The very same idea, expressed virtually in the same words, we meet a quarter of a century later in connection with the Kirov assassination.

The very fact of individual acts of terror is an infallible token of the political backwardness of a country and the feebleness of the progressive forces there. The revolution of 1905, which disclosed the vast strength of the proletariat, put an end to the romanticism of the single combat between a handful of intellectuals and Tsarism. "Terrorism in Russia is dead," I reiterated in a number of articles. ". . . Terror has migrated far to the East—to the provinces of Punjab and Bengal. . . . It may be that in other countries of the Orient terrorism is still destined to pass through an epoch of flowering. But in Russia it is already a part of the heritage of history."

In 1907 I found myself again in exile. The whip of counter-revolution was savagely at work, and the Russian colonies in European cities became very numerous. The entire period of my second emigration was devoted to reports and articles against the terror of vengeance and despair. In 1909 it was revealed that at the head of the terrorist organization of the so-called "Social Revolutionists" stood an *agent provocateur,* Azef. "In the blind alley of terrorism," I wrote, "the hand of provocation rules with assurance" (January, 1910). Terrorism has always remained for me nothing but a "blind alley."

During the same period I wrote: "The irreconcilable attitude of the Russian Social Democracy towards the bureaucratized terror of the revolution as a means of struggle against the terrorist bureaucracy of Tsarism has met with bewilderment and condemnation not only among the Russian liberals but also among the European Socialists." Both the latter and the former accused us of "doctrinairism." On our part, we, the Russian Marxists, attributed this sympathy for Russian terrorism to the opportunism of the leaders of European Social Democracy who had become accustomed to transferring their hopes from the masses to the ruling summits. "Whoever stalks a ministerial portfolio . . . as well as those who, clasping an infernal machine beneath a cloak, stalk the Minister himself, must equally *overestimate* the Minister—his personality and his post. For them the *system* itself disappears or recedes far away, and there remains only the *individual* invested with power." We shall presently, in connection with the Kirov assassination, meet once again with this thought, which runs through the decades of my activity.

In 1911 terrorist moods arose among certain groups of Austrian workers. Upon the request of Friedrich Adler, editor of *Der Kampf,* the theoretical monthly of the Austrian Social Democracy, I wrote in November, 1911, an article on terrorism for this publication.

> Whether or not a terrorist attempt, even if "successful," introduces confusion in the ruling circles depends upon the concrete political circumstances. In any case

> this confusion can be only of short duration. The capitalist state does not rest upon ministers and cannot be destroyed together with them. The classes whom the state serves will always find new men—the mechanism remains intact and continues to function. But much deeper is that confusion which the terrorist attempts introduce into the ranks of the working masses. If it is enough to arm oneself with a revolver to reach the goal, then to what end are the endeavors of the class struggle? If a pinch of powder and a slug of lead are ample to shoot the enemy through the neck, where is the need of a class organization? If there is any rhyme or reason in scaring titled personages with the noise of an explosion, what need is there for a party? What is the need of meetings, mass agitation, elections, when it is so easy to take aim at the Ministerial bench from the Parliamentary gallery? Individual terrorism in our eyes is inadmissible precisely for the reason that it *lowers the masses in their own consciousness,* reconciles them to impotence, and directs their glances and hopes towards the great avenger and emancipator who will some day come and accomplish his mission.

Five years later, in the heat of the imperialist war, Friedrich Adler, who had spurred me to write this article, killed the Austrian Minister-President Stuergkh in a Vienna restaurant. The heroic skeptic and opportunist was unable to find any other outlet for his indignation and despair. My sympathies were, naturally, not on the side of the Hapsburg dignitary. However, to the individualist action of Friedrich Adler I counterposed the form of activity of Karl Liebknecht who, during war-time, went out into a Berlin square to distribute a revolutionary manifesto to the workers.

On the 28th of December, 1934, four weeks after the Kirov assassination, at a time when the Stalinist judiciary did not know as yet in which direction to aim the barb of their "justice," I wrote in the *Bulletin of the Opposition:*

> . . . If Marxists have categorically condemned individual terrorism . . . even when the shots were directed against the agents of the Tsarist Government and of capitalist exploitation, then all the more relentlessly will they condemn and reject the criminal adventurism of terrorist acts directed against the bureaucratic representatives of the first workers' state in history. The subjective motivations of Nikolayev and his associates are a matter of indifference to us. The road to hell is paved with good intentions. So long as the Soviet bureaucracy has not been removed by the proletariat—a task which will eventually be accomplished—it fulfills a necessary function in the defense of the workers' state. Should terrorism of the Nikolayev type spread, it could, given other unfavorable circumstances, render service only to the fascist counter-revolution.
>
> Only political fakers who bank on imbeciles would endeavor to lay Nikolayev at the door of the Left Opposition, even if only in the guise of the Zinoviev group as it existed in 1926–1927. The terrorist organization of the Communist youth is fostered not by the Left Opposition but by the bureaucracy, by its internal decomposition. *Individual terrorism in its very essence is bureaucratism turned inside out.* For Marxists this law was not discovered yesterday. Bureaucratism has no confidence in the masses, and endeavors to substitute itself for the masses. Terrorism behaves in the same manner; it wants to make the masses happy without asking their participation. The Stalinist bureaucracy has created a revolting leader-cult, endowing leaders with divine attributes. The "hero" cult is also the religion of terrorism, only with a minus sign. The Nikolayevs imagine that

> all that is necessary is to remove a few leaders by means of revolvers, in order for history to take another course. Communist-terrorists, as an ideological grouping, are of the same flesh and blood as the Stalinist bureaucracy. [January, 1935, No. 41.]

These lines, as you have had the opportunity to convince yourselves, were not written *ad hoc.* They summarize the experience of a whole lifetime, which was in turn fed by the experience of two generations.

Already in the epoch of Tsarism, a young Marxist who went over to the ranks of the terrorist party was a comparatively rare phenomenon—rare enough to cause people to point their fingers. But at that time there was at least taking place an unceasing theoretical struggle between two tendencies; the publications of the two parties were waging a bitter polemic; public disputes did not cease for a single day. Now, on the other hand, they want to force us to believe that not young revolutionists, but old leaders of Russian Marxism, with the tradition of three revolutions behind them, have suddenly, without criticism, without discussion, without a single word of explanation, turned their faces toward the terrorism which they had always rejected, as a method of political suicide. The very possibility of such an accusation shows to what depths of debasement the Stalinist bureaucracy has dragged the official theoretical and political thought, not to mention Soviet justice. To political convictions gained through experience, sealed by theory, tempered in the white heat of the history of mankind, the falsifiers counterpose inchoate, contradictory, and utterly unsubstantiated testimonies of suspicious nonentities.

"Yes," said Stalin and his agents, "we cannot deny that Trotsky did warn with the very same insistence against terrorist adventurism, not only in Russia but also in other countries in various stages of political development and under different conditions. But we have discovered in his lifetime a few instances which constitute an exception to the rule: In a conspiratorial letter he wrote to one Dreitzer [and which nobody ever saw]; in a conversation with Holtzman who was brought to Trotsky in Copenhagen by his son [who was at the time in Berlin]; in a conversation with Berman-Yurin and David [of whom I never heard prior to the first reports of the court proceedings], in these four or five instances Trotsky issued to his followers [who were in reality my bitterest opponents] terrorist instructions [without making any attempt either to justify them or to tie them up with the cause to which my entire life has been devoted]. If Trotsky had imparted his programmatic views on terror orally and in writing to hundreds of thousands and millions in the course of forty years, it was only in order to deceive them. His real views he expounded in strictest secrecy to the Bermans and the Davids." And then a miracle came to pass! These inarticulate "instructions," which rest wholly on the mental level of the Messrs. Vyshinsky, proved sufficient for this: That hundreds of old Marxists—automatically, without any objections, without uttering a syllable—turned to the path of terror. Such is the political basis of the trial of the sixteen (Zinoviev et al.). In other words, the trial of the sixteen completely lacks a political basis.

X. THE KIROV ASSASSINATION

In the Moscow trials much was said about vast projects, plans, and criminal preparations. But all this took place in the realm of conversation, or rather of reminiscences of conversation, which the defendants had allegedly had with one another in the past. As we have already said, the trial record consists of nothing but conversation about conversations. The only real crime was the assassination of Kirov. But this very crime was committed neither by Oppositionists nor by capitulators passed off for Oppositionists by the G.P.U., but by one, perhaps by two or three, young Communists who fell into a trap baited by the G.P.U. provocateurs. Regardless of whether the provocateurs intended to carry things to the point of assassination, the responsibility for the crime falls upon the G.P.U., which could not have acted in so serious a matter without direct orders from Stalin.

On what are these assertions based? All the materials needed for the answer are to be found in the official documents of Moscow. An analysis of these was made in my pamphlet, "The Kirov Assassination and the Soviet Bureaucracy" (1935), in Leon Sedov's "Livre Rouge," and in other works. Here I will briefly summarize the conclusions of this analysis:

1. Zinoviev, Kamenev and the others could not have organized the assassination of Kirov, because this assassination was utterly meaningless politically. Kirov was of the second rank, without any significance by himself. Who in the world had heard of Kirov before he was assassinated? Even if one were to admit the absurd notion that Zinoviev, Kamenev and the others had taken the path of individual terror, they could not but have understood that the murder of Kirov, promising no political results whatever, would provoke furious reprisals against all those suspected and mistrusted, and make further oppositional activity of any kind—especially terrorism—more difficult. Real terrorists would have begun with Stalin, as a matter of course. Among the accused were members of the Central Committee and of the Government, who had free access everywhere. The assassination of Stalin would have presented no difficulties for them. If the "capitulators" did not commit this act, it was only because they were serving Stalin, and were not struggling against him or seeking to assassinate him.

2. The assassination of Kirov threw the ruling caste into a state of panicky confusion. Although Nikolayev's identity was immediately established, the first Government announcement did not link the assassination with the Opposition, but with White Guards who allegedly had entered the U.S.S.R. from Poland, Rumania and other border states. No fewer than 104 "White Guards" were shot, according to the official figures. Over a period of more than two weeks, the Government found it necessary by means of summary executions to turn public attention in another direction and to efface certain clues. The White Guard version was abandoned only on the sixteenth day. No official explanation has yet been given of the first period of Government panic signalized by more than a hundred corpses.

3. In the Soviet press nothing whatever was said about how and under what circumstances Nikolayev killed Kirov, or about the post Nikolayev held, or his relations with Kirov, etc. Everything concrete, whether concerning the political or the purely external facts of the assassination, still remains shrouded in darkness. The G.P.U. cannot tell what happened without revealing its initiative in the organization of the Kirov assassination.

4. Although Nikolayev and the thirteen other executed men said everything that was asked of them (and I assume that Nikolayev and his companions were subjected to physical torture), they did not have a word to say about the participation of Zinoviev, Bakayev, Kamenev, or any other "Trotskyite" in the assassination. The G.P.U., obviously, never once questioned them along these lines. All the circumstances of the affair were still too fresh, the role of provocation still too obvious, and the G.P.U. was less concerned about hunting for traces of the Opposition than with covering up its own tracks.

5. While the Radek-Pyatakov trial, which directly involved the governments of foreign states, took place publicly,

the trial of the Komsomol Nikolayev, who killed Kirov, was conducted on December 28–29th, 1934, behind closed doors. Why? Apparently not for diplomatic, but for internal reasons; the G.P.U. could not make a public display of its own work. It was necessary, first, quietly to exterminate the direct participants in the assassination and those closely connected with them; carefully to clean the hands of the G.P.U., and only then to fall upon the Opposition.

6. The Kirov assassination aroused such alarm within the bureaucracy itself that Stalin, on whom the shadow of suspicion had to fall in the circles of the initiated, was compelled to find a scapegoat. On January 23d, 1935, the trial of twelve leading functionaries of the Leningrad department of the G.P.U., headed by Medved, took place. The indictment admitted that Medved and his collaborators had "information about the preparation of the assassination of Kirov" in advance. The verdict declared that they "took no measures for the timely exposure and prevention" of the work of the terrorist group, *"although they had every possibility of so doing."* Greater candor one cannot ask. All the accused were condemned to from two to ten years at hard labor. It is plain that: the G.P.U., through its provocateurs, played with Kirov's head in order to involve the Opposition in the affair and then expose the conspiracy. Nikolayev, however, fired his shot without waiting for Medved's permission, and thereby cruelly compromised the amalgam. Stalin used Medved as a scapegoat.

7. Our analysis finds complete confirmation in the role of the Latvian Consul Bisseneks, an obvious agent of the G.P.U. The Consul, according to Nikolayev's confession, was in direct touch with him, gave him 5,000 rubles for carrying out his terroristic deed, and for no reason asked Nikolayev for a letter to Trotsky. Vyshinsky, in order to link my name at least indirectly to the Kirov case, introduced this astonishing episode into the indictment (Janu-

ary, 1935), and thereby completely revealed the provocative role of the Consul. The name of the Consul was made public, however, only at the direct insistence of the diplomatic corps. Thereupon he disappeared from the scene without leaving a trace. In subsequent trials, Bisseneks was not once mentioned, although he had been in direct contact with the assassin and had financed the assassination. All the other "organizers" of the terrorist act against Kirov (Bakayev, Kamenev, Zinoviev, Mrachkovsky, etc.) knew nothing about the Consul Bisseneks and did not once mention his name. It is difficult to imagine a cruder, more confused, more shameless provocation!

8. Only after the real terrorists and their friends and accomplices—doubtless including the G.P.U. agents involved in the conspiracy—had been wiped out, did Stalin consider it possible to go after the Opposition in earnest. The G.P.U. arrested the leaders of the former Zinovievists and divided them into two groups. The Tass agency, on December 22d, said that there was not "sufficient basis for turning over to the court" the seven leading personalities, former members of the Central Committee. The less important members of the group, in accordance with the traditional technique of the G.P.U., were left beneath the suspended sword of Damocles. Under the threat of death, some of them testified against Zinoviev, Kamenev and the others. The testimony, it is true, did not deal with terror, but with "counter-revolutionary activity" in general (dissatisfaction, criticism of Stalin's policies, etc.). But this testimony sufficed to force Zinoviev, Kamenev and the others to confess their "moral" responsibility for the terrorist act. At this price, Zinoviev and Kamenev (temporarily!) bought themselves off from the charge of direct participation in the assassination of Kirov.

9. On January 26th, 1935, I wrote to American friends (the letter was printed in the *Bulletin of the Opposition*, No.

42, February, 1935): "The strategy developed around Kirov's corpse won Stalin no great laurels. But just for this reason he can neither stop nor retreat. *Stalin will have to cover up the misbegotten amalgam by new, more extensive and . . . more successful amalgams. We must meet them well armed!*" The trials of 1936–37 confirmed this warning.

XI. WHO DREW UP THE LIST OF 'VICTIMS' OF THE TERROR? (THE MOLOTOV 'AFFAIR')

The Zinoviev-Kamenev trial (August, 1936) was constructed entirely on the basis of terror. The task of the so-called "center" consisted in destroying the Government through the assassination of the "leaders," and seizing power. With a careful comparison of the two trials, that of Zinoviev-Kamenev and that of Pyatakov-Radek, it is not difficult to convince oneself that the list of leaders who were doomed to extermination was drawn up not by terrorists but by their supposed victims—that is, above all by Stalin. His personal authorship emerges in a most revealing fashion in the question of Molotov.

According to the indictment in the case of Zinoviev et al, "the united Trotskyite-Zinovievite terrorist center, after it had killed Comrade *Kirov,* did not confine itself to organizing the assassination of Comrade *Stalin* alone. The terrorist Trotskyite-Zinovievite center simultaneously carried on work to organize assassinations of other leaders of the Party, namely, Comrades *Voroshilov, Zhdanov, Kaganovich, Kossior, Orjonikidze* and *Postyshev.*" Molotov's name is absent from this list. The listing of the victims singled out by the Trotskyites varied in the mouths of the several defendants at various stages of the preliminary investigation and the trial. But on one point it remained unaltered; none of the defendants named Molotov. According to Reingold's statement during the preliminary investigation, "*Zinoviev's* main instructions amounted to the following: The blow must be directed against *Stalin, Kaganovich* and *Kirov.*" At the evening session of August 19th, 1936, the same Reingold testified: "That is why the only method of struggle available is terroristic acts against Stalin and his closest comrades-in-arms, Kirov, Voroshilov, Kaganovich, Orjonikidze, Postyshev, Kossior and the others." Molotov does not figure amongst the "closest comrades-in-arms." Mrachkovsky testified: ". . . We were to kill *Stalin, Voroshilov* and *Kaganovich.* Stalin was to be killed first." Again Molotov is not mentioned.

The matter is not otherwise with my "terrorist directives." ". . . Dreitzer's group . . . received instructions to murder *Voroshilov* directly from *Trotsky,*" says the indictment. According to Mrachkovsky, Trotsky in the autumn of 1932 "once again emphasized the necessity of killing Stalin, Voroshilov and Kirov." In December, 1934, Mrachkovsky, through Dreitzer, received a letter from Trotsky urging him "to accelerate the assassination of Stalin and Voroshilov." Dreitzer testifies to the same thing. Berman-Yurin states: "Trotsky also said that in addition to Stalin it was necessary to assassinate Kaganovich and Voroshilov." Thus, in the course of some three years I gave instructions to assassinate Stalin, Voroshilov, Kirov and Kaganovich. There was no mention of Molotov. This circumstance is all the more remarkable because during the last years of my participation in the Political Bureau neither Kirov nor Kaganovich was a member of that body, and nobody considered them political figures, while Molotov occupied the first place after Stalin in the leading group. But Molotov is not only a member of the Political Bureau; he is also the head of the Government. His signature, alongside Stalin's, adorns the most important Government orders. Despite all that, the terrorists of the "unified center," as we have seen, obstinately ignore Molotov's existence. But—and this is the most astonishing thing—

Prosecutor Vyshinsky not only fails to evince surprise at this omission, but, on the contrary, himself considers that it is quite in the order of things. Thus, at the morning session of August 19th, Vyshinsky asked Zinoviev, as regards the prepared terrorist acts: "Against whom?"

"*Zinoviev:* Against the leaders.

"*Vyshinsky:* That is, against Comrades Stalin, Voroshilov and Kaganovich?"

The words "that is" leave no room for doubt: the Prosecutor officially excludes the head of the Government from the ranks of the leaders of the Party and the country. Finally, in drawing up the balance-sheet of the court hearings, the same Prosecutor, in his summation, thunders against the "Trotskyites," "who raised their hand against the leaders of our Party, against Comrades Stalin, Voroshilov, Zhdanov, Kaganovich, Orjonikidze, Kossior and Postyshev, against our leaders, the leaders of the Soviet state" (Session of Aug. 22d). The word "leaders" is repeated three times, but here again Molotov is not mentioned.

It is thus clearly indisputable that at the time of the lengthy preparation of the trial of the "unified center" there must have existed certain serious reasons for excluding Molotov from the list of "leaders." The uninitiated in the secrets of the heads of the Government are completely at a loss to understand why the terrorists deemed it necessary to kill Kirov, Postyshev, Kossior, Zhdanov—"leaders" of provincial stature—and to ignore Molotov, who, as is generally recognized, looms one head, if not two, above these candidates for killing. Already, in the "Livre Rouge," devoted to the Zinoviev-Kamenev trial, Sedov called attention to the ostracism of Molotov. Sedov writes: "Among the leaders listed by Stalin as those whom the terrorists allegedly intended to kill were included not only leaders of the first magnitude but even the Zhdanovs, the Kossiors and the Postyshevs. *But Molotov is not included.* In matters of this kind Stalin never makes slips . . ."

Where does the secret lie? In connection with the renunciation of the policies of the "third period," there circulated persistent and stubborn rumors of friction between Stalin and Molotov. These rumors found an indirect but unmistakable reflection in the Soviet press; Molotov was not quoted, extolled, or photographed, and at times was not even mentioned. The *Bulletin of the Opposition* remarked upon this fact more than once. It is incontestable in any case that in August, 1936, Stalin's chief comrade-in-arms in the struggle with all the Oppositionist groups was publicly and rudely ejected from the staff of the ruling heads of the state. Thus it is impossible to avoid the conclusion that the confessions of the accused, as well as my "directives," were intended to assist in resolving a specific episodic task: to elevate Kaganovich, Zhdanov and others to the rank of "leaders," and to discredit the old "leader," Molotov.

Perhaps, however, the matter is explained simply by the fact that at the time of the Zinoviev trial the judicial authorities did not yet have at their disposal the evidence on the attempts against Molotov? Such a hypothesis will not withstand the least criticism. The "evidence" in these trials, as has been said, does not exist in general; the verdict of August 23d, 1936, speaks of attempts (against Postyshev and Kossior) about which there is not a word in the court record. This consideration, however, which is not without importance of and by itself, is entirely overshadowed by comparison with the fact that the accused—and, above all, the members of the "center"—speak in their confessions not so much of attempts as of *plans* for attempts. It was exclusively a question of which persons the conspirators deemed it necessary to assassinate. The composition of the list of victims was consequently determined not by the materials of the preliminary investigation, but by a political appraisal of the leading figures. All the more astonishing is the fact that in the plans of the "center," as well as in my "directives," there entered all the possible and impossible candidates for martyrdom—except Molotov. Yet nobody ever considered Molotov a decorative figure like Kalinin. On the contrary, if one poses the question of who could replace Stalin, it is impossible to avoid answering that Molotov has incomparably greater chances than all the others.

Perhaps, however, the terrorists, on the basis of rumored discords among the leaders of the state, had simply decided to spare Molotov? As we shall see, this hypothesis will likewise not survive the test of examination. As a matter of fact, it was not the "terrorists" who spared Molotov, but it was Stalin who wished to create the impression that the terrorists did spare Molotov and thereby definitely break his opponent. Facts indicate that Stalin's design was crowned with complete success. Even before the August trial there could be observed a reconciliation between Stalin and Molotov. This immediately found a reflection in the pages of the Soviet press, which, at a signal from above, set about restoring Molotov in his former authority. One could, on the basis of *Pravda,* give a very clear and convincing picture of the gradual rehabilitation of Molotov in the course of the year 1936. In remarking upon this fact, the *Bulletin of the Opposition* (No. 50, May, 1936) said: "After the liquidation of the 'third period,' Molotov, as is well enough known, fell into semi-disgrace . . ." But finally he managed to get back into line. "During the last weeks he has delivered himself of several panegyrics of Stalin . . . By way of compensation . . . his name occupies the second place, and he himself is called the closest 'comrade-in-arms.'" In this question, as in many others, comparison of the official publications of the bureaucracy with the *Bulletin of the Opposition* resolves many enigmas.

The Zinoviev-Kamenev trial reflected the period which preceded the reconciliation; it was impossible at a moment's notice to change all the materials of the preliminary investigation! Furthermore, Stalin was not precipitate about a complete amnesty; Molotov had to be given an effective lesson. That is why Vyshinsky was still obliged in August to adhere to the former directive. On the other hand, the preparation of the Pyatakov-Radek trial took place already *after* the reconciliation. In conformity therewith, the list of victims is also changed, *not only as concerns the future but also as regards the past.* In his testimony of January 24th, Radek, referring to his interview with Mrachkovsky dating back to 1932, stated that he "did not have the slightest doubt that the acts were to be directed against Stalin and his immediate colleagues, against Kirov, Molotov, Voroshilov and Kaganovich." According to the testimony of the witness Loginov, at the morning session of January 25th, Pyatakov, at the beginning of the summer of 1935, "said that the Trotskyite parallel center . . . must quite definitely make preparations for terrorist acts against Stalin, Molotov, Voroshilov and Kaganovich . . ." Naturally, Pyatakov does not fail to confirm the deposition of Loginov. The defendants in the last trial, in contradistinction to the members of the unified "center," thus not only name Molotov among the intended victims, but also accord him first place after Stalin.

Who, then, drew up the list of proposed victims—the terrorists or the G.P.U.? The answer is plain: Stalin, through the G.P.U.! The hypothesis mentioned above, that the "Trotskyites" were aware of the friction between Stalin and Molotov and spared Molotov for political reasons, might be invested with a semblance of truth solely in the event that the "Trotskyites" engaged in the preparation of terrorist acts against Molotov only *after* his reconciliation with Stalin. But the "Trotskyites," it seems, were striving to kill Molotov as far back as 1932: they had merely "forgotten" to speak about it in August, 1936, and the Prosecutor "forgot" to remind them of it.

But no sooner had Molotov obtained political amnesty from Stalin than the memories of both the Prosecutor and the accused were instantly refreshed. And that is why we are witnesses to a miracle; despite the fact that Mrachkovsky himself in his testimony had spoken of the preparation of terrorist acts only against Stalin, Kirov, Voroshilov and Kaganovich, Radek, on the basis of a conversation with Mrachkovsky in 1932, retrospectively included Molotov's name in this list. Pyatakov spoke, supposedly to Loginov, about the preparation of attempts on Molotov at the beginning of the summer of 1935—that is, more than a year before the Zinoviev trial. Finally, the defendants Muralov, Shestov and Arnold spoke about the "actual" attempt on Molotov, which took place in the year 1934—more than two years before the trial of the "unified center"! The conclusions are absolutely clear; the defendants had as little freedom in their choice of "victims" as in all other respects. The list of those selected as the targets of the terrorists was in fact a list of leaders officially recommended to the masses. It was altered in accordance with the combinations at the top. It only remained for the defendants, as also for the Prosecutor, Vyshinsky, to conform to the totalitarian instructions.

There remains one more possible objection: But does not this whole machination appear too crude? To that we must reply: It is no more crude than all the other machinations in these infamous trials. The stage manager appeals to neither reason nor criticism. He aims to crush the authority of reason by the massiveness of the frame-up, signed and sealed by the firing squad.

XII. THE POLITICAL BASIS OF THE ACCUSATION: 'SABOTAGE'

The crudest part of the judicial frame-up, alike in design and execution, is the charge of sabotage against the "Trotskyites." This aspect of the trial, which constitutes one of the most important elements of the whole amalgam, has convinced nobody (if one excludes gentlemen of the type of Duranty and Company). The world learned, from the indictment and the proceedings, that all Soviet industry was virtually in the control of "a handful of Trotskyites." Nor were matters any better as regards transportation. But of what did the Trotskyite acts of sabotage really consist? In Pyatakov's confessions, corroborated by the testimony of his former subordinates who sat beside him on the prisoners' bench, it was revealed that: (a) plans for new factories were too slowly drafted, and revised time and again; (b) the construction of factories took far too long, and caused the immobilization of colossal sums; (c) enterprises were put into operation in an unfinished state and consequently were quickly ruined; (d) there were disproportions among the various sections of new plants, with the result that the productive capacity of the factories was reduced in the extreme; (e) the plants accumulated superfluous reserves of raw materials and supplies, thus transforming living capital into dead capital; (f) supplies were wildly squandered, etc. All these phenomena, long known as the *chronic diseases* of Soviet economic life, are now put forward as the fruits of a malicious conspiracy which Pyatakov led—naturally, under my orders.

However, it remains perfectly incomprehensible what, while all this went on, was the role of the state organs of industry and finance, and of the accounting authorities, not to speak of the Party, which has its nuclei in all institutions and enterprises. If one believes the indictment, the leadership of economy was not in the hands of the "genial, infallible leader," nor in the hands of his closest collaborators, the members of the Politburo and of the Government, but in the hands of an isolated man, already nine years in banishment and exile. How is one to understand this? According to a Moscow dispatch to the *New York Times* (March 25th, 1937), the new chief of heavy industry, V. Mezhlauk, at a meeting of his subordinates, revealed the criminal role of the saboteurs in the drawing up of *false plans*. But up to the time of Orjonikidze's death (February 18th, 1937), Mezhlauk himself was at the head of the State Planning Commission, whose special task was precisely to examine economic plans and projects. Thus, in its pursuit of frame-ups, the Soviet Government issues to itself a degrading certificate of bankruptcy. Not for nothing does the *Temps,* semi-official mouthpiece of the French ally, remark that it would have been better never to have let this part of the trial see daylight.

What has just been said about industry applies wholly to transportation as well. Railroad specialists calculate that the carrying capacity of a railroad has certain technical limits. From the time when Kaganovich took over the management of the transportation system, the "theory of limits" was officially declared to be a bourgeois prejudice; worse yet, the invention of saboteurs. Hundreds of engineers and technicians had to atone for their direct or indirect support of the "theory of limits." Undoubtedly many old specialists, trained under the conditions of capitalist economy, flagrantly underestimated the possibilities inherent in planned methods, and were consequently inclined to set extremely low norms. But that does not at all mean that the tempos of the economy depend solely on the inspiration and energy of the bureaucracy. The general industrial equipment of the country, the reciprocal interdependence of the various branches of industry, transportation and agriculture, the level of skill of the workers, the percentage of experienced engineers, and, lastly, the general material and cultural level of the population—these are the essential factors which have the last word in the fixing of limits. The effort of the bureaucracy to violate these factors by naked commands, reprisals and premiums ("Stakhanovism") inevitably exacts harsh penalties in the form of disorganization of plants, damage of machinery, a high proportion of damaged goods, accidents and disasters.

There is not the slightest ground for dragging a "Trotskyite conspiracy" into this matter.

The task of the prosecution is extremely complicated by the additional fact that from February, 1930, onwards, I exposed in the press, systematically and persistently, year in and year out, from one month to the next, the self-same vices of bureaucratized economy which are now being charged against a fantastic "Trotskyist" organization. I proved that Soviet industry required not *maximum* but *optimum* tempos—i.e., such tempos as would, by resting upon mutual correspondence among various sections of one and the same enterprise and among various enterprises, insure the uninterrupted growth of economy in the future. I wrote in the *Bulletin of the Opposition* on February 13th, 1930:

> Industry is racing towards a crisis, above all because of the monstrous bureaucratic methods of collating the plan. A five-year plan can be drafted, preserving the necessary proportions and guarantees, only on the condition of a free discussion of the tempos and the terms set, with the participation in the discussion of all the interested forces in industry, the working class, all its organizations, and above all the Party itself; with the free verification of the entire experience of Soviet economy in the recent period, including the monstrous mistakes of the leadership . . . A plan of socialist construction cannot be arrived at in the guise of an *a priori* departmental directive.

The "Trotskyites," we are told at every step, constitute an insignificant handful, isolated from and hated by the masses. It is for this very reason that they allegedly resorted to the methods of individual terror. The picture alters completely, however, when we come to sabotage. To be sure, a single man can throw sand into a machine or blow up a bridge.

But in the court we hear of such methods of sabotage as would be possible only if the entire administrative apparatus were in the hands of the saboteurs. Thus, the accused Shestov, a transparent *agent provocateur*, at the session of January 25th:

> And finally, at all the mines—the Prokopyevsk, the Anzherka and the Lenin Mines—the Stakhanov movement was sabotaged. Instructions were issued to worry the life out of the workers. Before a worker reached his place of work, he must be made to heap two hundred curses on the heads of the pit management. Impossible conditions of work were created. Normal work was rendered impossible, not only for Stakhanov methods but even for ordinary methods.

All that was done by the "Trotskyites"! Obviously, the whole administration from top to bottom was composed of "Trotskyites."

Not content with this, the prosecution also lists acts of sabotage which would be unrealizable without the active or at least passive support of the workers themselves. Thus, the President of the Court cites the following statement of the accused Muralov who, in his turn, cites the accused Boguslavsky: "Trotskyites on the railways . . . were putting locomotives out of commission, disrupting the traffic schedule and causing jams at the stations, thereby delaying the transportation of urgent freight." The crimes enumerated simply mean that the railroads were in the hands of the "Trotskyites." Not satisfied with this excerpt from Muralov's testimony, the President asks him:

> And quite lately Boguslavsky carried on wrecking activities on the construction of the Eiche-Sokol line?
>
> *Muralov:* Yes.

The President: And as a result disrupted the construction job?

Muralov: Yes.

And that is all. How Boguslavsky and two or three other "Trotskyites," without the support of the employees and workers, could have disrupted the construction work of a whole railroad line, remains entirely incomprehensible.

The dates of the sabotage are contradictory in the extreme. According to the most important testimony, sabotage in 1934 was "something new." But the aforementioned Shestov places the beginning of sabotage at the end of the year 1931. In the course of the court proceedings the dates are shifted, now forward, now backward. The mechanism of these shiftings is quite clear. Most of the concrete accusations of sabotage or "diversion" are based upon some mishap, failure or disaster which really occurred in industry or transportation. Beginning with the first Five-Year Plan there were not a few failures and accidents. The indictment chooses those which can be linked to one or another of the defendants. Hence flow the interminable jumps in the chronology of the sabotage. In any case, as far as one can make out, the general "directive" was first given by me only in 1934.

The most vicious manifestations of "sabotage" are now discovered in the chemical industry, where the internal proportions were especially grossly violated. Yet seven years ago, when the Soviet power first really began building this branch of industry, I wrote:

> For example, the solution of the question as to what place the *chemical industry* should occupy in the plan for the years immediately ahead can be prepared only by an open struggle among the various economic groupings and various branches of industry for their share of chemistry in the national economy. Soviet democracy is not

the demand of abstract politics, and still less of morality. It has become a matter of economic necessity.

What was the real situation in this respect? "Industrialization," I wrote in the same article, "is more and more kept going by the administrative whip. *Equipment and labor forces are being strained. The disproportions between the individual branches of industry are accumulating.*" Knowing only too well the Stalinist methods of self-defense, I added: "It is not difficult to forecast the response our analysis will evoke in official circles. Functionaries will say that we are speculating on a crisis. Scoundrels will add that we seek the downfall of the Soviet power . . . That will not stop us. Slanders pass, facts remain."

I do not intend to burden the record with citations. But I am ready to demonstrate with a collection of my articles in my hand that for seven years, on the basis of the official Soviet press reports, I untiringly warned against the ruinous consequences of skipping the period of laboratory preparation, of putting incomplete plants into operation, of supplanting technical training and correct organization by frantic and senseless reprisals, and, not infrequently, fantastic premiums. All the economic "crimes" referred to at the last trial were analyzed by me countless times—beginning in February, 1930, and ending in my latest book, "The Revolution Betrayed"—as the inevitable consequences of the bureaucratic system. I have not the slightest ground for boasting of my perspicacity. All I had to do was to follow attentively the official reports and draw rudimentary conclusions from the incontestable facts.

If the "sabotage" of Pyatakov and the others, as the indictment states, began actively only around the year 1934, how is one to explain the fact that already in the four preceding years I demanded the radical remedying of those diseases of Soviet industry which are now represented as due to the malicious activities of "Trotskyites"? But perhaps my critical work was mere "camouflage"? According to the real sense of that term, such camouflage could only have been intended to *conceal* crimes. Yet my criticism, on the contrary, *exposed* them. It thus transpires that while secretly organizing sabotage, I did everything in my power to draw the attention of the Government to the acts of "sabotage" and thereby—to the perpetrators. All this would have been extremely clever—if it were not so utterly nonsensical.

The system of Stalin and his police and prosecution agents is quite simple. For major accidents in plants, and especially for train wrecks, usually several employees were shot, often those who shortly before had been decorated for achieving high tempos. The result has been universal distrust and discontent. The last trial was intended to personify in Trotsky the causes for the accidents and disasters. Against Ormuzd, the spirit of good, was to be set the evil spirit Ahriman. Following the unchanging course of current Soviet legal procedure, all the accused naturally confessed their guilt. Is it any wonder? For the G.P.U. it is no great labor to place before a certain number of their victims the alternative: Either be shot immediately, or preserve a shadow of hope on the condition that you agree to appear in court in the guise of "Trotskyites," conscious saboteurs of industry and transportation. The rest requires no commentary.

The conduct of the Prosecutor in court constitutes in itself deadly evidence against the real conspirators. Vyshinsky limits himself to simple questions: "Do you confess yourself guilty of sabotage? Of organizing accidents and wrecks? Do you confess that the directives came from Trotsky?" But he never asks how the accused carried out their crimes in practice: how they succeeded in getting their wrecking plans adopted by the highest state institutions; in hiding the sabotage for years from their superiors and subordinates; in procuring the silence of local authorities, specialists, workers, etc. As always, Vyshinsky is the chief accomplice of the G.P.U. in the frame-up and the deception of public opinion.

The extent of the shamelessness of the inquisitors, moreover, is seen in the fact that the accused, on the persistent demand of the prosecution, declared—though, to be sure, not without reluctance—that they deliberately strove to cause as many human victims as possible, in order thus to inspire discontent among the workers. But that is not all. On March 24th—that is, just a few days ago—a dispatch from Moscow related the shooting of three "Trotskyites" for malicious arson of a school in Novosibirsk in which many children were burned to death. Permit me also to recall that my younger son, Sergei Sedov, was arrested on the charge of attempting the mass poisoning of workers. Let us for a moment imagine that the Government of the United States had, on the heels of the Texas school disaster which shocked the entire world, launched throughout the country a rabid campaign against the Comintern and charged it with the malicious extermination of children, and we get an approximate notion of the current policy of Stalin. Such vile charges, possible only in the polluted atmosphere of a totalitarian régime, bear their refutation within themselves.

XIII. THE POLITICAL BASIS OF THE ACCUSATION: THE ALLIANCE WITH HITLER AND THE MIKADO

To bolster up the all too improbable accusation of an alliance of the "Trotskyites" with Germany and Japan, the foreign attorneys of the G.P.U. are circulating the following versions:

1. Lenin, with the agreement of Ludendorff, crossed Germany during the war, in order to be able to carry out his revolutionary tasks.

2. The Bolshevik Government did not shrink from ced-

ing enormous territory and paying indemnity to Germany, in order to save the Soviet régime.

Conclusion: Why not admit that Trotsky entered into agreement with the same German General Staff in order to secure, through the cession of territory, the possibility of realizing his aims in the rest of the country?

This analogy represents, in reality, the most monstrous and poisonous slander against Lenin and the Bolshevik Party as a whole.

1. Lenin actually crossed Germany by utilizing the false hopes of Ludendorff that Russia would disintegrate as a result of internal struggle. But how did Lenin proceed in this matter?

(a) He did not conceal for a moment either his program or the purpose of his trip;

(b) He called in Switzerland a small conference of internationalists from various countries who fully approved his plan to travel to Russia through Germany;

(c) Lenin did not enter into any political agreement with the German authorities, and made the condition that no one was to enter his car during the passage across Germany;

(d) Immediately upon his arrival in Petrograd, Lenin explained before the Soviet and the laboring masses the purport and nature of his trip through Germany.

Audacity of decision and carefulness of preparation characterize Lenin also in this episode; but no less is he characterized by full and unconditional honesty towards the working class, to whom he is ready at any moment to render an accounting for each of his political steps.

2. The Bolshevik Government really did cede great territory to Germany after the peace of Brest-Litovsk, in order to save the Soviet régime in the rest of the country. But:

(a) The Soviet Government had no other choice;

(b) The decision was adopted not behind the backs of the people, but only after an open and public discussion;

(c) The Bolshevik Government did not for one moment conceal from the popular masses that the Brest-Litovsk peace signified a transitory and partial capitulation of the proletarian revolution to capitalism.

In this case, too, we have a full concordance of aims and methods and an unconditional honesty of the leadership before the public opinion of the toiling masses.

Now, let us see what sense there is in the accusation against me.

I have allegedly concluded an agreement with fascism and militarism on the following basis:

(a) I agree to renounce Socialism in favor of capitalism;

(b) I give the signal to destroy Soviet economy and exterminate workers and soldiers;

(c) I conceal from the whole world my real aims as well as my methods;

(d) My entire public political activity serves only to fool the working masses about my real plans, into which Hitler, the Mikado and their agents are initiated.

The activity ascribed to me has consequently nothing in common with the above-mentioned example of Lenin's activity, but in every respect represents its direct opposite.

The Brest-Litovsk peace was a temporary retreat, a compulsory compromise, with the object of saving the Soviet power and realizing the revolutionary program. A secret alliance with Hitler and the Mikado is a betrayal of the interests of the working class for the sake of personal power, or rather the illusion of power—i.e., the basest of all possible crimes.

To be sure, some attorneys of the G.P.U. are inclined to dilute with water the over-potent wine of Stalin. It may be, they say, that Trotsky agreed only verbally to restore capitalism, but in reality was preparing to realize in the remaining territory a policy in the spirit of his program. In the first place, this variant contradicts the confessions of Radek,

Pyatakov and others. But, independently of this fact, it is just as senseless as the official version given in the indictment. The program of the Opposition is the program of international Socialism. How could an experienced adult imagine that Hitler and the Mikado, possessing a complete list of his treasons and abominable crimes, would permit him to realize a revolutionary program? How could one hope, anyway, to achieve power at the price of acts of high treason in the service of a foreign general staff? Is it not clear in advance that Hitler and the Mikado, after using such an agent to the limit, would fling him aside like a squeezed lemon? Could the conspirators, headed by six members of Lenin's Political Bureau, have failed to understand this? The accusation is thus internally meaningless in both its variants—the official variant, which speaks of the restoration of capitalism, and the semi-official variant, which concedes to the conspirators a hidden design—to fool Hitler and the Mikado.

To this it is necessary to add that it must have been clear in advance to the conspirators that the conspiracy could in no case remain undiscovered. At the Zinoviev-Kamenev trial, Olberg and others testified that the "collaboration" of the "Trotskyites" with the Gestapo was not an exception but a "system." Consequently, scores and hundreds of people must have been initiated into this system. The commission of terrorist acts—and especially sabotage—would, in its turn, require hundreds and even thousands of agents. Discovery, therefore, would be absolutely unavoidable—with simultaneous exposure of the alliance of the "Trotskyites" with the fascist and Japanese spies. Could anyone but a lunatic hope to arrive at power in this way?

But that is still not all. The acts of sabotage, like acts of terror, presuppose on the part of their executors a readiness for self-sacrifice. When a German fascist or a Japanese agent risks his head in the U.S.S.R., he is impelled by such powerful stimuli as patriotism, nationalism, chauvinism. By what stimuli could the "Trotskyites" have been driven? Let us grant that the "leaders," having lost their senses, hoped to seize power by such methods. But what were the driving motives of Berman-Yurin, David, Olberg, Arnold and many others who, taking the actual path of terrorism and sabotage, thereby condemned themselves to certain death? A man is capable of sacrificing his life only for the sake of some high ideal, even though it be a mistaken one. What high ideal did the "Trotskyites" have? The desire to dismember the U.S.S.R.? The desire to give Trotsky power for the sake of the restoration of capitalism? Sympathy for German fascism? The desire to supply Japan with oil for a war against the United States? Neither the official nor the semi-official version furnishes any answer whatever to the question: For the sake of what were the hundreds of "executors" ready to stake their heads? The whole construction of the indictment is mechanical. It ignores the psychology of living men. In this sense, the indictment is the logical product of a totalitarian régime, with its disregard and contempt for men when they do not happen to be "leaders."

The second fantastic theory which is put into circulation by the friends of the G.P.U. declares that in view of my general position I am presumably politically interested in expediting war. The usual line of argument is as follows: Trotsky is for the international revolution. It is well known that war often produces revolution. Ergo, Trotsky must be interested in expediting war.

People who believe this, or who ascribe such ideas to me, have a very feeble conception of revolution, war, and their interdependence.

War has in fact often expedited revolution. But precisely for this reason it has often led to abortive results. War sharpens social contradictions and mass discontent. But that is insufficient for the *triumph* of the proletarian revolution.

Without a revolutionary party rooted in the masses, the revolutionary situation leads to the most cruel defeats. The task is not to "expedite" war—for this, unfortunately, the imperialists of all countries are working, not unsuccessfully. The task is to utilize the time which the imperialists still leave to the working masses for the building of a revolutionary party and revolutionary trade unions.

It is in the vital interest of the proletarian revolution that the outbreak of war be delayed as long as possible, that the maximum possible time be gained for preparation. The more firm, the more courageous, the more revolutionary the conduct of the toilers, the more the imperialists will hesitate, the more surely will it be possible to postpone war, the greater will be the chances that the revolution will occur *prior to* war and perhaps make war itself *impossible.*

It is precisely because the Fourth International stands for the international revolution that it is one of the factors working *against* war; for—I repeat—the only check to a new world war is the fear, among the propertied classes, of revolution.

War, we are told, creates a revolutionary situation. But have we had a lack of revolutionary situations in the period from 1917 until today? Let us glance briefly at the post-war period:

A revolutionary situation in Germany, 1918–1919.

A revolutionary situation in Austria and Hungary at the same time.

A revolutionary situation in Germany in 1923 (the Ruhr occupation).

A revolutionary situation in China, 1925–1927, which was not immediately preceded by a war.

Profound revolutionary convulsions in Poland in 1926.

A revolutionary situation in Germany, 1931–1933.

A revolution in Spain, 1931–1937.

A pre-revolutionary situation in France, beginning in 1934.

A pre-revolutionary situation in Belgium at present.

Despite the superabundance of revolutionary situations, the toiling masses have not carried off any revolutionary victory in any of the enumerated cases. What is lacking? A party capable of utilizing the revolutionary situation.

The Social Democracy has sufficiently demonstrated in Germany that it is hostile to the revolution. It now demonstrates this anew in France (Léon Blum). The Comintern, for its part, having usurped the authority of the October Revolution, disorganizes the revolutionary movement in all countries. The Comintern has, in reality, regardless of its intentions, become the best assistant of fascism and reaction in general.

Precisely for this reason there rises before the proletariat the iron necessity of building new parties and a new international which correspond to the character of our epoch—an epoch of great social convulsions and permanent war danger.

If, in the event of a new war, the masses are not headed by a bold, courageous, consistent revolutionary party, tested through experience and enjoying the confidence of the masses, a new revolutionary situation would throw society back. A war may, under such circumstances, terminate not with a victorious revolution, but with the crumbling of our whole civilization. One would have to be pathetically blind not to see this danger.

War and revolution are the gravest and most tragic phenomena in human history. You cannot joke with them. They do not tolerate dilettantism. We must understand clearly the interrelationship of war and revolution. We must understand no less clearly the interrelationship of the *objective* revolutionary factors, which cannot be induced at will, and the *subjective* factor of the revolution—the conscious vanguard of the proletariat, its party. It is necessary to prepare this party with the utmost energy.

Can one admit for a moment that the so-called "Trotskyites," the extreme left wing, hounded and persecuted by all other tendencies, would devote their forces to contemptible adventures, sabotage and war provocation, instead of building a new revolutionary party capable of meeting the revolutionary situation well armed? Only the cynical contempt of Stalin and his school for world public opinion, together with Stalin's primitive police cunning, are capable of creating such a monstrous and nonsensical accusation!

I have explained in scores of articles and hundreds of letters that a military defeat of the U.S.S.R. would inevitably signify the restoration of capitalism in a semi-colonial form under a fascist political régime, the dismemberment of the country, and the wrecking of the October Revolution. Indignant at the policy of the Stalinist bureaucracy, many of my former political friends in various countries arrived at the conclusion that we cannot take upon ourselves the obligation *"unconditionally"* to defend the U.S.S.R. Opposing this attitude, I argued that it is impermissible to identify the bureaucracy with the U.S.S.R.; that the new social foundation of the U.S.S.R. must be unconditionally defended against imperialism; that the Bonapartist bureaucracy will be overthrown by the toiling masses only on condition that the foundation of the new economic régime of the U.S.S.R. is preserved. On this question I broke publicly and demonstratively with dozens of old and hundreds of new friends. My archives contain an enormous correspondence devoted to the question of the defense of the U.S.S.R. Finally, my latest book, "The Revolution Betrayed," gives a detailed analysis of the military and diplomatic policies of the U.S.S.R., expressly from the standpoint of the defense of the country. Now, by the grace of the G.P.U., it appears that while breaking with many close friends who did not understand the necessity of *unconditional* defense of the U.S.S.R. against imperialism, I was actually concluding alliances with the imperialists and urging the destruction of the economic foundation of the U.S.S.R.

It is impossible to discern, moreover, exactly what Germany and Japan contributed in practice to the alliance. The "Trotskyites" sold their heads to the Mikado and Hitler; what did they receive in exchange? Money is the sinews of war; did the "Trotskyites" at least receive money from Germany and Japan? Not a word of this in the trial. The Prosecutor is not even interested in this question. At the same time it appears, from references to other financial sources, that neither Germany nor Japan gave any money. What, then, *did* they give to the "Trotskyites"? Throughout the trial this question receives not a shadow of an answer. The alliance with Germany and Japan rests wholly in the domain of metaphysics. To this I would add that it is the most dastardly of all the police metaphysics in the history of mankind!

XIV. COPENHAGEN

The "Copenhagen" chapter of the trial of the sixteen (Zinoviev and others) is, by virtue of the accumulation of contradictions and absurdities, the most monstrous of all its chapters. The facts relating to Copenhagen have been established and analyzed long since in a number of books, beginning with "Le Livre Rouge" by L. Sedov. I have presented to the Commission the most important documents and evidence, and I reserve the right to present supplementary material in the further course of the investigation. That is why I will be as brief as possible concerning the "terrorist week" in Copenhagen.

I accepted the invitation of the Danish students to lecture in Copenhagen, in the hope that I would succeed in remaining in Denmark or in securing admission to another European country. This hope was not realized because of pressure exerted by the Soviet Government on the Danish Government (threat of economic boycott). In order to deter other countries from offering me their hospitality, the G.P.U. decided to transform my week's stay in Copenhagen into a week of "terrorist plotting." Holtzman, Berman-Yurin and David allegedly visited me in the Danish capital. All three arrived independently of one another, and each one received separate terrorist instructions from me. Olberg, who was in Berlin, received similar instructions from me from Copenhagen, but in the shape of a letter.

The most important witness against myself and Leon Sedov is *Holtzman,* an old member of the party and personally known to both of us. Holtzman's confessions during the preliminary investigation, and at the trial itself, are distinguished from the confessions of most of the defendants by their extreme meagerness. Suffice it to say that, despite the insistence of the Prosecutor, Holtzman denied any participation whatever in the terrorist activity. Holtzman's testimony must be regarded as the least common denominator of all the depositions. Holtzman agreed to admit only the terrorist plans of *Trotsky* and the participation in them of *Leon Sedov.* It is precisely the meagerness of Holtzman's confessions which at first glance invests them with exceptional weight. Yet it is precisely the testimony of Holtzman which crumbles into dust upon contact with facts. The documents and affidavits presented by me, which I refrain from enumerating again, establish with certainty that, contrary to Holtzman's declaration, Sedov was *not* in Copenhagen, and consequently could not have brought Holtzman to me, especially from a Hotel Bristol demolished in 1917. Moreover, the statements of the three other "terrorists"—Berman-Yurin, David, and

Olberg—improbable in themselves, undermine one another and conclusively invalidate the testimony of Holtzman.

Holtzman, Berman-Yurin and David were, one and all, according to their own words, sent to Copenhagen by Leon Sedov. But the presence of Sedov in Copenhagen is mentioned by neither Berman nor David. Only Holtzman was supposed to have met Sedov in the vestibule of a razed hotel.

Berman-Yurin and David, who, according to their own admissions were utter strangers to me, are supposed to have been first recommended to me by my son, at the time a twenty-six year old student. Thus it follows that I concealed my terrorist views from those closest to me, while issuing terrorist instructions to chance acquaintances. This perplexing fact can be explained only in one way—those who were "chance acquaintances" *to me* were not at all "chance acquaintances" *to the G.P.U.*

A fourth terrorist, Olberg, declared at the evening session of August 20th, 1936: "Before my departure for the Soviet Union, I intended to go to Copenhagen with Sedov to see Trotsky. *Our trip did not materialize, but Suzanna, Sedov's wife, went there.* On her return she brought a letter from Trotsky addressed to Sedov, in which Trotsky agreed to my going to the U.S.S.R. . . ." (My emphasis.)

My Berlin friends, the Pfemferts, as appears from their letter of April 30th, 1930, already at that period regarded Olberg, if not as a G.P.U. agent, at least as a candidate for the job. I rejected his proposal that he come to Prinkipo from Berlin as my Russian secretary. It is all the more inconceivable that two years later I should have given him "terrorist instructions." But Olberg, unlike Berman-Yurin and David, did really engage in correspondence with me at one time, made Sedov's personal acquaintance in Berlin, met him several times, was acquainted with Sedov's friends—in short, to a certain degree moved in his circle. Olberg had the opportunity to learn and, as his testimony shows, really did learn, that the attempts of my son to reach Copenhagen proved unsuccessful, but that his wife, who had a French passport, did go there.

All the four "terrorists" declare, as you observe, that it was Sedov who put them in touch with me. But from that point on their testimony diverges. According to Holtzman, Sedov himself was in Copenhagen. Berman-Yurin and David make no mention of Sedov's presence in Copenhagen. Finally, Olberg categorically insists that Sedov was unable to make the trip to Copenhagen. The most astonishing thing of all is that the Prosecutor pays not the least attention to these contradictions.

At the disposal of the Commission there is, as I have stated, documentary proof that Sedov was not in Copenhagen. The testimony of Olberg and the silence of Berman-Yurin and David corroborate this fact. The most imposing testimony against Sedov and myself, that of Holtzman, thus crumbles into dust. There is nothing astonishing in the fact that the friends of the G.P.U. seek at any price to save the testimony of Holtzman, on which hangs the whole story of the Copenhagen "terrorist week." Hence the hypothesis: Sedov might have gone to Copenhagen illegally without the knowledge of Olberg and the others. In order to deprive my adversaries of their last loophole, I shall dwell briefly on this hypothesis.

What need had Sedov to risk an illegal journey? All that we know about his alleged stay in Copenhagen is reduced to this: That he brought Holtzman from the Hotel Bristol to my apartment and during my conversation with Holtzman "very often Trotsky's son Sedov came in and out of the room." That is all! Was it worth while to make an illegal journey from Berlin just for that?

Berman-Yurin and David, who, according to their own admissions, had never met me before, were able to locate me in Copenhagen without the help of Sedov who, as can be gathered from their own statements, gave them all the necessary directions in Berlin. It was all the easier for Holtzman, who had met me in the past, to ascertain my whereabouts. No sensible person will believe that Sedov traveled with a false passport from Berlin to Copenhagen in order to bring Holtzman to my apartment, while leaving Berman-Yurin and David, whom he had also sent from Berlin and whom I did not know personally, without any attention.

But perhaps Sedov came to Copenhagen illegally to meet his parents? This supposition might, at first glance, seem a trifle more plausible if Sedov had not, several days later, journeyed to France quite legally for the same purpose—that is, for a meeting with his parents.

But, persist the friends of the G.P.U., could not Sedov have made a second and legal trip solely to hide the first illegal trip? Let us for a moment picture this combination in all its concreteness. Entirely openly, in the view of all, Sedov busies himself with the preparations for his trip to Copenhagen. In other words, he hides from nobody his intention of meeting us. All our friends in Copenhagen know that we expect our son. His wife and attorney arrive in Copenhagen, and tell their friends of his unsuccessful efforts. Now they ask us to believe that, failing to secure a visa, Sedov procures a false passport and arrives secretly in Copenhagen unbeknown to any of our friends. There he meets Holtzman in the vestibule of a hotel which does not exist, brings him to a meeting with me without being seen by my guards, and during my conversation with Holtzman keeps coming "in and out of the room." Thereafter, he disappears from Copenhagen as miraculously as he appeared. Upon returning to Berlin, he manages to obtain a French visa, and already on December 5th meets us again in Paris at the Gare du Nord. And all this to what end?

On the one hand, we have the testimony of Holtzman, who has not a single word to say regarding the kind of passport he used for his journey to Copenhagen (the state Prosecutor does not, of course, question him on this point), and who, as the crowning misfortune, indicates a nonexistent hotel as his meeting place with the absent Sedov. On the other hand, we have the silence of Berman-Yurin and David about Sedov, the absolutely true assertion that Olberg and Sedov remained in Berlin, upwards of a score of affidavits corroborating the statements of Sedov, his mother and myself, and, for added measure, plain common sense, whose authority cannot be denied.

To sum up: Sedov was not in Copenhagen; the testimony of Holtzman is false. Holtzman is the chief witness for the prosecution. The whole "Copenhagen week" crumbles into dust.

I can state a number of supplementary arguments, which ought to dispel the last shred of doubt, if any is at all possible in this matter.

1. None of my pretended visitors names either my address or the section of the city where the meeting took place.

2. The small villa which we occupied belonged to a danseuse who had gone abroad. All the furnishings of the house evidenced the owner's profession, and could not have failed to attract the attention of any visitor. Had Holtzman, Berman-Yurin and David visited me, they would unfailingly have mentioned the furnishings of the apartment.

3. During our stay in Copenhagen, a rumor of Zinoviev's death circulated through the world press. The rumor proved false. But it made an impression on all of us. Can one imagine that my visitors, who came to receive "terrorist" instructions, either heard nothing from me or others about the death of Zinoviev, or else forgot all about it?

4. None of my pretended visitors said a word about my secretaries, my guards, etc.

5. Berman-Yurin and David said nothing about the passports with which they traveled, how they found me, where they lodged, etc.

The judges and the state Prosecutor do not raise a single concrete question, for fear that an incautious gesture might topple the flimsy structure.

The organ of the Danish governmental party, *Sozialdemokraten,* immediately after the trial of Zinoviev and Kamenev, on September 1st, 1936, stated that the Hotel Bristol, in which the alleged meeting between Holtzman and Sedov took place, was demolished in the year 1917. Moscow justice met this not unimportant revelation with a deep silence. One of the G.P.U. lawyers, presumably the irreplaceable Pritt, advanced the supposition that the stenographer in writing the name "Bristol" made a slip of the pen. If one considers that the trials were conducted in Russian, then it is entirely incomprehensible how a Russian stenographer could have made a mistake with such an un-Russian word as "Bristol." The carefully corrected reports of the court proceedings were, furthermore, read by the judges and the public. Foreign journalists attended the trial. No one noticed the "slip of the pen" before the revelation of *Sozialdemokraten.* The episode naturally became widely known. The Stalinists kept silent for five months.

Only in February of this year did the Comintern make a saving discovery: There really was no Hotel Bristol in Copenhagen, but there is, however, a confectioner's shop named "Bristol" which is contiguous to a hotel by virtue of a joint wall. To be sure, this hotel is called the "Grand Hotel Copenhagen," but it is, nevertheless, a hotel. To be sure, the confectioner's shop is not a hotel; still, its name is "Bristol." According to Holtzman, the meeting took place in the *vestibule* of the hotel. To be sure, the confectioner's shop has no vestibule; but on the other hand, the hotel, which is not called the "Bristol," does have a vestibule. To this it must be added that, as it appears even in the diagrams published in the Comintern press, the entrances to the shop and to the hotel are on different streets. Now, where did the meeting really take place? In the vestibule without the "Bristol" or in the "Bristol" without the vestibule?

Let us, however, assume for a moment that Holtzman had confused the shop and the hotel in arranging the meeting with Sedov in Berlin. How, then, did Sedov discover the place of the meeting? Let us meet the authors of the hypothesis more than half way and let us suppose that Sedov had demonstrated an unusual resourcefulness, that he turned into the other street and there found an entrance to a hotel of another name and met Holtzman in the vestibule. But it is self-evident that Holtzman could have made a mistake as regards the name of the hotel only *before* the meeting. *During* the meeting the error must have been cleared up and imprinted all the more sharply in the memories of both parties. *After* the meeting Holtzman could in no case have spoken of the vestibule—of the Bristol confectioner's shop. The hypothesis thus collapses at the very first touch.

But in order to confuse the situation still further, the Comintern press asserts that the Bristol shop has served for a long time as a meeting-place for Danish and transient "Trotskyites." There is an obvious anachronism here. In November, 1932, we were unable to find a single "Trotskyite" in Denmark. German "Trotskyites" appeared in Copenhagen only after Hitler's triumph—that is, in the year 1933. Yet, even if we suppose for a moment that there not only were "Trotskyites" there in 1932, but that the Bristol shop was already being utilized by them, the new hypothesis appears still more senseless. Let us turn to Holtzman's testimony, as given in the official report:

> . . . Sedov said to me: "As you are going to the U.S.S.R., it would be a good thing if you came with me to Copenhagen where my father is. . . ." I agreed. But I told him *that we could not go together, for reasons of secrecy* [my

> emphasis]. I arranged with Sedov to be in Copenhagen within two or three days, to put up at the Hotel Bristol and meet him there . . .

It is clear that the old revolutionist, who did not want to make the trip together with Sedov because his life would be endangered if his Copenhagen trip were discovered, would not be likely to fix a meeting place which, according to the Comintern press, "had for years [!] been the meeting place for the Danish Trotskyites, and for those in their circle, as well as for meetings between the Danish and foreign Trotskyites." In the latter circumstance, which, as has already been said, is a sheer invention, the over-zealous agents of the Comintern see a confirmation of their hypothesis. According to them, it follows that Holtzman fixed a meeting place in a shop sufficiently well known to the Stalinists as a "Trotskyite hangout." One absurdity is piled upon another. If the shop was generally known to the Danish and foreign "Trotskyites," especially to Holtzman, then he could not in the first place have mistaken it for the "Grand Hotel Copenhagen," and secondly, he would have shunned it precisely because of its "Trotskyite" reputation, as he would a plague. In such a manner do these people correct the stenographer's "slip of the pen"!

The Commission knows from the documents submitted by me that Sedov could not have been in the "Trotskyite" confectioner's shop because he was not in Copenhagen at all. In Sedov's "Livre Rouge" the Hotel Bristol episode is treated as a curiosity which characterizes the G.P.U.'s extremely slovenly methods of work. Main attention is concentrated on proving that Sedov was in Berlin in November, 1932. Innumerable documents and affidavits leave no room for any doubt on that score. They want us to believe that Sedov's ghost found its way into the ghostly vestibule of the confectioner's shop, which, after some delay, was transformed into a hotel by the fantasy of the agents of the G.P.U.

Holtzman made his alleged trip separately from Sedov and, naturally, with a false passport in order to leave no traces. The entry of foreigners is nowadays registered in all countries. Holtzman's testimony could be verified immediately if we knew what passport he used in journeying from Berlin to Copenhagen. Can one imagine a court procedure in which the Prosecutor, under such circumstances, does not question the defendant about his passport? It is well known that Holtzman categorically denied connection with the Gestapo. All the more reason for the Prosecutor to ask Holtzman who, then, procured the false passport for him. However, Vyshinsky, naturally, did not put this question, in order not to sabotage his own work. From all indications, Holtzman must have passed the night in Copenhagen. Where? Perhaps in the "Bristol" confectionery? Vyshinsky is not interested in this question, either. His function consists in protecting the defendants from a verification of their own testimony.

Naturally, the error in the matter of the Hotel Bristol discredits the accusation. The error regarding the meeting with the absent Sedov doubly discredits the trial. But what most discredits the trial, and Vyshinsky himself, is the circumstance that the latter did not interrogate the defendant about his passport, the source from which he obtained it, or his place of lodging, although these questions clamor for answer. Vyshinsky's silence exposes him in this case, also, as an accomplice in the judicial frame-up.

XV. RADEK

In his summation (January 28th), Prosecutor Vyshinsky said: "Radek is one of the most outstanding, and, to do him justice, one of the most able and persistent Trotskyites . . . He is incorrigible. . . . He is one of the men who is most trusted by and intimate with the big chief of this gang, Trotsky." All the elements of this characterization are false, with the possible exception of the reference to Radek's talent; but even here it is necessary to add, *talent as a journalist.* And only that! It is possible to speak of Radek's "persistency," of his "incorrigibility" as an Oppositionist, and of his intimacy with me, only by way of inept jesting.

Radek's outstanding characteristics, as a matter of fact, are impulsiveness, instability, undependability, a predisposition toward falling into panic at the first sign of danger, and exhibiting extreme loquacity when all is well. These qualities make him a journalistic Figaro of first-rate skill, an invaluable guide for foreign correspondents and tourists, but utterly unsuited for the role of conspirator. Among informed persons it is simply unthinkable to speak of Radek as an inspirer of terrorist attempts or the organizer of an international conspiracy!

However, it is not by accident that the Prosecutor attributes to Radek traits which are in direct contradiction to his real character; otherwise it would be impossible to create even the semblance of a psychological basis for the accusation. As a matter of fact, had I chosen Radek as the political leader of the "purely Trotskyite" center, and had I initiated none other than Radek into my negotiations with Germany and Japan, it would be perfectly self-evident that Radek must have been not only a "persistent" and "incorrigible" Trotskyite, but also one of my "most trusted and intimate" men. The characterization of Radek in the summation of the prosecutor is an indispensable constituent of the judicial frame-up.

According to the Prosecutor, Radek was the "holder of the portfolio of foreign affairs" in the "Trotskyite" center. Indeed, Radek was closely occupied with questions of foreign policy, but exclusively in the capacity of journalist. True, in the first years after the October Revolution he was for a time a member of the Council of the People's Commissariat of Foreign Affairs. But the Soviet diplomats complained to the Politburo that "anything said in Radek's presence is spread all over Moscow by the next morning." Radek was quickly removed from the Council.

At one time he was a member of the Central Committee, and in that capacity he had a right to attend the sessions of the Politburo. On Lenin's initiative, matters requiring secrecy were invariably discussed in Radek's absence. Lenin appreciated Radek as a journalist, but could not tolerate his lack of self-restraint, his light-minded attitude towards serious questions, his cynicism.

One cannot avoid recalling the estimate of Radek which Lenin gave at the Seventh Party Congress (1918), during the controversy over the Brest-Litovsk Treaty. Referring to Radek's remark, "Lenin yields space to gain time," Lenin said, "I return to what Comrade Radek said, and take this opportunity to emphasize that he has *accidentally* succeeded in uttering a serious thought." And, further on, "This time it has happened that Comrade Radek has delivered himself of a thoroughly serious thought." This twice-repeated remark well expresses the very essence of the attitude toward Radek not only of Lenin himself, but also of Lenin's closest collaborators. I note here that even six years later, in January, 1924, at the Party Conference which was called shortly before Lenin's death, Stalin said: "Most men's heads control their tongues; Radek's tongue controls his head." For all their rudeness, these words are not misdirected. In any case, they astonished no one, least of all Radek himself; he was accustomed to such appraisals. Who will believe that I placed at the head of a grandiose plot an individual whose tongue controls his head and who is in consequence capable of expressing serious ideas only "by accident"?

Radek's attitude towards me underwent two stages of development. In 1923 he wrote a panegyric about me ("Leon Trotsky—Organizer of Victory," *Pravda,* March 14th, 1923) which astonished me by its exalted tone. In the days of the Moscow trial (August 21st, 1936), Radek wrote about me the most slanderous and cynical of all his articles. The interval between these two articles is divided midway by Radek's capitulation. The year 1929 was the breaking-point in his political life as in his attitude towards me. The story of our relations before and after 1929 can be followed without difficulty from year to year through articles and letters. In this question, as in others, to reestablish the basic facts is to refute the accusation.

From 1923 to 1926 Radek vacillated between the Left Opposition in Russia and the Right Communist Opposition in Germany (Brandler, Thalheimer, etc.). At the time of the open break between Stalin and Zinoviev (beginning of 1926) Radek sought in vain to draw the Left Opposition into a bloc with Stalin. Thereafter Radek belonged for almost three years (an unusual period for him!) to the Left Opposition. But within the Opposition he kept swinging now to the right, now to the left.

Developing, in August, 1927, the idea of the menace of Thermidor, Radek wrote in his programmatic theses:

> The tendency toward Thermidorian degeneration of the Party and its leading institutions is exemplified in the following instances: . . . (d) in the line of augmenting the weight of the Party apparatus as against the organizations at the base of the Party, which line finds its classic expression in the declaration of Stalin to the Plenum (August, 1927): "These cadres can be removed only by civil war"—a declaration which is . . . the classic formula of the Bonapartist *coup d'état;* (e) in the foreign policy formulated by Sokolnikov. It is necessary to designate

> these tendencies openly as Thermidorian . . . and to say openly that they find their complete expression in the right wing of the Central Committee (Rykov, Kalinin, Voroshilov, Sokolnikov) and partly in the center (Stalin). It is necessary to say openly that the Thermidorian tendencies are growing . . .

This quotation is important in two respects:

(a) It shows, in the first place, that already in 1927 Stalin proclaimed that the bureaucracy ("these cadres") were irremovable, and pronounced that all opposition to it was equivalent to civil war (Radek, together with the whole Opposition, designated this open declaration as a manifestation of Bonapartism).

(b) It unequivocally characterizes *Sokolnikov,* not as an ideological adherent, but as a representative of the Thermidorian Right Wing. Yet in the last trial Sokolnikov figures as a member of the "Trotskyite" center.

At the end of 1927 Radek, along with hundreds of other Oppositionists, was expelled from the Party and banished to Siberia. Zinoviev, Kamenev and then Pyatakov made declarations of repentance. By the spring of 1928 Radek began to hesitate, but still for about a year he tried to stand erect.

Thus, on May 10th, Radek writes to Preobrazhensky from Tobolsk: "I reject Zinovievism and Pyatakovism as I reject Dostoievskyism. Doing violence to their convictions, they recant. It is impossible to help the working class by falsehood. Those who remain must speak the truth."

On June 24th, replying to my apprehensions, Radek wrote to me as follows: "None of us proposes to renounce his views. Such a renunciation would be all the more ridiculous since the test of history has brilliantly demonstrated their correctness."

For Radek, there was, thus, not the slightest doubt that the Oppositionists could recant only for the purpose of restoring themselves to the good graces of the bureaucracy. It never entered his head that behind the recantations there might lurk some diabolical design.

On July 3d, Radek wrote to the capitulator Vardine: "Zinoviev and Kamenev have recanted, if you please, in order to bring aid to the Party, but as a matter of fact the only thing they are bold enough to do is to write articles against the Opposition. That is the logic of their position, for the penitent must give proof of his repentance." These lines throw a glaring light on the trials to come, in which not only Zinoviev and Kamenev, but also Radek, were to "prove" the sincerity of all their preceding repentances.

In the summer of 1928, Radek, together with Smilga, elaborated political theses in which, among other things, they state: "Those who, like Pyatakov, make haste *to bury their pasts through betrayal* are gravely mistaken." Thus does Radek express himself about his future collaborator in the mythical "parallel center." At that very time Radek was himself already vacillating. But psychologically he was unable to appraise Pyatakov's capitulation as anything but treason.

However, Radek's urge to make his peace with the bureaucracy had already become so transparent in his letters that F. Dingelstedt, one of the most prominent exiles of the younger generation, openly stigmatized Radek's "capitulationist" tendencies. On August 8th Radek replied to Dingelstedt:

> The circulation of letters about my capitulation is a piece of lightmindedness, an action which can only sow panic, and which is unworthy of an old revolutionist . . . When you have thought the matter over, when your nerves have regained their balance (and we need strong nerves, for exile is a trifle in comparison with what we are destined to see in the days to come), then you, an old member of the Party, will be ashamed that you lost your head. Communist greetings, K.R.

Especially noteworthy in this letter is the remark that exile to Siberia is a mere trifle by comparison with the repressions ahead. It is as if Radek foresaw the future trials.

On September 16th Radek wrote to the exiles in the village of Kolpashev:

> Stalin demands that we acknowledge our "errors" and forget his errors—this formula is a demand for our capitulation as a special tendency and our submission to the center . . . On this condition he is ready to offer us clemency. We cannot accept this condition. [*Bulletin of the Opposition*, Nos. 3–4, September, 1929.]

That same day Radek wrote to Vrachev concerning the blows heaped upon him by the firmer Oppositionists: "The outcry will not hinder me from doing my duty. And whoever, on the basis of these criticisms [the criticisms of Radek] continues to babble about preparing for Pyatakovism will only give proof of his mental deficiency."

Pyatakov still remains for Radek the measure of extreme political bankruptcy.

These quotations alone, which describe the real process of differentiation within the Opposition and the desertion of its unstable and opportunist wing to the camp of the bureaucracy, completely destroy the indictment's police-manufactured version of the capitulations as a calculated method of conspiracy against the Party.

In October, 1928, Radek made an attempt to appeal to the Central Committee to stop or at least soften the persecution of the Opposition. "Despite the fact that the older ones among us have struggled for Communism for a quarter of a century," he wrote from Siberia to Moscow, "you expel us from the Party and banish us as counter-revolutionaries . . . on the basis of an accusation which dishonors not us, but those who make it." (Article 58 of the Penal Code.) Radek enumerates a series of instances of the cruel treatment of the exiles—Sibiriakov, Alski, Khorechko—and continues: "But the circumstances surrounding Trotsky's illness exhaust one's patience. We cannot remain silent and passive while malaria eats away the strength of the fighter who all his life has served the working class and who was the sword of the October Revolution."

Such was one of the last declarations of Radek, the Oppositionist, and his last positive judgment of me. At the beginning of 1929 he already refused to conceal his vacillations. In the middle of June, after negotiations with Party committees and the G.P.U., Radek, the capitulator, returned to Moscow, though to be sure still under guard. At one of the railroad stations in Siberia he had a conversation with the exiles, which one of the participants recounted in a letter abroad (*Bulletin of the Opposition,* No. 6, October, 1929):

> *Question:* And what is your attitude towards L.D. [Trotsky]?
>
> *Radek:* I have completely broken with L.D. From now on we are political adversaries . . . With the collaborator of Lord Beaverbrook we have nothing in common.
>
> *Question:* Do you demand the abolition of Article 58?
>
> *Radek:* Emphatically, no! For those who come along with us it will be automatically inapplicable. But we will not abolish Article 58 for those who continue to undermine the Party and who engage in organizing discontent among the masses.
>
> The agents of the G.P.U. would not allow the conversation to continue. They shoved Karl [Radek] into the train, accusing him of agitating against Trotsky's deportation. Radek shouted from the train: "I agitate against Trotsky's deportation? Ha! Ha! . . . I am agitating for comrades to return to the Party!" The G.P.U. agents listened

in silence and shoved Karl further into the train. The express began to move . . .

Regarding this vivid narrative, which paints Radek as he is in the flesh, I wrote an editorial note: "Our correspondent says that at bottom [of the capitulation] is 'cowardice.' This formulation may seem over-simplified. But in essence it is correct. Naturally, it is a question of political cowardice—personal cowardice does not necessarily enter here, although often enough they happily coincide." This characterization harmonizes completely with my appraisal of Radek.

Somewhat earlier, on June 14th, no sooner had the telegraph brought the news of Radek's "sincere repentance" than I wrote:

> In capitulating, Radek strikes himself from the roll of the living. He will fall into the category of the half-doomed, half-pardoned, headed by Zinoviev. These people fear to utter a single syllable aloud, fear to have minds of their own, and thus live in constant dread of their own shadows. [*Bulletin of the Opposition,* Nos. 1–2, July, 1929.]

Less than a month later (July 7th), I wrote, in another article on the subject of the capitulations: "Generally speaking, no one ever yet accused Radek of constancy or consistency" (*Bulletin of the Opposition,* Nos. 1–2, July, 1929). These words seem like a polemical retort to Prosecutor Vyshinsky, who seven years later was to be the first to accuse Radek of being "constant" and "consistent."

At the end of July, I again returned to the same theme, this time in a broader perspective:

> The capitulation of Radek, Smilga, Preobrazhensky, is in its way a major political fact. It shows above all how

> completely a great and heroic generation of revolutionists, whose destiny it was to pass through the experiences of the war and the October Revolution, has spent itself. Three old and meritorious revolutionists have removed their names from the roll of the living. They have deprived themselves of the most important thing, the right to command confidence. This they can never regain.

From the middle of 1929 Radek's name became, in the ranks of the Opposition, the symbol of the most degrading forms of capitulation and the knifing of yesterday's friends. The aforementioned Dingelstedt, in order to outline Stalin's difficulties more clearly, asks ironically, "Will he receive any aid from the renegade Radek?" To emphasize his contempt for the document of a recent capitulator, Dingelstedt adds, "You have cleared for yourself a road to Radek" (September 22d, 1929).

Another exiled Oppositionist writes from Siberia on October 27th (*Bulletin of the Opposition,* No. 7, November–December, 1929): "Radek's work has taken on an exceptionally despicable character—there is no other word for it. He lives on petty intrigues and gossip; he rabidly besmirches his own past."

In the autumn of 1929 Rakovsky describes how Preobrazhensky and Radek entered the path of capitulation: "The former did it with a certain measure of consistency, the latter, as always, with evasions and jumps from extreme left to extreme right, and vice versa." (*Bulletin of the Opposition,* No. 7, November–December, 1929.) Rakovsky observes sarcastically that each capitulator, on deserting the Opposition, is obliged "to kick at Trotsky with hoofs" shod with "Radekist nails." All these citations speak for themselves. No, the capitulations are not a military ruse of "Trotskyism"!

In the summer of 1929 a former member of my military secretariat, Blumkin, who was in Turkey at the time, paid me a visit in Constantinople. Upon his return to Moscow, Blumkin told Radek of the meeting. Radek immediately betrayed him. At that time, the G.P.U. had not yet descended to accusations of "terrorism." Nevertheless, Blumkin was shot, secretly and without trial. Here is what I then stated in the *Bulletin,* on December 25th, 1929, on the basis of letters received from Moscow: "Radek's nervous babbling is well known. Now he is absolutely demoralized, like the majority of the capitulators . . . Having lost the last remnants of moral equilibrium, Radek stops before no vileness." Further on, Radek is called an "empty hysteric." The letters give a detailed account of how Blumkin was betrayed after his meeting with Radek. From then on Radek was held in greatest scorn by the Opposition; he was not only a capitulator, but a traitor as well.

Seven years later—I am forced here to anticipate—Radek, in an article which demanded death for Zinoviev and the others, wrote in *Isvestia* on August 21st, 1936, that in 1929 I ordered Blumkin "to organize raids on Trade Representations abroad to obtain money that [Trotsky] needed for anti-Soviet operations." I will not stop to discuss the absurdity of this "order": the Trade Representations, one would think, keep funds not on their premises, but in banks! We are interested in another aspect of this matter: In August, 1936, Radek was still, according to his words, a member of the "Trotskyite center." In the course of the four months after his arrest he denied, according to his own statement in court, any participation whatsoever in the plot—that is, according to the prosecutor's characterization, he showed himself to be a stubborn and incorrigible "Trotskyite." Why, then, on August 21st, 1936—without any apparent reason—did he ascribe monstrous and nonsensical crimes to me, the "leader" of the plot? Let someone invent an explanation which can be made to fit into Vyshinsky's *schema.* For my part, I refuse to make any such attempt.

The bitter hostility between Radek and the Opposition can be traced year by year. I am forced to limit myself to a selection of examples.

Thirteen exiled Oppositionists in Kansk, Siberia, addressing a protest to the Praesidium of the Sixteenth Party Congress (June, 1930), wrote, among other things: "The Council of the G.P.U. of the U.S.S.R., basing itself on treacherous information received from the renegade Karl Radek, has condemned Comrade Blumkin, member of the C.P.S.U., to the supreme penalty."

An exiled Oppositionist, characterizing the political and moral degeneration of the capitulators in the *Bulletin of the Opposition* (No. 19, March, 1931), did not forget to add:

> The one who has degenerated most rapidly is Radek. The capitulators from the other groups, not only among the rank and file but also among the leaders, endeavor to make it clear that not only politically but also personally they have nothing in common with him. The frankest of them say, plainly: "Radek is playing a filthy, treacherous role," . . . I communicate [adds the correspondent] only a minor fact, but one indicative of Radek's cynicism. In response to a request to help an exiled Bolshevik who was gravely ill, Radek refused, adding, "He will return all the sooner." Radek measures everything with his dirty little yardstick!

The following, written from Moscow, appeared in the *Bulletin* on November 15th, 1931:

> All quiet on the capitulation "front." Zinoviev is writing a book on the Second International. Politically, neither he nor Kamenev exists. About the others, nothing to report. One exception: Radek; he is beginning to play a "role." Radek really directs *Isvestia.* He has become quite

notorious in his new role as "Stalin's personal friend." And this is no joke! In every conversation Radek tries with all his might to create the impression that he is on the most intimate terms with Stalin. "Yesterday, when I was having tea with Stalin," etc. [*Bulletin of the Opposition*, Nos. 25–26, November–December, 1931.]

Radek, unlike the other capitulators, began to play a certain "role" only because through his whole conduct he regained the confidence of the rulers. I might point out that the correspondence which has just been cited was published precisely at the time when, according to the accusation, I was taking the necessary measures to induce Radek to enter the path of terror. Evidently I was forcing my left hand to destroy what my right was doing.

The discussion revolving around Radek took on an international character. Thus, the German oppositional organization, the *Leninbund*, published the declaration of Radek, Smilga and Preobrazhensky, and offered to print my declaration. In October, 1929, I answered the leadership of the *Leninbund:* "Isn't it monstrous? In my brochure I defend the point of view of the Russian Opposition. Radek, Smilga and Preobrazhensky are renegades, bitter enemies of the Russian Opposition, and furthermore Radek does not stop at any calumny." In the publications of the Left Opposition during those years one can find, in several languages, not a few scornful articles and comments flaying Radek.

The American journalist, Max Shachtman, one of my co-thinkers, well informed about the internal relations of the Russian Opposition, sent me from New York on March 13th, 1932, several old remarks by Radek about me with the following comment: "In view of the Stalinist chorus in which Radek is now singing, would it not be interesting to remind the Communist workers again that about twelve years ago, before fighting against 'Trotskyism' became a profitable business, Radek sang a different song?"

During the trial, Radek testified: ". . . in February, 1932, I received a letter from Trotsky . . . Trotsky further wrote that since he knew me to be an active person he was convinced that I would return to the struggle." Three months after this alleged letter, on May 24th, 1932, I wrote to Albert Weisbord in New York: ". . . The ideological and moral degeneration of Radek testifies to the fact that not only is Radek not made of first-grade stuff, but also that the Stalinist régime must support itself either on depersonalized functionaries or demoralized people." Such was my real appraisal of this "active person"!

In May, 1932, the German liberal paper, *Berliner Tageblatt,* in a special issue devoted to economic construction in the U.S.S.R., published an article by Radek which for the one-hundred-and-first time condemned me for my disbelief in the possibility of building Socialism in one country. "This thesis is denied not only by the avowed enemies of the Soviet Union," wrote Radek, "but is also disputed by Leon Trotsky." I answered him in the *Bulletin* (No. 28, July, 1932) by a brief note entitled: "A Lightminded Man on a Weighty Question." Let me remind you that it was in the spring of that year that Radek went to Geneva, where he supposedly received, through Romm, a letter from me proposing the earliest possible extermination of the Soviet leaders. It turns out that I entrusted rather "weighty" missions to "a lightminded man"!

During the years 1933–1936 my ties with Radek, if one believes his testimony, became firmly welded. This did not prevent him from passionately revising the history of the Revolution in the personal interests of Stalin. On November 21st, 1935, three weeks before Pyatakov's "flight" to Oslo, Radek recounted in *Pravda* his interview with some foreigner: "I related to him how Lenin's closest comrade-in-arms, Stalin, directed the organization of the fronts and elaborated the strategic plans, on the basis of which we were victorious." I was thus completely excluded from the history of the Civil War. Yet the very same Radek once knew how to write in a different vein. I have already mentioned his article, "Leon Trotsky—Organizer of Victory" (*Pravda*, March 14th, 1923)—I am now compelled to quote from it:

> The need of the hour was for a man who would incarnate the call to struggle, a man who, subordinating himself completely to the requirements of the struggle, would become the ringing summons to arms, the will which exacts from all unconditional submission to a great, sacrificial necessity. Only a man with Trotsky's capacity for work, only a man so unsparing of himself as Trotsky, only a man who knew how to speak to the soldiers as Trotsky did—only such a man could have become the standard bearer of the armed toilers. He was all things rolled into one.

In 1923 I was "all"; in 1935, I became, for Radek, "nothing." In the lengthy article of 1923 Stalin is not once mentioned. In 1935 he turns out to be "the organizer of victory."

Radek thus has in his possession two diametrically opposite histories of the Civil War: One for the year 1923, the other for the year 1935. The two versions, regardless of which happens to be true, unmistakably characterize the degree of Radek's honesty as well as his attitude toward myself and Stalin at various times. While supposedly linking his fate with mine by the bonds of a plot, Radek indefatigably defames and blackens me. On the other hand, having decided to kill Stalin, he ecstatically shines his boots for seven years.

But this is still not all. In January, 1935, Zinoviev, Kamenev and others were sentenced, in connection with the Kirov assassination, to some years of imprisonment. During the trial they confessed a desire "to restore capitalism." In the

Bulletin of the Opposition I stigmatized this self-accusation as a rude and nonsensical frame-up. Who hastened to Vyshinsky's defense? Radek! "It is not a question of whether capitalism is the ideal of Messrs. Trotsky and Zinoviev," he wrote in *Pravda,* "but whether the building of Socialism is possible in our country . . . ," etc. I answered in the *Bulletin* (No 43, April, 1935): "Radek blurts out that Zinoviev and Kamenev did not engage in any plots with the aim of reestablishing capitalism—contrary to what the official statement so shamelessly affirms—but merely rejected the theory of Socialism in one country."

Radek's article of January, 1935, entering as a logical link into the chain of his calumnies against the Opposition, prepared the way for his article of August, 1936, captioned: "The Zinovievite-Trotskyite Fascist Gang and Its Hetman Trotsky." This, in its turn, was nothing else but a prelude to Radek's court testimony in January, 1937. Each succeeding step developed from the preceding one. This is precisely why absolutely no one would have believed Radek had he figured in the trial only as a witness for the Prosecution. For his testimony against me to carry any weight, it was necessary to transform Radek into a defendant, suspending above him the Damocles sword of the death penalty. The manner in which Radek was transformed into a defendant is a special question which, in essence, belongs in the domain of inquisitorial technique. Here it suffices for us that Radek took his seat on the defendants' bench, not as my co-thinker, collaborator and friend of yesteryear, but as an old capitulator, the betrayer of Blumkin, demoralized agent of Stalin and the G.P.U., as the most perfidious of all my enemies.

At this point we may anticipate the question: How, in view of these facts and documents, could the Government represent Radek as the leader of a "Trotskyite" plot?

This question, however, relates not to Radek himself, but

rather to the trial as a whole. Radek is transformed into a "Trotskyite" by the same methods which transformed me into an ally of the Mikado—and for the self-same political motives. To the question posed above, a brief answer would be the following: 1. For the system of "confessions" only capitulators, who had passed through the school of recantation, self-abasement and self-vilification, were suitable; 2. the organizers of the trial did not and could not find a better candidate for the role assigned to Radek; 3. the whole calculation of the organizers is constructed on the summary effect of public confessions and executions, which were intended to stifle all criticism. Such is the method of Stalin. Such is the present political system in the U.S.S.R. The case of Radek is only the most striking example.

XVI. VLADIMIR ROMM—'WITNESS'

The whole tissue of the trial is rotten. We shall see this now in the testimony of Vladimir Romm, a most important witness, who, moreover, was brought to court from jail under guard. If we leave aside Pyatakov's flight to Oslo in the mythical airplane, then Romm—according to the design of the indictment—serves as the chief connecting link between myself and the "parallel center" (Pyatakov-Radek-Sokolnikov-Serebryakov). Through Romm, letters were supposedly conveyed from me to Radek, and from Radek to me. Romm, allegedly, met personally not only Leon Sedov, my son, but also me. Who is this witness? What did he do and what did he see? What are the motives behind his participation in the conspiracy? Let us listen to him most attentively.

Romm is, of course, a "Trotskyite." Without Trotskyites by special appointment of the G.P.U., there would never have been any "Trotskyite conspiracy." We should like to learn, however, the exact date of Romm's adherence to the

"Trotskyists," granting that he ever did join them. But even to this first and, it would seem, not unimportant, question we hear a very suspicious answer:

"*Vyshinsky:* What were your ties with Radek in the past?"

"*Romm:* At first I was acquainted with him in connection with literary work and later, in 1926–1927, I was connected with him in joint Trotskyite anti-Party work."

And that exhausts the answer to Vyshinsky's leading question! What strikes one's attention first of all is the manner of expression. The witness makes no reference to his Oppositionist activity; he does not utter a single word to characterize its content; no, he immediately applies to it a criminal qualification: "Trotskyite anti-Party work"—and nothing more. Romm simply proffers the court, in ready-made form, the formula required for the report of the court proceedings. It is in this way that each disciplined accused and witness conducts himself during the trials of Stalin-Vyshinsky—the undisciplined are shot before the trial. In recognition of services rendered, the Prosecutor refrains altogether from embarrassing the witness by questioning him about the circumstances under which he joined the Opposition and the manner in which his "anti-Party" work expressed itself. Vyshinsky's fundamental rule is: Thou shalt not place witnesses and defendants in an embarrassing position! But even without the assistance of the Prosecutor it is not difficult to gather that in his very first statement Romm is telling an untruth. The years 1926–1927 embrace a period in which Oppositionist activity attained its widest sweep. The extended platform of the Opposition was elaborated and multigraphed; within the Party there was heated discussion; large meetings of the Opposition took place, attended by tens of thousands of workers in Moscow and Leningrad alone; finally, the Opposition participated in the November demonstration with its own banners and slogans. If Romm had really belonged to the Opposition during that period, he must have been connected with numerous individuals. But, no; he cautiously names only Radek. While Troyanovsky was assuring everybody in New York that Romm "really" was a "Trotskyite," the verbatim report of the trial definitely refuted the false statement of the diplomat. Radek says about Romm: "I knew Romm since 1925. . . . He was not a worker in a general sense, but he was with us on the Chinese question." This means, in other words, that Romm stood apart from the Opposition on all other questions. So this man who, even according to Radek's testimony, was only episodically with him on the Chinese question (1927), is dragged into the light of day in the guise of—terrorist!

Just why did it fall to Romm's lot to masquerade as the contact man? Because in his capacity of foreign correspondent he traveled to Geneva, Paris, the United States, and, in consequence, possessed the technical facilities for the fulfillment of the commission foisted upon him retroactively by the G.P.U. And inasmuch as after the tenfold purgings to which all the foreign delegations and institutions of the U.S.S.R. had been subjected since the end of 1927, it was impossible to locate even with a lantern any "Trotskyite" or even capitulator abroad, Yezhov was compelled to appoint Romm as "Trotskyite," while Vyshinsky had to content himself in silence with Romm's answer concerning the "anti-Party" connection with Radek in 1926–1927.

But what did Romm do *after* 1927? Did he break with the Opposition or did he remain loyal to it? Did he recant or had he nothing to recant? Not a word about all this. The prosecutor is interested not in political psychology but in geography.

"*Vyshinsky:* Were you ever in Geneva?

"*Romm:* Yes, I was Tass correspondent in Geneva, also in Paris. In Geneva from 1930 to 1934."

Did Romm read the *Bulletin of the Opposition* during the years of his stay abroad? Did he contribute funds to it? Did he even make a single attempt to establish connections with me personally? About all this—not a word. Yet it would have been no very great labor to write me a letter from Geneva or Paris. To have done so, one need only have been interested in the Opposition, and in my activity in particular. Romm makes no reference at all to any such interest on his part, and the prosecutor naturally asks him no questions about it. It follows that Romm terminated in 1927 his "anti-Party" work, which was known only to Radek—that is to say, if we admit for a moment that he had ever begun it. It must be borne in mind that it is not customary to send the first chance stranger as a Tass correspondent to Geneva or Paris. The G.P.U. carefully hand-picks individuals, and, at the same time, makes sure of their complete readiness to cooperate. Small wonder, then, that Romm, while abroad, did not evince the slightest "Oppositionist" interest in me or my activity!

But Vyshinsky is in urgent need of a contact man between Radek and myself. There is no candidate more suitable. That is why it suddenly turns out that in the summer of 1931, while passing through Berlin, Romm met Putna, who offered to "put him in touch with" Sedov. Who is Putna? A prominent officer of the General Staff, participant in the Civil War, and later military attaché in London. For a certain period of time Putna, as I learned even before my exile in Central Asia (1928), really did sympathize with the Opposition, and perhaps even participated in it. I had very little occasion to meet him personally, and then only on military matters. I never had any discussion with him on Opposition topics. I do not know whether he was later obliged to repent officially. At any rate, when I read in Prinkipo about Putna's appointment to the important post of military attaché in London, I drew the conclusion that he had fully restored himself in the confidence of the authorities. In such circumstances, neither I nor my son could have had any connection with Putna abroad. From the report of the court proceedings, however, I learn, among other extraordinary things, that it was none other than Putna himself who offered to put Romm "in touch with" Sedov. To what end? Romm did not even bother to ask. He simply accepted the offer of Putna, with whom he had had no previous political connections—at any rate he mentions none. Thus, after a lapse of four years Romm, for reasons unknown, consents to renew his "Trotskyite anti-Party work." Faithful to his system, he does not, in court, refer by so much as a single word to his political motives. Did he aim to seize power? Was he striving to restore capitalism? Was he consumed with hatred toward Stalin? Was he seduced by the connection with fascism? Or was he simply guided by his old friendship for Radek, who had, incidentally, contrived to repent and who had already been cursing the Opposition on all the highways and byways for more than two years? The Prosecutor, of course, does not annoy the witness with disconcerting questions. Romm is not in duty bound to possess a political psychology. His task is to effect a connection between Radek and Trotsky, and incidentally to compromise Putna, who is, meanwhile, being trained in the G.P.U. prison for future "confessions."

"I met Sedov," continues Romm, "and in reply to his question as to whether I was prepared, if necessary [!], to serve as liaison man with Radek, I consented . . ." When answering, Romm unfailingly gives his consent, without explaining his motives. Yet Romm could not but have known that for having met me in 1929 in Stamboul, and for having attempted to transmit a letter of mine to friends in Russia, Blumkin was shot. This letter, by the way, is at this very moment in the archives of the G.P.U., but it is so extremely ill-suited to the aims of Vyshinsky and Stalin that they would never even entertain the idea of publishing it. In any case, to have ventured, after the shooting of Blumkin, to take upon himself the mission of contact man, Romm must have been an extraordinarily self-sacrificing and heroic Oppositionist. Why did he keep silent for four years? Why did he wait for a chance meeting with Putna, and why did he wait to be "put in touch" with Sedov? And why, on the other hand, did a single meeting suffice for Romm to take upon himself, then and there, without any objection, this extremely perilous job? There is not a single element of human psychology in this trial. The witnesses, like the accused, tell only of those "actions" which are needful to Prosecutor Vyshinsky. The connection between the fictitious "actions" is provided not by the thoughts and feelings of living men, but by the *a priori* pattern of the indictment.

In the spring of the following year, when Radek arrived in Geneva, Romm "handed him a letter from Trotsky which I [Romm] had received from Sedov not long before that in Paris." So, in the spring of 1931, Sedov had hypothetically posed the question of making contact with Radek—"if necessary." Did Sedov, perhaps, foresee Radek's coming to Geneva? Obviously not, because in the summer of 1931 Radek himself could not have foreseen his future journey. By hook or crook, three-quarters of a year after a conversation in Berlin, Sedov obtained the opportunity to avail himself of a promise made him by Romm. But what took place in the recesses of Romm's mind in the interval between the summer of 1931, when he in principle took the path of "conspiracy," and the spring of 1932, when he took the first practical step? Did he attempt, even then, to establish connections with me? Did he become interested in my books, publications and friends? Did he have political discussions with Sedov? Nothing of the kind. Romm merely took upon himself a minor commission, which might have cost him his head. As for the rest, he was not interested. Does Romm bear any resemblance at all to a confirmed Trotskyist? Hardly; instead, he is as like a G.P.U. *agent provocateur* as one drop of water is to another, provided—provided he really did commit the acts he describes. As a matter of fact, all these acts were thought up retroactively. We shall have ample opportunity to become convinced of this.

In what circumstances did Sedov, in the spring of 1932, convey to Romm a letter for Radek? The answer to this question is truly remarkable: "A few days before my departure for Geneva," says Romm, "while in Paris, I received a letter posted in Paris, containing a short note from Sedov asking me to convey a letter enclosed in the envelope to Radek." And so, some nine to ten months after his one and only meeting with Romm—how many recantations, betrayals, and provocations were there during these very months!—Sedov, without any preliminary check-up, sends Romm a conspirative letter. For the sake of adding a second piece of giddiness to the first, he resorts to the services of the "city post." Why not from hand to hand? Vyshinsky naturally refrains from raising this ticklish question. But we, on our part, have an explanation to offer. Neither the G.P.U. nor Vyshinsky, nor, in consequence, Romm, knows with certainty Sedov's precise whereabouts in the spring of 1932—in Berlin or in Paris. Arrange the meeting in the Tiergarten? Choose Montparnasse as the rendezvous? No; it is safest to circumnavigate the submarine reefs. To be sure, a letter by city post somehow seems to hint that Sedov was in Paris. But "if necessary," it will always be possible to say that Sedov sent the letter from Berlin to some Parisian agent of his, and that it was really the latter who used the city post to convey the letter to Romm. How careless, how impotent are these "Trotskyist" conspirators! But it may be that Trotsky wrote his letter in code and with invisible ink? Let us listen to the witness on this point:

"*Romm:* I took this letter with me to Geneva and handed it to Radek when I met him. . . .

"*Vyshinsky:* Did Radek read the letter in your presence or after you had gone?

"*Romm:* He glanced through it quickly in my presence and put it in his pocket."

What inimitable detail! Radek did not swallow the letter, did not fling it into the gutter, and did not hand it over to the Secretariat of the League of Nations, but without much ado . . . "put it in his pocket." All the confessions abound in such "concrete" platitudes, of which the most incompetent writer of detective stories would be ashamed. In any case, we do learn that Radek quickly "glanced through" the letter in Romm's presence. It is impossible quickly to "glance through," then and there, in full view of an intermediary, a letter that is in code—all the more so in the case of a letter written with invisible ink. Consequently the letter, which went by city post, must have been written in the same fashion as birthday greetings. But perhaps this first letter at least did not contain any particular secrets. Let us listen further:

"*Vyshinsky:* What did Radek tell you about the contents of that letter?

"*Romm:* That it contained instructions about uniting with the Zinovievites, about adopting terrorist methods of struggle against the leaders of the C.P.S.U., in the first place against Stalin and Voroshilov."

We perceive that the communication was not at all innocent in content. It "contained instructions" to kill, as a beginning, Stalin and Voroshilov, and then all the others. It was precisely this little letter that Sedov allegedly sent by city post to Romm, whom he hardly knew, ten months after his first and only meeting with him. Our perplexity, however, does not end here. Vyshinsky, as we have just heard, puts a direct question to the witness: "What did Radek tell you about the contents of that letter?" It is as though Radek was *obliged* to impart the contents of an ultra-secret letter to an ordinary contact man! The most elementary conspiratorial rule reads that each participant in an illegal organization must be informed only about that which relates to his personal duties. Inasmuch as Romm remained abroad, and was, obviously, not engaged in preparations to assassinate Stalin, Voroshilov, or any of the others (at any rate, he himself tells nothing about such intentions), Radek, if he was in full possession of his senses, did not have the slightest ground for informing Romm about the contents of the letter. There were no grounds—from the standpoint of an Oppositionist, a conspirator, or a terrorist. But the question appears in a totally different light when viewed from the standpoint of the G.P.U. Had Radek told Romm nothing about the contents of the letter, Romm could not have revealed the terrorist directive of Trotsky, and his entire testimony on this score would have been pointless. We already know that the witnesses, like the accused, testify not to that which flows from the conspiratorial nature of their activities and from their individual psychology, but to that which is needful to Mr. Prosecutor, whom nature has endowed with very sluggish brains. In addition, the accused and the witnesses are under instructions to concern themselves with the verisimilitude of the report of the court proceedings.

What happened, the reader will ask, to the Tass correspondent when he suddenly heard Trotsky's directive to annihilate with the greatest speed imaginable the "leaders" of the Soviet Union? Was he horror-stricken? Did he swoon? Did he give vent to indignation? Or, on the contrary, did he pass into a state of exaltation? Not a word about all this. No psychology is demanded of the witnesses or the accused. Romm "incidentally" handed the letter to Radek. Radek "incidentally" informed him about the terrorist directive. "Then Radek left for Moscow and I did not see him until the autumn of 1932." That is all! They simply passed on to their routine tasks.

But on this point Radek, perturbed by the vividness of

the dialogue, incautiously corrects Romm: "In Trotsky's first letter," said he, "the names of Stalin and Voroshilov were not mentioned, since we never mentioned names in our letters." For correspondence with me, it appears that at that time Radek did not yet have a code. "Trotsky," he insists, "could not possibly have mentioned the names of Stalin and Voroshilov. . . ." We ask: How did Romm come upon them? And if he invented such a "trifle" as the names of Stalin and Voroshilov as the first victims of terror, perhaps he invented the whole letter? The Prosecutor does not concern himself with this at all.

In the autumn of 1932, Romm came to Moscow on official business and met Radek, who did not fail to seize the occasion to inform him that "in pursuance of Trotsky's directives a Trotskyite-Zinovievite *bloc* had been organized, but that he and Pyatakov had not joined that center." Again we perceive that Radek can hardly wait for the occasion to reveal some most important secret to Romm, not at all out of light-mindedness and altruistic loquacity, so peculiar to him in general, but rather for the sake of the supreme goal: The need to help Prosecutor Vyshinsky patch up the looming gaps in the confessions of Zinoviev, Kamenev and others. In fact, no one has been able to comprehend to this day how and why Radek and Pyatakov, who had already been exposed as "accomplices" by the accused during the preliminary investigation in the case of the sixteen, were not brought to trial at the proper time. No one has been able to comprehend how it happened that Zinoviev, Kamenev, Smirnov and Mrachkovsky knew nothing of the international plans of Radek and Pyatakov (expediting war, dismembering the U.S.S.R., etc.). People, not without some perspicacity, have reckoned that these grandiose plans, as well as the very idea of a "parallel center," originated in the G.P.U. only after the shooting of the sixteen, in order that one falsification might be propped up by a second. It turns out otherwise. Radek, well in advance, as far back as the autumn of 1932, had told Romm that the Trotskyite-Zinovievite center had already been formed but that he (Radek) and Pyatakov had not joined this center, saving themselves for the "parallel center on which the Trotskyites were to predominate." Thus, Radek's talkativeness is providential. This does not mean, however, that Radek really did speak to Romm about the parallel center in the autumn of 1932 as if in forecast of the worries which were to beset Vyshinsky in 1937. No; the matter is much more simple. In 1937, Radek and Romm, under the supervision of the G.P.U., constructed retroactively the schema of events for 1932. And to tell the truth, they constructed it very poorly.

While telling Romm about the principal and parallel centers, Radek did not let slip the opportunity to add, then and there, that "he wanted to get directives from Trotsky on this matter." Failing this, Romm's testimony would not have had any real value. "In pursuance of Trotsky's directives," the terrorist center had been formed. Trotsky's directives are now indispensable for the formation of the parallel center. These people are incapable of taking a single step without Trotsky—or rather, they seek to inform the universe through every channel that all crimes are committed only in pursuance of Trotsky's directives.

Availing himself of Romm's journey, Radek, naturally, wrote a letter to Trotsky.

"*Vyshinsky:* What was written in that letter? Did you know?

"*Romm:* Yes, because the letter was handed to me, and then [!] concealed in the cover of a German book before my departure back to Geneva . . ."

The Prosecutor has no anticipatory doubts about Romm's familiarity with the contents of the letter. After all, it is precisely for this reason that the ill-starred Tass correspondent has been converted into a witness! Nevertheless, there is more docility than sense in Romm's reply. The letter was first "handed" to him, and later put in the cover of a German book. What does "handed" mean in such a context? And by whom was it put in the cover of a book? If Radek had simply concealed the letter in the binding and instructed Romm to deliver the book to its destination—as was always done by revolutionists familiar with the ABC of conspiracy—then Romm would have been unable to tell the court anything except that he had delivered a "German book" to such and such address. This is naturally not enough for Vyshinsky. Therefore, the letter was first "handed" to Romm—so that he could read it?—and then inserted in the cover so that the Prosecutor would have no need to torture his faculties any further. In this way mankind learned without much trouble that Radek wrote to Trotsky not about spectral analysis but about the self-same terrorist center.

Passing through Berlin, Romm sent the book by parcel post to an address which Sedov had given him, "*poste restante* at one of the Berlin post offices." These gentlemen have burned their fingers during the trial of the sixteen, and therefore proceed with caution. Romm did not pay a personal visit either to Sedov or any individual designated by Sedov, for in that case it would have been necessary to state the latter's name and address, and that was far too risky. Nor did Romm send the book to the address of some German connected with Sedov. Such procedure, to be sure, would have been wholly in accord with conspiratorial tradition; but in that case, sad to say, one has to know the German's name and address. It is, therefore, far more cautious (not from the standpoint of conspiracy, but from the standpoint of falsification) to send the book "*poste restante* at one of the Berlin post offices."

Romm's next meeting with Sedov took place "in July 1933." Let us make note of this date. We are approaching the central point in the testimony. And here I, too, am called to appear on the scene.

"*Vyshinsky:* What was the occasion, where and how did you meet again?

"*Romm:* In Paris. I had arrived from Geneva and a few days after Sedov telephoned me . . ."

It remains unknown how Sedov learned about Romm's arrival. At first glance, this remark might seem captious. As a matter of fact, it once again reveals to us the system of cowardly reticence. In order to have informed Sedov of his arrival, Romm had to know Sedov's address or telephone number. Romm knew neither the one nor the other. It is safest to leave the initiative to Sedov. Romm is, in any case, acquainted with his own address. Sedov made an appointment for the meeting in a café on the Boulevard Montparnasse, and said that "he wanted to arrange for me [Romm] to meet Trotsky." We know that Romm, while devotedly risking his life as a contact man, had not evinced, up to this time, the slightest desire either to meet me or to enter into correspondence with me. But in answer to Sedov's proposal, he gave immediate consent. In exactly the same way, he went two years previously to meet Sedov on Putna's proposal. In exactly the same way he consented to convey letters to Radek the moment that Sedov opened his mouth. Romm's function is: Consent to everything, but display initiative in nothing. He has obviously agreed with the G.P.U. upon this "minimum" of criminal activity, in the hope of thus saving his life. Whether or not he will save it—that is another question.

A few days after the first telephone call, Sedov met Romm "in the same café." Out of caution, the café is not named. Suppose it suddenly turns out that the café had burned down on the eve of the meeting! The incident with the Hotel Bristol in Copenhagen has been well assimilated by these people. "From there [from the nameless café] we went to the Bois de Boulogne, where I met Trotsky."

"*Vyshinsky:* When was that?

"*Romm:* At the end of July 1933."

Assuredly, Vyshinsky could not have asked a more unseasonable question! Romm, to be sure, had somewhat earlier assigned this episode to July, 1933. But he might have been mistaken, or he might have qualified his statement. He might have been shot, and later one of the Pritts might have been entrusted with rectifying this error. But, upon the insistence of the Prosecutor, Romm repeats and states more explicitly that the meeting took place "at the end of July 1933." Here Vyshinsky throws caution to the wind! Romm specified a truly fatal date, which alone buries not only Romm's evidence, but the whole trial. I must, however, ask the Commission to be indulgent. We shall deal shortly with the fatal chronological error and its sources. But, before doing so, let us investigate further the court dialogue—or rather, the duet.

Romm's meeting with me in the Bois de Boulogne—the first time he had ever met me in his life, as follows from his own story—should have left, it seems, an imprint on his memory. But we hear him tell nothing—either about the first moment of acquaintance, his first impressions, or the course of the conversation. Did we walk along the allée? Did we sit on a bench? Was I smoking a cigarette, a cigar, or a pipe? How did I look? There is not a single living trace, not a single subjective experience, not a single visual impression. Trotsky in an allée of the Bois de Boulogne remains for Romm a phantom, an abstraction, a puppet from the folders of the G.P.U. Romm remarks only that the conversation lasted "twenty to twenty-five minutes."

"*Vyshinsky:* For what purpose did Trotsky meet you?

"*Romm:* As far as I could understand [!], in order verbally to confirm the instructions contained in the letter I was taking to Moscow."

Remarkable words these, "as far as I could understand"! The purpose of the meeting was, apparently, so indeterminate that Romm is only able to guess at it, and, indeed, only in retrospect. In fact, after I had written Radek a letter filled with the ritualistic instructions about annihilating the leaders, wrecking activities, etc., I could not have had any grounds for conversing with a contact agent unknown to me. There are cases when oral directives are confirmed by letter. There are cases when directives given to a subordinate are confirmed through a more authoritative person. But it remains entirely incomprehensible why I should have had to confirm orally those directives which I had communicated by letter to Radek—through Romm, who was an authority for nobody. But while such behavior is incomprehensible from the standpoint of a conspirator, the situation becomes immediately transformed if we take into account the interests of the Prosecutor. Failing a meeting with me, Romm could only have testified that he had brought Radek a letter concealed in the binding of a book. This letter is, of course, not in the possession of Radek, Romm or the Prosecutor. Romm could not have read a letter concealed in a binding. Could it be that the letter was not at all from me? It may even be that there was no letter at all? In order to extricate Romm from a difficult situation, I, instead of conveying a book for Radek to a contact man through some invulnerable intermediary, say, a Frenchman—as would have been done by any conspirator over the age of fifteen—I, who have passed the age of fifty, took the diametrically opposite course, namely: Not only did I involve my son in this operation—which alone would have been the grossest error—but I appeared in person to consummate the performance, for the sake of drilling into Romm's head, for twenty to twenty-five minutes, his future testimony at the trial. The methodology of the frame-up is not distinguished by refinement.

In the course of the conversation, I declared, of course, that I "agreed with the idea of the parallel center but only on the imperative condition that the *bloc* with the Zinovievites was preserved and also on the condition that the parallel center shall not be inactive but shall actively engage in gathering around itself the most stalwart cadres." What profound and fruitful ideas! I could not, of course, have failed to demand "that the *bloc* with the Zinovievites [be] preserved," for otherwise Stalin would not have had the possibility of shooting Zinoviev, Kamenev, Smirnov and the others. But I also approved the formation of the parallel center, so as to provide Stalin with the opportunity to shoot Pyatakov, Serebryakov and Muralov. Passing to the question of the necessity of applying not only terror but also wrecking activities in industry, I recommended disregard for the human victims. In reply, Romm declared himself "somewhat perplexed," for, after all, this "would undermine the defense capacity of the country . . ."! Thus, in the Bois de Boulogne, I supposedly bared my innermost thoughts to an unknown young man who did not even share my "defeatist" position. And all this on the basis of the fact that, in 1927, Romm supposedly agreed with Radek "on the Chinese question"!

The expeditious Romm, of course, delivered to its destination a letter which was never written, and, therewith told Radek about his imaginary conversation with me—so as to enable Vyshinsky to base himself upon at least two testimonies. At the end of September, 1933, Radek entrusted Romm with his reply. This time Romm has nothing to say about the contents of the letter. There is, incidentally, hardly any need for that, since all the letters in this trial are as like one another as the exorcisms of Siberian sorcerers. Romm gave the book containing the letter to Sedov "in Paris in November 1933." Their next meeting took place in April, 1934, once again in the Bois de Boulogne. Romm arrived with the news that he was soon to receive an appointment to America. Sedov "expressed regret at this," but requested him to bring back from Radek "a detailed report on the situation . . ."

"*Vyshinsky:* Did you convey this message?

"*Romm:* Yes, I did. . . ."

How could Romm have failed to convey the message? In May, 1934, he delivered to Sedov in Paris an Anglo-Russian technical dictionary (what a wealth of detail!) containing "a detailed report from the active center, as well as from the parallel center . . ." Let us bear in mind this precious circumstance! Not one of the sixteen defendants, from Zinoviev down to Reingold, who knew everything and "snitched" on everybody, knew anything at all in August, 1936, of the existence of the parallel center. On the other hand, Romm, as far back as the autumn of 1932, was kept fully informed of the idea of the parallel center and its future realization. No less remarkable is the fact that Radek, who did not belong to the principal center, nevertheless did send out "a detailed report from the active center, as well as from the parallel center." Romm had nothing to say concerning these reports, and Vyshinsky naturally refrains from annoying him. After all, what could Romm say? In May, 1934, Kirov had not yet been assassinated by Nikolayev, with the closest participation of the G.P.U. and its agent, the Latvian consul, Bisseneks. Romm would have had to say that the activity of the "active and parallel centers" consisted of requesting and receiving "directives" from me. But we already know this without him. Let us, therefore, leave Radek's "detailed reports" in the recesses of the technical dictionary!

Further on, Vyshinsky becomes interested in the context of the conversation with Sedov in connection with Romm's appointment to America. Romm immediately reveals a request from Trotsky, transmitted to him through Sedov, that Trotsky "be informed in case there was anything interesting in the sphere of Soviet-American relations." The request appears at first glance innocent enough in itself. As politician and writer, I, of course, could not but be interested in Soviet-American relations—all the more so since I had had more than one occasion during the previous years to write articles in the American press and to issue statements in favor of the recognition of the Soviets by the United States. But Romm, who had expressed no surprise when instructions on terror and wrecking were conveyed through him, felt it his duty to become surprised over this point. "When I asked why this was so interesting [!], Sedov told me: 'This follows from Trotsky's line on the defeat of the U.S.S.R.'" Here is another dot on the letter "i." In my articles, to be sure, I invariably came out for the defense of the U.S.S.R. I publicly broke with all those alleged co-thinkers of mine who entertained doubts about the duty of every revolutionist, despite the Stalinist régime, to defend the U.S.S.R. Nothing else remains than to concede that my "defeatism," which is in complete contradiction with my journalistic activity, has been kept a strict secret except from a handful of initiates. Needless to say, such a hypothesis is politically and psychologically absurd. In any case, the accusation rests wholly upon it, and must fall or flourish with it. But Vyshinsky, who is so "cautious" with regard to details (dates, addresses), is totally witless with respect to the fundamental problems of the trial. When Romm asks Sedov why I am "interested" in Soviet-American relations (the question is in itself nonsensical!) Sedov, instead of referring to my literary activity, with a rash haste blurts out: "This follows from Trotsky's line on the defeat of the U.S.S.R." But if that is the case, it turns out that I never made a secret of my "defeatism." Wherefore, then, my entire intense theoretical and journalistic work? Messrs. Accusers do not bother to think about this fact. They are incapable of thinking about it. Their frame-up unfolds upon a much lower plane. They manage to get along without psychology. They are satisfied with the inquisitorial machine.

To a subsequent question by Vyshinsky, Romm replies: "Yes. I agreed to send Trotsky information which interested him." But Romm carried out his "last commission" in May, 1934. After the murder of Kirov he resolved "to stop active work." Precisely because of that he did not send me information from the United States. I must confess that it quite escaped my notice. Among my American friends there are men highly qualified in science and politics, ready at any time to supply me with information on all questions within the orbit of my interests. In consequence, I had no grounds for turning to Romm for information—provided one discounts, of course, my urgent need to tell him about my "defeatist" program.

This entire episode was apparently included in Romm's testimony—and it may be that Romm in person was injected into the trial—only after it had become clear that I was migrating to America. The imagination of the G.P.U. sought to overtake in its flight the oil tanker transporting me from Oslo to Tampico. In this way the United States Government received immediate warning that in Washington itself a "Trotskyist" agent had been operating—Romm by name, who had "agreed" to send me information. What information? It is clear as noonday; such as threatens the vital interests of the United States. Radek deepened this warning. According to him, it was part of my program "to guarantee to supply Japan with oil in case of war with the United States." (Session of January 23.) Obviously, it is for this reason that I selected as my means of transportation from Oslo to Tampico the oil tanker, an indispensable vehicle for further operations in oil. At the next trial, Romm will probably recall that I had instructed him to plug up the Panama Canal and divert Niagara to flood New York—all this during his hours off duty as correspondent of *Isvestia*. . . . Can it be that all these people are so stupid? No; of course not. They are not stupid at all, but their minds have been totally demoralized by the régime of totalitarian irresponsibility.

Any careful reading will show that every question put

by Vyshinsky discredits beforehand the answer of Romm. Every answer of Romm constitutes evidence against Vyshinsky. The dialogue as a whole blots out the trial. The series of these trials irreparably covers Stalin's system with ignominy. But we have still not spoken of the most important matter. That Romm's testimony is false is self-evident, from the testimony itself, to every one who is not blind and deaf. But we have at our disposal proofs that are apt even for the blind and the deaf. I was not in the Bois de Boulogne at the end of July, 1933. I couldn't have been there. At that time I was a sick man living on the Atlantic coast 500 kilometers away from Paris. I have already issued a brief account of this fact to the *New York Times* (February 17th, 1937). I wish here to recount this entire episode in somewhat greater detail. It merits it!

On July 24, 1933, the Italian steamer "Bulgaria," with myself, my wife and four associates (two Americans, Sarah Weber, Max Shachtman; the Frenchman, Van Heijenoort; and the German émigré, Adolphe) aboard, was about to dock in the harbor of Marseilles. After more than four years' stay in Turkey, we were migrating to western Europe. Our coming to France was preceded by lengthy negotiations, and by solicitudes chief among which was concern about my health. In issuing the permit of entry, the Daladier Government proceeded, however, with caution. They feared attempts at assassination, demonstrations, and other incidents, especially in the capital. On June 29, 1933, Chautemps, the Minister of the Interior, wrote in a letter to Deputy Henri Guernut that I was "authorized on account of health to sojourn in one of the Southern departments and then establish residence in Corsica." (I had myself tentatively suggested Corsica in one of my letters.) Thus, from the very outset, it was not the capital that was under consideration, but one of the distant departments. I could not have had the slightest motive for violating this condition, since I was myself sufficiently interested in avoiding during my stay in France any complications whatsoever. One ought, therefore, to reject in advance, as fantastic, the very idea that I could, immediately upon setting foot on French soil, have violated the agreement by disappearing from under the very eyes of the police and departing secretly for Paris—for an unnecessary meeting with Romm! No; what actually took place was altogether different.

Encouraged by Hitler's victory in Germany, reaction in France was raising its head. Against my entry into the country a rabid campaign was waged by such newspapers as *le Matin, le Journal, la Liberté, l'Echo de Paris,* etc. In this chorus, the voice of *l'Humanité* rang most shrilly. The French Stalinists had not yet received orders to recognize Socialists and Radicals as their "brothers." Oh, no! Daladier was at that time treated by the Comintern as a Radical-Fascist, Léon Blum, who supported Daladier, was branded as a Social-Fascist. As concerns me, I was, by special appointment of Moscow, fulfilling the functions of an agent of American, British and French imperialism. How short is human memory! The assumed name under which we booked our passage was naturally discovered en route. There was reason to fear demonstrations at the Marseilles harbor on the part of fascists, and all the more so on the part of the Stalinists. Our friends in France had every reason to be concerned lest my entry be accompanied by incidents which might complicate my further stay in the country. To evade the vigilance of enemies, our friends—among them my son, who had succeeded in getting to Paris from Hitler's Germany—worked out a stratagem which was brilliantly successful, as proved by the last Moscow trial. By radio order from France, the "Bulgaria" was stopped a few kilometers outside the Marseilles harbor, to meet a motor boat in which were my son, the Frenchman Raymond Molinier, the Commissioner of the *Sûreté Générale,* and two boatmen. If I remember rightly, the sum of one thousand francs was paid for delaying the boat for three minutes. This incident is, of course, recorded in the ship's log. Moreover, it was at that time remarked upon by the entire world press. My son came aboard and handed to one of my associates, the Frenchman Van Heijenoort, written instructions. Only my wife and I descended to the motor boat. While our four fellow-travellers continued their journey to Marseilles with all our baggage, the motor boat docked at the tidy little village of Cassis, where two automobiles and two French friends, Leprince and Laste, awaited us. Without a moment's delay, we immediately proceeded westward from Marseilles, bearing in a northerly direction, to the mouth of the Gironde, in the Department of Charente-Inférieure, where a country house in the village of Saint Palais, near Royan, had previously been rented for us in the name of Molinier. On the road we stayed over night at a hotel. Our registrations at the hotel have been verified and presented by me to the Commission.

I might add that, for the sake of preserving the secret of our identity, all our baggage was checked in Turkey in the name of Max Shachtman. His initials have been preserved to this day on the wooden boxes in which my books and papers arrived in Mexico. But in view of the discovery of our incognito, it could no longer have been a secret to the G.P.U. agents in Marseilles that the baggage was really mine; and inasmuch as my associates, together with the baggage, headed toward Paris, the G.P.U. agents proceeded on the supposition that my wife and I had also gone to the French capital, by automobile or airplane. It should be borne in mind that at that period the relations between the Soviet and the French Governments were still very strained. The Comintern press even asserted that I came to France on a special mission—to assist the then Premier Daladier, now Minister of War, in preparing military intervention in the U.S.S.R. How short is human memory! Between the G.P.U. and the French police there could not, consequently, have been close relations. The G.P.U. knew about me only that which was published in the papers. Romm could know only that which was known to the G.P.U. Meanwhile, the press immediately lost track of us after our landing.

After checking the dispatches of their own correspondent for that period, the editors of the *New York Times* wrote on February 17th last:

> The ship that brought Mr. Trotsky from Turkey to Marseilles in 1933 docked after he had slipped secretly ashore, according to a Marseilles dispatch to the *New York Times* of July 25th, 1933. He had been taken aboard a tugboat three miles outside the harbor and landed at Cassis, where an automobile was waiting. At that time Mr. Trotsky was variously reported bound for Corsica, the curative waters of Royat, in the center of France near Vichy, or the latter place itself . . .

This report, which does credit to the accuracy of the *Times* correspondent, completely confirms the foregoing account. As early as July 24th the press was lost in speculation as to what had happened to us. The position of the G.P.U., one must admit, was extremely difficult.

The organizers of the frame-up reasoned approximately as follows: Trotsky could not have failed to spend at least a few days in Paris, in order to arrange things and find himself a domicile in the provinces. The G.P.U. did not know that all these details had been taken care of in advance, and that our country house had been rented prior to our arrival. On the other hand, Stalin, Yezhov, Vyshinsky feared to postpone the meeting with Romm to the month of August or thereafter. It was necessary to forge the iron while it was hot. In this way, these cautious and calculating men selected the end of July for the meeting, at a time when, according to all their suppositions, I could not have failed to be in Paris. But it was precisely in this supposition that they miscalculated. We were not in Paris. Accompanied by our son and three French friends, we arrived, as I have already stated, in Saint Palais, near Royan, on July 25th. As if in order to complicate further the position of the G.P.U., the day of our arrival was marked by a fire in our country house. An arbor burned down, also a section of the wooden fence, and a number of trees were scorched. The fire was caused by sparks from the smokestack of a locomotive. In the local newspapers for July 26th, accounts of this incident can be found. The landlord's niece arrived a few hours later to check up on the consequences of the fire. Many neighbors saw me during the fire. The testimony of both persons who served us on the journey as chauffeurs, Leprince and R. Molinier, as well as the testimony of Laste, who accompanied us, describes the journey in minute detail. A certification issued by the fire department corroborates the date of the fire. The reporter, Albert Bardon, who wrote up the fire in the press, saw me in an automobile and made a deposition to this effect. The above-mentioned niece of the landlord also made a deposition. In the country house, there were waiting for us Vera Lanis, who assumed the functions of housekeeper, and Segal, who was helping us to get settled. They spent the last part of July with us, and were witnesses to the fact that I arrived in Saint Palais suffering from lumbago and high fever, and that I scarcely left my bed.

The Prefect of the Department of Charente-Inférieure was immediately informed of our arrival, by a coded telegram from Paris. We lived near Royan, as in France generally, incognito. Our passports were stamped only by the highest officials of the *Sûreté Générale* in Paris. One can doubtless find there traces of our itinerary.

I remained in Saint Palais more than two months in a state of infirmity, under a physician's care. I wrote in the *New York Times* that I received as visitors in Saint Palais more than thirty friends. Subsequent recollections and researches among documents indicate that I really had some fifty visitors—more than thirty Frenchmen (mainly Parisians), seven Hollanders, two Belgians, two Germans, two Italians, three Englishmen, one Swiss, etc. Among the visitors were men with well known names; for instance, the French writer, Andre Malraux; the translator of my books, the writer Parijanine; the Dutch parliamentary Deputy, Sneevliet; the Dutch journalists, Schmidt and de Kadt; the former secretary of the British Independent Labor Party, Paton; the German émigré, V.; the German writer, G.; etc. (I refrain from giving the names of the émigrés in order not to cause them any difficulties, but all of them, of course, will be able to testify before the Commission.) Had I spent the end of July in Paris, most of the visitors would not have had to undertake a journey to Royan. They all knew that I was not and could not have been in Paris. Of the four associates who accompanied us, three came from Paris to Royan. Only Max Shachtman went from Havre to New York, without having an opportunity to bid me farewell. I have presented to the Commission his letter, dated August 8th, 1933, in which he expresses his disappointment at having been separated from us on the way and being unable even to say good-bye. No; there is no lack of proofs.

Towards the beginning of October, my physical condition improved, and my friends brought me by automobile to Bagnères in the Pyrenees, still further removed from Paris, where my wife and I passed the month of October. It was solely owing to the fact that our stay near Royan, like our stay in the Pyrenees, passed without any complications, that the Government agreed to permit us to settle nearer to the capital, but still recommended that we settle beyond the confines of the Seine Department. At the beginning of November we went to Barbizon, where a country house had been rented for us. From Barbizon, I did actually pay a few visits to the capital, always accompanied by two or three friends. Moreover, in every instance my day's activities were rigorously arranged beforehand, and those few homes that I visited can be accurately established, together with the list of my visitors. All this, however, pertains to the winter of 1933. Yet the G.P.U. arranged a meeting with me for Romm in July, 1933. There was no such meeting. There could have been none. If, in general, there exists in this world such a thing as an alibi, then in the given instance it receives its most complete and consummate expression. The unfortunate Romm lied. The G.P.U. compelled him to lie. Vyshinsky veiled his lie. For the sake of precisely this lie, Romm was arrested and included among the witnesses.

XVII. PYATAKOV'S FLIGHT TO NORWAY

Even on January 24th, the day following the opening of the last trial and Pyatakov's first statements to the court, when it was necessary to rely on the brief news dispatches, I wrote in a statement for the world press:

> If Pyatakov traveled [to Oslo] under his own name, the whole Norwegian press would have been informed of it. Consequently, he traveled under a false name. What was it? All Soviet dignitaries, when abroad, are in constant touch by telegraph or telephone with their embassies or trade representations, and not for an hour do they escape the surveillance of the G.P.U. How was Pyatakov able to accomplish his trip unknown to the Soviet institutions in Germany and Norway? Let him describe the interior appearance of my apartment. Did he see my wife? Did I or did I not have a beard? How was I dressed? The entrance to my work room was through the apartment of the Knudsens, and all our visitors, without exception,

were introduced to our host's family. Did Pyatakov meet them? Did they see Pyatakov? These are some of the questions with the aid of which it would be easy to demonstrate before any honest court that Pyatakov only repeats the inventions of the G.P.U.

On January 27th, 1937, on the eve of the Prosecutor's delivery of his summation, through the medium of the telegraph agencies, I addressed thirteen questions to the court at Moscow on the subject of Pyatakov's pretended interview with me in Norway. I explained the urgency of my questions as follows:

> Involved here is the testimony of Pyatakov. He stated that he met me in Norway in December, 1935, for conspiratorial talks. Pyatakov was supposed to have come from Berlin to Oslo by airplane. The immense importance of this testimony is self-evident. I have declared more than once, and I declare again, that Pyatakov, like Radek, for the past nine years was not my friend but one of my bitterest and most treacherous enemies, and that there could have been no question of negotiations and meetings between us. If it were proven that Pyatakov actually visited me, my position would be hopelessly compromised. On the contrary, if I prove that the account of the visit is false from beginning to end, it is the system of "voluntary confessions" which will be compromised. Even if one were to admit that the Moscow court is above suspicion, the accused Pyatakov would still remain suspect. His testimony must be verified. That is not difficult. Pyatakov is not yet shot. He should immediately be presented with the following series of precise questions.

I note again that these questions, presented by me to the Commission, are based upon the first news dispatches, and that is why they are not exact in certain secondary details. But in the main, even now, they retain their full strength.

My first questions regarding Pyatakov were already at the disposal of the court on January 25th. No later than January 28th—that is, the day when the Prosecutor delivered his summation—the court had my later questions. Not later than January 26th, the Prosecutor had received telegraphic information that the Norwegian press categorically denied Pyatakov's testimony about his flight. In the Prosecutor's address, there is an indirect allusion to this denial. However, not one of the thirteen concrete questions posed by me was presented to the accused, for whom the Prosecutor demanded death. The Prosecutor did not make the attempt, obligatory for him, to verify the main testimony of the principal accused and thereby reinforce the accusation against me and all the others in the eyes of the whole world. If the telegrams from Oslo and my telegraphic questions did not exist, it would still be possible to speak of the remissness, negligence, and intellectual poverty of the Prosecutor and the judges. In the light of the above circumstances, there can be no question of a judicial error. The Prosecutor, like the President of the Court, consciously avoided posing questions which flowed inescapably from the very nature of Pyatakov's testimony. They opposed the verification, not because it was impossible—on the contrary, it was exceedingly simple—but because, due to the whole role they were playing, they could not allow a verification. Instead, they hastened to shoot Pyatakov. However, the verification was made without them. It has completely and irrefutably demonstrated the falseness of the testimony of the principal accused in the principal question, and thus has demolished the entire indictment.

We now have at our disposal the so-called "verbatim" report of the trial of Pyatakov and the others. A careful study of the examination of Pyatakov and of the witness for the prosecution, Bukhartsev, demonstrates by itself that the Prosecutor's task in this completely artificial, untrue and rehearsed judicial dialogue was to help Pyatakov present, without too obvious absurdities, the fantastic tale which the G.P.U. had forced upon him. That is why we shall follow a double road in our analysis: First, we shall demonstrate on the basis of the official report itself the internal falseness of Pyatakov's examination by Vyshinsky; then we shall present objective proofs of the material impossibility of Pyatakov's flight and of his meeting with me. In this way we shall uncover not only the falseness of the principal testimony of the principal defendant, but also the participation of Prosecutor Vyshinsky and the judges in the frame-up.

"In the first half of December," 1935, Pyatakov made his mythical flight to Oslo, via Berlin. Bukhartsev, Berlin correspondent of *Isvestia,* acted as a sort of intermediary in the arrangement of the trip, just as V. Romm, *Isvestia* correspondent in Washington, had served as intermediary between Radek and me. The Government paper, strangely enough, appointed "Trotskyite" liaison agents to posts as correspondents in the most important places. Would it not be more accurate to assume that they were agents of the G.P.U.? Pyatakov's declaration that Bukhartsev "had connections with Trotsky" is pure and simple invention. I never had the slightest knowledge, personally or from his writings, of either Bukhartsev or Romm. I rarely see *Isvestia,* and I do not as a rule read the foreign correspondence in the Soviet press.

There is no reason to doubt that Pyatakov was really in Berlin on December 10th, 1935, on the official business of his department. The fact is easy to verify through the German and Soviet press, which must have noted Pyatakov's arrival in the German capital as well as his return to Moscow.* The G.P.U. was afterwards forced to adapt Pyatakov's mythical trip to Oslo to his real trip to Berlin; hence the unfortunate choice of the month of December.

On arriving in Berlin, Pyatakov, according to his own words, immediately ("the same day or the next"—that is, the 11th or 12th) met Bukhartsev. The latter allegedly informed me in advance of Pyatakov's impending arrival. By letter? By prearranged telegram? How worded? To what address? Nobody embarrasses Bukhartsev with these questions. In this court room dates and addresses are generally avoided like a plague. Having received Bukhartsev's information, I, in turn, immediately send a trustworthy messenger to Berlin with this note: "Y.L., the bearer of this note can be fully trusted." The word "fully" was underlined. This not very original detail will, as we shall see, have to compensate us for the absence of other, more substantial information. The messenger sent by me, with a name "either Heinrich or Gustav" (Pyatakov's testimony), took upon himself the arrangement of the flight to Oslo. The meeting between "Heinrich-Gustav" and Pyatakov took place in the Tiergarten (the 11th or 12th) and lasted altogether "literally for a couple of minutes." The second precious detail! Pyatakov was prepared to go to Oslo, although, as he twice repeats, "for me it meant taking a very great risk of discovery, exposure and anything you like." In the Russian report these words were omitted, and not inadvertently. The watch maintained over Soviet functionaries abroad is extremely strict. Pyatakov had *no possibility* of absenting himself from Berlin for

---

* The *Berliner Tageblatt* of December 21st, 1935, reports: "Among the current visitors to Berlin there is the first Vice Commissar of Heavy Industry of the Soviet Union, Mr. Pyatakov, and also the head of the import division of the Commissariat of Foreign Trade of the Soviet Union, Mr. Smolensky."

forty-eight hours, without indicating to the Soviet institutions where he was going and at what address they could communicate with him; as a member of the Central Committee and of the Government, Pyatakov could at any moment receive an inquiry or be charged with a mission by Moscow. The rules which exist on this subject are well known to the Prosecutor and to the judges. Moreover, on January, 24th, I already asked the court by telegraph: "How was Pyatakov able to complete his journey without the knowledge of the Soviet institutions in Germany and Norway?" On January 27th, I repeated: "How was Pyatakov able to conceal himself from the Soviet institutions in Berlin and Oslo? How did he explain his disappearance after his return?" No one, of course, bothered the defendant with such questions.

Pyatakov arranged with "Heinrich-Gustav" to meet "the next morning" (the 12th or 13th) at the Tempelhof Airport. The Prosecutor, who in questions which have no importance and cannot be subjected to verification demands sometimes a demonstrative display of precision, is entirely unconcerned about rendering precise a date of such exceptional importance! However, by means of the records of the Soviet trade representation in Berlin, it should be possible without difficulty to establish a day-to-day calendar of Pyatakov's activities. But that is precisely what must be avoided.

"Early next morning, I went straight to the entrance of the airdrome." Early in the morning? We should like to know at what hour. In matters of this nature, the hour is set in advance. But Pyatakov's inspirers were evidently afraid of erring with regard to the meteorological calendar. At the airport Pyatakov met "Heinrich-Gustav": "He was waiting at the entrance and led the way. He first showed me a passport which had been prepared for me. The passport was a German one. He saw to all the customs formalities himself, so that all I had to do was to sign my name. We got into an airplane and set off. . . ." No one so much as interrupted the defendant at this point. The Prosecutor—unbelievable though it may seem—is not even interested in the question of the passport. That the passport was "German" is enough for him. However, a German passport, like any other, is made out in a definite *name*. Precisely in whose name, in this instance? *Nomina sunt odiosa.* The Prosecutor is preoccupied with giving Pyatakov the opportunity to slide past this ticklish point as swiftly as possible. "The customs formalities?" "Heinrich-Gustav" took care of them. All Pyatakov had to do was "to sign [his] name." One would imagine that at this point the Prosecutor could not possibly have failed to ask Pyatakov what name he signed. Presumably the name that was on the German passport. But the Prosecutor considers this none of his business. The President of the Court also keeps his silence. So do the judges. A collective oversight, due to fatigue? But I took timely steps to refresh the memories of these gentlemen. As early as January 24th, I asked the court under what name Pyatakov arrived in Oslo. Three days later I returned to this point. Of the thirteen questions posed by me, the fourth was: "With what passport did Pyatakov depart from Berlin? Did he receive a Norwegian visa?" My questions were reproduced by newspapers throughout the world. If Vyshinsky still did not question Pyatakov about the passport and visa, it was because he knew that it was necessary to keep quiet about them. This silence alone is entirely sufficient to allow us to say: We have before us a frame-up!

Let us, however, continue to trace Pyatakov's steps: "We got into an airplane and set off. We did not stop anywhere, and at approximately 3 p.m. we landed at the airdrome in Oslo. There an automobile awaited us. We got in and drove off. We drove for about thirty minutes, and came to a country suburb. We got out, entered a small house that was not badly furnished, and there I saw Trotsky, whom I had not seen since 1928." Doesn't this narrative completely betray a man who has nothing to disclose? Not a trace of living reality! "We got into an airplane, and set off. . . . We got in and drove off. . . ." Pyatakov saw nothing, spoke with no one. He is unable to communicate anything whatsoever about "Heinrich-Gustav," who accompanied him from Berlin to my door.

What occurred when the plane landed at the airdrome? The Norwegian authorities could not have failed to evince interest in a foreign plane. They could not have failed to examine the passports of Pyatakov and his fellow travelers. However, on that subject, too, we hear not one word. The flight was made, so to speak, in the realm of dreams, where people glide noiselessly, untroubled by police or customs officials.

In the "small" and "not badly furnished" house, Pyatakov saw Trotsky, "whom [he] had not seen since 1928." (In reality, since the end of 1927.) Immediately after these stereotyped commonplaces follows an equally stereotyped description of the interview, seemingly predestined to adorn police records. Does any of this bear any resemblance to life and to living beings? After all, according to the sense of the amalgam, Pyatakov flew to visit me as a cothinker, as a friend, after many years of separation. For several years, approximately from 1923 to 1928, he really was fairly close to me, knew my family, always received a cordial welcome from my wife. He must, evidently, have preserved an entirely exceptional confidence in me if, on the basis of a single letter from me, he became a terrorist, a saboteur and a defeatist and, at the first signal, flew to see me at the risk of his life. It would seem that in such circumstances Pyatakov could not, after a separation of eight years, have failed to manifest some interest in the conditions of my life. But there is not a trace of that. Where did the meeting take place? In my apartment or in another house? Nobody knows. Where was my wife? Nobody knows. To a question by the Prosecutor, Pyatakov replies that absolutely nobody was present during the interview; even "Heinrich-Gustav" remained outside. And that's all! Yet, even by the interior furnishings, the presence or absence of Russian books or newspapers, the appearance of the writing table, Pyatakov could not but have determined at a single glance whether he was in my work room or in someone else's room. On the other hand, I could not have had the slightest reason for concealing such innocent information from my guest, to whom I confided my most secret designs and plans. Pyatakov could not have failed to inquire about my wife. On January 24th, I asked: "Did he see my wife?" On January 27th, I repeated my question: "Did Pyatakov see my wife? Was she at home that day?" (My wife's trips to her doctor and dentist in Oslo can easily be verified.) But, precisely in order to prevent a verification, Pyatakov's mentors taught him elastic formulas and noncommittal modes of expression. That is less risky. However, this excess of caution betrays the frame-up from another angle.

The airplane landed at 3:00 o'clock in the afternoon of the 12th or 13th. Pyatakov arrived at my house approximately at 3:30 p.m. The interview lasted about two hours. My guest must have been hungry. Did I give him something to eat? That, it would seem, was the elementary duty of a host. But I could not do that without the help of my wife or the mistress of the "not badly furnished" house. Not a word on that matter during the trial. Pyatakov left me at 5:30 in the evening. Where did he go from the country suburb, with the German passport in his pocket? The Prosecutor does not inquire about that. Where did he pass the December night? Hardly in the open air. Still less can one assume that he spent the night in the Soviet Embassy. Hardly in the German Embassy, either. In a hotel, then? In exactly which one? Among the thirteen questions which I put to the court was this one: "Pyatakov could not have avoided passing one night in Norway. Where? In what hotel?" The Prosecutor does not question the defendant about this. The President maintains silence.

If an old friend came to visit me—especially a fellow-conspirator—I, like anybody else similarly situated, would do everything to protect my guest from unpleasant surprises and needless risks. After the two-hour interview I would give him something to eat and arrange a suitable lodging. Such petty matters obviously could not have presented the slightest difficulty, since I had been able to send a "trustworthy person" to Berlin and to send a "special" automobile to the airport when the "special" airplane arrived. To avoid appearing in a hotel or in the streets of Oslo, Pyatakov would naturally have been interested in spending the night with us. Moreover, after a long separation, we would have had much to talk about! But the G.P.U. feared that version, because Pyatakov would then have had to go into details concerning my living conditions. Better to slide over these prosaic details. As a matter of fact, I lived, as is known, not in a country suburb near Oslo, but in a secluded village; not thirty minutes' travel from the airport, but at least two hours', especially in winter, when chains must be put on the tires. No; better to suffer a lapse of memory about the food, the December night, the danger of meeting someone connected with the Soviet Embassy. Better to hold one's tongue. Just as previously, during the trip, so now, in Norway, Pyatakov is like the immaterial shadow of a dream. Let fools take this shadow for reality!

Through the examination of the witness Bukhartsev, correspondent of *Isvestia,* we learn some not unimportant supplementary details about Pyatakov's trip. "Heinrich-Gustav," so he affirms, was Gustav Stirner. This name conveys absolutely nothing to me, although, according to Bukhartsev, Stirner had been my trusted man. In any event, my mysterious emissary deemed it necessary to reveal his exact identity to the Prosecutor's witness. Shall we meet a Stirner, in flesh and blood, in some future trial? Or is he a pure product of the imagination? I don't know. The German name, in any case, is food for some reflection.

At times, Pyatakov tried to picture the meeting with me almost as an unavoidable evil; the instinct of self-preservation timidly peeps through the confessions of the accused. On the other hand, according to Bukhartsev, Pyatakov, when apprised of my invitation, said that "he was pleased to hear this, that it fully coincided with his intentions, and that he would willingly agree to this meeting." What needless expansiveness for a conspirator! But needful indeed to the Prosecutor. The task of the witness is to deepen the guilt of the accused, while the task of the accused is to shift the main burden of guilt on to me. The task of the Prosecutor, finally, is to exploit the lies of both.

From the standpoint of the conspiracy, and even the airplane trip to Oslo, Bukhartsev is an entirely superfluous personage; even Vyshinsky is forced, as we shall see, to recognize that. But Gustav Stirner, if such a person exists, is apparently inaccessible to the prosecution. However, if there is no Stirner, there is also no witness. The story of how Pyatakov got into and alighted from the airplane would in that case be based on Pyatakov alone. That is insufficient. While Bukhartsev, who was called to testify by the Prosecutor, did not take part in the march of events, at least he fulfilled the function of the "messenger" in a classical tragedy, who announces the events which are occurring behind the scenes. Consequently, Pyatakov did not fail to inform the "messenger" on the eve of his departure from Berlin for Moscow (on which date?) that "he had been and seen." There was no reason to tell Bukhartsev any of this. In needlessly imparting such information to an outsider, Pyatakov was guilty of inexcusable lightmindedness. But he could not act differently without depriving Bukhartsev of the opportunity of serving as a useful witness for the prosecution.

At this point, the Prosecutor suddenly becomes aware of an omission. "Did you give your photograph?" he unexpectedly asks Pyatakov, interrupting the questioning of Bukhartsev. Vyshinsky resembles a school-boy who has skipped a line in a poem. Pyatakov answers laconically, "I did." Apparently involved here is a passport photograph. A photograph is essential for every passport, even the German variety. While thus showing his alertness, the Prosecutor risks nothing. Naturally, he keeps quiet now, too, about the name and the visa. Whereupon the guardian of the law again goes to work on Bukhartsev. "Do you know where Stirner obtained the passport, where he obtained the airplane? How is it so easy to do this in Germany?" Bukhartsev answers to the effect that Stirner did not go into the details, but requested him, Bukhartsev, not to worry—one of the few answers that sound natural and rational. The Prosecutor, however, is not to be deterred:

> *Vyshinsky:* And were you not curious about this?
> *Bukhartsev:* He did not tell me anything, did not go into details.
> *Vyshinsky:* But were you curious about this?
> *Bukhartsev:* Since he did not reply . . .
> *Vyshinsky:* But did you try to ask him?
> *Bukhartsev:* I did, but he did not reply.

And so on, in the same vein. But here we interrupt this instructive dialogue, to subject the Prosecutor himself to an examination.

"You just asked, Mr. Prosecutor, about a passport photograph. But does not the passport itself interest you? Did not the examining magistrate question Pyatakov about this? Have you, too, forgotten to fulfill your duty? Twice, on January 24th and on January 27th, I reminded you about it telegraphically. Did you pay any attention to my question? Were you, too, not interested in my address, my residence, my living conditions? Why have you not asked Pyatakov where he spent the night? Who recommended the hotel to him? How did he register there? Do not all these circumstances merit your attention? Bukhartsev at least could justify himself by saying that Gustav Stirner refused to let him into his secrets. You, Mr. Guardian of Justice, have not this justification, because Pyatakov keeps no secrets from the Prosecutor. Pyatakov maintains silence only as regards that about which he is forbidden to talk. But you, too, Mr. Prosecutor, did not accidentally shirk your plain duty to bring Pyatakov down from the fourth dimension on to this sinful earth with its customs officials, restaurants, hotels, and other troublesome details. You kept quiet about all this because you are one of the chief organizers of the frame-up!"

Vyshinsky is not to be mollified: "And the airplane?"

"*Bukhartsev:* I asked him [Stirner] how Pyatakov could travel and he told me a special airplane would take Pyatakov to Oslo and back."

It is to be observed that Stirner is not at all reticent. After all, he could simply have told the obtrusive Bukhartsev: "That's none of your business; Pyatakov himself knows what he has to do." But Stirner apparently recalled that before him stood the messenger from a tragedy, and therefore told him that Pyatakov would travel in a "special" plane—in other words, implied that the plane would be provided by the German Government.

Vyshinsky utilizes this prearranged indiscretion of Stirner and Bukhartsev: "But it was not Trotsky who arranged for the flight across the frontier?" Bukhartsev answers with eloquent modesty, "That I do not know."

"*Vyshinsky:* You are an experienced journalist; you know that a flight across a frontier from one country to another is not a simple matter?" (Alas, alas, that is something the

Prosecutor himself completely forgets when it is a question of landing at an airport, obtaining a passport, a visa, a night's lodging, a hotel, etc.) Bukhartsev takes another step to meet the Prosecutor: "I understood that Stirner was able to do this through German official persons." Q.E.D.

But at this point Vyshinsky appears suddenly to regain his senses: "Could they not dispense with you in this matter? Why did you take part in this operation?"

The risky question is put to give Bukhartsev the chance to tell the court how Radek, "some time before" (exactly when?) had forewarned him, a "Trotskyite," that he would have to carry out various commissions, and at the same time told him that "Pyatakov was a member of the center." As we see, Radek foresaw everything and, in any event, had armed the future witness with all the necessary data.

One way or another, thanks to Bukhartsev, we learn that Pyatakov not only flew to Oslo in a "special plane," but that he also returned to Berlin in the same way. This remarkably important declaration implies that the airplane did not simply land for a few minutes, but that it remained the rest of the day and overnight—that is, at least fifteen hours—at the Oslo airport. Probably it was also refueled there. As we shall soon see, Bukhartsev's declaration does us a greater service than it does the Prosecutor. We now arrive at the crux of Pyatakov's testimony, and of the whole trial.

The conservative Norwegian paper *Aftenposten*, immediately after Pyatakov's first day's testimony, made an investigation at the airport and, in its evening edition of January 25th, carried the information that in December, 1935, *not a single foreign airplane* landed in Oslo. This news immediately circulated around the world. Vyshinsky was forced to take into account the unpleasant news from Oslo. He did so in his own manner. At the session of January 27th, the Prosecutor asked Pyatakov whether he really landed at an airport in Norway, and if so, which one. Pyatakov answered:

"Near Oslo." He did not remember the name. Were there no difficulties in landing? Pyatakov, we were told, was so excited that he noticed nothing unusual.

"*Vyshinsky:* You confirm that you landed in an airdrome near Oslo?

"*Pyatakov:* Near Oslo, that I remember."

The only thing lacking was that he should forget such a detail! Thereupon the Prosecutor read into the court record a document which many newspapers mildly characterized as surprising—a communication from the Soviet Embassy in Norway that "the Kjellere Airdrome near Oslo receives all the year round, in accordance with international regulations, airplanes of other countries, and that the arrival and departure of airplanes is possible also in Winter months." That is all! The Prosecutor asks to have this valuable document entered as an exhibit. Thus he considers the question closed!

No; the question is just opened. The Norwegian agencies did not at all assert that air travel is impossible in Norway in the Winter months. Why, then, is it the job of the Moscow court to compile a meteorological handbook for aviators? The question is much more concrete: Did a foreign plane land in Oslo during the month of December, 1935, or not?

Konrad Knudsen, member of the Storting, on January 29th, 1937, sent the following telegram to Moscow:

> To Prosecutor Vyshinsky, Military Collegium of the Supreme Court, Moscow:
>
> I inform you that today it was officially confirmed that in December, 1935, no foreign or private airplane landed at the Oslo airdrome. As Leon Trotsky's host, I also confirm that in December, 1935, no conversation could have taken place in Norway between Trotsky and Pyatakov.
>
> KONRAD KNUDSEN, MEMBER OF STORTING.

On the same day, January 29th, the *Arbeiderbladet,* organ of the Government Party, undertook a new investigation of the "special airplane." It may not be inappropriate to mention that this paper not only approved my internment by the Norwegian Government, but also published extremely hostile articles about me during my imprisonment. I give the report of the *Arbeiderbladet* textually:

PYATAKOV'S MIRACULOUS TRIP TO KJELLER

No Foreign Airplane at Kjeller
from September, 1935, to May, 1936

Director Gulliksen Issues Categorical Denial

Pyatakov insists on his confession to the effect that he arrived by airplane in Norway and landed at the Kjeller Airdrome in December, 1935. The Russian Commissariat for Foreign Affairs has undertaken an investigation intended to confirm this evidence.

The authorities at the Kjeller Airdrome have already categorically denied that any foreign airplane landed there in December, 1935, while Konrad Knudsen, Trotsky's host and a member of the Storting, has issued a declaration that Trotsky received no visitors at all during that period.

A representative of the *Arbeiderbladet* made another inquiry today at the Kjeller Airdrome, and Director Gulliksen confirmed by telephone that no foreign airplane landed at Kjeller in December, 1935. During this month only *one* airplane landed there, and that was a Norwegian plane from Linkoping. But this plane carried no passengers.

Director Gulliksen examined the day-by-day customs register prior to issuing this statement to us, and in reply to our question he added that it is absolutely out of question for any plane to have landed without being observed. Throughout the night a military guard patrols the field.

"When was the last time, *prior* to December, 1935,

that a foreign plane landed at Kjeller?" our representative asked Director Gulliksen.

"On September 19th. It was an English plane, S.A.C.S.F., from Copenhagen. It was piloted by the English aviator, Mr. Robertson, with whom I am well acquainted."

"And *after* December, 1935, when did the first foreign plane land at Kjeller?"

"May 1st, 1936."

"In other words, according to the records kept at the airdrome, this would establish that no foreign plane landed at Kjeller in the interval between September 19th, 1935 and May 1st, 1936?"

"Yes."

In order to leave no room for any doubt, let me introduce the official confirmation of the newspaper interview. In reply to an inquiry made by my Norwegian attorney, the same Mr. Gulliksen, Director of the only airport at or near Oslo, replied on February 14th as follows:

KJELLER, FEBRUARY 14TH, 1937

Andreas Stoeylen,
Attorney-at-Law,
Ovre Slottagt 8V,
Oslo.

Sir: In reply to your letter of the 10th instant, I beg to inform you that my statement in the *Arbeiderbladet* was published accurately. . . .

Yours very truly,
GULLIKSEN, DIRECTOR, KJELLER AIRPORT.

In other words, even if we extend to the credit of the G.P.U. not simply thirty-one days (December) but 224 days (September 19th to May 1st) for Pyatakov's flight, even then Stalin could not save the situation. The question of Pyatakov's flight to Oslo may consequently, I hope, be considered closed for all time.

On January 29th the sentence had not yet been pronounced. The statements of Knudsen and the *Arbeiderbladet* were of such extraordinary importance that they called for a supplementary inquiry. But the Moscow Themis is not the sort to permit facts to halt her movements. It is quite probable—almost certain—that in the preliminary negotiations Pyatakov, like Radek, was promised his life. The keeping of this promise to Pyatakov, the "organizer" of the alleged "sabotage," was not at all easy. But if Stalin had any hesitation left in this respect, the news from Oslo must have terminated it. On January 29th I said to the press in my daily statement: "The first steps of the inquiry in Norway have enabled the Storting Deputy, K. Knudsen, to establish that in December no foreign airplane at all landed in Oslo. . . . I am very much afraid that the G.P.U. will make haste to shoot Pyatakov in order to forestall further disconcerting questions and deprive the future international commission of inquiry of the opportunity to demand further clarification from Pyatakov." The next day, January 30th, Pyatakov was condemned to death, and on February 1st, he was shot.

Through the medium of the Norwegian "yellow journal" *Tidens Tegn,* similar in character to the Hearst publications in America, the friends of the G.P.U. are seeking to establish a new version of Pyatakov's flight. Perhaps the German airplane did not land on a flying field, but on a frozen fjord? Perhaps Pyatakov did not visit Trotsky in a suburb of Oslo, but in a forest? Not in a house "not badly furnished," but in a little hut in the forest? Not thirty minutes but three hours from Oslo? Perhaps Pyatakov did not come in an automobile, but on a sleigh or on skis? Perhaps this interview took place, not on December 12th or 13th, but on December 21st or 22d? This creative effort is neither better nor worse than the attempt to pass off a Copenhagen confectioner's shop as the Hotel Bristol. The hypotheses of *Tidens Tegn* suffer from this defect: They leave not a shred of Pyatakov's confession, and at the same time they themselves crumble in face of the facts. These fantasies have long since been refuted by the Norwegian press, especially by the liberal *Dagbladet,* on the basis of an examination of the essential facts—i.e., the circumstances of time and place. The Storting Deputy, Konrad Knudsen, has subjected the belated fictions to a no less annihilating criticism in the columns of the same yellow newspaper, which in the meantime has become the oracle of the Comintern. If, for its part, the Commission deems it necessary to subject to an examination not only the data of the official report but also the literary versions brought forward by the friends of the G.P.U. after the shooting of Pyatakov, I will place all the necessary material at its disposal.

I wish here to add that at the beginning of March the Danish author, Andersen Nexo, visited Oslo for a special lecture. By a happy coincidence Nexo (like Pritt, like Duranty, like several others) happened to be in Moscow during the trial and "with his own ears" heard Pyatakov's confession. Whether Nexo knows Russian or not is inconsequential; it is enough that this Scandinavian knight of the truth "does not doubt" the credibility of Pyatakov's confession. If Romain Rolland undertakes degrading assignments which testify to a complete loss of moral and psychological sensitivity, why shall not Mr. Nexo do the same?

The corruption introduced by the G.P.U. among certain circles of radical writers and politicians the world over has reached truly frightful proportions. I shall not here inquire into the means the G.P.U. may use in each individual case. It is sufficiently well known that these means do not always have an "ideological" character—the Irish author O'Flaherty has already revealed this, with his peculiar cynicism. One of the reasons for my break with Stalin and his comrades-in-arms was, incidentally, that they resorted to bribery of functionaries of the European labor movement from 1924 on. An indirect but very important result of the work of the Commission will be, I hope, the cleansing of the radical ranks of "Left" sycophants, political parasites, "revolutionary" courtiers, or those gentlemen who remain Friends of the Soviet Union in so far as they are friends of the Soviet State Publishing House or ordinary pensioners of the G.P.U.

XVIII. WHAT HAS BEEN REFUTED IN THE LAST TRIAL?

The agents of Moscow have lately resorted to the following argument: "Since his arrival in Mexico, Trotsky has not presented any evidence. There is no reason to believe that he will present any in the future. By that very fact the Commission is doomed beforehand to impotence." How, I ask, can one refute a frame-up prepared and fabricated for a number of years, without examining the facts and documents? I really do not possess any "voluntary confessions" from Stalin, Yagoda, Yezhov or Vyshinsky—this I confess at the outset. But if I have not up to now presented a magic formula encompassing *all* the evidence, it is not true that I have not presented *any* evidence. During the last trial I issued daily statements to the press containing specific refutations. The newspapers published only parts of my statements, often in distorted form. I place at the disposal of the Commission the exact texts of these statements. I am also writing a book which will furnish the key to the most important political and psychological "enigmas" of the Moscow trials. I received the verbatim report of the second trial only two weeks ago. Under these circumstances it is, naturally, impossible to speak of an exhaustive refutation. However, despite the fact that I did not have at my disposal a daily or even a weekly paper in which I could freely express myself, I completely refuted those facts of the last trial which were directed against me personally, and thereby broke down the whole judicial amalgam.

Radek, defending himself in his final plea against the insults of the Prosecutor, who characterized the accused only as crooks and bandits (Prosecutor Vyshinsky, a cynical careerist, former Right-Wing Menshevik—what an incarnation of the régime!), obviously overstepped the previously fixed limits of defense, and said more than was necessary or than he wished to say himself. That is one of Radek's distinctive traits! This time, however, he said things of exceptional value. I beg every member of the Commission to read with particular care the final plea of this defendant.

The terrorist activity and the connection of the "Trotskyites" with organizations of counter-revolutionaries and saboteurs are, according to Radek, fully demonstrated. "But," he continues:

> The trial is bicentric, and it has another important significance. It has revealed the smithy of war, and has shown that the Trotskyite organization became an agency of the forces which are fomenting a new world war. What proofs are there in support of this fact? In support of this fact there is the evidence of two people—the testimony of myself, who received the directives and the letters from Trotsky (which, unfortunately, I burned), and the testimony of Pyatakov, who spoke to Trotsky. All the testimony of the other accused rests on our testimony. If you are dealing with mere criminals and spies, on what can you base your conviction that what we have said is the truth, the firm truth?

One can hardly believe one's eyes when one reads these cynically frank lines in the record. Neither the Prosecutor nor the President even tried to refute or correct Radek—it was too risky! Yet his astonishing words batter down the whole trial. Yes; the entire accusation against me rests only on the testimony of Radek and Pyatakov. There is not even a trace of material evidence. The letters which Radek allegedly received from me were "unfortunately" burned by him (nevertheless, the indictment was published in the *Russian* version of the court proceedings as if quoting my actual letters). The Prosecutor treats Radek and Pyatakov as unprincipled liars, pursuing only one aim—to deceive the authorities. The sum and substance of Radek's reply is: "If our testimony is false (both Radek and the Prosecutor know well enough that the testimony is false!), then what other proof do you have that Trotsky concluded an alliance with Germany and Japan, with the object of precipitating war and dismembering the U.S.S.R.? You have nothing left. There are no documents. The testimony of the other accused rests upon our testimony." Not a word from the Prosecutor. Not a word from the President. Silent, too, are the "friends" abroad. A damning silence! Such is the true face of the trial—a face of shame!

Let us recall the factual side of the testimony of Radek and Pyatakov. Radek was supposed to have maintained communication with me through Vladimir Romm. The latter allegedly saw me the first and only time at the end of July, 1933, in the Bois de Boulogne, in Paris. By precise references to dates, facts and witnesses, including the French police, I have proved that I was not and could not have been in the Bois de Boulogne, since, being ill, I went directly from Marseilles to Saint Palais near Royan, several hundred kilometers from Paris.

Pyatakov testified that he flew in a German airplane to see me in Oslo in December, 1935. However, the Norwegian authorities have stated publicly that not a single foreign airplane landed at Oslo between September 19th, 1935, and May 1st, 1936. From this evidence there is no appeal. Pyatakov no more flew to see me in Oslo than Romm met me in the Bois de Boulogne. Yet Radek's sole alleged contact with me was through Romm. The destruction of Romm's testimony leaves nothing of Radek's testimony. Nor does anything remain of Pyatakov's testimony. However, according to Radek's confession, confirmed by the court's silence, the accusation against me rests exclusively on the testimony of Radek and Pyatakov. All the other testimony is of an accessory, auxiliary character, designed to bolster up Radek and Pyatakov, the principal accused—more exactly, Stalin's principal witnesses—against me. The function of Radek and Pyatakov was to demonstrate the direct connection between the criminals and myself. "All the testimony of the other accused rests on our testimony," Radek confesses. In other words, it rests upon nothing. The main charge has been demolished. It has crumbled into dust. It is hardly necessary to demolish a building brick by brick, once the two basic columns on which it rests are thrown down. Messrs. Accusers, crawl on your bellies in the wreckage and gather up the chips of your masonry!

XIX. THE PROSECUTOR-FALSIFIER

My "terrorist" and "defeatist" activity, as is known, was supposed to be a matter of the utmost secrecy, into which I initiated only those who were most trustworthy. On the other hand, my public activity, hostile to terror and defeatism, was supposedly only "camouflage." The Prosecutor, however, does not maintain this position throughout, and sometimes succumbs to the temptation to discover terrorist and defeatist propaganda in my public activity as well. We shall demonstrate by certain cardinal examples that the literary frauds of Vyshinsky represent only an auxiliary to the judicial frame-ups.

I

On February 20th, 1932, the Central Executive Committee of the U.S.S.R., by a special decree, deprived me and the members of my family who were abroad of Soviet citizenship. Even the text of the decree, I note in passing, represented an amalgam. I was referred to not only by the name of Trotsky, but also by my father's name, Bronstein, although this name had never before been used in any Soviet document. Moreover, they hunted up Mensheviks named Bronstein and included them in the decree of deprivation of citizenship. Such is the political style of Stalin!

I replied by an "Open Letter to the Praesidium of the Central Executive Committee of the U.S.S.R.," on March 1st, 1932 (*Bulletin of the Opposition,* No. 27). This "Open Letter" mentioned a series of frauds perpetrated by the Soviet press on command from above, for the purpose of discrediting me in the eyes of the toiling masses of the U.S.S.R. Recounting the principal errors of Stalin in the questions of home and foreign policy, the "Open Letter" branded his Bonapartist tendencies. ". . . Under the lash of the Stalinist clique," the "Open Letter" went on to say, "the sorry, confused, frightened, demoralized Central Committee of the German Communist Party helps with all its might—and cannot but help—the leaders of the German Social Democracy to hand over the German working class to Hitler for crucifixion." Less than a year later this prediction, unfortunately, was entirely confirmed! Furthermore, the "Open Letter" contained the following proposal: ". . . Stalin has led you into a blind alley. Without liquidating Stalinism there is no way out. You must trust in the working class, give the proletarian vanguard the possibility of reviewing the whole Soviet system and pitilessly cleansing it of the accumulated rubbish. *It is time, finally, to fulfill the last urgent advice of Lenin—to remove Stalin.*" The proposal "to remove Stalin" I motivated with the following words: "You know Stalin as well as I do. . . . The strength of Stalin was never in himself but in the apparatus; or, rather, in himself in so far as he was the most consummate embodiment of bureaucratic automatism. Apart from the apparatus, counterposed to the apparatus, Stalin is nothing, a mere cipher . . . It is high time to abandon the Stalin myth." It is plain that in question here is not the physical extermination of Stalin, but only the liquidation of his apparatus power.

Incredible though it seems, it is precisely this document, the "Open Letter to the Central Executive Committee," that was to form part of the basis of the Stalin-Vyshinsky judicial frame-ups.

At the court session of August 20th, 1936, the accused Olberg deposed:

> The first time Sedov spoke to me about my journey [to the U.S.S.R.] was after Trotsky's message in connection with Trotsky's being deprived of the citizenship of the U.S.S.R. In this message Trotsky developed the idea that it was necessary to assassinate Stalin. This idea was expressed in the following words: "Stalin must be removed." Sedov showed me the typewritten text of this message and said: "Well, now you see, it cannot be expressed in a clearer way. It is a diplomatic wording." . . . it was then that Sedov proposed that I should go to the U.S.S.R.

The "Open Letter" is called by Olberg, for the sake of prudence, a "message." Olberg gives only a partial citation. The Prosecutor does not ask for details. The words *"remove* Stalin" are interpreted to mean that it was necessary to *assassinate* Stalin.

On August 21st, according to the record, the accused Holtzman testified that "in the course of the conversation Trotsky said that it was 'necessary to remove Stalin.'"

"*Vyshinsky:* What does 'Remove Stalin' mean? Explain it." Holtzman naturally proceeds to explain it according to the requirements of Vyshinsky.

Seemingly in order to dissipate all doubts concerning the source of his own fraud, Vyshinsky declared on August 22d, 1936, in his summation: ". . . in March 1932, in a fit of counter-revolutionary fury, Trotsky burst out in an open letter with an appeal to 'put Stalin out of the way' (this letter was found between the double walls of Holtzman's suitcase and figured as an exhibit in this case)."

The Prosecutor speaks flatly of an "open letter" written in March, 1932, about withdrawal of my citizenship and containing the call "to remove Stalin." This document is nothing else but my "Open Letter to the Central Executive Committee"! According to the Prosecutor, it was "found between the double walls of Holtzman's suitcase." It is possible that, returning from abroad, Holtzman concealed in his suitcase a copy of the *Bulletin* containing my "Open Letter"; such means of concealment are in accord with traditional practice among Russian revolutionists. In any case, the specific indications given by the Prosecutor: (a) reference to the name ("Open Letter"); (b) the date (March, 1932); (c) the theme (decree depriving me of citizenship); finally, (d) the slogan ("remove Stalin"), point with absolute certainty to my "Open Letter to the Central Executive Committee," and to the fact that the testimony of Olberg and Holtzman, as well as the Prosecutor's summation in the Zinoviev-Kamenev case, revolved precisely around this document.

In his summation in the Pyatakov-Radek case (January 28th, 1937), Vyshinsky again turns to the "Open Letter" as the basic terrorist directive: "We are in possession of documents proving that Trotsky, at least twice, and, moreover, in a fairly open and undisguised form, gave a line for terrorism, documents which their author has proclaimed *urbi et orbi.* I refer, firstly, to that letter of 1932, in which Trotsky issued his treacherous and shameful call, 'Remove Stalin,' . . ."*

Permit me, at this point, to interrupt the quotation, from which we learn again that the terrorist directive was supposedly given by me openly or, as the Prosecutor puts it, proclaimed *urbi et orbi.* In a word, it is a question of the same "Open Letter" in which, invoking Lenin's Testament, I recommended the removal of Stalin from his post as General Secretary.

The situation is clear, esteemed Commissioners! In the two principal trials of the "Zinovievites" and "Trotskyites" the point of departure of the indictment on the question of terror is a consciously falsified interpretation of an article of mine published in various languages and accessible to verification by every literate person. Such are the methods of Vyshinsky! Such are the methods of Stalin!

II

In the same summation (January 28th, 1937), the Prosecutor continues: ". . . and secondly, to a later document, the Trotskyite *Bulletin of the Opposition,* Nos. 36–37, of October, 1933, in which we find a number of direct references to terrorism as a method of fighting the Soviet government." Then follows a quotation from the *Bulletin:* "It would be childish to think that the Stalin bureaucracy can be removed by means of a Party or Soviet Congress. Normal, constitutional means are no longer available for the removal of the

---

* In the English edition of the record of the second trial (page 507) it says: "Remove Stalin." In the English edition of the record of the first trial (page 127) the same phrase is translated: "Put Stalin out of the way." In the French edition of the record of the second trial the phrase reads: "Supprimez Staline," i.e., "Destroy Stalin." The great frame-up is shot through with hundreds of petty frame- ups, including even fraudulent translations.

ruling clique. . . . They can be compelled to hand over power to the proletarian vanguard only by force."

"What else can it be called," the Prosecutor concludes, "if not a direct call for terrorism? I cannot call it anything else." In order to prepare this conclusion, Vyshinsky declares in advance: "An opponent of *terrorism,* and opponent of *violence,* should have said: 'Yes, peaceful means [of reforming the state] are possible on the basis, say, of the constitution.'" Precisely so: "On the basis, *say,* of the constitution"!

The entire argument rests upon the identification of revolutionary violence with individual terror. Even the Tsarist prosecutors seldom stooped to such methods! I never passed myself off as a pacifist, a Tolstoyan, a follower of Gandhi. Serious revolutionists never play with violence. But neither do they refuse to have recourse to revolutionary violence if history does not permit of other methods. From 1923 to 1933 I defended the idea of "reforming" the Soviet state apparatus. That is precisely why, even in March, 1932, I advised the Central Executive Committee to "remove Stalin." Only gradually and under the pressure of irresistible facts did I arrive at the conclusion that the popular masses cannot overthrow the bureaucracy except by *revolutionary violence.* In accordance with the fundamental principle of my activity, I immediately expressed this conclusion publicly. Yes, ladies and gentlemen of the Commission, I think that the system of Stalinist Bonapartism can be liquidated only by means of a new political revolution. However, revolutions are not made to order. They spring from the development of society. They cannot be evoked artificially. It is even less possible to replace revolution by the adventurism of terrorist acts. When Vyshinsky identifies, instead of counterposing, these two methods—that of individual terror and that of mass insurrection—he blots out the entire history of the Russian Revolution and the entire philosophy of Marxism. What does he put in their place? A frame-up!

III

Ambassador Troyanovsky, following Vyshinsky, did exactly the same thing: During the last trial he discovered, as is well known, that in one of my statements to the press I had admitted my terrorist views. Troyanovsky's discovery was printed; it was discussed; it had to be refuted. Is this not degrading to human reason? It appears that, on the one hand, in my books, articles and statements on the latest trials, I categorically denied the charge of terrorism, founding my denials on theoretical, political and factual arguments. On the other hand, I am supposed to have given the Hearst papers a statement in which, contradicting all my other statements, I openly confessed to the Soviet Ambassador my terroristic crimes. Are there any limits to absurdity? If Troyanovsky commits, in full view of the whole civilized world, falsifications so unprecedented in their crudeness and cynicism, it is not difficult to imagine what the G.P.U. does in its cellars.

IV

Nor can Vyshinsky do any better as regards my *defeatism.* The foreign attorneys of the G.P.U. continue to torture their faculties over the question of how the former leader of the Red Army became a "defeatist." For Vyshinsky and the other falsifiers of Moscow, this question ceased to exist a long time ago—Trotsky was *always* a defeatist, they say, even during the period of the Civil War. A whole literature already exists on this subject. Educated on this literature, the Prosecutor says in his summation:

> We must remember that ten years ago Trotsky justified his defeatist position in regard to the U.S.S.R. by referring to the famous Clemenceau thesis. Trotsky then

> wrote: "We must restore the tactics of Clemenceau, who, as is well known [!!], rose against the French Government at a time when the Germans were 80 kms. from Paris."*
> . . . It was not an accident that Trotsky and his accomplices advanced the Clemenceau thesis. They reverted to this thesis once again, but this time advancing it not as a theoretical proposition, but as practical preparation, real preparation, in alliance with foreign intelligence services, for the defeat of the U.S.S.R. in war.

It is hard to believe that the text of this speech was printed in foreign languages, including the French. One would imagine that the French were not unastonished to learn that Clemenceau, during the war, "rose against the French Government." The French never suspected that Clemenceau was a defeatist and an ally of "foreign intelligence services." On the contrary, they call him "the father of victory." Exactly what is meant by the gibberish of the Prosecutor? The fact is that the Stalinist bureaucracy, to justify violence against the Soviets and the party, has, since 1926, appealed to the war danger—classic subterfuge of Bonapartism! In opposing this, I always expressed myself in the sense that freedom of criticism is indispensable for us not only in time of peace but also in time of war. I referred to the fact that even in bourgeois countries, France in particular, the ruling class did not dare, despite all its fear of the masses, completely to suppress criticism during the war. In this connection I adduced the example of Clemenceau, who, despite the proximity of the war front to Paris—or rather, precisely because of it—de-

---

* In the English edition these words are placed in quotation marks, which might lead the members of the Commission to mistake them for a quotation. In reality, the sentence is invented out of whole cloth by the Prosecutor. Vyshinsky's judicial "citations" have the same authenticity as Stalin's literary "citations"; in this school there is uniformity of style.

nounced in his paper the worthlessness of the military policy of the French Government. In the end, Clemenceau, as is well known, convinced Parliament, took over the leadership of the Government, and assured victory. Where is the "uprising" here? Where is the "defeatism"? Where is the connection with foreign intelligence services? I repeat: The reference to Clemenceau was made by me at a time when I judged it still possible to accomplish by peaceful means the transformation of the governmental system of the U.S.S.R. Today I can no longer invoke Clemenceau, because the Bonapartism of Stalin has barred the road to legal reform. But even today I stand completely for the defense of the U.S.S.R.—that is to say, for the defense of its social bases, both against foreign imperialism and domestic Bonapartism.

In the question of "defeatism," the Prosecutor based himself first on Zinoviev, then on Radek, as the principal witnesses against me. I am here going to cite Zinoviev and Radek as witnesses against the Prosecutor. I shall cite their free and unfalsified opinions.

Speaking of the revolting persecution of the Opposition, Zinoviev wrote to the Central Committee on September 6th, 1927: "It is enough to point to the article of the not unknown N. Kuzmin in the *Komsomolskaya Pravda* in which this 'teacher' of our military youth . . . interprets Comrade Trotsky's reference to Clemenceau as a demand for the shooting of peasants at the front in case of war. What is this, if not a downright Thermidorian, not to say Black Hundred agitation?"

At the same period as the letter of Zinoviev (September, 1927), Radek wrote in his programmatic thesis:

> . . . On the question of war, it is necessary to repeat in our platform things said in our various public speeches, and to bring them together; that is to say: Our state is a workers' state, despite strong tendencies working to change

> its nature. *The defense of that state is the defense of the proletarian dictatorship. . . .* The question posed by Stalin's group—by distorting Comrade Trotsky's reference to Clemenceau—cannot be lightly tossed aside, but must be answered clearly: We will defend the dictatorship of the proletariat, even with the false leadership of the present majority, as we have declared; but the pledge of victory is in the correction of errors of this leadership and in the acceptance by the party of our platform.

These testimonials from Zinoviev and Radek are doubly precious. On the one hand, they establish in an entirely correct manner the attitude of the Opposition toward the defense of the U.S.S.R.; on the other hand, they show that since 1927 the Stalinist group has distorted in every way imaginable my reference to Clemenceau, with the object of imputing defeatist tendencies to the Opposition. It is worth noting that this same Zinoviev, in one of his latter-day recantations, also docilely included in his arsenal the official falsification relating to Clemenceau. ". . . The whole party, as one man," Zinoviev wrote in *Pravda* of May 8th, 1933, "will fight under the banner of Lenin and Stalin . . . Only contemptible renegades will, perhaps, try to recall here the notorious Clemenceau thesis." Undoubtedly, one could find similar quotations from Radek. Thus, this time also, the Prosecutor has invented nothing new. He has merely given a juridical twist to the traditional Thermidorian hounding of the Opposition. And it is of such shoddy tricks that the whole accusation is made up. Lies and frame-ups! Frame-ups and lies! Sum total—the firing squad.

XX. THE THEORY OF 'CAMOUFLAGE'

Some "jurists," of the sort who swallow camels and strain at gnats, are fond of arguing that my correspondence can have no "juridical" value as evidence, because there always remains room for the possibility that it was conducted with the anticipated aim of camouflaging my real manner of thinking and acting. This argument, which has its roots in commonplace criminal practice, has absolutely no application to a political trial of vast proportions. For the purpose of camouflage, one can compose five, ten, a hundred letters. But one cannot carry on an intensive correspondence on the most diverse questions over a period of years, with the most diverse people, near and distant, with the sole aim of fooling them all. To the letters must be added the articles and books. One can devote to the task of "camouflage" the energy and time which remain over after one's main work is done. But one can carry on an enormous correspondence only on the condition of a profound concern for its content and results. Precisely for this reason, the innumerable letters, which are permeated through and through with the proselytizing spirit, must inevitably reflect the true face of the author, and in no case a mask assumed temporarily. I hope that the Commission will estimate the letters, articles and books in their reciprocal connections.

When I appeared in Norway on December 11th, 1936, as a witness in the case which arose from the unsuccessful fascist raid on my archives, I tried to explain to the judges and jurors the meaning of my papers as a means of defense against false accusations.

> You will perhaps permit me [I said], to give an example from a field in which the jurors are more at home. Let us imagine a religious, God-fearing man who strives to live his whole life in strict conformity with the teachings of the Bible. At some point, his enemies raise—with the aid of false documents and false witnesses—the charge that this man secretly carries on atheistic propaganda. What would the victim of the slander say? "Here is my

family, here are my friends, here is my library, here is my correspondence of many years, here is my entire life. Read my letters, addressed to the most diverse people on the most diverse occasions, ask the hundreds of people who over the course of years have been in contact with me, and you will be convinced that I *could not* have carried on a work in conflict with my whole moral nature." This argument will convince every intelligent and honest man.

Let us take another example from the field of art: Let us suppose that somebody were to declare that Diego Rivera is a secret agent of the Catholic Church. If I were to participate in an inquiry into such a slander, I would first of all propose to all the participants that they inspect Rivera's frescoes. One could hardly find expressed anywhere a more impassioned or more intense hatred of the Church. Will some jurist try to object that perhaps Rivera painted these frescoes with the aim of camouflaging his real role? Serious people would only laugh contemptuously at such an objection, and proceed with their business.

For the purpose of camouflaging crimes (I speak now of the crimes of the G.P.U.), it is possible, with the help of a venal apparatus, to fabricate an indictment, to exact a series of monotonous confessions, and at state expense to print a "verbatim" report. The inner contradictions and crudenesses of this concoction sufficiently expose, by and of themselves, this bureaucratic "creation" made to order. But one cannot without conviction and intellectual passion paint tremendous frescoes which in the language of art lash the oppression of man by man, or year after year under countless blows of enemies develop the ideas of international revolution. One cannot pour out "heart's blood and nerve's sap" (Börne) in scientific, artistic or political work, with the object of "camouflage." People who know what creative work is, and all intelligent and sensitive people in general, will laugh derisively at bureaucratic and "juridical" casuists, and proceed to serious business.

Let us, finally, bring dispassionate arithmetic to bear on this case. According to the statements in both trials, the content of my criminal work was as follows: Three meetings in Copenhagen, two letters of Mrachkovsky and others, three letters to Radek, a letter to Pyatakov, another to Muralov, a meeting with Romm lasting twenty to twenty-five minutes, a meeting with Pyatakov lasting two hours. That is all! Altogether, the conversations and correspondence with the conspirators, according to their own testimony, did not take more than twelve or thirteen hours of my time. I do not know how much time was taken up by my conversations with Hess and the Japanese diplomats. Let us add twelve more hours. Altogether, this totals a maximum of three working days. Meanwhile, I calculate that the eight years of my most recent exile comprise 2,920 possible working days. That I did not expend my time uselessly is proven by my books published during these years, by innumerable articles, and by the still more numerous letters which in size and content not infrequently are comparable to articles. In this way we come to a rather paradoxical conclusion: During 2,917 working days I wrote books, articles and letters and held conversations devoted to the defense of Socialism, the proletarian revolution and the struggle against fascist and all other forms of reaction. On the other hand, I devoted three days—three whole days!—to a conspiracy in the interests of fascism. Not even my adversaries have denied that my books and articles, written in the spirit of the Communist revolution, possess some merit. On the other hand, my letters and verbal directives inspired by interest in fascism, are, to judge by the Moscow reports, distinguished by an extraordinary stupidity. Between the two branches of my activity, the public and the secret, there is observable an extreme disproportion. The public—that is, the "hypocritical"—activity, which served only as "camouflage," surpassed my secret—that is, the "genuine"—activity almost a thousand times in quantity and, I venture to assert, equally in quality. One gets the impression that I built a skyscraper to "camouflage" a dead rat. No, it is not convincing!

The same thing applies to the testimony of my witnesses. Naturally, I lived in a circle of political friends, and associated chiefly, though not exclusively, with my co-thinkers. It is a simple matter, therefore, to try to discredit the testimony of my witnesses as coming from persons connected with an interested party *(ex parte).* Such an attempt, however, must from the outset be regarded as untenable. Today there are in some thirty countries smaller or larger organizations which were founded and have developed during the past eight years in close connection with my theoretical works and political articles. Hundreds of members of these organizations carried on personal correspondence with me, entered into discussions with me, and visited me whenever they could. Everyone of them afterwards shared his impressions with scores, if not hundreds, of other persons. Thus there is involved no closed circle, bound together by family pride or mutual material interests, but a broad international movement, nourished exclusively from ideological sources. To this it must be added that in all these thirty organizations, during all these years, there occurred an intensive ideological struggle, which not infrequently led to splits and expulsions. The internal life of each of these organizations was reflected, in its turn, in bulletins, circular letters and polemical articles. In all this work I took an active part. The question arises: Did the international organization of the "Trotskyites" know about my "genuine" plans and intentions (terrorism, war, defeat of the U.S.S.R., fascism)? If *so,* then it is altogether incomprehensible why this secret failed to leak out, either through carelessness or bad faith, especially in view of the numerous conflicts and splits. If *not*, that means that I succeeded in calling into existence a growing international movement based on ideas which were not mine, but which served me only as camouflage for directly opposite ideas. But such an assumption is really preposterous! I would like to add that I propose to call as witnesses dozens of persons who have broken with the Trotskyist organization or have been expelled from it, and have become my political opponents, sometimes extremely bitter ones. To apply the narrow term *"ex parte"* to such broad dimensions—the quantity here, too, passes into quality—means to ignore reality and clutch at a shadow.

XXI. WHY AND WHEREFORE THESE TRIALS?

An American writer complained to me in a conversation: "It is difficult for me to believe," he said, "that you entered into an alliance with fascism; but it is equally difficult for me to believe that Stalin carried out such horrible frame-ups." I can only pity the author of this remark. It is, in fact, difficult to find a solution if one approaches the question exclusively from an individual psychological and not political viewpoint. I do not wish to deny by this the importance of the individual element in history. Neither Stalin nor I find ourselves in our present positions by accident. But we did not create these positions. Each of us is drawn into this drama as the representative of definite ideas and principles. In their turn, the ideas and principles do not fall from the sky, but have profound social roots. That is why one must take, not the psychological abstraction of Stalin as a "man," but his concrete, historical personality as leader of the Soviet bureaucracy. One can understand the acts of Stalin only by starting from the conditions of existence of the new privileged stratum, greedy for power, greedy for material comforts, apprehensive for its positions, fearing the masses, and mortally hating all opposition.

The position of a privileged bureaucracy in a society which that bureaucracy itself calls Socialist is not only contradictory, but also false. The more precipitate the jump from the October overturn—which laid bare all social falsehood—to the present situation, in which a caste of upstarts is forced to cover up its social ulcers, the cruder the Thermidorian lies. It is, consequently, a question not simply of the individual depravity of this or that person, but of the corruption lodged in the position of a whole social group for whom lying has become a vital political necessity. In the struggle for its newly gained positions, this caste has reeducated itself and simultaneously reeducated—or rather, demoralized—its leaders. It raised upon its shoulders the man who best, most resolutely and most ruthlessly expresses its interests. Thus Stalin, who was once a revolutionist, became the leader of the Thermidorian caste.

The formulas of Marxism, expressing the interests of the masses, more and more inconvenienced the bureaucracy, in so far as they were inevitably directed against its interests. From the time that I entered into opposition to the bureaucracy, its courtier-theoreticians began to call the revolutionary essence of Marxism—*"Trotskyism."* At the same time, the official conception of *Leninism* changed from year to year, becoming more and more adapted to the needs of the ruling caste. Books devoted to Party history, to the October Revolution, or to the theory of Leninism, were revised annually. I have adduced an example from the literary activity of Stalin himself. In 1918 he wrote that the victory of the October insurrection was "principally and above all" assured by Trotsky's leadership. In 1924 Stalin wrote that Trotsky could not have played any special role in the October Revolution. To this tune the whole historiography was adjusted.

This signifies in practice that hundreds of young scholars and thousands of journalists were systematically trained in the spirit of falsification. Whoever resisted was stifled. This applies in a still greater measure to the propagandists, functionaries, judges, not to speak of the examining magistrates of the G.P.U. The incessant Party purges were directed above all toward the uprooting of "Trotskyism," and during these purges not only discontented workers were called "Trotskyites," but also all writers who honestly presented historical facts or citations which contradicted the latest official standardization. Novelists and artists were subject to the same régime. The spiritual atmosphere of the country became completely impregnated with the poison of conventionalities, lies and direct frame-ups.

All the possibilities along this road were soon exhausted. The theoretical and historical falsifications no longer attained their aims—people grew too accustomed to them. It was necessary to give to bureaucratic repression a more massive foundation. To bolster up the literary falsifications, accusations of a criminal character were brought in.

My exile from the U.S.S.R. was officially motivated by the allegation that I had prepared an "armed insurrection." However, the accusation launched against me was not even published in the press. Today it may seem incredible, but already in 1929 we were confronted with accusations against the Trotskyites of "sabotage," "espionage," "preparation of railroad wrecks," etc., in the Soviet press. However, there was not a single trial involving these accusations. The matter was limited to a literary calumny which represented, nevertheless, the first link in the preparation of the future judicial frame-ups. To justify the repressions, it was necessary to have framed accusations. To give weight to the false accusations, it was necessary to reinforce them with more brutal repressions. Thus the logic of the struggle drove Stalin along the road of gigantic judicial amalgams.

They also became necessary to him for international reasons. If the Soviet bureaucracy does not want revolutions and fears them, it cannot, at the same time, openly renounce the revolutionary traditions without definitely undermining its prestige within the U.S.S.R. However, the obvious bankruptcy of the Comintern opens the way for a new International. Since 1933, the idea of new revolutionary parties under the banner of the Fourth International has met with great success in the Old and New Worlds. Only with difficulty can an outside observer appreciate the real dimensions of this success. It cannot be measured by membership statistics alone. The general tendency of development is of much greater importance. Deep, internal fissures are spreading throughout all the sections of the Comintern, which at the first historic shock will result in splits and debacles. If Stalin fears the little *Bulletin of the Opposition* and punishes its introduction into the U.S.S.R. with death, it is not difficult to understand what fright seizes the bureaucracy at the possibility that news of the self-sacrificing work of the Fourth International in the service of the working class may penetrate into the U.S.S.R.

The moral authority of the leaders of the bureaucracy and, above all, of Stalin, rests in large measure upon the Tower of Babel of slanders and falsifications erected over a period of thirteen years. The moral authority of the Comintern rests entirely and exclusively on the moral authority of the Soviet bureaucracy. In its turn, the authority of the Comintern as well as its support, is necessary for Stalin before the Russian workers. This Tower of Babel, which frightens its own builders, is maintained inside the U.S.S.R. with the aid of more and more terrible repressions, and outside the U.S.S.R. with the aid of a gigantic apparatus which, through resources drawn from the labor of the Soviet workers and peasants, poisons world public opinion with the virus of lies, falsifications and blackmail. Millions of people throughout the world identify the October Revolution with the Thermidorian bureaucracy, the Soviet Union with Stalin's clique, the revolutionary workers with the utterly demoralized Comintern apparatus.

The first great breach in this Tower of Babel will necessarily cause it to collapse entirely, and bury beneath its débris the authority of the Thermidorian chiefs. That is why it is for Stalin a life-and-death question to kill the Fourth International while it is still in embryo! Now, as we are here examining the Moscow trials, the Executive Committee of the Comintern, according to information in the press, is sitting in Moscow. Its agenda is: *The struggle against world Trotskyism*. The session of the Executive Committee of the Comintern is not only a link in the long chain of the Moscow frame-ups, but also the projection of the latter on the world arena. Tomorrow we shall hear about new misdeeds of the Trotskyites in Spain, of their direct or indirect support of the fascists. Echoes of this base calumny, indeed, have already been heard in this room. Tomorrow we shall hear how the Trotskyites in the United States are preparing railroad wrecks and the obstruction of the Panama Canal, in the interests of Japan. We shall learn the day after tomorrow how the Trotskyites in Mexico are preparing measures for the restoration of Porfirio Diaz. You say Diaz died a long time ago? The Moscow creators of amalgams do not stop before such trifles. They stop before nothing—nothing at all. Politically and morally, it is a question of life and death for them. Emissaries of the G.P.U. are prowling in all countries of the Old and the New World. They do not lack money. What does it mean to the ruling clique to spend twenty or fifty millions of dollars more or less, to sustain its authority and its power? These gentlemen buy human consciences like sacks of potatoes. We shall see this in many instances.

Fortunately, not everybody can be bought. Otherwise humanity would have rotted away a long time ago. Here, in the person of the Commission, we have a precious cell of unmarketable public conscience. All those who thirst for purification of the social atmosphere will turn instinctively toward the Commission. In spite of intrigues, bribes and calumny, it will be rapidly protected by the armor of the sympathy of broad, popular masses.

Ladies and gentlemen of the Commission! Already for five years—I repeat, five years!—I have incessantly demanded the creation of an international commission of inquiry. The day I received the telegram about the creation of your sub-commission was a great holiday in my life. Some friends anxiously asked me: Will not the Stalinists penetrate into the Commission, as they at first penetrated into the Committee for the Defense of Trotsky? I answered: Dragged into the light of day, the Stalinists are not fearsome. On the contrary, I will welcome the most venomous questions from the Stalinists; to break them down I have only to tell what actually happened. The world press will give the necessary publicity to my replies. I knew in advance that the G.P.U. would bribe individual journalists and whole newspapers. But I did not doubt for one moment that the conscience of the world cannot be bribed and that it will score, in this case as well, one of its most splendid victories.

Esteemed Commissioners! The experience of my life, in which there has been no lack either of successes or of failures, has not only not destroyed my faith in the clear, bright future of mankind, but, on the contrary, has given it an indestructible temper. This faith in reason, in truth, in human solidarity, which at the age of eighteen I took with me into the workers' quarters of the provincial Russian town of Nikolaiev—this faith I have preserved fully and completely. It has become more mature, but not less ardent. In the very fact of your Commission's formation—in the fact that, at its head, is a man of unshakable moral authority, a man who by virtue of his age should have the right to remain outside of the skirmishes in the political arena—in this fact I see a new and truly magnificent reinforcement of the revolutionary optimism which constitutes the fundamental element of my life.

Ladies and gentlemen of the Commission! Mr. Attorney Finerty! and you, my defender and friend, Goldman! Allow me to express to all of you my warm gratitude, which in this case does not bear a personal character. And allow me, in conclusion, to express my profound respect to the educator, philosopher and personification of genuine American idealism, the scholar who heads the work of your Commission. (Applause)

DEWEY: Anything I can say will be an anti-climax. But I still have to repeat an announcement I made before, that in adjourning today we are only adjourning the sessions of the Preliminary Commission which might be regarded even as opening the investigation of the larger and complete Commission. I wish only to add that several members of the Commission will remain here for a few days—we have been so occupied that we have not had sufficient time to examine the archives and all the letters—and that one member of this Preliminary Commission has been appointed as a sub-commission and will remain to make a thorough examination of the documents, for the purpose of both the examination and the verification of the translations.

TROTSKY: The English, and including the Russian.

DEWEY: The hearings of the Preliminary Commission of Inquiry are now ended.

End of Thirteenth Session—Eight Forty-five o'clock P.M.

SUPPLEMENTARY STATEMENT BY ALBERT M. GLOTZER

On May 12th, 1937, upon my return from the hearings of the Preliminary Commission of Inquiry in Coyoacan, Mexico, I received the following letter from Mr. Albert Goldman, the attorney for Leon Trotsky, and copies of two additional letters dealing with the question of entering into the record additional exhibits which arrived from Europe after the close of the hearings. Following is an exact copy of the letter of Mr. Goldman, and his enclosures:

ALBERT GOLDMAN
ATTORNEY-AT-LAW
105 W. MADISON STREET,
CHICAGO.

MAY 12, 1937

Albert Glotzer,
155 N. Clark St.,
Chicago, Illinois.
Dear Sir:

I am enclosing a copy of a letter which I addressed to the sub-commission that took Mr. Trotsky's testimony at Coyoacan, Mexico, asking permission to introduce as a supplementary exhibit a certain document which we received after the hearings were closed. I am also sending you a copy of a letter which I received from Miss Suzanne LaFollette granting my request, on behalf of the sub-commission.

If you have not as yet completed the typing of the record will you kindly insert the material I am now sending you and show the introduction into the evidence of a document written by Windfeld-Hansen and having reference to the testimony of alleged sabotage introduced at the Radek-Pyatakov trial by Hrasche, one of the defendants?

Sincerely yours,
[Signed] ALBERT GOLDMAN

*

(Copy of letter of Mr. Goldman to the Commission and Mr. John Finerty, Attorney for the Commission.)

MAY 5, 1937

To the Members of the Commission and to John Finerty, Attorney for the Commission:

We have received a deposition from Windfeld-Hansen, a Danish engineer who was mentioned by one of the defendants in the Radek-Pyatakov trial as one who was implicated in acts of sabotage. During the hearings I mentioned that such a deposition was on the way from Denmark, and since it deals with an exceedingly important aspect of the whole case I would like to have your permission to introduce it as a supplementary exhibit. This will enable you to include it among the printed exhibits in case you decided to publish the exhibits together with the testimony and speeches.

I would appreciate your acting on the matter at your earliest convenience. You can either sign this letter indicating your consent or grant it in a more formal manner if you deem it best. I am assuming that there will be no objection to my request. I have taken steps to get the consent of Otto Ruehle.

Sincerely,
[Signed] ALBERT GOLDMAN

*

(Copy of letter from Suzanne LaFollette.)

222 WEST 23RD STREET
NEW YORK
10 MAY, 1937

Mr. Albert Goldman,
Attorney-at-Law,
105 West Madison St.,
Chicago, Illinois.
Dear Mr. Goldman:

With reference to the deposition from Windfeld-Hansen which you have asked permission to introduce as a supplementary exhibit in Mr. Trotsky's case, I am authorized by the sub-commission to say that we are willing to have it so introduced.

Yours sincerely,
[Signed] SUZANNE LAFOLLETTE,
Secretary.

(By order of the sub-commission the deposition of Windfeld-Hansen was added to the evidence as Exhibit No. 34.—Ed.)

Appendix I

In re *Copenhagen*

LONDRES 127,
COYOACAN,
D.F.,MEXICO.
MAY 29, 1937.

To the Commission of Inquiry:
(Copy to Attorney Goldman)

I am enclosing a document of exceptional importance, a letter from me to my son, written December 3, 1932, in the cabin of the boat en route from Denmark to France. This letter alone suffices to overthrow Holtzman's deposition about his alleged visit to me in Copenhagen. I present here the first part of the letter which bears directly on the question of showing whether Leon Sedov was or was not in Copenhagen at the end of November, 1932:

> Dear Liovoussiatka, so it seems that we shall not succeed in meeting: between the arrival of the boat at Dunquerke and the departure of the boat from Marseilles,

> there is just time to cross France. To wait for the next boat (a whole week!) will not, of course, be permitted us. . . . Mother is very, very dejected that the meeting did not take place, and I also. . . . Nothing to be done. . . .

Then follows advice of a political nature, which, through the intermediacy of my son, I transmitted to third persons. The letter ended thus:

> Let us hope that Jeanne returned home safely.
>
> I clasp you in my arms and embrace you. Yours. 3/12/1932. Cabin on board ship. Mother embraces you (she is still asleep; it is seven o'clock in the morning). She will probably write you today.

This letter requires some explanations.

1. Unlike the overwhelming majority of the other letters, it is not written by machine but by hand, on two pages torn from a notebook. This is explained by the fact that on the boat I had neither a Russian collaborator with me, nor a Russian typewriter.

2. It is precisely because the letter was written by hand that no copy was preserved in my archives; consequently I could not present the letter to the Commission at a more timely moment. As far as the papers of my son are concerned, they are not kept by him in a classified and orderly form as mine are; furthermore not in his apartment because he is constantly in fear of a raid by the agents of the G.P.U. This explains how my son happened upon this exceptionally precious document only recently, while going through old papers.

3. From the text of the letter it is absolutely clear that my son was not in Copenhagen, and that his wife, Jeanne, was.

4. Since the question might be raised whether the letter might have been written recently, in the interests of the de-

fense, I ask that the letter be subjected to a chemical analysis which will establish with certainty that it was written several years ago.

LEON TROTSKY

*

222 WEST 23D ST.,
NEW YORK,
JUNE 9, 1937.

Mr. Leon Trotsky,
127 Avenida de Londres,
Coyoacan, D.F.,
Mexico.

Dear Mr. Trotsky:

This is to acknowledge your letter of May 29, enclosing and commenting upon a letter written by you to Leon Sedov, dated 3/12/1932. I am authorized by the Commission to accept in evidence the letter to Leon Sedov, and to include both that and your explanatory letter in the exhibit labelled "Copenhagen."

Yours sincerely,
SUZANNE LAFOLLETTE
Secretary of the Commission.

*

AVENIDA LONDRES 127,
COYOACAN, D.F.
MEXICO.
JUNE 30, 1937.

To the Commission of Inquiry:

I am sending you, directly and simultaneously with this letter, some very important documents, consisting of two notebooks and one separate exercise-sheet. These belonged to Leon Sedov during his studies at the *Technische Hochschule* in Berlin. Student attendance at the *Hochschule* was noted by the professors with stamps on the exercises submitted. You will see that there are three stamps from the 25th, 26th, and 27th of November, 1932, that is, just the time of my sojourn in Copenhagen. In the coming days you will receive a new official document (a student "passport") with three stamps confirming Leon Sedov's presence at the *Hochschule* on November 29. That all these documents belong to that period can be established by chemical analysis. Now, I believe, the Commission has at its disposal a whole documentation confirming that in the last week of November, 1932, Sedov was in Berlin and not in Copenhagen. Permit me to express the opinion that an alibi of such fullness and incontestability has perhaps never been established.

LEON TROTSKY

*

222 WEST 23D ST.,
NEW YORK,
JULY 13, 1937

Mr. Leon Trotsky,
127 Avenida de Londres,
Coyoacan, D.F.,
Mexico.

Dear Mr. Trotsky:

The notebooks and separate exercise sheet of Leon Sedov, to which you referred in your letter of June 30, arrived several days ago, and I am authorized by the Commission to accept them in evidence. They will be included in the exhibit labelled "Copenhagen."

Yours sincerely,
SUZANNE LAFOLLETTE
Secretary of the Commission.

Appendix II

Factual corrections

LONDRES 127,
COYOACAN, D.F.
MEXICO,
JUNE 29, 1937.

To the Commission of Inquiry:

The depositions which I made before the sub-commission in Coyoacan contain some factual inaccuracies. Actually not one of them has any direct bearing on the object of the Commission's inquiry, or can influence its conclusions. Nevertheless, in the interests of exactitude, I believe it necessary to correct here the errors which I overlooked.

1. To a question regarding Holtzman I replied that after my departure from Russia I had neither "directly or indirectly" any communication with him (Session 3, page 91). In fact, Holtzman met my son, Sedov, in Berlin in 1932 and communicated to him, as I subsequently learned, some factual reports about the situation in the U.S.S.R. These reports were published in the Russian *Bulletin of the Opposition* (No. 31, November, 1932). This fact can be interpreted as an

"indirect" communication between Holtzman and myself.

2. To the question of Defense Attorney Goldman as to whether Blumkin had capitulated, I answered: "In a very modest manner" (Session 4, page 134). This statement is apparently erroneous. At least, I have found no evidence of Blumkin's capitulation. He worked abroad in the counterespionage system of the G.P.U. His work had a strictly individual character. His chiefs, Menzhinsky and Trilisser, considered him an irreplaceable worker and for that reason, despite Blumkin's Oppositionist convictions, they retained him in an extremely responsible post.

3. Regarding the question of the return from Copenhagen of my son's wife, Jeanne Martin des Pallières, it is stated in the report (Session 4, page 141) that she made the trip from Denmark to France on the same boat as my wife and myself. This is an error. The shortest and cheapest route from Copenhagen to Paris is through Hamburg. This is the itinerary which was followed by several of our friends for whom the question of a German visa presented no difficulties. Jeanne Martin des Pallières, since she was a French citizen, went to Paris through Hamburg. I am presenting to the Commission a post-card sent by Jeanne from Hamburg to her mother. Since Jeanne left Copenhagen at the same time as we; since many friends accompanied us on the boat; since my wife and I remained continually in our cabin; and since Jeanne rejoined us in Paris, I had the incorrect impression that she left on the same boat as we.

4. We arrived at Paris from Copenhagen, not December 5th, 1932, as is indicated incorrectly in the report (Session 4, page 140 and Session 5, page 159), but December 6th. It was precisely on this day that we met our son, Leon Sedov, who had succeeded in coming from Germany.

5. Regarding the time of Radek's arrival in Russia (Session 3, page 100), I indicated the end of the year 1918. This is an obvious mistake. Radek took part in the Brest-Litovsk

discussions at the beginning of the year 1918. He came from Stockholm to Petersburg, it seems, at the end of 1917; in any case after the October insurrection.

6. As regards Victor Serge's wife, it is stated in the report that she was arrested (Session 2, page 43). Actually she was sentenced to one month of forced labor with the right to spend the night in her home. The information to the effect that she became insane as a result of the repressions against her family is absolutely correct. At present she is still mentally ill in Paris.

As has already been said, none of these corrections basically affects my depositions or the conclusions which flow from them. I reserve for myself the right to correct further inaccuracies as well, to the extent that I discover them.

LEON TROTSKY

*

222 WEST 23D ST.,
NEW YORK,
JULY 6, 1937

Mr. Leon Trotsky,
127 Avenida de Londres,
Coyoacan, D.F.,
Mexico.

Dear Mr. Trotsky:

Your letter of June 29, making certain factual corrections in your testimony before the Preliminary Commission of Inquiry, has been received. I am authorized by the Commission to append this letter to the Record. The post-card which was enclosed, addressed to Mme. des Pallières and signed "Jeanne," will be included in the exhibit labelled "Copenhagen."

Sincerely yours,
SUZANNE LAFOLLETTE
Secretary of the commission.

Appendix III

Correspondence

The invitations and answers reproduced below are appended to the record in pursuance of the Chairman's announcement that they would be so appended.—Editor.

LETTER

NEW YORK,
MARCH 30, 1937

Hon. Alexander A. Troyanovsky,
Ambassador of the U.S.S.R. to the U.S.A.,
Embassy of the U.S.S.R.
1119 16th St., N.W.
Washington, D.C.
Sir:

We request that you communicate to your Government the following message:

"Having constituted a preliminary Commission of Inquiry into the charges made against Leon Trotsky and his son, Lev Sedov, in the trials held before the Military Collegium of the Supreme Court of the U.S.S.R. on August 19–24th, 1936, and on January 23–30th, 1937, we are proceeding to Mexico City to hold formal hearings, at which we shall take the testimony of Leon Trotsky, cross examine him and all available witnesses.

"We extend to your Government an invitation to send a representative to such hearings. Your representative will have full rights to cross examine Trotsky and his witnesses.

"To facilitate a thorough examination of the accused, Leon Trotsky, we respectfully request that your Government make available to us verbatim reports of all proceedings in the trials and the volumes of preliminary examination; and whatever other documents may be helpful to us in our work."

[Signed] JOHN DEWEY, Chairman
[Signed] JOHN FINERTY, Counsel

*

DAY LETTERS

NEW YORK,
MARCH 30, 1937

The Communist Party of the U.S.
50 East 13th St.,
New York City

We intend to go to Mexico with preliminary commission of inquiry to take evidence from Leon Trotsky relative to recent Moscow trials stop we shall examine and cross examine Trotsky to the best of our ability stop naturally we feel that our efforts would prove more effective if attorney appointed by the Communist Party appeared before Commission with full powers of cross examination stop if this is not possible will you provide us with material for cross examination stop our only purpose is to help ascertain the truth and we shall appreciate any help you can give us.

[Signed] JOHN DEWEY, Chairman,
[Signed] JOHN FINERTY, Counsel.

*

NEW YORK,
MARCH 30, 1937

Joseph R. Brodsky, Esq.
100 Fifth Avenue,
New York City

We intend to go to Mexico with preliminary Commission of Inquiry to take evidence Leon Trotsky relative recent Moscow trials we shall examine and cross examine Trotsky to the best of our ability stop the Communist Party has been requested to send a lawyer to appear before the Commission with full powers of cross examination with preference expressed that they appoint you stop will you as the outstanding Communist attorney in this country either as a representative of the Communist Party or personally in your professional capacity representing the Communist point of view on the Moscow trials go to Mexico and participate in cross examination stop if this is not possible will you provide us with material for cross examination stop the group will probably leave on Friday April second stop needless to say we are not going as propagandists our only purpose being to help ascertain the truth we will appreciate any help you can give us.

[Signed] JOHN DEWEY, Chairman
[Signed] JOHN FINERTY, Counsel

*

LETTERS

AMBERES 65,
MÉXICO, D.F.,
7 DE ABRIL DE 1937

Luis Sañchez Ponton,
Miembro Correspondiente del
Secretariado de la Sociedad de Naciones
Seville 30,
México, D.F.

La Comisión Preliminar de encuesta e investigación sobre los cargos lanzados contra León Trotsky en los procesos de Moscú, invita a la organización de Uds. a nombrar un representante acreditado para las audiencias que tendrán lugar en la casa No. 127 de la Avenida Londres en Coyoacán, D.F. y que principiaran a las 10 hs. a.m. del sábado 10 de abril, continuando por varios días.

Las sesiones seran diarias, de 10 a.m. a 1 p.m. y de 4 p.m. a 6.30 p.m.

Permítannos ustedes preguntarles si su organización podrá delegar a un miembro representativo y en caso de ser así les rogamos enviarnos inmediatamente el nombre de su representante con objeto de proporcionarle una tarjeta de admisión, requisito que será, sin excepción alguna, requisito indispensable absolutamente para la admisión a las audiencias.

Muy atentamente,
El Presidente de la Comisión.
[Signed] JOHN DEWEY

Letters identical with the above were sent to the following organizations:

Confederación General de Trabajadores (C.G.T.)
Confederación Regional Obrera Mexicana (C.R.O.M.)
Federación de Sindicatos Obreros del Distrito Federal

Sindicato Único de Trabajadores de Construcción del D.F.
Casa del Pueblo
Sindicato de Trabajadores Petroleros de la República Mexicana
Federación Nacional de Trabajadores de la Industria Eléctrica
Liga Cultural Israelita

The following answers were received:

*

SOCIEDAD DE LAS NACIONES
OFICINA DEL MIEMBRO CORRESPONDIENTE
DE LA SECRETARÍA GENERAL

SEVILLA 30
MÉXICO, D.F.
9 DE ABRIL DE 1937

Dr. John Dewey,
Presidente de la Comisión Investigadora en el Caso Trotsky,
Ciudad.

De conformidad con los términos de la atenta invitación que esa Comisión dignamente presidida por Ud. se ha servido hacer a esta Organización en su nota fecha 7 de este mes a fin de acudir a las audiencias preliminares sobre investigación de los cargos lanzados contra León Trotsky en los procesos de Moscú, le manifiesto que el suscrito Miembro Correspondiente de la S.D.N. concurrirá personalmente en vista del interés que ofrece para dicha Sociedad el trabajo que va a desarrollar esa Comisión.

Ruego a Ud. por lo tanto se sirva enviarme la tarjeta de admisión a las sesiones respectivas.

Me es grato ofrecerle mi consideración distinguida.

[Signed] LUIS SÁNCHEZ PONTÓN

*

CONFEDERACIÓN GENERAL DE TRABAJADORES
AV. INDEPENDENCIA NÚM. 8
DESPACHOS: 1, 2 Y 3
MÉXICO, D.F.

Sr. John Dewey
Calle Amberes 65
Ciudad.

En contestación a su atenta carta de fecha 7 del actual en la cual hacen formal invitación a esta Confederación para nombrar un Representante debidamente acreditado de esta Central para concurrir las audiencias que tendrán lugar en la casa 127 de la Avenida Londres de Coyoacán, D. F., y en las que se tratará lo relativo a los cargos lanzados en los procesos verificados en Moscú Rusia, en contra del camarada León Trotsky nos es grato hacer de su conocimiento que en junta plenaria del Comité Confederal fué nombrado Representante de esta Confederación General de Trabajadores el camarada Alberto Araoz de Léon.

Al comunicar a Ud. lo anterior le rogamos se faciliten a nuestro representante todos los datos o informaciones que el caso requiera para que pueda normar su criterio al respecto de proceder de acuerdo con las circunstancias.

Aprovechamos la ocasión para suscribirnos fraternalmente de Ud. por la conquista de la jornada máxima de seis horas de labor con pago de ocho.

Salud y Revolución Proletaria.
MÉXICO, D.F.
10 DE ABRIL DE 1937.
P. el Comité Confederal.
[Signed] JULIO RAMÍREZ
El Srio. del Exterior.
[Signed] ALFONSO FERNANDES Z.

✵

CONFEDERACIÓN REGIONAL OBRERA MEXICANA
REPÚBLICA DE CUBA NÚM. 60
MÉXICO, D.F.
ABRIL 9 DE 1937

Sr. John Dewey,
Presente.

Agradecemos la invitación que se ha servido Ud. hacernos en su carta de fecha 8 del actual, para nombrar una persona que en representación de nuestra Organización asista a las sesiones de encuesta e investigación sobre los cargos lanzados contra León Trotsky en los procesos de Moscú.

En contestación nos permitimos informarle que hemos designado para asistir a las citadas sesiones, a nuestro compañero Emilio Mujica, quien entregará personalmente esta carta. Igualmente participamos a Ud. que nuestro Delegado tendrá exclusivamente el carácter de observador, pues nuestra Organización no participa de los cargos contra León Trotsky, ni tiene elementos de información bastante, con este motivo, para poder juzgar acerca de lo mismo.

Atentamente
Salud y Revolución Social.
Comité Central. Secretario General.
[Signed] RICARDO TREVIÑO

✵

FEDERACIÓN DE SINDICATOS OBREROS
DEL DISTRITO FEDERAL
BELISARIO DOMÍNGUEZ 64,
MÉXICO, D.F.

Al Sr. John Dewey,
Presidente de la Comisión de Investigación,
Amberes No. 65,
Ciudad.
Muy señor nuestro:

En nuestro poder su atenta de fecha 8 de los corrientes por la cual se nos invita para asistir a las Audiencias que del jurado en contra de León Trotski, tendrán verificativo en la casa No. 127 de la Av. Londres, en Coyoacán, D.F.

En debida contestación participamos a usted que es de bastante interés para nosotros el caso, por lo que, de ser posible, pedimos se nos extiendan dos Tarjetas de Admisión a nombre de los CC. Emiliano B. Esqueda y Francisco Castillo, si no fuere posible otorgar las dos Tarjetas de Admisión, en este caso deberá extenderse una en favor del C. Esqueda.

Hemos de merecer de usted nos remita por correo las Tarjetas de referencia, y si hubiere necesidad de acudir a recogerlas, suplicamos también se nos avise por nuestros teléfonos: Eric. 6-80-47 y Mex. J. 28-78.

Muy agradecidos por la Invitación que se nos hizo, aprovechamos esta oportunidad para suscribirnos de usted atenta y fraternalmente.

"Salud y Revolución Social"
MÉXICO, D.F., A 9 DE ABRIL DE 1937.
Por el Comité Ejecutivo.
El Srio. General:
[Signed] EMILIANO B. ESQUEDA.

SINDICATO ÚNICO DE TRABAJADORES
DE CONSTRUCCIÓN DEL D.F.
REP. DEL SALVADOR 11-A

Mr. John Dewey.
Amberes No. 65.
Ciudad.

En atención a la invitación de ustedes para que este Sindicato se haga representar en el jurado que se está llevando a cabo al compañero León Trotsky, participamos a ustedes que este Sindicato ha designado al compañero Raymundo Romo para que lo represente en dicho acto.

Quedamos de usted fraternalmente.
"Por la emancipación del proletariado"
MÉXICO, D.F., ABRIL 12 DE 1937
Por el Comité Ejecutivo.
El. Srio. General.
[Signed] JUAN R. DE LA CRUZ

✱

SINDICATO DE OBREROS PANADEROS,
BIZCOCHEROS Y REPOSTEROS
CASA DEL PUEBLO DEL DISTRITO FEDERAL
BOLÍVAR 238

Sr. John Dewey
Amberes 65
Ciudad.

Atendiendo la invitación que se ha servido formular a la Central de Obreros y Campesinos del Distrito Federal "Casa del Pueblo," la Comisión preliminar de encuesta e investigación sobre los cargos lanzados contra León Trotsky en los procesos de Moscú; se tiene a bien comunicar a usted que se acredita Delegado por ésta Central de trabajadores, al compañero Genaro Gómez.

Lo que se hace de su conocimiento para los fines a que haya lugar.

Por la Causa del Proletariado Internacional.

MÉXICO, D.F., ABRIL 10 DE 1937.
Unión y Emancipación.
Por el Comité Ejecutivo.
El Secretario.
[Signed] MANUEL DE LA SERNA

⁕

EL TIEMPO
PERIÓDICO BISEMANAL
ARTÍCULO 123 NO. 47.
MÉXICO, D.F.

Sr. John Dewey
Presidente de la Comisión.
Calle Amberes 65
Muy señor nuestro:

La Liga Cultural Israelita y el Periódico Bisemanal "El Tiempo" agradecen la atención que la Comisión Investigadora por conducto de su Presidente, el Señor John Dewey, se ha servido dispensarnos invitando a dichas organizaciones para enviar un representante al Jurado contra León Trotsky, que desde el día 10 de abril se celebrará en esta Capital.

Tomando en consideración el interés mundial que reviste el mencionado Jurado, estas Agrupaciones agradecen su atención y para el efecto queda nombrado el Sr. Jacobo Abrams para que concurra a ellas con el carácter de nuestro representante legalmente autorizado por estas Agrupaciones, y a quien estimaremos se sirvan acreditar, enviándole por nuestro conducto la Tarjeta de admisión que lo acredite como tal, y que será necesaria para que pueda desempeñar la comisión que le hemos dado.

Dándole nuestras más expresivas gracias por su fineza nos repetimos suyos afmos. attos. y Ss.Ss.

"LIGA CULTURAL ISRAELITA"
El Presidente
[Signed] A. JESIOV
PERIÓDICO "EL TIEMPO"
Gerente
[Signed] JACOBO ABRAMS

Cards of admission were also issued to the following: Ramón Garibay, representing the Sindicato de Panaderos, Bizcocheros y Reposteros del Distrito Federal; Ingeniero Francisco Briera-Alvirez, representing the Sindicato de Electricistas del D.F.

*

AMBERES 65,
MEXICO, D.F.,
APRIL 8, 1937.

Secretario General,
Partido Nacional Revolucionario,
Paseo de la Reforma 18,
Mexico, D.F.
Dear Sir:

On behalf of the Preliminary Commission to Inquire into the Charges Made Against Leon Trotsky in the Moscow trials, I take pleasure in inviting you, as representative of the Partido Nacional, to be present at its hearings.

This Preliminary Commission has only one function: To gather all available evidence bearing on the charges made against Mr. Trotsky. It will confine itself to this function.

The hearings will be held from ten to one and from four to seven daily, including Sunday, beginning on Saturday, April 10, at Avenida de Londres 127, Coyoacan, D.F. May we ask you to inform us immediately whether or not you can be present, in order that we may send you a card of admission? In case you are unable to attend, we shall be glad to send a card to any representative of your party whom you may designate.

With the assurance of my highest personal regard, I am,

Yours sincerely,
[Signed] JOHN DEWEY,
Chairman.

*

AMBERES 65,
MEXICO, D.F.,
APRIL 11, 1937.

Secretario General,
Partido Nacional Revolucionario,
Paseo de la Reforma 18,
Mexico, D.F.
Dear Sir:

Since I have had no reply to my letter of the eighth, a copy of which is enclosed, I am writing you once more to invite you to represent the Partido Nacional at the hearings of the Preliminary Commission to Inquire into the Charges Made Against Leon Trotsky in the Moscow Trials. Our receipt for the original of this letter is numbered 0073983.

In order to save time, I suggest that in case you wish to come or send a representative, the presentation of this letter at the entrance will secure a card of admission.

With the assurance of my highest personal regard, I am,

Yours sincerely,
[Signed] JOHN DEWEY, Chairman.

⁕

AMBERES 65,
MEXICO, D.F.,
APRIL 8, 1937.

Lic. Vicente Lombardo Toledano,
Secretario General de la C.T.M.,
Mexico, D.F.

Dear Mr. Toledano:

On behalf of the Preliminary Commission to Inquire into the Charges Made Against Leon Trotsky in the Moscow Trials, I take pleasure in inviting you to be present at its hearings. We are inviting you as the head of the dominant labor movement in Mexico; and also because of your well known and clear position on this historic issue.

This Preliminary Commission has only one function: To gather all available evidence bearing on the charges made against Mr. Trotsky. It will confine itself to this function. We would welcome your cooperation in the cross examination of Mr. Trotsky or any other witness who may appear before us, on the evidence and documents submitted at the hearings.

The hearings will be held from ten to one and from four to seven daily, including Sunday, beginning on Saturday, April 10, at Avenida de Londres 127, Coyoacan, D.F. May we ask you to inform us immediately whether or not you can be present, in order that we may send you a card of admission?

In the hope that you will consent to facilitate the work of our Commission within the logic of its function, I am, with the highest personal regard,

Yours sincerely,
[Signed] JOHN DEWEY, Chairman.

⁕

CONFEDERACIÓN DE TRABAJADORES DE MÉXICO
BALDERAS NÚM. 27,
MÉXICO, D.F.

Señor doctor
John Dewey,
Amberes #65.
México, D.F.

Por la seriedad y el prestigio de que merecidamente goza la Confederación de Trabajadores de México ante el proletariado internacional, me veo en el caso de no aceptar la amable invitación de usted para asistir al llamado jurado de Trotsky.

Hago presente a usted las seguridades de mi consideración más distinguida.

"Por una sociedad sin clases"
MÉXICO, D.F., 9 DE ABRIL DE 1937.
Por el Comité Nacional de la Confederación de Trabajadores de México,
El Secretario General,
[Signed] VICENTE LOMBARDO TOLEDANO

*

AMBERES 65,
MEXICO, D.F.,
APRIL 8, 1937.

Mr. Hernan Laborde, Secretary,
The Communist Party of Mexico,
4, Calle de Soto 83,
Mexico, D.F.

Dear Mr. Laborde:

On behalf of the Preliminary Commission to Inquire into the Charges Made Against Leon Trotsky in the Moscow Trials, I take pleasure in inviting you, as official representative of the Communist Party of Mexico, to be present at its hearings.

This Preliminary Commission has only one function: To gather all available evidence bearing on the charges made against Mr. Trotsky. It will confine itself to this function. We would welcome your cooperation in the cross examination of Mr. Trotsky or any other witness who may appear before us, on the evidence and documents submitted at the hearings.

The hearings will be held from ten to one and from four to seven daily, including Sunday, beginning on Saturday, April 10, at Avenida Londres 127, Coyoacan, D.F. May we ask you to inform us immediately whether or not you can be present, in order that we may send you a card of admission?

In the hope that you will consent to facilitate the work of our Commission within the logic of its function, I am, with the highest personal regard,

Yours sincerely,
[Signed] JOHN DEWEY,
Chairman.

*

PARTIDO COMUNISTA DE MÉXICO
(SECCIÓN DE LA INTERNACIONAL COMUNISTA)
COMITÉ CENTRAL

4, DE SOTO 83.
MÉXICO, D.F.
8 DE ABRIL DE 1937

Sr. John Dewey
Amberes #65
México, D.F.

Recibimos su atenta carta de hoy en la que tiene usted a bien invitarnos a presenciar las audiencias de la Comisión que usted preside y que se propone investigar los cargos hechos (y probados) al Sr. Trotsky en los Procesos de Moscú.

El Buró Político del Comité Central de nuestro Partido ha resuelto declinar la invitación, por considerar que se trata evidentemente de un grupo parcial formado por amigos declarados o encubiertos de Trotsky, previamente decididos a absolverlo de sus crímenes y a ofrecerle una ocasión de reanudar sus ataques a la Unión Soviética y su campaña contra el frente único popular anti-fachista.

Concurrir a las audiencias de la Comisión que usted preside sería tanto como dar valor a lo que no tiene ninguno.

Esperamos que todas las organizaciones serias y responsables rehusarán su participación en esta comedia trotskista.

De usted muy atentamente.

Proletarios de todos los países, uníos

Por el Buró Político del Comité Central del Partido Comunista

[Signed] HERNÁN LABORDE,
Secretario General.

*

AMBERES 65,
MEXICO, D.F.
APRIL 9, 1937

Professor David Vilches, President,
Asociación de Profesores Mexicanos,
Basilio Vadillo, 9
Mexico, D.F.

Dear Professor Vilches:

The Preliminary Commission to Inquire into the Charges Made Against Leon Trotsky in the Moscow Trials invites you to be present at the hearings to be held at Avenida de Londres 127, Coyoacan, D.F., beginning at 10 A.M., Saturday, April 10. The hearings will be held daily (including Sundays)

from 10 A.M. to 1 P.M. and from 4 P.M. to 7 P.M.

May we ask you to inform us immediately whether or not you can be present in order that we may send you a ticket of admission?

Very sincerely,
[Signed] JOHN DEWEY,
Chairman.

❋

FEDERACIÓN DE TRABAJADORES DE LA ENSEÑANZA
DEL DISTRITO FEDERAL
SAN ILDEFONSO 36.
MÉXICO, D.F.

Señor Profesor John Dewey,
Chairman de la Comisión para investigar sobre los cargos hechos contra León Trotsky en el Jurado de Moscú.
Avenida Londres 127.
Coyoacán, D.F.
Estimado señor profesor:

Siendo el Secretario General de la Federación de Trabajadores de la Enseñanza del Distrito Federal, miembro de la FROC y de la CTM, por un deber de lealtad y por mis convicciones personales, me veo en la pena de no aceptar la atenta invitación de usted para asistir a las audiencias de la investigación.

Agradeciendo mucho su invitación, quedo de usted atento y seguro servidor.

POR UNA SOCIEDAD SIN CLASES
MÉXICO, D.F., 9 DE ABRIL DE 1937.
Por El Comité Ejecutivo.
El Secretario General.
[Signed] DAVID VILCHES

*

AMBERES 65,
MEXICO, D.F.,
APRIL 11, 1937

Mr. Santiago R. De la Vega,
Palacio de Bellas Artes,
Ciudad.

My dear Mr. De la Vega:

The Preliminary Commission to Inquire into the Charges made Against Leon Trotsky in the Moscow Trials invites you to be present at the hearings which are now being held at Avenida de Londres 127, Coyoacan, D.F. The hearings will be held daily from 10 A.M. to 1 P.M. and from 4 P.M. to 7 P.M.

If you will present this letter at the door you will receive a ticket of admission to all the sessions.

Very sincerely,
[Signed] JOHN DEWEY,
Chairman.

*

Letters identical with the above were sent to Sr. Francisco Zamora, Sr. Aurelio Manrique, and Sr. Antonio Hidalgo.

Index

Revolution in the United States

Is Socialist Revolution in the U.S. Possible?

A Necessary Debate

MARY-ALICE WATERS

In two talks, presented as part of a wide-ranging debate at the Venezuela International Book Fairs in 2007 and 2008, Waters explains why a socialist revolution in the United States is possible. Why revolutionary struggles by working people are inevitable, forced upon us by the crisis-driven assaults of the propertied classes. As solidarity grows among a fighting vanguard of working people, the outlines of coming class battles can already be seen. $7. Also in Spanish and French.

Cuba and the Coming American Revolution

JACK BARNES

The Cuban Revolution of 1959 had a worldwide political impact, including on working people and youth in the imperialist heartland. As the mass, proletarian-based struggle for Black rights was already advancing in the U.S., the social transformation fought for and won by the Cuban toilers set an example that socialist revolution is not only necessary—it can be made and defended.

This second edition, with a new foreword by Mary-Alice Waters, should be read alongside *Is Socialist Revolution in the U.S. Possible?* $10. Also in Spanish and French.

www.pathfinderpress.com

From the dictatorship of capital . . .

The Communist Manifesto

Karl Marx, Frederick Engels

Why is all recorded history "the history of class struggles"? Why is the capitalist state "but a committee for managing the common affairs of the whole bourgeoisie"? How does the fight for "the proletariat organized as the ruling class" open the only way forward for humanity? The answers to these questions, addressed in the founding document of the modern working-class movement in 1848, remain as vital today as they were at the time. $5. Also in Spanish, French, and Arabic.

The Civil War in France

Karl Marx

In 1871 insurgent working people in Paris rose up and established the first workers government in history, one crushed in blood 72 days later by troops of the French bourgeoisie. In his 20th anniversary introduction to Marx's contemporary account of the Paris Commune, Engels wrote that middle-class misleaders in the workers movement have "been filled with wholesome terror at the words: Dictatorship of the Proletariat. Well and good, gentlemen, do you want to know what this dictatorship looks like? Look at the Paris Commune." $5

State and Revolution

V.I. Lenin

"The relation of the socialist proletarian revolution to the state is acquiring not only practical political importance," wrote V.I. Lenin in the preface to this booklet, finished just months before the October 1917 Russian Revolution. It also addresses the "most urgent problem of the day: explaining to the masses what they will have to do to free themselves from capitalist tyranny." In *Essential Works of Lenin.* $12.95

...to the dictatorship of the proletariat

Their Trotsky and Ours

Jack Barnes

To lead the working class in a successful revolution, a mass proletarian party is needed whose cadres, well beforehand, have absorbed a world communist program, are proletarian in life and work, derive deep satisfaction from doing politics, and have forged a leadership with an acute sense of what to do next. This book is about building such a party. $16. Also in Spanish and French.

The History of the Russian Revolution

Leon Trotsky

A classic account of the social and political dynamics of the first socialist revolution, told by one of its central leaders. Trotsky describes how, under Lenin's guidance, the Bolshevik Party led the working class, peasantry, and oppressed nationalities to overturn the monarchist regime of the landlords and capitalists and bring to power a workers and peasants republic that set an example for toilers the world over. Unabridged, 3 vols. in one. $36. Also in Russian.

The Transitional Program for Socialist Revolution

Leon Trotsky

In this 1938 founding document drafted for the Socialist Workers Party in the U.S. and the world movement it is part of, Bolshevik leader Leon Trotsky explains an interconnected program of slogans and demands that "lead to one and the same political conclusion: the workers need to break with all traditional parties of the bourgeoisie in order, jointly with the farmers, to establish their own power." $20

www.pathfinderpress.com

Building a PROLETARIAN PARTY

The Changing Face of U.S. Politics

Working-Class Politics and the Trade Unions

JACK BARNES

Building the kind of party working people need to prepare for coming class battles through which they will revolutionize themselves, their unions, and all society. A handbook for those seeking the road toward effective action to overturn the exploitative system of capitalism and join in reconstructing the world on new, socialist foundations. $24. Also in Spanish, French, and Swedish.

Revolutionary Continuity

Marxist Leadership in the U.S.

FARRELL DOBBS

How successive generations took part in struggles of the U.S. labor movement, seeking to build a leadership that could advance the class interests of workers and small farmers and link up with fellow toilers around the world. Two volumes:

The Early Years, 1848–1917, $20; *Birth of the Communist Movement 1918–1922*, $19.

The History of American Trotskyism, 1928–38

Report of a Participant

JAMES P. CANNON

"Trotskyism is not a new movement, a new doctrine," Cannon says, "but the restoration, the revival of genuine Marxism as it was expounded and practiced in the Russian revolution and in the early days of the Communist International." In twelve talks given in 1942, Cannon recounts a decisive period in efforts to build a proletarian party in the United States. $22. Also in Spanish and French.

What Is To Be Done?

V.I. LENIN

The stakes in creating a disciplined organization of working-class revolutionaries capable of acting as a "tribune of the people, able to react to every manifestation of tyranny and oppression, no matter where it appears, to clarify for all and everyone the world-historic significance of the struggle for the emancipation of the proletariat." Written in 1902. In *Essential Works of Lenin.* $12.95

In Defense of Marxism

Against the Petty-Bourgeois Opposition in the Socialist Workers Party

LEON TROTSKY

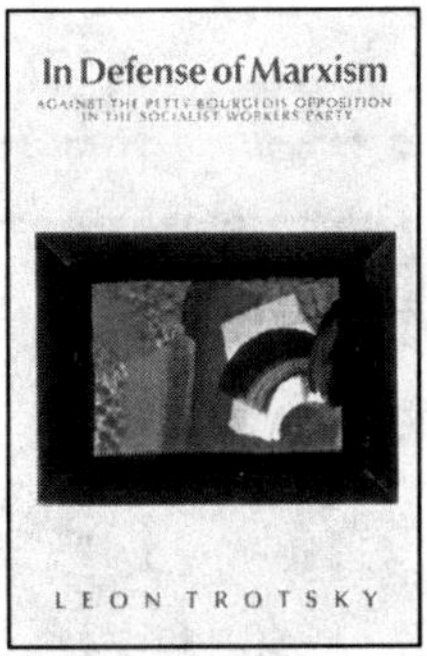

Writing in 1939–40, Leon Trotsky replies to those in the revolutionary workers movement beating a retreat from defense of the Soviet Union in face of the looming imperialist assault. Why only a party that fights to bring growing numbers of workers into its ranks and leadership can steer a steady revolutionary course. $25. Also in Spanish.

The Struggle for a Proletarian Party

JAMES P. CANNON

"The workers of America have power enough to topple the structure of capitalism at home and to lift the whole world with them when they rise," Cannon asserts. On the eve of World War II, a founder of the communist movement in the U.S. and leader of the Communist International in Lenin's time defends the program and party-building norms of Bolshevism. $22

Socialism on Trial

JAMES P. CANNON

The basic ideas of socialism, explained in testimony during the 1941 trial of leaders of the Minneapolis Teamsters union and the Socialist Workers Party framed up and imprisoned under the notorious Smith "Gag" Act during World War II. $16. Also in Spanish.

The Cuban Revolution and

Our History Is Still Being Written

THE STORY OF THREE CHINESE-CUBAN GENERALS IN THE CUBAN REVOLUTION

In Cuba, the greatest measure against racial discrimination "was the revolution itself," says Gen. Moisés Sío Wong, "the triumph of a socialist revolution." Armando Choy, Gustavo Chui, and Sío Wong talk about the historic place of Chinese immigration to Cuba, as well as more than five decades of revolutionary action and internationalism, from Cuba to Angola and Venezuela today. Through their stories we see how millions of ordinary men and women changed the course of history, becoming different human beings in the process. $20. Also in Spanish and Chinese.

From the Escambray to the Congo

IN THE WHIRLWIND OF THE CUBAN REVOLUTION

Víctor Dreke

The author describes how easy it became after the Cuban Revolution to take down a rope segregating blacks from whites in the town square, yet how enormous was the battle to transform social relations underlying all the "ropes" inherited from capitalism and Yankee domination. Dreke, second in command of the internationalist column in the Congo led by Che Guevara in 1965, recounts the creative joy with which working people have defended their revolutionary course—from Cuba's Escambray mountains to Africa and beyond. $17. Also in Spanish.

Renewal or Death

Fidel Castro

"To really establish total equality takes more than declaring it in law," Fidel Castro told delegates to the 1986 congress of the Cuban Communist Party, pointing to the revolution's enormous conquests in the fight against anti-black racism. "We can't leave it to chance to correct historical injustices," he said. "We have to straighten out what history has twisted." In *New International* no. 6. $16

World Politics

The First and Second Declarations of Havana

Nowhere are the questions of revolutionary strategy that today confront men and women on the front lines of struggles in the Americas addressed with greater truthfulness and clarity than in these two documents, adopted by million-strong assemblies of the Cuban people in 1960 and 1962. These uncompromising indictments of imperialist plunder and "the exploitation of man by man" continue to stand as manifestos of revolutionary struggle by working people the world over. $10. Also in Spanish, French, and Arabic.

Che Guevara Talks to Young People

The Argentine-born revolutionary leader challenges youth of Cuba and the world to study, to work, to become disciplined. To join the front lines of struggles, small and large. To politicize themselves and the work of their organizations. To become a different kind of human being as they strive with working people of all lands to transform the world. Eight talks from 1959 to 1964. $15. Also in Spanish.

The Inevitable Battle

FROM THE BAY OF PIGS TO PLAYA GIRÓN

Juan Carlos Rodríguez

The U.S.-led invasion of Cuba in April 1961 was defeated in 66 hours by militia battalions composed of worker and peasant volunteers, along with soldiers from the Cuban armed forces. Cuban historian Juan Carlos Rodríguez explains that the human material available to Washington could not match the courage and determination of a people fighting to defend what they had gained through the continent's first socialist revolution. $20. Also in Spanish.

www.pathfinderpress.com

Also from Pathfinder

CAPITALISM'S WORLD DISORDER

Jack Barnes

The social devastation and financial panic, the coarsening of politics, the cop brutality and acts of imperialist aggression accelerating around us—all are the product not of something gone wrong but of the lawful workings of capitalism. Yet the future can be changed by the united struggle and selfless action of workers and farmers conscious of their power to transform the world. $25. Also in Spanish and French.

LENIN'S FINAL FIGHT

SPEECHES AND WRITINGS, 1922–23

V.I. Lenin

In 1922 and 1923, V.I. Lenin, central leader of the world's first socialist revolution, waged what was to be his last political battle. At stake was whether that revolution would remain on the proletarian course that had brought workers and peasants to power in October 1917—and laid the foundations for a truly worldwide revolutionary movement of toilers organizing to emulate the Bolsheviks' example. *Lenin's Final Fight* brings together the reports, articles, and letters through which Lenin waged this political battle. $20. Also in Spanish.

PROBLEMS OF WOMEN'S LIBERATION

Evelyn Reed

Six articles explore the social and economic roots of women's oppression from prehistoric society to modern capitalism and point the road forward to emancipation. $15

CAPITALISM AND THE TRANSFORMATION OF AFRICA

REPORTS FROM EQUATORIAL GUINEA

Mary-Alice Waters, Martín Koppel

An account of the transformation of production and class relations in this Central African country, as it is drawn deeper into the world market and both a capitalist class and modern proletariat are born. Here also the example of Cuba's socialist revolution comes alive in the collaboration of Cuban volunteer medical brigades helping to transform social conditions. Woven together, the outlines of a future to be fought for today can be seen—a future in which the toilers of Africa have more weight in world politics than ever before. $10. Also in Spanish.

THE WORKING CLASS AND THE TRANSFORMATION OF LEARNING

THE FRAUD OF EDUCATION REFORM UNDER CAPITALISM

Jack Barnes

"Until society is reorganized so that education is a human activity from the time we are very young until the time we die, there will be no education worthy of working, creating humanity." $3. Also in Spanish, French, Swedish, Icelandic, Farsi, and Greek.

IMPERIALISM, THE HIGHEST STAGE OF CAPITALISM

V.I. Lenin

"I trust that this pamphlet will help the reader to understand the fundamental economic question, that of the economic essence of imperialism," Lenin wrote in 1917. "For unless this is studied, it will be impossible to understand and appraise modern war and modern politics." $10. Also in Spanish.

THE FIGHT AGAINST FASCISM

The Struggle against Fascism in Germany

Leon Trotsky

Writing in the heat of struggle against the rising Nazi movement, a central leader of the Russian revolution examines the class roots of fascism and advances a revolutionary strategy to combat it. $32

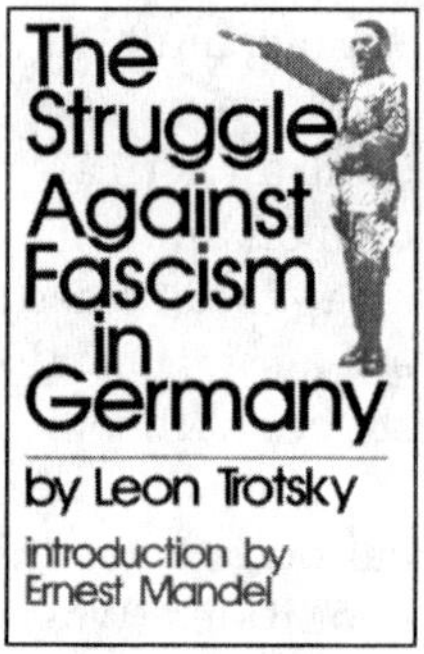

The Socialist Workers Party in World War II

WRITINGS AND SPEECHES, 1940–43

James P. Cannon

Preparing the communist movement in the United States to stand against the patriotic wave inside the workers movement supporting the imperialist slaughter and to campaign against wartime censorship, repression, and antiunion assaults. $24.95

The Jewish Question

A MARXIST INTERPRETATION

Abram Leon

Traces the historical rationalizations of anti-Semitism to the fact that Jews—in the centuries preceding the domination of industrial capitalism—emerged as a "people-class" of merchants and moneylenders. Leon explains why the propertied rulers incite renewed Jew-hatred today. $22

What Is American Fascism?

James P. Cannon and Joseph Hansen

Analyzing examples from the 20th century—Father Charles Coughlin, Jersey City mayor Frank Hague, and Sen. Joseph McCarthy—this collection looks at the features distinguishing fascist movements and demagogues in the U.S. from the 1930s to today. $8

THE COMMUNIST INTERNATIONAL IN LENIN'S TIME

TO SEE THE DAWN

Baku, 1920—First Congress of the Peoples of the East

How can peasants and workers in the colonial world achieve freedom from imperialist exploitation? By what means can working people overcome divisions incited by their national ruling classes and act together for their common class interests? These questions were addressed by 2,000 delegates to the 1920 Congress of the Peoples of the East. $24

WORKERS OF THE WORLD AND OPPRESSED PEOPLES, UNITE!

Proceedings and Documents of the Second Congress, 1920

The debate among delegates from 37 countries takes up key questions of working-class strategy and program and offers a vivid portrait of social struggles in the era of the October revolution. 2 vol. set, $65

LENIN'S STRUGGLE FOR A REVOLUTIONARY INTERNATIONAL

Documents, 1907–1916; The Preparatory Years

The debate among revolutionary working-class leaders, including V.I. Lenin and Leon Trotsky, on a socialist response to World War I. $35.95

Other volumes in the series:

The German Revolution and the Debate on Soviet Power (1918–1919)

Founding the Communist International (March 1919)

WWW.PATHFINDERPRESS.COM

New International

A MAGAZINE OF MARXIST POLITICS AND THEORY

NEW INTERNATIONAL NO. 12

CAPITALISM'S LONG HOT WINTER HAS BEGUN

Jack Barnes

and "Their Transformation and Ours," Resolution of the Socialist Workers Party

Today's sharpening interimperialist conflicts are fueled both by the opening stages of what will be decades of economic, financial, and social convulsions and class battles, and by the most far-reaching shift in Washington's military policy and organization since the U.S. buildup toward World War II. Class-struggle-minded working people must face this historic turning point for imperialism, and draw satisfaction from being "in their face" as we chart a revolutionary course to confront it. $16

NEW INTERNATIONAL NO. 14

REVOLUTION, INTERNATIONALISM, AND SOCIALISM: THE LAST YEAR OF MALCOLM X

Jack Barnes

"To understand Malcolm's last year is to see how, in the imperialist epoch, revolutionary leadership of the highest political capacity, courage, and integrity converges with communism. That truth has even greater weight today as billions around the world, in city and countryside, from China to Brazil, are being hurled into the modern class struggle by the violent expansion of world capitalism."—Jack Barnes

Also in No. 14: "The Clintons' Antilabor Legacy: Roots of the 2008 World Financial Crisis"; "The Stewardship of Nature Also Falls to the Working Class"; and "Setting the Record Straight on Fascism and World War II." $14

ALL THESE ISSUES ARE ALSO AVAILABLE IN SPANISH AND MOST IN FRENCH AT WWW.PATHFINDERPRESS.COM

NEW INTERNATIONAL NO. 13

OUR POLITICS START WITH THE WORLD

Jack Barnes

The huge economic and cultural inequalities between imperialist and semicolonial countries, and among classes within almost every country, are produced, reproduced, and accentuated by the workings of capitalism. For vanguard workers to build parties able to lead a successful revolutionary struggle for power in our own countries, says Jack Barnes in the lead article, our activity must be guided by a strategy to close this gap.

Also in No. 13: "Farming, Science, and the Working Classes" *by Steve Clark.* $14

NEW INTERNATIONAL NO. 11

U.S. IMPERIALISM HAS LOST THE COLD WAR

Jack Barnes

Contrary to imperialist expectations at the opening of the 1990s in the wake of the collapse of regimes across Eastern Europe and the USSR claiming to be communist, the workers and farmers there have not been crushed. The toilers remain an intractable obstacle to imperialism's advance, one the exploiters will have to confront in class battles and war. $16

NEW INTERNATIONAL NO. 8

CHE GUEVARA, CUBA, AND THE ROAD TO SOCIALISM

Articles by Ernesto Che Guevara, Carlos Rafael Rodríguez, Carlos Tablada, Mary-Alice Waters, Steve Clark, Jack Barnes

Exchanges from the opening years of the Cuban Revolution and today on the political perspectives defended by Guevara as he helped lead working people to advance the transformation of economic and social relations in Cuba. $10

NEW INTERNATIONAL NO. 5

THE COMING REVOLUTION IN SOUTH AFRICA

Jack Barnes

Writing a decade before the white supremacist regime fell, Barnes explores the social roots of apartheid in South African capitalism and tasks of urban and rural toilers in dismantling it, as they forge a communist leadership of the working class. $14

PATHFINDER AROUND THE WORLD

Visit our website for a complete list of titles and to place orders

www.pathfinderpress.com

PATHFINDER DISTRIBUTORS

UNITED STATES
(and Caribbean, Latin America, and East Asia)

Pathfinder Books, 306 W. 37th St., 10th Floor, New York, NY 10018

CANADA

Pathfinder Books, 7107 St. Denis, Suite 204, Montreal, QC H2S 2S5

UNITED KINGDOM
(and Europe, Africa, Middle East, and South Asia)

Pathfinder Books, First Floor, 120 Bethnal Green Road (entrance in Brick Lane), London E2 6DG

SWEDEN

Pathfinder böcker, Bildhuggarvägen 17, S-121 44 Johanneshov

AUSTRALIA
(and Southeast Asia and the Pacific)

Pathfinder, Level 1, 3/281-287 Beamish St., Campsie, NSW 2194
Postal address: P.O. Box 164, Campsie, NSW 2194

NEW ZEALAND

Pathfinder, 4/125 Grafton Road, Grafton, Auckland
Postal address: P.O. Box 3025, Auckland 1140

Join the Pathfinder Readers Club
to get 15% discounts on all Pathfinder titles and bigger discounts on special offers. Sign up at www.pathfinderpress.com or through the distributors above.